Prediction, Learning, and Games

This important new text and reference for researchers and students in machine learning, game theory, statistics, and information theory offers the first comprehensive treatment of the problem of predicting individual sequences. Unlike standard statistical approaches to forecasting, prediction of individual sequences does not impose any probabilistic assumption on the data-generating mechanism. Yet, prediction algorithms can be constructed that work well for all possible sequences, in the sense that their performance is always nearly as good as the best forecasting strategy in a given reference class.

The central theme is the model of prediction using expert advice, a general framework within which many related problems can be cast and discussed. Repeated game playing, adaptive data compression, sequential investment in the stock market, sequential pattern analysis, and several other problems are viewed as instances of the experts' framework and analyzed from a common nonstochastic standpoint that often reveals new and intriguing connections. Old and new forecasting methods are described in a mathematically precise way in order to characterize their theoretical limitations and possibilities.

Nicolò Cesa-Bianchi is Professor of Computer Science at the University of Milan, Italy. His research interests include learning theory, pattern analysis, and worst-case analysis of algorithms. He is an action editor of the journal *Machine Learning*.

Gábor Lugosi has been working on various problems in pattern classification, nonparametric statistics, statistical learning theory, game theory, probability, and information theory. He is coauthor of the monographs *A Probabilistic Theory of Pattern Recognition* and *Combinatorial Methods of Density Estimation*. He has been an associate editor of various journals, including the *IEEE Transactions of Information Theory, Test, ESAIM: Probability and Statistics*, and *Statistics and Decisions*.

Prediction, Learning, and Games

NICOLÒ CESA-BIANCHI
Università degli Studi di Milano

GÁBOR LUGOSI
Universitat Pompeu Fabra, Barcelona

CAMBRIDGE
UNIVERSITY PRESS

CAMBRIDGE UNIVERSITY PRESS
Cambridge, New York, Melbourne, Madrid, Cape Town, Singapore,
São Paulo, Delhi, Dubai, Tokyo, Mexico City

Cambridge University Press
32 Avenue of the Americas, New York, NY 10013-2473, USA

www.cambridge.org
Information on this title: www.cambridge.org/9780521841085

First published 2006
Reprinted 2010 (thrice)

A catalog record for this publication is available from the British Library.

Library of Congress Cataloging in Publication Data

Cesa-Bianchi, Nicolò, 1963–
Prediction, learning, and games / Nicolò Cesa-Bianchi, Gábor Lugosi.
    p.   cm.
Includes bibliographical references and index.
ISBN 0-521-84108-9 (hardback)
1. Game theory.   2. Machine learning.   3. Computer algorithms.
I. Lugosi, Gábor. II. Title.
QA269.C45   2006
519.3–dc22   2005034788

ISBN 978-0-521-84108-5 Hardback

to Betta, Silvia, and Luca – NCB

to Arrate, Dani, and Frida
to the memory of my parents – GL

Contents

Preface

. . . beware of mathematicians, and all those who make empty prophecies.

St. Augustine, *De Genesi ad Litteram libri duodecim.*
Liber Secundus, 17, 37.

Prediction of individual sequences, the main theme of this book, has been studied in various fields, such as statistical decision theory, information theory, game theory, machine learning, and mathematical finance. Early appearances of the problem go back as far as the 1950s, with the pioneering work of Blackwell, Hannan, and others. Even though the focus of investigation varied across these fields, some of the main principles have been discovered independently. Evolution of ideas remained parallel for quite some time. As each community developed its own vocabulary, communication became difficult. By the mid-1990s, however, it became clear that researchers of the different fields had a lot to teach each other.

When we decided to write this book, in 2001, one of our main purposes was to investigate these connections and help ideas circulate more fluently. In retrospect, we now realize that the interplay among these many fields is far richer than we suspected. For this reason, exploring this beautiful subject during the preparation of the book became a most exciting experience – we really hope to succeed in transmitting this excitement to the reader. Today, several hundreds of pages later, we still feel there remains a lot to discover. This book just shows the first steps of some largely unexplored paths. We invite the reader to join us in finding out where these paths lead and where they connect.

The book should by no means be treated as an encyclopedia of the subject. The selection of the material reflects our personal taste. Large parts of the manuscript have been read and constructively criticized by Gilles Stoltz, whose generous help we greatly appreciate. Claudio Gentile and András György also helped us with many important and useful comments. We are equally grateful to the members of a seminar group in Budapest who periodically gathered in Laci Györfi's office at the Technical University and unmercifully questioned every line of the manuscript they had access to, and to György Ottucsák who diligently communicated to us all these questions and remarks. The members of the group are András Antos, Balázs Csanád Csáji, Laci Györfi, András György, Levente Kocsis, György Ottucsák, Márti Pintér, Csaba Szepesvári, and Kati Varga. Of course, all remaining errors are our responsibility.

We thank all our friends and colleagues who, often without realizing it, taught us many ideas, tricks, and points of view that helped us understand the subtleties of the material.

The incomplete list includes Peter Auer, Andrew Barron, Peter Bartlett, Shai Ben-David, Stéphane Boucheron, Olivier Bousquet, Miklós Csürös, Luc Devroye, Meir Feder, Paul Fischer, Dean Foster, Yoav Freund, Claudio Gentile, Fabrizio Germano, András György, Laci Györfi, Sergiu Hart, David Haussler, David Helmbold, Marcus Hutter, Sham Kakade, Adam Kalai, Balázs Kégl, Jyrki Kivinen, Tamás Linder, Phil Long, Yishay Mansour, Andreu Mas-Colell, Shahar Mendelson, Neri Merhav, Jan Poland, Hans Simon, Yoram Singer, Rob Schapire, Kic Udina, Nicolas Vayatis, Volodya Vovk, Manfred Warmuth, Marcelo Weinberger, and Michael 'Il Lupo' Wolf.

We gratefully acknowledge the research support of the Italian Ministero dell'Istruzione, Università e Ricerca, the Generalitat de Catalunya, the Spanish Ministry of Science and Technology, and the IST Programme of the European Community under the PASCAL Network of Excellence.

Many thanks to Elisabetta Parodi-Dandini for creating the cover art, which is inspired by the work of Alighiero Boetti (1940–1994).

Finally, a few grateful words to our families. Nicolò thanks Betta, Silvia, and Luca for filling his life with love, joy, and meaning. Gábor wants to thank Arrate for making the last ten years a pleasant adventure and Dani for so much fun, and to welcome Frida to the family.

Have as much fun reading this book as we had writing it!

Nicolò Cesa-Bianchi, Milano
Gábor Lugosi, Barcelona

1

Introduction

1.1 Prediction

Prediction, as we understand it in this book, is concerned with guessing the short-term evolution of certain phenomena. Examples of prediction problems are forecasting tomorrow's temperature at a given location or guessing which asset will achieve the best performance over the next month. Despite their different nature, these tasks look similar at an abstract level: one must predict the next element of an unknown sequence given some knowledge about the past elements and possibly other available information. In this book we develop a formal theory of this general prediction problem. To properly address the diversity of potential applications without sacrificing mathematical rigor, the theory will be able to accommodate different formalizations of the entities involved in a forecasting task, such as the elements forming the sequence, the criterion used to measure the quality of a forecast, the protocol specifying how the predictor receives feedback about the sequence, and any possible side information provided to the predictor.

In the most basic version of the sequential prediction problem, the predictor – or forecaster – observes one after another the elements of a sequence $y_1, y_2, \ldots$ of symbols. At each time $t = 1, 2, \ldots$, before the tth symbol of the sequence is revealed, the forecaster guesses its value y_t on the basis of the previous $t - 1$ observations.

In the classical statistical theory of sequential prediction, the sequence of elements, which we call outcomes, is assumed to be a realization of a stationary stochastic process. Under this hypothesis, statistical properties of the process may be estimated on the basis of the sequence of past observations, and effective prediction rules can be derived from these estimates. In such a setup, the *risk* of a prediction rule may be defined as the expected value of some *loss function* measuring the discrepancy between predicted value and true outcome, and different rules are compared based on the behavior of their risk.

This book looks at prediction from a quite different angle. We abandon the basic assumption that the outcomes are generated by an underlying stochastic process and view the sequence $y_1, y_2, \ldots$ as the product of some unknown and unspecified mechanism (which could be deterministic, stochastic, or even adversarially adaptive to our own behavior). To contrast it with stochastic modeling, this approach has often been referred to as prediction of *individual sequences*.

Without a probabilistic model, the notion of risk cannot be defined, and it is not immediately obvious how the goals of prediction should be set up formally. Indeed, several possibilities exist, many of which are discussed in this book. In our basic model, the performance of the forecaster is measured by the loss accumulated during many rounds of prediction, where loss is scored by some fixed loss function. Since we want to avoid any assumption on the way the sequence to be predicted is generated, there is no obvious baseline against which to measure the forecaster's performance. To provide such a baseline, we introduce a class of *reference forecasters*, also called *experts*. These experts make their prediction available to the forecaster before the next outcome is revealed. The forecaster can then make his own prediction depend on the experts' "advice" in order to keep his cumulative loss close to that of the best reference forecaster in the class.

The difference between the forecaster's accumulated loss and that of an expert is called *regret*, as it measures how much the forecaster regrets, in hindsight, of not having followed the advice of this particular expert. Regret is a basic notion of this book, and a lot of attention is payed to constructing forecasting strategies that guarantee a small regret with respect to *all* experts in the class. As it turns out, the possibility of keeping the regrets small depends largely on the size and structure of the class of experts, and on the loss function. This model of prediction using expert advice is defined formally in Chapter 2 and serves as a basis for a large part of the book.

The abstract notion of an "expert" can be interpreted in different ways, also depending on the specific application that is being considered. In some cases it is possible to view an expert as a black box of unknown computational power, possibly with access to private sources of side information. In other applications, the class of experts is collectively regarded as a statistical model, where each expert in the class represents an optimal forecaster for some given "state of nature." With respect to this last interpretation, the goal of minimizing regret on arbitrary sequences may be thought of as a robustness requirement. Indeed, a small regret guarantees that, even when the model does not describe perfectly the state of nature, the forecaster does almost as well as the best element in the model fitted to the particular sequence of outcomes. In Chapters 2 and 3 we explore the basic possibilities and limitations of forecasters in this framework.

Models of prediction of individual sequences arose in disparate areas motivated by problems as different as playing repeated games, compressing data, or gambling. Because of this diversity, it is not easy to trace back the first appearance of such a study. But it is now recognized that Blackwell, Hannan, Robbins, and the others who, as early as in the 1950s, studied the so-called *sequential compound decision* problem were the pioneering contributors in the field. Indeed, many of the basic ideas appear in these early works, including the use of randomization as a powerful tool of achieving a small regret when it would otherwise be impossible. The model of randomized prediction is introduced in Chapter 4. In Chapter 6 several variants of the basic problem of randomized prediction are considered in which the information available to the forecaster is limited in some way.

Another area in which prediction of individual sequences appeared naturally and found numerous applications is information theory. The influential work of Cover, Davisson, Lempel, Rissanen, Shtarkov, Ziv, and others gave the information-theoretic foundations of sequential prediction, first motivated by applications for data compression and "universal" coding, and later extended to models of sequential gambling and investment. This theory mostly concentrates on a particular loss function, the so-called *logarithmic* or *self-information* loss, as it has a natural interpretation in the framework of *sequential probability assignment*. In this version of the prediction problem, studied in Chapters 9 and 10, at each time instance the forecaster determines a probability distribution over the set of possible outcomes. The total likelihood assigned to the entire sequence of outcomes is then used to score the forecaster. Sequential probability assignment has been studied in different closely related models in statistics, including bayesian frameworks and the problem of *calibration* in various forms. Dawid's "prequential" statistics is also close in spirit to some of the problems discussed here.

In computer science, algorithms that receive their input sequentially are said to operate in an *online* modality. Typical application areas of online algorithms include tasks that involve sequences of decisions, like when one chooses how to serve each incoming request in a stream. The similarity between decision problems and prediction problems, and the fact that online algorithms are typically analyzed on arbitrary sequences of inputs, has resulted in a fruitful exchange of ideas and techniques between the two fields. However, some crucial features of sequential decision problems that are missing in the prediction framework (like the presence of states to model the interaction between the decision maker and the mechanism generating the stream of requests) has so far prevented the derivation of a general theory allowing a unified analysis of both types of problems.

1.2 Learning

Prediction of individual sequences has also been a main topic of research in the theory of machine learning, more concretely in the area of *online learning*. In fact, in the late 1980s–early 1990s the paradigm of prediction with expert advice was first introduced as a model of online learning in the pioneering papers of De Santis, Markowski, and Wegman; Littlestone and Warmuth; and Vovk, and it has been intensively investigated ever since. An interesting extension of the model allows the forecaster to consider other information apart from the past outcomes of the sequence to be predicted. By considering *side information* taking values in a vector space, and experts that are linear functions of the side information vector, one obtains classical models of online pattern recognition. For example, Rosenblatt's Perceptron algorithm, the Widrow-Hoff rule, and ridge regression can be naturally cast in this framework. Chapters 11 and 12 are devoted to the study of such online learning algorithms.

Researchers in machine learning and information theory have also been interested in the computational aspects of prediction. This becomes a particularly important problem when very large classes of reference forecasters are considered, and various tricks need to be invented to make predictors feasible for practical applications. Chapter 5 gathers some of these basic tricks illustrated on a few prototypical examples.

1.3 Games

The online prediction model studied in this book has an intimate connection with game theory. First of all, the model is most naturally defined in terms of a repeated game played between the forecaster and the "environment" generating the outcome sequence, thus offering a convenient way of describing variants of the basic theme. However, the connection is much deeper. For example, in Chapter 7 we show that classical minimax theorems of game theory can be recovered as simple applications of some basic bounds for the performance of sequential prediction algorithms. On the other hand, certain generalized minimax theorems, most notably *Blackwell's approachability theorem* can be used to define forecasters with good performance on individual sequences.

Perhaps surprisingly, the connection goes even deeper. It turns out that if all players in a repeated normal form game play according to certain simple regret-minimizing prediction strategies, then the induced dynamics leads to equilibrium in a certain sense. This interesting line of research has been gaining terrain in game theory, based on the pioneering work of Foster, Vohra, Hart, Mas-Colell, and others. In Chapter 7 we discuss the possibilities and limitations of strategies based on regret minimizing forecasting algorithms that lead to various notions of equilibria.

1.4   A Gentle Start

To introduce the reader to the spirit of the results contained in this book, we now describe in detail a simple example of a forecasting procedure and then analyze its performance on an arbitrary sequence of outcomes.

Consider the problem of predicting an unknown sequence $y_1, y_2, \ldots$ of bits $y_t \in \{0, 1\}$. At each time t the forecaster first makes his guess $\widehat{p}_t \in \{0, 1\}$ for y_t. Then the true bit y_t is revealed and the forecaster finds out whether his prediction was correct. To compute $\widehat{p}_t$ the forecaster listens to the advice of N experts. This advice takes the form of a binary vector $(f_{1,t}, \ldots, f_{N,t})$, where $f_{i,t} \in \{0, 1\}$ is the prediction that expert i makes for the next bit y_t. Our goal is to bound the number of time steps t in which $\widehat{p}_t \neq y_t$, that is, to bound the number of mistakes made by the forecaster.

To start with an even simpler case, assume we are told in advance that, on this particular sequence of outcomes, there is some expert i that makes no mistakes. That is, we know that $f_{i,t} = y_t$ for some i and for all t, but we do not know for which i this holds. Using this information, it is not hard to devise a forecasting strategy that makes at most $\lfloor \log_2 N \rfloor$ mistakes on the sequence. To see this, consider the forecaster that starts by assigning a weight $w_j = 1$ to each expert $j = 1, \ldots, N$. At every time step t, the forecaster predicts with $\widehat{p}_t = 1$ if and only if the number of experts j with $w_j = 1$ and such that $f_{j,t} = 1$ is bigger than those with $w_j = 1$ and such that $f_{j,t} = 0$. After y_t is revealed, if $\widehat{p}_t \neq y_t$, then the forecaster performs the assignment $w_k \leftarrow 0$ on the weight of all experts k such that $f_{k,t} \neq y_t$. In words, this forecaster keeps track of which experts make a mistake and predicts according to the majority of the experts that have been always correct.

The analysis is immediate. Let W_m be the sum of the weights of all experts after the forecaster has made m mistakes. Initially, $m = 0$ and $W_0 = N$. When the forecaster makes his mth mistake, at least half of the experts that have been always correct so far make their first mistake. This implies that $W_m \leq W_{m-1}/2$, since those experts that were incorrect for the first time have their weight zeroed by the forecaster. Since the above inequality holds for all $m \geq 1$, we have $W_m \leq W_0/2^m$. Recalling that expert i never makes a mistake, we know that $w_i = 1$, which implies that $W_m \geq 1$. Using this together with $W_0 = N$, we thus find that $1 \leq N/2^m$. Solving for m (which must be an integer) gives the claimed inequality $m \leq \lfloor \log_2 N \rfloor$.

We now move on to analyze the general case, in which the forecaster does not have any preliminary information on the number of mistakes the experts will make on the sequence. Our goal now is to relate the number of mistakes made by the forecaster to the number of mistakes made by the best expert, irrespective of which sequence is being predicted.

Looking back at the previous forecasting strategy, it is clear that setting the weight of an incorrect expert to zero makes sense only if we are sure that some expert will never make a mistake. Without this guarantee, a safer choice could be performing the assignment $w_k \leftarrow \beta\, w_k$ every time expert k makes a mistake, where $0 < \beta < 1$ is a free parameter. In other words, every time an expert is incorrect, instead of zeroing its weight we shrink it by a constant factor. This is the only modification we make to the old forecaster, and this makes its analysis almost as easy as the previous one. More precisely, the new forecaster compares the total weight of the experts that recommend predicting 1 with those that recommend 0 and predicts according to the weighted majority. As before, at the time the forecaster makes his mth mistake, the overall weight of the incorrect experts must be at least $W_{m-1}/2$. The weight of these experts is then multiplied by β, and the weight of the other experts, which is at most $W_{m-1}/2$, is left unchanged. Hence, we have $W_m \leq W_{m-1}/2 + \beta\, W_{m-1}/2$. As this holds for all $m \geq 1$, we get $W_m \leq W_0(1 + \beta)^m/2^m$. Now let k be the expert that has made the fewest mistakes when the forecaster made his mth mistake. Denote this minimal number of mistakes by m^*. Then the current weight of this expert is $w_k = \beta^{m^*}$, and thus we have $W_m \geq \beta^{m^*}$. This provides the inequality $\beta^{m^*} \leq W_0(1 + \beta)^m/2^m$. Using this, together with $W_0 = N$, we get the final bound

$$m \leq \left\lfloor \frac{\log_2 N + m^* \log_2(1/\beta)}{\log_2 \frac{2}{1+\beta}} \right\rfloor .$$

For any fixed value of β, this inequality establishes a linear dependence between the mistakes made by the forecaster, after any number of predictions, and the mistakes made by the expert that is the best after that same number of predictions. Note that this bound holds irrespective of the choice of the sequence of outcomes.

The fact that m and m^* are linearly related means that, in some sense, the performance of this forecaster gracefully degrades as a function of the "misfit" m^* between the experts and the outcome sequence. The bound also exhibits a mild dependence on the number of experts: the $\log_2 N$ term implies that, apart from computational considerations, doubling the number of experts causes the bound to increase by a small additive term.

Notwithstanding its simplicity, this example contains some of the main themes developed in the book, such as the idea of computing predictions using weights that are functions of the experts' past performance. In the subsequent chapters we develop this and many other ideas in a rigorous and systematic manner with the intent of offering a comprehensive view on the many facets of this fascinating subject.

1.5 A Note to the Reader

The book is addressed to researchers and students of computer science, mathematics, engineering, and economics who are interested in various aspects of prediction and learning. Even though we tried to make the text as self-contained as possible, the reader is assumed to be comfortable with some basic notions of probability, analysis, and linear algebra. To help the reader, we collect in the Appendix some technical tools used in the book. Some of this material is quite standard but may not be well known to all potential readers.

In order to minimize interruptions in the flow of the text, we gathered bibliographical references at the end of each chapter. In these references we intend to trace back the origin of the results described in the text and point to some relevant literature. We apologize for any possible omissions. Some of the material is published here for the first time. These results are not flagged. Each chapter is concluded with a list of exercises whose level of difficulty varies between distant extremes. Some of the exercises can be solved by an easy adaptation of the material described in the main text. These should help the reader in mastering the material. Some others resume difficult research results. In some cases we offer guidance to the solution, but there is no solution manual.

Figure 1.1 describes the dependence structure of the chapters of the book. This should help the reader to focus on specific topics and teachers to organize the material of various possible courses.

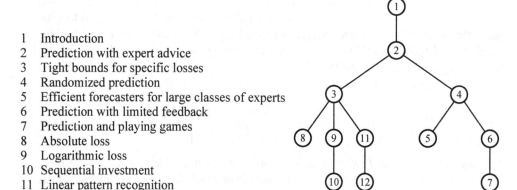

1   Introduction
2   Prediction with expert advice
3   Tight bounds for specific losses
4   Randomized prediction
5   Efficient forecasters for large classes of experts
6   Prediction with limited feedback
7   Prediction and playing games
8   Absolute loss
9   Logarithmic loss
10 Sequential investment
11 Linear pattern recognition
12 Linear classification

Figure 1.1. The dependence structure of the chapters.

2

Prediction with Expert Advice

The model of prediction with expert advice, introduced in this chapter, provides the foundations to the theory of prediction of individual sequences that we develop in the rest of the book.

Prediction with expert advice is based on the following protocol for sequential decisions: the decision maker is a forecaster whose goal is to predict an unknown sequence $y_1, y_2 \ldots$ of elements of an *outcome space* $\mathcal{Y}$. The forecaster's predictions $\widehat{p}_1, \widehat{p}_2 \ldots$ belong to a *decision space* $\mathcal{D}$, which we assume to be a convex subset of a vector space. In some special cases we take $\mathcal{D} = \mathcal{Y}$, but in general $\mathcal{D}$ may be different from $\mathcal{Y}$.

The forecaster computes his predictions in a sequential fashion, and his predictive performance is compared to that of a set of reference forecasters that we call *experts*. More precisely, at each time t the forecaster has access to the set $\{f_{E,t} : E \in \mathcal{E}\}$ of expert predictions $f_{E,t} \in \mathcal{D}$, where $\mathcal{E}$ is a fixed set of indices for the experts. On the basis of the experts' predictions, the forecaster computes his own guess $\widehat{p}_t$ for the next outcome y_t. After $\widehat{p}_t$ is computed, the true outcome y_t is revealed.

The predictions of forecaster and experts are scored using a nonnegative *loss function* $\ell : \mathcal{D} \times \mathcal{Y} \to \mathbb{R}$.

This prediction protocol can be naturally viewed as the following repeated game between "forecaster," who makes guesses $\widehat{p}_t$, and "environment," who chooses the expert advice $\{f_{E,t} : E \in \mathcal{E}\}$ and sets the true outcomes y_t.

PREDICTION WITH EXPERT ADVICE

Parameters: decision space $\mathcal{D}$, outcome space $\mathcal{Y}$, loss function ℓ, set $\mathcal{E}$ of expert indices.

For each round $t = 1, 2, \ldots$

    (1) the environment chooses the next outcome y_t and the expert advice $\{f_{E,t} \in \mathcal{D} : E \in \mathcal{E}\}$; the expert advice is revealed to the forecaster;
    (2) the forecaster chooses the prediction $\widehat{p}_t \in \mathcal{D}$;
    (3) the environment reveals the next outcome $y_t \in \mathcal{Y}$;
    (4) the forecaster incurs loss $\ell(\widehat{p}_t, y_t)$ and each expert E incurs loss $\ell(f_{E,t}, y_t)$.

The forecaster's goal is to keep as small as possible the *cumulative regret* (or simply *regret*) with respect to each expert. This quantity is defined, for expert E, by the sum

$$R_{E,n} = \sum_{t=1}^{n} \left(\ell(\widehat{p}_t, y_t) - \ell(f_{E,t}, y_t) \right) = \widehat{L}_n - L_{E,n},$$

where we use $\widehat{L}_n = \sum_{t=1}^{n} \ell(\widehat{p}_t, y_t)$ to denote the forecaster's cumulative loss and $L_{E,n} = \sum_{t=1}^{n} \ell(f_{E,t}, y_t)$ to denote the cumulative loss of expert E. Hence, $R_{E,n}$ is the difference between the forecaster's total loss and that of expert E after n prediction rounds. We also define the instantaneous regret with respect to expert E at time t by $r_{E,t} = \ell(\widehat{p}_t, y_t) - \ell(f_{E,t}, y_t)$, so that $R_{E,n} = \sum_{t=1}^{n} r_{E,t}$. One may think about $r_{E,t}$ as the regret the forecaster feels of not having listened to the advice of expert E right after the tth outcome y_t has been revealed.

Throughout the rest of this chapter we assume that the number of experts is finite, $\mathcal{E} = \{1, 2, \ldots, N\}$, and use the index $i = 1, \ldots, N$ to refer to an expert. The goal of the forecaster is to predict so that the regret is as small as possible for all sequences of outcomes. For example, the forecaster may want to have a vanishing per-round regret, that is, to achieve

$$\max_{i=1,\ldots,N} R_{i,n} = o(n) \quad \text{or, equivalently,} \quad \frac{1}{n} \left(\widehat{L}_n - \min_{i=1,\ldots,N} L_{i,n} \right) \overset{n \to \infty}{\longrightarrow} 0,$$

where the convergence is uniform over the choice of the outcome sequence and the choice of the expert advice. In the next section we show that this ambitious goal may be achieved by a simple forecaster under mild conditions.

The rest of the chapter is structured as follows. In Section 2.1 we introduce the important class of weighted average forecasters, describe the subclass of potential-based forecasters, and analyze two important special cases: the polynomially weighted average forecaster and the exponentially weighted average forecaster. This latter forecaster is quite central in our theory, and the following four sections are all concerned with various issues related to it: Section 2.2 shows certain optimality properties, Section 2.3 addresses the problem of tuning dynamically the parameter of the potential, Section 2.4 investigates the problem of obtaining improved regret bounds when the loss of the best expert is small, and Section 2.5 investigates the special case of differentiable loss functions. Starting with Section 2.6, we discover the advantages of rescaling the loss function. This simple trick allows us to derive new and even sharper performance bounds. In Section 2.7 we introduce and analyze a weighted average forecaster for rescaled losses that, unlike the previous ones, is not based on the notion of potential. In Section 2.8 we return to the exponentially weighted average forecaster and derive improved regret bounds based on rescaling the loss function. Sections 2.9 and 2.10 address some general issues in the problem of prediction with expert advice, including the definition of minimax values. Finally, in Section 2.11 we discuss a variant of the notion of regret where discount factors are introduced.

2.1 Weighted Average Prediction

A natural forecasting strategy in this framework is based on computing a *weighted average* of experts' predictions. That is, the forecaster predicts at time t according to

$$\widehat{p}_t = \frac{\sum_{i=1}^{N} w_{i,t-1} f_{i,t}}{\sum_{j=1}^{N} w_{j,t-1}},$$

where $w_{1,t-1}, \ldots, w_{N,t-1} \geq 0$ are the weights assigned to the experts at time t. Note that $\widehat{p}_t \in \mathcal{D}$, since it is a convex combination of the expert advice $f_{1,t}, \ldots, f_{N,t} \in \mathcal{D}$ and $\mathcal{D}$ is convex by our assumptions. As our goal is to minimize the regret, it is reasonable to choose the weights according to the regret up to time $t - 1$. If $R_{i,t-1}$ is large, then we assign a large weight $w_{i,t-1}$ to expert i, and vice versa. As $R_{i,t-1} = \widehat{L}_{t-1} - L_{i,t-1}$, this results in weighting more those experts i whose cumulative loss $L_{i,t-1}$ is small. Hence, we view the weight as an arbitrary increasing function of the expert's regret. For reasons that will become apparent shortly, we find it convenient to write this function as the derivative of a nonnegative, convex, and increasing function $\phi : \mathbb{R} \to \mathbb{R}$. We write ϕ' to denote this derivative. The forecaster uses ϕ' to determine the weight $w_{i,t-1} = \phi'(R_{i,t-1})$ assigned to the ith expert. Therefore, the prediction $\widehat{p}_t$ at time t of the weighted average forecaster is defined by

$$\widehat{p}_t = \frac{\sum_{i=1}^{N} \phi'(R_{i,t-1}) f_{i,t}}{\sum_{j=1}^{N} \phi'(R_{j,t-1})} \qquad \text{(weighted average forecaster).}$$

Note that this is a legitimate forecaster as $\widehat{p}_t$ is computed on the basis of the experts' advice at time t and the cumulative regrets up to time $t - 1$.

We start the analysis of weighted average forecasters by a simple technical observation.

Lemma 2.1. *If the loss function ℓ is convex in its first argument, then*

$$\sup_{y_t \in \mathcal{Y}} \sum_{i=1}^{N} r_{i,t} \phi'(R_{i,t-1}) \leq 0.$$

Proof. Using Jensen's inequality, for all $y \in \mathcal{Y}$,

$$\ell(\widehat{p}_t, y) = \ell\left(\frac{\sum_{i=1}^{N} \phi'(R_{i,t-1}) f_{i,t}}{\sum_{j=1}^{N} \phi'(R_{j,t-1})}, y\right) \leq \frac{\sum_{i=1}^{N} \phi'(R_{i,t-1}) \ell(f_{i,t}, y)}{\sum_{j=1}^{N} \phi'(R_{j,t-1})}.$$

Rearranging, we obtain the statement. ∎

The simple observation of the lemma above allows us to interpret the weighted average forecaster in an interesting way. To do this, introduce the *instantaneous regret vector*

$$\mathbf{r}_t = (r_{1,t}, \ldots, r_{N,t}) \in \mathbb{R}^N$$

and the corresponding *regret vector* $\mathbf{R}_n = \sum_{t=1}^{n} \mathbf{r}_t$. It is convenient to introduce also a *potential function* $\Phi : \mathbb{R}^N \to \mathbb{R}$ of the form

$$\Phi(\mathbf{u}) = \psi \left(\sum_{i=1}^{N} \phi(u_i) \right) \qquad \text{(potential function)},$$

where $\phi : \mathbb{R} \to \mathbb{R}$ is any nonnegative, increasing, and twice differentiable function, and $\psi : \mathbb{R} \to \mathbb{R}$ is any nonnegative, strictly increasing, concave, and twice differentiable auxiliary function.

Using the notion of potential function, we can give the following equivalent definition of the weighted average forecaster

$$\widehat{p}_t = \frac{\sum_{i=1}^{N} \nabla \Phi(\mathbf{R}_{t-1})_i \, f_{i,t}}{\sum_{j=1}^{N} \nabla \Phi(\mathbf{R}_{t-1})_j}$$

where $\nabla \Phi(\mathbf{R}_{t-1})_i = \partial \Phi(\mathbf{R}_{t-1}) / \partial R_{i,t-1}$. We say that a forecaster defined as above is *based on the potential* Φ. Even though the definition of the weighted average forecaster is independent of the choice of ψ (the derivatives ψ' cancel in the definition of $\widehat{p}_t$ above), the proof of the main result of this chapter, Theorem 2.1, reveals that ψ plays an important role in the analysis. We remark that convexity of ϕ is not needed to prove Theorem 2.1, and this is the reason why convexity is not mentioned in the above definition of potential function. On the other hand, all forecasters in this book that are based on potential functions and have a vanishing per-round regret are constructed using a convex ϕ (see also Exercise 2.2).

The statement of Lemma 2.1 is equivalent to

$$\sup_{y_t \in \mathcal{Y}} \mathbf{r}_t \cdot \nabla \Phi(\mathbf{R}_{t-1}) \leq 0 \qquad \text{(Blackwell condition)}.$$

The notation $\mathbf{u} \cdot \mathbf{v}$ stands for the the inner product of two vectors defined by $\mathbf{u} \cdot \mathbf{v} = u_1 v_1 + \cdots + u_N v_N$. We call the above inequality *Blackwell condition* because of its similarity to a key property used in the proof of the celebrated Blackwell's approachability theorem. The theorem, and its connection to the above inequality, are explored in Sections 7.7 and 7.8. Figure 2.1 shows an example of a prediction satisfying the Blackwell condition.

The Blackwell condition shows that the function Φ plays a role vaguely similar to the potential in a dynamical system: the weighted average forecaster, by forcing the regret vector to point away from the gradient of Φ irrespective to the outcome y_t, tends to keep the point $\mathbf{R}_t$ close to the minimum of Φ. This property, in fact, suggests a simple analysis because the increments of the potential function Φ may now be easily bounded by Taylor's theorem. The role of the function ψ is simply to obtain better bounds with this argument.

The next theorem applies to any forecaster satisfying the Blackwell condition (and thus not only to weighted average forecasters). However, it will imply several interesting bounds for different versions of the weighted average forecaster.

Theorem 2.1. *Assume that a forecaster satisfies the Blackwell condition for a potential* $\Phi(\mathbf{u}) = \psi \left(\sum_{i=1}^{N} \phi(u_i) \right)$. *Then, for all* $n = 1, 2, \ldots,$

$$\Phi(\mathbf{R}_n) \leq \Phi(\mathbf{0}) + \frac{1}{2} \sum_{t=1}^{n} C(\mathbf{r}_t),$$

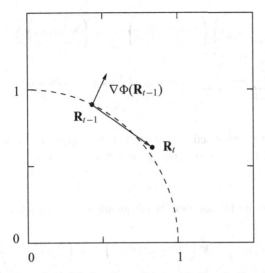

Figure 2.1. An illustration of the Blackwell condition with $N = 2$. The dashed line shows the points in regret space with potential equal to 1. The prediction at time t changed the potential from $\Phi(\mathbf{R}_{t-1}) = 1$ to $\Phi(\mathbf{R}_t) = \Phi(\mathbf{R}_{t-1} + \mathbf{r}_t)$. Though $\Phi(\mathbf{R}_t) > \Phi(\mathbf{R}_{t-1})$, the inner product between $\mathbf{r}_t$ and the gradient $\nabla\Phi(\mathbf{R}_{t-1})$ is negative, and thus the Blackwell condition holds.

where

$$C(\mathbf{r}_t) = \sup_{\mathbf{u} \in \mathbb{R}^N} \psi'\left(\sum_{i=1}^{N} \phi(u_i)\right) \sum_{i=1}^{N} \phi''(u_i) r_{i,t}^2.$$

Proof.   We estimate $\Phi(\mathbf{R}_t)$ in terms of $\Phi(\mathbf{R}_{t-1})$ using Taylor's theorem. Thus, we obtain

$$\Phi(\mathbf{R}_t) = \Phi(\mathbf{R}_{t-1} + \mathbf{r}_t)$$

$$= \Phi(\mathbf{R}_{t-1}) + \nabla\Phi(\mathbf{R}_{t-1}) \cdot \mathbf{r}_t + \frac{1}{2}\sum_{i=1}^{N}\sum_{j=1}^{N} \frac{\partial^2 \Phi}{\partial u_i \partial u_j}\bigg|_{\xi} r_{i,t} r_{j,t}$$

(where ξ is some vector in $\mathbb{R}^N$)

$$\leq \Phi(\mathbf{R}_{t-1}) + \frac{1}{2}\sum_{i=1}^{N}\sum_{j=1}^{N} \frac{\partial^2 \Phi}{\partial u_i \partial u_j}\bigg|_{\xi} r_{i,t} r_{j,t}$$

where the inequality follows by the Blackwell condition. Now straightforward calculation shows that

$$\sum_{i=1}^{N}\sum_{j=1}^{N} \frac{\partial^2 \Phi}{\partial u_i \partial u_j}\bigg|_{\xi} r_{i,t} r_{j,t}$$

$$= \psi''\left(\sum_{i=1}^{N}\phi(\xi_i)\right)\sum_{i=1}^{N}\sum_{j=1}^{N}\phi'(\xi_i)\phi'(\xi_j)r_{i,t}r_{j,t}$$

$$+ \psi'\left(\sum_{i=1}^{N}\phi(\xi_i)\right)\sum_{i=1}^{N}\phi''(\xi_i)r_{i,t}^2$$

$$= \psi'' \left(\sum_{i=1}^{N} \phi(\xi_i) \right) \left(\sum_{i=1}^{N} \phi'(\xi_i) r_{i,t} \right)^2 + \psi' \left(\sum_{i=1}^{N} \phi(\xi_i) \right) \sum_{i=1}^{N} \phi''(\xi_i) r_{i,t}^2$$

$$\leq \psi' \left(\sum_{i=1}^{N} \phi(\xi_i) \right) \sum_{i=1}^{N} \phi''(\xi_i) r_{i,t}^2 \quad \text{(since } \psi \text{ is concave)}$$

$$\leq C(\mathbf{r}_t)$$

where at the last step we used the definition of $C(\mathbf{r}_t)$. Thus, we have obtained $\Phi(\mathbf{R}_t) - \Phi(\mathbf{R}_{t-1}) \leq C(\mathbf{r}_t)/2$. The proof is finished by summing this inequality for $t = 1, \ldots, n$. ∎

Theorem 2.1 can be used as follows. By monotonicity of ψ and ϕ,

$$\psi \left(\phi \left(\max_{i=1,\ldots,N} R_{i,n} \right) \right) = \psi \left(\max_{i=1,\ldots,N} \phi(R_{i,n}) \right) \leq \psi \left(\sum_{i=1}^{N} \phi(R_{i,n}) \right) = \Phi(\mathbf{R}_n).$$

Note that ψ is invertible by the definition of the potential function. If ϕ is invertible as well, then we get

$$\max_{i=1,\ldots,N} R_{i,n} \leq \phi^{-1} \left(\psi^{-1} (\Phi(\mathbf{R}_n)) \right),$$

where $\Phi(\mathbf{R}_n)$ is replaced with the bound provided by Theorem 2.1. In the first of the two examples that follow, however, ϕ is not invertible, and thus $\max_{i=1,\ldots,N} R_{i,n}$ is directly majorized using a function of the bound provided by Theorem 2.1.

Polynomially Weighted Average Forecaster

Consider the *polynomially weighted average forecaster* based on the potential

$$\Phi_p(\mathbf{u}) = \left(\sum_{i=1}^{N} (u_i)_+^p \right)^{2/p} = \|\mathbf{u}_+\|_p^2 \qquad \text{(polynomial potential)},$$

where $p \geq 2$. Here $\mathbf{u}_+$ denotes the vector of positive parts of the components of $\mathbf{u}$. The weigths assigned to the experts are then given by

$$w_{i,t-1} = \nabla \Phi_p(\mathbf{R}_{t-1})_i = \frac{2(R_{i,t-1})_+^{p-1}}{\|(\mathbf{R}_{t-1})_+\|_p^{p-2}}$$

and the forecaster's predictions are just the weighted average of the experts predictions

$$\widehat{p}_t = \frac{\sum_{i=1}^{N} \left(\sum_{s=1}^{t-1} (\ell(\widehat{p}_s, y_s) - \ell(f_{i,s}, y_s)) \right)_+^{p-1} f_{i,t}}{\sum_{j=1}^{N} \left(\sum_{s=1}^{t-1} (\ell(\widehat{p}_s, y_s) - \ell(f_{j,s}, y_s)) \right)_+^{p-1}}.$$

Corollary 2.1. *Assume that the loss function ℓ is convex in its first argument and that it takes values in $[0, 1]$. Then, for any sequence $y_1, y_2, \ldots \in \mathcal{Y}$ of outcomes and for any $n \geq 1$, the* *regret of the polynomially weighted average forecaster satisfies*

$$\widehat{L}_n - \min_{i=1,\ldots,N} L_{i,n} \le \sqrt{n(p-1)N^{2/p}}.$$

This shows that, for all $p \ge 2$, the per-round regret converges to zero at a rate $O(1/\sqrt{n})$ uniformly over the outcome sequence and the expert advice. The choice $p = 2$ yields a particularly simple algorithm. On the other hand, the choice $p = 2 \ln N$ (for $N > 2$), which approximately minimizes the upper bound, leads to

$$\widehat{L}_n - \min_{i=1,\ldots,N} L_{i,n} \le \sqrt{ne(2\ln N - 1)}$$

yielding a significantly better dependence on the number of experts N.

Proof of Corollary 2.1. Apply Theorem 2.1 using the polynomial potential. Then $\phi(x) = x_+^p$ and $\psi(x) = x^{2/p}$, $x \ge 0$. Moreover

$$\psi'(x) = \frac{2}{px^{(p-2)/p}} \quad \text{and} \quad \phi''(x) = p(p-1)x_+^{p-2}.$$

By Hölder's inequality,

$$\sum_{i=1}^{N} \phi''(u_i)r_{i,t}^2 = p(p-1)\sum_{i=1}^{N}(u_i)_+^{p-2} r_{i,t}^2$$

$$\le p(p-1)\left(\sum_{i=1}^{N}\left((u_i)_+^{p-2}\right)^{p/(p-2)}\right)^{(p-2)/p}\left(\sum_{i=1}^{N}|r_{i,t}|^p\right)^{2/p}.$$

Thus,

$$\psi'\left(\sum_{i=1}^{N}\phi(u_i)\right)\sum_{i=1}^{N}\phi''(u_i)r_{i,t}^2 \le 2(p-1)\left(\sum_{i=1}^{N}|r_{i,t}|^p\right)^{2/p}$$

and the conditions of Theorem 2.1 are satisfied with $C(\mathbf{r}_t) \le 2(p-1)\|\mathbf{r}_t\|_p^2$. Since $\Phi_p(\mathbf{0}) = 0$, Theorem 2.1, together with the boundedness of the loss function, implies that

$$\left(\sum_{i=1}^{N}\left(R_{i,n}\right)_+^p\right)^{2/p} = \Phi_p(\mathbf{R}_n) \le (p-1)\sum_{t=1}^{n}\|\mathbf{r}_t\|_p^2 \le n(p-1)N^{2/p}.$$

Finally, since

$$\widehat{L}_n - \min_{i=1,\ldots,N} L_{i,n} = \max_{i=1,\ldots,N} R_{i,n} \le \left(\sum_{i=1}^{N}\left(R_{i,n}\right)_+^p\right)^{1/p}$$

the result follows. ■

Remark 2.1. We have defined the polynomial potential as $\Phi_p(\mathbf{u}) = \|\mathbf{u}_+\|_p^2$, which corresponds to taking $\psi(x) = x^{2/p}$. Recall that ψ does not have any influence on the prediction, it only has a role in the analysis. The particular form analyzed here is chosen by convenience, but there are other possibilities leading to similar results. For example, one may argue that it is more natural to take $\psi(x) = x^{1/p}$, which leads to the potential function $\Phi(\mathbf{u}) = \|\mathbf{u}_+\|_p$.

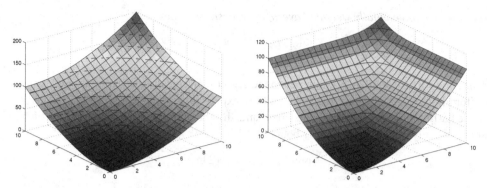

Figure 2.2. Plots of the polynomial potential function $\Phi_p(\mathbf{u})$ for $N = 2$ experts with exponents $p = 2$ and $p = 10$.

We leave it as an exercise to work out a bound similar to that of Corollary 2.1 based on this choice.

Exponentially Weighted Average Forecaster

Our second main example is the *exponentially weighted average forecaster* based on the potential

$$\Phi_\eta(\mathbf{u}) = \frac{1}{\eta} \ln \left(\sum_{i=1}^{N} e^{\eta u_i} \right) \qquad \text{(exponential potential)},$$

where η is a positive parameter. In this case, the weigths assigned to the experts are of the form

$$w_{i,t-1} = \nabla \Phi_\eta(\mathbf{R}_{t-1})_i = \frac{e^{\eta R_{i,t-1}}}{\sum_{j=1}^{N} e^{\eta R_{j,t-1}}},$$

and the weighted average forecaster simplifies to

$$\widehat{p}_t = \frac{\sum_{i=1}^{N} \exp\left(\eta\left(\widehat{L}_{t-1} - L_{i,t-1}\right)\right) f_{i,t}}{\sum_{j=1}^{N} \exp\left(\eta\left(\widehat{L}_{t-1} - L_{j,t-1}\right)\right)} = \frac{\sum_{i=1}^{N} e^{-\eta L_{i,t-1}} f_{i,t}}{\sum_{j=1}^{N} e^{-\eta L_{j,t-1}}}.$$

The beauty of the exponentially weighted average forecaster is that it only depends on the past performance of the experts, whereas the predictions made using other general potentials depend on the past predictions $\widehat{p}_s, s < t$, as well. Furthermore, the weights that the forecaster assigns to the experts are computable in a simple incremental way: let $w_{1,t-1}, \ldots, w_{N,t-1}$ be the weights used at round t to compute the prediction $\widehat{p}_t = \sum_{i=1}^{N} w_{i,t-1} f_{i,t}$. Then, as one can easily verify,

$$w_{i,t} = \frac{w_{i,t-1} e^{-\eta \ell(f_{i,t}, y_t)}}{\sum_{j=1}^{N} w_{j,t-1} e^{-\eta \ell(f_{j,t-1}, y_t)}}.$$

A simple application of Theorem 2.1 reveals the following performance bound for the exponentially weighted average forecaster.

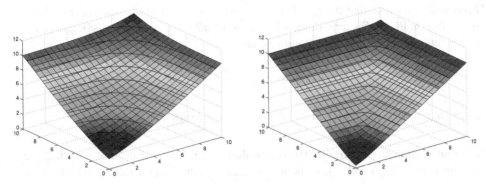

Figure 2.3. Plots of the exponential potential function $\Phi_\eta(\mathbf{u})$ for $N = 2$ experts with $\eta = 0.5$ and $\eta = 2$.

Corollary 2.2. *Assume that the loss function ℓ is convex in its first argument and that it takes values in $[0, 1]$. For any n and $\eta > 0$, and for all $y_1, \ldots, y_n \in \mathcal{Y}$, the regret of the exponentially weighted average forecaster satisfies*

$$\widehat{L}_n - \min_{i=1,\ldots,N} L_{i,n} \leq \frac{\ln N}{\eta} + \frac{n\eta}{2}.$$

Optimizing the upper bound suggests the choice $\eta = \sqrt{2 \ln N / n}$. In this case the upper bound becomes $\sqrt{2n \ln N}$, which is slightly better than the best bound we obtained using $\phi(x) = x_+^p$ with $p = 2 \ln N$. In the next section we improve the bound of Corollary 2.2 by a direct analysis. The disadvantage of the exponential weighting is that optimal tuning of the parameter η requires knowledge of the horizon n in advance. In the next two sections we describe versions of the exponentially weighted average forecaster that do not suffer from this drawback.

Proof of Corollary 2.2. Apply Theorem 2.1 using the exponential potential. Then $\phi(x) = e^{\eta x}$, $\psi(x) = (1/\eta) \ln x$, and

$$\psi' \left(\sum_{i=1}^N \phi(u_i) \right) \sum_{i=1}^N \phi''(u_i) r_{i,t}^2 \leq \eta \max_{i=1,\ldots,N} r_{i,t}^2 \leq \eta.$$

Using $\Phi_\eta(\mathbf{0}) = (\ln N)/\eta$, Theorem 2.1 implies that

$$\max_{i=1,\ldots,N} R_{i,n} \leq \Phi_\eta(\mathbf{R}_n) \leq \frac{\ln N}{\eta} + \frac{n\eta}{2}$$

as desired. ∎

2.2 An Optimal Bound

The purpose of this section is to show that, even for general convex loss functions, the bound of Corollary 2.2 may be improved for the exponentially weighted average forecaster. The following result improves Corollary 2.2 by a constant factor. In Section 3.7 we see that the bound obtained here cannot be improved further.

Theorem 2.2. *Assume that the loss function ℓ is convex in its first argument and that it takes values in $[0, 1]$. For any n and $\eta > 0$, and for all $y_1, \ldots, y_n \in \mathcal{Y}$, the regret of the exponentially weighted average forecaster satisfies*

$$\widehat{L}_n - \min_{i=1,\ldots,N} L_{i,n} \leq \frac{\ln N}{\eta} + \frac{n\eta}{8}.$$

In particular, with $\eta = \sqrt{8 \ln N / n}$, the upper bound becomes $\sqrt{(n/2) \ln N}$.

The proof is similar, in spirit, to that of Corollary 2.2, but now, instead of bounding the evolution of $(1/\eta) \ln \left(\sum_i e^{\eta R_{i,t}} \right)$, we bound the related quantities $(1/\eta) \ln(W_t / W_{t-1})$, where

$$W_t = \sum_{i=1}^{N} w_{i,t} = \sum_{i=1}^{N} e^{-\eta L_{i,t}}$$

for $t \geq 1$, and $W_0 = N$. In the proof we use the following classical inequality due to Hoeffding [161].

Lemma 2.2. *Let X be a random variable with $a \leq X \leq b$. Then for any $s \in \mathbb{R}$,*

$$\ln \mathbb{E} \left[e^{sX} \right] \leq s \, \mathbb{E} X + \frac{s^2 (b-a)^2}{8}.$$

The proof is in Section A.1 of the Appendix.

Proof of Theorem 2.2. First observe that

$$\ln \frac{W_n}{W_0} = \ln \left(\sum_{i=1}^{N} e^{-\eta L_{i,n}} \right) - \ln N$$

$$\geq \ln \left(\max_{i=1,\ldots,N} e^{-\eta L_{i,n}} \right) - \ln N$$

$$= -\eta \min_{i=1,\ldots,N} L_{i,n} - \ln N. \tag{2.1}$$

On the other hand, for each $t = 1, \ldots, n$,

$$\ln \frac{W_t}{W_{t-1}} = \ln \frac{\sum_{i=1}^{N} e^{-\eta \ell(f_{i,t}, y_t)} e^{-\eta L_{i,t-1}}}{\sum_{j=1}^{N} e^{-\eta L_{j,t-1}}}$$

$$= \ln \frac{\sum_{i=1}^{N} w_{i,t-1} e^{-\eta \ell(f_{i,t}, y_t)}}{\sum_{j=1}^{N} w_{j,t-1}}.$$

Now using Lemma 2.2, we observe that the quantity above may be upper bounded by

$$-\eta \frac{\sum_{i=1}^{N} w_{i,t-1} \ell(f_{i,t}, y_t)}{\sum_{j=1}^{N} w_{j,t-1}} + \frac{\eta^2}{8} \leq -\eta \ell \left(\frac{\sum_{i=1}^{N} w_{i,t-1} f_{i,t}}{\sum_{j=1}^{N} w_{j,t-1}}, y_t \right) + \frac{\eta^2}{8}$$

$$= -\eta \ell(\widehat{p}_t, y_t) + \frac{\eta^2}{8},$$

where we used the convexity of the loss function in its first argument and the definition of the exponentially weighted average forecaster. Summing over $t = 1, \ldots, n$, we get

$$\ln \frac{W_n}{W_0} \le -\eta \widehat{L}_n + \frac{\eta^2}{8} n.$$

Combining this with the lower bound (2.1) and solving for $\widehat{L}_n$, we find that

$$\widehat{L}_n \le \min_{i=1,\ldots,N} L_{i,n} + \frac{\ln N}{\eta} + \frac{\eta}{8} n$$

as desired.　■

2.3 Bounds That Hold Uniformly over Time

As we pointed out in the previous section, the exponentially weighted average forecaster has the disadvantage that the regret bound of Corollary 2.2 does not hold uniformly over sequences of any length, but only for sequences of a given length n, where n is the value used to choose the parameter η. To fix this problem one can use the so-called "doubling trick." The idea is to partition time into periods of exponentially increasing lengths. In each period, the weighted average forecaster is used with a parameter η chosen optimally for the length of the interval. When the period ends, the weighted average forecaster is reset and then is started again in the next period with a new value for η. If the doubling trick is used with the exponentially weighted average forecaster, then it achieves, for any sequence $y_1, y_2, \ldots \in \mathcal{Y}$ of outcomes and for any $n \ge 1$,

$$\widehat{L}_n - \min_{i=1,\ldots,N} L_{i,n} \le \frac{\sqrt{2}}{\sqrt{2}-1} \sqrt{\frac{n}{2} \ln N}$$

(see Exercise 2.8). This bound is worse than that of Theorem 2.2 by a factor of $\sqrt{2}/(\sqrt{2}-1)$, which is about 3.41.

Considering that the doubling trick resets the weights of the underlying forecaster after each period, one may wonder whether a better bound could be obtained by a more direct argument. In fact, we can avoid the doubling trick altogether by using the weighted average forecaster with a time-varying potential. That is, we let the parameter η of the exponential potential depend on the round number t. As the best nonuniform bounds for the exponential potential are obtained by choosing $\eta = \sqrt{8(\ln N)/n}$, a natural choice for a time-varying exponential potential is thus $\eta_t = \sqrt{8(\ln N)/t}$. By adapting the approach used to prove Theorem 2.2, we obtain for this choice of η_t a regret bound whose main term is $2\sqrt{(n/2)\ln N}$ and is therefore better than the doubling trick bound. More precisely, we prove the following result.

Theorem 2.3. *Assume that the loss function ℓ is convex in its first argument and takes values in $[0, 1]$. For all $n \ge 1$ and for all $y_1, \ldots, y_n \in \mathcal{Y}$, the regret of the exponentially weighted average forecaster with time-varying parameter $\eta_t = \sqrt{8(\ln N)/t}$ satisfies*

$$\widehat{L}_n - \min_{i=1,\ldots,N} L_{i,n} \le 2\sqrt{\frac{n}{2} \ln N} + \sqrt{\frac{\ln N}{8}}.$$

The exponentially weighted average forecaster with time-varying potential predicts with $\widehat{p}_t = \sum_{i=1}^{N} f_{i,t} w_{i,t-1} / W_{t-1}$, where $W_{t-1} = \sum_{j=1}^{N} w_{j,t-1}$ and $w_{i,t-1} = e^{-\eta_t L_{i,t-1}}$. The potential parameter is chosen as $\eta_t = \sqrt{a(\ln N)/t}$, where $a > 0$ is determined by the analysis. We use $w'_{i,t-1} = e^{-\eta_{t-1} L_{i,t-1}}$ to denote the weight $w_{i,t-1}$, where the parameter η_t is replaced by η_{t-1}. Finally, we use k_t to denote the expert whose loss after the first t rounds is the lowest (ties are broken by choosing the expert with smallest index). That is, $L_{k_t,t} = \min_{i \leq N} L_{i,t}$. In the proof of the theorem, we also make use of the following technical lemma.

Lemma 2.3. *For all $N \geq 2$, for all $\beta \geq \alpha \geq 0$, and for all $d_1, \ldots, d_N \geq 0$ such that $\sum_{i=1}^{N} e^{-\alpha d_i} \geq 1$,*

$$\ln \frac{\sum_{i=1}^{N} e^{-\alpha d_i}}{\sum_{j=1}^{N} e^{-\beta d_j}} \leq \frac{\beta - \alpha}{\alpha} \ln N.$$

Proof.   We begin by writing

$$\ln \frac{\sum_{i=1}^{N} e^{-\alpha d_i}}{\sum_{j=1}^{N} e^{-\beta d_j}} = \ln \frac{\sum_{i=1}^{N} e^{-\alpha d_i}}{\sum_{j=1}^{N} e^{(\alpha-\beta)d_j} e^{-\alpha d_j}} = -\ln \mathbb{E}\left[e^{(\alpha-\beta)D} \right] \leq (\beta - \alpha)\mathbb{E}\, D$$

by Jensen's inequality, where D is a random variable taking value d_i with probability $e^{-\alpha d_i} / \sum_{j=1}^{N} e^{-\alpha d_j}$ for each $i = 1, \ldots, N$. Because D takes at most N distinct values, its entropy $H(D)$ is at most $\ln N$ (see Section A.2 in the Appendix). Therefore,

$$\ln N \geq H(D)$$
$$= \sum_{i=1}^{N} e^{-\alpha d_i} \left(\alpha d_i + \ln \sum_{k=1}^{N} e^{-\alpha d_k} \right) \frac{1}{\sum_{j=1}^{N} e^{-\alpha d_j}}$$
$$= \alpha \mathbb{E}\, D + \ln \sum_{k=1}^{N} e^{-\alpha d_k}$$
$$\geq \alpha \mathbb{E}\, D,$$

where the last inequality holds because $\sum_{i=1}^{N} e^{-\alpha d_i} \geq 1$. Hence $\mathbb{E}\, D \leq (\ln N)/\alpha$. As $\beta > \alpha$ by hypothesis, we can substitute the upper bound on $\mathbb{E}\, D$ in the first derivation above and conclude the proof.   ∎

We are now ready to prove the main theorem.

Proof of Theorem 2.3. As in the proof of Theorem 2.2, we study the evolution of $\ln(W_t/W_{t-1})$. However, here we need to couple this with $\ln(w_{k_{t-1},t-1}/w_{k_t,t})$, including in both terms the time-varying parameter η_t. Keeping track of the currently best expert, k_t is used to lower bound the weight $\ln(w_{k_t,t}/W_t)$. In fact, the weight of the overall best expert (after n rounds) could get arbitrarily small during the prediction process. We thus write the following:

$$\frac{1}{\eta_t} \ln \frac{w_{k_{t-1},t-1}}{W_{t-1}} - \frac{1}{\eta_{t+1}} \ln \frac{w_{k_t,t}}{W_t}$$

$$= \underbrace{\left(\frac{1}{\eta_{t+1}} - \frac{1}{\eta_t} \right) \ln \frac{W_t}{w_{k_t,t}}}_{(A)} + \underbrace{\frac{1}{\eta_t} \ln \frac{w'_{k_t,t}/W'_t}{w_{k_t,t}/W_t}}_{(B)} + \underbrace{\frac{1}{\eta_t} \ln \frac{w_{k_{t-1},t-1}/W_{t-1}}{w'_{k_t,t}/W'_t}}_{(C)}.$$

We now bound separately the three terms on the right-hand side. The term (A) is easily bounded by noting that $\eta_{t+1} < \eta_t$ and using the fact that k_t is the index of the expert with the smallest loss after the first t rounds. Therefore, $w_{k_t,t}/W_t$ must be at least $1/N$. Thus we have

$$(A) = \left(\frac{1}{\eta_{t+1}} - \frac{1}{\eta_t} \right) \ln \frac{W_t}{w_{k_t,t}} \le \left(\frac{1}{\eta_{t+1}} - \frac{1}{\eta_t} \right) \ln N.$$

We proceed to bounding the term (B) as follows:

$$(B) = \frac{1}{\eta_t} \ln \frac{w'_{k_t,t}/W'_t}{w_{k_t,t}/W_t} = \frac{1}{\eta_t} \ln \frac{\sum_{i=1}^{N} e^{-\eta_{t+1}(L_{i,t} - L_{k_t,t})}}{\sum_{j=1}^{N} e^{-\eta_t(L_{j,t} - L_{k_t,t})}}$$

$$\le \frac{\eta_t - \eta_{t+1}}{\eta_t \eta_{t+1}} \ln N = \left(\frac{1}{\eta_{t+1}} - \frac{1}{\eta_t} \right) \ln N,$$

where the inequality is proven by applying Lemma 2.3 with $d_i = L_{i,t} - L_{k_{t+1},t}$. Note that $d_i \ge 0$ because k_t is the index of the expert with the smallest loss after the first t rounds and $\sum_{i=1}^{N} e^{-\eta_{t+1} d_i} \ge 1$ as for $i = k_{t+1}$ we have $d_i = 0$. The term (C) is first split as follows:

$$(C) = \frac{1}{\eta_t} \ln \frac{w_{k_{t-1},t-1}/W_{t-1}}{w'_{k_t,t}/W'_t} = \frac{1}{\eta_t} \ln \frac{w_{k_{t-1},t-1}}{w'_{k_t,t}} + \frac{1}{\eta_t} \ln \frac{W'_t}{W_{t-1}}.$$

We treat separately each one of the two subterms on the right-hand side. For the first one, we have

$$\frac{1}{\eta_t} \ln \frac{w_{k_{t-1},t-1}}{w'_{k_t,t}} = \frac{1}{\eta_t} \ln \frac{e^{-\eta_t L_{k_{t-1},t-1}}}{e^{-\eta_t L_{k_t,t}}} = L_{k_t,t} - L_{k_{t-1},t-1}.$$

For the second subterm, we proceed similarly to the proof of Theorem 2.2 by applying Hoeffding's bound (Lemma 2.2) to the random variable Z that takes the value $\ell(f_{i,t}, y_t)$ with probability $w_{i,t-1}/W_{t-1}$ for each $i = 1, \ldots, N$:

$$\frac{1}{\eta_t} \ln \frac{W'_t}{W_{t-1}} = \frac{1}{\eta_t} \ln \sum_{i=1}^{N} \frac{w_{i,t-1}}{W_{t-1}} e^{-\eta_t \ell(f_{i,t}, y_t)}$$

$$\le -\sum_{i=1}^{N} \frac{w_{i,t-1}}{W_{t-1}} \ell(f_{i,t}, y_t) + \frac{\eta_t}{8}$$

$$\le -\ell(\widehat{p}_t, y_t) + \frac{\eta_t}{8},$$

where in the last step we used the convexity of the loss ℓ. Finally, we substitute back in the main equation the bounds on the first two terms (A) and (B), and the bounds on the two subterms of the term (C). Solving for $\ell(\widehat{p}_t, y_t)$, we obtain

$$
\ell(\widehat{p}_t, y_t) \leq \left(L_{k_t,t} - L_{k_{t-1},t-1}\right) + \frac{\sqrt{a \ln N}}{8} \frac{1}{\sqrt{t}}
$$

$$
+ \frac{1}{\eta_{t+1}} \ln \frac{w_{k_t,t}}{W_t} - \frac{1}{\eta_t} \ln \frac{w_{k_{t-1},t-1}}{W_{t-1}}
$$

$$
+ 2 \left(\frac{1}{\eta_{t+1}} - \frac{1}{\eta_t} \right) \ln N.
$$

We apply the above inequality to each $t = 1, \dots, n$ and sum up using $\sum_{t=1}^{n} \ell(\widehat{p}_t, y_t) = \widehat{L}_n$, $\sum_{t=1}^{n} \left(L_{k_t,t} - L_{k_{t-1},t-1}\right) = \min_{i=1,\dots,N} L_{i,n}$, $\sum_{t=1}^{n} 1/\sqrt{t} \leq 2\sqrt{n}$, and

$$
\sum_{t=1}^{n} \left(\frac{1}{\eta_{t+1}} \ln \frac{w_{k_t,t}}{W_t} - \frac{1}{\eta_t} \ln \frac{w_{k_{t-1},t-1}}{W_{t-1}} \right) \leq -\frac{1}{\eta_1} \ln \frac{w_{k_0,0}}{W_0} = \sqrt{\frac{\ln N}{a}}
$$

$$
\sum_{t=1}^{n} \left(\frac{1}{\eta_{t+1}} - \frac{1}{\eta_t} \right) = \sqrt{\frac{n+1}{a(\ln N)}} - \sqrt{\frac{1}{a(\ln N)}}.
$$

Thus, we can write the bound

$$
\widehat{L}_n \leq \min_{i=1,\dots,N} L_{i,n} + \frac{\sqrt{an \ln N}}{4} + 2\sqrt{\frac{(n+1)\ln N}{a}} - \sqrt{\frac{\ln N}{a}}.
$$

Finally, by overapproximating and choosing $a = 8$ to trade off the two main terms, we get

$$
\widehat{L}_n \leq \min_{i=1,\dots,N} L_{i,n} + 2\sqrt{\frac{n}{2} \ln N} + \sqrt{\frac{\ln N}{8}}
$$

as desired. ∎

2.4 An Improvement for Small Losses

The regret bound for the exponentially weighted average forecaster shown in Theorem 2.2 may be improved significantly whenever it is known beforehand that the cumulative loss of the best expert will be small. In some cases, as we will see, this improvement may even be achieved without any prior knowledge.

To understand why one can hope for better bounds for the regret when the cumulative loss of the best expert is small, recall the simple example described in the introduction when $\mathcal{Y} = \mathcal{D} = \{0, 1\}$ and $\ell(\widehat{p}, y) = |\widehat{p} - y| \in \{0, 1\}$ (this example violates our assumption that $\mathcal{D}$ is a convex set but helps understand the basic phenomenon). If the forecaster knows in advance that one of the N experts will suffer zero loss, that is, $\min_{i=1,\dots,N} L_{i,n} = 0$, then he may predict using the following simple "majority vote." At time $t = 1$ predict $\widehat{p}_1 = 0$ if and only if at least half of the N experts predict 0. After the first bit y_1 is revealed, discard all experts with $f_{i,1} \neq y_1$. At time $t = 2$ predict $\widehat{p}_2 = 0$ if and only if at least half of the N remaining experts predict 0, discard all incorrectly predicting experts after y_2 is revealed, and so on. Hence, each time the forecaster makes a mistake, at least half of the surviving experts are discarded (because the forecaster always votes according to the majority of the remaining experts). If only one expert remains, the forecaster does not make any further mistake. Thus, the total number of mistakes of the forecaster (which, in this case, coincides with his regret) is at most $\lfloor \log_2 N \rfloor$.

In this section we show that regret bounds of the form $O(\ln N)$ are possible for all bounded and convex losses on convex decision spaces whenever the forecaster is given the information that the best expert will suffer no loss. Note that such bounds are significantly better than $\sqrt{(n/2)\ln N}$, which holds independently of the loss of the best expert.

For simplicity, we write $L_n^* = \min_{i=1,\dots,N} L_{i,n}$. We now show that whenever L_n^* is known beforehand, the parameter η of the exponentially weighted average forecaster can be chosen so that his regret is bounded by $\sqrt{2L_n^* \ln N} + \ln N$, which equals to $\ln N$ when $L_n^* = 0$ and is of order $\sqrt{n \ln N}$ when L_n^* is of order n. Our main tool is the following refinement of Theorem 2.2.

Theorem 2.4. *Assume that the loss function ℓ is convex in its first argument and that it takes values in $[0, 1]$. Then for any $\eta > 0$ the regret of the exponentially weighted average forecaster satisfies*

$$\widehat{L}_n \leq \frac{\eta L_n^* + \ln N}{1 - e^{-\eta}}.$$

It is easy to see that, in some cases, an uninformed choice of η can still lead to a good regret bound.

Corollary 2.3. *Assume that the exponentially weighted average forecaster is used with $\eta = 1$. Then, under the conditions of Theorem 2.4,*

$$\widehat{L}_n \leq \frac{e}{e-1}\left(L_n^* + \ln N\right).$$

This bound is much better than the general bound of Theorem 2.2 if $L_n^* \ll \sqrt{n}$, but it may be much worse otherwise.

We now derive a new bound by tuning η in Theorem 2.4 in terms of the total loss L_n^* of the best expert.

Corollary 2.4. *Assume the exponentially weighted average forecaster is used with $\eta = \ln\left(1 + \sqrt{(2\ln N)/L_n^*}\right)$, where $L_n^* > 0$ is supposed to be known in advance. Then, under the conditions of Theorem 2.4,*

$$\widehat{L}_n - L_n^* \leq \sqrt{2L_n^* \ln N} + \ln N.$$

Proof. Using Theorem 2.4, we just need to show that, for our choice of η,

$$\frac{\ln N + \eta L_n^*}{1 - e^{-\eta}} \leq L_n^* + \ln N + \sqrt{2L_n^* \ln N}. \qquad (2.2)$$

We start from the elementary inequality $(e^{\eta} - e^{-\eta})/2 = \sinh(\eta) \geq \eta$, which holds for all $\eta \geq 0$. Replacing the η in the numerator of the left-hand side of (2.2) with this upper bound, we find that (2.2) is implied by

$$\frac{\ln N}{1 - e^{-\eta}} + \frac{1 + e^{-\eta}}{2e^{-\eta}}L_n^* \leq L_n^* + \ln N + \sqrt{2L_n^* \ln N}.$$

The proof is concluded by noting that the above inequality holds with equality for our choice of η. ∎

Of course, the quantity L_n^* is only available after the nth round of prediction. The lack of this information may be compensated by letting η change according to the loss of the currently best expert, similarly to the way shown in Section 2.3 (see Exercise 2.10). The regret bound that is obtainable via this approach is of the form $2\sqrt{2L_n^* \ln N} + c \ln N$, where $c > 1$ is a constant. Note that, similarly to Theorem 2.3, the use of a time-varying parameter η_t leads to a bound whose leading term is twice the one obtained when η is fixed and chosen optimally on the basis of either the horizon n (as in Theorem 2.2) or the loss L_n^* of the best expert (as in Corollary 2.4).

Proof of Theorem 2.4. The proof is a simple modification of that of Theorem 2.2. The only difference is that Hoeffding's inequality is now replaced by Lemma A.3 (see the Appendix). Recall from the proof of Theorem 2.2 that

$$-\eta L_n^* - \ln N \leq \ln \frac{W_n}{W_0} = \sum_{t=1}^{n} \ln \frac{W_t}{W_{t-1}} = \sum_{t=1}^{n} \ln \frac{\sum_{i=1}^{N} w_{i,t-1} e^{-\eta \ell(f_{i,t}, y_t)}}{\sum_{j=1}^{N} w_{j,t-1}}.$$

We apply Lemma A.3 to the random variable X_t that takes value $\ell(f_{i,t}, y_t)$ with probability $w_{i,t-1}/W_{t-1}$ for each $i = 1, \ldots, N$. Note that by convexity of the loss function and Jensen's inequality, $\mathbb{E} X_t \geq \ell(\widehat{p}_t, y_t)$ and therefore, by Lemma A.3,

$$\ln \frac{\sum_{i=1}^{N} w_{i,t-1} e^{-\eta \ell(f_{i,t}, y_t)}}{\sum_{j=1}^{N} w_{j,t-1}} = \ln \mathbb{E}\left[e^{-\eta X_t}\right] \leq \left(e^{-\eta} - 1\right) \mathbb{E} X_t \leq \left(e^{-\eta} - 1\right) \ell(\widehat{p}_t, y_t).$$

Thus,

$$-\eta L_n^* - \ln N \leq \sum_{t=1}^{n} \ln \frac{\sum_{i=1}^{N} w_{i,t-1} e^{-\eta \ell(f_{i,t}, y_t)}}{\sum_{j=1}^{N} w_{j,t-1}} \leq \left(e^{-\eta} - 1\right) \widehat{L}_n.$$

Solving for $\widehat{L}_n$ yields the result. ∎

2.5 Forecasters Using the Gradient of the Loss

Consider again the exponentially weighted average forecaster whose predictions are defined by

$$\widehat{p}_t = \frac{\sum_{i=1}^{N} w_{i,t-1} f_{i,t}}{\sum_{j=1}^{N} w_{j,t-1}},$$

where the weight $w_{i,t-1}$ for expert i at round t is defined by $w_{i,t-1} = e^{-\eta L_{i,t-1}}$. In this section we introduce and analyze a different exponentially weighted average forecaster in which the cumulative loss $L_{i,t-1}$ appearing at the exponent of $w_{i,t-1}$ is replaced by the gradient of the loss summed up to time $t - 1$. This new class of forecasters will be generalized in Chapter 11, where we also provide extensive analysis and motivation.

Recall that the decision space $\mathcal{D}$ is a convex subset of a linear space. Throughout this section, we also assume that $\mathcal{D}$ is finite dimensional, though this assumption can be relaxed easily. If ℓ is differentiable, we use $\nabla \ell(\widehat{p}, y)$ to denote its gradient with respect to the first argument $\widehat{p} \in \mathcal{D}$.

Define the *gradient-based exponentially weighted average forecaster* by

$$\widehat{p}_t = \frac{\sum_{i=1}^{N} \exp\left(-\eta \sum_{s=1}^{t-1} \nabla \ell(\widehat{p}_s, y_s) \cdot f_{i,s}\right) f_{i,t}}{\sum_{j=1}^{N} \exp\left(-\eta \sum_{s=1}^{t-1} \nabla \ell(\widehat{p}_s, y_s) \cdot f_{j,s}\right)}.$$

To understand the intuition behind this predictor, note that the weight assigned to expert i is small if the sum of the inner products $\nabla \ell(\widehat{p}_s, y_s) \cdot f_{i,s}$ has been large in the past. This inner product is large if expert i's advice $f_{i,s}$ points in the direction of the largest increase of the loss function. Such a large value means that having assigned a little bit larger weight to this expert would have increased the loss suffered at time s. According to the philosophy of the gradient-based exponentially weighted average forecaster, the weight of such an expert has to be decreased.

The predictions of this forecaster are, of course, generally different from those of the standard exponentially weighted average forecaster. However, note that in the special case of binary prediction with absolute loss (i.e., if $\mathcal{D} = [0, 1]$, $\mathcal{Y} = \{0, 1\}$ and $\ell(x, y) = |x - y|$), a setup that we study in detail in Chapter 8, the predictions of the two forecasters are identical (see the exercises).

We now show that, under suitable conditions on the norm of the gradient of the loss, the regret of the new forecaster can be bounded by the same quantity that was used to bound the regret of the standard exponentially weighted average forecaster in Corollary 2.2.

Corollary 2.5. *Assume that the decision space $\mathcal{D}$ is a convex subset of the euclidean unit ball $\{q \in \mathbb{R}^d : \|q\| \leq 1\}$, the loss function ℓ is convex in its first argument and that its gradient $\nabla \ell$ exists and satisfies $\|\nabla \ell\| \leq 1$. For any n and $\eta > 0$, and for all $y_1, \ldots, y_n \in \mathcal{Y}$, the regret of the gradient-based exponentially weighted average forecaster satisfies*

$$\widehat{L}_n - \min_{i=1,\ldots,N} L_{i,n} \leq \frac{\ln N}{\eta} + \frac{n\eta}{2}.$$

Proof. The weight vector $\mathbf{w}_{t-1} = (w_{1,t-1}, \ldots, w_{N,t-1})$ used by this forecaster has components

$$w_{i,t-1} = \exp\left(-\eta \sum_{s=1}^{t-1} \nabla \ell(\widehat{p}_s, y_s) \cdot f_{i,s}\right).$$

Observe that these weights correspond to the exponentially weighted average forecaster based on the loss function ℓ', defined at time t by

$$\ell'(q, y_t) = q \cdot \nabla \ell(\widehat{p}_t, y_t), \quad q \in \mathcal{D}.$$

By assumption, ℓ' takes values in $[-1, 1]$. Applying Theorem 2.2 after rescaling ℓ' in $[0, 1]$ (see Section 2.6), we get

$$\max_{i=1,\ldots,N} \sum_{i=1}^{n} (\widehat{p}_t - f_{i,t}) \cdot \nabla \ell(\widehat{p}_t, y_t) = \sum_{t=1}^{n} \ell'(\widehat{p}_t, y_t) - \min_{i=1,\ldots,N} \sum_{t=1}^{n} \ell'(f_{i,t}, y_t)$$

$$\leq \frac{\ln N}{\eta} + \frac{n\eta}{2}.$$

The proof is completed by expanding $\ell(f_{i,t}, y_t)$ around $\ell(\widehat{p}_t, y_t)$ as follows:

$$\ell(\widehat{p}_t, y_t) - \ell(f_{i,t}, y_t) \leq (\widehat{p}_t - f_{i,t}) \cdot \nabla \ell(\widehat{p}_t, y_t),$$

which implies that

$$\widehat{L}_n - \min_{i=1,\dots,N} L_{i,n} \leq \sum_{t=1}^{n} \ell'(\widehat{p}_t, y_t) - \min_{i=1,\dots,N} \sum_{t=1}^{n} \ell'(f_{i,t}, y_t). \quad \blacksquare$$

2.6 Scaled Losses and Signed Games

Up to this point we have always assumed that the range of the loss function ℓ is the unit interval $[0, 1]$. We now investigate how scalings and translations of this range affect forecasting strategies and their performance.

Consider first the case of a loss function $\ell \in [0, M]$. If M is known, we can run the weighted average forecaster on the scaled losses ℓ/M and apply without any modification the analysis developed for the $[0, 1]$ case. For instance, in the case of the exponentially weighted average forecaster, Corollary 2.4, applied to these scaled losses, yields the regret bound

$$\widehat{L}_n - L_n^* \leq \sqrt{2 L_n^* M \ln N} + M \ln N.$$

The additive term $M \ln N$ is necessary. Indeed, if ℓ is such that for all $p \in \mathcal{D}$ there exist $p' \in \mathcal{D}$ and $y \in \mathcal{Y}$ such that $\ell(p, y) = M$ and $\ell(p', y) = 0$, then the expert advice can be chosen so that any forecaster incurs a cumulative loss of at least $M \log N$ on some outcome sequence with $L_n^* = 0$.

Consider now the translated range $[-M, 0]$. If we interpret negative losses as gains, we may introduce the regret $G_n^* - \widehat{G}_n$ measuring the difference between the cumulative gain $G_n^* = -L_n^* = \max_{i=1,\dots,N}(-L_{i,n})$ of the best expert and the cumulative gain $\widehat{G}_n = -\widehat{L}_n$ of the forecaster. As before, if M is known we can run the weighted average forecaster on the scaled gains $(-\ell)/M$ and apply the analysis developed for $[0, 1]$-valued loss functions. Adapting Corollary 2.4 we get a bound of the form

$$G_n^* - \widehat{G}_n \leq \sqrt{2 G_n^* M \ln N} + M \ln N.$$

Note that the regret now scales with the largest cumulative gain G_n^*.

We now turn to the general case in which the forecasters are scored using a generic *payoff function* $h : \mathcal{D} \times \mathcal{Y} \to \mathbb{R}$, concave in its first argument. The goal of the forecaster is to maximize his cumulative payoff. The corresponding regret is defined by

$$\max_{i=1,\dots,N} \sum_{t=1}^{n} h(f_{i,t}, y_t) - \sum_{t=1}^{n} h(\widehat{p}_t, y_t) = H_n^* - \widehat{H}_n.$$

If the payoff function h has range $[0, M]$, then it is a gain function and the forecaster plays a *gain game*. Similarly, if h has range in $[-M, 0]$, then it is the negative of a loss function and the forecaster plays a *loss game*. Finally, if the range of h includes a neighborhood of 0, then the game played by the forecaster is a *signed game*.

Translated to this terminology, the arguments proposed at the beginning of this section say that in any unsigned game (i.e., any loss game $[-M, 0]$ or gain game $[0, M]$), rescaling of the payoffs yields a regret bound of order $\sqrt{|H_n^*|M \ln N}$ whenever M is known. In the case of signed games, however, scaling is not sufficient. Indeed, if $h \in [-M, M]$, then the reduction to the [0, 1] case is obtained by the linear transformation $h \mapsto (h + M)/(2M)$. Applying this to the analysis leading to Corollary 2.4, we get the regret bound

$$H_n^* - \widehat{H}_n \le \sqrt{4(H_n^* + Mn)(M \ln N)} + 2M \ln N = O\left(M\sqrt{n \ln N}\right).$$

This shows that, for signed games, reducing to the [0, 1] case might not be the best thing to do. Ideally, we would like to replace the factor n in the leading term with something like $|h(f_{i,1}, y_1)| + \cdots + |h(f_{i,n}, y_n)|$ for an arbitrary expert i. In the next sections we show that, in certain cases, we can do even better than that.

2.7 The Multilinear Forecaster

Potential functions offer a convenient tool to derive weighted average forecasters. However, good forecasters for signed games can also be designed without using potentials, as shown in this section.

Fix a signed game with payoff function $h : \mathcal{D} \times \mathcal{Y} \to \mathbb{R}$, and consider the weighted average forecaster that predicts, at time t,

$$\widehat{p}_t = \frac{\sum_{i=1}^N w_{i,t-1} f_{i,t}}{W_{t-1}},$$

where $W_{t-1} = \sum_{j=1}^N w_{j,t-1}$. The weights $w_{i,t-1}$ of this forecaster are recursively defined as follows

$$w_{i,t} = \begin{cases} 1 & \text{if } t = 0 \\ w_{i,t-1}\big(1 + \eta h(f_{i,t}, y_t)\big) & \text{otherwise,} \end{cases}$$

where $\eta > 0$ is a parameter of the forecaster. Because $w_{i,t}$ is a multilinear form of the payoffs, we call this the *multilinear forecaster*.

Note that the weights $w_{1,t}, \ldots, w_{N,t}$ cannot be expressed as functions of the regret $\mathbf{R}_t$ of components $H_{i,n} - \widehat{H}_n$. On the other hand, since $(1 + \eta h) \approx e^{\eta h}$, the regret of the multilinear forecaster can be bounded via a technique similar to the one used in the proof of Theorem 2.2 for the exponentially weighted average forecaster. We just need the following simple lemma (proof is left as exercise).

Lemma 2.4. *For all $z \ge -1/2$, $\ln(1 + z) \ge z - z^2$.*

The next result shows that the regret of the multilinear forecaster is naturally expressed in terms of the squared sum of the payoffs of an arbitrary expert.

Theorem 2.5. *Assume that the payoff function h is concave in its first argument and satisfies $h \in [-M, \infty)$. For any n and $0 < \eta < 1/(2M)$, and for all $y_1, \ldots, y_n \in \mathcal{Y}$, the regret of the multilinear forecaster satisfies*

$$H_{i,n} - \widehat{H}_n \le \frac{\ln N}{\eta} + \eta \sum_{t=1}^n h(f_{i,t}, y_t)^2 \quad \text{for each } i = 1, \ldots, N.$$

Proof. For any $i = 1, \ldots, N$, note that $h(f_{i,t}, y_t) \geq -M$ and $\eta \leq 1/(2M)$ imply that $\eta h(f_{i,t}, y_t) \geq -1/2$. Hence, we can apply Lemma 2.4 to $\eta h(f_{i,t}, y_t)$ and get

$$\ln \frac{W_n}{W_0} = -\ln N + \ln \prod_{t=1}^{n} \left(1 + \eta h(f_{i,t}, y_t)\right)$$

$$= -\ln N + \sum_{t=1}^{n} \ln\left(1 + \eta h(f_{i,t}, y_t)\right)$$

$$\geq -\ln N + \sum_{t=1}^{n} \left(\eta h(f_{i,t}, y_t) - \eta^2 h(f_{i,t}, y_t)^2\right)$$

$$= -\ln N + \eta H_{i,n} - \eta^2 \sum_{t=1}^{n} h(f_{i,t}, y_t)^2.$$

On the other hand,

$$\ln \frac{W_n}{W_0} = \sum_{t=1}^{n} \ln \frac{W_t}{W_{t-1}}$$

$$= \sum_{t=1}^{n} \ln \left(\sum_{i=1}^{N} \widehat{p}_{i,t} \left(1 + \eta h(f_{i,t}, y_t)\right)\right)$$

$$\leq \eta \sum_{t=1}^{n} \sum_{i=1}^{N} \widehat{p}_{i,t} \, h(f_{i,t}, y_t) \quad (\text{since } \ln(1 + x) \leq x \text{ for } x > -1)$$

$$\leq \eta \widehat{H}_n \quad (\text{since } h(\cdot, y) \text{ is concave}).$$

Combining the upper and lower bounds of $\ln(W_n/W_0)$, and dividing by $\eta > 0$, we get the claimed bound. ∎

Let $Q_n^* = h(f_{k,1}, y_1)^2 + \cdots + h(f_{k,n}, y_n)^2$ where k is such that $H_{k,n} = H_n^* = \max_{i=1,\ldots,N} H_{i,n}$. If η is chosen using Q_n^*, then Theorem 2.5 directly implies the following.

Corollary 2.6. *Assume the multilinear forecaster is run with*

$$\eta = \min\left\{\frac{1}{2M}, \sqrt{\frac{\ln N}{Q_n^*}}\right\},$$

where $Q_n^* > 0$ is supposed to be known in advance. Then, under the conditions of Theorem 2.5,

$$H_n^* - \widehat{H} \leq 2\sqrt{Q_n^* \ln N} + 4M \ln N.$$

To appreciate this result, consider a loss game with $h \in [-M, 0]$ and let $L_n^* = -\max_i H_{i,n}$. As $Q_n^* \leq ML_n^*$, the performance guarantee of the multilinear forecaster is at most a factor of $\sqrt{2}$ larger than that of the exponentially weighted average forecaster, whose regret in this case has the leading term $\sqrt{2L_n^* M \ln N}$ (see Section 2.4). However, in some cases Q_n^* may be significantly smaller than ML_n^*, so that the bound of Corollary 2.6 presents a real improvement. In Section 2.8, we show that a more careful analysis of the exponentially weighted average forecaster yields similar (though noncomparable) second-order regret bounds.

It is still an open problem to obtain regret bounds of order $\sqrt{Q_n^* \ln N}$ without exploiting some prior knowledge on the sequence $y_1, \ldots, y_n$ (see Exercise 2.14). In fact, the analysis of adaptive tuning techniques, such as the doubling trick or the time-varying η, rely on the monotonicity of the quantity whose evolution determines the tuning strategy. On the other hand, the sequence $Q_1^*, Q_2^*, \ldots$ is not necessarily monotone as Q_t^* and Q_{t+1}^* cannot generally be related when the experts achieving the largest cumulative payoffs at rounds t and $t+1$ are different.

2.8 The Exponential Forecaster for Signed Games

A slight modification of our previous analysis is sufficient to show that the exponentially weighted average forecaster also is able to achieve a small regret in signed games. Like the multilinear forecaster of Section 2.7, this new bound is expressed in terms of sums of quadratic terms that are related to the variance of the experts' losses with respect to the distribution induced by the forecaster's weights. Furthermore, the use of a time-varying potential allows us to dispense with the need of any preliminary knowledge of the best cumulative payoff H_n^*.

We start by redefining, for the setup where payoff functions are used, the exponentially weighted average forecaster with time-varying potential introduced in Section 2.3. Given a payoff function h, this forecaster predicts with $\widehat{p}_t = \sum_{i=1}^N f_{i,t} w_{i,t-1} / W_{t-1}$, where $W_{t-1} = \sum_{j=1}^N w_{j,t-1}$, $w_{i,t-1} = e^{\eta_t H_{i,t-1}}$, $H_{i,t-1} = h(f_{i,1}, y_1) + \cdots + h(f_{i,t-1}, y_{t-1})$, and we assume that the sequence $\eta_1, \eta_2, \ldots$ of parameters is positive. Note that the value of η_1 is immaterial because $H_{i,0} = 0$ for all i.

Let $X_1, X_2, \ldots$ be random variables such that $X_t = h(f_{i,t}, y_t)$ with probability $w_{i,t-1}/W_{t-1}$ for all i and t. The next result, whose proof is left as an exercise, bounds the regret of the exponential forecaster for any nonincreasing sequence of potential parameters in terms of the process $X_1, \ldots, X_n$. Note that this lemma does not assume any boundedness condition on the payoff function.

Lemma 2.5. *Let h be a payoff function concave in its first argument. The exponentially weighted average forecaster, run with any nonincreasing sequence $\eta_1, \eta_2, \ldots$ of parameters satisfies, for any $n \geq 1$ and for any sequence $y_1, \ldots, y_n$ of outcomes,*

$$H_n^* - \widehat{H}_n \leq \left(\frac{2}{\eta_{n+1}} - \frac{1}{\eta_1} \right) \ln N + \sum_{t=1}^n \frac{1}{\eta_t} \ln \mathbb{E} \left[e^{\eta_t (X_t - \mathbb{E} X_t)} \right].$$

Let

$$V_t = \sum_{s=1}^t \mathrm{var}(X_s) = \sum_{s=1}^t \mathbb{E} \left[(X_s - \mathbb{E} X_s)^2 \right].$$

Our next result shows that, with an appropriate choice of the sequence η_t, the regret of the exponential forecaster at time n is at most of order $\sqrt{V_n \ln N}$. Note, however, that the bound is not in closed form as V_n depends on the forecaster's weights $w_{i,t}$ for all i and t.

Theorem 2.6. *Let h be a $[-M, M]$-valued payoff function concave in its first argument. Suppose the exponentially weighted average forecaster is run with*

$$\eta_t = \min \left\{ \frac{1}{2M}, \sqrt{\frac{2(\sqrt{2} - 1)}{e - 2}} \sqrt{\frac{\ln N}{V_{t-1}}} \right\}, \qquad t = 2, 3, \ldots.$$

Then, for any $n \geq 1$ and for any sequence $y_1, \ldots, y_n$ of outcomes,

$$H_n^* - \widehat{H}_n \leq 4\sqrt{V_n \ln N} + 4M \ln N + (e - 2)M.$$

Proof. For brevity, write

$$C = \sqrt{\frac{2(\sqrt{2} - 1)}{e - 2}}.$$

We start by applying Lemma 2.5 (with, say, $\eta_1 = \eta_2$)

$$H_n^* - \widehat{H}_n \leq \left(\frac{2}{\eta_{n+1}} - \frac{1}{\eta_1} \right) \ln N + \sum_{t=1}^{n} \frac{1}{\eta_t} \ln \mathbb{E} \left[e^{\eta_t(X_t - \mathbb{E} X_t)} \right]$$

$$\leq 2 \max \left\{ 2M \ln N, \frac{1}{C} \sqrt{V_n \ln N} \right\} + \sum_{t=1}^{n} \frac{1}{\eta_t} \ln \mathbb{E} \left[e^{\eta_t(X_t - \mathbb{E} X_t)} \right].$$

Since $\eta_t \leq 1/(2M)$, $\eta_t(X_t - \mathbb{E} X_t) \leq 1$ and we may apply the inequality $e^x \leq 1 + x + (e - 2)x^2$ for all $x \leq 1$. We thus find that

$$H_n^* - \widehat{H}_n \leq 2 \max \left\{ 2M \ln N, \frac{1}{C} \sqrt{V_n \ln N} \right\} + (e - 2) \sum_{t=1}^{n} \eta_t \, \text{var}(X_t).$$

Now denote by T the first time step t when $V_t > M^2$. Using $\eta_t \leq 1/(2M)$ for all t and $V_T \leq 2M^2$, we get

$$\sum_{t=1}^{n} \eta_t \, \text{var}(X_t) \leq M + \sum_{t=T+1}^{n} \eta_t \, \text{var}(X_t).$$

We bound the sum using $\eta_t \leq C\sqrt{(\ln N)/V_{t-1}}$ for $t \geq 2$ (note that, for $t > T$, $V_{t-1} \geq V_T > M^2 > 0$). This yields

$$\sum_{t=T+1}^{n} \eta_t \, \text{var}(X_t) \leq C\sqrt{\ln N} \sum_{t=T+1}^{n} \frac{V_t - V_{t-1}}{\sqrt{V_{t-1}}}.$$

Let $v_t = \text{var}(X_t) = V_t - V_{t-1}$. Since $V_t \leq V_{t-1} + M^2$ and $V_{t-1} \geq M^2$, we have

$$\frac{v_t}{\sqrt{V_{t-1}}} = \frac{\sqrt{V_t} + \sqrt{V_{t-1}}}{\sqrt{V_{t-1}}} \left(\sqrt{V_t} - \sqrt{V_{t-1}} \right) \leq (\sqrt{2} + 1) \left(\sqrt{V_t} - \sqrt{V_{t-1}} \right).$$

Therefore,

$$\sum_{t=T+1}^{n} \eta_t \text{var}(X_t) \leq \frac{C\sqrt{\ln N}}{\sqrt{2} - 1} \left(\sqrt{V_n} - \sqrt{V_T} \right) \leq \frac{C}{\sqrt{2} - 1} \sqrt{V_n \ln N}.$$

Substituting our choice of C and performing trivial overapproximations concludes the proof. ∎

Remark 2.2. The analyses proposed by Theorem 2.5, Corollary 2.6, and Theorem 2.6 show that the multilinear forecaster and the exponentially weighted average forecaster work, with no need of translating payoffs, in both unsigned and signed games. In addition, the regret bounds shown in these results are potentially much better than the invariant bound $M\sqrt{n \ln N}$ obtained via the explicit payoff transformation $h \mapsto (h + M)/(2M)$ from signed to unsigned games (see Section 2.6). However, none of these bounds applies to the case when no preliminary information is available on the sequence of observed payoffs.

The main term of the bound stated in Theorem 2.6 contains V_n. This quantity is smaller than all quantities of the form

$$\sum_{t=1}^{n} \sum_{i=1}^{N} \frac{w_{i,t-1}}{W_{t-1}} \left(h(f_{i,t}, y_t) - \mu_t \right)^2$$

where $\mu_1, \mu_2, \ldots$ is any sequence of real numbers that may be chosen in *hindsight*, as it is not required for the definition of the forecaster. This gives us a whole family of upper bounds, and we may choose for the analysis the most convenient sequence of μ_t.

To provide a concrete example, denote the effective range of the payoffs at time t by $R_t = \max_{i=1,\ldots,N} h(f_{i,t}, y_t) - \min_{j=1,\ldots,N} h(f_{j,t}, y_t)$ and consider the choice $\mu_t = \min_{j=1,\ldots,N} h(f_{j,t}, y_t) + R_t/2$.

Corollary 2.7. *Under the same assumptions as in Theorem 2.6,*

$$H_n^* - \widehat{H}_n \leq 2 \sqrt{(\ln N) \sum_{t=1}^{n} R_t^2 + 4M \ln N + (e - 2)M}.$$

In a loss game, where h has the range $[-M, 0]$, Corollary 2.7 states that the regret is bounded by a quantity dominated by the term $2M\sqrt{n \ln N}$. A comparison with the bound of Theorem 2.3 shows that we have only lost a factor $\sqrt{2}$ to obtain a much more general result.

2.9 Simulatable Experts

So far, we have viewed experts as unspecified entities generating, at each round t, an advice to which the forecaster has access. A different setup is when the experts themselves are accessible to the forecaster, who can make arbitrary experiments to reveal their future behavior. In this scenario we may define an expert E using a sequence of functions $f_{E,t} : \mathcal{Y}^{t-1} \to \mathcal{D}$, $t = 1, 2, \ldots$ such that, at every time instant t, the expert predicts according to $f_{E,t}(y^{t-1})$. We also assume that the forecaster has access to these functions and therefore can, at any moment, hypothesize future outcomes and compute all experts' future predictions for that specific sequence of outcomes. Thus, the forecaster can "simulate" the experts' future reactions, and we call such experts *simulatable*. For example, a simulatable expert for a prediction problem where $\mathcal{D} = \mathcal{Y}$ is the expert E such that $f_{E,t}(y^{t-1}) = (y_1 + \cdots + y_{t-1})/(t-1)$. Note that we have assumed that at time t the prediction of a simulatable expert only depends on the sequence y^{t-1} of past observed outcomes. This is not true for the more general type of experts, whose advice might depend on arbitrary sources of information also hidden from the forecaster. More importantly, while the prediction of a general expert, at time t, may depend on the past moves $\widehat{p}_1, \ldots, \widehat{p}_{t-1}$ of the forecaster (just recall the protocol of the game of prediction with expert advice), the values a simulatable expert outputs only depend on the past sequence of outcomes. Because here we are not concerned with computational issues, we allow $f_{E,t}$ to be an arbitrary function of y^{t-1} and assume that the forecaster may always compute such a function.

A special type of simulatable expert is a *static* expert. An expert E is static when its predictions $f_{E,t}$ only depend on the round index t and not on y^{t-1}. In other words, the functions $f_{E,t}$ are all constant valued. Thus, a static expert E is completely described by the sequence $f_{E,1}, f_{E,2}, \ldots$ of its predictions at each round t. This sequence is fixed irrespective of the actual observed outcomes. For this reason we use $f = (f_1, f_2, \ldots)$ to denote an arbitrary static expert. Abusing notation, we use f also to denote simulatable experts.

Simulatable and static experts provide the forecaster with additional power. It is then interesting to consider whether this additional power could be exploited to reduce the forecaster's regret. This is investigated in depth for specific loss functions in Chapters 8 and 9.

2.10   Minimax Regret

In the model of prediction with expert advice, the best regret bound obtained so far, which holds for all $[0, 1]$-valued convex losses, is $\sqrt{(n/2)\ln N}$. This is achieved (for any fixed $n \geq 1$) by the exponentially weighted average forecaster. Is this the best possible uniform bound? Which type of forecaster achieves the best regret bound for each specific loss? To address these questions in a rigorous way we introduce the notion of minimax regret. Fix a loss function ℓ and consider N general experts. Define the *minimax regret at horizon* n by

$$
V_n^{(N)} = \sup_{(f_{1,1},\ldots,f_{N,1})\in\mathcal{D}^N} \; \inf_{\widehat{p}_1\in\mathcal{D}} \; \sup_{y_1\in\mathcal{Y}} \; \sup_{(f_{1,2},\ldots,f_{N,2})\in\mathcal{D}^N} \; \inf_{\widehat{p}_2\in\mathcal{D}} \; \sup_{y_2\in\mathcal{Y}}
$$

$$
\cdots \sup_{(f_{1,n},\ldots,f_{N,n})\in\mathcal{D}^N} \; \inf_{\widehat{p}_n\in\mathcal{D}} \; \sup_{y_n\in\mathcal{Y}} \left(\sum_{t=1}^n \ell(\widehat{p}_t, y_t) - \min_{i=1,\ldots,N} \sum_{t=1}^n \ell(f_{i,t}, y_t) \right).
$$

An equivalent, but simpler, definition of minimax regret can be given using static experts. Define a strategy for the forecaster as a prescription for computing, at each round t, the prediction $\widehat{p}_t$ given the past $t-1$ outcomes $y_1, \ldots, y_{t-1}$ and the expert advice $(f_{1,s}, \ldots, f_{N,s})$ for $s = 1, \ldots, t$. Formally, a forecasting strategy P is a sequence $\widehat{p}_1, \widehat{p}_2, \ldots$ of functions

$$
\widehat{p}_t : \mathcal{Y}^{t-1} \times \left(\mathcal{D}^N\right)^t \to \mathcal{D}.
$$

Now fix any class $\mathcal{F}$ of N static experts and let $\widehat{L}_n(P, \mathcal{F}, y^n)$ be the cumulative loss on the sequence y^n of the forecasting strategy P using the advice of the experts in $\mathcal{F}$. Then the minimax regret $V_n^{(N)}$ can be equivalently defined as

$$V_n^{(N)} = \inf_{P} \sup_{\{\mathcal{F}\,:\,|\mathcal{F}|=N\}} \sup_{y^n \in \mathcal{Y}^n} \max_{i=1,\dots,N} \left(\widehat{L}_n(P, \mathcal{F}, y^n) - \sum_{t=1}^{n} \ell(f_{i,t}, y_t) \right),$$

where the infimum is over all forecasting strategies P and the first supremum is over all possible classes of N static experts (see Exercise 2.18).

The minimax regret measures the best possible performance guarantee one can have for a forecasting algorithm that holds for all possible classes of N experts and all outcome sequences of length n. An upper bound on $V_n^{(N)}$ establishes the existence of a forecasting strategy achieving a regret not larger than the upper bound, regardless of what the class of experts and the outcome sequence are. On the other hand, a lower bound on $V_n^{(N)}$ shows that for any forecasting strategy there exists a class of N experts and an outcome sequence such that the regret of the forecaster is at least as large as the lower bound.

In this chapter and in the next, we derive minimax regret upper bounds for several losses, including $V_n^{(N)} \leq \ln N$ for the logarithmic loss $\ell(x, y) = -\mathbb{I}_{\{y=1\}} \ln x - \mathbb{I}_{\{y=0\}} \ln(1 - x)$, where $x \in [0, 1]$ and $y \in \{0, 1\}$, and $V_n^{(N)} \leq \sqrt{(n/2) \ln N}$ for all $[0, 1]$-valued convex losses, both achieved by the exponentially weighted average forecaster. In Chapters 3, 8, and 9 we complement these results by proving, among other related results, that $V_n^{(N)} = \ln N$ for the logarithmic loss provided that $n \geq \log_2 N$ and that the minimax regret for the absolute loss $\ell(x, y) = |x - y|$ is asymptotically $\sqrt{(n/2) \ln N}$, matching the upper bound we derived for convex losses. This entails that the exponentially weighted average forecaster is minimax optimal, in an asymptotic sense, for both the logarithmic and absolute losses.

The notion of minimax regret defined above is based on the performance of any forecaster in the case of the worst possible class of experts. However, often one is interested in the best possible performance a forecaster can achieve compared with the best expert in a *fixed* class. This leads to the definition of minimax regret for a fixed class of (simulatable) experts as follows. Fix some loss function ℓ and let $\mathcal{F}$ be a (not necessarily finite) class of simulatable experts. A forecasting strategy P based on $\mathcal{F}$ is now just a sequence $\widehat{p}_1, \widehat{p}_2, \dots$ of functions $\widehat{p}_t : \mathcal{Y}^{t-1} \to \mathcal{D}$. (Note that $\widehat{p}_t$ implicitly depends on $\mathcal{F}$, which is fixed. Therefore, as the experts in $\mathcal{F}$ are simulatable, $\widehat{p}_t$ need not depend explicitly on the expert advice.) The *minimax regret with respect to* $\mathcal{F}$ at horizon n is then defined by

$$V_n(\mathcal{F}) = \inf_{P} \sup_{y^n \in \mathcal{Y}^n} \left(\sum_{t=1}^{n} \ell\big(\widehat{p}_t(y^{t-1}), y_t\big) - \inf_{f \in \mathcal{F}} \sum_{t=1}^{n} \ell\big(f_t(y^{t-1}), y_t\big) \right).$$

This notion of regret is studied for specific losses in Chapters 8 and 9.

Given a class $\mathcal{F}$ of simulatable experts, one may also define the closely related quantity

$$U_n(\mathcal{F}) = \sup_{Q} \inf_{P} \int_{\mathcal{Y}^n} \left(\sum_{t=1}^{n} \ell\big(\widehat{p}_t(y^{t-1}), y_t\big) - \inf_{f \in \mathcal{F}} \sum_{t=1}^{n} \ell\big(f_t(y^{t-1}), y_t\big) \right) dQ(y^n),$$

where the supremum is taken over all probability measures over the set $\mathcal{Y}^n$ of sequences of outcomes of length n. $U_n(\mathcal{F})$ is called the *maximin regret with respect to* $\mathcal{F}$. Of course, to define probability measures over $\mathcal{Y}^n$, the set $\mathcal{Y}$ of outcomes should satisfy certain regularity properties. For simplicity, assume that $\mathcal{Y}$ is a compact subset of $\mathbb{R}^d$. This assumption is satisfied for most examples that appear in this book and can be significantly weakened if necessary. A general minimax theorem, proved in Chapter 7, implies that if the decision space $\mathcal{D}$ is convex and the loss function ℓ is convex and continuous in its first argument, then

$$V_n(\mathcal{F}) = U_n(\mathcal{F}).$$

This equality follows simply by the fact that the function

$$F(P, Q) = \int_{\mathcal{Y}^n} \left(\sum_{t=1}^{n} \ell(\widehat{p}_t(y^{t-1}), y_t) - \inf_{f \in \mathcal{F}} \sum_{t=1}^{n} \ell(f_t(y^{t-1}), y_t) \right) dQ(y^n)$$

is convex in its first argument and concave (actually linear) in the second. Here we define a convex combination $\lambda P^{(1)} + (1 - \lambda)P^{(2)}$ of two forecasting strategies $P^{(1)} = (\widehat{p}_1^{(1)}, \widehat{p}_2^{(1)}, \ldots)$ and $P^{(2)} = (\widehat{p}_1^{(2)}, \widehat{p}_2^{(2)}, \ldots)$ by a forecaster that predicts, at time t, according to

$$\lambda \widehat{p}_t^{(1)}(y^{t-1}) + (1 - \lambda)\widehat{p}_t^{(2)}(y^{t-1}).$$

We leave the details of checking the conditions of Theorem 7.1 to the reader (see Exercise 2.19).

2.11 Discounted Regret

In several applications it is reasonable to assume that losses in the past are less significant than recently suffered losses. Thus, one may consider *discounted regrets* of the form

$$\rho_{i,n} = \sum_{t=1}^{n} \beta_{n-t} r_{i,t},$$

where the discount factors β_t are typically decreasing with t and $r_{i,t} = \ell(\widehat{p}_t, y_t) - \ell(f_{i,t}, y_t)$ is the instantaneous regret with respect to expert i at round t. In particular, we assume that $\beta_0 \geq \beta_1 \geq \beta_2 \geq \cdots$ is a nonincreasing sequence and, without loss of generality, we let $\beta_0 = 1$. Thus, at time $t = n$, the actual regret $r_{i,t}$ has full weight while regrets suffered in the past have smaller weight; the more distant the past, the less its weight.

In this setup the goal of the forecaster is to ensure that, regardless of the sequence of outcomes, the average discounted cumulative regret

$$\max_{i=1,\ldots,N} \frac{\sum_{t=1}^{n} \beta_{n-t} r_{i,t}}{\sum_{t=1}^{n} \beta_{n-t}}$$

is as small as possible. More precisely, one would like to bound the average discounted regret by a function of n that converges to zero as $n \to \infty$. The purpose of this section is to explore for what sequences of discount factors it is possible to achieve this goal. The case when $\beta_t = 1$ for all t corresponds to the case studied in the rest of this chapter. Other natural choices include the exponential discount sequence $\beta_t = a^{-t}$ for some $a > 1$ or sequences of the form $\beta_t = (t + 1)^{-a}$ with $a > 0$.

First we observe that if the discount sequence decreases too quickly, then, except for trivial cases, there is no hope to prove any meaningful bound.

Theorem 2.7. *Assume that there is a positive constant c such that for each n there exist outcomes $y_1, y_2 \in \mathcal{Y}$ and two experts $i \neq i'$ such that $i = \text{argmin}_j \ell(f_{j,n}, y_1)$,*

$i' = \text{argmin}_j \ell(f_{j,n}, y_2)$, *and* $\min_{y=y_1,y_2} |\ell(f_{i,n}, y) - \ell(f_{i',n}, y)| \geq c$. *If* $\sum_{t=0}^{\infty} \beta_t < \infty$, *then there exists a constant C such that, for any forecasting strategy, there is a sequence of outcomes such that*

$$\max_{i=1,\ldots,N} \frac{\sum_{t=1}^{n} \beta_{n-t} r_{i,t}}{\sum_{t=1}^{n} \beta_{n-t}} \geq C$$

for all n.

Proof. The lower bound follows simply by observing that the weight of the regrets at the last time step $t = n$ is too large: it is comparable with the total weight of the whole past. Formally,

$$\max_{i=1,\ldots,N} \sum_{t=1}^{n} \beta_{n-t} r_{i,t} \geq \max_{i=1,\ldots,N} \beta_0 r_{i,n} = \ell(\widehat{p}_n, y_n) - \min_{i=1,\ldots,N} \ell(f_{i,n}, y_n).$$

Thus,

$$\sup_{y^n \in \mathcal{Y}^n} \max_{i=1,\ldots,N} \frac{\sum_{t=1}^{n} \beta_{n-t} r_{i,t}}{\sum_{t=1}^{n} \beta_{n-t}}$$

$$\geq \frac{\sup_{y \in \mathcal{Y}} \left(\ell(\widehat{p}_n, y) - \min_{i=1,\ldots,N} \ell(f_{i,n}, y) \right)}{\sum_{t=0}^{\infty} \beta_t}$$

$$\geq \frac{C}{2 \sum_{t=0}^{\infty} \beta_t}. \quad \blacksquare$$

Next we contrast the result by showing that whenever the discount factors decrease sufficiently slowly such that $\sum_{t=0}^{\infty} \beta_t = \infty$, it is possible to make the average discounted regret vanish for large n. This follows from an easy application of Theorem 2.1. We may define weighted average strategies on the basis of the discounted regrets simply by replacing $r_{i,t}$ by $\widetilde{r}_{i,t} = \beta_{n-t} r_{i,t}$ in the definition of the weighted average forecaster. Of course, to use such a predictor, one needs to know the time horizon n in advance. We obtain the following.

Theorem 2.8. *Consider a discounted polynomially weighted average forecaster defined, for $t = 1, \ldots, n$, by*

$$\widehat{p}_t = \frac{\sum_{i=1}^{N} \phi'\left(\sum_{s=1}^{t-1} \widetilde{r}_{i,s}\right) f_{i,s}}{\sum_{j=1}^{N} \phi'\left(\sum_{s=1}^{t-1} \widetilde{r}_{j,s}\right)} = \frac{\sum_{i=1}^{N} \phi'\left(\sum_{s=1}^{t-1} \beta_{n-s} r_{i,s}\right) f_{i,s}}{\sum_{j=1}^{N} \phi'\left(\sum_{s=1}^{t-1} \beta_{n-s} r_{j,s}\right)},$$

where $\phi'(x) = (p-1)x^p$, with $p = 2 \ln N$. Then the average discounted regret satisfies

$$\max_{i=1,\ldots,N} \frac{\sum_{t=1}^{n} \beta_{n-t} r_{i,t}}{\sum_{t=1}^{n} \beta_{n-t}} \leq \sqrt{2e \ln N} \frac{\sqrt{\sum_{t=1}^{n} \beta_{n-t}^2}}{\sum_{t=1}^{n} \beta_{n-t}}.$$

(A similar bound may be proven for the discounted exponentially weighted average forecaster as well.) In particular, if $\sum_{t=0}^{\infty} \beta_t = \infty$, then

$$\max_{i=1,\ldots,N} \frac{\sum_{t=1}^{n} \beta_{n-t} r_{i,t}}{\sum_{t=1}^{n} \beta_{n-t}} = o(1).$$

Proof.   Clearly the forecaster satisfies the Blackwell condition, and for each t, $|\widetilde{r}_{i,t}| \le \beta_{n-t}$. Then Theorem 2.1 implies, just as in the proof of Corollary 2.1,

$$\max_{i=1,\dots,N} \rho_{i,n} \le \sqrt{2e \ln N} \sqrt{\sum_{t=1}^{n} \beta_{n-t}^2}$$

and the first statement follows. To prove the second, just note that

$$\begin{aligned}
\sqrt{2e \ln N} \frac{\sqrt{\sum_{t=1}^{n} \beta_{n-t}^2}}{\sum_{t=1}^{n} \beta_{n-t}} &= \sqrt{2e \ln N} \frac{\sqrt{\sum_{t=1}^{n} \beta_{t-1}^2}}{\sum_{t=1}^{n} \beta_{t-1}} \\
&\le \sqrt{2e \ln N} \frac{\sqrt{\sum_{t=1}^{n} \beta_{t-1}}}{\sum_{t=1}^{n} \beta_{t-1}} \\
&= \frac{\sqrt{2e \ln N}}{\sqrt{\sum_{t=1}^{n} \beta_{t-1}}} = o(1). \quad \blacksquare
\end{aligned}$$

It is instructive to consider the special case when $\beta_t = (t+1)^{-a}$ for some $0 < a \le 1$. (Recall from Theorem 2.7 that for $a > 1$, no meaningful bound can be derived.) If $a = 1$, Theorem 2.8 implies that

$$\max_{i=1,\dots,N} \frac{\sum_{t=1}^{n} \beta_{n-t} r_{i,t}}{\sum_{t=1}^{n} \beta_{n-t}} \le \frac{C}{\log n}$$

for a constant $C > 0$. This slow rate of convergence to zero is not surprising in view of Theorem 2.7, because the series $\sum_t 1/(t+1)$ is "barely nonsummable." In fact, this bound cannot be improved substantially (see Exercise 2.20). However, for $a < 1$ the convergence is faster. In fact, an easy calculation shows that the upper bound of the theorem implies that

$$\max_{i=1,\dots,N} \frac{\sum_{t=1}^{n} \beta_{n-t} r_{i,t}}{\sum_{t=1}^{n} \beta_{n-t}} = \begin{cases} O\left(1/\log n\right) & \text{if } a = 1 \\ O\left(n^{a-1}\right) & \text{if } 1/2 < a < 1 \\ O\left(\sqrt{(\log n)/n}\right) & \text{if } a = 1/2 \\ O\left(1/\sqrt{n}\right) & \text{if } a < 1/2. \end{cases}$$

Not surprisingly, the slower the discount factor decreases, the faster the average discounted cumulative regret converges to zero. However, it is interesting to observe the "phase transition" occurring at $a = 1/2$: for all $a < 1/2$, the average regret decreases at a rate $n^{-1/2}$, a behavior quantitatively similar to the case when no discounting is taken into account.

2.12   Bibliographic Remarks

Our model of sequential prediction with expert advice finds its roots in the theory of repeated games. Zero-sum repeated games with fixed loss matrix are a classical topic of game theory. In these games, the regret after n plays is defined as the excess loss of the row player with respect to the smallest loss that could be incurred had he known in advance the empirical distribution of the column player actions during the n plays. In his pioneering work, Hannan [141] devises a randomized playing strategy whose per-round expected regret grows at rate $N\sqrt{3nm/2}$, where N is the number of rows, m is the number of columns in the loss matrix, and n is the number of plays. As shown in Chapter 7, our polynomially and exponentially weighted average forecasters can be used to play zero-sum repeated games achieving the regret $\sqrt{(n/2)\ln N}$. We obtain the same dependence on the number n of plays Compared with Hannan's regret, but we significantly improve the dependence on the dimensions, N and m, of the loss matrix. A different randomized player with a vanishing per-round regret can be also derived from the celebrated Blackwell's approachability theorem [28], generalizing von Neumann's minimax theorem to vector-valued payoffs. This result, which we re-derive in Chapter 7, is based on a mixed strategy equivalent to our polynomially weighted average forecaster with $p = 2$. Exact asymptotical constants for the minimax regret (for a special case) were first shown by Cover [68]. In our terminology, Cover investigates the problem of predicting a sequence of binary outcomes with two static experts, one always predicting 0 and the other always predicting 1. He shows that the minimax regret for the absolute loss in this special case is $(1 + o(1))\sqrt{n/(2\pi)}$.

The problem of sequential prediction, deprived of any probabilistic assumption, is deeply connected with the information-theoretic problem of compressing an individual data sequence. A pioneering research in this field was carried out by Ziv [317, 318] and Lempel and Ziv [197, 317, 319], who solved the problem of compressing an individual data sequence almost as well as the best finite-state automaton. As shown by Feder, Merhav, and Gutman [95], the Lempel–Ziv compressor can be used as a randomized forecaster (for the absolute loss) with a vanishing per-round regret against the class of all finite-state experts, a surprising result considering the rich structure of this class. In addition, Feder, Merhav, and Gutman devise, for the same expert class, a forecaster with a convergence rate better than the rate provable for the Lempel–Ziv forecaster (see also Merhav and Feder [213] for further results along these lines). In Section 9 we continue the investigation of the relationship between prediction and compression showing simple conditions under which prediction with logarithmic loss is minimax equivalent to adaptive data compression. Connections between prediction with expert advice and information content of an individual sequence have been explored by Vovk and Watkins [303], who introduced the notion of predictive complexity of a data sequence, a quantity that, for the logarithmic loss, is related to the Kolmogorov complexity of the sequence. We refer to the book of Li and Vitányi [198] for an excellent introduction to the algorithmic theory of randomness.

Approximately at the same time when Hannan and Blackwell were laying down the foundations of the game-theoretic approach to prediction, Solomonoff had the idea of formalizing the phenomenon of inductive inference in humans as a sequential prediction process. This research eventually led him to the introduction of a *universal prior probability* [273–275], to be used as a prior in bayesian inference. An important "side product" of Solomonoff's universal prior is the notion of algorithmic randomess, which he introduced independently of Kolmogorov. Though we acknowledge the key role played by Solomonoff in the field of sequential prediction theory, especially in connection with Kolmogorov complexity, in this book we look at the problem of forecasting from a different angle. Having said this, we certainly think that exploring the connections between algorithmic randomness and game theory, through the unifying notion of prediction, is a surely exciting research plan.

The field of inductive inference investigates the problem of sequential prediction when experts are functions taken from a large class, possibly including all recursive languages or all partial recursive functions, and the task is that of eventually identifying an expert that is consistent (or nearly consistent) with an infinite sequence of observations. This learning paradigm, introduced in 1967 by Gold [130], is still actively studied. Unlike the theory described in this book, whose roots are game theoretic, the main ideas and analytical tools used in inductive inference come from recursion theory (see Odifreddi [227]).

In computer science, an area related to prediction with experts is competitive analysis of online algorithms (see the monograph of Borodin and El-Yaniv [36] for a survey). A good example of a paper exploring the use of forecasting algorithms in competitive analysis is the work by Blum and Burch [32].

The paradigm of prediction with expert advice was introduced by Littlestone and Warmuth [203] and Vovk [297], and further developed by Cesa-Bianchi, Freund, Haussler, Helmbold, Schapire, and Warmuth [48] and Vovk [298], although some of its main ingredients already appear in the papers of De Santis, Markowski, and Wegman [260], Littlestone [200], and Foster [103]. The use of potential functions in sequential prediction is due to Hart and Mas-Colell [146], who used Blackwell's condition in a game-theoretic context, and to Grove, Littlestone, and Schuurmans [133], who used exactly the same condition for the analysis of certain variants of the Perceptron algorithm (see Chapter 11). Our Theorem 2.1 is inspired by, and partially builds on, Hart and Mas-Colell's analysis of Λ-strategies for playing repeated games [146] and on the analysis of the quasi-additive algorithm of Grove, Littlestone, and Schuurmans [133]. The unified framework for sequential prediction based on potential functions that we describe here was introduced by Cesa-Bianchi and Lugosi [54]. Forecasting based on the exponential potential has been used in game theory as a variant of smooth fictitious play (see, e.g., the book of Fudenberg and Levine [119]). In learning theory, exponentially weighted average forecasters were introduced and analyzed by Littlestone and Warmuth [203] (the weighted majority algorithm) and by Vovk [297] (the aggregating algorithm). The trick of setting the parameter p of the polynomial potential to $2 \ln N$ is due to Gentile [123]. The analysis in Section 2.2 is based on Cesa-Bianchi's work [46]. The idea of doubling trick of Section 2.3 appears in the articles of Cesa-Bianchi, Freund, Haussler, Helmbold, Schapire, and Warmuth [48] and Vovk [298], whereas the analysis of Theorem 2.3 is adapted from Auer, Cesa-Bianchi, and Gentile [13]. The data-dependent bounds of Section 2.4 are based on two sources: Theorem 2.4 is from the work of Littlestone and Warmuth [203] and Corollary 2.4 is due to Freund and Schapire [112]. A more sophisticated analysis of the exponentially weighted average forecaster with time-varying η_t is due to Yaroshinski, El-Yaniv, and Seiden [315]. They show a regret bound of the order $(1 + o(1))\sqrt{2L_n^* \ln N}$, where $o(1) \to 0$ for $L_n^* \to \infty$. Hutter and Poland [165] prove a result similar to Exercise 2.10 using follow-the-perturbed-leader, a randomized forecaster that we analyze in Chapter 4.

The multilinear forecaster and the results of Section 2.8 are due to Cesa-Bianchi, Mansour, and Stoltz [57]. A weaker version of Corollary 2.7 was proven by Allenberg-Neeman and Neeman [7].

The gradient-based forecaster of Section 2.5 was introduced by Kivinen and Warmuth [181]. The proof of Corollary 2.5 is due to Cesa-Bianchi [46]. The notion of simulatable experts and worst-case regret for the experts' framework was first investigated by Cesa-Bianchi et al. [48]. Results for more general loss functions are contained in Chung's paper [60]. Fudenberg and Levine [121] consider discounted regrets is a somewhat different model than the one discussed here.

The model of prediction with expert advice is connected to bayesian decision theory. For instance, when the absolute loss is used, the normalized weights of the weighted average forecaster based on the exponential potential closely approximate the posterior distribution of a simple stochastic generative model for the data sequence (see Exercise 2.7). From this viewpoint, our regret analysis shows an example where the Bayes decisions are robust in a strong sense, because their performance can be bounded not only in expectation with respect to the random draw of the sequence but also for each individual sequence.

2.13 Exercises

2.1 Assume that you have to predict a sequence $Y_1, Y_2, \ldots \in \{0, 1\}$ of i.i.d. random variables with unknown distribution, your decision space is $[0, 1]$, and the loss function is $\ell(\widehat{p}, y) = |\widehat{p} - y|$. How would you proceed? Try to estimate the cumulative loss of your forecaster and compare it to the cumulative loss of the best of the two experts, one of which always predicts 1 and the other always predicts 0. Which are the most "difficult" distributions? How does your (expected) regret compare to that of the weighted average algorithm (which does not "know" that the outcome sequence is i.i.d.)?

2.2 Consider a weighted average forecaster based on a potential function

$$\Phi(\mathbf{u}) = \psi\left(\sum_{i=1}^{N} \phi(u_i)\right).$$

Assume further that the quantity $C(\mathbf{r}_t)$ appearing in the statement of Theorem 2.1 is bounded by a constant for all values of $\mathbf{r}_t$ and that the function $\psi(\phi(u))$ is strictly convex. Show that there exists a nonnegative sequence $\varepsilon_n \to 0$ such that the cumulative regret of the forecaster satisfies, for every n and for every outcome sequence y^n,

$$\frac{1}{n}\left(\max_{i=1,\ldots,N} R_{i,n}\right) \leq \varepsilon_n.$$

2.3 Analyze the polynomially weighted average forecaster using Theorem 2.1 but using the potential function $\Phi(\mathbf{u}) = \|\mathbf{u}_+\|_p$ instead of the choice $\Phi_p(\mathbf{u}) = \|\mathbf{u}_+\|_p^2$ used in the proof of Corollary 2.1. Derive a bound of the same form as in Corollary 2.1, perhaps with different constants.

2.4 Let $\mathcal{Y} = \{0, 1\}$, $\mathcal{D} = [0, 1]$, and $\ell(\widehat{p}, y) = |\widehat{p} - y|$. Prove that the cumulative loss $\widehat{L}$ of the exponentially weighted average forecaster is always at least as large as the cumulative loss $\min_{i \leq N} L_i$ of the best expert. Show that for other loss functions, such as the square loss $(\widehat{p} - y)^2$, this is not necessarily so. *Hint:* Try to reverse the proof of Theorem 2.2.

2.5 (*Nonuniform initial weights*) By definition, the weighted average forecaster uses uniform initial weights $w_{i,0} = 1$ for all $i = 1, \ldots, N$. However, there is nothing special about this choice, and the analysis of the regret for this forecaster can be carried out using any set of nonnegative numbers for the initial weights.

Consider the exponentially weighted average forecaster run with arbitrary initial weights $w_{1,0}, \ldots, w_{N,0} > 0$, defined, for all $t = 1, 2, \ldots$, by

$$\widehat{p}_t = \frac{\sum_{i=1}^{N} w_{i,t-1} f_{i,t}}{\sum_{j=1}^{N} w_{j,t-1}}, \quad w_{i,t} = w_{i,t-1} e^{-\eta \ell(f_{i,t}, y_t)}.$$

Under the same conditions as in the statement of Theorem 2.2, show that for every n and for every outcome sequence y^n,

$$\widehat{L}_n \leq \min_{i=1,\ldots,N}\left(L_{i,n} + \frac{1}{\eta} \ln \frac{1}{w_{i,0}}\right) + \frac{\ln W_0}{\eta} + \frac{\eta}{8} n,$$

where $W_0 = w_{1,0} + \cdots + w_{N,0}$.

2.6 (*Many good experts*)   Sequences of outcomes on which many experts suffer a small loss are intuitively easier to predict. Adapt the proof of Theorem 2.2 to show that the exponentially weighted forecaster satistifies the following property: for every n, for every outcome sequence y^n, and for all $L > 0$,

$$\widehat{L}_n \le L + \frac{1}{\eta} \ln \frac{N}{N_L} + \frac{\eta}{8} n,$$

where N_L is the cardinality of the set $\{1 \le i \le N : L_{i,n} \le L\}$.

2.7 (*Random generation of the outcome sequence*)   Consider the exponentially weighted average forecaster and define the following probabilistic model for the generation of the sequence $y^n \in \{0, 1\}^n$, where we now view each bit y_t as the realization of a Bernoulli random variable Y_t. An expert I is drawn at random from the set of N experts. For each $t = 1, \ldots, n$, first $X_t \in \{0, 1\}$ is drawn so that $X_t = 1$ with probability $f_{I,t}$. Then Y_t is set to X_t with probability β and is set to $1 - X_t$ with probability $1 - \beta$, where $\beta = 1/(1 + e^{-\eta})$. Show that the forecaster weights $w_{i,t}/(w_{1,t} + \cdots + w_{N,t})$ and are equal to the posterior probability $P[I = i \mid Y_1 = y_1, \ldots, Y_{t-1} = y_{t-1}]$ that expert i is drawn given that the sequence $y_1, \ldots, y_{t-1}$ has been observed.

2.8 (*The doubling trick*)   Consider the following forecasting strategy ("doubling trick"): time is divided in periods $(2^m, \ldots, 2^{m+1} - 1)$, where $m = 0, 1, 2, \ldots$. In period $(2^m, \ldots, 2^{m+1} - 1)$ the strategy uses the exponentially weighted average forecaster initialized at time 2^m with parameter $\eta_m = \sqrt{8(\ln N)/2^m}$. Thus, the weighted average forecaster is reset at each time instance that is an integer power of 2 and is restarted with a new value of η. Using Theorem 2.2 prove that, for any sequence $y_1, y_2, \ldots \in \mathcal{Y}$ of outcomes and for any $n \ge 1$, the regret of this forecaster is at most

$$\widehat{L}_n - \min_{i=1,\ldots,N} L_{i,n} \le \frac{\sqrt{2}}{\sqrt{2} - 1} \sqrt{\frac{n}{2} \ln N}.$$

2.9 (*The doubling trick, continued*)   In Exercise 2.8, quite arbitrarily, we divided time into periods of length 2^m, $m = 1, 2, \ldots$. Investigate what happens if instead the period lengths are of the form $\lfloor a^m \rfloor$ for some other value of $a > 0$. Which choice of a minimizes, asymptotically, the constant in the bound? How much can you gain compared with the bound given in the text?

2.10   Combine Theorem 2.4 with the doubling trick of Exercise 2.8 to construct a forecaster that, without any previous knowledge of L^*, achieves, for all n,

$$\widehat{L}_n - L_n^* \le 2\sqrt{2 L_n^* \ln N} + c \ln N$$

whenever the loss function is bounded and convex in its first argument, and where c is a positive constant.

2.11 (*Another time-varying potential*)   Consider the adaptive exponentially weighted average forecaster that, at time t, uses

$$\eta_t = c \sqrt{\frac{\ln N}{\min_{i=1,\ldots,N} L_{i,t-1}}},$$

where c is a positive constant. Show that whenever ℓ is a $[0, 1]$-valued loss function convex in its first argument, then there exists a choice of c such that

$$\widehat{L}_n - L_n^* \le 2\sqrt{2 L_n^* \ln N} + \kappa \ln N,$$

where $\kappa > 0$ is an appropriate constant (Auer, Cesa-Bianchi, and Gentile [13]). *Hint:* Follow the outline of the proof of Theorem 2.3. This exercise is not easy.

2.12   Consider the prediction problem with $\mathcal{Y} = \mathcal{D} = [0, 1]$ with the absolute loss $\ell(\widehat{p}, y) = |\widehat{p} - y|$. Show that in this case the gradient-based exponentially weighted average forecaster coincides with the exponentially weighted average forecaster. (Note that the derivative of the loss does not exist for $\widehat{p} = y$ and the definition of the gradient-based exponentially weighted average forecaster needs to be adjusted appropriately.)

2.13 Prove Lemma 2.4.

2.14 Use the doubling trick to prove a variant of Corollary 2.6 in which no knowledge about the outcome sequence is assumed to be preliminarily available (however, as in the corollary, we still assume that the payoff function h has range $[-M, M]$ and is concave in its first argument). Express the regret bound in terms of the smallest monotone upper bound on the sequence $Q_1^*, Q_2^*, \ldots$ (see Cesa-Bianchi, Mansour, and Stoltz [57]).

2.15 Prove a variant of Theorem 2.6 in which no knowledge about the range $[-M, M]$ of the payoff function is assumed to be preliminarily available (see Cesa-Bianchi, Mansour, and Stoltz [57]). *Hint:* Replace the term $1/(2M)$ in the definition of η_t with $2^{-(1+k_t)}$, where k is the smallest nonnegative integer such that $\max_{s=1,\ldots,t-1} \max_{i=1,\ldots,N} |h(f_{i,s}, y_s)| \leq 2^k$.

2.16 Prove a regret bound for the multilinear forecaster using the update $w_{i,t} = w_{i,t-1}(1 + \eta r_{i,t})$, where $r_{i,t} = h(f_{i,t}, y_t) - h(\widehat{p}_t, y_t)$ is the instantaneous regret. What can you say about the evolution of the total weight $W_t = w_{1,t} + \cdots + w_{N,t}$ of the experts?

2.17 Prove Lemma 2.5. *Hint:* Adapt the proof of Theorem 2.3.

2.18 Show that the two expressions of the minimax regret $V_n^{(N)}$ in Section 2.10 are equivalent.

2.19 Consider a class $\mathcal{F}$ of simulatable experts. Assume that the set $\mathcal{Y}$ of outcomes is a compact subset of $\mathbb{R}^d$, the decision space $\mathcal{D}$ is convex, and the loss function ℓ is convex and continuous in its first argument. Show that $V_n(\mathcal{F}) = U_n(\mathcal{F})$. *Hint:* Check the conditions of Theorem 7.1.

2.20 Consider the discount factors $\beta_t = 1/(t + 1)$ and assume that there is a positive constant c such that for each n there exist outcomes $y_1, y_2 \in \mathcal{Y}$ and two experts $i \neq i'$ such that $i = \operatorname{argmin}_j \ell(f_{j,n}, y_1)$, $i' = \operatorname{argmin}_j \ell(f_{j,n}, y_2)$, and $\min_{y=y_1,y_2} |\ell(f_{i,n}, y) - \ell(f_{i',n}, y)| \geq c$. Show that there exists a constant C such that for any forecasting strategy, there is a sequence of outcomes such that

$$\max_{i=1,\ldots,N} \frac{\sum_{t=1}^n \beta_{n-t} r_{i,t}}{\sum_{t=1}^n \beta_{n-t}} \geq \frac{C}{\log n}$$

for all n.

3

Tight Bounds for Specific Losses

3.1 Introduction

In Chapter 2 we established the existence of forecasters that, under general circumstances, achieve a worst-case regret of the order of $\sqrt{n \ln N}$ with respect to any finite class of N experts. The only condition we required was that the decision space $\mathcal{D}$ be a convex set and the loss function ℓ be bounded and convex in its first argument. In many cases, under specific assumptions on the loss function and/or the class of experts, significantly tighter performance bounds may be achieved. The purpose of this chapter is to review various situations in which such improvements can be made. We also explore the limits of such possible improvements by exhibiting lower bounds for the worst-case regret.

In Section 3.2 we show that in some cases a myopic strategy that simply chooses the best expert on the basis of past performance achieves a rapidly vanishing worst-case regret under certain smoothness assumptions on the loss function and the class of experts.

Our main technical tool, Theorem 2.1, has been used to bound the potential $\Phi(\mathbf{R}_n)$ of the weighted average forecaster in terms of the initial potential $\Phi(\mathbf{0})$ plus a sum of terms bounding the error committed in taking linear approximations of each $\Phi(\mathbf{R}_t)$ for $t = 1, \ldots, n$. In certain cases, however, we can bound $\Phi(\mathbf{R}_n)$ directly by $\Phi(\mathbf{0})$, without the need of taking any linear approximation. To do this we can exploit simple geometrical properties exhibited by the potential when combined with specific loss functions. In this chapter we develop several techniques of this kind and use them to derive tighter regret bounds for various loss functions.

In Section 3.3 we consider a basic property of a loss function, exp-concavity, which ensures a bound of $(\ln N)/\eta$ for the exponentially weighted average forecaster, where η must be smaller than a critical value depending on the specific exp-concave loss. In Section 3.4 we take a more extreme approach by considering a forecaster that chooses predictions minimizing the worst-case increase of the potential. This "greedy" forecaster is shown to perform not worse than the weighted average forecaster. In Section 3.5 we focus on the exponential potential and refine the analysis of the previous sections by introducing the aggregating forecasters, a family that includes the greedy forecaster. These forecasters, which apply to exp-concave losses, are designed to achieve a regret of the form $c \ln N$, where c is the best possible constant for each loss for which such bounds are possible. In the course of the analysis we characterize the important subclass of mixable losses. These losses are, in some sense, the easiest to work with. Finally, in Section 3.7 we prove a lower bound of the form $\Omega(\log N)$ for generic losses and a lower bound for the absolute loss that matches (constants included) the upper bound achieved by the exponentially weighted average forecaster.

3.2 Follow the Best Expert

In this section we study possibly the simplest forecasting strategy. This strategy chooses, at time t, an expert that minimizes the cumulative loss over the past $t - 1$ time instances. In other words, the forecaster always follows the expert that has had the smallest cumulative loss up to that time. Perhaps surprisingly, this simple predictor has a good performance under general conditions on the loss function and the experts.

Formally, consider a class $\mathcal{E}$ of experts and define the forecaster that predicts the same as the expert that minimizes the cumulative loss in the past, that is,

$$\widehat{p}_t = f_{E,t} \quad \text{if} \quad E = \operatorname*{argmin}_{E' \in \mathcal{E}} \sum_{s=1}^{t-1} \ell(f_{E',s}, y_s).$$

$\widehat{p}_1$ is defined as an arbitrary element of $\mathcal{D}$. Throughout this section we assume that the minimum is always achieved. In case of multiple minimizers, E can be chosen arbitrarily.

Our goal is, as before, to compare the performance of $\widehat{p}$ with that of the best expert in the class; that is, to derive bounds for the regret

$$\widehat{L}_n - \inf_{E \in \mathcal{E}} L_{E,n} = \sum_{t=1}^{n} \ell(\widehat{p}, y_t) - \inf_{E \in \mathcal{E}} \sum_{t=1}^{n} \ell(f_{E,t}, y_t).$$

Consider the hypothetical forecaster defined by

$$p_t^* = f_{E,t} \quad \text{if} \quad E = \operatorname*{argmin}_{E' \in \mathcal{E}} \sum_{s=1}^{t} \ell(f_{E',s}, y_s).$$

Note that p_t^* is defined like $\widehat{p}_t$, with the only difference that p_t^* also takes the losses suffered at time t into account. Clearly, p_t^* is not a "legal" forecaster, because it is allowed to peek into the future; it is defined as a tool for our analysis. The following simple lemma states that p_t^* "performs" at least as well as the best expert.

Lemma 3.1. *For any sequence* $y_1, \ldots, y_n$ *of outcomes,*

$$\sum_{t=1}^{n} \ell(p_t^*, y_t) \le \sum_{t=1}^{n} \ell(p_n^*, y_t) = \min_{E \in \mathcal{E}} L_{E,n}.$$

Proof. The proof goes by induction. The statement is obvious for $n = 1$. Assume now that

$$\sum_{t=1}^{n-1} \ell(p_t^*, y_t) \le \sum_{t=1}^{n-1} \ell(p_{n-1}^*, y_t).$$

Since by definition $\sum_{t=1}^{n-1} \ell(p_{n-1}^*, y_t) \leq \sum_{t=1}^{n-1} \ell(p_n^*, y_t)$, the inductive assumption implies

$$\sum_{t=1}^{n-1} \ell(p_t^*, y_t) \leq \sum_{t=1}^{n-1} \ell(p_n^*, y_t).$$

Add $\ell(p_n^*, y_n)$ to both sides to obtain the result. ∎

This simple property implies that the regret of the forecaster $\widehat{p}$ may be upper bounded as

$$\widehat{L}_n - \inf_{E \in \mathcal{E}} L_{E,n} \leq \sum_{t=1}^{n} \big(\ell(\widehat{p}_t, y_t) - \ell(p_t^*, y_t)\big).$$

By recalling the definitions of $\widehat{p}_t$ and p_t^*, it is reasonable to expect that in some situations $\widehat{p}_t$ and p_t^* are close to each other. For example, if one can guarantee that for every t,

$$\sup_{y \in \mathcal{Y}} \big(\ell(\widehat{p}_t, y) - \ell(p_t^*, y)\big) \leq \varepsilon_t$$

for a sequence of real numbers $\varepsilon_t > 0$, then the inequality shows that

$$\widehat{L}_n - \inf_{E \in \mathcal{E}} L_{E,n} \leq \sum_{t=1}^{n} \varepsilon_t. \tag{3.1}$$

In what follows, we establish some general conditions under which $\varepsilon_t \sim 1/t$, which implies that the regret grows as slowly as $O(\ln n)$.

In all these examples we consider "constant" experts; that is, we assume that for each $E \in \mathcal{E}$ and $y \in \mathcal{Y}$, the loss of expert E is independent of time. In other words, for any fixed y, $\ell(f_{E,1}, y) = \cdots = \ell(f_{E,n}, y)$. To simplify notation, we write $\ell(E, y)$ for the common value, where now each expert is characterized by an element $E \in \mathcal{D}$.

Square Loss

As a first example consider the square loss in a general vector space. Assume that $\mathcal{D} = \mathcal{Y}$ is the unit ball $\{p : \|p\| \leq 1\}$ in a Hilbert space $\mathcal{H}$, and consider the loss function

$$\ell(p, y) = \|p - y\|^2, \qquad p, y \in \mathcal{H}.$$

Let the expert class $\mathcal{E}$ contain all constant experts indexed by $E \in \mathcal{D}$. In this case it is easy to determine explicitly the forecaster $\widehat{p}$. Indeed, because for any $p \in \mathcal{D}$,

$$\frac{1}{t-1} \sum_{s=1}^{t-1} \|p - y_s\|^2 = \frac{1}{t-1} \sum_{s=1}^{t-1} \left\| \frac{1}{t-1} \sum_{r=1}^{t-1} y_r - y_s \right\|^2 + \left\| \frac{1}{t-1} \sum_{r=1}^{t-1} y_r - p \right\|^2$$

(easily checked by expanding the squares), we have

$$\widehat{p}_t = \frac{1}{t-1} \sum_{s=1}^{t-1} y_s.$$

Similarly,

$$p_t^* = \frac{1}{t} \sum_{s=1}^{t} y_s.$$

Then, for any $y \in \mathcal{D}$,

$$\ell(\widehat{p}_t, y) - \ell(p_t^*, y) = \|\widehat{p}_t - y\|^2 - \|p_t^* - y\|^2$$
$$= (\widehat{p}_t - p_t^*) \cdot (\widehat{p}_t + p_t^* - 2y)$$
$$\leq 4 \|\widehat{p}_t - p_t^*\|$$

by boundedness of the set $\mathcal{D}$. The norm of the difference can be easily bounded by writing

$$\widehat{p}_t - p_t^* = \frac{1}{t-1} \sum_{s=1}^{t-1} y_s - \frac{1}{t} \sum_{s=1}^{t} y_s = \left(\frac{1}{t-1} - \frac{1}{t} \right) \sum_{s=1}^{t-1} y_s - \frac{y_t}{t}$$

so that, clearly, regardless of the sequence of outcomes, $\|\widehat{p}_t - p_t^*\| \leq 2/t$. We obtain

$$\ell(\widehat{p}_t, y) - \ell(p_t^*, y) \leq \frac{8}{t},$$

and therefore, by (3.1), we have

$$\widehat{L}_n - \inf_{E \in \mathcal{E}} L_{E,n} \leq \sum_{t=1}^{n} \frac{8}{t} \leq 8 \left(1 + \ln n \right),$$

where we used $\sum_{t=1}^{n} 1/t \leq 1 + \int_1^n dx/x = 1 + \ln n$. Observe that this performance bound is significantly smaller than the general bounds of the order of $\sqrt{n}$ obtained in Chapter 2. Also, remarkably, the "size" of the class of experts is not reflected in the upper bound. The class of experts in the example considered is not only infinite but can be a ball in an infinite-dimensional vector space!

Convex Losses, Constant Experts

In the rest of this section we generalize the example of square loss described earlier by deriving general sufficient conditions for convex loss functions when the class of experts contains constant experts. For the simplicity of exposition we limit the discussion to the finite-dimensional case, but it is easy to generalize the results.

Let $\mathcal{D}$ be a bounded convex subset of $\mathbb{R}^d$, and assume that an expert E is assigned to each element of $\mathcal{D}$ so that the loss of expert E at time t is $\ell(E, y_t)$. Using our convention of denoting vectors by bold letters, we write $\widehat{\mathbf{p}}_t = (\widehat{p}_{1,t}, \ldots, \widehat{p}_{d,t})$ for the follow-the-best-expert forecaster, and similarly $\mathbf{p}_t^* = (p_{1,t}^*, \ldots, p_{d,t}^*)$ for the corresponding hypothetical forecaster. We make the following assumptions on the loss function:

1. ℓ is convex in its first argument and takes its values in $[0, 1]$;
2. for each fixed $y \in \mathcal{Y}$, $\ell(\cdot, y)$ is Lipschitz in its first argument, with constant B;
3. for each fixed $y \in \mathcal{Y}$, $\ell(\cdot, y)$ is twice differentiable. Moreover, there exists a constant $C > 0$ such that for each fixed $y \in \mathcal{Y}$, the Hessian matrix

$$\left(\frac{\partial^2 \ell(\mathbf{p}, y)}{\partial p_i \partial p_j} \right)_{d \times d}$$

   is positive definite with eigenvalues bounded from below by C;
4. for any $y_1, \ldots, y_t$, the minimizer $\mathbf{p}_t^*$ is such that $\nabla \Psi_t(\mathbf{p}_t^*) = 0$, where, for each $\mathbf{p} \in \mathcal{D}$,

$$\Psi_t(\mathbf{p}) = \frac{1}{t} \sum_{s=1}^{t} \ell(\mathbf{p}, y_s).$$

Theorem 3.1. *Under the assumptions described above, the per-round regret of the follow-the-best-expert forecaster satisfies*

$$\frac{1}{n}\left(\widehat{L}_n - \inf_{E \in \mathcal{E}} L_{E,n}\right) \le \frac{4B^2\,(1 + \ln n)}{Cn}.$$

Proof. First, by a Taylor series expansion of Ψ_t around its minimum value $\mathbf{p}_t^*$, we have

$$\Psi_t(\widehat{\mathbf{p}}_t) - \Psi_t(\mathbf{p}_t^*) = \frac{1}{2}\sum_{i=1}^{d}\sum_{j=1}^{d} \frac{\partial^2 \ell(\mathbf{p}, y)}{\partial p_i \partial p_j}\bigg|_{\mathbf{p}} (\widehat{p}_{i,t} - p_{i,t}^*)(\widehat{p}_{j,t} - p_{j,t}^*)$$

(for some $\mathbf{p} \in \mathcal{D}$)

$$\ge \frac{C}{2}\left\|\widehat{\mathbf{p}}_t - \mathbf{p}_t^*\right\|^2,$$

where we used the fact that $\nabla \Psi_t(\mathbf{p}_t^*) = 0$ and the assumption on the Hessian of the loss function. On the other hand,

$$\begin{aligned}
\Psi_t(\widehat{\mathbf{p}}_t) &- \Psi_t(\mathbf{p}_t^*) \\
&= \left(\Psi_{t-1}(\widehat{\mathbf{p}}_t) - \Psi_t(\mathbf{p}_t^*)\right) + \left(\Psi_t(\widehat{\mathbf{p}}_t) - \Psi_{t-1}(\widehat{\mathbf{p}}_t)\right) \\
&\le \left(\Psi_{t-1}(\mathbf{p}_t^*) - \Psi_t(\mathbf{p}_t^*)\right) + \left(\Psi_t(\widehat{\mathbf{p}}_t) - \Psi_{t-1}(\widehat{\mathbf{p}}_t)\right) \\
&\quad \text{(by the definition of } \widehat{\mathbf{p}}_t) \\
&= \frac{1}{t(t-1)}\sum_{s=1}^{t-1}\left(\ell(\mathbf{p}_t^*, y_s) - \ell(\widehat{\mathbf{p}}_t, y_s)\right) + \frac{1}{t}\left(\ell(\widehat{\mathbf{p}}_t, y_t) - \ell(\mathbf{p}_t^*, y_t)\right) \\
&\le \frac{2B}{t}\left\|\widehat{\mathbf{p}}_t - \mathbf{p}_t^*\right\|,
\end{aligned}$$

where at the last step we used the Lipschitz property of $\ell(\cdot, y)$. Comparing the upper and lower bounds derived for $\Psi_t(\widehat{\mathbf{p}}_t) - \Psi_t(\mathbf{p}_t^*)$, we see that for every $t = 1, 2, \ldots,$

$$\left\|\widehat{\mathbf{p}}_t - \mathbf{p}_t^*\right\| \le \frac{4B}{Ct}.$$

Therefore,

$$\widehat{L}_n - \inf_{E \in \mathcal{E}} L_{E,n} \le \sum_{t=1}^{n}\left(\ell(\widehat{\mathbf{p}}_t, y) - \ell(\mathbf{p}_t^*, y)\right) \le \sum_{t=1}^{n} B\left\|\widehat{\mathbf{p}}_t - \mathbf{p}_t^*\right\| \le \frac{4B^2}{C}\sum_{t=1}^{n}\frac{1}{t}$$

as desired. ■

Theorem 3.1 establishes general conditions for the loss function under which the regret grows at the slow rate of $\ln n$. Just as in the case of the square loss, the size of the class of experts does not appear explicitly in the upper bound. In particular, the upper bound is independent of the dimension. The third condition basically requires that the loss function have an approximately quadratic behavior around the minimum. The last condition is satisfied for many smooth strictly convex loss functions. For example, if $\mathcal{Y} = \mathcal{D}$ and $\ell(\mathbf{p}, \mathbf{y}) = \|\mathbf{p} - \mathbf{y}\|^\alpha$ for some $\alpha \in (1, 2]$, then all assumptions are easily seen to be satisfied. Other general conditions under which the follow-the-best-expert forecaster achieves logarithmic regret have been thoroughly studied. Pointers to the literature are given at the end of the chapter.

3.3 Exp-concave Loss Functions

Now we return to the scenario of Section 2.1. Thus, we consider a finite class of N experts. In this section we introduce a class of loss functions that enjoys some useful properties when used in conjunction with the exponential potential $\Phi_\eta(\mathbf{u}) = \frac{1}{\eta} \ln \left(\sum_{i=1}^N e^{\eta u_i} \right)$. A loss function ℓ is *exp-concave* for a certain $\eta > 0$ if the function $F(z) = e^{-\eta \ell(z,y)}$ is concave for all $y \in \mathcal{Y}$. Exp-concavity is a stronger property than convexity of ℓ in the first argument (see the exercises). The larger the value of η, the more stringent the assumption of exp-concavity is. The following result shows a key property of exp-concave functions. Recall that the exponentially weighted average forecaster is defined by $\widehat{p}_t = \sum_{i=1}^N w_{i,t-1} f_{i,t} / \sum_{j=1}^N w_{j,t-1}$, where $w_{i,t-1} = e^{-\eta L_{i,t-1}}$.

Theorem 3.2. *If the loss function ℓ is exp-concave for $\eta > 0$, then the regret of the exponentially weighted average forecaster (used with the same value of η) satisfies, for all $y_1, \ldots, y_n \in \mathcal{Y}$, $\Phi_\eta(\mathbf{R}_n) \leq \Phi_\eta(\mathbf{0})$.*

Proof. It suffices to show that the value of the potential function can never increase; that is, $\Phi_\eta(\mathbf{R}_t) \leq \Phi_\eta(\mathbf{R}_{t-1})$ or, equivalently,

$$\sum_{i=1}^N e^{-\eta L_{i,t-1}} e^{\eta r_{i,t}} \leq \sum_{i=1}^N e^{-\eta L_{i,t-1}}.$$

This may be rewritten as

$$\exp\left(-\eta \ell(\widehat{p}_t, y_t)\right) \geq \frac{\sum_{i=1}^N w_{i,t-1} \exp\left(-\eta \ell(f_{i,t}, y_t)\right)}{\sum_{j=1}^N w_{j,t-1}}. \tag{3.2}$$

But this follows from the definition of $\widehat{p}$, the concavity of $F(z)$, and Jensen's inequality. ∎

The fact that a forecaster is able to guarantee $\Phi_\eta(\mathbf{R}_n) \leq \Phi_\eta(\mathbf{0})$ immediately implies that his regret is bounded by a constant independently of the sequence length n.

Proposition 3.1. *If, for some loss function ℓ and for some $\eta > 0$, a forecaster satisfies $\Phi_\eta(\mathbf{R}_n) \leq \Phi_\eta(\mathbf{0})$ for all $y_1, \ldots, y_n \in \mathcal{Y}$, then the regret of the forecaster is bounded by*

$$\widehat{L}_n - \min_{i=1,\ldots,N} L_{i,n} \leq \frac{\ln N}{\eta}.$$

Proof. Using $\Phi_\eta(\mathbf{R}_n) \leq \Phi_\eta(\mathbf{0})$ we immediately get

$$\widehat{L}_n - \min_{i=1,\ldots,N} L_{i,n} = \max_{i=1,\ldots,N} R_{i,n} \leq \frac{1}{\eta} \ln \sum_{j=1}^N e^{\eta R_{j,n}} = \Phi_\eta(\mathbf{R}_n) \leq \Phi_\eta(\mathbf{0}) = \frac{\ln N}{\eta}. \quad ∎$$

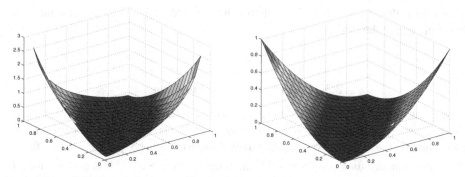

Figure 3.1. The relative entropy loss and the square loss plotted for $\mathcal{D} = \mathcal{Y} = [0, 1]$.

Clearly, the larger the η, the better is the bound guaranteed by Proposition 3.1. For each loss function ℓ there is a maximal value of η for which ℓ is exp-concave (if such an η exists at all). To optimize performance, the exponentially weighted average forecaster should be run using this largest value of η.

For the exponentially weighted average forecaster, combining Theorem 3.2 with Proposition 3.1 we get the regret bounded by $(\ln N)/\eta$ for all exp-concave losses (where η may depend on the loss), a quantity which is independent of the length n of the sequence of outcomes. Note that, apart from the assumption of exp-concavity, we do not assume anything else about the loss function. In particular, we do not explicitly assume that the loss function is bounded. The examples that follow show that some simple and important loss functions are exp-concave (see the exercises for further examples).

Relative Entropy Loss

Let $\mathcal{D} = \mathcal{Y} = [0, 1]$, and consider, the relative entropy loss $\ell(\widehat{p}, y) = y \ln(y/\widehat{p}) + (1 - y) \ln\big((1 - y)/(1 - \widehat{p})\big)$. With an easy calculation one can check that for $\eta = 1$ the function $F(z)$ is concave for all values of y. Note that this is an unbounded loss function. A special case of this loss function, for $\mathcal{Y} = \{0, 1\}$ and $\mathcal{D} = [0, 1]$, is the logarithmic loss $\ell(z, y) = -\mathbb{I}_{\{y=1\}} \ln z - \mathbb{I}_{\{y=0\}} \ln(1 - z)$. The logarithmic loss function plays a central role in several applications, and we devote a separate chapter to it (Chapter 9).

Square Loss

This loss function is defined by $\ell(z, y) = (z - y)^2$, where $\mathcal{D} = \mathcal{Y} = [0, 1]$. Straightforward calculation shows that $F(z)$ is concave if and only if, for all z, $(z - y)^2 \leq 1/(2\eta)$. This is clearly guaranteed if $\eta \leq 1/2$.

Absolute Loss

Let $\mathcal{D} = \mathcal{Y} = [0, 1]$, and consider the absolute loss $\ell(z, y) = |z - y|$. It is easy to see that $F(z)$ is not concave for any value of η. In fact, as is shown in Section 3.7, for this loss function there is no forecaster whose cumulative excess loss can be bounded independently of n.

Exp-concave losses also make it easy to prove regret bounds that hold for countably many experts. The only modification we need is that the exponential potential $\Phi_\eta(\mathbf{R}) = \frac{1}{\eta} \ln \left(\sum_{i=1}^{N} e^{\eta R_i} \right)$ be changed to $\Phi_\eta(\mathbf{R}) = \frac{1}{\eta} \ln \left(\sum_{i=1}^{\infty} q_i e^{\eta R_i} \right)$, where $\{q_i : i = 1, 2 \ldots\}$ is any probability distribution over the set of positive integers. This ensures convergence of the series. Equivalently, q_i represents the initial weight of expert i (as in Exercise 2.5).

Corollary 3.1. *Assume that (ℓ, η) satisfy the assumption of Theorem 3.2. For any countable class of experts and for any probability distribution $\{q_i : i = 1, 2 \ldots\}$ over the set of positive integers, the exponentially weighted average forecaster defined above satisfies, for all $n \geq 1$ and for all $y_1, \ldots, y_n \in \mathcal{Y}$,*

$$\widehat{L}_n \leq \inf_{i \geq 1} \left(L_{i,n} + \frac{1}{\eta} \ln \frac{1}{q_i} \right).$$

Proof. The proof is almost identical to that of Theorem 3.2; we merely need to redefine $w_{i,t-1}$ in that proof as $q_i e^{-\eta L_{i,t-1}}$. This allows us to conclude that $\Phi_\eta(\mathbf{R}_n) \leq \Phi_\eta(\mathbf{0})$. Hence, for all $i \geq 1$,

$$q_i e^{\eta R_{i,n}} \leq \sum_{j=1}^{\infty} q_j e^{\eta R_{j,n}} = e^{\eta \Phi_\eta(\mathbf{R}_n)} \leq e^{\eta \Phi_\eta(\mathbf{0})} = 1.$$

Solving for $R_{i,n}$ yields the desired bound. ∎

Thus, the cumulative loss of the forecaster exceeds the loss of each expert by at most a constant, but the constant depends on the expert. If we write the exponentially weighted forecaster for countably many experts in the form

$$\widehat{p}_t = \frac{\sum_{i=1}^{\infty} f_{i,t} \exp\left(-\eta \left(L_{i,t-1} + \frac{1}{\eta} \ln \frac{1}{q_i} \right) \right)}{\sum_{j=1}^{\infty} \exp\left(-\eta \left(L_{j,t-1} + \frac{1}{\eta} \ln \frac{1}{q_j} \right) \right)},$$

then we see that the quantity $\frac{1}{\eta} \ln(1/q_i)$ may be regarded as a "penalty" we add to the cumulative loss of expert i at each time t. Corollary 3.1 is a so-called "oracle inequality," which states that the mixture forecaster achieves a cumulative loss matching the best penalized cumulative loss of the experts (see also Section 3.5).

A Mixture Forecaster for Exp-concave Losses

We close this section by showing how the exponentially weighted average predictor can be extended naturally to handle certain uncountable classes of experts. The class we consider is given by the convex hull of a finite number of "base" experts. Thus, the goal of the forecaster is to predict as well as the best convex combination of the base experts. The formal model is described as follows: consider N (base) experts whose predictions, at time t, are given by $f_{i,t} \in \mathcal{D}, i = 1, \ldots, N, t = 1, \ldots, n$. We denote by $\mathbf{f}_t$ the vector $(f_{1,t}, \ldots, f_{N,t})$ of expert advice at time t. The decision space $\mathcal{D}$ is assumed to be a convex set, and we assume that the loss function ℓ is exp-concave for a certain value $\eta > 0$. Define the regret of a forecaster, with respect to the convex hull of the N base experts, by

$$\widehat{L}_n - \inf_{\mathbf{q} \in \Delta} L_{\mathbf{q},n} = \sum_{t=1}^{n} \ell(\widehat{p}_t, y_t) - \inf_{\mathbf{q} \in \Delta} \sum_{t=1}^{n} \ell(\mathbf{q} \cdot \mathbf{f}_t, y_t),$$

where $\widehat{L}_n$ is the cumulative loss of the forecaster, Δ denotes the simplex of N-vectors $\mathbf{q} = (q_1, \ldots, q_N)$, with $q_i \geq 0$, $\sum_{i=1}^{N} q_i = 1$, and $\mathbf{q} \cdot \mathbf{f}_t$ denotes the element of $\mathcal{D}$ given by the convex combination $\sum_{i=1}^{N} q_i f_{i,t}$. Finally, $L_{\mathbf{q},n}$ denotes the cumulative loss of the expert associated with $\mathbf{q}$.

Next we analyze the regret (in the sense defined earlier) of the exponentially weighted average forecaster defined by the "mixture"

$$\widehat{p} = \frac{\int_\Delta w_{\mathbf{q},t-1} \mathbf{q} \cdot \mathbf{f} \, d\mathbf{q}}{\int_\Delta w_{\mathbf{q},t-1} d\mathbf{q}},$$

where for each $\mathbf{q} \in \Delta$, $w_{\mathbf{q},t-1} = \exp\left(-\eta \sum_{s=1}^{t-1} \ell(\mathbf{q} \cdot \mathbf{f}_s, y_s)\right)$. Just as before, the value of η used in the definition of the weights is such that the loss function is exp-concave. Thus, the forecaster calculates a weighted average over the whole simplex Δ, exponentially weighted by the past performance corresponding to each vector $\mathbf{q}$ of convex coefficients. At this point we are not concerned with computational issues, but in Section 9 we will see that the forecaster can be computed easily in certain special cases. The next theorem shows that the regret is bounded by a quantity of the order of $N \ln(n/N)$. This is not always optimal; just consider the case of the square loss and constant experts studied in Section 3.2 for which we derived a bound independent of N. However, the bound shown here is much more general and can be seen to be tight in some cases; for example, for the logarithmic loss studied in Chapter 9. To keep the argument simple, we assume that the loss function is bounded, though this condition can be relaxed in some cases.

Theorem 3.3. *Assume that the loss function ℓ is exp-concave for η and it takes values in $[0, 1]$. Then the exponentially weighted mixture forecaster defined above satisfies*

$$\widehat{L}_n - \inf_{\mathbf{q}\in\Delta} L_{\mathbf{q},n} \le \frac{N}{\eta} \ln \frac{e\eta n}{N}.$$

Proof.   Defining, for all $\mathbf{q}$, the regret

$$R_{\mathbf{q},n} = \widehat{L}_n - L_{\mathbf{q},n}$$

we may write $\mathbf{R}_n$ for the function $\mathbf{q} \mapsto R_{\mathbf{q},n}$. Introducing the potential

$$\Phi_\eta(\mathbf{R}_n) = \int_\Delta e^{\eta R_{\mathbf{q},n}} d\mathbf{q}$$

we see, by mimicking the proof of Theorem 3.2, that $\Phi_\eta(\mathbf{R}_n) \le \Phi_\eta(\mathbf{0}) = 1/(N!)$. It remains to relate the excess cumulative loss to the value $\Phi_\eta(\mathbf{R}_n)$ of the potential function.

Denote by $\mathbf{q}^*$ the vector in Δ for which

$$L_{\mathbf{q}^*,n} = \inf_{\mathbf{q}\in\Delta} L_{\mathbf{q},n}.$$

Since the loss function is convex in its first argument (see Exercise 3.4), for any $\mathbf{q}' \in \Delta$ and $\lambda \in (0, 1)$,

$$L_{(1-\lambda)\mathbf{q}^*+\lambda\mathbf{q}',n} \le (1-\lambda)L_{\mathbf{q}^*,n} + \lambda L_{\mathbf{q}',n} \le (1-\lambda)L_{\mathbf{q}^*,n} + \lambda n,$$

where we used the boundedness of the loss function. Therefore, for any fixed $\lambda \in (0, 1)$,

$$
\begin{aligned}
\Phi_\eta(\mathbf{R}_n) &= \int_\Delta e^{\eta R_{\mathbf{q},n}} \, d\mathbf{q} \\
&= e^{\eta \widehat{L}_n} \int_\Delta e^{-\eta L_{\mathbf{q},n}} \, d\mathbf{q} \\
&\geq e^{\eta \widehat{L}_n} \int_{\{\mathbf{q}\,:\,\mathbf{q}=(1-\lambda)\mathbf{q}^*+\lambda\mathbf{q}',\mathbf{q}'\in\Delta\}} e^{-\eta L_{\mathbf{q},n}} \, d\mathbf{q} \\
&\geq e^{\eta \widehat{L}_n} \int_{\{\mathbf{q}\,:\,\mathbf{q}=(1-\lambda)\mathbf{q}^*+\lambda\mathbf{q}',\mathbf{q}'\in\Delta\}} e^{-\eta\left((1-\lambda)L_{\mathbf{q}^*,n}+\lambda n\right)} \, d\mathbf{q} \\
&\qquad \text{(by the above inequality)} \\
&= e^{\eta \widehat{L}_n} e^{-\eta\left((1-\lambda)L_{\mathbf{q}^*,n}+\lambda n\right)} \int_{\{\mathbf{q}\,:\,\mathbf{q}=(1-\lambda)\mathbf{q}^*+\lambda\mathbf{q}',\mathbf{q}'\in\Delta\}} \, d\mathbf{q}.
\end{aligned}
$$

The integral on the right-hand side is the volume of the simplex, scaled by λ and centered at $\mathbf{q}^*$. Clearly, this equals λ^N times the volume of Δ, that is, $\lambda^N/(N!)$. Using $\Phi_\eta(\mathbf{R}_n) \leq 1/(N!)$, and rearranging the obtained inequality, we get

$$
\widehat{L}_n - \inf_{\mathbf{q}\in\Delta} L_{\mathbf{q},n} \leq \widehat{L}_n - (1-\lambda)L_{\mathbf{q}^*,n} \leq \frac{1}{\eta}\ln\lambda^{-N} + \lambda n.
$$

The minimal value on the right-hand side is achieved by $\lambda = N/\eta n$, which yields the bound of the theorem. ∎

3.4 The Greedy Forecaster

In several arguments we have seen so far for analyzing the performance of weighted average forecasters, the key of the proof is bounding the increase of the value of the potential function $\Phi(\mathbf{R}_t)$ on the regret at time t with respect to the previous value $\Phi(\mathbf{R}_{t-1})$. In Theorem 2.1 we do this using the Blackwell condition. In some cases special properties of the loss function may be used to derive sharper bounds. For example, in Section 3.3 it is shown that for some loss functions the exponential potential in fact *decreases* at each step (see Theorem 3.2). Thus, one may be tempted to construct prediction strategies which, at each time instance, minimize the worst-case increase of the potential. The purpose of this section is to explore this possibility.

The first idea one might have is to construct a forecaster $\widehat{p}$ that, at each time instant t, predicts to minimize the worst-case regret, that is,

$$
\begin{aligned}
\widehat{p}_t &= \operatorname*{argmin}_{p\in\mathcal{D}} \sup_{y_t\in\mathcal{Y}} \max_{i=1,\dots,N} R_{i,t} \\
&= \operatorname*{argmin}_{p\in\mathcal{D}} \sup_{y_t\in\mathcal{Y}} \max_{i=1,\dots,N} \left(R_{i,t-1} + \ell(p_t, y_t) - \ell(f_{i,t}, y_t)\right).
\end{aligned}
$$

It is easy to see that the minimum in $\widehat{p}_t$ exists whenever the loss function ℓ is bounded and convex in its first argument. However, the minimum may not be unique. In such cases we may choose a minimizer by any pre-specified rule. Unfortunately, this strategy, known as fictitious play in the context of playing repeated games (see Chapter 7), fails to guarantee a vanishing per-round regret (see the exercises).

A next attempt may be to minimize, instead of $\max_{i \leq N} R_{i,t}$, a "smooth" version of the same such as the exponential potential

$$\Phi_\eta(\mathbf{R}_t) = \frac{1}{\eta} \ln \left(\sum_{i=1}^{N} e^{\eta R_{i,t}} \right).$$

Note that if $\eta \max_{i \leq N} R_{i,t}$ is large, then $\Phi_\eta(\mathbf{R}_t) \approx \max_{i \leq N} R_{i,t}$; but Φ_η is now a smooth function of its components. The quantity η is a kind of smoothing parameter. For large values of η the approximation is tighter, though the level curves of Φ_η become less smooth (see Figure 2.3).

On the basis of the potential function Φ, we may now introduce the forecaster $\widehat{p}$ that, at every time instant, greedily minimizes the largest possible increase of the potential function for all possible outcomes y_t. That is,

$$\widehat{p}_t = \operatorname*{argmin}_{p \in \mathcal{D}} \ \sup_{y_t \in \mathcal{Y}} \ \Phi(\mathbf{R}_{t-1} + \mathbf{r}_t) \qquad \text{(the greedy forecaster)}.$$

Recall that the ith component of the regret vector $\mathbf{r}_t$ is $\ell(p, y_t) - \ell(f_{i,t}, y_t)$. Note that, for the exponential potential, the previous condition is equivalent to

$$\widehat{p}_t = \operatorname*{argmin}_{p \in \mathcal{D}} \ \sup_{y_t \in \mathcal{Y}} \ \left(\ell(p, y_t) + \frac{1}{\eta} \ln \sum_{i=1}^{N} e^{-\eta L_{i,t}} \right).$$

In what follows, we show that the greedy forecaster is well defined, and, in fact, has the same performance guarantees as the weighted average forecaster based on the same potential function.

Assume that the potential function Φ is convex. Then, because the supremum of convex functions is convex, $\sup_{y_t \in \mathcal{Y}} \Phi(\mathbf{R}_{t-1} + \mathbf{r}_t)$ is a convex function of p if ℓ is convex in its first argument. Thus, the minimum over p exists, though it may not be unique. Once again, a minimizer may be chosen by any pre-specified rule. To compute the predictions $\widehat{p}_t$, a convex function has to be minimized at each step. This is computationally feasible in many cases, though it is, in general, not as simple as computing, for example, the predictions of a weighted average forecaster. In some cases, however, the predictions may be given in a closed form. We provide some examples.

The following obvious result helps analyze greedy forecasters. Better bounds for certain losses are derived in Section 3.5 (see Proposition 3.3).

Theorem 3.4. *Let $\Phi : \mathbb{R}^N \to \mathbb{R}$ be a nonnegative, twice differentiable convex function. Assume that there exists a forecaster whose regret vector satisfies*

$$\Phi(\mathbf{R}'_t) \leq \Phi(\mathbf{R}'_{t-1}) + c_t$$

for any sequence $\mathbf{r}'_1, \ldots, \mathbf{r}'_n$ of regret vectors and for any $t = 1, \ldots, n$, where c_t is a constant depending on t only. Then the regret $\mathbf{R}_t$ of the greedy forecaster satisfies

$$\Phi(\mathbf{R}_n) \leq \Phi(\mathbf{0}) + \sum_{t=1}^{n} c_t.$$

Proof. It suffices to show that, for every $t = 1, \ldots, n$,

$$\Phi(\mathbf{R}_t) \leq \Phi(\mathbf{R}_{t-1}) + c_t.$$

By the definition of the greedy forecaster, this is equivalent to saying that there exists a $\widehat{p}_t \in \mathcal{D}$ such that

$$\sup_{y_t \in \mathcal{Y}} \Phi\left(\mathbf{R}_{t-1} + \mathbf{r}_t\right) \leq \Phi(\mathbf{R}_{t-1}) + c_t,$$

where $\mathbf{r}_t$ is the vector with components $\ell(\widehat{p}_t, y_t) - \ell(f_{i,t}, y_t)$, $i = 1, \ldots, N$. The existence of such a $\widehat{p}_t$ is guaranteed by assumption. ∎

The weighted average forecasters analyzed in Sections 2.1 and 3.3 all satisfy the condition of Theorem 3.4, and therefore the corresponding greedy forecasters inherit their properties proven in Theorems 2.1 and 3.2. Some simple examples of greedy forecasters using the exponential potential Φ_η follow.

Absolute Loss
Consider the absolute loss $\ell(\widehat{p}, y) = |\widehat{p} - y|$ in the simple case when $\mathcal{Y} = \{0, 1\}$ and $\mathcal{D} = [0, 1]$. Consider the greedy forecaster based on the exponential potential Φ_η. Since y_t is binary valued, determining $\widehat{p}_t$ amounts to minimizing the maximum of two convex functions. After trivial simplifications we obtain

$$\widehat{p}_t = \underset{p \in [0,1]}{\operatorname{argmin}} \max \left\{ \sum_{i=1}^{N} e^{\eta\left(\ell(p,0) - \ell(f_{i,t},0) - L_{i,t-1}\right)}, \sum_{i=1}^{N} e^{\eta\left(\ell(p,1) - \ell(f_{i,t},1) - L_{i,t-1}\right)} \right\}.$$

(Recall that $L_{i,t} = \ell(f_{i,1}, y_1) + \cdots + \ell(f_{i,t}, y_t)$ denotes the cumulative loss of expert i at time t.) To determine the minimum, just observe that the maximum of two convex functions achieves its minimum either at a point where the two functions are equal or at the minimum of one of the two functions. Thus, $\widehat{p}$ either equals 0 or 1, or

$$\frac{1}{2} + \frac{1}{2\eta} \ln \frac{\sum_{i=1}^{N} e^{-\eta L_{i,t-1} - \eta \ell(f_{i,t},1)}}{\sum_{j=1}^{N} e^{-\eta L_{j,t-1} - \eta \ell(f_{j,t},0)}}$$

depending on which of the three values gives a smaller worst-case value of the potential function. Now it follows by Theorems 3.4 and 2.2 that the cumulative loss of this greedy forecaster is bounded as

$$\widehat{L}_n - \min_{i=1,\ldots,N} L_{i,n} \leq \frac{\ln N}{\eta} + \frac{n\eta}{8}.$$

Square Loss
Consider next the setup of the previous example with the only difference that the loss function now is $\ell(\widehat{p}, y) = (\widehat{p} - y)^2$. The calculations may be repeated the same way, and, interestingly, it turns out that the greedy forecaster $\widehat{p}_t$ has exactly the same form as before; that is, it equals either 0 or 1, or

$$\frac{1}{2} + \frac{1}{2\eta} \ln \frac{\sum_{i=1}^{N} e^{-\eta L_{i,t-1} - \eta \ell(f_{i,t},1)}}{\sum_{j=1}^{N} e^{-\eta L_{j,t-1} - \eta \ell(f_{j,t},0)}}$$

depending on which of the three values gives a smaller worst-case value of the potential function. In Theorem 3.2 it is shown that special properties of the square loss imply that if the exponentially weighted average forecaster is used with $\eta = 1/2$, then the potential function cannot increase in any step. Theorem 3.2, combined with the previous result shows that if $\eta = 1/2$, then the greedy forecaster satisfies

$$\widehat{L}_n - \min_{i=1,\dots,N} L_{i,n} \leq 2 \ln N.$$

Logarithmic Loss

Again let $\mathcal{Y} = \{0, 1\}$ and $\mathcal{D} = [0, 1]$, and consider the logarithmic loss $\ell(\widehat{p}, y) = -\mathbb{I}_{\{y=1\}} \ln \widehat{p} - \mathbb{I}_{\{y=0\}} \ln(1 - \widehat{p})$ and the exponential potential. It is interesting that in this case, for $\eta = 1$, the greedy forecaster coincides with the exponentially weighted average forecaster (see the exercises).

3.5   The Aggregating Forecaster

The analysis based on exp-concavity from Section 3.3 hinges on finding, for a given loss, some $\eta > 0$ such that the exponential potential $\Phi_\eta(\mathbf{R}_n)$ remains bounded by the initial potential $\Phi_\eta(\mathbf{0})$ when the predictions are computed by the exponentially weighted average forecaster. If such an η is found, then Proposition 3.1 entails that the regret remains uniformly bounded by $(\ln N)/\eta$. However, as we show in this section, for all losses for which such an η exists, one might obtain an even better regret bound by finding a forecaster (not necessarily based on weighted averages) guaranteeing $\Phi_\eta(\mathbf{R}_n) \leq \Phi_\eta(\mathbf{0})$ for a larger value of η than the largest η that the weighted average forecaster can afford. Thus, we look for a forecaster whose predictions $\widehat{p}_t$ satisfy $\Phi_\eta(\mathbf{R}_{t-1} + \mathbf{r}_t) \leq \Phi_\eta(\mathbf{R}_{t-1})$ irrespective of the choice of the next outcome $y_t \in \mathcal{Y}$ (recall that, as usual, $\mathbf{r}_t = (r_{1,t}, \dots, r_{N,t})$, where $r_{i,t} = \ell(\widehat{p}_t, y_t) - \ell(f_{i,t}, y_t)$). It is easy to see that this is equivalent to the condition

$$\ell(\widehat{p}_t, y_t) \leq -\frac{1}{\eta} \ln \left(\sum_{i=1}^{N} e^{-\eta \ell(f_{i,t}, y_t)} \mathbf{q}_{i,t-1} \right) \qquad \text{for all } y_t \in \mathcal{Y}.$$

The distribution $q_{1,t-1}, \dots, q_{N,t-1}$ is defined via the weights associated with the exponential potential. That is, $q_{i,t-1} = e^{-\eta L_{i,t-1}} / \left(\sum_{j=1}^{N} e^{-\eta L_{j,t-1}} \right)$. To allow the analysis of losses for which no forecaster is able to prevent the exponential potential from ever increasing, we somewhat relax the previous condition by replacing the factor $1/\eta$ with $\mu(\eta)/\eta$. The real-valued function μ is called the *mixability curve* for the loss ℓ, and it is formally defined as follows. For all $\eta > 0$, $\mu(\eta)$ is the infimum of all numbers c such that for all N, for all probability distributions $(q_1, \dots, q_N)$, and for all choices of the expert advice $f_1, \dots, f_N \in \mathcal{D}$, there exists a $\widehat{p} \in \mathcal{D}$ such that

$$\ell(\widehat{p}, y) \leq -\frac{c}{\eta} \ln \left(\sum_{i=1}^{N} e^{-\eta \ell(f_i, y)} \mathbf{q}_i \right) \qquad \text{for all } y \in \mathcal{Y}. \qquad (3.3)$$

Using the terminology introduced by Vovk, we call *aggregating forecaster* any forecaster that, when run with input parameter η, predicts using $\widehat{p}$, which satisfies (3.3), with $c = \mu(\eta)$.

The mixability curve can be used to obtain a bound on the loss of the aggregating forecaster for all values $\eta > 0$.

Proposition 3.2. *Let μ be the mixability curve for an arbitrary loss function ℓ. Then, for all $\eta > 0$, the aggregating forecaster achieves*

$$\widehat{L}_n \leq \mu(\eta) \min_{i=1,\dots,N} L_{i,n} + \frac{\mu(\eta)}{\eta} \ln N$$

for all $n \geq 1$ and for all $y_1, \dots, y_n \in \mathcal{Y}$.

Proof.   Let $W_t = \sum_{i=1}^{N} e^{-\eta L_{i,t}}$. Then, by definition of mixability, for each t there exists a $\widehat{p}_t \in \mathcal{D}$ such that

$$\ell(\widehat{p}_t, y_t) \le -\frac{\mu(\eta)}{\eta} \ln \left(\frac{\sum_{i=1}^{N} e^{-\eta L_{i,t-1}} e^{-\eta \ell(f_{i,t}, y_t)}}{\sum_{j=1}^{N} e^{-\eta L_{j,t-1}}} \right) = -\frac{\mu(\eta)}{\eta} \ln \left(\frac{W_t}{W_{t-1}} \right).$$

Summing the leftmost and rightmost members of this inequality for $t = 1, \dots, n$ we get

$$
\begin{aligned}
\widehat{L}_n &\le -\frac{\mu(\eta)}{\eta} \ln \left(\prod_{t=1}^{n} \frac{W_t}{W_{t-1}} \right) \\
&= -\frac{\mu(\eta)}{\eta} \ln \frac{W_n}{W_0} \\
&= -\frac{\mu(\eta)}{\eta} \ln \left(\frac{\sum_{j=1}^{N} e^{-\eta L_{j,n}}}{N} \right) \\
&\le \frac{\mu(\eta)}{\eta} \left(\eta L_{i,n} + \ln N \right)
\end{aligned}
$$

for any expert $i = 1, \dots, N$. ■

In the introduction to Chapter 2 we described the problem of prediction with expert advice as an iterated game between the forecaster and the environment. To play this game, the environment must use some strategy for choosing expert advice and outcome at each round based on the forecaster's past predictions. Fix such a strategy for the environment and fix a strategy for the forecaster (e.g., the weighted average forecaster). For a pair $(a, b) \in \mathbb{R}_+^2$, say that the forecaster wins if his strategy achieves

$$\widehat{L}_n \le a \min_{i=1,\dots,N} L_{i,n} + b \ln N$$

for all n, $N \ge 1$; otherwise the environment wins (suppose that the number N of experts is chosen by the environment at the beginning of the game).

This game was introduced and analyzed through the notion of mixability curve in the pioneering work of Vovk [298]. Under mild conditions on $\mathcal{D}$, $\mathcal{Y}$, and ℓ, Vovk shows the following result:

- For each pair $(a, b) \in \mathbb{R}_+^2$ the game is determined. That is, either there exists a forecasting strategy that wins irrespective of the strategy used by the environment or the environment has a strategy that defeats any forecasting strategy.
- The forecaster wins exactly for those pairs $(a, b) \in \mathbb{R}_+^2$ such that there exists some $\eta \ge 0$ satisfying $\mu(\eta) \le a$ and $\mu(\eta)/\eta \le b$.

Vovk's result shows that the mixability curve is exactly the boundary of the set of all pairs (a, b) such that the forecaster can always guarantee that $\widehat{L}_n \le a \min_{i \le N} L_{i,n} + b \ln N$. It can be shown, under mild assumptions on ℓ, that $\mu \ge 1$. The largest value of η for which $\mu(\eta) = 1$ is especially relevant to our regret minimization goal. Indeed, for this η we can get the strong regret bounds of the form $(\ln N)/\eta$.

We call η-*mixable* any loss function for which there exists an η satisfying $\mu(\eta) = 1$ in the special case $\mathcal{D} = [0, 1]$ and $\mathcal{Y} = \{0, 1\}$ (the choice of 0 and 1 is arbitrary; the theorem can be proven for any two real numbers a, b, with $a < b$). The next result characterizes mixable losses.

Theorem 3.5 (Mixability Theorem). *Let $\mathcal{D} = [0, 1]$, $\mathcal{Y} = \{0, 1\}$, and choose a loss function ℓ. Consider the set $S \subseteq [0, 1]^2$ of all pairs (x, y) such that there exists some $p \in [0, 1]$ satisfying $\ell(p, 0) \leq x$ and $\ell(p, 1) \leq y$. For each $\eta > 0$, introduce the homeomorphism $H_\eta : [0, 1]^2 \to [e^{-\eta}, 1]^2$ defined by $H_\eta(x, y) = (e^{-\eta x}, e^{-\eta y})$. Then ℓ is η-mixable if and only if the set $H_\eta(S)$ is convex.*

Proof.   We need to find, for some $\eta > 0$, for all $y \in \{0, 1\}$, for all probability distributions $q_1, \ldots, q_N$, and for any expert advice $f_1, \ldots, f_N \in [0, 1]$, a number $p \in [0, 1]$ satisfying

$$\ell(p, y) \leq -\frac{1}{\eta} \ln \left(\sum_{i=1}^{N} e^{-\eta \ell(f_i, y)} q_i \right).$$

This condition can be rewritten as

$$e^{-\eta \ell(p, y)} \geq \sum_{i=1}^{N} e^{-\eta \ell(f_i, y)} q_i$$

and, recalling that $y \in \{0, 1\}$, as

$$e^{-\eta \ell(p, 0)} \geq \sum_{i=1}^{N} e^{-\eta \ell(f_i, 0)} q_i \quad \text{and} \quad e^{-\eta \ell(p, 1)} \geq \sum_{i=1}^{N} e^{-\eta \ell(f_i, 1)} q_i.$$

The condition says that a prediction p must exist so that each coordinate of $H_\eta\big(\ell(p, 0), \ell(p, 1)\big)$ is not smaller than the corresponding coordinate of the convex combination $\sum_{i=1}^{N} H_\eta\big(\ell(f_i, 0), \ell(f_i, 1)\big) q_i$. If $H_\eta(S)$ is convex, then the convex combination belongs to $H_\eta(S)$. Therefore such a p always exists by definition of S (see Figure 3.2). This condition is easily seen to be also necessary. ∎

Remark 3.1.   Assume that $\ell_0(p) = \ell(p, 0)$ and $\ell_1(p) = \ell(p, 1)$ are twice differentiable so that $\ell_0(0) = \ell_1(1) = 0$, $\ell_0'(p) > 0$, $\ell_1'(p) < 0$ for all $0 < p < 1$. Then, for each $\eta > 0$, there exists a twice differentiable function h_η such that $y_\eta(p) = h_\eta\big(x_\eta(p)\big)$ and, by Theorem 3.5, ℓ is η-mixable if and only if h_η is concave. Using again the assumptions on ℓ, the concavity of h_η is equivalent to (see Exercise 3.11)

$$\eta \leq \inf_{0 < p < 1} \frac{\ell_0'(p)\ell_1''(p) - \ell_0''(p)\ell_1'(p)}{\ell_0'(p)\ell_1'(p)\big(\ell_1'(p) - \ell_0'(p)\big)}.$$

Remark 3.2.   We can extend the mixability theorem to provide a condition sufficient for mixability in the cases where $\mathcal{D} = \mathcal{Y} = [0, 1]$. To do this, we must verify that $e^{-\eta \ell(p, 0)} \geq \sum_{i=1}^{N} e^{-\eta \ell(f_i, 0)} q_i$ and $e^{-\eta \ell(p, 1)} \geq \sum_{i=1}^{N} e^{-\eta \ell(f_i, 1)} q_i$ together imply that $e^{-\eta \ell(p, y)} \geq \sum_{i=1}^{N} e^{-\eta \ell(f_i, y)} q_i$ for all $0 \leq y \leq 1$. This implication is satisfied whenever

$$e^{-\eta \ell(p, y)} - \sum_{i=1}^{N} e^{-\eta \ell(f_i, y)} q_i \tag{3.4}$$

is a concave function of $y \in [0, 1]$ for each fixed $p \in [0, 1]$, f_i, and q_i, $i = 1 \ldots, N$.

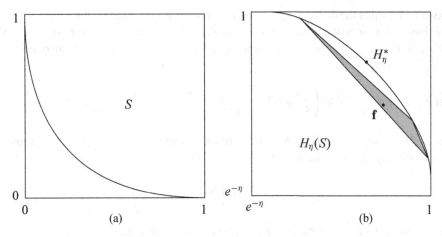

Figure 3.2. Mixability for the square loss. (a) Region S of points (x, y) satisfying $(p - 0)^2 \leq x$ and $(p - 1)^2 \leq y$ for some $p \in [0, 1]$. (b) Prediction p must correspond to a point $H_\eta^* = H_\eta\big(\ell(p, 0), \ell(p, 1)\big)$ to the north-east of $\mathbf{f} = \sum_{i=1}^{N} H_\eta\big(\ell(f_i, 0), \ell(f_i, 1)\big) q_i$. Note that $\mathbf{f}$ is in the convex hull (the shaded region) whose vertices are in $H_\eta(S)$. Therefore, if $H_\eta(S)$ is convex, then $\mathbf{f} \in H_\eta(S)$, and finding such a p is always possible by definition of S.

The next result proves a simple relationship between the aggregating forecaster and the greedy forecaster of Section 3.4.

Proposition 3.3. *For any η-mixable loss function ℓ, the greedy forecaster using the exponential potential Φ_η is an aggregating forecaster.*

Proof. If a loss ℓ is mixable, then for each t and for all $y_t \in \mathcal{Y}$ there exists $\widehat{p}_t \in \mathcal{D}$ satisfying

$$\ell(\widehat{p}_t, y_t) \leq -\frac{1}{\eta} \ln \frac{\sum_{i=1}^{N} e^{-\eta L_{i,t-1} - \eta \ell(f_{i,t}, y_t)}}{\sum_{j=1}^{N} e^{-\eta L_{j,t-1}}}.$$

Such a $\widehat{p}_t$ may then be defined by

$$\widehat{p}_t = \operatorname*{argmin}_{p \in \mathcal{D}} \sup_{y_t \in \mathcal{Y}} \left(\ell(p, y_t) + \frac{1}{\eta} \ln \frac{\sum_{i=1}^{N} e^{-\eta L_{i,t-1} - \eta \ell(f_{i,t}, y_t)}}{\sum_{j=1}^{N} e^{-\eta L_{j,t-1}}} \right)$$

$$= \operatorname*{argmin}_{p \in \mathcal{D}} \sup_{y_t \in \mathcal{Y}} \left(\ell(p, y_t) + \frac{1}{\eta} \ln \sum_{i=1}^{N} e^{-\eta L_{i,t}} \right),$$

which is exactly the definition of the greedy forecaster using the exponential potential. ∎

Oracle Inequality for Mixable Losses

The aggregating forecaster may be extended, in a simple way, to handle countably infinite classes of experts. Consider a sequence $f_1, f_2, \ldots$ of experts such that, at time t, the prediction of expert f_i is $f_{i,t} \in \mathcal{D}$. The goal of the forecaster is to predict as well as any of the experts f_i. In order to do this, we assign, to each expert, a positive number $\pi_i > 0$ such that $\sum_{i=1}^{\infty} \pi_i = 1$. The numbers π_i may be called *prior probabilities*.

Assume now that the decision space $\mathcal{D}$ is a compact metric space and the loss function ℓ is continuous. Let μ be the mixability curve of ℓ. By the definition of μ, for every $y_t \in \mathcal{Y}$, every sequence $q_1, q_2, \ldots$ of positive numbers with $\sum_i q_i = 1$, and $N > 0$, there exists a $\widehat{p}^{(N)} \in \mathcal{D}$ such that

$$\ell(\widehat{p}^{(N)}, y_t) \leq -\frac{\mu(\eta)}{\eta} \ln \left(\sum_{i=1}^{N} e^{-\eta \ell(f_i, y_t)} \frac{q_i}{\sum_{j=1}^{N} q_j} \right) \leq -\frac{\mu(\eta)}{\eta} \ln \left(\sum_{i=1}^{N} e^{-\eta \ell(f_i, y_t)} q_i \right).$$

Because $\mathcal{D}$ is compact, the sequence $\{\widehat{p}^{(N)}\}$ has an accumulation point $\widehat{p} \in \mathcal{D}$. Moreover, by the continuity of ℓ, this accumulation point satisfies

$$\ell(\widehat{p}, y_t) \leq -\frac{\mu(\eta)}{\eta} \ln \left(\sum_{i=1}^{\infty} e^{-\eta \ell(f_i, y_t)} q_i \right).$$

In other words, the aggregating forecaster, defined by $\widehat{p}_t$ satisfying

$$\ell(\widehat{p}_t, y_t) \leq -\frac{\mu(\eta)}{\eta} \ln \frac{\sum_{i=1}^{\infty} \pi_i \, e^{-\eta L_{i,t-1} - \eta \ell(f_{i,t}, y_t)}}{\sum_{j=1}^{\infty} \pi_j \, e^{-\eta L_{j,t-1}}}$$

is well defined. Then, by the same argument as in Corollary 3.1, for all $\eta > 0$, we obtain

$$\widehat{L}_n \leq \mu(\eta) \min_{i=1,2,\ldots} \left(L_{i,n} + \frac{1}{\eta} \ln \frac{1}{\pi_i} \right)$$

for all $n \geq 1$ and for all $y_1, \ldots, y_n \in \mathcal{Y}$.

By writing the forecaster in the form

$$\ell(\widehat{p}_t, y_t) \leq -\frac{\mu(\eta)}{\eta} \ln \frac{\sum_{i=1}^{\infty} \exp\left(-\eta \left(L_{i,t-1} + \frac{1}{\eta} \ln \frac{1}{\pi_i} \right) - \eta \ell(f_{i,t}, y_t) \right)}{\sum_{j=1}^{\infty} \exp\left(-\eta \left(L_{j,t-1} + \frac{1}{\eta} \ln \frac{1}{\pi_j} \right) \right)}$$

we see that the quantity $\frac{1}{\eta} \ln(1/\pi_i)$ may be regarded as a "penalty" added to the cumulative loss of expert i at each time t. The performance bound for the aggregating forecaster is a so-called "oracle inequality," which states that it achieves a cumulative loss matching the best penalized cumulative loss of the experts.

3.6 Mixability for Certain Losses

In this section, we examine the mixability properties of various loss functions of special importance.

The Relative Entropy Loss Is 1-Mixable
Recall that this loss is defined by

$$\ell(p, y) = y \ln \frac{y}{p} + (1 - y) \ln \frac{1 - y}{1 - p}, \qquad \text{where } p, y \in [0, 1].$$

Let us first consider the special case when $y \in \{0, 1\}$ (logarithmic loss). It is easy to see that the conditions of the mixability theorem are satisfied with $\eta = 1$. Note that for this choice of η, the unique prediction $\widehat{p}$ satisfying definition (3.3) of the aggregating forecaster with $c = 1$ is exactly the prediction of the exponentially weighted average forecaster. Therefore, in the case of logarithmic loss, this approach does not offer any advantage with respect to the analysis based on exp-concavity from Section 3.3. Also recall from Section 3.4 that for $\eta = 1$ the exponentially weighted average forecaster is the unique greedy minimizer of the potential function. Thus, for the logarithmic loss, this predictor has various interesting properties. Indeed, in Chapter 9 we show that when the set of experts is finite, the exponentially weighted average forecaster is the best possible forecaster.

Returning to the relative entropy loss, the validity of (3.3) for $c = 1$, $\eta = 1$, and $\widehat{p} = \sum_{i=1}^{N} f_i q_i$ (i.e., when $\widehat{p}$ is the weighted average prediction) is obtained directly from the exp-concavity of the function $F(z) = e^{-\eta \ell(z,y)}$, which we proved in Section 3.3. Therefore, the exponentially weighted average forecaster with $\eta = 1$ satisfies the conditions of the mixability theorem also for the relative entropy loss. Again, on the other hand, we do not get any improvement with respect to the analysis based on exp-concavity.

The Square Loss Is 2-Mixable

For the square loss $\ell(p, y) = (p - y)^2$, $p, y \in [0, 1]$, we begin again by assuming $y \in \{0, 1\}$. Then the conditions of the mixability theorem are easily verified with $\eta = 2$. With a bit more work, we can also verify that function (3.4) is concave in $y \in [0, 1]$ (Exercise 3.12). Therefore, the conditions of the mixability theorem are satisfied also when $\mathcal{D} = \mathcal{Y} = [0, 1]$. Note that, unlike in the case of the relative entropy loss, here we gain a factor of 4 in the regret bound with respect to the analysis based on exp-concavity. This gain is real, because it can be shown that the conditions of the mixability theorem cannot be satisfied, in general, by the exponentially weighted average forecaster. Moreover, it can be shown that no prediction of the form $\widehat{p} = g\left(\sum_{i=1}^{N} f_i q_i\right)$ satisfies (3.3) with $c = 1$ and $\eta = 2$ no matter which function g is picked (Exercise 3.13).

We now derive a closed-form expression for the prediction $\widehat{p}_t$ of the aggregating forecaster. Since the square loss is mixable, by Proposition 3.3 the greedy forecaster is an aggregating forecaster. Recalling from Section 3.4 the prediction of the greedy forecaster for the square loss, we get

$$\widehat{p}_t = \begin{cases} 0 & \text{if } r_t < 0 \\ r_t & \text{if } 0 \le r_t \le 1 \\ 1 & \text{if } r_t > 1 \end{cases}$$

where

$$r_t = \frac{1}{2} + \frac{1}{2\eta} \ln \frac{\sum_{i=1}^{N} e^{-\eta L_{i,t-1} - \eta \ell(f_{i,t}, 1)}}{\sum_{j=1}^{N} e^{-\eta L_{j,t-1} - \eta \ell(f_{j,t}, 0)}}.$$

The Absolute Loss Is Not Mixable

The absolute loss, defined by $\ell(p, y) = |p - y|$ for $p, y \in [0, 1]$, does not satisfy the conditions of the mixability theorem. Hence, we cannot hope to find $\eta > 0$ such that $\mu(\eta) = 1$. However, we can get a bound for the loss for all $\eta > 0$ by applying Proposition 3.2. To do this, we need to find the mixability function for the absolute loss, that is, the smallest function

$\mu : \mathbb{R}_+ \to \mathbb{R}_+$ such that, for all distributions $q_1, \ldots, q_N$, for all $f_1, \ldots, f_N \in [0, 1]$, and for all outcomes y, there exists a $\widehat{p} \in [0, 1]$ satisfying

$$|\widehat{p} - y| \leq -\frac{\mu(\eta)}{\eta} \ln \left(\sum_{i=1}^{N} e^{-\eta|f_i - y|} q_i \right). \tag{3.5}$$

Here we only consider the simple case when $y \in \{0, 1\}$ (prediction of binary outcomes). In this case, the prediction $\widehat{p}$ achieving mixability is expressible as a (nonlinear) function of the exponentially weighted average forecaster. In the more general case, when $y \in [0, 1]$, no prediction of the form $\widehat{p} = g\left(\sum_{i=1}^{N} f_i q_i \right)$ achieves mixability no matter how function g is chosen (Exercise 3.14).

Using the linear interpolation $e^{-\eta x} \leq 1 - (1 - e^{-\eta}) x$, which holds for all $\eta > 0$ and $0 \leq x \leq 1$, we get

$$-\frac{\mu(\eta)}{\eta} \ln \left(\sum_{i=1}^{N} e^{-\eta|f_i - y|} q_i \right)$$

$$\geq -\frac{\mu(\eta)}{\eta} \ln \left(1 - \sum_{i=1}^{N} (1 - e^{-\eta}) |f_i - y| q_i \right) \tag{3.6}$$

$$= -\frac{\mu(\eta)}{\eta} \ln \left(1 - (1 - e^{-\eta}) \left| \sum_{i=1}^{N} f_i q_i - y \right| \right),$$

where in the last step we used the assumption $y \in \{0, 1\}$. Hence, using the notation $r = \sum_{i=1}^{N} f_i q_i$, it is sufficient to prove that

$$|\widehat{p} - y| \leq -\frac{\mu(\eta)}{\eta} \ln\left(1 - (1 - e^{-\eta})|r - y|\right)$$

or equivalently, using again the assumption $y \in \{0, 1\}$,

$$1 + \frac{\mu(\eta)}{\eta} \ln\left(1 - (1 - e^{-\eta})(1 - r)\right) \leq \widehat{p} \leq -\frac{\mu(\eta)}{\eta} \ln\left(1 - (1 - e^{-\eta})r\right). \tag{3.7}$$

By setting $r = 1/2$ in inequality (3.7), we get

$$1 + \frac{\mu(\eta)}{\eta} \ln \left(\frac{1 + e^{-\eta}}{2} \right) \leq -\frac{\mu(\eta)}{\eta} \ln \left(\frac{1 + e^{-\eta}}{2} \right), \tag{3.8}$$

which is satisfied only by the assignment

$$\mu(\eta) = \frac{\eta/2}{\ln\left(2/(1 + e^{-\eta})\right)}.$$

Note that for this assignment, (3.8) holds with equality. Simple calculations show that the choice of μ above satisfies (3.7) for all $0 \leq r \leq 1$. Note further that for $f_1, \ldots, f_N \in \{0, 1\}$ the linear approximation (3.6) is tight. If in addition $r = \sum_{i=1}^{N} f_i q_i = 1/2$, then there exists only one function μ such that (3.5) holds. Therefore, μ is indeed the mixability curve for the absolute loss with binary outcomes. It can be proven (Exercise 3.15) that this function is also the mixability curve for the more general case when $y \in [0, 1]$. In Figure 3.3 we show, as a function of r, the upper and lower bounds (3.7) on the prediction $\widehat{p}$

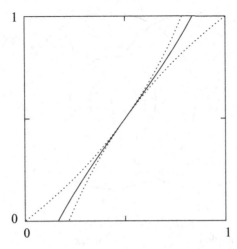

Figure 3.3. The two dashed lines show, as a function of the weighted average r, the upper and lower bounds (3.7) on the mixability-achieving prediction $\widehat{p}$ for the absolute loss when $\eta = 2$; the solid line in between is a mixability-achieving prediction $\widehat{p}$ obtained by taking the average of the upper and lower bounds. Note that, in this case, $\widehat{p}$ can be expressed as a (nonlinear) function of the weighted average.

achieving mixability and the curve $\widehat{p} = \widehat{p}(r)$ obtained by taking the average of the upper and lower bounds. Comparing the regret bound for the mixability-achieving forecaster obtained via Proposition 3.2 with the bound of Theorem 2.2 for the weighted average forecaster, one sees that the former has a better dependence on η than the latter. However, as we show in Section 3.7 the bound of Theorem 2.2 is asymptotically tight. Hence, the benefit of using the more complicated mixability-achieving forecaster vanishes as n grows to infinity.

The relationships between the various losses examined so far are summarized in Figure 3.4.

3.7 General Lower Bounds

We now address the question of the tightness of the upper bounds obtained so far in this and the previous chapters. Our purpose here is to derive lower bounds for the worst-case regret. More precisely, we investigate the behavior of the minimax regret $V_n^{(N)}$. Recall from Section 2.10 that, given a loss function ℓ, $V_n^{(N)}$ is defined as the regret of the best possible forecasting strategy for the worst possible choice of n outcomes and advice $f_{i,t}$ for N experts, where $i = 1, \ldots, N$ and $t = 1, \ldots, n$.

The upper bound of Theorem 2.2 shows that if the loss function is bounded between 0 and 1 then $V_n^{(N)} \le \sqrt{(n/2) \ln N}$. On the other hand, the mixability theorem proven in this chapter shows that for any mixable loss ℓ, the significantly tighter upper bound $V_n^{(N)} \le c_\ell \ln N$ holds, where c_ℓ is a parameter that depends on the specific mixable loss. (See Remark 3.1 for an analytic characterization of this parameter.) In this section we show that, in some sense, both of these upper bounds are tight. The next result shows that, apart from trivial and uninteresting cases, the minimax loss is at least proportional to the logarithm of the number N of experts. The theorem provides a lower bound for *any*

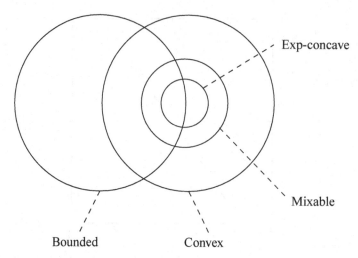

Figure 3.4. A Venn diagram illustrating the hierarchy of losses examined so far. The minimax regret for bounded and convex losses is $O(\sqrt{n \ln N})$, and this value is achieved by the weighted average forecaster. Mixable losses, which are not always bounded, have a minimax regret of the form $c \ln N$. This regret is not necessarily achieved by the weighted average forecaster. Exp-concave losses are those mixable losses for which the weighted average forecaster does guarantee a regret $c \ln N$. Such losses are properly included in the set of mixable losses in the following sense: for certain values of η, some losses are η-mixable but not exp-concave (e.g., the square loss). The minimax regret for bounded losses that are not necessarily convex is studied in Chapter 4 using randomized forecasters.

loss function. When applied to mixable losses, this lower bound captures the logarithmic dependence on N, but it does not provide a matching constant.

Theorem 3.6. *Fix any loss function ℓ. Then $V_{n\lfloor \log_2 N \rfloor}^{(N)} \geq \lfloor \log_2 N \rfloor V_n^{(2)}$ for all $N \geq 2$ and all $n \geq 1$.*

Proof. Without loss of generality, assume that there are $N = 2^M$ experts for some $M \geq 1$. For any $m \leq N/2$, we say that the expert advice $f_{1,t}, \ldots, f_{N,t}$ at time t is *m-coupled* if $f_{i,t} = f_{m+i,t}$ for all $i = 1, \ldots, m$. Similarly, we say that the expert advice at time t is *m-simple* if $f_{1,t} = \cdots = f_{m,t}$ and $f_{m+1,t} = \cdots = f_{2m,t}$. Note that these definitions impose no constraints on the advice of experts with index $i > 2m$. We break time in M stages of n time steps each. We say that the expert advice is m-simple (m-coupled) in stage s if it is m-simple (m-coupled) on each time step in the stage. We choose the expert advice so that

1. the advice is 2^{s-1}-simple for each stage $s = 1, \ldots, M$;
2. for each $s = 1, \ldots, M-1$, the advice is 2^s-coupled in all time steps up to stage s included.

Note that we can obtain such an advice simply by choosing, at each stage $s = 1, \ldots, M$, an arbitrary 2^{s-1}-simple expert advice for the first 2^s experts, and then copying this advice onto the remaining experts (see Figure 3.5).

$$
\begin{array}{cccc}
 & s=1 & s=2 & s=3 \\
1 & 0 & 0 & 0 \\
2 & 1 & 0 & 0 \\
3 & 0 & 1 & 0 \\
4 & 1 & 1 & 0 \\
5 & 0 & 0 & 1 \\
6 & 1 & 0 & 1 \\
7 & 0 & 1 & 1 \\
8 & 1 & 1 & 1
\end{array}
$$

Figure 3.5. An assignment of expert advice achieving the lower bound of Theorem 3.6 for $N = 8$ and $n = 1$. Note that the advice is 1-simple for $s = 1$, 2-simple for $s = 2$, and 4-simple for $s = 3$. In addition, the advice is also 2-coupled for $s = 1$ and 4-coupled for $s = 1, 2$.

Consider an arbitrary forecasting strategy P. For any fixed sequence $y_1, \ldots, y_M$ on which P is run, and for any pair of stages $1 \le r \le s \le M$, let

$$
R_i(y_r^s) = \sum_{t=n(r-1)+1}^{ns} \left(\ell(\widehat{p}_t, y_t) - \ell(f_{i,t}, y_t) \right),
$$

where $\widehat{p}_t$ is the prediction computed by P at time t.

For the sake of simplicity, assume that $n = 1$. Fix some arbitrary expert i and pick any expert j (possibly equal to i). If $i, j \le 2^{M-1}$ or $i, j > 2^{M-1}$, then $R_i(y_1^M) = R_i(y_1^{M-1}) + R_j(y_M)$ because the advice at $s = M$ is 2^{M-1}-simple. Otherwise, assume without loss of generality that $i \le 2^{M-1}$ and $j > 2^{M-1}$. Since the advice at $s = 1, \ldots, M - 1$ is 2^{M-1}-coupled, there exists $k > 2^{M-1}$ such that $R_i(y_1^{M-1}) = R_k(y_1^{M-1})$. In addition, since the advice at $t = M$ is 2^{M-1}-simple, $R_j(y_M) = R_k(y_M)$. We have thus shown that for any i and j there always exists k such that $R_i(y_1^M) = R_k(y_1^{M-1}) + R_j(y_M)$. Repeating this argument, and using our recursive assumptions on the expert advice, we obtain

$$
R_i(y_1^M) = \sum_{s=1}^{M} R_{j_s}(y_s),
$$

where $j_1, \ldots, j_M = j$ are *arbitrary* experts. This reasoning can be easily extended to the case $n \ge 1$, obtaining

$$
R_i\left(y_1^{nM}\right) = \sum_{s=1}^{M} R_{j_s}\left(y_{n(s-1)+1}^{ns}\right).
$$

Now note that the expert advice at each stage $s = 1, \ldots, M$ is 2^{s-1}-simple, implying that we have a pool of at least two "uncommitted experts" at each time step. Hence, using the fact that the sequence $y_1, \ldots, y_{nM}$ is arbitrary and

$$
V_n^{(N)} = \inf_P \sup_{\{\mathcal{F} : |\mathcal{F}| = N\}} \sup_{y^n \in \mathcal{Y}^n} \max_{i=1,\ldots,N} \sum_{t=1}^{n} \left(\ell(\widehat{p}_t, y_t) - \ell(f_{i,t}, y_t) \right),
$$

where $\mathcal{F}$ are classes of *static* experts (see Section 2.10), we have, for each stage s,

$$
R_{j_s}\left(y_{n(s-1)+1}^{ns}\right) \ge V_n^{(2)}.
$$

for some choices of outcomes y_t, expert index j_s, and static expert advice. To conclude the proof note that, trivially, $V_M^{(N)} \geq R_i(y_1^M)$.   ∎

Using a more involved argument, it is possible to prove a parametric lower bound that asymptotically (for both $N, n \to \infty$) matches the upper bound $c_\ell \ln N$, where c_ℓ is the best constant achieved by the mixability theorem.

What can be said about $V_n^{(N)}$ for nonmixable losses? Consider, for example, the absolute loss $\ell(p, y) = |p - y|$. By Theorem 2.2, the exponentially weighted average forecaster has a regret bounded by $\sqrt{(n/2)\ln N}$, which implies that, for all n and N,

$$\frac{V_n^{(N)}}{\sqrt{(n/2)\ln N}} \leq 1.$$

The next result shows that, in a sense, this bound cannot be improved further. It also shows that the exponentially weighted average forecaster is asymptotically optimal.

Theorem 3.7. *If* $\mathcal{Y} = \{0, 1\}$, $\mathcal{D} = [0, 1]$ *and* ℓ *is the absolute loss* $\ell(p, y) = |p - y|$, *then*

$$\sup_{n, N} \frac{V_n^{(N)}}{\sqrt{(n/2)\ln N}} \geq 1.$$

Proof. Clearly, $V_n^{(N)} \geq \sup_{\mathcal{F} : |\mathcal{F}| = N} V_n(\mathcal{F})$, where we take the supremum over classes of N *static* experts (see Section 2.9 for the definition of a static expert). We start by lower bounding $V_n(\mathcal{F})$ for a fixed $\mathcal{F}$. Recall that the minimax regret $V_n(\mathcal{F})$ for a fixed class of experts is defined as

$$V_n(\mathcal{F}) = \inf_P \sup_{y^n \in \{0, 1\}^n} \sup_{f \in \mathcal{F}} \sum_{t=1}^{n} (|\widehat{p}_t - y_t| - |f_t - y_t|),$$

where the infimum is taken over all forecasting strategies P. Introducing i.i.d. symmetric Bernoulli random variables $Y_1, \ldots, Y_n$ (i.e., $\mathbb{P}[Y_t = 0] = \mathbb{P}[Y_t = 1] = 1/2$), one clearly has

$$V_n(\mathcal{F}) \geq \inf_P \mathbb{E} \sup_{f \in \mathcal{F}} \sum_{t=1}^{n} (|\widehat{p}_t - Y_t| - |f_t - Y_t|)$$

$$= \inf_P \mathbb{E} \sum_{t=1}^{n} |\widehat{p}_t - Y_t| - \mathbb{E} \inf_{f \in \mathcal{F}} \sum_{t=1}^{n} |f_t - Y_t|.$$

(In Chapter 8 we show that this actually holds with equality.) Since the sequence $Y_1, \ldots, Y_n$ is completely random, for all forecasting strategies one obviously has $\mathbb{E} \sum_{t=1}^{n} |\widehat{p}_t - Y_t| = n/2$. Thus,

$$V_n(\mathcal{F}) \geq \frac{n}{2} - \mathbb{E}\left[\inf_{f \in \mathcal{F}} \sum_{t=1}^{n} |f_t - Y_t| \right]$$

$$= \mathbb{E}\left[\sup_{f \in \mathcal{F}} \sum_{t=1}^{n} \left(\frac{1}{2} - |f_t - Y_t| \right) \right]$$

$$= \mathbb{E}\left[\sup_{f \in \mathcal{F}} \sum_{t=1}^{n} \left(\frac{1}{2} - f_t \right) \sigma_t \right],$$

where $\sigma_t = 1 - 2Y_t$ are i.i.d. *Rademacher* random variables (i.e., with $\mathbb{P}[\sigma_t = 1] = \mathbb{P}[\sigma_t = -1] = 1/2$). We lower bound $\sup_{\mathcal{F}\,:\,|\mathcal{F}|=N} V_n(\mathcal{F})$ by taking an average over an appropriately chosen set of expert classes containing N experts. This may be done by replacing each expert $f = (f_1, \ldots, f_n)$ by a sequence of symmetric i.i.d. Bernoulli random variables. More precisely, let $\{Z_{i,t}\}$ be an $N \times n$ array of i.i.d. Rademacher random variables with distribution $\mathbb{P}[Z_{i,t} = -1] = \mathbb{P}[Z_{i,t} = 1] = 1/2$. Then

$$
\begin{aligned}
\sup_{\mathcal{F}\,:\,|\mathcal{F}|=N} V_n(\mathcal{F}) &\geq \sup_{\mathcal{F}\,:\,|\mathcal{F}|=N} \mathbb{E}\left[\sup_{f \in \mathcal{F}} \sum_{t=1}^{n} \left(\frac{1}{2} - f_t \right) \sigma_t \right] \\
&\geq \frac{1}{2}\mathbb{E}\left[\max_{i=1,\ldots,N} \sum_{t=1}^{n} Z_{i,t}\sigma_t \right] \\
&= \frac{1}{2}\mathbb{E}\left[\max_{i=1,\ldots,N} \sum_{t=1}^{n} Z_{i,t} \right].
\end{aligned}
$$

By the central limit theorem, for each $i = 1, \ldots, N$, $n^{-1/2} \sum_{t=1}^{n} Z_{i,t}$ converges to a standard normal random variable. In fact, it is not difficult to show (see Lemma A.11 in the Appendix for the details) that

$$
\lim_{n \to \infty} \mathbb{E}\left[\max_{i=1,\ldots,N} \frac{1}{\sqrt{n}} \sum_{t=1}^{n} Z_{i,t} \right] = \mathbb{E}\left[\max_{i=1,\ldots,N} G_i \right],
$$

where $G_1, \ldots, G_N$ are independent standard normal random variables. But it is well known (see Lemma A.12 in the Appendix) that

$$
\lim_{N \to \infty} \frac{\mathbb{E}\left[\max_{i=1,\ldots,N} G_i \right]}{\sqrt{2 \ln N}} = 1,
$$

and this concludes the proof. ∎

3.8 Bibliographic Remarks

The follow-the-best-expert forecaster and its variants have been thoroughly studied in a somewhat more general framework, known as the *sequential compound decision problem* first put forward by Robbins [244]; see also Blackwell [28, 29], Gilliland [127], Gilliland and Hannan [128], Hannan [141], Hannan and Robbins [142], Merhav and Feder [213], van Ryzin [254], and Samuel [256, 257]. In these papers general conditions may be found that guarantee that the per-round regret converges to 0. Lemma 3.1 is due to Hannan [141]. The example of the square loss with constant experts has been studied by Takimoto and Warmuth [284], who show that the minimax regret is $\ln n - \ln \ln n + o(1)$.

Exp-concave loss functions were studied by Kivinen and Warmuth [182]. Theorem 3.3 is a generalization of an argument of Blum and Kalai [33]. The mixability curve of Section 3.5 was introduced by Vovk [298, 300], and also studied by Haussler, Kivinen, and Warmuth [151], who characterize the loss functions for which $\Theta(\ln N)$ regret bounds are possible. The characterization of the optimal η for mixable functions given in Remark 3.1 is due to Haussler, Kivinen, and Warmuth [151]. The examples of mixability are taken from Cesa-Bianchi, Freund, Haussler, Helmbold, Schapire, and Warmuth [48], Haussler,

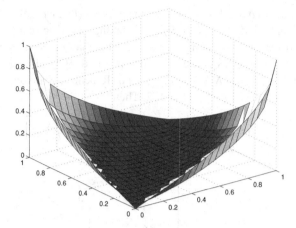

Figure 3.6. The Hellinger loss.

Kivinen, and Warmuth [151], and Vovk [298, 300]. The mixability curve of Section 3.5 is equivalent to the notion of "extended stochastic complexity" introduced by Yamanishi [313]. This notion generalizes Rissanen's stochastic complexity [240, 242].

In the case of binary outcomes $\mathcal{Y} = \{0, 1\}$, mixability of a loss function ℓ is equivalent to the existence of the predictive complexity for ℓ, as shown by Kalnishkan, Vovk and Vyugin [178], who also provide an analytical characterization of mixability in the binary case. The predictive complexity for the logarithmic loss is equivalent to Levin's version of Kolmogorov complexity, see Zvonkin and Levin [320]. In this sense, predictive complexity may be viewed as a generalization of Kolmogorov complexity.

Theorem 3.6 is due to Haussler, Kivinen, and Warmuth [151]. In the same paper, they also prove a lower bound that, asymptotically for both $N, n \to \infty$, matches the upper bound $c_\ell \ln N$ for any mixable loss ℓ. This result was initially proven by Vovk [298] with a more involved analysis. Theorem 3.7 is due to Cesa-Bianchi, Freund, Haussler, Helmbold, Schapire, and Warmuth [48]. Similar results for other loss functions appear in Haussler, Kivinen, and Warmuth [151]. More general lower bounds for the absolute loss were proved by Cesa-Bianchi and Lugosi [51].

3.9 Exercises

3.1 Consider the follow-the-best-expert forecaster studied in Section 3.2. Assume that $\mathcal{D} = \mathcal{Y}$ is a convex subset of a topological vector space. Assume that the sequence of outcomes is such that $\lim_{n \to \infty} \frac{1}{n} \sum_{t=1}^{n} y_t = y$ for some $y \in \mathcal{Y}$. Establish weak general conditions that guarantee that the per-round regret of the forecaster converges to 0.

3.2 Let $\mathcal{Y} = \mathcal{D} = [0, 1]$, and consider the *Hellinger loss*

$$\ell(z, y) = \frac{1}{2} \left(\left(\sqrt{x} - \sqrt{y} \right)^2 + \left(\sqrt{1-x} - \sqrt{1-y} \right)^2 \right)$$

(see Figure 3.6). Determine the values of η for which the function $F(z)$ defined in Section 3.3 is concave.

3.3 Let $\mathcal{Y} = \mathcal{D}$ be the closed ball of radius $r > 0$, centered at the origin in $\mathbb{R}^d$, and consider the loss $\ell(z, y) = \|z - y\|^2$ (where $\| \cdot \|$ denotes the euclidean norm in $\mathbb{R}^d$). Show that $F(z)$ of Theorem 3.2 is concave whenever $\eta \leq 1/(8r^2)$.

3.4 Show that if for a $y \in \mathcal{Y}$ the function $F(z) = e^{-\eta \ell(z,y)}$ is concave, then $\ell(z, y)$ is a convex function of z.

3.5 Show that if a loss function is exp-concave for a certain value of $\eta > 0$, then it is also exp-concave for any $\eta' \in (0, \eta)$.

3.6 In classification problems, various versions of the so-called *hinge loss* have been used. Typically, $\mathcal{Y} = \{-, 1\}$, $\mathcal{D} = [-1, 1]$, and the loss function has the form $\ell(\widehat{p}, y) = c(-y\widehat{p})$, where c is a nonnegative, increasing, and convex *cost function*. Derive conditions for c and the parameter η under which the hinge loss is exp-concave.

3.7 (*Discounted regret for exp-concave losses*) Consider the discounted regret

$$\rho_{i,n} = \sum_{t=1}^{n} \beta_{n-t} \big(\ell(\widehat{p}_t, y_t) - \ell(f_{i,t}, y_t) \big)$$

defined in Section 2.11, where $1 = \beta_0 \geq \beta_1 \geq \cdots$ is a nonincreasing sequence of discount factors. Assume that the loss function ℓ is exp-concave for some $\eta > 0$, and consider the discounted exponentially weighted average forecaster

$$\widehat{p}_t = \frac{\sum_{i=1}^{N} f_{i,t} \exp\left(-\eta \sum_{s=1}^{t-1} \beta_{n-s} \ell(f_{i,s}, y_s)\right)}{\sum_{j=1}^{N} \exp\left(-\eta \sum_{s=1}^{t-1} \beta_{n-s} \ell(f_{j,s}, y_s)\right)}.$$

Show that the average discounted regret is bounded by

$$\max_{i=1,\dots,N} \frac{\sum_{t=1}^{n} \beta_{n-t} r_{i,t}}{\sum_{t=1}^{n} \beta_{n-t}} \leq \frac{\ln N}{\eta \sum_{t=1}^{n} \beta_{n-t}}.$$

In particular, show that the average discounted regret is $o(1)$ if and only if $\sum_{t=0}^{\infty} \beta_t = \infty$.

3.8 Show that the greedy forecaster based on "fictitious play" defined at the beginning of Section 3.4 does not guarantee that $n^{-1} \max_{i \leq N} R_{i,n}$ converge to 0 as $n \to \infty$ for all outcome sequences. *Hint:* It suffices to consider the simple example when $\mathcal{Y} = \mathcal{D} = [0, 1]$, $\ell(\widehat{p}, y) = |\widehat{p} - y|$, and $N = 2$.

3.9 Show that for $\mathcal{Y} = \{0, 1\}$, $\mathcal{D} = [0, 1]$ and the logarithmic loss function, the greedy forecaster based on the exponential potential with $\eta = 1$ is just the exponentially weighted average forecaster (also with $\eta = 1$).

3.10 Show that $\mu(\eta) \geq 1$ for all loss functions ℓ on $\mathcal{D} \times \mathcal{Y}$ satisfying the following conditions: (1) there exists $p \in \mathcal{D}$ such that $\ell(p, y) < \infty$ for all $y \in \mathcal{Y}$; (2) there exists no $p \in \mathcal{D}$ such that $\ell(p, y) = 0$ for all $y \in \mathcal{Y}$ (Vovk [298]).

3.11 Show the following: Let $C \subset \mathbb{R}^2$ be a curve with parametric equations $x = x(t)$ and $y = y(t)$, which are twice differentiable functions. If there exists a twice differentiable function h such that $y(t) = h(x(t))$ for t in some open interval, then

$$\frac{dy}{dx} = \frac{\frac{dy}{dt}}{\frac{dx}{dt}} \quad \text{and} \quad \frac{d^2 y}{dx^2} = \frac{\frac{d}{dt}\frac{dy}{dx}}{\frac{dx}{dt}}.$$

3.12 Check that for the square loss $\ell(p, y) = (p - y)^2$, $p, y \in [0, 1]$, function (3.4) is concave in y if $\eta \leq 1/2$ (Vovk [300]).

3.13 Prove that for the square loss there is no function g such that the prediction $\widehat{p} = g\left(\sum_{i=1}^{N} f_i q_i\right)$ satisfies (3.3) with $c = 1$. *Hint:* Consider $N = 2$ and find f_1, f_2, q_1, q_2 and f_1', f_2', q_1', q_2' such that $f_1 q_1 + f_2 q_2 = f_1' q_1' + f_2' q_2'$ but plugging these values in (3.3) yields a contradiction (Haussler, Kivinen, and Warmuth [151]).

3.14 Prove that for the absolute loss there is no function g for which the prediction $\widehat{p} = g\left(\sum_{i=1}^{N} f_i q_i\right)$ satisfies (3.5), where $\mu(\eta)$ is the mixability curve for the absolute loss. *Hint:* Set $\eta = 1$ and follow the hint in Exercise 3.13 (Haussler, Kivinen, and Warmuth [151]).

3.15 Prove that the mixability curve for the absolute loss with binary outcomes is also the mixability function for the case when the outcome space is [0, 1] (Haussler, Kivinen, and Warmuth [151]). *Warning:* This exercise is not easy.

3.16 Find the mixability curve for the following loss: $\mathcal{D}$ is the probability simplex in $\mathbb{R}^N$, $\mathcal{Y} = [0, 1]^N$, and $\ell(\widehat{p}, y) = \widehat{p} \cdot y$ (Vovk [298]). *Warning:* This exercise is not easy.

4

Randomized Prediction

4.1 Introduction

The results of Chapter 2 crucially build on the assumption that the loss function ℓ is convex in its first argument. While this assumption is natural in many applications, it is not satisfied in some important examples.

One such example is the case when both the decision space and the outcome space are $\{0, 1\}$ and the loss function is $\ell(p, y) = \mathbb{I}_{\{p \neq y\}}$. In this case it is clear that for any deterministic strategy of the forecaster, there exists an outcome sequence $y^n = (y_1, \ldots, y_n)$ such that the forecaster errs at every single time instant, that is, $\widehat{L}_n = n$. Thus, except for trivial cases, it is impossible to achieve $\widehat{L}_n - \min_{i=1,\ldots,N} L_{i,n} = o(n)$ uniformly over all outcome sequences. For example, if $N = 2$ and the two experts' predictions are $f_{1,t} = 0$ and $f_{2,t} = 1$ for all t, then $\min_{i=1,2} L_{i,n} \leq n/2$, and no matter what the forecaster does,

$$\max_{y^n \in \mathcal{Y}^n} \left(\widehat{L}_n(y^n) - \min_{i=1,\ldots,N} L_{i,n}(y^n) \right) \geq \frac{n}{2}.$$

One of the key ideas of the theory of prediction of individual sequences is that in such a situation randomization may help. Next we describe a version of the sequential prediction problem in which the forecaster has access, at each time instant, to an independent random variable uniformly distributed on the interval $[0, 1]$. The scenario is conveniently described in the framework of playing repeated games.

Consider a game between a player (the forecaster) and the environment. At each round of the game, the player chooses an action $i \in \{1, \ldots, N\}$, and the environment chooses an action $y \in \mathcal{Y}$ (in analogy with Chapters 2 and 3 we also call "outcome" the adversary's action). The player's loss $\ell(i, y)$ at time t is the value of a loss function $\ell : \{1, \ldots, N\} \times \mathcal{Y} \to [0, 1]$. Now suppose that, at the tth round of the game, the player chooses a probability distribution $\mathbf{p}_t = (p_{1,t}, \ldots, p_{N,t})$ over the set of actions and plays action i with probability $p_{i,t}$. Formally, the player's action I_t at time t is defined by

$$I_t = i \quad \text{if and only if} \quad U_t \in \left[\sum_{j=1}^{i-1} p_{j,t}, \sum_{j=1}^{i} p_{j,t} \right)$$

so that

$$\mathbb{P}[I_t = i \mid U_1, \ldots, U_{t-1}] = p_{i,t}, \qquad i = 1, \ldots, N,$$

where $U_1, U_2, \ldots$ are independent random variables, uniformly distributed in the interval $[0, 1]$. Adopting a game-theoretic terminology, we often call an action a *pure strategy* and a probability distribution over actions a *mixed strategy*. Suppose the environment chooses action $y_t \in \mathcal{Y}$. The loss of the player is then $\ell(I_t, y_t)$.

If $I_1, I_2, \ldots$ is the sequence of forecaster's actions and $y_1, y_2, \ldots$ is the sequence of outcomes chosen by the environment, the player's goal is to minimize the cumulative regret

$$\widehat{L}_n - \min_{i=1,\ldots,N} L_{i,n} = \sum_{t=1}^{n} \ell(I_t, y_t) - \min_{i=1,\ldots,N} \sum_{t=1}^{n} \ell(i, y_t),$$

that is, the realized difference between the cumulative loss and the loss of the best pure strategy.

Remark 4.1 (*Experts vs. actions*). Note that, unlike for the game of prediction with expert advice analyzed in Chapter 2, here we define the regret in terms of the forecaster's best constant prediction rather than in terms of the best expert. Hence, as experts can be arbitrarily complex prediction strategies, this game appears to be easier for the forecaster than the game of Chapter 2. However, as our forecasting algorithms make assumptions neither on the structure of the outcome space $\mathcal{Y}$ nor on the structure of the loss function ℓ, we can prove for the expert model the same bounds proven in this chapter. This is done via a simple reduction in which we use $\{1, \ldots, N\}$ to index the set of experts and define the loss $\ell'(i, y_t) = \ell(f_{i,t}, y_t)$, where ℓ is the loss function used to score predictions in the expert game.

Before moving on, we point out an important subtlety brought in by allowing the forecaster to randomize. The actions y_t of the environment are now random variables Y_t as they may depend on the past (randomized) plays $I_1, \ldots, I_{t-1}$ of the forecaster. One may even allow the environment to introduce an independent randomization to determine the outcomes Y_t, but this is irrelevant for the material of this section; so, for simplicity, we exclude this possibility. We explicitly deal with such situations in Chapter 7.

A slightly less powerful model is obtained if one does not allow the actions of the environment to depend on the predictions I_t of the forecaster. In this model, which we call the *oblivious opponent*, the whole sequence $y_1, y_2, \ldots$ of outcomes is determined before the game starts. Then, at time t, the forecaster makes its (randomized) prediction I_t and the environment reveals the tth outcome y_t. Thus, in this model, the y_t's are nonrandom fixed values. The model of an oblivious opponent is realistic whenever it is reasonable to believe that the actions of the forecaster do not have an effect on future outcomes of the sequence to be predicted. This is the case in many applications, such as weather forecasting or predicting a sequence of bits of a speech signal for encoding purposes. However, there are important cases when one cannot reasonably assume that the opponent is oblivious. The main example is when a player of a game predicts the other players' next move and bases his action on such a prediction. In such cases the other players' future actions may depend on the action (and therefore on the forecast) of the player in any complicated way. The stock market comes to mind as an obvious example. Such game-theoretic applications are discussed in Chapter 7.

Formally, an oblivious opponent is defined by a fixed sequence $y_1, y_2, \ldots$ of outcomes, whereas a nonoblivious opponent is defined by a sequence of functions $g_1, g_2, \ldots$, with

$g_t : \{1, \ldots, N\}^{t-1} \to \mathcal{Y}$, and each outcome Y_t is given by $Y_t = g_t(I_1, \ldots, I_{t-1})$. Thus Y_t is measurable with respect to the σ-algebra generated by the random variables $U_1, \ldots, U_{t-1}$.

Interestingly, any forecaster that is guaranteed to work well against an oblivious opponent also works well in the general model against any strategy of a nonoblivious opponent, in a certain sense. To formulate this fact, we introduce the *expected loss*

$$\overline{\ell}(\mathbf{p}_t, Y_t) \overset{\text{def}}{=} \mathbb{E}\big[\ell(I_t, Y_t) \,\big|\, U_1, \ldots, U_{t-1}\big] = \mathbb{E}_t \, \ell(I_t, Y_t) = \sum_{i=1}^{N} \ell(i, Y_t) p_{i,t}.$$

Here the "expected value" $\mathbb{E}_t$ is taken only with respect to the random variable I_t. More precisely, $\overline{\ell}(\mathbf{p}_t, Y_t)$ is the conditional expectation of $\ell(I_t, Y_t)$ given the past plays $I_1, \ldots, I_{t-1}$ (we use $\mathbb{E}_t$ to denote this conditional expectation). Since $Y_t = g_t(I_1, \ldots, I_{t-1})$, the value of $\overline{\ell}(\mathbf{p}_t, Y_t)$ is determined solely by $U_1, \ldots, U_{t-1}$.

An important property of the forecasters investigated in this chapter is that the probability distribution $\mathbf{p}_t$ of play is fully determined by the past outcomes $Y_1, \ldots, Y_{t-1}$; that is, it does not explicitly depend on the past plays $I_1, \ldots, I_{t-1}$. Formally, $\mathbf{p}_t : \mathcal{Y}^{t-1} \to \mathcal{D}$ is a function taking values in the simplex $\mathcal{D}$ of probability distributions over N actions.

Note that the next result, which assumes that the forecaster is of the above form, is in terms of the cumulative expected loss $\sum_{t=1}^{n} \overline{\ell}(\mathbf{p}_t, Y_t)$, and not in terms of its expected value

$$\mathbb{E}\left[\sum_{t=1}^{n} \overline{\ell}(\mathbf{p}_t, Y_t) \right] = \mathbb{E}\left[\sum_{t=1}^{n} \ell(I_t, Y_t) \right].$$

Exercise 4.1 describes a closely related result about the expected value of the cumulative losses.

Lemma 4.1. *Let B, C be positive constants. Consider a randomized forecaster such that, for every $t = 1, \ldots, n$, $\mathbf{p}_t$ is fully determined by the past outcomes $y_1, \ldots, y_{t-1}$. Assume the forecaster's expected regret against an oblivious opponent satisfies*

$$\sup_{y^n \in \mathcal{Y}^n} \mathbb{E}\left[\sum_{t=1}^{n} \ell(I_t, y_t) - C \sum_{t=1}^{n} \ell(i, y_t) \right] \le B, \qquad i = 1, \ldots, N.$$

If the same forecaster is used against a nonoblivious opponent, then

$$\sum_{t=1}^{n} \overline{\ell}(\mathbf{p}_t, Y_t) - C \sum_{t=1}^{n} \ell(i, Y_t) \le B, \qquad i = 1, \ldots, N$$

holds. Moreover, for all $\delta > 0$, with probability at least $1 - \delta$ the actual cumulative loss satisfies, for any (nonoblivious) strategy of the opponent,

$$\sum_{t=1}^{n} \ell(I_t, Y_t) - C \min_{i=1,\ldots,N} \sum_{t=1}^{n} \ell(i, Y_t) \le B + \sqrt{\frac{n}{2} \ln \frac{1}{\delta}}.$$

Proof. Observe first that if the opponent is oblivious, that is, the sequence $y_1, \ldots, y_n$ is fixed, then $\mathbf{p}_t$ is also fixed and thus for each $i = 1, \ldots, N$,

$$\mathbb{E}\left[\sum_{t=1}^{n} \ell(I_t, y_t) - C \sum_{t=1}^{n} \ell(i, y_t) \right] = \sum_{t=1}^{n} \overline{\ell}(\mathbf{p}_t, y_t) - C \sum_{t=1}^{n} \ell(i, y_t),$$

which is bounded by B by assumption. If the opponent is nonoblivious, then for each $i = 1, \ldots, N$,

$$\sum_{t=1}^{n} \overline{\ell}(\mathbf{p}_t, Y_t) - C \sum_{t=1}^{n} \ell(i, Y_t)$$

$$\leq \sup_{y_1 \in \mathcal{Y}} \mathbb{E}_1\big[\ell(I_1, y_1) - C\ell(i, y_1)\big] + \cdots + \sup_{y_n \in \mathcal{Y}} \mathbb{E}_n\big[\ell(I_n, y_n) - C\ell(i, y_n)\big]$$

$$= \sup_{y^n \in \mathcal{Y}^n} \Big(\mathbb{E}_1\big[\ell(I_1, y_1) - C\ell(i, y_1)\big] + \cdots + \mathbb{E}_n\big[\ell(I_n, y_n) - C\ell(i, y_n)\big]\Big).$$

To see why the last equality holds, consider $n = 2$. Since the quantity $\mathbb{E}_1[\ell(I_1, y_1) - C\ell(i, y_1)]$ does not depend on the value of y_2, and since y_2, owing to our assumptions on $\mathbf{p}_2$, does not depend on the realization of I_1, we have

$$\sup_{y_1 \in \mathcal{Y}} \mathbb{E}_1\big[\ell(I_1, y_1) - C\ell(i, y_1)\big] + \sup_{y_2 \in \mathcal{Y}} \mathbb{E}_2\big[\ell(I_2, y_2) - C\ell(i, y_2)\big]$$

$$= \sup_{y_1 \in \mathcal{Y}} \sup_{y_2 \in \mathcal{Y}} \Big(\mathbb{E}_1\big[\ell(I_1, y_1) - C\ell(i, y_1)\big] + \mathbb{E}_2\big[\ell(I_2, y_2) - C\ell(i, y_2)\big]\Big).$$

The proof for $n > 2$ follows by repeating the same argument. By assumption,

$$\sup_{y^n \in \mathcal{Y}^n} \Big(\mathbb{E}_1\big[\ell(I_1, y_1) - C\ell(i, y_1)\big] + \cdots + \mathbb{E}_n\big[\ell(I_n, y_n) - C\ell(i, y_n)\big]\Big) \leq B,$$

which concludes the proof of the first statement of the lemma.

To prove the second statement just observe that the random variables $\ell(I_t, Y_t) - \overline{\ell}(\mathbf{p}_t, Y_t)$, $t = 1, 2, \ldots$ form a sequence of bounded martingale differences (with respect to the sequence $U_1, U_2, \ldots$ of randomizing variables). Thus, a simple application of the Hoeffding–Azuma inequality (see Lemma A.7 in the Appendix) yields that for every $\delta > 0$, with probability at least $1 - \delta$,

$$\sum_{t=1}^{n} \ell(I_t, Y_t) \leq \sum_{t=1}^{n} \overline{\ell}(\mathbf{p}_t, Y_t) + \sqrt{\frac{n}{2} \ln \frac{1}{\delta}}.$$

Combine this inequality with the first statement to complete the proof. ∎

Most of the results presented in this and the next two chapters (with the exception of those of Section 6.10) are valid in the general model of the nonoblivious opponent. So, unless otherwise specified, we allow the actions of environment to depend on the randomized predictions of the forecaster.

In Section 4.2 we show that the techniques of Chapter 2 may be used in the setup of randomized prediction as well. In particular, a simple adaptation of the weighted average forecaster guarantees that the actual regret becomes negligible as n grows. This property is known as *Hannan consistency*.

In Section 4.3 we describe and analyze a randomized forecaster suggested by Hannan. This forecaster adds a small random "noise" to the observed cumulative losses of all strategies and selects the one achieving the minimal value. We show that this simple method achieves a regret comparable to that of weighted average predictors. In particular, the forecaster is Hannan consistent.

In Section 4.4, a refined notion of regret, the so-called *internal regret*, is introduced. It is shown that even though control of internal regret is more difficult than achieving Hannan consistency, the results of Chapter 2 may be used to construct prediction strategies with small internal regret.

An interesting application of no-internal-regret prediction is described in Section 4.5. The forecasters considered there predict a $\{0, 1\}$-valued sequence with numbers between $[0, 1]$. Each number is interpreted as the predicted "chance" of the next outcome being 1. A forecaster is *well calibrated* if at those time instances in which a certain percentage is predicted, the fraction of 1's indeed turns out to be the predicted value. The main result of the section is the description of a randomized forecaster that is well calibrated for all possible sequences of outcomes.

In Section 4.6 we introduce a general notion of regret that contains both internal and external regret as special cases, as well as a number of other applications.

The chapter is concluded by describing, in Section 4.7, a significantly stronger notion of calibration, by introducing *checking rules*. The existence of a calibrated forecaster, in this stronger sense, follows by a simple application of the general setup of Section 4.6.

4.2 Weighted Average Forecasters

In order to understand the randomized prediction problem described above, we first consider a simplified version in which we only consider the *expected loss* $\mathbb{E}_t \ell(I_t, Y_t) = \overline{\ell}(\mathbf{p}_t, Y_t)$. If the player's goal is to minimize the difference between the cumulative expected loss

$$\overline{L}_n \overset{\text{def}}{=} \sum_{t=1}^{n} \overline{\ell}(\mathbf{p}_t, Y_t)$$

and the loss of the best pure strategy, then the problem becomes a special case of the problem of prediction using expert advice described in Chapter 2. To see this, define the decision space $\mathcal{D}$ of the forecaster (player) as the simplex of probability distributions in $\mathbb{R}^N$. Then the instantaneous regret for the player is the vector $\mathbf{r}_t \in \mathbb{R}^N$, whose ith component is

$$r_{i,t} = \overline{\ell}(\mathbf{p}_t, Y_t) - \ell(i, Y_t).$$

This quantity measures the expected change in the player's loss if it were to deterministically choose action i and the environment did not change its action. Observe that the "expected" loss function is linear (and therefore convex) in its first argument, and Lemma 2.1 may be applied in this situation. To this end, we recall the weighted average forecaster of Section 2.1 based on the potential function

$$\Phi(\mathbf{u}) = \psi \left(\sum_{i=1}^{N} \phi(u_i) \right),$$

where $\phi : \mathbb{R} \to \mathbb{R}$ is any nonnegative, increasing, and twice differentiable function and $\psi : \mathbb{R} \to \mathbb{R}$ is any nonnegative, strictly increasing, concave, and twice differentiable auxiliary function (which only plays a role in the analysis but not in the definition of the forecasting strategy). The general potential-based weighted average strategy $\mathbf{p}_t$ is now

$$p_{i,t} = \frac{\nabla \Phi(\mathbf{R}_{t-1})_i}{\sum_{k=1}^{N} \nabla \Phi(\mathbf{R}_{t-1})_k} = \frac{\phi'(R_{i,t-1})}{\sum_{k=1}^{N} \phi'(R_{k,t-1})}$$

for $t > 1$ and $p_{i,1} = 1/N$ for $i = 1, \ldots, N$.

By Lemma 2.1, for any $y_t \in \mathcal{Y}$, the Blackwell condition holds, that is,

$$\mathbf{r}_t \cdot \nabla \Phi(\mathbf{R}_{t-1}) \leq 0. \tag{4.1}$$

In fact, by the linearity of the loss function, it is immediate to see that inequality (4.1) is satisfied with equality. Thus, because the loss function ranges in $[0, 1]$, then choosing $\phi(x) = x_+^p$ (with $p \geq 2$) or $\phi(x) = e^{\eta x}$, the respective performance bounds of Corollaries 2.1 and 2.2 hold in this new setup as well. Also, Theorem 2.2 may be applied, which we recall here for completeness: consider the exponentially weighted average player given by

$$p_{i,t} = \frac{\exp\left(-\eta \sum_{s=1}^{t} \ell(i, Y_s)\right)}{\sum_{k=1}^{N} \exp\left(-\eta \sum_{s=1}^{t} \ell(k, Y_s)\right)} \qquad i = 1, \ldots, N,$$

where $\eta > 0$. Then

$$\overline{L}_n - \min_{i=1,\ldots,N} L_{i,n} \leq \frac{\ln N}{\eta} + \frac{n\eta}{8}.$$

With the choice $\eta = \sqrt{8 \ln N / n}$ the upper bound becomes $\sqrt{(n \ln N)/2}$. We remark here that this bound is essentially unimprovable in this generality. Indeed, in Section 3.7 we prove the following.

Corollary 4.1. *Let* $n, N \geq 1$. *There exists a loss function ℓ such that for any randomized forecasting strategy,*

$$\sup_{y^n \in \mathcal{Y}^n} \left(\overline{L}_n - \min_{i=1,\ldots,N} L_{i,n} \right) \geq \left(1 - \varepsilon_{N,n}\right) \sqrt{\frac{n \ln N}{2}},$$

where $\lim_{N \to \infty} \lim_{n \to \infty} \varepsilon_{N,n} = 0$.

Thus the expected cumulative loss of randomized forecasters may be effectively bounded by the results of Chapter 2. On the other hand, it is more interesting to study the behavior of the actual (random) cumulative loss $\ell(I_1, Y_1) + \cdots + \ell(I_n, Y_n)$. As we have already observed in the proof of Lemma 4.1, the random variables $\ell(I_t, Y_t) - \overline{\ell}(\mathbf{p}_t, Y_t)$, for $t = 1, 2, \ldots$, form a sequence of bounded martingale differences, and a simple application of the Hoeffding–Azuma inequality yields the following.

Corollary 4.2. *Let* $n, N \geq 1$ *and* $\delta \in (0, 1)$. *The exponentially weighted average forecaster with* $\eta = \sqrt{8 \ln N / n}$ *satisfies, with probability at least* $1 - \delta$,

$$\sum_{t=1}^{n} \ell(I_t, Y_t) - \min_{i=1,\ldots,N} \sum_{t=1}^{n} \ell(i, Y_t) \leq \sqrt{\frac{n \ln N}{2}} + \sqrt{\frac{n}{2} \ln \frac{1}{\delta}}.$$

The relationship between the forecaster's cumulative loss and the cumulative loss of the best possible action appears in the classical notion of *Hannan consistency*, first established by Hannan [141]. A forecaster is said to be Hannan consistent if

$$\limsup_{n \to \infty} \frac{1}{n} \left(\sum_{t=1}^{n} \ell(I_t, Y_t) - \min_{i=1,\ldots,N} \sum_{t=1}^{n} \ell(i, Y_t) \right) = 0, \qquad \text{with probability } 1,$$

where "probability" is understood with respect to the randomization of the forecaster. A simple modification of Corollary 4.2 leads to the following.

Corollary 4.3. *Consider the exponentially weighted average forecaster defined above. If the parameter $\eta = \eta_t$ is chosen by $\eta_t = \sqrt{(8 \ln N)/t}$ (as in Section 2.8), then the forecaster is Hannan consistent.*

The simple proof is left as an exercise. In the exercises some other modifications are described as well.

In the definition of Hannan consistency the number of pure strategies N is kept fixed while we let the number n of rounds of the game grow to infinity. However, in some cases it is more reasonable to set up the asymptotic problem by allowing the number of comparison strategies to grow with n. Of course, this may be done in many different ways. Next we briefly describe such a model. The nonasymptotic nature of the performance bounds described above may be directly used to address this general problem. Let $\ell : \{1, \ldots, N\} \times \mathcal{Y} \to [0, 1]$ be a loss function, and consider the forecasting game defined above. A *dynamic strategy s* is simply a sequence of indices $s_1, s_2, \ldots$, where $s_t \in \{1, \ldots, N\}$ marks the guess a forecaster predicting according to this strategy makes at time t. Given a class $\mathcal{S}$ of dynamic strategies, the forecaster's goal is to achieve a cumulative loss not much larger than the best of the strategies in $\mathcal{S}$ regardless of the outcome sequence, that is, to keep the difference

$$\sum_{t=1}^{n} \ell(I_t, Y_t) - \min_{s \in \mathcal{S}} \sum_{t=1}^{n} \ell(s_t, Y_t)$$

as small as possible. The weighted average strategy described earlier may be generalized to this situation in a straightforward way, and repeating the same proof we thus obtain the following.

Theorem 4.1. *Let $\mathcal{S}$ be an arbitrary class of dynamic strategies and, for each $t \geq 1$, denote by N_t the number of different vectors $s = (s_1, \ldots, s_t) \in \{1, \ldots, N\}^t$, $s \in \mathcal{S}$. For any $\eta > 0$ there exists a randomized forecaster such that for all $\delta \in (0, 1)$, with probability at least $1 - \delta$,*

$$\sum_{t=1}^{n} \ell(I_t, Y_t) - \min_{s \in \mathcal{S}} \sum_{t=1}^{n} \ell(s_t, Y_t) \leq \frac{\ln N_n}{\eta} + \frac{n\eta}{8} + \sqrt{\frac{n}{2} \ln \frac{1}{\delta}}.$$

Moreover, there exists a strategy such that if $n^{-1} \ln N_n \to 0$ as $n \to \infty$, then

$$\frac{1}{n} \sum_{t=1}^{n} \ell(I_t, Y_t) - \frac{1}{n} \min_{s \in \mathcal{S}} \sum_{t=1}^{n} \ell(s_t, Y_t) \to 0, \qquad \text{with probability } 1.$$

The details of the proof are left as an easy exercise. As an example, consider the following class of dynamic strategies. Let $k_1, k_2, \ldots$ be a monotonically increasing sequence of positive integers such that $k_n \leq n$ for all $n \geq 1$. Let $\mathcal{S}$ contain all dynamic strategies such that each strategy changes actions at most $k_n - 1$ times between time 1 and n, for all n. In other words, each $s \in \mathcal{S}$ is such that the sequence $s_1, \ldots, s_n$ consists of k_n constant segments. It is easy to see that, for each n, $N_n = \sum_{k=1}^{k_n} \binom{n-1}{k-1} N(N-1)^{k-1}$. Indeed, for each k, there are $\binom{n-1}{k-1}$ different ways of dividing the time segment $1, \ldots, n$ into k pieces, and for a division with segment lengths $n_1, \ldots, n_k$, there are $N(N-1)^{k-1}$ different ways of assigning actions to the segments such that no two consecutive segments have the same actions assigned.

Thus, Theorem 4.1 implies that, whenever the sequence $\{k_n\}$ is such that $k_n \ln n = o(n)$, we have

$$\frac{1}{n} \sum_{t=1}^{n} \ell(I_t, Y_t) - \frac{1}{n} \min_{s \in S} \sum_{t=1}^{n} \ell(s_t, Y_t) \to 0, \qquad \text{with probability 1.}$$

Of course, calculating the weighted average forecaster for a large class of dynamic strategies may be computationally prohibitive. However, in many important cases (such as the concrete example given above), efficient algorithms exist. Several examples are described in Chapter 5.

Corollary 4.2 is based on the Hoeffding–Azuma inequality, which asserts that, with probability at least $1 - \delta$,

$$\sum_{t=1}^{n} \ell(I_t, Y_t) - \sum_{t=1}^{n} \overline{\ell}(\mathbf{p}_t, Y_t) \leq \sqrt{\frac{n}{2} \ln \frac{1}{\delta}}.$$

This inequality is combined with the fact that the cumulative expected regret is bounded as $\sum_{t=1}^{n} \overline{\ell}(\mathbf{p}_t, Y_t) - \min_{i=1,\dots,N} \sum_{t=1}^{n} \ell(i, Y_t) \leq \sqrt{(n/2) \ln N}$. The term bounding the random fluctuations is thus about the same order of magnitude as the bound for the expected regret. However, it is pointed out in Section 2.4 that if the cumulative loss $\min_{i=1,\dots,N} \sum_{t=1}^{n} \ell(i, Y_t)$ is guaranteed to be bounded by a quantity $L_n^* \ll n$, then significantly improved performance bounds, of the form $\sqrt{2L_n^* \ln N} + \ln N$, may be achieved. In this case the term $\sqrt{(n/2) \ln(1/\delta)}$ resulting from the Hoeffding–Azuma inequality becomes dominating. However, in such a situation improved bounds may be established for the difference between the "actual" and "expected" cumulative losses. This may be done by invoking Bernstein's inequality for martingales (see Lemma A.8 in the Appendix). Indeed, because

$$\mathbb{E}_t \left[\ell(I_t, Y_t) - \overline{\ell}(\mathbf{p}_t, Y_t) \right]^2 = \mathbb{E}_t \ell(I_t, Y_t)^2 - \left(\overline{\ell}(\mathbf{p}_t, Y_t) \right)^2$$
$$\leq \mathbb{E}_t \ell(I_t, Y_t)^2 \leq \mathbb{E}_t \ell(I_t, Y_t) = \overline{\ell}(\mathbf{p}_t, Y_t),$$

the sum of the conditional variances is bounded by the expected cumulative loss $\overline{L}_n = \sum_{t=1}^{n} \overline{\ell}(\mathbf{p}_t, Y_t)$. Then by Lemma A.8, with probability at least $1 - \delta$,

$$\sum_{t=1}^{n} \ell(I_t, Y_t) - \sum_{t=1}^{n} \overline{\ell}(\mathbf{p}_t, Y_t) \leq \sqrt{2\overline{L}_n \ln \frac{1}{\delta}} + \frac{2\sqrt{2}}{3} \ln \frac{1}{\delta}.$$

If the cumulative loss of the best action is bounded by a number L_n^* known in advance, then $\overline{L}_n$ can be bounded by $L_n^* + \sqrt{2L_n^* \ln N} + \ln N$ (see Corollary 2.4), and the effect of the random fluctuations is comparable with the bound for the expected regret.

4.3 Follow the Perturbed Leader

One may wonder whether "following the leader," that is, predicting at time t according to the action i whose cumulative loss $L_{i,t-1}$ up to that time is minimal, is a reasonable algorithm. In Section 3.2 we saw that under certain conditions for the loss function, this is quite a powerful strategy. However, it is easy to see that in the setup of this chapter this strategy, also known as *fictitious play*, does not achieve Hannan consistency. To see this, just consider $N = 2$ actions such that the sequence of losses $\ell(1, y_t)$ of the first action is $(1/2, 0, 1, 0, 1, 0, 1, \ldots)$ while the values of $\ell(2, y_t)$ are $(1/2, 1, 0, 1, 0, 1, 0, \ldots)$. Then $L_{i,n}$ is about $n/2$ for both $i = 1$ and $i = 2$, but fictitious play suffers a loss close to n. (See also Exercises 3.8 and 4.6.) However, as it was pointed out by Hannan [141], a simple modification suffices to achieve a significantly improved performance. One merely has to add a small random perturbation to the cumulative losses and follow the "perturbed" leader.

Formally, let $\mathbf{Z}_1, \mathbf{Z}_2, \ldots$ be independent, identically distributed random N-vectors with components $Z_{i,t}$ $(i = 1, \ldots, N)$. For simplicity, assume that $\mathbf{Z}_t$ has an absolutely continuous distribution (with respect to the N-dimensional Lebesgue measure) and denote its density by f. The follow-the-perturbed-leader forecaster selects, at time t, an action

$$I_t = \operatorname*{argmin}_{i=1,\ldots,N} \left(L_{i,t-1} + Z_{i,t} \right).$$

(Ties may be broken, say, in favor of the smallest index.)

Unlike in the case of weighted average predictors, the definition of the forecaster does not explicitly specify the probabilities $p_{i,t}$ of selecting action i at time t. However, it is clear from the definition that given the past sequence of plays and outcomes, the value of $p_{i,t}$ only depends on the joint distribution of the random variables $Z_{i,t}$ but not on their random values. Therefore, by Lemma 4.1 it suffices to consider the model of oblivious opponent and derive bounds for the expected regret in that case.

To state the main result of this section, observe that the loss $\ell(I_t, y_t)$ suffered at time t is a function of the random vector $\mathbf{Z}_t$ and denote this function by $F_t(\mathbf{Z}_t) = \ell(I_t, y_t)$. The precise definition of $F_t : \mathbb{R}^N \to [0, 1]$ is given by

$$F_t(\mathbf{z}) = \ell \left(\operatorname*{argmin}_{i=1,\ldots,N} \left(L_{i,t-1} + z_i \right), y_t \right), \qquad \mathbf{z} = (z_1, \ldots, z_N).$$

Denoting by $\boldsymbol{\ell}_t = \left(\ell(i, y_t), \ldots, \ell(N, y_t) \right)$ the vector of losses of the actions at time t, we have the following general result.

Theorem 4.2. *Consider the randomized prediction problem with an oblivious opponent. The expected cumulative loss of the follow-the-perturbed-leader forecaster is bounded by*

$$\overline{L}_n - \min_{i=1,\ldots,N} L_{i,n}$$

$$\leq \mathbb{E} \max_{i=1,\ldots,N} Z_{i,1} + \mathbb{E} \max_{i=1,\ldots,N} (-Z_{i,1}) + \sum_{t=1}^{n} \int F_t(\mathbf{z}) \big(f(\mathbf{z}) - f(\mathbf{z} - \boldsymbol{\ell}_t) \big) \mathrm{d}\mathbf{z}$$

and also

$$\overline{L}_n \leq \sup_{\mathbf{z},t} \frac{f(\mathbf{z})}{f(\mathbf{z} - \boldsymbol{\ell}_t)} \left(\min_{i=1,\ldots,N} L_{i,n} + \mathbb{E} \max_{i=1,\ldots,N} Z_{i,1} + \mathbb{E} \max_{i=1,\ldots,N} (-Z_{i,1}) \right).$$

Even though in this chapter we only consider losses taking values in $[0, 1]$, it is worth pointing out that Theorem 4.2 holds for all, not necessarily bounded, loss functions. Before proving the general statement, we illustrate its meaning by the following immediate corollary. (Boundedness of ℓ is necessary for the corollary.)

Corollary 4.4. *Assume that the random vector $\mathbf{Z}_t$ has independent components $Z_{i,t}$ uniformly distributed on $[0, \Delta]$, where $\Delta > 0$. Then the expected cumulative loss of the follow-the-perturbed-leader forecaster with an oblivious opponent satisfies*

$$\overline{L}_n - \min_{i=1,\dots,N} L_{i,n} \le \Delta + \frac{Nn}{\Delta}.$$

In particular, if $\Delta = \sqrt{nN}$, then

$$\overline{L}_n - \min_{i=1,\dots,N} L_{i,n} \le 2\sqrt{nN}.$$

Moreover, with any (nonoblivious) opponent, with probability at least $1 - \delta$, the actual regret satisfies

$$\sum_{t=1}^{n} \ell(I_t, Y_t) - \min_{i=1,\dots,N} \sum_{t=1}^{n} \ell(i, Y_t) \le 2\sqrt{nN} + \sqrt{\frac{n}{2} \ln \frac{1}{\delta}}.$$

Proof. On the one hand, we obviously have

$$\mathbb{E} \max_{i=1,\dots,N} (-Z_{i,1}) \le 0 \quad \text{and} \quad \mathbb{E} \max_{i=1,\dots,N} |Z_{i,1}| \le \Delta.$$

On the other hand, because $f(\mathbf{z}) = \Delta^{-N} \mathbb{I}_{\{\mathbf{z} \in [0, \Delta]^N\}}$ and F_t is between 0 and 1,

$$
\begin{aligned}
\int F_t(\mathbf{z})\big(f(\mathbf{z}) - f(\mathbf{z} - \boldsymbol{\ell}_t)\big) d\mathbf{z} &\le \int_{\{\mathbf{z} : f(\mathbf{z}) > f(\mathbf{z} - \boldsymbol{\ell}_t)\}} f(\mathbf{z}) \, d\mathbf{z} \\
&= \frac{1}{\Delta^N} \text{Volume}\big(\{\mathbf{z} : f(\mathbf{z}) > f(\mathbf{z} - \boldsymbol{\ell}_t)\}\big) \\
&= \frac{1}{\Delta^N} \text{Volume}\big(\{\mathbf{z} : (\exists i)\, z_i \le \ell(i, y_t)\}\big) \\
&\le \frac{1}{\Delta^N} \sum_{i=1}^{N} \ell(i, y_t) \Delta^{N-1} \\
&\le \frac{N}{\Delta}
\end{aligned}
$$

as desired. The last statement follows by applying Lemma 4.1. ■

Note that in order to achieve the bound $2\sqrt{nN}$, previous knowledge of n is required. This may be easily avoided by choosing a time-dependent value of Δ. In fact, by choosing $\Delta_t = \sqrt{tN}$, the bound $2\sqrt{2nN}$ is achieved (see Exercise 4.7). Thus the price of not knowing the horizon n in advance is at most a factor of $\sqrt{2}$ in the upper bound.

The dependence of the upper bound $\sqrt{nN}$ derived above on the number N of actions is significantly worse than that of the $O(\sqrt{n \ln N})$ bounds derived in the previous section for certain weighted average forecasters. Bounds of the optimal order may be achieved by the follow-the-perturbed-leader forecaster if the distribution of the perturbations $\mathbf{Z}_t$ is chosen more carefully. Such an example is described in the following corollary.

Corollary 4.5. *Assume that the $Z_{i,t}$ are independent with two-sided exponential distribution of parameter $\eta > 0$, so that the joint density of $\mathbf{Z}_t$ is $f(\mathbf{z}) = (\eta/2)^N e^{-\eta\|\mathbf{z}\|_1}$, where $\|\mathbf{z}\|_1 = \sum_{i=1}^N |z_i|$. Then the expected cumulative loss of the follow-the-perturbed-leader forecaster against an oblivious opponent satisfies*

$$\overline{L}_n \le e^\eta \left(L_n^* + \frac{2(1 + \ln N)}{\eta} \right),$$

where $L_n^* = \min_{i=1,\ldots,N} L_{i,n}$.
  In particular, if $\eta = \min\left\{1, \sqrt{2(1 + \ln N)/((e-1)L_n^*)}\right\}$, then

$$\overline{L}_n - L_n^* \le 2\sqrt{2(e-1)L_n^*(1 + \ln N)} + 2(e+1)(1 + \ln N).$$

Remark 4.2 (*Nonoblivious opponent*). Just as in Corollary 4.4, an analogous result may be established for the actual regret under any nonoblivious opponent. Using Lemma 4.1 (and $L_n^* \le n$) it is immediate to see that with probability at least $1 - \delta$, the actual regret satisfies

$$\sum_{t=1}^n \ell(I_t, Y_t) - \min_{i=1,\ldots,N} \sum_{t=1}^n \ell(i, Y_t)$$

$$\le 2\sqrt{2(e-1)n(1 + \ln N)} + 2(e+1)(1 + \ln N) + \sqrt{\frac{n}{2} \ln \frac{N}{\delta}}.$$

Proof of Corollary 4.5. Applying the theorem directly does not quite give the desired result. However, the following simple observation makes it possible to obtain the optimal dependence in terms of N. Consider the performance of the follow-the-perturbed-leader forecaster on a related prediction problem, which has the property that, in each step, at most one action has a nonzero loss. Observe that any prediction problem may be converted to satisfy this property by replacing each round of play with loss vector $\boldsymbol{\ell}_t = \big(\ell(1, y_t), \ldots, \ell(N, y_t)\big)$ by N rounds so that in the ith round only the ith action has a positive loss, namely $\ell(i, y_t)$. The new problem has nN rounds of play, the total cumulative loss of the best action does not change, and the follow-the-perturbed-leader has an expected cumulative loss at least as large as in the original problem. To see this, consider time t of the original problem in which the expected loss is $\overline{\ell}(\mathbf{p}_t, y_t) = \sum_i \ell(i, y_t)p_{i,t}$. This corresponds to steps $N(t-1) + 1, \ldots, Nt$ of the converted problem. At the beginning of this period of length N, the cumulative losses of all actions coincide with the cumulative losses of the actions at time $t - 1$ in the original problem. At time $N(t-1) + 1$ the expected loss is $\ell(1, y_t)p_{1,t}$ (where $p_{i,t}$ denotes the probability of i assigned by the follow-the-perturbed-leader forecaster at time t in the original problem). At time $N(t-1) + 2$ in the converted problem the cumulative losses of all actions stay the same as in the previous time instant, except for the first action whose loss has increased. Thus the probabilities assigned by the follow-the-perturbed-leader forecaster increase except for that of the first action. This implies that at time $N(t-1) + 2$ the expected loss is at least $\ell(2, y_t)p_{2,t}$. By repeating the argument N times we see that the expected loss accumulated during these N periods of the converted problem is at least $\ell(1, y_t)p_{1,t} + \cdots + \ell(N, y_t)p_{N,t} = \overline{\ell}(\mathbf{p}_t, y_t)$. Therefore, it suffices to prove the corollary for prediction problems satisfying $\|\boldsymbol{\ell}_t\|_1 \le 1$ for all t.

We apply the second inequality of Theorem 4.2. First note that

$$
\mathbb{E} \max_{i=1,\ldots,N} Z_{i,1} + \mathbb{E} \max_{i=1,\ldots,N} (-Z_{i,1})
$$

$$
\leq 2\,\mathbb{E} \max_{i=1,\ldots,N} Z_{i,1}
$$

$$
= 2 \int_0^\infty \mathbb{P}\left[\max_{i=1,\ldots,N} Z_{i,1} > u \right] du
$$

$$
\leq 2v + 2N \int_v^\infty \mathbb{P}\left[Z_{1,1} > u \right] du \quad \text{(for any } v > 0\text{)}
$$

$$
= 2v + \frac{2N}{\eta} e^{-\eta v}
$$

$$
= \frac{2(1 + \ln N)}{\eta} \qquad \text{(by choosing } v = \ln N / \eta\text{)}.
$$

On the other hand, for each $\mathbf{z}$ and t the triangle inequality implies that,

$$
\frac{f(\mathbf{z})}{f(\mathbf{z} - \boldsymbol{\ell}_t)} = \exp\left(-\eta \big(\|\mathbf{z}\|_1 - \|\mathbf{z} - \boldsymbol{\ell}_t\|_1 \big) \right) \leq \exp\big(\eta \|\boldsymbol{\ell}_t\|_1 \big) \leq e^\eta,
$$

where we used the fact that $\|\boldsymbol{\ell}_t\| \leq 1$ in the converted prediction problem. This proves the first inequality. To derive the second, just note that $e^\eta \leq 1 + (e - 1)\eta$ for $\eta \in [0, 1]$, and substitute the given value of η in the first inequality. ∎

The follow-the-perturbed-leader forecaster with exponentially distributed perturbations has thus a performance comparable to that of the best weighted average predictors (see Section 2.4). If L_n^* is not known in advance, the adaptive techniques described in Chapter 2 may be used.

It remains to prove Theorem 4.2.

***Proof of Theorem* 4.2.** The proof is based on an adaptation of the arguments of Section 3.2. First we investigate a related "forecaster" defined by

$$
\widehat{I}_t = \operatorname*{argmin}_{i=1,\ldots,N} \left(L_{i,t} + Z_{i,t} \right) = \operatorname*{argmin}_{i=1,\ldots,N} \sum_{s=1}^t \big(\ell(i, y_s) + Z_{i,s} - Z_{i,s-1} \big),
$$

where we define $Z_{i,0} = 0$ for all i. Observe that $\widehat{I}_t$ is not a legal forecaster because it uses the unknown values of the losses at time t. However, we show in what follows that I_t and $\widehat{I}_t$ have a similar behavior. To bound the performance of $\widehat{I}_t$ we apply Lemma 3.1 for the losses $\ell(i, y_s) + Z_{i,s} - Z_{i,s-1}$. We obtain

$$
\sum_{t=1}^n \big(\ell(\widehat{I}_t, y_t) + Z_{\widehat{I}_t,t} - Z_{\widehat{I}_t,t-1} \big) \leq \min_{i=1,\ldots,N} \sum_{t=1}^n \big(\ell(i, y_t) + Z_{i,t} - Z_{i,t-1} \big)
$$

$$
= \min_{i=1,\ldots,N} \left(\sum_{t=1}^n \ell(i, y_t) + Z_{i,n} \right)
$$

$$
\leq \min_{i=1,\ldots,N} L_{i,n} + Z_{i^*,n},
$$

where i^* is the index of the overall best action. Rearranging, we obtain

$$\sum_{t=1}^{n} \ell(\widehat{I}_t, y_t) \leq \min_{i=1,\ldots,N} L_{i,n} + Z_{i^*,n} + \sum_{t=1}^{n} \left(Z_{\widehat{I}_t,t-1} - Z_{\widehat{I}_t,t} \right)$$

$$\leq \min_{i=1,\ldots,N} L_{i,n} + \max_{i=1,\ldots,N} Z_{i,n} + \sum_{t=1}^{n} \max_{i=1,\ldots,N} \left(Z_{i,t-1} - Z_{i,t} \right).$$

Our next aim is to bound the expected value

$$\mathbb{E} \sum_{t=1}^{n} \ell(\widehat{I}_t, y_t) = \sum_{t=1}^{n} \mathbb{E}\, \ell(\widehat{I}_t, y_t).$$

The key observation is that, because the opponent is oblivious, for each t, the value $\mathbb{E}\, \ell(\widehat{I}_t, y_t)$ only depends on the vector $\mathbf{Z}_t = (Z_{1,t}, \ldots, Z_{N,t})$ but not on $\mathbf{Z}_s, s \neq t$. Therefore, $\mathbb{E} \sum_{t=1}^{n} \ell(\widehat{I}_t, y_t)$ remains unchanged if the $Z_{i,t}$ are replaced by $Z'_{i,t}$ in the definition of $\widehat{I}_t$ as long as the marginal distribution of the vector $\mathbf{Z}'_t = (Z'_{1,t}, \ldots, Z'_{N,t})$ remains the same as that of $\mathbf{Z}_t$. In particular, unlike $\mathbf{Z}_1, \ldots, \mathbf{Z}_n$, the new vectors $\mathbf{Z}'_1, \ldots, \mathbf{Z}'_n$ do not need to be independent. The convenient choice is to take them all equal so that $\mathbf{Z}'_1 = \mathbf{Z}'_2 = \cdots = \mathbf{Z}'_n$. Then the inequality derived above implies that

$$\mathbb{E} \sum_{t=1}^{n} \ell(\widehat{I}_t, y_t) \leq \mathbb{E} \left[\min_{i=1,\ldots,N} L_{i,n} + \max_{i=1,\ldots,N} Z'_{i,n} + \sum_{t=1}^{n} \max_{i=1,\ldots,N} \left(Z'_{i,t-1} - Z'_{i,t} \right) \right]$$

$$= \min_{i=1,\ldots,N} L_{i,n} + \mathbb{E} \max_{i=1,\ldots,N} Z_{i,n} + \mathbb{E} \max_{i=1,\ldots,N} (-Z_{i,1}).$$

The last step is to relate $\mathbb{E} \sum_{t=1}^{n} \ell(\widehat{I}_t, y_t)$ to the expected loss $\mathbb{E} \sum_{t=1}^{n} \ell(I_t, y_t)$ of the follow-the-perturbed-leader forecaster. To this end, just observe that

$$\mathbb{E}\, \ell(\widehat{I}_t, y_t) = \int F_t(\mathbf{z} + \boldsymbol{\ell}_t) f(\mathbf{z}) d\mathbf{z} = \int F_t(\mathbf{z}) f(\mathbf{z} - \boldsymbol{\ell}_t)\, d\mathbf{z}.$$

Thus,

$$\mathbb{E} \sum_{t=1}^{n} \ell(I_t, y_t) - \mathbb{E} \sum_{t=1}^{n} \ell(\widehat{I}_t, y_t) = \sum_{t=1}^{n} \int F_t(\mathbf{z}) \big(f(\mathbf{z}) - f(\mathbf{z} - \boldsymbol{\ell}_t) \big)\, d\mathbf{z}$$

and the first inequality follows. To obtain the second, simply observe that

$$\mathbb{E}\, \ell(I_t, y_t) = \int F_t(\mathbf{z}) f(\mathbf{z}) d\mathbf{z}$$

$$\leq \sup_{\mathbf{z},t} \frac{f(\mathbf{z})}{f(\mathbf{z} - \boldsymbol{\ell}_t)} \int F_t(\mathbf{z}) f(\mathbf{z} - \boldsymbol{\ell}_t)\, d\mathbf{z}$$

$$= \sup_{\mathbf{z},t} \frac{f(\mathbf{z})}{f(\mathbf{z} - \boldsymbol{\ell}_t)} \mathbb{E}\, \ell(\widehat{I}_t, y_t). \quad \blacksquare$$

4.4 Internal Regret

In this section we design forecasters able to minimize a notion of regret, which we call "internal," strictly stronger than the regret for randomized prediction analyzed in this chapter. A game-theoretic motivation for the study of internal regret is offered in Section 7.4.

Recall the following randomized prediction problem: at each time instance t the forecaster (or player) determines a probability distribution $\mathbf{p}_t = (p_{1,t} \ldots, p_{N,t})$ over the set of N possible actions and chooses an action randomly according to this distribution. In this section, for simplicity, we focus our attention on the expected loss $\bar{\ell}(\mathbf{p}_t, Y_t) = \sum_{i=1}^{N} \ell(i, Y_t) p_{i,t}$ and not on the actual random loss to which we return in Section 7.4.

Up to this point we have always compared the (expected) cumulative loss of the forecaster to the cumulative loss of each action, and we have investigated prediction schemes, such as the exponentially weighted average forecaster, guaranteeing that the forecaster's cumulative expected loss is not much larger than the cumulative loss of the best action. The difference

$$\sum_{t=1}^{n} \bar{\ell}(\mathbf{p}_t, Y_t) - \min_{i=1,\ldots,N} \sum_{t=1}^{n} \ell(i, Y_t)$$

$$= \max_{i=1,\ldots,N} \sum_{t=1}^{n} \sum_{j=1}^{N} p_{j,t}\big(\ell(j, Y_t) - \ell(i, Y_t)\big)$$

is sometimes called the *external regret* of the forecaster. Next we investigate a closely related but different notion of regret.

Roughly speaking, a forecaster has a small internal regret if, for each pair of experts (i, j), the forecaster does not regret of not having followed expert j each time he followed expert i.

The *internal cumulative regret* of a forecaster $\mathbf{p}_t$ is defined by

$$\max_{i,j=1,\ldots,N} R_{(i,j),n} = \max_{i,j=1,\ldots,N} \sum_{t=1}^{n} p_{i,t}\big(\ell(i, Y_t) - \ell(j, Y_t)\big).$$

Thus, $r_{(i,j),t} = p_{i,t}(\ell(i, Y_t) - \ell(j, Y_t)) = \mathbb{E}_t \mathbb{I}_{\{I_t=i\}}(\ell(I_t, Y_t) - \ell(j, Y_t))$ expresses the forecaster's expected regret of having taken action i instead of action j. Equivalently, $r_{(i,j),t}$ is the forecaster's regret of having put the probability mass $p_{i,t}$ on the ith expert instead of on the jth one. Now, clearly, the external regret of the forecaster $\mathbf{p}_t$ equals

$$\max_{i=1,\ldots,N} \sum_{j=1}^{N} R_{(i,j),n} \leq N \max_{i,j=1,\ldots,N} R_{(i,j),n},$$

which shows that any algorithm with a small (i.e., sublinear in n) internal regret also has a small external regret. On the other hand, it is easy to see that a small external regret does not imply small internal regret. In fact, as it is shown in the following example, even the exponentially weighted average algorithm defined in Section 4.2 may have a linearly growing internal regret.

Example 4.1 (*Weighted average forecaster has a large internal regret*). Consider the following example with three actions A, B, and C. Let n be a large multiple of 3, and assume that time is divided in three equally long regimes characterized by a constant loss for each action. These losses are summarized in Table 4.1. We claim that the regret $R_{(B,C),n}$ of B versus C grows linearly with n, that is,

$$\liminf_{n\to\infty} \frac{1}{n} \sum_{t=1}^{n} p_{B,t}\big(\ell(B, y_t) - \ell(C, y_t)\big) = \gamma > 0,$$

Table 4.1. *Example of a problem in which the exponentially
weighted average forecaster has a large internal regret.*

Regimes	$\ell(A, y_t)$	$\ell(B, y_t)$	$\ell(C, y_t)$
$1 \le t \le n/3$	0	1	5
$n/3 + 1 \le t \le 2n/3$	1	0	5
$2n/3 + 1 \le t \le n$	1	0	-1

where $p_{B,t}$ denotes the weight assigned by the exponentially weighted average forecaster to action B:

$$p_{B,t} = \frac{e^{-\eta L_{B,t-1}}}{e^{-\eta L_{A,t-1}} + e^{-\eta L_{B,t-1}} + e^{-\eta L_{C,t-1}}},$$

where $L_{i,t} = \sum_{s=1}^{t} \ell(i, y_s)$ denotes the cumulative loss of action i and η is chosen as usual, that is,

$$\eta = \frac{1}{6}\sqrt{\frac{8 \ln 3}{n}} = \frac{K}{\sqrt{n}},$$

with $K = \sqrt{8 \ln 3}/6$. The intuition behind this example is that at the end of the second regime the forecaster quickly switches from A to B, and the weight of action C can never recover because of its disastrous behavior in the first two regimes. But since action C behaves much better than B in the third regime, the weighted average forecaster will regret of not having chosen C each time it chose B. Figure 4.1 illustrates the behavior of the weight of action B.

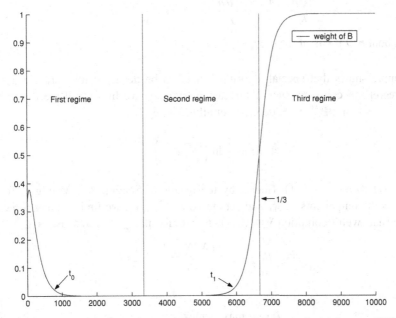

Figure 4.1. The evolution of the weight assigned to B in Example 4.1 for $n = 10000$.

More precisely, we show that during the first two regimes the number of times when $p_{B,t}$ is more than ε is of the order of $\sqrt{n}$ and that, in the third regime, $p_{B,t}$ is always more than a fixed constant ($1/3$, say). In the first regime, a sufficient condition for $p_{B,t} \leq \varepsilon$ is $e^{-\eta L_{B,t-1}} \leq \varepsilon$. This occurs whenever $t \geq t_0 = (-\ln \varepsilon)\sqrt{n}/K$. For the second regime, we lower bound the time instant t_1 when $p_{B,t}$ gets larger than ε. To this end, note that $p_{B,t} \geq \varepsilon$ is equivalent to

$$(1 - \varepsilon)e^{-\eta L_{B,t-1}} \geq \varepsilon\left(e^{-\eta L_{A,t-1}} + e^{-\eta L_{C,t-1}}\right).$$

Thus, $p_{B,t} \geq \varepsilon$ implies that $(1 - \varepsilon)e^{-\eta L_{B,t-1}} \geq \varepsilon e^{-\eta L_{A,t-1}}$, which leads to

$$t_1 \leq \frac{2n}{3} + \frac{\sqrt{n}}{K} \ln \frac{1 - \varepsilon}{\varepsilon}.$$

Finally, in the third regime, we have at each time instant $L_{B,t-1} \leq L_{A,t-1}$ and $L_{B,t-1} \leq L_{C,t-1}$, so that $p_{B,t} \geq 1/3$. Putting these three steps together, we obtain the following lower bound for the internal regret of B versus C

$$\sum_{t=1}^{n} p_{B,t}\left(\ell(B, y_t) - \ell(C, y_t)\right)$$

$$= \sum_{t=1}^{n/3} p_{B,t}\left(\ell(B, y_t) - \ell(C, y_t)\right) + \sum_{t=n/3+1}^{2n/3} p_{B,t}\left(\ell(B, y_t) - \ell(C, y_t)\right)$$

$$+ \sum_{t=2n/3+1}^{n} p_{B,t}\left(\ell(B, y_t) - \ell(C, y_t)\right)$$

$$\geq -4\left(\frac{n}{3} - \frac{\sqrt{n}}{K} \ln \frac{1}{\varepsilon}\right)\varepsilon - 5\left(\frac{n}{3} + \frac{\sqrt{n}}{K} \ln \frac{1 - \varepsilon}{\varepsilon}\right)\varepsilon + \frac{n}{9}$$

$$= -3n\varepsilon - \frac{\varepsilon\sqrt{n}}{K} \ln \frac{1}{\varepsilon} - 5\frac{\varepsilon\sqrt{n}}{K} \ln(1 - \varepsilon) + \frac{n}{9},$$

which is about $n/9$ if ε is of the order of $n^{-1/2}$. □

This example shows that special algorithms need to be designed to guarantee a small internal regret. To construct such a forecasting strategy, we first recall the *exponential potential function* $\Phi : \mathbb{R}^M \to \mathbb{R}$ defined, for all $\eta > 0$, by

$$\Phi(\mathbf{u}) = \frac{1}{\eta} \ln\left(\sum_{i=1}^{M} e^{\eta u_i}\right),$$

where we set $M = N(N - 1)$. Hence, by the results of Section 2.1, writing $\mathbf{r}_t$ for the M-vector with components $r_{(i,j),t}$ and setting $\mathbf{R}_t = \sum_{s=1}^{t} \mathbf{r}_s$, we find that any forecaster satisfying Blackwell's condition $\nabla\Phi(\mathbf{R}_{t-1}) \cdot \mathbf{r}_t \leq 0$, for all $t \geq 1$, also satisfies

$$\max_{i,j=1,\ldots,N} R_{(i,j),t} \leq \frac{\ln N(N - 1)}{\eta} + \frac{\eta}{2} t B^2,$$

where

$$B = \max_{i,j=1,\ldots,N} \max_{s=1,\ldots,t} r_{(i,j),s}^2.$$

By choosing η optimally, one then obtains an internal regret bounded by $2B\sqrt{n \ln N}$ (see Corollary 2.2).

To design a forecaster satisfying the Blackwell condition, observe that the following simple exchange of the order of summation yields

$$\nabla \Phi(\mathbf{R}_{t-1}) \cdot \mathbf{r}_t$$

$$= \sum_{i,j=1}^{N} \nabla_{(i,j)} \Phi(\mathbf{R}_{t-1}) p_{i,t} \big(\ell(i, Y_t) - \ell(j, Y_t) \big)$$

$$= \sum_{i=1}^{N} \sum_{j=1}^{N} \nabla_{(i,j)} \Phi(\mathbf{R}_{t-1}) p_{i,t} \ell(i, Y_t) - \sum_{i=1}^{N} \sum_{j=1}^{N} \nabla_{(i,j)} \Phi(\mathbf{R}_{t-1}) p_{i,t} \ell(j, Y_t)$$

$$= \sum_{i=1}^{N} \sum_{j=1}^{N} \nabla_{(i,j)} \Phi(\mathbf{R}_{t-1}) p_{i,t} \ell(i, Y_t) - \sum_{j=1}^{N} \sum_{i=1}^{N} \nabla_{(j,i)} \Phi(\mathbf{R}_{t-1}) p_{j,t} \ell(i, Y_t)$$

$$= \sum_{i=1}^{N} \ell(i, Y_t) \left(\sum_{j=1}^{N} \nabla_{(i,j)} \Phi(\mathbf{R}_{t-1}) p_{i,t} - \sum_{k=1}^{N} \nabla_{(k,i)} \Phi(\mathbf{R}_{t-1}) p_{k,t} \right).$$

To guarantee that this quantity is nonpositive, it suffices to require that

$$p_{i,t} \sum_{j=1}^{N} \nabla_{(i,j)} \Phi(\mathbf{R}_{t-1}) - \sum_{k=1}^{N} \nabla_{(k,i)} \Phi(\mathbf{R}_{t-1}) p_{k,t} = 0$$

for all $i = 1, \ldots, N$. The existence of such a vector $\mathbf{p}_t = (p_{1,t}, \ldots, p_{N,t})$ may be proven by noting that $\mathbf{p}_t$ satisfies $\mathbf{p}_t^\top A = \mathbf{0}$, where A is an $N \times N$ matrix whose entries are

$$A_{k,i} = \begin{cases} -\nabla_{(k,i)} \Phi(\mathbf{R}_{t-1}) & \text{if } i \neq k, \\ \sum_{j \neq i} \nabla_{(k,j)} \Phi(\mathbf{R}_{t-1}) & \text{otherwise.} \end{cases}$$

To this end, first note that $\nabla_{(i,j)} \Phi(\mathbf{R}_{t-1}) \geq 0$ for all i, j. Let $a_{\max} = \max_{i,j} |A_{i,j}|$ and let I be the $N \times N$ identity matrix. Then $I - A/a_{\max}$ is a nonnegative row-stochastic matrix, and the Perron–Frobenius theorem (see, e.g., Seneta [263]) implies that a probability vector $\mathbf{q}$ exists such that $\mathbf{q}^\top (I - A/a_{\max}) = \mathbf{q}^\top$.

As such a $\mathbf{q}$ also satisfies $\mathbf{q}^\top A = \mathbf{0}^\top$, the choice $\mathbf{p}_t = \mathbf{q}$ leads to a forecaster satisfying the Blackwell condition. Foster and Vohra [107] suggest a gaussian elimination method for the practical computation of $\mathbf{p}_t$.

We remark that instead of the exponential potential defined above, other potential functions may also be used with success. For example, polynomial potentials of the form

$$\Phi(\mathbf{u}) = \left(\sum_{i=1}^{N} (u_i)_+^p \right)^{2/p}$$

for $p \geq 2$ lead to the bound $\max_{i,j=1,\ldots,N} R_{(i,j),t} \leq B\sqrt{2(p-1)t N^{4/p}}$.

From Small External Regret to Small Internal Regret

We close this section by describing a simple way of converting any external-regret-minimizing (i.e., Hannan consistent) forecaster into a strategy to minimize the internal regret. Such a method may be defined recursively as follows. At time $t = 1$, let

$\mathbf{p}_1 = (1/N, \ldots, 1/N)$ be the uniform distribution over N actions. Consider now $t > 1$ and assume that at time $t - 1$ the forecaster chose an action according to the distribution $\mathbf{p}_{t-1} = (p_{1,t-1}, \ldots, p_{N,t-1})$. For each pair (i, j) of actions $(i \neq j)$ define the probability distribution $\mathbf{p}_{t-1}^{i \to j}$ by the vector whose components are the same as those of $\mathbf{p}_{t-1}$, except that the ith component of $\mathbf{p}_{t-1}^{i \to j}$ equals zero and the jth component equals $p_{i,t-1} + p_{j,t-1}$. Thus, $\mathbf{p}_{t-1}^{i \to j}$ is obtained from $\mathbf{p}_{t-1}$ by transporting the probability mass from i to j. We call these the $i \to j$ *modified strategies*. Consider now any external-regret-minimizing strategy that uses the $i \to j$ modified strategies as experts. More precisely, let $\mathbf{\Delta}_t$ be a probability distribution over the pairs $i \neq j$ that has the property that its cumulative expected loss is almost as small as that of the best modified strategy, that is,

$$\frac{1}{n} \sum_{t=1}^{n} \sum_{i \neq j} \overline{\ell}(\mathbf{p}_t^{i \to j}, Y_t) \Delta_{(i,j),t} \leq \min_{i \neq j} \frac{1}{n} \sum_{t=1}^{n} \overline{\ell}(\mathbf{p}_t^{i \to j}, Y_t) + \varepsilon_n$$

for some $\varepsilon_n \to 0$. For example, the exponentially weighted average strategy

$$\Delta_{(i,j),t} = \frac{\exp\left(-\eta \sum_{s=1}^{t-1} \overline{\ell}(\mathbf{p}_s^{i \to j}, Y_s)\right)}{\sum_{(k,l): k \neq l} \exp\left(-\eta \sum_{s=1}^{t-1} \overline{\ell}(\mathbf{p}_s^{k \to l}, Y_s)\right)}$$

guarantees that $\varepsilon_n = \sqrt{\ln(N(N-1))/(2n)} \leq \sqrt{(\ln N)/n}$ by Theorem 2.2 and for a properly chosen value of η.

Given such a "meta-forecaster," we define the forecaster $\mathbf{p}_t$ by the fixed point equality

$$\mathbf{p}_t = \sum_{(i,j): i \neq j} \mathbf{p}_t^{i \to j} \Delta_{(i,j),t}. \tag{4.2}$$

The existence of a solution of the defining equation may be seen by an argument similar to the one we used to prove the existence of the potential-based internal-regret-minimizing forecaster defined earlier in this section. It follows from the defining equality that for each t,

$$\overline{\ell}(\mathbf{p}_t, Y_t) = \sum_{i \neq j} \overline{\ell}(\mathbf{p}_t^{i \to j}, Y_t) \Delta_{(i,j),t}$$

and therefore the cumulative loss of the forecaster $\mathbf{p}_t$ is bounded by

$$\frac{1}{n} \sum_{t=1}^{n} \overline{\ell}(\mathbf{p}_t, Y_t) \leq \min_{i \neq j} \frac{1}{n} \sum_{t=1}^{n} \overline{\ell}(\mathbf{p}_t^{i \to j}, Y_t) + \varepsilon_n$$

or, equivalently,

$$\frac{1}{n} \max_{i \neq j} R_{(i,j),n} \leq \varepsilon_n.$$

Observe that if the meta-forecaster $\mathbf{\Delta}_t$ is a potential-based weighted average forecaster, then the derived forecaster $\mathbf{p}_t$ and the one introduced earlier in this section coincide (just note that the latter forecaster satisfies Blackwell's condition). The bound obtained here improves the earlier one by a factor of 2.

4.5 Calibration

In the practice of forecasting binary sequences it is common to form the prediction in terms of percentages. For example, weather forecasters often publish their prevision in statements like "the chance of rain tomorrow is 30%." The quality of such forecasts may be assessed in various ways. In Chapters 8 and 9 we define and study different notions of quality of such *sequential probability assignments*. Here we are merely concerned with a simple notion known as *calibration*. While predictions of binary sequences in terms of "chances" or "probabilities" may not be obvious to interpret, a forecaster is definitely not doing his job well if, on a long run, the proportion of all rainy days for which the chance of rain was predicted to be 30% does not turn out to be about 30%. In such cases we say that the predictor is not well calibrated.

One may formalize the setup and the notion of calibration as follows. We consider a sequence of binary-valued outcomes $y_1, y_2, \ldots \in \{0, 1\}$. Assume that, at each time instant, the forecaster selects a decision q_t from the interval $[0, 1]$. The value of q_t may be interpreted as the prediction of the "probability" that $y_t = 1$. In this section, instead of defining a "loss" of predicting q_t when the outcome is y_t, we only require that for any fixed $x \in [0, 1]$ of the time instances when q_t is close to x, the proportion of times with $y_t = 1$ should be approximately x. To quantify this notion, for all $\varepsilon > 0$ define $\rho_n^\varepsilon(x)$ to be the average of outcomes y_t at the times $t = 1, \ldots, n$ when a value q_t close to x was predicted. Formally,

$$\rho_n^\varepsilon(x) = \frac{\sum_{t=1}^n y_t \, \mathbb{I}_{\{q_t \in (x-\varepsilon, x+\varepsilon)\}}}{\sum_{s=1}^n \mathbb{I}_{\{q_s \in (x-\varepsilon, x+\varepsilon)\}}}.$$

If $\sum_{t=1}^n \mathbb{I}_{\{q_t \in (x-\varepsilon, x+\varepsilon)\}} = 0$, we say $\rho_n^\varepsilon(x) = 0$.

The forecaster is said to be *ε-calibrated* if, for all $x \in [0, 1]$ for which $\limsup_{n \to \infty} \frac{1}{n} \sum_{t=1}^n \mathbb{I}_{\{q_t \in (x-\varepsilon, x+\varepsilon)\}} > 0$,

$$\limsup_{n \to \infty} \left| \rho_n^\varepsilon(x) - x \right| \le \varepsilon.$$

A forecaster is *well calibrated* if it is ε-calibrated for all $\varepsilon > 0$.

For some sequences it is very easy to construct well-calibrated forecasters. For example, if the outcome sequence happens to be stationary in the sense that the limit $\lim_{n \to \infty} \frac{1}{n} \sum_{t=1}^n y_t$ exists, then the forecaster

$$q_t = \frac{1}{t - 1} \sum_{s=1}^{t-1} y_s$$

is well calibrated. (The proof is left as an easy exercise.)

However, for arbitrary sequences of outcomes, constructing a calibrated forecaster is not a trivial issue. In fact, it is not difficult to see that no deterministic forecaster can be calibrated for all possible sequences of outcomes (see Exercise 4.9). Interestingly, however, if the forecaster is allowed to randomize, well-calibrated prediction is possible. Of the several known possibilities the one we describe next is based on the minimization of the internal regret of a suitably defined associated prediction problem. The existence of internal regret minimizing strategies, proved in the previous section, will then immediately imply the existence of well-calibrated forecasters for all possible sequences.

In what follows, we assume that the forecaster is allowed to randomize. We adopt the model described at the beginning of this chapter. That is, at each time instance t, before making his prediction q_t, the forecaster has access to a random variable U_t, where $U_1, U_2, \ldots$ is a sequence of independent random variables uniformly distributed in $[0, 1]$. These values remain hidden from the opponent who sets the outcomes $y_t \in \{0, 1\}$, where y_t may depend on the predictions of the forecaster up to time $t - 1$.

Remark 4.3. Once one allows randomized forecasters, it has to be clarified whether the opponent is oblivious or not. As noted earlier, we allow nonoblivious opponents. To keep the notation coherent, in this section we continue using lower-case y_t to denote the outcomes, but we keep in mind that y_t is a random variable, measurable with respect to $U_1, \ldots, U_{t-1}$.

The first step of showing the existence of a well-calibrated randomized forecaster is noting that it suffices to construct ε-calibrated forecasters. This observation may be proved by a simple application of a doubling trick whose details are left as an exercise.

Lemma 4.2. *Suppose for each $\varepsilon > 0$ there is a forecaster that is ε-calibrated for all possible sequences of outcomes. Then a well-calibrated forecaster can be constructed.*

To construct an ε-calibrated forecaster for a fixed positive ε, it is clearly sufficient to consider strategies whose predictions are restricted to a sufficiently fine grid of the unit interval $[0, 1]$. In the sequel we consider forecasters whose prediction takes the form $q_t = I_t/N$, where N is a fixed positive integer and I_t takes its values from the set $\{0, 1, \ldots, N\}$. At each time instance t, the forecaster determines a probability distribution $\mathbf{p}_t = (p_{0,t}, \ldots, p_{N,t})$ and selects prediction I_t randomly according to this distribution. The quality of such a predictor may be assessed by means of the discretized version of the function ρ_n defined as

$$\rho_n(i/N) = \frac{\sum_{t=1}^{n} y_t \, \mathbb{I}_{\{I_t=i\}}}{\sum_{s=1}^{n} \mathbb{I}_{\{I_s=i\}}} \qquad \text{for } i = 0, 1, \ldots, N.$$

Define the quantity C_n, often called the *Brier score*, as

$$C_n = \sum_{i=0}^{N} \left(\rho_n(i/N) - \frac{i}{N} \right)^2 \left(\frac{1}{n} \sum_{t=1}^{n} \mathbb{I}_{\{I_t=i\}} \right).$$

The following simple lemma shows that it is enough to make sure that the Brier score remains small asymptotically. The routine proof is again left to the reader.

Lemma 4.3. *Let $\varepsilon > 0$ be fixed and assume that $(N + 1)/N^2 > 1/\varepsilon^2$. If a discretized forecaster is such that*

$$\limsup_{n \to \infty} C_n \leq \frac{N + 1}{N^2} \qquad \text{almost surely,}$$

then the forecaster is almost surely ε-calibrated.

According to Lemmas 4.2 and 4.3, to prove the existence of a randomized forecaster that is well calibrated for all possible sequences of outcomes it suffices to exhibit, for each fixed N, a "discretized" forecaster I_t such that $\limsup_{n \to \infty} C_n \leq (N + 1)/N^2$ almost surely. Such a forecaster may be constructed by a simple application of the techniques shown in the previous chapter. To this end, define a loss function by

$$\ell(i, y_t) = \left(y_t - \frac{i}{N} \right)^2, \qquad i = 0, 1, \ldots, N.$$

Then, by the results of Section 4.4, one may define a forecaster whose randomizing distribution $\mathbf{p}_t = (p_{0,t}, \ldots, p_{N,t})$ is such that the average internal regret

$$\max_{i,j=0,1,\ldots,N} \frac{R_{(i,j),n}}{n} = \max_{i,j=0,1,\ldots,N} \frac{1}{n} \sum_{t=1}^{n} r_{(i,j),t}$$

$$= \max_{i,j=0,1,\ldots,N} \frac{1}{n} \sum_{t=1}^{n} p_{i,t} \big(\ell(i, y_t) - \ell(j, y_t) \big)$$

converges to zero for all possible sequences of outcomes. The next result guarantees that any such predictor has the desired property.

Lemma 4.4. *Consider the loss function defined above and assume that* $\mathbf{p}_1, \mathbf{p}_2, \ldots$ *is such that, for all sequences of outcomes,*

$$\lim_{n \to \infty} \max_{i,j=0,1,\ldots,N} \frac{1}{n} R_{(i,j),n} = 0.$$

If the forecaster is such that I_t *is drawn, at each time instant, randomly according to the distribution* $\mathbf{p}_t$*, then*

$$\limsup_{n \to \infty} C_n \le \frac{N+1}{N^2} \qquad \text{almost surely.}$$

Proof. Define, for each $n = 1, 2, \ldots$ and $i = 0, 1, \ldots, N$,

$$\tilde{p}_n(i/N) = \frac{\sum_{t=1}^{n} y_t p_{i,t}}{\sum_{t=1}^{n} p_{i,t}}$$

and also

$$\tilde{C}_n = \sum_{i=0}^{N} \left(\tilde{p}_n(i/N) - \frac{i}{N} \right)^2 \left(\frac{1}{n} \sum_{t=1}^{n} p_{i,t} \right).$$

By martingale convergence (e.g., by Lemma A.7 and the Borel–Cantelli lemma) we have

$$\lim_{n \to \infty} \left| \frac{1}{n} \sum_{t=1}^{n} y_t \, \mathbb{I}_{\{I_t=i\}} - \frac{1}{n} \sum_{t=1}^{n} y_t p_{i,t} \right| = 0 \qquad \text{almost surely}$$

and, similarly,

$$\lim_{n \to \infty} \left| \frac{1}{n} \sum_{t=1}^{n} \mathbb{I}_{\{I_t=i\}} - \frac{1}{n} \sum_{t=1}^{n} p_{i,t} \right| = 0 \qquad \text{almost surely.}$$

This implies that

$$\lim_{n\to\infty} \left|C_n - \tilde{C}_n\right| = 0 \qquad \text{almost surely}$$

and therefore it suffices to prove that

$$\limsup_{n\to\infty} \tilde{C}_n \le \frac{N+1}{N^2}.$$

To this end, observe that

$$r_{(i,j),t} = p_{i,t}\left(\left(y_t - \frac{i}{N}\right)^2 - \left(y_t - \frac{j}{N}\right)^2\right) = p_{i,t}\frac{j-i}{N}\left(2y_t - \frac{i+j}{N}\right)$$

and therefore

$$R_{(i,j),n} = \sum_{t=1}^{n} r_{(i,j),t}$$

$$= \frac{2(j-i)}{N}\sum_{t=1}^{n} p_{i,t}\left(y_t - \frac{i+j}{2N}\right)$$

$$= \frac{2(j-i)}{N}\left(\sum_{t=1}^{n} p_{i,t}\right)\left(\tilde{\rho}_n(i/N) - \frac{i+j}{2N}\right)$$

$$= \left(\sum_{t=1}^{n} p_{i,t}\right)\left[\left(\tilde{\rho}_n(i/N) - \frac{i}{N}\right)^2 - \left(\tilde{\rho}_n(i/N) - \frac{j}{N}\right)^2\right].$$

For any fixed $i = 0, 1, \ldots, N$, the quantity $R_{(i,j),n}$ is maximized for the value of j minimizing $(\tilde{\rho}_n(i/N) - j/N)^2$. Thus,

$$\left(\sum_{t=1}^{n} p_{i,t}\right)\left(\tilde{\rho}_n(i/N) - \frac{i}{N}\right)^2$$

$$= \max_{j=0,1,\ldots,N} R_{(i,j),n} + \min_{j=0,1,\ldots,N}\left(\sum_{t=1}^{n} p_{i,t}\right)\left(\tilde{\rho}_n(i/N) - \frac{j}{N}\right)^2$$

$$\le \max_{j=0,1,\ldots,N} R_{(i,j),n} + \frac{n}{N^2}.$$

This implies that

$$\tilde{C}_n = \frac{1}{n}\sum_{i=0}^{N}\left(\sum_{t=1}^{n} p_{i,t}\right)\left(\tilde{\rho}_n(i/N) - \frac{i}{N}\right)^2$$

$$\le \sum_{i=0}^{N}\left(\max_{j=0,1,\ldots,N}\frac{1}{n}R_{(i,j),n} + \frac{1}{N^2}\right)$$

$$\le (N+1)\max_{i,j=0,1,\ldots,N}\frac{1}{n}R_{(i,j),n} + \frac{N+1}{N^2},$$

which concludes the proof. ■

In summary, if N is sufficiently large, then any forecaster designed to keep the cumulative internal regret small, based on the loss function $\ell(i, y_t) = (y_t - i/N)^2$, is guaranteed to be ε-calibrated. Because internal-regret-minimizing algorithms are not completely straightforward (see Section 4.4), the resulting forecaster is somewhat complex.

Interestingly, the form of the quadratic loss function is important. For example, forecasters that keep the internal regret based on the "absolute loss" $\ell(i, y_t) = |y_t - i/N|$ small cannot be calibrated (see Exercise 4.14).

We remark here that the forecaster constructed above has some interesting extra features. In fact, apart from being ε-calibrated, it is also a good predictor in the sense that its cumulative squared loss is not much larger than that of the best constant predictor. Indeed, since external regret is at most N times the internal regret $\max_{i,j=0,1,\dots,N} R_{(i,j),n}$, we immediately find that the forecaster constructed in the proof of Lemma 4.4 satisfies

$$\frac{1}{n}\left(\sum_{t=1}^{n}\left(y_t - \frac{I_t}{N}\right)^2 - \min_{i=0,1,\dots,N}\sum_{t=1}^{n}\left(y_t - \frac{i}{N}\right)^2\right) \to 0 \qquad \text{almost surely.}$$

(See, however, Exercise 4.13.)

In fact, no matter what algorithm is used, calibrated forecasters must have a low excess squared error in the above sense. Just note that the proof of Lemma 4.4 reveals that

$$\widetilde{C}_n \geq \sum_{i=0}^{N}\left(\max_{j=0,1,\dots,N}\frac{1}{n}R_{(i,j),n}\right) \geq \max_{i,j=0,1,\dots,N}\frac{1}{n}R_{(i,j),n}.$$

Thus, any forecaster that keeps $\widetilde{C}_n$ small has a small internal regret (defined on the basis of the quadratic losses $\ell(i, y_t) = (y_t - i/N)^2$) and therefore has a small external regret as well.

We conclude by pointing out that all results of this section may be extended to forecasting nonbinary sequences. Assume that the outcomes y_t take their values in the finite set $\mathcal{Y} = \{1, 2, \dots, m\}$. Then at time t the forecaster outputs a vector $\mathbf{q}_t \in \mathcal{D}$ in the probability simplex

$$\mathcal{D} = \left\{\mathbf{p} = (p_1, \dots, p_m) : \sum_{j=1}^{m} p_j = 1, \ p_j \geq 0, \ j = 1, \dots, m\right\} \subset \mathbb{R}^m.$$

Analogous to the case of binary outcomes, in this setup we may define, for all $\mathbf{x} \in \mathcal{D}$,

$$\rho_n^\varepsilon(\mathbf{x}) = \frac{\sum_{t=1}^{n} \mathbf{y}_t \, \mathbb{I}_{\{\mathbf{q}_t \, : \, \|\mathbf{x}-\mathbf{q}_t\|<\varepsilon\}}}{\sum_{t=1}^{n} \mathbb{I}_{\{\mathbf{q}_t \, : \, \|\mathbf{x}-\mathbf{q}_t\|<\varepsilon\}}}$$

(with $\rho_n^\varepsilon(\mathbf{x}) = \mathbf{0}$ if $\sum_{t=1}^{n} \mathbb{I}_{\{\mathbf{q}_t \, : \, \|\mathbf{x}-\mathbf{q}_t\|<\varepsilon\}} = 0$), where $\|\cdot\|$ denotes the euclidean distance and $\mathbf{y}_t$ denotes the m-vector $(\mathbb{I}_{\{y_t=1\}}, \dots, \mathbb{I}_{\{y_t=m\}})$.

The forecaster is now ε-*calibrated* if we have

$$\limsup_{n \to \infty} \left\|\rho_n^\varepsilon(\mathbf{x}) - \mathbf{x}\right\| \leq \varepsilon$$

for all $\mathbf{x} \in \mathcal{D}$ with $\limsup_{n\to\infty} \frac{1}{n}\sum_{t=1}^{n} \mathbb{I}_{\{\mathbf{q}_t \, : \, \|\mathbf{x}-\mathbf{q}_t\|<\varepsilon\}} > 0$. The forecaster is well calibrated if it is ε-calibrated for all $\varepsilon > 0$. The procedure of constructing a well-calibrated forecaster may be extended in a straightforward way to this more general setup. The details are left to the reader.

Remark 4.4. We introduced the notion of ε-*calibratedness* by requiring

$$\limsup_{n\to\infty} \left| \rho_n^{\varepsilon}(x) - x \right| \le \varepsilon \tag{4.3}$$

for all $x \in [0, 1]$ satisfying $\limsup_{n\to\infty} \frac{1}{n} \sum_{t=1}^{n} \mathbb{I}_{\{q_t \in (x-\varepsilon, x+\varepsilon)\}} > 0$. A simple inspection of the proof of the existence of well-calibrated forecasters reveals, in fact, the existence of a forecaster satisfying (4.3) for all $x \in [0, 1]$ with $\limsup_{n\to\infty} n^{-\alpha} \sum_{t=1}^{n} \mathbb{I}_{\{q_t \in (x-\varepsilon, x+\varepsilon)\}} > 0$, where α is any number greater than $1/2$. Some authors consider an even stronger definition by requiring (4.3) to hold for all x for which $\sum_{t=1}^{n} \mathbb{I}_{\{q_t \in (x-\varepsilon, x+\varepsilon)\}}$ tends to infinity. See the bibliographical comments for references to works proving that calibration is possible under this stricter definition as well.

4.6 Generalized Regret

In this section we consider a more general notion of regret that encompasses internal and external regret encountered in previous sections and makes it possible to treat, in a unified framework, a variety of other notions of regret.

We still work within the framework of randomized prediction in which the forecaster determines, at every time instant $t = 1, \ldots, n$, a probability distribution $\mathbf{p}_t = (p_{1,t}, \ldots, p_{N,t})$ over N actions and chooses an action I_t according to this distribution. Similarly to the model introduced in Chapter 2, we compare the performance of the forecaster to the performance of the best expert in a given set of m experts. However, as forecasters here use randomization, we allow the predictions of experts at each time t to depend also on the forecaster's random action I_t. We use $f_{i,t}(I_t) \in \{1, \ldots, N\}$ to denote the action taken by expert i at time t when I_t is the forecaster's action. In this model, the expert advice at time t thus consists of m vectors $\left(f_{i,t}(1), \ldots, f_{i,t}(N) \right)$ for $i = 1, \ldots, m$.

For each expert $i = 1, \ldots, m$ and time t we also define an *activation function* $A_{i,t} : \{1, \ldots, N\} \to \{0, 1\}$. The activation function determines whether the corresponding expert is active at the current prediction step. At each time instant t the values $A_{i,t}(k)$ $(i = 1, \ldots, m, k = 1, \ldots, N)$ of the activation function and the expert advice are revealed to the forecaster who then computes $\mathbf{p}_t = (p_{1,t}, \ldots, p_{N,t})$. Define the (expected) *generalized regret* of a randomized forecaster with respect to expert i at round t by

$$r_{i,t} = \sum_{k=1}^{N} p_{k,t} \, A_{i,t}(k) \big(\ell(k, Y_t) - \ell(f_{i,t}(k), Y_t) \big)$$

$$= \mathbb{E}_t \left[A_{i,t}(I_t) \big(\ell(I_t, Y_t) - \ell(f_{i,t}(I_t), Y_t) \big) \right].$$

Hence, the generalized regret with respect to expert i is nonzero only if expert i is active, and the expert is active based on the current step t and, possibly, on the forecaster's guess k. In this model we allow that the functions $f_{i,t}$ and $A_{i,t}$ depend on the past random choices $I_1, \ldots, I_{t-1}$ of the forecaster (determined by a possibly nonoblivious adversary) and are revealed to the forecaster just before round t.

The following examples show that special cases of the generalized regret include external and internal regret and extend beyond these notions.

Example 4.2 (External regret). Taking $m = N$, $f_{i,t}(k) = i$ for all $k = 1, \ldots, N$, and letting $A_{i,t}(k)$ to be the constant function 1, the generalized regret becomes

$$r_{i,t} = \sum_{k=1}^{N} p_{k,t}\big(\ell(k, Y_t) - \ell(i, Y_t)\big),$$

which is just the (external) regret introduced in Section 4.2. $\square$

Example 4.3 (Internal regret). To see how the notion of internal regret may be recovered as a special case, consider $m = N(N - 1)$ experts indexed by pairs (i, j) for $i \neq j$. For each t expert (i, j) predicts as follows: $f_{(i,j),t}(k) = k$ if $k \neq i$ and $f_{(i,j),t}(i) = j$ otherwise. Thus, if $A_{(i,j),t} \equiv 1$, component (i, j) of the generalized regret vector $\mathbf{r}_t \in \mathbb{R}^m$ becomes

$$r_{(i,j),t} = p_{i,t}\big(\ell(i, Y_t) - \ell(j, Y_t)\big)$$

which coincides with the definition of internal regret in Section 4.4. $\square$

Example 4.4 (Swap regret). A natural extension of internal regret is obtained by letting the experts $f_1, \ldots, f_m$ compute all N^N functions $\{1, \ldots, N\} \to \{1, \ldots, N\}$ defined on the set of actions. In other words, for each $i = 1, \ldots, m = N^N$ the sequence $(f_i(1), \ldots, f_i(N))$ takes its values in $\{1, \ldots, N\}$. Note that, in this case, the prediction of the experts depends on t only through I_t. The resulting regret is called *swap regret*. It is easy to see (Exercise 4.8) that

$$\max_{\sigma \in \Sigma} R_{\sigma,n} \leq N \max_{i \neq j} R_{(i,j),n},$$

where Σ is the set of all functions $\{1, \ldots, N\} \to \{1, \ldots, N\}$ and R_σ is the regret against the expert indexed by σ. Thus, any forecaster whose average internal regret converges to zero also has a vanishing swap regret. Note that the forecaster of Theorem 4.3, run with the exponential potential, has a swap regret bounded by $O\big(\sqrt{n(N \ln N)}\big)$. This improves on the bound $O\big(N\sqrt{n \ln N}\big)$, which we obtain by combining the bound of Exercise 4.8 with the regret bound for the exponentially weighted average forecaster of Section 4.2. $\square$

This more general formulation permits us to consider an even wider family of prediction problems. For example, by defining the activation function $A_{i,t}(k)$ to depend on t and i but not on k, one may model "specialists," that is, experts that occasionally abstain from making a prediction. In the next section we describe an application in which the activation functions play an important role. See also the bibliographic remarks for other variants of the problem.

The basic question now is whether it is possible to define a forecaster guaranteeing that the generalized regret $R_{i,n} = r_{i,1} + \cdots + r_{i,n}$ grows slower than n for all $i = 1, \ldots, m$, regardless of the sequence of outcomes, the experts, and the activation functions. Let $\mathbf{R}_n = (R_{1,n}, \ldots, R_{m,n})$ denote the vector of regrets. By Theorem 2.1, it suffices to show the existence of a predictor $\mathbf{p}_t$ satisfying the Blackwell condition $\nabla \Phi(\mathbf{R}_{t-1}) \cdot \mathbf{r}_t \leq 0$ for an appropriate potential function Φ. The existence of such $\mathbf{p}_t$ is shown in the following result. For such a predictor we may then apply Theorem 2.1 and its corollaries to obtain performance bounds without further work.

Theorem 4.3. *Fix a potential* Φ *with* $\nabla \Phi \geq \mathbf{0}$. *Then a randomized forecaster satisfying the Blackwell condition for the generalized regret is defined by the unique solution to the set of* N *linear equations*

$$p_{k,t} = \frac{\sum_{j=1}^{N} p_{j,t} \sum_{i=1}^{m} \mathbb{I}_{\{f_{i,t}(j)=k\}} A_{i,t}(j) \nabla_i \Phi(\mathbf{R}_{t-1})}{\sum_{i=1}^{m} A_{i,t}(k) \nabla_i \Phi(\mathbf{R}_{t-1})}, \qquad k = 1, \ldots, N.$$

Observe that in the special case of external regret (i.e., $m = N$, $f_{i,t}(k) = i$ for all $k = 1, \ldots, N$, and $A_{i,t} \equiv 1$), the predictor of Theorem 4.3 reduces to the usual weighted average forecaster of Section 4.2. Also, in the case of internal regret described in Example 4.3, the forecaster of Theorem 4.3 reduces to the forecaster studied in Section 4.4.

Proof. The proof is a generalization of the argument we used for the internal regret in Section 4.4. We may rewrite the left-hand side of the Blackwell condition as follows:

$$\nabla \Phi(\mathbf{R}_{t-1}) \cdot \mathbf{r}_t$$

$$= \sum_{i=1}^{m} \nabla_i \Phi(\mathbf{R}_{t-1}) \sum_{k=1}^{N} p_{k,t} A_{i,t}(k) \big(\ell(k, Y_t) - \ell(f_{i,t}(k), Y_t) \big)$$

$$= \sum_{k=1}^{N} \sum_{j=1}^{N} \sum_{i=1}^{m} \mathbb{I}_{\{f_{i,t}(k)=j\}} \nabla_i \Phi(\mathbf{R}_{t-1}) p_{k,t} A_{i,t}(k) \big(\ell(k, Y_t) - \ell(f_{i,t}(k), Y_t) \big)$$

$$= \sum_{k=1}^{N} \sum_{j=1}^{N} \sum_{i=1}^{m} \mathbb{I}_{\{f_{i,t}(k)=j\}} \nabla_i \Phi(\mathbf{R}_{t-1}) p_{k,t} A_{i,t}(k) \ell(k, Y_t)$$

$$- \sum_{k=1}^{N} \sum_{j=1}^{N} \sum_{i=1}^{m} \mathbb{I}_{\{f_{i,t}(k)=j\}} \nabla_i \Phi(\mathbf{R}_{t-1}) p_{k,t} A_{i,t}(k) \ell(j, Y_t)$$

$$= \sum_{k=1}^{N} \sum_{j=1}^{N} \sum_{i=1}^{m} \mathbb{I}_{\{f_{i,t}(k)=j\}} \nabla_i \Phi(\mathbf{R}_{t-1}) p_{k,t} A_{i,t}(k) \ell(k, Y_t)$$

$$- \sum_{k=1}^{N} \sum_{j=1}^{N} \sum_{i=1}^{m} \mathbb{I}_{\{f_{i,t}(j)=k\}} \nabla_i \Phi(\mathbf{R}_{t-1}) p_{j,t} A_{i,t}(j) \ell(k, Y_t)$$

$$= \sum_{k=1}^{N} \ell(k, Y_t) \left[\sum_{i=1}^{m} \nabla_i \Phi(\mathbf{R}_{t-1}) p_{k,t} A_{i,t}(k) \right.$$

$$\left. - \sum_{j=1}^{N} \sum_{i=1}^{m} \mathbb{I}_{\{f_{i,t}(j)=k\}} \nabla_i \Phi(\mathbf{R}_{t-1}) p_{j,t} A_{i,t}(j) \right].$$

Because the $\ell(k, Y_t)$ are arbitrary and nonnegative, the last expression is guaranteed to be nonpositive whenever

$$p_{k,t} \sum_{i=1}^{m} \nabla_i \Phi(\mathbf{R}_{t-1}) A_{i,t}(k) - \sum_{j=1}^{N} \sum_{i=1}^{m} \mathbb{I}_{\{f_{i,t}(j)=k\}} \nabla_i \Phi(\mathbf{R}_{t-1}) p_{j,t} A_{i,t}(j) = 0$$

for each $k = 1, \ldots, N$. Solving for $p_{k,t}$ yields the result. It remains to check that such a predictor always exists. For clarity, let $c_{i,j} = \nabla_i \Phi(\mathbf{R}_{t-1}) A_{i,t}(j)$, so that the above condition can be written as

$$p_{k,t} \sum_{i=1}^{m} c_{i,k} - \sum_{j=1}^{N} p_{j,t} \sum_{i=1}^{m} \mathbb{I}_{\{f_{i,t}(j)=k\}} c_{i,j} = 0 \qquad \text{for } k = 1, \ldots, N.$$

Now note that this condition is equivalent to $\mathbf{p}_t^\top H = \mathbf{0}$, where $\mathbf{p}_t = (p_{1,t}, \ldots, p_{N,t})$ and H is an $N \times N$ matrix whose entries are

$$H_{j,k} = \begin{cases} -\sum_{i=1}^{m} \mathbb{I}_{\{f_{i,t}(k)=j\}} c_{i,k} & \text{if } k \neq j, \\ \sum_{i=1}^{m} \mathbb{I}_{\{f_{i,t}(j)\neq j\}} c_{i,j} & \text{otherwise.} \end{cases}$$

As in the argument in Section 4.4, let $h_{\max} = \max_{i,j} |H_{i,j}|$ and let I be the $N \times N$ identity matrix. Since $\nabla \Phi \geq \mathbf{0}$, matrix $I - H/h_{\max}$ is nonnegative and row stochastic. The Perron–Frobenius theorem then implies that there exists a probability vector $\mathbf{q}$ such that $\mathbf{q}^\top (I - H/h_{\max}) = \mathbf{q}$. Because such a $\mathbf{q}$ also satisfies $\mathbf{q}^\top H = \mathbf{0}^\top$, the choice $\mathbf{p}_t = \mathbf{q}$ leads to a forecaster satisfying the Blackwell condition. ■

4.7 Calibration with Checking Rules

The notion of calibration has some important weaknesses. While calibratedness is an important basic property one expects from a probability forecaster, a well-calibrated forecaster may have very little predictive power. To illustrate this, consider the sequence of outcomes $\{y_t\}$ formed by alternating 0's and 1's: $01010101\ldots$. The forecaster $q_t \equiv 1/2$ is well calibrated but unsatisfactory, as any sensible forecaster should, intuitively, predict something close to 0 at time $t = 2 \times 10^6 + 1$ after having seen the pattern "01" repeated a million times.

A way of strengthening the definition of calibration is by introducing so-called *checking rules*. Consider the randomized forecasting problem described in Section 4.5. In this problem, at each time instance $t = 1, 2, \ldots$ the forecaster determines his randomized prediction q_t and then observes the outcome Y_t. A checking rule A assigns, to each time instance t, an indicator function $A_t(x) = \mathbb{I}_{\{x \in S_t\}}$ of a set $S_t \in [0, 1]$ and reveals it to the forecaster *before* making a prediction q_t. The set S_t may depend on the past sequence of outcomes and forecasts $q_1, Y_1, \ldots, q_{t-1}, Y_{t-1}$. (Formally, A_t is measurable with respect to the filtration generated by the past forecasts and outcomes.) The role of checking rules is the same as that of the activation functions introduced in Section 4.6. Given a countable family $\{A^{(1)}, A^{(2)}, \ldots\}$ of checking rules, the goal of the forecaster now is to guarantee that, for all checking rules $A^{(k)}$ with $\limsup_{n \to \infty} \frac{1}{n} \sum_{t=1}^{n} A_t^{(k)}(q_t) > 0$,

$$\lim_{n \to \infty} \left| \frac{\sum_{t=1}^{n} y_t A_t^{(k)}(q_t)}{\sum_{s=1}^{n} A_s^{(k)}(q_s)} - \frac{\sum_{t=1}^{n} q_t A_t^{(k)}(q_t)}{\sum_{s=1}^{n} A_s^{(k)}(q_s)} \right| = 0.$$

We call a forecaster satisfying this property *well calibrated under checking rules*.

Thus, any checking rule selects, on the basis of the past, a subset of $[0, 1]$, and we calculate the average of the forecasts only over those periods in which the checking rule was active at q_t. Before making the prediction, the forecaster is warned on what sets the checking rules are active at that period. The goal of the predictor is to force the average of his forecasts, computed over the periods in which a checking rule was active, to be close to the average of the outcomes over the same periods. By considering checking rules of the form $A_t(q) = \mathbb{I}_{\{q \in (x-\varepsilon, x+\varepsilon)\}}$ we recover the original notion of calibration introduced in Section 4.5. However, by introducing checking rules that depend on the time instance t and/or on the past, one may obtain much more interesting notions of calibration. For example, one may include checking rules that are active only at even periods of time, others that are active at odd periods of time, others that are only active if the last three outcomes were 0, etc. One may even consider a checking rule that is only active when the average of past outcomes is far away from the average of the past forecasts, calculated over the time instances in which the rule was active in the past.

By a simple combination of Theorem 4.3 and the arguments of Section 4.5, it is now easy to establish the existence of well calibrated forecasters under a wide class of checking rules. Just like in Section 4.5, the first step of the argument is a discretization. Fix an $\varepsilon > 0$ and consider first a division of the unit interval $[0, 1]$ into intervals of length $N = \lfloor 1/\varepsilon \rfloor$. Consider checking rules A such that, for all t and histories $q_1, Y_1, \ldots, q_{t-1}, Y_{t-1}, A_t$ is an indicator function of a union of some of these N intervals. Call a checking rule satisfying this property an ε-*checking rule*. The proof of the following result is left as an exercise.

Theorem 4.4. *Let $\varepsilon > 0$. For any countable family $\{A^{(1)}, A^{(2)}, \ldots\}$ of ε-checking rules, there exists a randomized forecaster such that, almost surely, for all $A^{(k)}$ with* $\limsup_{n\to\infty} \frac{1}{n} \sum_{t=1}^{n} A_t^{(k)}(q_t) > 0$,

$$\limsup_{n\to\infty} \left| \frac{\sum_{t=1}^{n} y_t A_t^{(k)}(q_t)}{\sum_{s=1}^{n} A_s^{(k)}(q_s)} - \frac{\sum_{t=1}^{n} q_t A_t^{(k)}(q_t)}{\sum_{s=1}^{n} A_s^{(k)}(q_s)} \right| = 0.$$

4.8   Bibliographic Remarks

Randomized forecasters have been considered in various different setups; see, for example, Feder, Merhav, and Gutman [95], Foster and Vohra [107], Cesa-Bianchi and Lugosi [51]. For surveys we refer to Foster and Vohra [107], Vovk [300], Merhav and Feder [214]. The first Hannan consistent forecasters were proposed by Hannan [141] and Blackwell [29]. Hannan's original forecaster is based on the idea of "following the perturbed leader," as described in Section 4.3. Blackwell's procedure is, instead, in same the spirit as the weighted average forecasters based on the quadratic potential. (This is described in detail in Section 7.5.)

The analysis of Hannan's forecaster presented in Section 4.3 is due to Kalai and Vempala [174]. Hutter and Poland [164] provide a refined analysis. Hart and Mas-Colell [146] characterize the whole class of potentials for which the Blackwell condition (4.1) yields a Hannan consistent player.

The existence of strategies with small internal regret was first shown by Foster and Vohra [105], see also Fudenberg and Levine [118, 121] and Hart and Mas Colell [145, 146]. The forecaster described here is based on Hart and Mas Colell [146] and is taken from Cesa-Bianchi and Lugosi [54]. The example showing that simple weighted average predictors are not sufficient appears in Stoltz and Lugosi [279]. The method of converting forecasters with small external regret into the ones with small internal regret described here was suggested by Stoltz and Lugosi [279] – see also Blum and Mansour [34] for a related result. The swap regret was introduced in [34], where a polynomial time algorithm is introduced that achieves a bound of the order of $\sqrt{nN \ln N}$ for the swap regret.

The notion of calibration was introduced in the weather forecasting literature by Brier [42], after whom the Brier score is named. It was Dawid [80] who introduced the problem to the literature of mathematical statistics – see also Dawid's related work on calibration and "prequential" statistics [81, 82, 84]. Oakes [226] and Dawid [83] pointed out the impossibility of deterministic calibration. The fact that randomized calibrated forecasters exist was proved by Foster and Vohra [106], and the construction of the forecaster of Section 4.5 is based on their paper. Foster [104], Hart (see [106]), and Fudenberg and Levine [120] also introduce calibrated forecasters. The constructions of Hart and Fudenberg and Levine are based on von Neumann's minimax theorem. The notion of calibration discussed in Section 4.5 has been strengthened by Lehrer [194], Sandroni, Smorodinsky, and Vohra [259], and Vovk and Shafer [301]. These last references also consider checking rules and establish results in the spirit of the one presented in Section 4.7. These last two papers construct well-calibrated forecasters using even stronger notions of checking rules. Kakade and Foster [171] and Vovk, Takemura, and Shafer [302] independently define a weaker notion of calibration by requiring that for all nonnegative Lipschitz functions w,

$$\lim_{n \to \infty} \frac{1}{n} \sum_{t=1}^{n} w(q_t)(y_t - q_t) = 0.$$

They show the existence of a deterministic weakly calibrated forecaster and use this to define an "almost deterministic" calibrated forecaster. Calibration is also closely related to the notion of "merging" originated by Blackwell and Dubins [30]. Kalai, Lehrer, and Smorodinsky [177] show that, in fact, these two notions are equivalent in some sense, see Kalai and Lehrer [176], Lehrer, and Smorodinsky [196], Sandroni and Smorodinsky [258] for related results.

Generalized regret (Section 4.6) was introduced by Lehrer [195] (see also Cesa-Bianchi and Lugosi [54]). The "specialist" algorithm of Freund, Schapire, Singer, and Warmuth [115] is a special case of the forecaster for generalized regret defined in Theorem 4.3. The framework of specialists has been applied by Cohen and Singer [65] to a text categorization problem.

4.9 Exercises

4.1 Let $B_n : \mathcal{Y}^n \to [0, \infty]$ be a function that assigns a nonnegative number to any sequence $y^n = (y_1, \ldots, y_n)$ of outcomes, and consider a randomized forecaster whose expected cumulative loss satisfies

$$\sup_{y^n} \left(\mathbb{E} \sum_{t=1}^{n} \ell(I_t, y_t) - B_n(y^n) \right) \leq 0.$$

Show that if the same forecaster is used against a nonoblivious opponent, then its expected performance satisfies

$$\mathbb{E}\left[\sum_{t=1}^{n} \ell(I_t, Y_t) - B_n(Y^n) \right] \leq 0$$

(Hutter and Poland [164]). *Hint:* Show that when the forecaster is used against a nonoblivious opponent, then

$$\sup_{y_1 \in \mathcal{Y}} \mathbb{E}_1 \sup_{y_2 \in \mathcal{Y}} \mathbb{E}_2 \ldots \sup_{y_n \in \mathcal{Y}} \mathbb{E}_n \left[\sum_{t=1}^{n} \ell(I_t, y_t) - B_n(y^n) \right] \leq 0.$$

Proceed as in Lemma 4.1.

4.2 Prove Corollary 4.3. First show that the difference between the cumulative loss $\sum_{t=1}^{n} \ell(I_t, Y_t)$ and its expected value $\sum_{t=1}^{n} \bar{\ell}(\mathbf{p}_t, Y_t)$ is, with overwhelming probability, not larger than something of the order of $\sqrt{n}$. *Hint:* Use the Hoeffding–Azuma inequality and the Borel–Cantelli lemma.

4.3 Investigate the same problem as in the previous exercise but now for the modification of the randomized forecaster defined as

$$p_{i,t} = \frac{\phi'(\tilde{R}_{i,t-1})}{\sum_{j=1}^{N} \phi'(\tilde{R}_{j,t-1})},$$

where $\tilde{R}_{i,t} = \sum_{s=1}^{t} \left(\ell(I_s, Y_s) - \ell(f_{i,s}, Y_s) \right)$. *Warning:* There is an important difference here between different choices of ϕ. $\phi(x) = e^{\eta x}$ is the easiest case.

4.4 Consider the randomized forecasters of Section 4.2. Prove that the cumulative loss $\hat{L}_n$ of the exponentially weighted average forecaster is always at least as large as the cumulative loss $\min_{i=1,\ldots,N} L_{i,n}$ of the best pure strategy. *Hint:* Reverse the proof of Theorem 2.2.

4.5 Prove Theorem 4.1. *Hint:* The first statement is straightforward after defining appropriately the exponentially weighted average strategy. To prove the second statement, combine the first part with the results of Section 2.8.

4.6 Show that the regret of the follow-the-leader algorithm (i.e., fictitious play) mentioned at the beginning of Section 4.3 is bounded by the number of times the "leader" (i.e., the action with minimal cumulative loss) is changed during the sequence of plays.

4.7 Consider the version of the follow-the-perturbed-leader forecaster in which the distribution of $\mathbf{Z}_t$ is uniform on the cube $[0, \Delta_t]^N$ where $\Delta_t = \sqrt{tN}$. Show that the expected cumulative loss after n rounds is bounded as

$$\bar{L}_n - \min_{i=1,\ldots,N} L_{i,n} \leq 2\sqrt{2nN}.$$

Conclude that the forecaster is Hannan consistent (Hannan [141], Kalai and Vempala [174]).

4.8 Show that the swap regret is bounded by N times the internal regret.

4.9 Consider the setup of Section 4.5. Show that if $\varepsilon < 1/3$, then for any deterministic forecaster, that is, for any sequence of functions $q_t : \{0, 1\}^{t-1} \to [0, 1]$, $t = 1, 2, \ldots$, there exists a sequence of outcomes $y_1, y_2, \ldots$ such that the forecaster $q_t = q_t(y_1^{t-1})$ is not ε-calibrated (Oakes [226], Dawid [83]).

4.10 Show that if $\lim_{n \to \infty} \frac{1}{n} \sum_{t=1}^{n} y_t$ exists, then the deterministic forecaster

$$q_t = \frac{1}{t-1} \sum_{s=1}^{t-1} y_s$$

is well calibrated.

4.11 Prove Lemma 4.2.

4.12 Prove Lemma 4.3.

4.13 This exercise points out that calibrated forecasters are necessarily bad in a certain sense. Show that for any well-calibrated forecaster q_t there exists a sequence of outcomes such that

$$\liminf_{n\to\infty} \frac{1}{n}\left(\sum_{t=1}^{n}|y_t - q_t| - \min\left\{\sum_{t=1}^{n}|y_t - 0|, \sum_{t=1}^{n}|y_t - 1|\right\}\right) > 0.$$

4.14 Let $N > 0$ be fixed and consider any forecaster that keeps the internal regret based on the absolute loss

$$\max_{i,j=0,1,\ldots,N} \frac{1}{n}R_{(i,j),n} = \max_{i,j=0,1,\ldots,N} \frac{1}{n}\sum_{t=1}^{n}p_{i,t}\big(|y_t - i/N| - |y_t - j/N|\big)$$

small (i.e., it converges to 0). Show that for any ε, if N is sufficiently large, such a forecaster cannot be ε calibrated. *Hint:* Use the result of the previous exercise.

4.15 *(Uniform calibration)* Recall the notation of Section 4.5. A forecaster is said to be *uniformly well calibrated* if for all $\varepsilon > 0$,

$$\limsup_{n\to\infty} \sup_{x\in[0,1]} |\rho_n^\varepsilon(x) - x| < \varepsilon.$$

Show that there exists a uniformly well-calibrated randomized forecaster.

4.16 *(Uniform calibration continued)* An even stronger notion of calibration is obtained if we define, for all sets $A \subset [0, 1]$,

$$\rho_n(A) = \frac{\sum_{t=1}^{n} y_t \,\mathbb{I}_{\{q_t \in A\}}}{\sum_{s=1}^{n} \mathbb{I}_{\{q_s \in A\}}}.$$

Let $A_\varepsilon = \{x : \exists y \in A \text{ such that } |x - y| < \varepsilon\}$ be the ε-blowup of set A and let λ denote the Lebesgue measure. Show that there exists a forecaster such that, for all $\varepsilon > 0$,

$$\limsup_{n\to\infty} \sup_{A}\left|\rho_n(A_\varepsilon) - \frac{\int_{A_\varepsilon} x\,\mathrm{d}x}{\lambda(A_\varepsilon)}\right| < \varepsilon,$$

where the supremum is taken over all subsets of $[0, 1]$. (Note that if the supremum is only taken over all singletons $A = \{x\}$, then we recover the notion of uniform calibration defined in the previous exercise.)

4.17 *(Uniform calibration of non-binary sequences)* We may extend the notion of uniform calibration to the case of forecasting non-binary sequences described at the end of Section 4.5. Here $y_t \in \mathcal{Y} = \{1, 2, \ldots, m\}$ and the forecaster outputs a vector $\mathbf{q}_t \in \mathcal{D}$. For any subset A of the probability simplex $\mathcal{D}$, define

$$\rho_n(A) = \frac{\sum_{t=1}^{n} \mathbf{y}_t \,\mathbb{I}_{\{\mathbf{q}_t \in A\}}}{\sum_{s=1}^{n} \mathbb{I}_{\{\mathbf{q}_s \in A\}}},$$

where $\mathbf{y}_t = (\mathbb{I}_{\{y_t=1\}}, \ldots, \mathbb{I}_{\{y_t=m\}})$. Writing $A_\varepsilon = \{\mathbf{x} : (\exists \mathbf{x}' \in A)\,\|\mathbf{x} - \mathbf{x}'\| < \varepsilon\}$ and λ for the uniform probability measure over $\mathcal{D}$, show that there exists a forecaster such that for all $A \subset \mathcal{D}$ and for all $\varepsilon > 0$,

$$\limsup_{n\to\infty} \left|\rho_n(A_\varepsilon) - \frac{\int_{A_\varepsilon} \mathbf{x}\,\mathrm{d}x}{\lambda(A_\varepsilon)}\right| < \varepsilon.$$

Prove the uniform version of this result by showing the existence of a forecaster such that, for all $\varepsilon > 0$,

$$\limsup_{n\to\infty} \sup_{A}\left|\rho_n(A_\varepsilon) - \frac{\int_{A_\varepsilon} \mathbf{x}\,\mathrm{d}x}{\lambda(A_\varepsilon)}\right| < \varepsilon,$$

where the supremum is taken over all subsets of $\mathcal{D}$.

4.18 *(Hannan consistency for discounted regret)* Consider the problem of randomized prediction described in Section 4.1. Let $\beta_0 \geq \beta_1 \geq \cdots$ be a sequence of positive discount factors. A forecaster is said to satisfy *discounted Hannan consistency* if

$$\limsup_{n \to \infty} \frac{\sum_{t=1}^{n} \beta_{n-t} \ell(I_t, Y_t) - \min_{i=1,\ldots,N} \sum_{t=1}^{n} \beta_{n-t} \ell(i, Y_t)}{\sum_{t=1}^{n} \beta_{n-t}} = 0$$

with probability 1. Derive sufficient and necessary conditions for the sequences of discount factors for which discounted Hannan consistency may be achieved.

4.19 Prove Theorem 4.4. *Hint:* First assume a finite class of ε-checking rules and show, by combining the arguments of Section 4.5 with Theorem 4.3, that for any interval of the form $(i/N, (i + 1)/N]$,

$$\limsup_{n \to \infty} \left| \frac{\sum_{t=1}^{n} (y_t - q_t) \mathbb{I}_{\{A_t^{(k)}(q_t) \in (i/N, (i+1)/N]\}}}{\sum_{s=1}^{n} \mathbb{I}_{\{A_s^{(k)}(q_s) \in (i/N, (i+1)/N]\}}} \right| = 0$$

whenever $\limsup_{n \to \infty} \frac{1}{n} \sum_{t=1}^{n} \mathbb{I}_{\{A_t^{(k)}(q_t) \in (i/N, (i+1)/N]\}} > 0$.

5

Efficient Forecasters for Large Classes of Experts

5.1 Introduction

The results presented in Chapters 2, 3, and 4 show that it is possible to construct algorithms for online forecasting that predict an arbitrary sequence of outcomes almost as well as the best of N experts. Namely, the per-round cumulative loss of the predictor is at most as large as that of the best expert plus a term proportional to $\sqrt{\ln N/n}$ for any bounded loss function, where n is the number of rounds in the prediction game. The logarithmic dependence on the number of experts makes it possible to obtain meaningful bounds even if the pool of experts is very large. However, the basic prediction algorithms, such as weighted average forecasters, have a computational complexity proportional to the number of experts, and they are therefore infeasible when the number of experts is very large.

On the other hand, in many applications the set of experts has a certain structure that may be exploited to construct efficient prediction algorithms. Perhaps the best known such example is the problem of *tracking the best expert*, in which there is a small number of "base" experts and the goal of the forecaster is to predict as well as the best "compound" expert. This expert is defined by a sequence consisting of at most $m+1$ blocks of base experts so that in each block the compound expert predicts according to a fixed base expert. If there are N base experts and the length of the prediction game is n, then the total number of compound experts is $\Theta\left(N(nN/m)^m\right)$, exponentially large in m. In Section 5.2 we develop a forecasting algorithm able to track the best expert on any sequence of outcomes while requiring only $O(N)$ computations in each time period.

Prototypical examples of structured classes of experts for which efficient algorithms have been constructed include classes that can be represented by discrete structures such as lists, trees, and paths in graphs. It turns out that many of the forecasters we analyze in this book can be efficiently calculated over large classes of such "combinatorial experts." Computational efficiency is achieved because combinatorial experts are generated via manipulation of a simple base structure (i.e., a class might include experts associated with all sublists of a given list or all subtrees of a given tree), and for this reason their predictions are tightly related.

Most of these algorithms are based on efficient implementations of the exponentially weighted average forecaster. We describe two important examples in Section 5.3, concerned with experts defined on binary trees, and in Section 5.4, devoted to experts defined by paths in a given graph. A different approach uses follow-the-perturbed-leader predictors (see Section 4.3) that may be used to obtain efficient algorithms for a large class of problems, including the shortest path problem. This application is described in Section 5.4. The purpose of Section 5.5 is to develop efficient algorithms to track the best expert in the case when the class of "base" experts is already very large and has some structure. This is, in a sense, a combination of the two types of problems described above.

For simplicity, we analyze combinatorial experts in the framework of randomized prediction (see Chapter 4). Most results of this chapter (with the exception of the algorithms using the follow-the-perturbed-leader forecaster) can also be presented in the deterministic framework developed in Chapters 2 and 3. Following the model and convention introduced in Chapter 4, we sometimes use the term *action* instead of *expert*. The two are synonymous in the context of this chapter.

5.2 Tracking the Best Expert

In the basic model of randomized prediction the forecaster's predictions are evaluated against the best performing single action. This criterion is formalized by the usual notion of regret

$$\sum_{t=1}^{n} \ell(I_t, Y_t) - \min_{i=1,\dots,N} \sum_{t=1}^{n} \ell(i, Y_t),$$

which expresses the excess cumulative loss of the forecaster when compared with strategies that use the same action all the time. In this section we are interested in comparing the cumulative loss of the forecaster with more flexible strategies that are allowed to switch actions a limited number of times. (Recall that in Section 4.2 we briefly addressed such comparison classes of "dynamic" strategies.) This is clearly a significantly richer class, because there may be many outcome sequences $Y_1, \dots, Y_n$ such that

$$\min_{i=1,\dots,N} \sum_{t=1}^{n} \ell(i, Y_t)$$

is large, but there is a partition of the sequence in blocks $Y_1^{t_1-1}, Y_{t_1}^{t_2-1}, \dots, Y_{t_m}^{n}$ of consecutive outcomes so that on each block $Y_{t_k}^{t_{k+1}-1} = (Y_{t_k}, \dots, Y_{t_{k+1}-1})$ some action i_k performs very well.

Forecasting strategies that are able to "track" the sequence $i_1, i_2, \dots, i_{m+1}$ of good actions would then perform substantially better than any individual action. This motivates the following generalization of regret. Fix a horizon n. Given any sequence $i_1, \dots, i_n$ of actions from $\{1, \dots, N\}$, define the *tracking regret* by

$$R(i_1, \dots, i_n) = \sum_{t=1}^{n} \ell(I_t, Y_t) - \sum_{t=1}^{n} \ell(i_t, Y_t),$$

where, as usual, $I_1, \dots, I_n$ is the sequence of randomized actions drawn by the forecaster. To simplify the arguments, throughout this chapter we study the "expected" regret

$$\overline{R}(i_1, \dots, i_n) = \sum_{t=1}^{n} \overline{\ell}(\mathbf{p}_t, Y_t) - \sum_{t=1}^{n} \ell(i_t, Y_t),$$

where, following the notation introduced in Chapter 4, $\mathbf{p}_t = (p_{1,t}, \dots, p_{N,t})$ denotes the distribution according to which the random action I_t is drawn at time t, and

$\overline{\ell}(\mathbf{p}_t, Y_t) = \sum_{i=1}^{N} p_{i,t} \ell(I_t, Y_t)$ is the expected loss of the forecaster at time t. Recall from Section 4.1 that, with probability at least $1 - \delta$,

$$\sum_{t=1}^{n} \ell(I_t, Y_t) \le \sum_{t=1}^{n} \overline{\ell}(\mathbf{p}_t, Y_t) + \sqrt{\frac{n}{2} \ln \frac{1}{\delta}}$$

and even tighter bounds can be established if $\sum_{t=1}^{n} \overline{\ell}(\mathbf{p}_t, Y_t)$ is small.

Clearly, it is unreasonable to require that a forecaster perform well against the best sequence of actions for any given sequence of outcomes. Ideally, the tracking regret should scale, with some measure of complexity, penalizing action sequences that are, in a certain sense, harder to track. To this purpose, introduce

$$\text{size}\,(i_1, \ldots, i_n) = \sum_{t=2}^{n} \mathbb{I}_{\{i_{t-1} \ne i_t\}}$$

counting how many switches (i_t, i_{t+1}) with $i_t \ne i_{t+1}$ occur in the sequence. Note that

$$\sum_{t=1}^{n} \overline{\ell}(\mathbf{p}_t, Y_t) - \min_{(i_1, \ldots, i_n)\,:\,\text{size}\,(i_1, \ldots, i_n)=0} \sum_{t=1}^{n} \ell(i_t, Y_t)$$

corresponds to the usual (nontracking) regret.

It is not difficult to modify the randomized forecasting strategies of Chapter 4 in order to achieve a good tracking regret against any sequence of actions with a bounded number of switches. We may simply associate a *compound action* with each action sequence $i_1, \ldots, i_n$ so that size $(i_1, \ldots, i_n) \le m$ for some m and fixed horizon n. We then run our randomized forecaster over the set of compound actions: at any time t the randomized forecaster draws a compound action $(I_1, \ldots, I_n)$ and plays action I_t. Denote by M the number of all compound actions with size bounded by m. If we use the randomized exponentially weighted forecaster over this set of all compound actions, then Corollary 4.2 implies that the tracking regret is bounded by $\sqrt{(n \ln M)/2}$. Hence, it suffices to count the number of compound actions: for each $k = 0, \ldots, m$ there are $\binom{n-1}{k}$ ways to pick k time steps $t = 1, \ldots, n-1$ where a switch $i_t \ne i_{t+1}$ occurs, and there are $N(N-1)^k$ ways to assign a distinct action to each of the $k + 1$ resulting blocks. This gives

$$M = \sum_{k=0}^{m} \binom{n-1}{k} N(N-1)^k \le N^{m+1} \exp\left((n-1)H\left(\frac{m}{n-1}\right)\right),$$

where $H(x) = -x \ln x - (1-x)\ln(1-x)$ is the binary entropy function defined for $x \in [0, 1]$. Substituting this bound in the above expression, we find that the tracking regret of the randomized exponentially weighted forecaster for compound actions satisfies

$$\overline{R}(i_1, \ldots, i_n) \le \sqrt{\frac{n}{2}\left((m+1)\ln N + (n-1)H\left(\frac{m}{n-1}\right)\right)}$$

on any action sequence $i_1, \ldots, i_n$ such that size $(i_1, \ldots, i_n) \le m$.

The Fixed Share Forecaster

In its straightforward implementation, the exponentially weighted average forecaster requires to explicitly manage an exponential number of compound actions. We now show how to efficiently implement a generalized version of this forecasting strategy that achieves the same performance bound for the tracking regret. This efficient forecaster is derived from a variant of the exponentially weighted forecaster where the initial weight distribution is not uniform. The basis of this argument is the next simple general result. Consider the randomized exponentially weighted average forecaster defined in Section 4.2, with the only difference that the initial weights $w_{i,0}$ assigned to the N actions are not necessarily uniform. Via a straightforward combination of the proof of Theorem 2.2 (see also Exercise 2.5) with the results of Section 4.2, we obtain the following result.

Lemma 5.1. *For all $n \geq 1$, if the randomized exponentially weighted forecaster is run using initial weights $w_{1,0}, \ldots, w_{N,0} \geq 0$ such that $W_0 = w_{1,0} + \cdots + w_{N,0} \leq 1$, then*

$$\sum_{t=1}^{n} \overline{\ell}(\mathbf{p}_t, Y_t) \leq \frac{1}{\eta} \ln \frac{1}{W_n} + \frac{\eta}{8} n,$$

where $W_n = \sum_{i=1}^{N} w_{i,n} = \sum_{i=1}^{N} w_{i,0} e^{-\eta \sum_{t=1}^{n} \ell(i, Y_t)}$ is the sum of the weights after n rounds.

Nonuniform initial weights may be interpreted to assign prior importance to the different actions. The weighted average forecaster gives more importance to actions with larger initial weight and is guaranteed to achieve a smaller regret with respect to these experts.

For the tracking application, we choose the initial weights of compound actions $(i_1, \ldots, i_n)$ so that their values correspond to a probability distribution parameterized by a real number $\alpha \in (0, 1)$. We show that our efficient forecaster achieves the same tracking regret bound as the (nonefficient) exponentially weighted forecaster run with uniform weights over all compound actions whose number of switches is bounded by a function of α.

We start by defining the initial weight assignment. Throughout the whole section we assume that the horizon n is fixed and known in advance. We write $w_t'(i_1, \ldots, i_n)$ to denote the weight assigned at time t by the exponentially weighted forecaster to the compound action $(i_1, \ldots, i_n)$. For any fixed choice of the parameter $\alpha \in (0, 1)$, the initial weights of the compound actions are defined by

$$w_0'(i_1, \ldots, i_n) = \frac{1}{N} \left(\frac{\alpha}{N} \right)^{\text{size } (i_1, \ldots, i_n)} \left(1 - \alpha + \frac{\alpha}{N} \right)^{n - \text{size } (i_1, \ldots, i_n)}.$$

Introducing the "marginalized" weights

$$w_0'(i_1, \ldots, i_t) = \sum_{i_{t+1}, \ldots, i_n} w_0'(i_1, \ldots, i_t, i_{t+1}, \ldots, i_n)$$

for all $t = 1, \ldots, n$, it is easy to see that the initial weights are recursively computed as follows:

$$w_0'(i_1) = 1/N$$

$$w_0'(i_1, \ldots, i_{t+1}) = w_0'(i_1, \ldots, i_t) \left(\frac{\alpha}{N} + (1 - \alpha) \mathbb{I}_{\{i_{t+1} = i_t\}} \right).$$

Note that, for any n, this assignment corresponds to a probability distribution over $\{1, \ldots, N\}^n$, the set of all compound actions of length n. In particular, the ratio $w_0'(i_1, \ldots, i_{t+1})/w_0'(i_1, \ldots, i_t)$ can be viewed as the conditional probability that a random compound action $(I_1, \ldots, I_n)$, drawn according to the distribution w_0', has $I_{t+1} = i_{t+1}$ given that $I_t = i_t$. Hence, w_0' is the joint distribution of a Markov process over the set

$\{1, \ldots, N\}$ such that I_1 is drawn uniformly at random, and each next action I_{t+1} is equal to the previous action I_t with probability $1 - \alpha + \alpha/N$, and is equal to a different action $j \neq I_t$ with probability α/N. Thus, choosing α small amounts to assigning a small initial weight to compound actions with a large number of switches.

At any time t, a generic weight of the exponentially weighted forecaster has the form

$$w'_t(i_1, \ldots, i_n) = w'_0(i_1, \ldots, i_n) \exp\left(-\eta \sum_{s=1}^{t} \ell(i_s, Y_s)\right)$$

and the forecaster draws action i at time $t+1$ with probability $w'_{i,t}/W'_t$, where $W'_t = w'_{1,t} + \cdots + w'_{N,t}$ and

$$w'_{i,t} = \sum_{i_1, \ldots, i_t, i_{t+2}, \ldots, i_n} w'_t(i_1, \ldots, i_t, i, i_{t+2}, \ldots, i_n) \qquad \text{for } t \geq 1 \quad \text{and} \quad w'_{i,0} = \frac{1}{N}.$$

We now define a general forecasting strategy for running efficiently the exponentially weighted forecaster with this choice of initial weights.

THE FIXED SHARE FORECASTER

Parameters: Real numbers $\eta > 0$ and $0 \leq \alpha \leq 1$.

Initialization: $\mathbf{w}_0 = (1/N, \ldots, 1/N)$.

For each round $t = 1, 2, \ldots$

   (1) draw an action I_t from $\{1, \ldots, N\}$ according to the distribution

$$p_{i,t} = \frac{w_{i,t-1}}{\sum_{j=1}^{N} w_{j,t-1}}, \qquad i = 1, \ldots, N.$$

   (2) obtain Y_t and compute

$$v_{i,t} = w_{i,t-1} \, e^{-\eta \ell(i, Y_t)} \qquad \text{for each } i = 1, \ldots, N.$$

   (3) let

$$w_{i,t} = \alpha \frac{W_t}{N} + (1 - \alpha) v_{i,t} \qquad \text{for each } i = 1, \ldots, N,$$

   where $W_t = v_{1,t} + \cdots + v_{N,t}$.

Note that with $\alpha = 0$ the fixed share forecaster reduces to the simple exponentially weighted average forecaster over N base actions. A positive value of α forces the weights to stay above a minimal level, which allows to track the best compound action. We will see shortly that if the goal is to track the best compound action with at most m switches, then the right choice of α is about m/n.

The following result shows that the fixed share forecaster is indeed an efficient version of the exponentially weighted forecaster.

Theorem 5.1. *For all $\alpha \in [0, 1]$, for any sequence of n outcomes, and for all $t = 1, \ldots, n$, the conditional (given the past) distribution of the action I_t, drawn at time t by the fixed share forecaster with input parameter α, is the same as the conditional distribution of* *action I_t' drawn at time t by the exponentially weighted forecaster run over the compound actions $(i_1, \ldots, i_n)$ using initial weights $w_0'(i_1, \ldots, i_n)$ set with the same value of α.*

Proof. It is enough to show that, for all i and t, $w_{i,t} = w_{i,t}'$. We proceed by induction on t. For $t = 0$, $w_{i,0} = w_{i,0}' = 1/N$ for all i. For the induction step, assume that $w_{i,s} = w_{i,s}'$ for all i and $s < t$. We have

$$
w_{i,t}' = \sum_{i_1, \ldots, i_t, i_{t+2}, \ldots, i_n} w_t'(i_1, \ldots, i_t, i, i_{t+2}, \ldots, i_n)
$$

$$
= \sum_{i_1, \ldots, i_t} \exp\left(-\eta \sum_{s=1}^{t} \ell(i_s, Y_s)\right) w_0'(i_1, \ldots, i_t, i)
$$

$$
= \sum_{i_1, \ldots, i_t} \exp\left(-\eta \sum_{s=1}^{t} \ell(i_s, Y_s)\right) w_0'(i_1, \ldots, i_t) \frac{w_0'(i_1, \ldots, i_t, i)}{w_0'(i_1, \ldots, i_t)}
$$

$$
= \sum_{i_1, \ldots, i_t} \exp\left(-\eta \sum_{s=1}^{t} \ell(i_s, Y_s)\right) w_0'(i_1, \ldots, i_t) \left(\frac{\alpha}{N} + (1 - \alpha)\mathbb{I}_{\{i_t = i\}}\right)
$$

(using the recursive definition of w_0')

$$
= \sum_{i_t} e^{-\eta\ell(i_t, Y_t)} w_{i_t, t-1}' \left(\frac{\alpha}{N} + (1 - \alpha)\mathbb{I}_{\{i_t = i\}}\right)
$$

$$
= \sum_{i_t} e^{-\eta\ell(i_t, Y_t)} w_{i_t, t-1} \left(\frac{\alpha}{N} + (1 - \alpha)\mathbb{I}_{\{i_t = i\}}\right)
$$

(by the induction hypothesis)

$$
= \sum_{i_t} v_{i_t, t} \left(\frac{\alpha}{N} + (1 - \alpha)\mathbb{I}_{\{i_t = i\}}\right) \qquad \text{(using step 2 of fixed share)}
$$

$$
= w_{i,t} \qquad \text{(using step 3 of fixed share).} \quad \blacksquare
$$

Note that n does not appear in the proof, and the choice of n is thus immaterial in the statement of the theorem. Hence, unless α and η are chosen in terms of n, the prediction at time t of the exponentially weighted forecaster can be computed without knowing the length of the compound actions.

We are now ready to state the tracking regret bound for the fixed share forecaster.

Theorem 5.2. *For all $n \geq 1$, the tracking regret of the fixed share forecaster satisfies*

$$
\overline{R}(i_1, \ldots, i_n) \leq \frac{m+1}{\eta} \ln N + \frac{1}{\eta} \ln \frac{1}{(\alpha/N)^m (1 - \alpha)^{n-m-1}} + \frac{\eta}{8} n
$$

for all action sequences $i_1, \ldots, i_n$, where $m = \text{size}(i_1, \ldots, i_n)$.

We emphasize that the bound of Theorem 5.2 is true for *all* sequences $i_1, \ldots, i_n$, and the bound on the regret depends on size $(i_1, \ldots, i_n)$, the complexity of the sequence. If the objective is to minimize the tracking regret for all sequences with size bounded by m, then the parameters α and η can be tuned to minimize the right-hand side. This is shown in the next result. We see that by tuning the parameters α and η we obtain a tracking regret bound exactly equal to the one proven for the exponentially weighted forecaster run with uniform weights over all compound actions of complexity bounded by m. The good choice of α turns out to be $m/(n-1)$. Observe that with this choice the compound actions with m switches have the largest initial weight. In fact, it is easy to see that the initial weight distribution is concentrated on the set of compound actions with about m switches. This intuitively explains why the next performance bound matches the one obtained for the exponentially weighted average algorithm run over the full set of compound actions.

Corollary 5.1. *For all n, m such that $0 \le m < n$, if the fixed share forecaster is run with parameters $\alpha = m/(n-1)$, where for $m = 0$ we let $\alpha = 0$, and*

$$\eta = \sqrt{\frac{8}{n}\left((m+1)\ln N + (n-1)H\left(\frac{m}{n-1}\right)\right)},$$

then

$$\overline{R}(i_1,\ldots,i_n) \le \sqrt{\frac{n}{2}\left((m+1)\ln N + (n-1)H\left(\frac{m}{n-1}\right)\right)}$$

for all action sequences $i_1,\ldots,i_n$ such that size $(i_1,\ldots,i_n) \le m$.

Proof. First of all, note that for $\alpha = m/(n-1)$

$$\ln\frac{1}{\alpha^m(1-\alpha)^{n-m-1}} \le -m\ln\frac{m}{n-1} - (n-m-1)\ln\frac{n-m-1}{n-1}$$
$$= (n-1)H\left(\frac{m}{n-1}\right).$$

Using our choice for η in the bound of Theorem 5.2 concludes the proof. ∎

In the special case $m = 0$, when the tracking regret reduces to the usual regret, the bound of Corollary 5.1 is $\sqrt{(n/2)\ln N}$, which is the bound for the exponentially weighted forecaster proven in Theorem 2.2.

Proof of Theorem 5.2. Recall that for an arbitrary compound action $i_1,\ldots,i_n$ we have

$$\ln w'_n(i_1,\ldots,i_n) = \ln w'_0(i_1,\ldots,i_n) - \eta\sum_{t=1}^{n}\ell(i_t, Y_t).$$

By definition of w'_0, if $m = $ size $(i_1,\ldots,i_n)$,

$$w'_0(i_1,\ldots,i_n) = \frac{1}{N}\left(\frac{\alpha}{N}\right)^m\left(\frac{\alpha}{N}+(1-\alpha)\right)^{n-m-1} \ge \frac{1}{N}\left(\frac{\alpha}{N}\right)^m(1-\alpha)^{n-m-1}.$$

Therefore, using this in the bound of Lemma 5.1 we get, for any sequence $(i_1, \ldots, i_n)$ with size $(i_1, \ldots, i_n) = m$,

$$
\sum_{t=1}^{n} \overline{\ell}(\mathbf{p}_t, Y_t)
$$

$$
\leq \frac{1}{\eta} \ln \frac{1}{W'_n} + \frac{\eta}{8} n
$$

$$
\leq \frac{1}{\eta} \ln \frac{1}{w'_n(i_1, \ldots, i_n)} + \frac{\eta}{8} n
$$

$$
\leq \sum_{t=1}^{n} \ell(i_t, Y_t) + \frac{1}{\eta} \ln N + \frac{m}{\eta} \ln \frac{N}{\alpha} - \frac{n - m - 1}{\eta} \ln(1 - \alpha) + \frac{\eta}{8} n,
$$

which concludes the proof. ∎

Hannan Consistency

A natural question is under what conditions Hannan consistency for the tracking regret can be achieved. In particular, if we assume that at time n the tracking regret is measured against the best compound action with at most $\mu(n)$ switches, we may ask what is the fastest rate of growth of $\mu(n)$ a Hannan consistent forecaster can tolerate. The following result shows that a growth slightly slower than linear is already sufficient.

Corollary 5.2. *Let* $\mu : \mathbb{N} \to \mathbb{N}$ *be any nondecreasing integer-valued function such that*

$$
\mu(n) = o\left(\frac{n}{\log(n) \log \log(n)} \right).
$$

Then there exists a randomized forecaster such that

$$
\limsup_{n \to \infty} \frac{1}{n} \left(\sum_{t=1}^{n} \ell(I_t, Y_t) - \min_{\mathcal{F}_n} \sum_{t=1}^{n} \ell(i_t, Y_t) \right) = 0 \quad \text{with probability 1,}
$$

where $\mathcal{F}_n$ *is the set of compound actions* $(i_1, \ldots, i_n)$ *whose size is at most* $\mu(n)$.

The proof of Corollary 5.2 goes along the same lines as the proof of Corollary 6.1, and we leave it as an exercise.

The Variable Share Forecaster

Recall that if the best action has a small cumulative loss, then improved regret bounds may be achieved that involve the loss of the best action (see Section 2.4). Next we show how this can be done in the tracking framework such that the resulting forecaster is still computationally feasible. This is achieved by a modification of the fixed share forecaster. All we have to do is to change the initial weight assignment appropriately.

A crucial feature of the choice of initial weights w'_0 when forecasting compound actions is that for any i and t, the weight $w'_{i,t}$ depends only on $w'_0(i_1, \ldots, i_t, i)$ and on the realized losses up to time t. That is, for computing the prediction at time $t + 1$ there is no need to know how $w'_0(i_1, \ldots, i_t, i)$ is split into $w'_0(i_1, \ldots, i_t, i, i_{t+2}, \ldots, i_n)$ for each continuation $i_{t+2}, \ldots, i_n \in \{1, \ldots, N\}$. This fact, which is the key to the proof of Theorem 5.1, can be exploited to define $w'_0(i_1, \ldots, i_t, i_{t+1})$ using information that is only made available at time t. For example, consider the following recursive definition

$$w_0'(i_1, \ldots, i_{t+1})$$
$$= w_0'(i_1, \ldots, i_t) \left(\frac{1 - (1 - \alpha)^{\ell(i_t, Y_t)}}{N - 1} \mathbb{I}_{\{i_t \neq i_{t+1}\}} + (1 - \alpha)^{\ell(i_t, Y_t)} \mathbb{I}_{\{i_t = i_{t+1}\}} \right).$$

This is similar to the definition of the Markov process associated with the initial weight distribution used by the fixed share forecaster. The difference is that here we see that, given $I_t = i_t$, the probability of $I_{t+1} \neq i_t$ grows with $\ell(i_t, Y_t)$, the loss incurred by action i_t at time t. Hence, this new distribution assigns a further penalty to compound actions that switch to a new action when the old one incurs a small loss.

On the basis of this new distribution, we introduce the *variable share forecaster*, replacing step 3 of the fixed share forecaster with

$$w_{i,t} = \frac{1}{N - 1} \sum_{j \neq i} \left(1 - (1 - \alpha)^{\ell(j, Y_t)} \right) v_{j,t} + (1 - \alpha)^{\ell(i, Y_t)} v_{i,t}.$$

Mimicking the proof of Theorem 5.1, it is easy to check that the weights $w_{i,t}'$ of the variable share forecaster satisfy

$$w_{i,t} = \sum_{i_1, \ldots, i_t, i_{t+2}, \ldots, i_n} w_t'(i_1, \ldots, i_t, i, i_{t+2}, \ldots, i_n).$$

Hence, the computation carried out by the variable share forecaster efficiently updates the weights $w_{i,t}'$.

Note that this initial weight distribution assigns a negligible weight w_0' to all compound actions $(i_1, \ldots, i_n)$ such that $i_{t+1} \neq i_t$ and $\ell(i_t, Y_t)$ is close to 0 for some t. In Theorem 5.3 we analyze the performance of the variable share forecaster under the simplifying assumption of binary losses $\ell \in \{0, 1\}$. Via a similar, but somewhat more complicated, argument, a regret bound slightly larger than the bound of Theorem 5.3 can be proven in the general setup where $\ell \in [0, 1]$ (see Exercise 5.4).

Theorem 5.3. *Fix a time horizon n. Under the assumption $\ell \in \{0, 1\}$, for all $\eta > 0$ and for all $\alpha \leq (N - 1)/N$ the tracking regret of the variable share forecaster satisfies*

$$\sum_{t=1}^n \overline{\ell}(\mathbf{p}_t, Y_t) - \sum_{t=1}^n \ell(i_t, Y_t)$$

$$\leq m + \frac{m + 1}{\eta} \ln N + \frac{m}{\eta} \ln \frac{1}{\alpha} + \frac{1}{\eta} \left(\sum_{t=1}^n \ell(i_t, Y_t) \right) \ln \frac{1}{1 - \alpha} + \frac{\eta}{8} n$$

for all action sequences $i_1, \ldots, i_n$, where $m = \text{size}(i_1, \ldots, i_n)$.

Observe that the performance bound guaranteed by the theorem is similar to that of Theorem 5.2 with the only exception that

$$\frac{n - m - 1}{\eta} \ln \frac{1}{1 - \alpha} \quad \text{is replaced by} \quad \frac{1}{\eta} \left(\sum_{t=1}^n \ell(i_t, Y_t) \right) \ln \frac{1}{1 - \alpha} + m.$$

Because the inequality holds for all sequences with size $(i_1, \ldots, i_n) \leq m$, this is a significant improvement if there exists a sequence $(i_1, \ldots, i_n)$ with at most m switches, with m not too large, that has a small cumulative loss. Of course, if the goal of the forecaster is to minimize the cumulative regret with respect to the class of all compound actions with size $(i_1, \ldots, i_n) \leq m$, then the optimal choice of α and η depends on the smallest such cumulative loss of the compound actions. In the lack of prior knowledge of the minimal loss, these parameters may be chosen adaptively to achieve a regret bound of the desired order. The details are left to the reader.

***Proof of Theorem* 5.3.** In its current form, Lemma 5.1 cannot be applied to the initial weights w_0' of the variable share distribution because these weights depend on the outcome sequence $Y_1, \ldots, Y_n$ that, in turn, may depend on the actions of the forecaster. (Recall that in the model of randomized prediction we allow nonoblivious opponents.) However, because the draw I_t of the variable share forecaster is conditionally independent (given the past outcomes $Y_1, \ldots, Y_{t-1}$) of the past random draws $I_1, \ldots, I_{t-1}$, Lemma 4.1 may be used, which states that, without loss of generality, we may assume that the opponent is oblivious. In other words, it suffices to prove our result for any fixed (nonrandom) outcome sequence $y_1, \ldots, y_n$. Once the outcome sequence is fixed, the initial weights are well defined and we can apply Lemma 5.1.

Introduce the notation $L(j_1, \ldots, j_n) = \ell(j_1, y_1) + \ldots + \ell(j_n, y_n)$. Fix any compound action $(i_1, \ldots, i_n)$. Let $m = \text{size}(i_1, \ldots, i_n)$ and $L^* = L(i_1, \ldots, i_n)$. If $m = 0$, then

$$\ln W_n' \geq \ln w_n'(i_1, \ldots, i_n) = \ln\left(\frac{1}{N} e^{-\eta L^*}(1 - \alpha)^{L^*}\right)$$

and the theorem follows from Lemma 5.1. Assume then $m \geq 1$. Denote by $\mathcal{F}_{L^*+m}$ the set of compound actions $(j_1, \ldots, j_n)$ with cumulative loss $L(j_1, \ldots, j_n) \leq L^* + m$. Then

$$
\begin{aligned}
\ln W_n' &= \ln\left(\sum_{(j_1, \ldots, j_n) \in \{1, \ldots, N\}^m} w_0'(j_1, \ldots, j_n) e^{-\eta L(j_1, \ldots, j_n)}\right) \\
&\geq \ln\left(\sum_{(j_1, \ldots, j_n) \in \mathcal{F}_{L^*+m}} w_0'(j_1, \ldots, j_n) e^{-\eta(L^*+m)}\right) \\
&= -\eta(L^* + m) + \ln\left(\sum_{(j_1, \ldots, j_n) \in \mathcal{F}_{L^*+m}} w_0'(j_1, \ldots, j_n)\right).
\end{aligned}
$$

We now show that $\mathcal{F}_{L^*+m}$ contains at least a compound action $(j_1, \ldots, j_n)$ with a large weight $w_0'(j_1, \ldots, j_n)$. This compound action $(j_1, \ldots, j_n)$ mimics $(i_1, \ldots, i_n)$ until the latter makes a switch. If the switch is made right after a step t where $\ell(i_t, y_t) = 0$, then $(j_1, \ldots, j_n)$ delays the switch (which would imply $w_0'(j_1, \ldots, j_n) = 0$) and keeps repeating action i_t until some later time step t' where $\ell(i_t, y_t') = 1$. Then, from time $t' + 1$ onward, $(j_1, \ldots, j_n)$ mimics $(i_1, \ldots, i_n)$ again until the next switch occurs.

We formalize the above argument as follows. Let t_1 be the time step where the first switch $i_{t_1} \neq i_{t_1+1}$ occurs. Set $j_t = i_t$ for all $t = 1, \ldots, t_1$. Then set $j_t = i_{t_1}$ for all $t = t_1 + 1, \ldots, t_1'$, where t_1' is the first step after t_1 such that $\ell(i_{t_1}, y_{t_1'}) = 1$. If no such t_1' exists, then let $t_1' = n$. Proceed by setting $j_t = i_t$ for all $t = t_1' + 1, t_1' + 2, \ldots$ until a new switch $i_{t_2} \neq i_{t_2+1}$ occurs for some $t_2 > t_1'$ (if there are no more switches after t_1', then set $j_t = i_t$ for all $t = t_1' + 1, \ldots, n$). Repeat the procedure described above until the end of the sequence is reached.

Call a sequence of steps $t_k' + 1, \ldots, t_{k+1} - 1$ (where t_k' may be 1 and $t_{k+1} - 1$ may be n) an *A-block*, and a sequence of steps $t_k, \ldots, t_k'$ (where t_k' may be n) a *B-block*. Note that

$(j_1, \ldots, j_n)$ never makes a switch within an A-block and makes at most one switch within each B-block. Also, $L(j_1, \ldots, j_n) \leq L^* + m$, because $j_t = i_t$ within A-blocks, $L(j_{t_k}, \ldots, j_{t'_k}) \leq 1$ within each B-block, and the number of B-blocks is at most m.

Introduce the notation

$$Q_t = \frac{1 - (1 - \alpha)^{\ell(i_t, y_t)}}{N - 1} \mathbb{I}_{\{i_t \neq i_{t+1}\}} + (1 - \alpha)^{\ell(i_t, y_t)} \mathbb{I}_{\{i_t = i_{t+1}\}}.$$

By definition of w_0' we have

$$w_0'(j_1, \ldots, j_n) = w_0'(j_1) \prod_{t=1}^{n-1} Q_t.$$

For all t in an A-block, $Q_t = (1 - \alpha)^{\ell(i_t, y_t)}$. Now fix any B-block $t_k, \ldots, t'_k$. Then $\ell(j_t, y_t) = 0$ for all $t = t_k, \ldots, t'_k - 1$ and $\ell(j_{t'_k}, y_{t'_k}) \leq 1$, as $\ell(j_{t'_k}, y_{t'_k})$ might be 0 when $t'_k = n$. We thus have

$$\prod_{t \in \text{B-block}} Q_t \geq (1 - \alpha)^0 \times \cdots \times (1 - \alpha)^0 \times \frac{1 - (1 - \alpha)^1}{N - 1} = \frac{\alpha}{N - 1}.$$

The factor $\left(1 - (1 - \alpha)^1\right)/(N - 1)$ appears under the assumption that $j_{t'_k} < n$ and $j_{t'_k + 1} \neq j_{t'_k}$. If $i_{t'_k + 1} = i_{t_k}$, implying $j_{t'_k + 1} = j_{t'_k}$, then $Q_{t'_k} = (1 - \alpha)^1$ and the above inequality still holds since $\alpha/(N - 1) \leq 1 - \alpha$ is implied by the assumption $\alpha \leq (N - 1)/N$.

Now, as explained earlier,

$$\sum_t \ell(j_t, y_t) \leq L^* \qquad \text{and} \qquad \sum_{t'} \ell(j_{t'}, y_{t'}) \leq m,$$

where the first sum is over all t in A-blocks and the second sum is over all t' in B-blocks (recall that there are at most m B-blocks). Thus, there exists a $(j_1, \ldots, j_n) \in \mathcal{F}_{L^* + m}$ with

$$w_0'(j_1, \ldots, j_n) = w_0'(j_1) \prod_{t=1}^{n-1} Q_t \geq \frac{1}{N}(1 - \alpha)^{L^*} \left(\frac{\alpha}{N - 1}\right)^m.$$

Hence,

$$\ln \sum_{\mathcal{F}_{L^* + m}} w_0'(j_1, \ldots, j_n) \geq \ln \left(\frac{1}{N}(1 - \alpha)^{L^*} \left(\frac{\alpha}{N - 1}\right)^m\right),$$

which concludes the proof. ∎

5.3 Tree Experts

An important example of structured classes of experts is obtained by representing experts (i.e., actions) by binary trees. We call such structured actions *tree experts*. A tree expert E is a finite ordered binary tree in which each node has either 2 child nodes (a left child and a right child) or no child nodes (if it is a leaf). The leaves of E are labeled with actions chosen from $\{1, \ldots, N\}$. We use λ to indicate the root of E and 0 and 1 to indicate the left and right children of λ. In general, $(x_1, \ldots, x_d) \in \{0, 1\}^d$ denotes the left (if $x_d = 0$) or right (if $x_d = 1$) child of the node $(x_1, \ldots, x_{d-1})$.

Like the frameworks studied in Chapters 9, 11, and 12, we assume that, at each prediction round, a piece of "side information" is made available to the forecaster. We do not make any assumptions on the source of this side information. In the case of tree

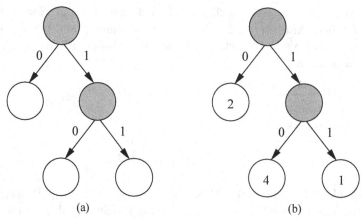

Figure 5.1. A binary tree (a) and a tree expert based on it (b). Given any side information vector with prefix $(1, 0, \ldots)$, this tree expert chooses action 4, the label of leaf $(1, 0)$.

experts the side information is represented, at each time step t, by an infinite binary vector $\mathbf{x}_t = (x_{1,t}, x_{2,t}, \ldots)$. In the example described in this section, however, we only make use of a finite number of components in the side information vector.

An expert E uses the side information to select a leaf in its tree and outputs the action labeling that leaf. Given side information $\mathbf{x} = (x_1, x_2, \ldots)$, let $\mathbf{v} = (v_1, \ldots, v_d)$ be the unique leaf of E such that $v_1 = x_1, \ldots, v_d = x_d$. The label of this leaf, denoted by $i_E(\mathbf{x}) \in \{1, \ldots, N\}$, is the action chosen by expert E upon observation of $\mathbf{x}$ (see Figure 5.1).

***Example* 5.1 (*Context trees*).** A simple application where unbounded side information occurs is the following: consider the set of actions $\{0, 1\}$, let $\mathcal{Y} = \{0, 1\}$, and define ℓ by $\ell(i, Y) = \mathbb{I}_{\{i \neq Y\}}$. This setup models a randomized binary prediction problem in which the forecaster is scored with the number of prediction mistakes. Define the side information at time t by $\mathbf{x}_t = (Y_{t-1}, Y_{t-2}, \ldots)$, where Y_t for $t \leq 0$ is defined arbitrarily, say, as $Y_t = 0$. Hence, the leaf of a tree expert E determining the expert's prediction $i_E(\mathbf{x}_t)$ is selected according to a suffix of the outcome sequence. However, depending on E, the length of the suffix used to determine $i_E(\mathbf{x}_t)$ may vary. This model of interaction between the outcome sequence and the expert predictions was originated in the area of information theory. Suffix-based tree experts are also known as *prediction suffix trees*, *context trees*, or *variable-length Markov models*.   □

We define the (expected) regret of a randomized forecaster against the tree expert E by

$$\overline{R}_{E,n} = \sum_{t=1}^{n} \overline{\ell}(\mathbf{p}_t, Y_t) - \sum_{t=1}^{n} \ell(i_E(\mathbf{x}_t), Y_t).$$

In this section we derive bounds for the maximal regret against any tree expert such that the depth of the corresponding binary tree (i.e., the depth of the node of maximum distance from the root) is bounded. As in Section 5.2, this is achieved by a version of the exponentially weighted average forecaster. Furthermore, we will see that the forecaster is easy to compute.

Before moving on to the analysis of regret for tree experts, we state and prove a general result about sums of functions associated with the leaves of a binary tree. We use T to denote a finite binary tree. Thus, a tree expert E is a binary tree T with an action labeling each

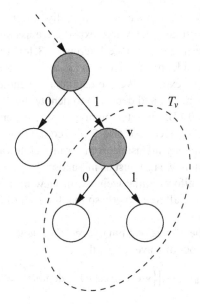

Figure 5.2. A fragment of a binary tree. The dashed line shows a subtree T_v rooted at **v**.

leaf. The size $\|T\|$ of a finite binary tree T is the number of nodes in T. In the following, we often consider binary subtrees rooted at arbitrary nodes **v** (see Figure 5.2).

Lemma 5.2. *Let* $g : \{0, 1\}^* \to \mathbb{R}$ *be any nonnegative function defined over the set of all binary sequences of finite length, and introduce the function* $G : \{0, 1\}^* \to \mathbb{R}$ *by*

$$G(\mathbf{v}) = \sum_{T_v} 2^{-\|T_v\|} \prod_{\mathbf{x} \in \text{leaves}(T_v)} g(\mathbf{x}),$$

where the sum is over all finite binary subtrees T_v *rooted at* $\mathbf{v} = (v_1, \ldots, v_d)$. *Then*

$$G(\mathbf{v}) = \frac{g(\mathbf{v})}{2} + \frac{1}{2} G(v_1, \ldots, v_d, 0) G(v_1, \ldots, v_d, 1).$$

Proof. Fix any node $\mathbf{v} = (v_1, \ldots, v_d)$ and let T_0 and T_1 range over all the finite binary subtrees rooted, respectively, at $(v_1, \ldots, v_d, 0)$ and $(v_1, \ldots, v_d, 1)$. The leaves of any subtree rooted at **v** can be split in three subsets: those belonging to the left subtree T_0 of **v**, those belonging to the right subtree T_1 of **v**, and the singleton set $\{\mathbf{v}\}$ belonging to the subtree containing only the leaf **v**. Thus we have

$$G(\mathbf{v}) = \frac{g(\mathbf{v})}{2} + \sum_{T_0} \sum_{T_1} 2^{-(1+\|T_0\|+\|T_1\|)} \left(\prod_{\mathbf{x} \in \text{leaves}(T_0)} g(\mathbf{x}) \right) \left(\prod_{\mathbf{x}' \in \text{leaves}(T_1)} g(\mathbf{x}') \right)$$

$$= \frac{g(\mathbf{v})}{2} + \frac{1}{2} \left(\sum_{T_0} 2^{-\|T_0\|} \prod_{\mathbf{x} \in \text{leaves}(T_0)} g(\mathbf{x}) \right) \left(\sum_{T_1} 2^{-\|T_1\|} \prod_{\mathbf{x}' \in \text{leaves}(T_1)} g(\mathbf{x}') \right)$$

$$= \frac{g(\mathbf{v})}{2} + \frac{1}{2} G(v_1, \ldots, v_d, 0) G(v_1, \ldots, v_d, 1). \quad \blacksquare$$

Our next goal is to define the randomized exponentially weighted forecaster for the set of tree experts. To deal with finitely many tree experts, we assume a fixed bound $D \geq 0$ on the maximum depth of a tree expert (see Exercise 5.8 for a more general analysis). Hence, the first D bits of the side information $\mathbf{x} = (x_1, x_2, \ldots)$ are sufficient to determine the predictions of all such tree experts. We use depth($\mathbf{v}$) to denote the depth d of a node $\mathbf{v} = (v_1, \ldots, v_d)$ in a binary tree T, and depth(T) to denote the maximum depth of a leaf in T. (We define depth(λ) = 0.) Because the number of tree experts based on binary trees of depth bounded by D is N^{2^D} (see Exercise 5.10), computing a weight separately for each tree expert is computationally infeasible even for moderate values of D. To obtain an easily calculable approximation, we use, just as in Section 5.2, the exponentially weighted average forecaster with nonuniform initial weights. In view of using Lemma 5.1, we just have to assign initial weights to all tree experts so that the sum of these weights is at most 1. This can be done as follows.

For $D \geq 0$ fixed, define the D-size of a binary tree T of depth at most D as the number of nodes in T minus the number of leaves at depth D:

$$\|T\|_D = \|T\| - \left|\left\{\mathbf{v} \in \text{leaves}(T) : \text{depth}(\mathbf{v}) = D\right\}\right|.$$

Lemma 5.3. *For any $D \geq 0$,*

$$\sum_{T : \text{depth}(T) \leq D} 2^{-\|T\|_D} = 1,$$

where the summation is over all trees rooted at λ, of depth at most D.

Proof. We proceed by induction on D. For $D = 0$ the lemma holds because $\|T\|_0 = 0$ for the single-node tree $\{\lambda\}$ of depth 0. For the induction step, fix $D \geq 1$ and define

$$g(\mathbf{v}) = \begin{cases} 0 & \text{if depth}(\mathbf{v}) > D \\ 2 & \text{if depth}(\mathbf{v}) = D \\ 1 & \text{otherwise.} \end{cases}$$

Then, for any tree T,

$$2^{-\|T\|} \prod_{\mathbf{x} \in \text{leaves}(T)} g(\mathbf{x}) = \begin{cases} 0 & \text{if depth}(T) > D \\ 2^{-\|T\|_D} & \text{if depth}(T) \leq D. \end{cases}$$

Applying Lemma 5.2 with $\mathbf{v} = \lambda$ we get

$$\sum_{T : \text{depth}(T) \leq D} 2^{-\|T\|_D} = \sum_T 2^{-\|T\|} \prod_{\mathbf{x} \in \text{leaves}(T)} g(\mathbf{x}) = \frac{g(\lambda)}{2} + \frac{1}{2} G(0) G(1).$$

Since λ has depth 0 and $D \geq 1$, $g(\lambda) = 1$. Furthermore, letting T_0 and T_1 range over the trees rooted at node 0 (the left child of λ) and node 1 (the right child of λ), for each $b \in \{0, 1\}$ we have

$$G(b) = \sum_{T_b : \text{depth}(T_b) \leq D-1} 2^{-\|T_b\|} \prod_{\mathbf{x} \in \text{leaves}(T_b)} g(\mathbf{x}) = \sum_{T : \text{depth}(T) \leq D-1} 2^{-\|T\|_{D-1}} = 1$$

by induction hypothesis. ∎

Using Lemma 5.3, we can define an initial weight over all tree experts E of depth at most D as follows:

$$w_{E,0} = 2^{-\|E\|_D} N^{-|\text{leaves}(E)|}$$

where, in order to simplify notation, we write $\|E\|_D$ and $\text{leaves}(E)$ for $\|T\|_D$ and $\text{leaves}(T)$ whenever the tree expert E has T as the underlying binary tree. (In general, when we speak about a leaf, node, or depth of a tree expert, we always mean a leaf, node, or depth of the underlying tree T.) The factor $N^{-|\text{leaves}(E)|}$ in the definition of $w_{E,0}$ accounts for the fact that there are $N^{|\text{leaves}(E)|}$ tree experts E for each binary tree T.

If $\mathbf{u} = (u_1, \ldots, u_d)$ is a prefix of $\mathbf{v} = (u_1, \ldots, u_d, \ldots, u_D)$, we write $\mathbf{u} \sqsubseteq \mathbf{v}$. In particular, $\mathbf{u} \sqsubset \mathbf{v}$ if $\mathbf{u} \sqsubseteq \mathbf{v}$ and $\mathbf{v}$ has at least one extra component v_{d+1} with respect to $\mathbf{u}$.

Define the weight $w_{E,t-1}$ of a tree expert E at time t by

$$w_{E,t-1} = w_{E,0} \prod_{\mathbf{v} \in \text{leaves}(E)} w_{E,\mathbf{v},t-1},$$

where $w_{E,\mathbf{v},t-1}$, the weight of leaf $\mathbf{v}$ in E, is defined as follows: $w_{E,\mathbf{v},0} = 1$ and

$$w_{E,\mathbf{v},t} = \begin{cases} w_{E,\mathbf{v},t-1} e^{-\eta \, \ell(i_E(\mathbf{v}), Y_t)} & \text{if } \mathbf{v} \sqsubseteq \mathbf{x}_t \\ w_{E,\mathbf{v},t-1} & \text{otherwise,} \end{cases}$$

where $i_E(\mathbf{v}) = i_E(\mathbf{x}_t)$ is the action labeling the leaf $\mathbf{v} \sqsubseteq \mathbf{x}_t$ of E. (Note that $\mathbf{v}$ is unique.) As no other leaf $\mathbf{v}' \neq \mathbf{v}$ of E is updated at time t, we have $w_{E,\mathbf{v}',t} = w_{E,\mathbf{v}',t-1}$ for all such $\mathbf{v}'$, and therefore

$$w_{E,t} = w_{E,t-1} e^{-\eta \, \ell(i_E(\mathbf{x}_t), Y_t)} \qquad \text{for all } t = 1, 2, \ldots$$

as $\mathbf{v} \sqsubseteq \mathbf{x}_t$ always holds for exactly one leaf of E. At time t, the randomized exponentially weighted forecaster draws action k with probability

$$p_{k,t} = \frac{\sum_E \mathbb{I}_{\{i_E(\mathbf{x}_t)=k\}} w_{E,t-1}}{\sum_{E'} w_{E',t-1}},$$

where the sums are over tree experts E with $\text{depth}(E) \leq D$. Using Lemma 5.1, we immediately get the following regret bound.

Theorem 5.4. *For all $n \geq 1$, the regret of the randomized exponentially weighted forecaster run over the set of tree experts of depth at most D satisfies*

$$\overline{R}_{E,n} \leq \frac{\|E\|_D}{\eta} \ln 2 + \frac{|\text{leaves}(E)|}{\eta} \ln N + \frac{\eta}{8} n$$

for all such tree experts E and for all sequences $\mathbf{x}_1, \ldots, \mathbf{x}_n$ of side information.

Observe that if the depth of the tree is at most D, then $\|E\|_D \leq 2^D - 1$ and $|\text{leaves}(E)| \leq 2^D$, leading to the regret bound

$$\max_{E:\text{depth}(E) \leq D} \overline{R}_{E,n} \leq \frac{2^D}{\eta} \ln(2N) + \frac{\eta}{8} n.$$

Thus, choosing η to minimize the upper bound yields a forecaster with

$$\max_{E:\text{depth}(E) \leq D} \overline{R}_{E,n} \leq \sqrt{n2^{D-1} \ln(2N)}.$$

We now show how to implement this forecaster using N weights for each node of the complete binary tree of depth D; thus $N(2^{D+1} - 1)$ weights in total. This is a substantial improvement with respect to using a weight for each tree expert because there are N^{2^D} tree experts with corresponding tree of depth at most D (see Exercise 5.10). The efficient forecaster, which we call the *tree expert forecaster*, is described in the following. Because we only consider tree experts of depth D at most, we may assume without loss of generality that the side information $\mathbf{x}_t$ is a string of D bits, that is, $\mathbf{x}_t \in \{0, 1\}^D$. This convention simplifies the notation that follows.

THE TREE EXPERT FORECASTER

Parameters: Real number $\eta > 0$, integer $D \geq 0$.

Initialization: $\overline{w}_{i,\mathbf{v},0} = 1$, $w_{i,\mathbf{v},0} = 1$ for each $i = 1, \ldots, N$ and for each node $\mathbf{v} = (v_1, \ldots, v_d)$ with $d \leq D$.

For each round $t = 1, 2, \ldots$

(1) draw an action I_t from $\{1, \ldots, N\}$ according to the distribution

$$p_{i,t} = \frac{\overline{w}_{i,\lambda,t-1}}{\sum_{j=1}^N \overline{w}_{j,\lambda,t-1}}, \qquad i = 1, \ldots, N;$$

(2) obtain Y_t and compute, for each $\mathbf{v}$ and for each $i = 1, \ldots, N$,

$$w_{i,\mathbf{v},t} = \begin{cases} w_{i,\mathbf{v},t-1}\, e^{-\eta\, \ell(i,Y_t)} & \text{if } \mathbf{v} \sqsubseteq \mathbf{x}_t \\ w_{i,\mathbf{v},t-1} & \text{otherwise;} \end{cases}$$

(3) recursively update each node $\mathbf{v} = (v_1, \ldots, v_d)$ with $d = D, D-1, \ldots, 0$

$$\overline{w}_{i,\mathbf{v},t} = \begin{cases} \frac{1}{2N} w_{i,\mathbf{v},t} & \text{if } \mathbf{v} = \mathbf{x}_t \\[2mm] \frac{1}{2N} \sum_{j=1}^N w_{j,\mathbf{v},t} & \text{if depth}(\mathbf{v}) = D \\ & \text{and } \mathbf{v} \neq \mathbf{x}_t \\[2mm] \frac{1}{2N} w_{i,\mathbf{v},t} + \frac{1}{2N}\left(\overline{w}_{i,\mathbf{v}_0,t} + \overline{w}_{i,\mathbf{v}_1,t}\right) & \text{if } \mathbf{v} \sqsubset \mathbf{x}_t \\[2mm] \overline{w}_{i,\mathbf{v},t-1} & \text{if depth}(\mathbf{v}) < D \\ & \text{and } \mathbf{v} \not\sqsubseteq \mathbf{x}_t \end{cases}$$

where $\mathbf{v}_0 = (v_1, \ldots, v_d, 0)$ and $\mathbf{v}_1 = (v_1, \ldots, v_d, 1)$.

With each weight $w_{i,\mathbf{v},t}$ the tree expert forecaster associates an auxiliary weight $\overline{w}_{i,\mathbf{v},t}$. As shown in the next theorem, the auxiliary weight $\overline{w}_{i,\lambda,t}$ equals

$$\sum_E \mathbb{I}_{\{i_E(\mathbf{x}_t)=i\}} w_{E,t}.$$

The computation of $w_{i,\mathbf{v},t}$ and $\overline{w}_{i,\mathbf{v},t}$ given $w_{i,\mathbf{v},t-1}$ and $\overline{w}_{i,\mathbf{v},t-1}$ for each $\mathbf{v}, i$ can be carried out in $O(D)$ time using a simple dynamic programming scheme. Indeed, only the weights associated with the D nodes $\mathbf{v} \sqsubseteq \mathbf{x}_t$ change their values from time $t - 1$ to time t.

Theorem 5.5. *Fix a nonnegative integer $D \geq 0$. For any sequence of outcomes and for all $t \geq 1$, the conditional distribution of the action I_t drawn at time t by the tree expert* *forecaster with input parameter D is the same as the conditional distribution of the action I'_t drawn at time t by the exponentially weighted forecaster run over the set of all tree experts of depth bounded by D using the initial weights $w_{E,0}$ defined earlier.*

Proof. We show that for each $t = 0, 1, \ldots$ and for each $k = 1, \ldots, N$,

$$\sum_E \mathbb{I}_{\{i_E(\mathbf{x}_t)=k\}} w_{E,t-1} = \overline{w}_{k,\lambda,t-1},$$

where the sum is over all tree experts E such that depth$(E) \le D$. We start by rewriting the left-hand side of the this expression as

$$\sum_E \mathbb{I}_{\{i_E(\mathbf{x}_t)=k\}} w_{E,t-1} = \sum_E 2^{-\|E\|_D} N^{-\text{leaves}(E)} \mathbb{I}_{\{i_E(\mathbf{x}_t)=k\}} \prod_{v \in \text{leaves}(E)} w_{E,v,t-1}$$

$$= \sum_E 2^{-\|E\|_D} \mathbb{I}_{\{i_E(\mathbf{x}_t)=k\}} \prod_{v \in \text{leaves}(E)} \frac{w_{E,v,t-1}}{N}$$

$$= \sum_T 2^{-\|T\|_D} \sum_{(i_1,\ldots,i_d)} \prod_{j=1}^d \frac{w_{i_j,v_j,t-1}}{N} \mathbb{I}_{\{v_j \sqsubseteq \mathbf{x}_t \Rightarrow i_j = k\}}$$

where in the last step we split the sum over tree experts E in a sum over trees T and a sum over all assignments $(i_1, \ldots, i_d) \in \{1, \ldots, N\}^d$ of actions to the leaves $\mathbf{v}_1, \ldots, \mathbf{v}_d$ of T. The indicator function selects those assignments $(i_1, \ldots, i_d)$ such that the unique leaf $\mathbf{v}_j$ satisfying $\mathbf{v}_j \sqsubseteq \mathbf{x}_t$ has the desired label k. We now proceed the above derivation by exchanging $\sum_{(i_1,\ldots,i_d)}$ with $\prod_{j=1}^d$. This gives

$$\sum_E \mathbb{I}_{\{i_E(\mathbf{x}_t)=k\}} w_{E,t-1} = \sum_T 2^{-\|T\|_D} \prod_{j=1}^d \sum_{i=1}^N \frac{w_{i,v_j,t-1}}{N} \mathbb{I}_{\{v_j \sqsubseteq \mathbf{x}_t \Rightarrow i=k\}}.$$

Note that this last expression is of the form

$$\sum_T 2^{-\|T\|_D} \prod_{v \in \text{leaves}(T)} g_{t-1}(\mathbf{v}) \qquad \text{for} \qquad g_{t-1}(\mathbf{v}) = \sum_{i=1}^N \frac{w_{i,v,t-1}}{N} \mathbb{I}_{\{v \sqsubseteq \mathbf{x}_t \Rightarrow i=k\}}.$$

Let

$$G_{t-1}(\mathbf{v}) = \sum_{T_\mathbf{v}} 2^{-\|T_\mathbf{v}\|_D} \prod_{x \in \text{leaves}(T_\mathbf{v})} g_{t-1}(\mathbf{x}),$$

where $T_\mathbf{v}$ ranges over all trees rooted at $\mathbf{v}$. By Lemma 5.2 (noting that the lemma remains true if $\|T_\mathbf{v}\|$ is replaced by $\|T_\mathbf{v}\|_D$), and using the definition of g_{t-1}, for all $\mathbf{v} = (v_1, \ldots, v_d)$,

$$G_{t-1}(\mathbf{v}) = \begin{cases} \frac{1}{2N} w_{k,\mathbf{v},t-1} & \text{if } \mathbf{v} = \mathbf{x}_t \\[2mm] \frac{1}{2N} \sum_{i=1}^N w_{i,v_j,t-1} & \text{if depth}(\mathbf{v}) = D \\ & \text{and } \mathbf{v} \ne \mathbf{x}_t \\[2mm] \frac{1}{2N} w_{k,\mathbf{v},t-1} + \frac{1}{2}\big(G_{t-1}(\mathbf{v}_0) + G_{t-1}(\mathbf{v}_1)\big) & \text{otherwise} \end{cases}$$

where $\mathbf{v}_0 = (v_1, \ldots, v_d, 0)$ and $\mathbf{v}_1 = (v_1, \ldots, v_d, 1)$. We now prove, by induction on $t \geq 1$, that $G_{t-1}(\lambda) = \overline{w}_{k,\lambda,t-1}$ for all t. For $t = 1$, $\overline{w}_{k,\lambda,0} = 1$. Also,

$$G_0(\lambda) = \sum_T 2^{-\|T\|_D} \prod_{v \in \text{leaves}(T)} \frac{1}{N} \sum_{i=1}^{N} w_{i,\mathbf{v},0} = 1$$

because $w_{i,\mathbf{v},0} = 1$ for all i and $\mathbf{v}$, and we used Lemma 5.3 to sum $2^{-\|T\|_D}$. Assuming the claim holds for $t - 1$, note that the definition of $G_t(\mathbf{v})$ and $\overline{w}_{k,\mathbf{v},t}$ is the same for the cases $\mathbf{v} = \mathbf{x}_t$, $\mathbf{v} \neq \mathbf{x}_t$, and $\mathbf{v} \sqsubseteq \mathbf{x}_t$. For the case $\mathbf{v} \not\sqsubseteq \mathbf{x}_t$ with depth$(\mathbf{v}) < D$, we have $\overline{w}_{i,\mathbf{v},t} = \overline{w}_{i,\mathbf{v},t-1}$. Furthermore, $w_{i,\mathbf{v},t} = w_{i,\mathbf{v},t-1}$ for all i. Thus $G_t(\mathbf{v}) = G_{t-1}(\mathbf{v})$ as all further $\mathbf{v}'$ involved in the recursion for $G_t(\mathbf{v})$ also satisfy $\mathbf{v}' \not\sqsubseteq \mathbf{x}_t$. By induction hypothesis, $G_{t-1}(\mathbf{v}) = \overline{w}_{i,\mathbf{v},t-1}$ and the proof is concluded. ∎

5.4 The Shortest Path Problem

In this section we discuss a representative example of structured expert classes that has received attention in the literature for its many applications. Our purpose is to describe the main ideas in the simplest form rather than to offer an exhaustive account of online prediction problems for which computationally efficient solutions exist. The shortest path problem is the ideal guinea pig for our purposes.

Consider a network represented by a set of nodes connected by edges, and assume that we have to send a stream of packets from a source node to a destination node. At each time instance a packet is sent along a chosen route connecting source and destination. Depending on traffic, each edge in the network may have a different delay, and the total delay the packet suffers on the chosen route is the sum of delays of the edges composing the route. The delays may vary in each time instance in an arbitrary way, and our goal is to find a way of choosing the route in each time instance such that the sum of the total delays over time is not much more than that of the best fixed route in the network.

Of course, this problem may be cast as a sequential prediction problem in which each possible route is represented by an expert. However, the number of routes is typically exponentially large in the number of edges, and therefore computationally efficient predictors are called for. In this section we describe two solutions of very different flavor. One of them is based on the follow-the-perturbed-leader forecaster discussed in Section 4.3, whereas the other is based on an efficient computation of the exponentially weighted average forecaster. Both solutions have different advantages and may be generalized in different directions. The key for both solutions is the additive structure of the loss, that is; the fact that the delay corresponding to each route may be computed as the sum of the delays of the edges on the route.

To formalize the problem, consider a (finite) directed acyclic graph with a set of edges $E = \{e_1, \ldots, e_{|E|}\}$ and set of vertices V. Thus, each edge $e \in E$ is an ordered pair of vertices (v_1, v_2). Let u and v be two distinguished vertices in V. A *path* from u to v is a sequence of edges $e^{(1)}, \ldots, e^{(k)}$ such that $e^{(1)} = (u, v_1)$, $e^{(j)} = (v_{j-1}, v_j)$ for all $j = 2, \ldots, k - 1$, and $e^{(k)} = (v_{k-1}, v)$. We identify a path with a binary vector $\mathbf{i} \in \{0, 1\}^{|E|}$ such that the jth component of $\mathbf{i}$ equals 1 if and only if the edge e_j is in the path. For simplicity, we assume that every edge in E is on some path from u to v and every vertex in V is an endpoint of an edge (see Figure 5.3 for examples).

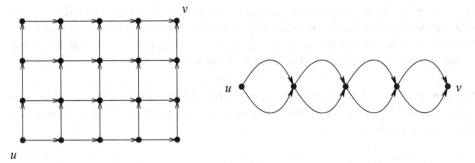

Figure 5.3. Two examples of directed acyclic graphs for the shortest path problem.

In each round $t = 1, \ldots, n$ of the forecasting game, the forecaster chooses a path $\mathbf{I}_t$ among all paths from u to v. Then a loss $\ell_{e,t} \in [0, 1]$ is assigned to each edge $e \in E$. Formally, we may identify the outcome Y_t with the vector $\boldsymbol{\ell}_t \in [0, 1]^{|E|}$ of losses whose jth component is $\ell_{e_j,t}$. The loss of a path $\mathbf{i}$ at time t equals the sum of the losses of the edges on the path, that is,

$$\ell(\mathbf{i}, Y_t) = \mathbf{i} \cdot \boldsymbol{\ell}_t.$$

Just as before, the forecaster is allowed to randomize and to choose $\mathbf{I}_t$ according to the distribution $\mathbf{p}_t$ over all paths from u to v. We study the "expected" regret

$$\sum_{t=1}^{n} \overline{\ell}(\mathbf{p}_t, Y_t) - \min_{\mathbf{i}} \sum_{t=1}^{n} \ell(\mathbf{i}, Y_t),$$

where the minimum is taken over all paths $\mathbf{i}$ from u to v and $\overline{\ell}(\mathbf{p}_t, Y_t) = \sum_{\mathbf{i}} p_{\mathbf{i},t} \ell(\mathbf{i}, Y_t)$. Note that the loss $\ell(\mathbf{i}, Y_t)$ is not bounded by 1 but rather by the length K of the longest path from u to v. Thus, by the Hoeffding–Azuma inequality, with probability at least $1 - \delta$, the difference between the actual cumulative loss $\sum_{t=1}^{n} \ell(\mathbf{I}_t, Y_t)$ and $\sum_{t=1}^{n} \overline{\ell}(\mathbf{p}_t, Y_t)$ is bounded by $K\sqrt{(n/2)\ln(1/\delta)}$.

We describe two different computationally efficient forecasters with similar performance guarantees.

Follow the Perturbed Leader

The first solution is based on selecting, at each time t, the path that minimizes the "perturbed" cumulative loss up to time $t - 1$. This is the idea of the forecaster analyzed in Section 4.3 that may be adapted to the shortest path problem easily as follows.

Let $\mathbf{Z}_1, \ldots, \mathbf{Z}_n$ be independent, identically distributed random vectors taking values in $\mathbb{R}^{|E|}$. The follow-the-perturbed-leader forecaster chooses the path

$$\mathbf{I}_t = \operatorname*{argmin}_{\mathbf{i}} \mathbf{i} \cdot \left(\sum_{s=1}^{t-1} \boldsymbol{\ell}_s + \mathbf{Z}_t \right).$$

Thus, at time t, the cumulative loss of each edge e_j is "perturbed" by the random quantity $Z_{j,t}$ and $\mathbf{I}_t$ is the path that minimizes the perturbed cumulative loss over all paths. Since efficient algorithms exist for finding the shortest path in a directed acyclic graph (for acyclic graphs linear-time algorithms are known), the forecaster may be computed efficiently. The following theorem bounds the regret of this simple algorithm when the perturbation vectors $\mathbf{Z}_t$ are uniformly distributed. An improved performance bound may be obtained by using two-sided exponential distribution instead (just as in Corollary 4.5). The straightforward details are left as an exercise (see Exercises 5.11 and 5.12).

Theorem 5.6. *Consider the follow-the-perturbed-leader forecaster for the shortest path problem such that the vectors* $\mathbf{Z}_t$ *are distributed uniformly in* $[0, \Delta]^{|E|}$. *Then, with probability at least* $1 - \delta$,

$$\sum_{t=1}^{n} \ell(\mathbf{I}_t, Y_t) - \min_{\mathbf{i}} \sum_{t=1}^{n} \ell(\mathbf{i}, Y_t) \le K\Delta + \frac{nK|E|}{\Delta} + K\sqrt{\frac{n}{2} \ln \frac{1}{\delta}},$$

where K *is the length of the longest path from* u *to* v. *With the choice* $\Delta = \sqrt{n|E|}$ *the upper bound becomes* $2K\sqrt{n|E|} + K\sqrt{(n/2)\ln(1/\delta)}$.

Proof. The proof mimics the arguments of Theorem 4.2 and Corollary 4.4: by Lemma 4.1, it suffices to consider an oblivious opponent and to show that in that case the expected regret satisfies

$$\mathbb{E}\sum_{t=1}^{n} \ell(\mathbf{I}_t, y_t) - \min_{\mathbf{i}} \sum_{t=1}^{n} \ell(\mathbf{i}, y_t) \le K\Delta + \frac{nK|E|}{\Delta}.$$

As in the proof of Theorem 4.2, we define the fictitious forecaster

$$\widehat{\mathbf{I}}_t = \arg\min_{\mathbf{i}} \mathbf{i} \cdot \left(\sum_{s=1}^{t} \boldsymbol{\ell}_s + \mathbf{Z}_t\right),$$

which differs from $\mathbf{I}_t$ in that the cumulative loss is now calculated up to time t (rather than $t - 1$). Of course, $\widehat{\mathbf{I}}_t$ cannot be calculated by the forecaster because he uses information not available at time t: it is defined merely for the purpose of the proof. Exactly as in Theorem 4.2, one has, for the expected cumulative loss of the fictitious forecaster,

$$\mathbb{E}\sum_{t=1}^{n} \ell(\widehat{\mathbf{I}}_t, y_t) \le \min_{\mathbf{i}} \sum_{t=1}^{n} \ell(\mathbf{i}, y_t) + \mathbb{E}\max_{\mathbf{i}}(\mathbf{i} \cdot \mathbf{Z}_n) + \mathbb{E}\max_{\mathbf{i}}(-\mathbf{i} \cdot \mathbf{Z}_1).$$

Since the components of $\mathbf{Z}_1$ are assumed to be nonnegative, the last term on the right-hand side may be dropped. On the other hand,

$$\mathbb{E}\max_{\mathbf{i}}(\mathbf{i} \cdot \mathbf{Z}_n) \le \max_{\mathbf{i}} \|\mathbf{i}\|_1 \, \mathbb{E}\|\mathbf{Z}_n\|_\infty \le K\Delta,$$

where $K = \max_{\mathbf{i}} \|\mathbf{i}\|_1$ is the length of the longest path from u to v. It remains to compare the cumulative loss of $\mathbf{I}_t$ with that of $\widehat{\mathbf{I}}_t$. Once again, this may be done just as in Theorem 4.2. Define, for any $\mathbf{z} \in \mathbb{R}^{|E|}$, the optimal path

$$\mathbf{i}^*(\mathbf{z}) = \arg\min_{\mathbf{i}} \mathbf{i} \cdot \mathbf{z}$$

and the function

$$F_t(\mathbf{z}) = \mathbf{i}^*\left(\sum_{s=1}^{t-1} \boldsymbol{\ell}_s + \mathbf{z}\right) \cdot \boldsymbol{\ell}_t.$$

Denoting the density function of the random vector $\mathbf{Z}_t$ by $f(\mathbf{z})$, we clearly have

$$\mathbb{E}\,\ell(\mathbf{I}_t, y_t) = \int_{\mathbf{R}^{|E|}} F_t(\mathbf{z}) f(\mathbf{z})\,d\mathbf{z} \quad \text{and} \quad \mathbb{E}\,\ell(\widehat{\mathbf{I}}_t, y_t) = \int_{\mathbf{R}^{|E|}} F_t(\mathbf{z}) f(\mathbf{z} - \boldsymbol{\ell}_t)\,d\mathbf{z}.$$

Therefore, for each $t = 1, \ldots, n$,

$$\mathbb{E}\,\ell(\mathbf{I}_t, y_t) - \mathbb{E}\,\ell(\widehat{\mathbf{I}}_t, y_t)$$

$$= \boldsymbol{\ell}_t \cdot \int_{\mathbf{R}^{|E|}} \mathbf{i}^* \left(\sum_{s=1}^{t-1} \boldsymbol{\ell}_s + \mathbf{z} \right) \big(f(\mathbf{z}) - f(\mathbf{z} - \boldsymbol{\ell}_t) \big)\,d\mathbf{z}$$

$$\leq \boldsymbol{\ell}_t \cdot \int_{\{\mathbf{z}:\, f(\mathbf{z}) > f(\mathbf{z} - \boldsymbol{\ell}_t)\}} \mathbf{i}^* \left(\sum_{s=1}^{t-1} \boldsymbol{\ell}_s + \mathbf{z} \right) f(\mathbf{z})\,d\mathbf{z}$$

$$\leq \|\boldsymbol{\ell}_t\|_\infty \left\| \int_{\{\mathbf{z}:\, f(\mathbf{z}) > f(\mathbf{z} - \boldsymbol{\ell}_t)\}} \mathbf{i}^* \left(\sum_{s=1}^{t-1} \boldsymbol{\ell}_s + \mathbf{z} \right) f(\mathbf{z})\,d\mathbf{z} \right\|_1$$

$$\leq K \int_{\{\mathbf{z}:\, f(\mathbf{z}) > f(\mathbf{z} - \boldsymbol{\ell}_t)\}} f(\mathbf{z})\,d\mathbf{z}$$

(since $\|\boldsymbol{\ell}_t\|_\infty \leq 1$ and all paths have length at most K)

$$\leq \frac{K|E|}{\Delta},$$

where the last inequality follows from the argument in Corollary 4.4. ∎

Theorem 5.6 asserts that the follow-the-perturbed-leader forecaster used with uniformly distributed perturbations has a cumulative regret of the order of $K\sqrt{n|E|}$. By using two-sided exponentially distributed perturbation, an alternative bound of the order of $\sqrt{L^*|E|K\ln|E|} \leq K\sqrt{n|E|\ln|E|}$ may be achieved (Exercise 5.11) or even $\sqrt{L^*|E|\ln M} \leq \sqrt{nK|E|\ln M}$, where M is the number of all paths in the graph leading from u to v (Exercise 5.12). Clearly, $M \leq \binom{|E|}{K}$, but in concrete cases (e.g., in the two examples of Figure 5.3) M may be significantly smaller than this upper bound. These bounds can be improved to $K\sqrt{n\ln M}$ by a fundamentally different solution, which we describe next.

Efficient Computation of the Weighted Average Forecaster

A conceptually different way of approaching the shortest path problem is to consider each path as an action (expert) and look for an efficient algorithm that computes the exponentially weighted average predictor over the set of these experts.

The exponentially weighted average forecaster, calculated over the set of experts given by all paths from u to v, selects, at time t, a path $\mathbf{I}_t$ randomly, according to the probability distribution

$$\mathbb{P}_t[\mathbf{I}_t = \mathbf{i}] = p_{\mathbf{i},t} = \frac{e^{-\eta \sum_{s=1}^{t-1} \mathbf{i}\cdot\boldsymbol{\ell}_s}}{\sum_{\mathbf{i}'} e^{-\eta \sum_{s=1}^{t-1} \mathbf{i}'\cdot\boldsymbol{\ell}_s}},$$

where $\eta > 0$ is a parameter of the forecaster and $\mathbb{P}_t$ denotes the conditional probability given the past actions.

In the remaining part of this section we show that it is possible to draw the random path $\mathbf{I}_t$ in an efficiently computable way. The main idea is that we select the edges of the path one by one, according to the appropriate conditional distributions generated by the distribution over the set of paths given above.

With an abuse of notation, we write $e \in \mathbf{i}$ if the edge $e \in E$ belongs to the path represented by the binary vector $\mathbf{i}$. Then observe that for any $t = 1, \ldots, n$ and path $\mathbf{i}$,

$$\mathbf{i} \cdot \boldsymbol{\ell}_t = \sum_{e \in \mathbf{i}} \ell_{e,t},$$

and therefore the cumulative loss of each expert $\mathbf{i}$ takes the additive form

$$\sum_{s=1}^{t} \mathbf{i} \cdot \boldsymbol{\ell}_s = \sum_{e \in \mathbf{i}} L_{e,t},$$

where $L_{e,t} = \sum_{s=1}^{t} \ell_{e,s}$ is the loss accumulated by edge e during the first t rounds of the game.

For any vertex $w \in V$, let $\mathcal{P}_w$ denote the set of paths from w to v. To each vertex w and $t = 1, \ldots, n$, we assign the value

$$G_t(w) = \sum_{\mathbf{i} \in \mathcal{P}_w} e^{-\eta \sum_{e \in \mathbf{i}} L_{e,t}}.$$

First observe that the function $G_t(w)$ may be computed efficiently. To this end, assume that the vertices $v_1, \ldots, v_{|V|}$ of the graph are labeled such that $u = v_1, v = v_{|V|}$, and if $i < j$, then there is no edge from z_j to z_i. (Note that such a labeling can be found in time $O(|E|)$.) Then $G_t(v) = 1$, and once $G_t(v_i)$ has been calculated for all v_i with $i = |V|, |V| - 1|, \ldots, j + 1$, then $G_t(v_j)$ is obtained, recursively, by

$$G_t(v_j) = \sum_{w : (v_j, w) \in E} G_t(w) e^{-\eta L_{(v_j, w), t}}.$$

Thus, at time t, all values of $G_t(w)$ may be calculated in time $O(|E|)$.

It remains to see how the values $G_{t-1}(w)$ may be used to generate a random path $\mathbf{I}_t$ according to the distribution prescribed by the exponentially weighted average forecaster. We may draw the path $\mathbf{I}_t$ by drawing its edges successively. Denote the kth vertex along a path $\mathbf{i} \in \mathcal{P}_u$ by $v_{\mathbf{i},k}$ for $k = 0, 1, \ldots, K_{\mathbf{i}}$, where $v_{\mathbf{i},0} = u$, $v_{\mathbf{i},K_{\mathbf{i}}} = v$, and $K_{\mathbf{i}} = \|\mathbf{i}\|_1$ denotes the length of the path $\mathbf{i}$. For each path $\mathbf{i}$, we may write

$$p_{\mathbf{i},t} = \mathbb{P}_t[\mathbf{I}_t = \mathbf{i}] = \prod_{k=1}^{K_{\mathbf{i}}} \mathbb{P}_t\big[v_{\mathbf{I}_t,k} = v_{\mathbf{i},k} \mid v_{\mathbf{I}_t,k-1} = v_{\mathbf{i},k-1}, \ldots, v_{\mathbf{I}_t,0} = v_{\mathbf{i},0}\big].$$

To generate a random path $\mathbf{I}_t$ with this distribution, it suffices to generate the vertices $v_{\mathbf{I}_t,k}$ successively for $k = 1, 2, \ldots$ such that the product of the conditional probabilities is just $p_{\mathbf{i},t}$.

Next we show that, for any k, the probability that the kth vertex in the path $\mathbf{I}_t$ is $v_{\mathbf{i},k}$, given that the previous vertices in the graph are $v_{\mathbf{i},0}, \ldots, v_{\mathbf{i},k-1}$, is

$$\mathbb{P}_t\big[v_{\mathbf{I}_t,k} = v_{\mathbf{i},k} \mid v_{\mathbf{I}_t,k-1} = v_{\mathbf{i},k-1}, \ldots, v_{\mathbf{I}_t,0} = v_{\mathbf{i},0}\big]$$

$$= \begin{cases} \dfrac{G_{t-1}(v_{\mathbf{i},k})}{G_{t-1}(v_{\mathbf{i},k-1})} & \text{if } (v_{\mathbf{i},k-1}, v_{\mathbf{i},k}) \in E \\ 0 & \text{otherwise.} \end{cases}$$

To see this, just observe that if $(v_{i,k-1}, v_{i,k}) \in E$,

$$\mathbb{P}_t\big[v_{I_t,k} = v_{i,k} \,\big|\, v_{I_t,k-1} = v_{i,k-1}, \ldots, v_{I_t,0} = v_{i,0}\big]$$

$$= \frac{\sum_{j \in \mathcal{P}_{v_{i,k}}} e^{-\eta \sum_{e \in j} L_{e,t-1}}}{\sum_{j' \in \mathcal{P}_{v_{i,k-1}}} e^{-\eta \sum_{e \in j'} L_{e,t-1}}} = \frac{G_{t-1}(v_{i,k})}{G_{t-1}(v_{i,k-1})}$$

as desired. Summarizing, we have the following.

Theorem 5.7. *The algorithm described above computes the exponentially weighted average forecaster over all paths between vertices u and v in a directed acyclic graph such that, at each time instance, the algorithm requires $O(|E|)$ operations. The regret is bounded, with probability at least $1 - \delta$, by*

$$\sum_{t=1}^{n} \ell(\mathbf{I}_t, Y_t) - \min_{\mathbf{i}} \sum_{t=1}^{n} \ell(\mathbf{i}, Y_t) \le K \left(\frac{\ln M}{\eta} + \frac{n\eta}{8} + \sqrt{\frac{n}{2} \ln \frac{1}{\delta}} \right),$$

where M is the total number of paths from u to v in the graph and K is the length of the longest path.

5.5 Tracking the Best of Many Actions

The purpose of this section is to develop efficient algorithms to track the best action in the case when the class of "base" experts is already very large but has some structure. Thus, in a sense, we consider a combination of the problem of tracking the best action described in Section 5.2 with predicting as well as the best in a large class of experts with a certain structure, such as the examples described in Sections 5.3 and 5.4.

Our approach is based on a reformulation of the fixed share tracking algorithm that allows one to apply it, in a computationally efficient way, over some classes of large and structured experts. We will illustrate the method on the problem of "tracking the shortest path."

The main step to this direction is an alternative expression of the weights of the fixed share forecaster.

Lemma 5.4. *Consider the fixed share forecaster of Section 5.2. For any $t = 2, \ldots, n$, the probability $p_{i,t}$ and the corresponding normalization factor W_{t-1} can be obtained as*

$$p_{i,t} = \frac{(1-\alpha)^{t-1}}{N W_{t-1}} e^{-\eta \sum_{s=1}^{t-1} \ell(i, Y_s)}$$

$$+ \frac{\alpha}{N W_{t-1}} \sum_{t'=2}^{t-1} (1-\alpha)^{t-t'} W_{t'-1} e^{-\eta \sum_{s=t'}^{t-1} \ell(i, Y_s)} + \frac{\alpha}{N}$$

$$W_{t-1} = \frac{\alpha}{N} \sum_{t'=2}^{t-1} (1-\alpha)^{t-1-t'} W_{t'-1} Z_{t',t-1} + \frac{(1-\alpha)^{t-2}}{N} Z_{1,t-1},$$

where $Z_{t',t-1} = \sum_{i=1}^{N} e^{-\eta \sum_{s=t'}^{t-1} \ell(i, Y_s)}$ is the sum of the (unnormalized) weights assigned to the experts by the exponentially weighted average forecaster method based on the partial past outcome sequence $(Y_{t'}, \ldots, Y_{t-1})$.

Proof. The expressions in the lemma follow directly from the recursive definition of the weights $w_{i,t-1}$. First we show that, for $t = 1, \ldots, n$,

$$
v_{i,t} = \frac{\alpha}{N} \sum_{t'=2}^{t} (1-\alpha)^{t-t'} W_{t'-1} e^{-\eta \sum_{s=t'}^{t} \ell(i,Y_s)}
$$
$$
+ \frac{(1-\alpha)^{t-1}}{N} e^{-\eta \sum_{s=1}^{t} \ell(i,Y_s)} \tag{5.1}
$$

and

$$
w_{i,t} = \frac{\alpha}{N} W_t + \frac{\alpha}{N} \sum_{t'=2}^{t} (1-\alpha)^{t+1-t'} W_{t'-1} e^{-\eta \sum_{s=t'}^{t} \ell(i,Y_s)}
$$
$$
+ \frac{(1-\alpha)^{t}}{N} e^{-\eta \sum_{s=1}^{t} \ell(i,Y_s)}. \tag{5.2}
$$

Clearly, for a given t, (5.1) implies (5.2) by the definition of the fixed share forecaster. Since $w_{i,0} = 1/N$ for every expert i, (5.1) and (5.2) hold for $t = 1$ and $t = 2$ (for $t = 1$ the summations are 0 in both equations). Now assume that they hold for some $t \geq 2$. We show that then (5.1) holds for $t + 1$. By definition,

$$
v_{i,t+1} = w_{i,t} e^{-\eta \ell(i,Y_{t+1})}
$$
$$
= \frac{\alpha}{N} W_t e^{-\eta \ell(i,Y_{t+1})} + \frac{\alpha}{N} \sum_{t'=2}^{t} (1-\alpha)^{t+1-t'} W_{t'-1} e^{-\eta \sum_{s=t'}^{t+1} \ell(i,Y_s)}
$$
$$
+ \frac{(1-\alpha)^{t}}{N} e^{-\eta \sum_{s=1}^{t+1} \ell(i,Y_s)}
$$
$$
= \frac{\alpha}{N} \sum_{t'=2}^{t+1} (1-\alpha)^{t+1-t'} W_{t'-1} e^{-\eta \sum_{s=t'}^{t+1} \ell(i,Y_s)} + \frac{(1-\alpha)^{t}}{N} e^{-\eta \sum_{s=1}^{t+1} \ell(i,Y_s)}
$$

and therefore (5.1) and (5.2) hold for all $t = 1, \ldots, n$. Now the expression for $p_{i,t}$ follows from (5.2) by normalization for $t = 2, \ldots, n+1$. Finally, the recursive formula for W_{t-1} can easily be proved from (5.1). Indeed, recalling that $\sum_i w_{i,t} = \sum_i v_{i,t}$, we have that for any $t = 2, \ldots, n$,

$$
W_{t-1} = \sum_{i=1}^{N} w_{i,t-1}
$$
$$
= \sum_{i=1}^{N} \left(\frac{\alpha}{N} \sum_{t'=2}^{t-1} (1-\alpha)^{t-1-t'} W_{t'-1} e^{-\eta \sum_{s=t'}^{t-1} \ell(i,Y_s)} + \frac{(1-\alpha)^{t-2}}{N} e^{-\eta \sum_{s=1}^{t-1} \ell(i,Y_s)} \right)
$$
$$
= \frac{\alpha}{N} \sum_{t'=2}^{t-1} (1-\alpha)^{t-1-t'} W_{t'-1} \sum_{i=1}^{N} e^{-\eta \sum_{s=t'}^{t-1} \ell(i,Y_s)} + \frac{(1-\alpha)^{t-2}}{N} \sum_{i=1}^{N} e^{-\eta \sum_{s=1}^{t-1} \ell(i,Y_s)}
$$
$$
= \frac{\alpha}{N} \sum_{t'=2}^{t-1} (1-\alpha)^{t-1-t'} W_{t'-1} Z_{t',t-1} + \frac{(1-\alpha)^{t-2}}{N} Z_{1,t-1}. \quad \blacksquare
$$

Examining the formula for $p_{i,t} = \mathbb{P}_t[I_t = i]$ given by Lemma 5.4, one may realize that I_t may be drawn by the following two-step procedure.

THE ALTERNATIVE FIXED SHARE FORECASTER

Parameters: Real numbers $\eta > 0$ and $0 \leq \alpha \leq 1$.

Initialization: For $t = 1$, choose I_1 uniformly from the set $\{1, \ldots, N\}$.

For each round $t = 2, 3 \ldots$

(1) draw τ_t randomly according to the distribution

$$\mathbb{P}_t[\tau_t = t'] = \begin{cases} \frac{(1-\alpha)^{t-1} Z_{1,t-1}}{N W_{t-1}} & \text{for } t' = 1 \\ \frac{\alpha(1-\alpha)^{t-t'} W_{t'-1} Z_{t',t-1}}{N W_{t-1}} & \text{for } t' = 2, \ldots, t, \end{cases}$$

where we define $Z_{t,t-1} = N$;

(2) given $\tau_t = t'$, choose I_t randomly according to the probabilities

$$\mathbb{P}_t[I_t = i | \tau_t = t'] = \begin{cases} \frac{e^{-\eta \sum_{s=t'}^{t-1} \ell(i,Y_s)}}{Z_{t',t-1}} & \text{for } t' = 1, \ldots, t-1 \\ 1/N & \text{for } t' = t. \end{cases}$$

Indeed, Lemma 5.4 immediately implies that

$$p_{i,t} = \sum_{t'=1}^{t} \mathbb{P}_t[I_t = i \mid \tau = t'] \mathbb{P}_t[\tau = t']$$

and therefore the alternative fixed share forecaster provides an equivalent implementation of the fixed share forecaster.

Theorem 5.8. *The fixed share forecaster and the alternative fixed share forecaster are equivalent in the sense that the generated forecasters have the same distribution. More precisely, the sequence $(I_1, \ldots, I_n)$ generated by the alternative fixed share forecaster satisfies*

$$\mathbb{P}_t[I_t = i] = p_{i,t}$$

for all t and i, where $p_{i,t}$ is the probability of drawing action i at time t computed by the fixed share forecaster.

Observe that once the value $\tau = t'$ is determined, the conditional probability of $I_t = i$ is equivalent to the weight assigned to expert i by the exponentially weighted average forecaster computed for the last $t - t'$ outcomes of the sequence, that is, for $(Y_{t'}, \ldots, Y_{t-1})$. Therefore, for $t \geq 2$, the randomized prediction I_t of the fixed share forecaster can be determined in two steps. First we choose a random time τ_t, which specifies how many of the most recent outcomes we use for the prediction. Then we choose I_t according to the exponentially weighted average forecaster based only on these outcomes.

It is not immediately obvious why the alternative implementation of the fixed share forecaster is more efficient. However, in many cases the probabilities $\mathbb{P}_t[I_t = i \mid \tau_t = t']$ and normalization factors $Z_{t',t-1}$ may be computed efficiently, and in all those cases, since W_{t-1} can be obtained via the recursion formula of Lemma 5.4, the alternative fixed share forecaster becomes feasible. Theorem 5.8 offers a general tool for obtaining such algorithms.

Rather than isolating a single theorem that summarizes conditions under which such an efficient computation is possible, we illustrate the use of this algorithm on the problem of "tracking the shortest path," that is, when the base experts are defined by paths in a directed acyclic graph between two fixed vertices. Thus, we are interested in an efficient forecaster that is able to choose a path at each time instant such that the cumulative loss is not much larger than the best forecaster that is allowed to switch paths m times. In other words, the class of (base) experts is the one defined in Section 5.4, and the goal is to track the best such expert. Because the number of paths is typically exponentially large in the number of edges of the graph, a direct implementation of the fixed share forecaster is infeasible. However, the alternative fixed share forecaster may be combined with the efficient implementation of the exponentially weighted average forecaster for the shortest path problem (see Section 5.4) to obtain a computationally efficient way of tracking the shortest path. In particular, we obtain the following result. Its straightforward, though somewhat technical, proof is left as an exercise (see Exercise 5.13).

Theorem 5.9. *Consider the problem of tracking the shortest path between two fixed vertices in a directed acyclic graph described above. The alternative fixed share algorithm can be implemented such that, at time t, computing the prediction I_t requires time $O(tK|E| + t^2)$. The expected tracking regret of the algorithm satisfies*

$$\overline{R}(\mathbf{i}_1, \ldots, \mathbf{i}_n) \leq K \sqrt{\frac{n}{2} \left((m+1) \ln M + m \ln \frac{e(n-1)}{m} \right)}$$

for all sequences of paths $\mathbf{i}_1, \ldots, \mathbf{i}_n$ such that size $(\mathbf{i}_1, \ldots, \mathbf{i}_n) \leq m$, *where M is the number of all paths in the graph between vertices u and v and K is the length of the longest path.*

Note that we extended, in the obvious way, the definition of size $(\cdot)$ to sequences $(\mathbf{i}_1, \ldots, \mathbf{i}_n)$.

5.6   Bibliographic Remarks

The notion of tracking regret, the fixed share forecaster, and the variable share forecaster were introduced by Herbster and Warmuth [159]. The tracking regret bounds stated in Theorem 5.2, Corollary 5.1, and Theorem 5.3 were originally proven in [159]. Vovk [299] has shown that the fixed and variable share forecasters correspond to efficient implementations of the exponentially weighted average forecaster run over the set of compound actions with a specific choice of the initial weights. Our proofs follow Vovk's analysis; The work [299] also provides an elegant solution to the problem of tuning the parameter α optimally (see Exercise 5.6).

Minimization of tracking regret is similar to the sequential allocation problems studied within the competitive analysis model (see Borodin and El-Yaniv [36]). Indeed, Blum and Burch [32] use tracking regret and the exponentially weighted average forecaster to solve a certain class of sequential allocation problems.

Bousquet and Warmuth [40] consider the tracking regret measured against all compound actions with at most m switches and including at most k distinct actions (out of the N available actions). They prove that a variant of the fixed share forecaster achieves, with high probability, the bound of Theorem 5.2 in which the factor $m \ln N$ is replaced by

$k \ln N + m \ln k$ (see Exercise 5.1). We also refer to Auer and Warmuth [15] and Herbster and Warmuth [160] for various extensions and powerful variants of the problem.

Tree-based experts are natural evolutions of tree sources, a probabilistic model intensively studied in information theory. Lemma 5.2 is due to Willems, Shtarkov, and Tjalkens [311], who were the first to show how to efficiently compute averages over all trees of bounded depth. Theorem 5.4 was proven by Helmbold and Schapire [156]. An alternative efficient forecaster for tree experts, also based on dynamic programming, is proposed and analyzed by Takimoto, Maruoka, and Vovk [283]. Freund Schapire, Singer, and Warmuth [115] propose a more general expert framework in which experts may occasionally abstain from predicting (see also Section 4.8). Their algorithm can be efficiently applied to tree experts, even though the resulting bound apparently has a quadratic (rather than linear) dependence on the number of leaves of the tree. Other closely related references include Pereira and Singer [233] and Takimoto and Warmuth [285], which consider planar decision graphs. The dynamic programming implementations of the forecasters for tree experts and for the shortest path problem, both involving computations of sums of products over the nodes of a directed acyclic graph, are special cases of the general sum–product algorithm of Kschischang, Frey, and Loeliger [187].

Kalai and Vempala [174] were the first to promote the use of follow-the-perturbed-leader type forecasters for efficiently computable prediction, described in Section 5.4. Their framework is more general, and the shortest path problem discussed here is just an example of a family of online optimization problems. The required property is that the loss has an additive form. Awerbuch and Kleinberg [19] and McMahan and Blum [211] extend the follow-the-perturbed-leader forecaster to the bandit setting. For a general framework of linear-time algorithms to find the shortest path in a directed acyclic graph, we refer to [219]. Takimoto and Warmuth [286] consider a family of algorithms based on the efficient computation of weighted average predictors for the shortest path problem. György, Linder, and Lugosi [137, 138] apply similar techniques to the ones described for the shortest path problem in online lossy data compression, where the experts correspond to scalar quantizers. The material in Section 5.5 is based on György, Linder, and Lugosi [139].

A further example of efficient forecasters for exponentially many experts is provided by Maass and Warmuth [207]. Their technique is used to learn the class of indicator functions of axis-parallel boxes when all "instances" $\mathbf{x}_t$ (i.e., side information elements) belong to the d-dimensional grid $\{1, \ldots, N\}^d$. Note that the complement of any such box is represented as the union of $2d$ axis-parallel halfspaces. This union can be learned by the Winnow algorithm (see Section 12.2) by mapping each original instance $\mathbf{x}_t$ to a transformed boolean instance whose components are the indicator functions of all $2Nd$ axis-parallel halfspaces in the grid. Maass an Warmuth show that Winnow can be run over the transformed instances in time polynomial in d and $\log N$, thus achieving an exponential speedup in N. In addition, they show that the resulting mistake bound is essentially the best possible, even if computational issues are disregarded.

5.7 Exercises

5.1 *(Tracking a subset of actions)* Consider the problem of tracking a small unknown subset of k actions chosen from the set of all N actions. That is, we want to bound the tracking regret

$$\sum_{t=1}^{n} \overline{\ell}(\mathbf{p}_t, Y_t) - \sum_{t=1}^{n} \ell(i_t, Y_t),$$

where size $(i_1, \ldots, i_n) \leq m$ and the compound action $(i_1, \ldots, i_n)$ contains at most k distinct actions, k being typically much smaller than m and N. Prove that by running the fixed share forecaster over a set of at most N^k meta-actions, and by tuning the parameter α in a suitable way, a tracking regret bound of order

$$\sqrt{n(k \ln N + m \ln k + m \ln n)}$$

is achieved (Bousquet and Warmuth [40].)

5.2 Prove Corollary 5.2.

5.3 (*Lower bound for tracking regret*) Show that there exists a loss function such that for any forecaster there exists a sequence of outcomes on which the tracking regret

$$\sup_{(i_1, \ldots, i_n) \,:\, \text{size}\,(i_1, \ldots, i_n) = m} \overline{R}(i_1, \ldots, i_n)$$

is lower bounded by a quantity of the order of $\sqrt{nm \ln N}$.

5.4 Prove that a slightly weaker version of the tracking regret bound established by Theorem 5.3 holds when $\ell \in [0, 1]$. *Hint:* Fix an arbitrary compound action $(i_1, \ldots, i_n)$ with size$(i_1, \ldots, i_n) = m$ and cumulative loss L^*. Prove a lower bound on the sum of the weights $w_0'(j_1, \ldots, j_n)$ of all compound actions $(j_1, \ldots, j_n)$ with cumulative loss bounded by $L^* + 2m$ (Herbster and Warmuth [159], Vovk [299]).

5.5 (*Tracking experts that switch very often*) In Section 5.2 we focused on tracking compound actions that can switch no more than m times, where $m \ll n$. This exercise shows that it is possible to track the best compound action that switches almost all times. Consider the problem of tracking the best action when $N = 2$. Construct a computationally efficient forecaster such that, for all action sequences $i_1, \ldots, i_n$ such that size $(i_1, \ldots, i_n) \geq n - m - 1$, the tracking regret is bounded by

$$\overline{R}(i_1, \ldots, i_n) \leq \sqrt{\frac{n}{2}\left((m+1)\ln 2 + m \ln \frac{e(n-1)}{m}\right)}.$$

Hint: Use the fixed share forecaster with appropriately chosen parameters.

5.6 (*Exponential forecaster with average weights*) In the problem of tracking the best expert, consider the initial assignment of weights where each compound action $(i_1, \ldots, i_n)$, with $m = $ size $(i_1, \ldots, i_n)$, gets a weight

$$w_{0,\alpha}'(i_1, \ldots, i_n) = \frac{1}{N}\left(\frac{\alpha}{N}\right)^m \left(\frac{\alpha}{N} + (1-\alpha)\right)^{n-m-1} \varepsilon \alpha^{\varepsilon - 1}$$

for each value of $\alpha \in (0, 1)$, where $\varepsilon > 0$. Using known facts on the Beta distribution (see Section A.1.9 in the Appendix) and the lower bound $B(a, b) \geq \Gamma(a)\left(b + (a-1)_+\right)^{-a}$ for all $a, b > 0$, prove a bound on the tracking regret $\overline{R}(i_1, \ldots, i_n)$ for the exponentially weighted average forecaster that predicts at time t based on the average weights

$$w_{t-1}'(i_1, \ldots, i_n) = \int_0^1 w_{t-1,\alpha}'(i_1, \ldots, i_n)\, d\alpha$$

(Vovk [299]).

5.7 (*Fixed share with automatic tuning*) Obtain an efficient implementation of the exponential forecaster introduced in Exercise 5.6 by a suitable modification of the fixed share forecaster. *Hint:* Each action i gets an initial weight $w_{i,0}(\alpha) = (\varepsilon \alpha^{\varepsilon - 1})/N$. At time t, predict with

$$p_{i,t} = \frac{w_{i,t-1}}{\sum_{j=1}^N w_{j,t-1}} \qquad i = 1, \ldots, N,$$

where

$$w_{i,t-1} = \int_0^1 w_{i,t-1}(\alpha)\, d\alpha \qquad \text{for } i = 1, \ldots, N.$$

Use the recursive representations of weights given in Lemma 5.4 and properties of the Beta distribution to show that $w_{i,t}$ can be updated in time $O(Nt)$ (Vovk [299].)

5.8 (*Arbitrary-depth tree experts*) Prove an oracle inequality of the form

$$\sum_{t=1}^n \overline{\ell}(\mathbf{p}_t, Y_t) \le \min_E \left(\sum_{t=1}^n \ell(i_E(\mathbf{x}_t), Y_t) + \frac{c}{\eta}\big(\|E\| + |\text{leaves}(E)|\ln N\big) \right) + \frac{\eta}{8}n,$$

Which holds for the randomized exponentially weighted forecaster run over the (infinite) set of all finite tree experts. Here c is a positive constant. *Hint:* Use the fact that the number of binary trees with $2k + 1$ nodes is

$$a_k = \frac{1}{k}\binom{2k}{k-1} \qquad \text{for } k = 1, 2, \ldots$$

(closely related to the Catalan numbers) and that the series $a_1^{-1} + a_2^{-1} + \cdots$ is convergent. Ignore the computability issues involved in storing and updating an infinite number of weights.

5.9 (*Continued*) Prove an oracle inequality of the same form as the one stated in Exercise 5.8 when the randomized exponentially weighted forecaster is only allowed to perform a finite amount of computation to select an action. *Hint:* Exploit the exponentially decreasing initial weights to show that, at time t, the probability of picking a tree expert E whose size $\|E\|$ is larger than some function of t is so small that can be safely ignored irrespective of the performance of the expert.

5.10 Show that the number of tree experts corresponding to the set of all ordered binary trees of depth at most D is N^{2^D}. Use this to derive a regret bound for the ordinary exponentially weighted average forecaster over this class of experts. Compare the bound with Theorem 5.4.

5.11 (*Exponential perturbation*) Consider the follow-the-perturbed-leader forecaster for the shortest path problem. Assume that the distribution of $\mathbf{Z}_t$ is such that it has independent components, all distributed according to the two-sided exponential distribution with parameter $\eta > 0$ so that the joint density of $\mathbf{Z}_t$ is $f(\mathbf{z}) = (\eta/2)^{|E|}e^{-\eta\|\mathbf{z}\|_1}$. Show that with a proper tuning of η, the regret of the forecaster satisfies, with probability at least $1 - \delta$,

$$\sum_{t=1}^n \ell(\mathbf{I}_t, y_t) - L^* \le c\left(\sqrt{L^*K|E|\ln|E|} + K|E|\ln|E|\right) + K\sqrt{\frac{n}{2}\ln\frac{1}{\delta}},$$

where $L^* = \min_i \sum_{t=1}^n \ell(\mathbf{i}, y_t) \le Kn$ and c is a constant. (Note that L^* may be as large as Kn in which case this bound is worse than that of Theorem 5.6.) *Hint:* Combine the proofs of Theorem 5.6 and Corollary 4.5.

5.12 (*Continued*) Improve the bound of the previous exercise to

$$\sum_{t=1}^n \ell(\mathbf{I}_t, y_t) - L^* \le c\left(\sqrt{L^*|E|\ln M} + |E|\ln M\right) + K\sqrt{\frac{n}{2}\ln\frac{1}{\delta}},$$

where M is the number of all paths from u to v in the graph. *Hint:* Bound $\mathbb{E}\max_i |\mathbf{i}\cdot\mathbf{Z}_n|$ more carefully. First show that for all $\lambda \in (0, \eta)$ and path $\mathbf{i}$, $\mathbb{E}\, e^{\lambda\mathbf{i}\cdot\mathbf{Z}_n} \le \big(2\eta^2/(\eta-\lambda)^2\big)^K$, and then use the technique of Lemma A.13.

5.13 Prove Theorem 5.9. *Hint:* The efficient implementation of the algorithm is obtained by combining the alternative fixed share forecaster with the techniques used to establish the computationally efficient implementation of the exponentially weighted average in Section 5.4. The regret bound is a direct application of Corollary 5.1 (György, Linder, and Lugosi [139].)

6

Prediction with Limited Feedback

6.1 Introduction

This chapter investigates several variants of the randomized prediction problem. These variants are more difficult than the basic version treated in Chapter 4 in that the forecaster has only limited information about the past outcomes of the sequence to be predicted. In particular, after making a prediction, the true outcome y_t is not necessarily revealed to the forecaster, and a whole range of different problems can be defined depending on the type of information the forecaster has access to.

One of the main messages of this chapter is that Hannan consistency may be achieved under significantly more restricted circumstances, a surprising fact in some of the cases described later. The price paid for not having full information about the outcomes is reflected in the deterioration of the rate at which the per-round regret approaches 0.

In the first variant, investigated in Sections 6.2 and 6.3, only a small fraction of the outcomes is made available to the forecaster. Surprisingly, even in this "label efficient" version of the prediction game, Hannan consistency may be achieved under the only assumption that the number of outcomes revealed after n prediction rounds grows faster than $\log(n) \log \log(n)$.

Section 6.4 formulates prediction problems with limited information in a general framework. In the setup of prediction under *partial monitoring*, the forecaster, instead of his own loss, only receives a feedback signal. The difficulty of the problem depends on the relationship between losses and feedbacks. We determine general conditions under which Hannan consistency can be achieved. The best achievable rates of convergence are determined in Section 6.5, while sufficient and necessary conditions for Hannan consistency are briefly described in Section 6.6.

Sections 6.7, 6.8, and 6.9 are dedicated to the *multi-armed bandit* problem, an important special case of forecasting with partial monitoring where the forecaster only gets to see his own loss $\ell(I_t, y_t)$ but not the loss $\ell(i, y_t)$ of the other actions $i \neq I_t$. In other words, the feedback received by the forecaster corresponds to his own loss. Hannan consistency may be achieved by the results of Section 6.4. The issue of rates of convergence is somewhat more delicate, and to achieve the fastest possible rate, appropriate modifications of the prediction method are necessary. These issues are treated in detail in Sections 6.8 and 6.9.

In another variant of the prediction problem, studied in Section 6.10, the forecaster observes the sequence of outcomes during a period whose length he decides and then selects a single action that cannot be changed for the rest of the game.

Perhaps the main message of this chapter is that randomization is a tool of unexpected power. All forecasters introduced in this chapter use randomization in a clever way to compensate for the reduction in the amount of information that is made available after each prediction. Surprisingly, being able to access independent uniform random variables offers a way of estimating this hidden information. These estimates can then be used to effectively construct randomized forecasters with nontrivial performance guarantees. Accordingly, the main technical tools build on probability theory. More specifically, martingale inequalities are at the heart of the analysis in many cases.

6.2   Label Efficient Prediction

Here we discuss a version of the sequential prediction problem in which obtaining the value of the outcome is costly. More precisely, after choosing a guess at time t, the forecaster decides whether to query the outcome (or "label") Y_t. However, the number $\mu(n)$ of queries that can be issued within a given time horizon n by the forecaster is limited. Formally, the "label efficient" prediction game is defined as follows:

LABEL EFFICIENT PREDICTION

Parameters: Number N of actions, outcome space $\mathcal{Y}$, loss function ℓ, query rate $\mu : \mathbb{N} \to \mathbb{N}$.

For each round $t = 1, 2, \ldots$

(1) the environment chooses the next outcome $Y_t \in \mathcal{Y}$ without revealing it;
(2) the forecaster chooses an action $I_t \in \{1, \ldots, N\}$;
(3) the forecaster incurs loss $\ell(I_t, Y_t)$ and each action i incurs loss $\ell(i, Y_t)$ where none of these values is revealed to the forecaster;
(4) if less than $\mu(t)$ queries have been issued so far, the forecaster may issue a new query to obtain the outcome Y_t; if no query is issued, then Y_t remains unknown.

The goal of the forecaster is to keep the difference

$$\widehat{L}_n - \min_{i=1,\ldots,N} L_{i,n} = \sum_{t=1}^{n} \ell(I_t, Y_t) - \min_{i=1,\ldots,N} \sum_{t=1}^{n} \ell(i, Y_t)$$

as small as possible regardless of the outcome sequence. We start by considering the finite-horizon case in which the forecaster's goal is to control the regret after n predictions, where n is fixed in advance. In this restricted setup we also assume that at most $m = \mu(n)$ queries can be issued, where μ is the query rate function. However, we do not impose any further restriction on the distribution of these m queries in the n time steps; that is, $\mu(t) = m$ for all $t = 1, \ldots, n$. For this setup we define a simple forecaster whose expected regret is bounded by $n\sqrt{2(\ln N)/m}$. Thus, if $m = n$, we recover the order of the optimal bound of Section 4.2.

It is easy to see that in order to achieve a nontrivial performance, a forecaster must use randomization in determining whether a label should be revealed or not. It turns out that a simple biased coin does the job.

LABEL EFFICIENT FORECASTER

Parameters: Real numbers $\eta > 0$ and $0 \le \varepsilon \le 1$.

Initialization: $\mathbf{w}_0 = (1, \ldots, 1)$.

For each round $t = 1, 2, \ldots$

    (1) draw an action I_t from $\{1, \ldots, N\}$ according to the distribution $p_{i,t} = w_{i,t-1}/(w_{1,t-1} + \cdots + w_{N,t-1})$ for $i = 1, \ldots, N$.

    (2) draw a Bernoulli random variable Z_t such that $\mathbb{P}[Z_t = 1] = \varepsilon$;

    (3) if $Z_t = 1$, then obtain Y_t and compute

$$w_{i,t} = w_{i,t-1}\, e^{-\eta\, \ell(i,Y_t)/\varepsilon} \qquad \text{for each } i = 1, \ldots, N;$$

    else, let $\mathbf{w}_t = \mathbf{w}_{t-1}$.

Our label efficient forecaster uses an i.i.d. sequence $Z_1, Z_2, \ldots, Z_n$ of Bernoulli random variables such that $\mathbb{P}[Z_t = 1] = 1 - \mathbb{P}[Z_t = 0] = \varepsilon$ and asks the label Y_t to be revealed whenever $Z_t = 1$. Here $\varepsilon > 0$ is a parameter and typically we take $\varepsilon \approx m/n$ so that the number of solicited labels during n rounds is about m (note that this way the forecaster may ask the value of more than m labels, but we ignore this detail as it can be dealt with by a simple adjustment). Because the forecasting strategy is randomized, we distinguish between oblivious and nonoblivious opponents. In particular, following the protocol introduced in Chapter 4, we use Y_t to denote outcomes generated by a nonoblivious opponent, thus emphasizing that the outcome Y_t may depend on the past actions $I_1, \ldots, I_{t-1}$ of the forecaster, as well as on $Z_1, \ldots, Z_{t-1}$.

The label efficient forecaster is an exponentially weighted average forecaster using the *estimated losses*

$$\widetilde{\ell}(i, Y_t) = \begin{cases} \ell(i, Y_t)/\varepsilon & \text{if } Z_t = 1 \\ 0 & \text{otherwise} \end{cases}$$

instead of the true losses. Note that

$$\mathbb{E}_t \widetilde{\ell}(i, Y_t) = \mathbb{E}\big[\widetilde{\ell}(i, Y_t) \,\big|\, I_1, Z_1, \ldots, I_{t-1}, Z_{t-1}\big] = \ell(i, Y_t),$$

where $I_1, \ldots, I_{t-1}$ is the sequence of previously chosen actions. Therefore, $\widetilde{\ell}(i, Y_t)$ may be considered as an unbiased estimate of the true loss $\ell(i, Y_t)$. The expected performance of this forecaster may be bounded as follows.

Theorem 6.1. *Fix a time horizon n and consider the label efficient forecaster run with parameters $\varepsilon = m/n$ and $\eta = (\sqrt{2m \ln N})/n$. Then the expected number of revealed labels equals m and*

$$\mathbb{E}\,\widehat{L}_n - \min_{i=1,\ldots,N} \mathbb{E}\, L_{i,n} \le n\sqrt{\frac{2 \ln N}{m}}.$$

Before proceeding to the proof we introduce the notation

$$\widetilde{\ell}(\mathbf{p}_t, Y_t) = \sum_{i=1}^{N} p_{i,t}\, \widetilde{\ell}(i, Y_t) \qquad \text{and} \qquad \widetilde{L}_{i,n} = \sum_{t=1}^{n} \widetilde{\ell}(i, Y_t) \quad \text{for } i = 1, \ldots, N.$$

Proof. The basis of the proof is a simple modification of the proof of Theorem 2.2. For $t \geq 0$ let $W_t = w_{1,t} + \cdots + w_{N,t}$. On the one hand,

$$
\begin{aligned}
\ln \frac{W_n}{W_0} &= \ln \left(\sum_{i=1}^{N} e^{-\eta \widetilde{L}_{i,n}} \right) - \ln N \\
&\geq \ln \left(\max_{i=1,\ldots,N} e^{-\eta \widetilde{L}_{i,n}} \right) - \ln N \\
&= -\eta \min_{i=1,\ldots,N} \widetilde{L}_{i,n} - \ln N.
\end{aligned}
$$

On the other hand, for each $t = 1, \ldots, n$,

$$
\begin{aligned}
\ln \frac{W_t}{W_{t-1}} &= \ln \sum_{i=1}^{N} p_{i,t} e^{-\eta \widetilde{\ell}(i, Y_t)} \\
&\leq \ln \sum_{i=1}^{N} p_{i,t} \left(1 - \eta \widetilde{\ell}(i, Y_t) + \frac{\eta^2}{2} \widetilde{\ell}^2(i, Y_t) \right) \\
&\leq -\eta \sum_{i=1}^{N} p_{i,t} \widetilde{\ell}(i, Y_t) + \frac{\eta^2}{2} \sum_{i=1}^{N} p_{i,t} \widetilde{\ell}^2(i, Y_t) \\
&\leq -\eta \widetilde{\ell}(\mathbf{p}_t, Y_t) + \frac{\eta^2}{2\varepsilon} \widetilde{\ell}(\mathbf{p}_t, Y_t),
\end{aligned}
$$

where we used the facts $e^{-x} \leq 1 - x + x^2/2$ for $x \geq 0$, $\ln(1 + x) \leq x$ for all $x \geq -1$, and $\widetilde{\ell}(i, Y_t) \in [0, 1/\varepsilon]$.

Summing this inequality over $t = 1, \ldots, n$, and using the obtained lower bound for $\ln(W_n / W_0)$, we get, for all $i = 1, \ldots, N$,

$$
\sum_{t=1}^{n} \widetilde{\ell}(\mathbf{p}_t, Y_t) - \widetilde{L}_{i,n} \leq \frac{\eta}{2\varepsilon} \sum_{t=1}^{n} \widetilde{\ell}(\mathbf{p}_t, Y_t) + \frac{\ln N}{\eta}. \tag{6.1}
$$

Now note that $\mathbb{E}\left[\sum_{t=1}^{n} \widetilde{\ell}(\mathbf{p}_t, Y_t) \right] = \mathbb{E}\,\widehat{L}_n \leq n$. Hence, taking the expected value of both sides, we obtain, for all $i = 1, \ldots, N$,

$$
\mathbb{E}\left[\widehat{L}_n - L_{i,n} \right] \leq \frac{n\eta}{2\varepsilon} + \frac{\ln N}{\eta}.
$$

Substituting the value $\eta = \sqrt{(2\varepsilon \ln N)/n}$ we conclude the proof. ∎

Remark 6.1 (*Switching to a new action not too often*). Theorem 6.1 (and similarly Theorem 6.2) can be strengthened by considering the following "lazy" forecaster.

LAZY LABEL EFFICIENT FORECASTER

Parameters: Real numbers $\eta > 0$ and $0 \le \varepsilon \le 1$.

Initialization: $\mathbf{w}_0 = (1, \ldots, 1)$, $Z_0 = 1$.

For each round $t = 1, 2, \ldots$

   (1) if $Z_{t-1} = 1$, then draw an action I_t from $\{1, \ldots, N\}$ according to the distribution
$$p_{i,t} = w_{i,t-1}/(w_{1,t-1} + \cdots + w_{N,t-1}), \quad i = 1, \ldots, N; \text{ otherwise, let } I_t = I_{t-1};$$
   (2) draw a Bernoulli random variable Z_t such that $\mathbb{P}[Z_t = 1] = \varepsilon$;

   (3) if $Z_t = 1$, then obtain Y_t and compute

$$w_{i,t} = w_{i,t-1}\, e^{-\eta\, \ell(i,Y_t)/\varepsilon} \qquad \text{for each } i = 1, \ldots, N;$$

       else, let $\mathbf{w}_t = \mathbf{w}_{t-1}$.

Note that this forecaster keeps choosing the same action as long as no new queries are issued. It can be proven (Exercise 6.2) that the bound of Theorem 6.1 holds for the lazy forecaster against any oblivious opponent with the additional statement that, with probability 1, the number of changes of an action (i.e., the number of steps where $I_t \ne I_{t+1}$) is at most the number of queried labels. (Note that Lemma 4.1 cannot be used to extend this result to nonoblivious opponents as the lemma is only valid for forecasters that use independent randomization at each time instant.) A similar result can be proven for Theorem 6.2 (Exercise 6.3).

Theorem 6.1 guarantees that the expected per-round regret converges to 0 whenever $m \to \infty$ as $n \to \infty$. However, a bound on the expected regret gives very limited information about the actual behavior of the (random) regret $\widehat{L}_t - \min_{i=1,\ldots,N} L_{i,t}$. Theorem 6.1 does not exclude the possibility that the regret has enormous fluctuations around its mean. Just note that the outcomes Y_t may depend, in any complicated way, on the past randomized actions of the forecaster, as well as on the random draws of the variables Z_s for $s < t$. The next result shows that the regret cannot exceed by much its expected value and it is, with overwhelming probability, bounded by a quantity proportional to $n\sqrt{(\ln N)/m}$.

Theorem 6.2. *Fix a time horizon n and a number $\delta \in (0, 1)$. Consider the label efficient forecaster run with parameters*

$$\varepsilon = \max\left\{0, \frac{m - \sqrt{2m \ln(4/\delta)}}{n}\right\} \qquad \text{and} \qquad \eta = \sqrt{\frac{2\varepsilon \ln N}{n}}.$$

Then, with probability at least $1 - \delta$, the number of revealed labels is at most m and

$$\forall t = 1, \ldots, n \quad \widehat{L}_t - \min_{i=1,\ldots,N} L_{i,t} \le 2n\sqrt{\frac{\ln N}{m}} + 6n\sqrt{\frac{\ln(4N/\delta)}{m}}.$$

Before proving Theorem 6.2 note that if $\delta \le 4Ne^{-m/8}$, then the right-hand side of the inequality is greater than n and therefore the statement is trivial. Thus we may assume throughout the proof that $\delta > 4Ne^{-m/8}$. This ensures that $\varepsilon \ge m/(2n) > 0$. We need a few of preliminary lemmas.

Lemma 6.1. *The probability that the label efficient forecaster asks for more than m labels is at most $\delta/4$.*

Proof.   Note that the number of labels $M = Z_1 + \cdots + Z_n$ asked is binomially distributed with parameters n and ε. Therefore, writing $\gamma = m/n - \varepsilon = n^{-1}\sqrt{2m \ln(4/\delta)}$ and using Bernstein's inequality (see Corollary A.3) we obtain

$$\mathbb{P}[M > m] = \mathbb{P}[M - \mathbb{E}\, M > n\gamma] \le e^{-n\gamma^2/(2\varepsilon + 2\gamma/3)} \le e^{-n^2\gamma^2/2m} \le \frac{\delta}{4}. \quad \blacksquare$$

The next lemma relates the "expected" loss $\overline{\ell}(\mathbf{p}_s, Y_s) = \sum_{i=1}^{N} p_{i,s}\ell(i, Y_s)$ to the estimated loss $\widetilde{\ell}(\mathbf{p}_s, Y_s) = \sum_{i=1}^{N} p_{i,s}\widetilde{\ell}(i, Y_s)$.

Lemma 6.2. *With probability at least $1 - \delta/4$, for all $t = 1, \ldots, n$,*

$$\sum_{s=1}^{t} \overline{\ell}(\mathbf{p}_s, Y_s) \le \sum_{s=1}^{t} \widetilde{\ell}(\mathbf{p}_s, Y_s) + \frac{4n}{\sqrt{3}}\sqrt{\frac{\ln(4/\delta)}{m}}.$$

Furthermore, with probability at least $1 - \delta/4$, for all $t = 1, \ldots, n$ and $i = 1, \ldots, N$,

$$\widetilde{L}_{i,t} \le L_{i,t} + \frac{4n}{\sqrt{3}}\sqrt{\frac{\ln(4N/\delta)}{m}}.$$

Proof.   The proof in both cases is based on Bernstein's inequality for martingales (see Lemma A.8). To prove the first inequality, introduce the martingale $S_t = X_1 + \cdots + X_t$, where $X_s = \overline{\ell}(\mathbf{p}_s, Y_s) - \widetilde{\ell}(\mathbf{p}_s, Y_s)$, $s = 1, \ldots, n$, is a martingale difference sequence with respect to the sequence (I_s, Z_s). For all $t = 1, \ldots, n$, define

$$\Sigma_t^2 = \sum_{s=1}^{t} \mathbb{E}\left[X_s^2 \mid Z^{s-1}, I^{s-1}\right].$$

Now note that, for all $s = 1, \ldots, n$,

$$\mathbb{E}\left[X_s^2 \mid Z^{s-1}, I^{s-1}\right] = \mathbb{E}\left[\left(\overline{\ell}(\mathbf{p}_s, Y_s) - \widetilde{\ell}(\mathbf{p}_s, Y_s)\right)^2 \mid Z^{s-1}, I^{s-1}\right]$$
$$\le \mathbb{E}\left[\widetilde{\ell}(\mathbf{p}_s, Y_s)^2 \mid Z^{s-1}, I^{s-1}\right] \le 1/\varepsilon,$$

which implies that $\Sigma_t^2 \le n/\varepsilon$ for all $t = 1, \ldots, n$. We now apply Lemma A.8. noting that $\max_t |X_t| \le 1/\varepsilon$ with probability 1. For $u > 0$ this yields

$$\mathbb{P}\left[\max_{t=1,\ldots,n} S_t > u\right] = \mathbb{P}\left[\max_{t=1,\ldots,n} S_t > u \text{ and } \Sigma_n^2 \le \frac{n}{\varepsilon}\right]$$
$$\le \exp\left(-\frac{u^2}{2(n/\varepsilon + u/(3\varepsilon))}\right).$$

Choosing $u = (4/\sqrt{3})n\sqrt{(1/m)\ln(4/\delta)}$, and using $\ln(4/\delta) \le m/8$ implied by the assumption $\delta > 4Ne^{-m/8}$, we see that $u \le n$. This, combined with $\varepsilon \ge m/(2n)$, shows that

$$\frac{u^2}{2(n/\varepsilon + u/(3\varepsilon))} \ge \frac{u^2}{(8/3)n/\varepsilon} \ge \frac{3u^2 m}{16 n^2} = \ln\frac{4}{\delta},$$

thus proving the first inequality.

To prove the second inequality note that, as just seen, for each fixed i, we have

$$\mathbb{P}\left[\max_{t=1,\ldots,n}\widetilde{L}_{i,t} - L_{i,t} > (4/\sqrt{3})\,n\sqrt{\frac{\ln(4N/\delta)}{m}}\right] \le \frac{\delta}{4N}.$$

An application of the union-of-events bound to $i = 1, \ldots, N$ concludes the proof. ∎

Proof of Theorem 6.2. When $m \le \ln N$, the bound of the theorem is trivial. Therefore, we only need to consider the case $m > \ln N$. In this case $\varepsilon \ge m/(2n)$ implies that $1 - \eta/(2\varepsilon) \ge 0$. Thus, a straightforward combination of Lemmas 6.1 and 6.2 with (6.1) shows that, with probability at least $1 - 3\delta/4$, the following events simultaneously hold (where $\overline{L}_t = \sum_{s=1}^{t}\overline{\ell}(\mathbf{p}_s, Y_s)$):

1. the strategy asks for at most m labels;
2. for all $t = 1, \ldots, n$

$$\left(1 - \frac{\eta}{2\varepsilon}\right)\overline{L}_t \le \min_{i=1,\ldots,N}L_{i,t} + \frac{8}{\sqrt{3}}n\sqrt{\frac{1}{m}\ln\frac{4N}{\delta}} + \frac{\ln N}{\eta}.$$

Since $\overline{L}_t \le n$ for all $t \le n$, the inequality implies that for all $t = 1\ldots, n$

$$\overline{L}_t - \min_{i=1,\ldots,N}L_{i,t} \le \frac{n\eta}{2\varepsilon} + \frac{8n}{\sqrt{3}}\sqrt{\frac{1}{m}\ln\frac{4N}{\delta}} + \frac{\ln N}{\eta}$$

$$= 2n\sqrt{\frac{\ln N}{m}} + \frac{8n}{\sqrt{3}}\sqrt{\frac{1}{m}\ln\frac{4N}{\delta}}$$

by our choice of η, and using $1/(2\varepsilon) \le n/m$ derived from $\varepsilon \ge m/(2n)$. The proof is finished by noting that the Hoeffding–Azuma inequality (see Lemma A.7) implies that, with probability at least $1 - \delta/4$, for all $t = 1, \ldots, n$,

$$\widehat{L}_t \le \overline{L}_t + \sqrt{\frac{n}{2}\ln\frac{4}{\delta}} \le \overline{L}_t + n\sqrt{\frac{1}{2m}\ln\frac{4N}{\delta}},$$

where we used $m \le n$ in the last step. ∎

Theorem 6.1 does not directly imply Hannan consistency of the associated forecasting strategy because the regret bound does not hold uniformly over the sequence length n. However, using standard dynamical tuning techniques (such as the "doubling trick" described in Chapter 2) Hannan consistency can be achieved. The main quantity that arises in the analysis is the query rate $\mu(n)$, which is the number of queries that can be issued up to time n. The next result shows that Hannan consistency is achievable whenever $\mu(n)/(\log(n)\log\log(n)) \to \infty$.

Corollary 6.1. *Let $\mu : \mathbb{N} \to \mathbb{N}$ be any nondecreasing integer-valued function such that*

$$\lim_{n\to\infty}\frac{\mu(n)}{\log_2(n)\log_2\log_2(n)} = \infty.$$

Then there exists a Hannan consistent randomized label efficient forecaster that issues at most $\mu(n)$ queries in the first n predictions for any $n \in \mathbb{N}$.

Proof.   The algorithm we consider divides time into consecutive epochs of increasing lengths $n_r = 2^r$ for $r = 0, 1, 2, \ldots$. In the rth epoch (of length 2^r) the algorithm runs the forecaster of Theorem 6.2 with parameters $n = 2^r$, $m = m_r$, and $\delta_r = 1/(1+r)^2$, where m_r will be determined by the analysis (without loss of generality, we assume that the forecaster always asks for at most m_r labels in each epoch r). Our choice of δ_r and the Borel–Cantelli lemma implies that the bound of Theorem 6.2 holds for all but finitely many epochs. Denote the (random) index of the last epoch in which the bound does not hold by $\hat{R}$. Let $L^{(r)}$ be cumulative loss of the best action in epoch r and let $\widehat{L}^{(r)}$ be the cumulative loss of the forecaster in the same epoch. Introduce $R(n) = \lfloor \log_2 n \rfloor$. Then, by Theorem 6.2 and by definition of $\hat{R}$, for each n and for each realization of I^n and Z^n, we have

$$\widehat{L}_n - L_n^* \le \sum_{r=0}^{R(n)-1} \left(\widehat{L}^{(r)} - L^{(r)} \right) + \sum_{t=2^{R(n)}}^{n} \ell(I_t, Y_t) - \min_{j=1,\ldots,N} \sum_{t=2^{R(n)}}^{n} \ell(j, Y_n)$$

$$\le \sum_{r=0}^{\hat{R}} 2^r + 8 \sum_{r=\hat{R}+1}^{R(n)} 2^r \sqrt{\frac{\ln(4N(r+1)^2)}{m_r}}.$$

This, the finiteness of $\hat{R}$ and $1/n \le 2^{-R(n)}$ imply that, with probability 1,

$$\limsup_{n \to \infty} \frac{\widehat{L}_n - L_n^*}{n} \le 8 \limsup_{R \to \infty} 2^{-R} \sum_{r=0}^{R} 2^r \sqrt{\frac{\ln(4N(r+1)^2)}{m_r}}.$$

Cesaro's lemma ensures that this lim sup equals 0 as soon as $m_r / \ln r \to +\infty$. It remains to see that the latter condition is satisfied under the additional requirement that the forecaster does not issue more than $\mu(n)$ queries up to time n. This is guaranteed whenever $m_0 + m_1 + \cdots + m_{R(n)} \le \mu(n)$ for each n. Denote by ϕ the largest nondecreasing function such that

$$\phi(t) \le \frac{\mu(t)}{(1 + \log_2 t) \log_2 (1 + \log_2 t)} \qquad \text{for all } t = 1, 2, \ldots.$$

As μ grows faster than $\log_2(n) \log_2 \log_2(n)$, we have that $\phi(t) \to +\infty$. Thus, choosing $m_0 = 0$, and $m_r = \lfloor \phi(2^r) \log_2(1+r) \rfloor$, we indeed ensure that $m_r / \ln r \to +\infty$. Furthermore, considering that m_r is nondecreasing as a function of r, and using the monotonicity of ϕ,

$$\sum_{r=0}^{R(n)} m_r \le (R(n) + 1)\phi(2^{R(n)}) \log_2(1 + R(n))$$

$$\le (1 + \log_2 n)\phi(n) \log_2(1 + \log_2 n) \le \mu(n).$$

This concludes the proof.   ∎

We also note here that in case the cumulative loss of the best action $L_n^* = \min_{i=1,\ldots,N} L_{i,n}$ is small, Theorem 6.2 may be improved by a more careful analysis. In particular, an upper bound of the order

$$\sqrt{\frac{nL_n^*(\ln Nn)}{m}} + \frac{n(\ln Nn)}{m}$$

holds. Thus, when $L_n^* = 0$, the rate of convergence becomes significantly faster. For the details we refer the reader to Exercise 6.4.

6.3 Lower Bounds

Here we show that the performance bounds proved in the previous section for the label efficient exponentially weighted average forecaster are essentially unimprovable in the strong sense that no other label efficient forecasting strategy can have a significantly better performance for all problems. The main result of the previous section is that there exists a randomized forecasting algorithm such that its regret is bounded by a quantity of the order of $n\sqrt{\ln N/m}$ if m is the maximum number of revealed labels during the n rounds. The next result shows that for all possible forecasters asking for at most m labels, there exists a prediction problem such that the expected excess cumulative loss is at least a constant times $n\sqrt{\ln N/m}$. In other words, the best achievable per-round regret is of the order $\sqrt{\ln N/m}$. Interestingly, this does not depend on the number n of rounds but only on the number m of revealed labels. Recall that in the "full information" case of Chapter 4 the best achievable per-round regret has the form $\sqrt{\ln N/n}$. Intuitively, m plays the role of the "sample size" in the problem of label efficient prediction.

To present the main ideas in a transparent way, first we assume that $N = 2$; that is, the forecaster has two actions to choose from at each time instance, and the outcome space is binary as well, for example, $\mathcal{Y} = \{0, 1\}$. The general result for $N > 2$ is shown subsequently. Consider the simple zero-one loss function given by $\ell(i, y) = \mathbb{I}_{\{i \neq y\}}$. Then we have the following lower bound.

Theorem 6.3. *Let $n \geq m$ and consider the setup described earlier. Then for any, possibly randomized, prediction strategy that asks for at most m labels,*

$$\sup_{y^n \in \{0,1\}^n} \left(\mathbb{E}\,\widehat{L}_n - \min_{i=0,1} L_{i,n} \right) \geq 0.14 \frac{n}{\sqrt{m}}$$

where the expectation is taken with respect to the randomization of the forecaster.

Proof.   As is usual in proofs of lower bounds, we construct a random outcome sequence and show that the expected value (with respect to the random choice of the outcome sequence) of the excess loss $\widehat{L}_n - \min_{i=0,1} L_{i,n}$ is bounded from below by $0.14\, n/\sqrt{m}$ for any prediction strategy, randomized not. This obviously implies the theorem, because the expected value can never exceed the supremum.

To this end, we define the outcome sequence $Y_1, \ldots, Y_n$ as a sequence of random variables whose joint distribution is defined as follows. Let σ be a symmetric Bernoulli random variable $\mathbb{P}[\sigma = 0] = \mathbb{P}[\sigma = 1] = 1/2$. Given the event $\sigma = 1$, the Y_t's are conditionally independent with distribution

$$\mathbb{P}[Y_t = 1 \mid \sigma = 1] = 1 - \mathbb{P}[Y_t = 0 \mid \sigma = 1] = \frac{1}{2} + \varepsilon,$$

where ε is a positive number specified later. Given $\sigma = 0$, the Y_t's are also conditionally independent with

$$\mathbb{P}[Y_t = 1 \mid \sigma = 0] = 1 - \mathbb{P}[Y_t = 0 \mid \sigma = 0] = \frac{1}{2} - \varepsilon.$$

Now it suffices to establish a lower bound for $\mathbb{E}\left[\widehat{L}_n - \min_{i=0,1} L_{i,n}\right]$ when the outcome sequence is $Y_1, \ldots, Y_n$ and the expected value is taken with respect to both the randomization of the forecaster and the distribution of the Y_i's. Note that we may assume at this point that the prediction strategy is deterministic. Since any randomized strategy may be regarded as a randomized choice from a class of deterministic strategies, if the lower bound is true for any deterministic strategy, by Fubini's theorem it must also hold for the average over all deterministic strategies according to the randomization. First note that

$$\mathbb{E} \min \{L_{0,n}, L_{1,n}\}$$

$$= \frac{1}{2} \left(\mathbb{E}[\min\{L_{0,n}, L_{1,n}\} \mid \sigma = 1] + \mathbb{E}[\min\{L_{0,n}, L_{1,n}\} \mid \sigma = 0] \right)$$

$$\leq \frac{1}{2} \left(\min\{\mathbb{E}[L_{0,n} \mid \sigma = 1], \mathbb{E}[L_{1,n} \mid \sigma = 1]\} \right.$$

$$\left. + \min\{\mathbb{E}[L_{0,n} \mid \sigma = 0], \mathbb{E}[L_{1,n} \mid \sigma = 0]\} \right)$$

$$= n \left(\frac{1}{2} - \varepsilon \right)$$

and therefore

$$\mathbb{E} \left[\widehat{L}_n - \min_{i=0,1} L_{i,n} \right] \geq \mathbb{E} \widehat{L}_n - n \left(\frac{1}{2} - \varepsilon \right).$$

It remains to prove a lower bound for $\mathbb{E} \widehat{L}_n = \sum_{t=1}^{n} \mathbb{E} \ell(I_t, Y_t)$, where I_t is the action chosen by the predictor at time t. Denote by $1 \leq T_1 \leq \ldots \leq T_K \leq n$ the prediction rounds when the forecaster queried a label, and let $Z_1 = Y_{T_1}, \ldots, Z_K = Y_{T_K}$ be the revealed labels. Here the random variable K denotes the number of labels queried by the forecaster in n rounds. By the label efficient assumption, $K \leq m$. Recall that we consider only deterministic prediction strategies. Since the predictions of the forecaster can only depend on the labels revealed up to that time, such a strategy may be formalized by a function $g_t : \{0, 1, \star\}^m \to \{0, 1\}$ so that at time t the forecaster outputs

$$I_t = g_t(Z_1, \ldots, Z_K, \underbrace{\star, \ldots, \star}_{m-K \text{ times}}).$$

Defining the random vector $\mathbf{Z} = (Z_1, \ldots, Z_K)$, by a slight abuse of notation we may simply write

$$I_t = g_t(\mathbf{Z}).$$

The expected loss at time t is then

$$\mathbb{E} \ell(I_t, Y_t) = \mathbb{P}[g_t(\mathbf{Z}) \neq Y_t] = \sum_{k=1}^{m} \mathbb{P}[K = k] \, \mathbb{P}[g_t(\mathbf{Z}) \neq Y_t \mid K = k].$$

To simplify notation, in the sequel we use

$$\mathbb{P}_k[\cdot] = \mathbb{P}[\cdot \mid K = k] \qquad \text{and} \qquad \mathbb{E}_k[\cdot] = \mathbb{E}[\cdot \mid K = k]$$

to denote the conditional distribution and expectation given that exactly k labels have been revealed up to time t. Since, for any t, the event $\{T_i = t\}$ is determined by the values taken by $Y_1, \ldots, Y_t$, a well-known fact of probability theory (see, e.g., Chow and Teicher [59, Lemma 2, p. 138]) implies that $Z_1 = Y_{T_1}, \ldots, Z_K = Y_{T_K}$ are independent and identically distributed, with the same distribution as Y_1. It follows by a basic identity of the theory of binary classification (see Lemma A.15) – by taking Y_t as Y and the pair $(\mathbf{Z}, \sigma)$ as X – that

$$\mathbb{P}_k[g_t(\mathbf{Z}) \neq Y_t] = \frac{1}{2} - \varepsilon + (2\varepsilon)\mathbb{P}_k[g_t(\mathbf{Z}) \neq \sigma].$$

Thus, it suffices to obtain a lower bound for $\mathbb{P}_k[g_t(\mathbf{Z}) \neq \sigma]$. By Lemmas A.14 and A.15, this probability is at least

$$\mathbb{E}_k \min\{\mathbb{P}_k[\sigma = 0 \mid \mathbf{Z}], \mathbb{P}_k[\sigma = 1 \mid \mathbf{Z}]\}.$$

Observe that for any $\mathbf{z} \in \{0, 1\}^k$,

$$\mathbb{P}_k[\sigma = 0 \mid \mathbf{Z} = \mathbf{z}] = \frac{\mathbb{P}_k[\sigma = 0]\,\mathbb{P}_k[\mathbf{Z} = \mathbf{z} \mid \sigma = 0]}{\mathbb{P}_k[\mathbf{Z} = \mathbf{z}]}$$

$$= \frac{(1/2 + \varepsilon)^{n_0}(1/2 - \varepsilon)^{n_1}}{2\mathbb{P}_k[\mathbf{Z} = \mathbf{z}]},$$

where n_0 and n_1 denote the number of 0's and 1's in the string $\mathbf{z} \in \{0, 1\}^k$. Similarly,

$$\mathbb{P}_k[\sigma = 1 \mid \mathbf{Z} = \mathbf{z}] = \frac{(1/2 - \varepsilon)^{n_0}(1/2 + \varepsilon)^{n_1}}{2\mathbb{P}_k[\mathbf{Z} = \mathbf{z}]}$$

and therefore

$$
\begin{aligned}
&\mathbb{P}_k[g_t(\mathbf{Z}) \neq \sigma] \\
&\geq \mathbb{E}_k \min\{\mathbb{P}_k[\sigma = 0 \mid \mathbf{Z}], \mathbb{P}_k[\sigma = 1 \mid \mathbf{Z}]\} \\
&= \sum_{\mathbf{z} \in \{0,1\}^k} \mathbb{P}_k[\mathbf{Z} = \mathbf{z}] \min\{\mathbb{P}_k[\sigma = 0 \mid \mathbf{Z} = \mathbf{z}], \mathbb{P}_k[\sigma = 1 \mid \mathbf{Z} = \mathbf{z}]\} \\
&= \frac{1}{2} \sum_{\mathbf{z} \in \{0,1\}^k} \min\{(1/2 - \varepsilon)^{n_0}(1/2 + \varepsilon)^{n_1}, (1/2 - \varepsilon)^{n_1}(1/2 + \varepsilon)^{n_0}\} \\
&= \frac{1}{2} \sum_{j=0}^{k} \binom{k}{j} \min\{(1/2 - \varepsilon)^j(1/2 + \varepsilon)^{k-j}, (1/2 - \varepsilon)^{k-j}(1/2 + \varepsilon)^j\} \\
&\geq \sum_{j=\lceil k/2 \rceil}^{k} \binom{k}{j}(1/2 - \varepsilon)^j(1/2 + \varepsilon)^{k-j} \\
&= \mathbb{P}\left[B \geq \frac{k}{2}\right],
\end{aligned}
$$

where B is a binomial random variable with parameters k and $1/2 - \varepsilon$. By the central limit theorem this probability may be bounded from below by a constant if ε is at most of the order $1/\sqrt{k}$. Since $k \leq m$, this may be achieved by taking, for example, $\varepsilon = 1/(4\sqrt{m})$.

To get a nonasymptotic bound, we use Slud's inequality (see Lemma A.10) implying that

$$\mathbb{P}\left[B \geq \frac{k}{2}\right] \geq 1 - \Phi\left(\frac{\varepsilon\sqrt{k}}{\sqrt{(1/2 - \varepsilon)(1/2 + \varepsilon)}}\right)$$

$$\geq 1 - \Phi\left(\frac{1/4}{\sqrt{1/4 - 1/(16m)}}\right) \geq 1 - \Phi(0.577) \geq 0.28,$$

where Φ is the distribution function of a standard normal random variable. Here we used the fact that $k \leq m$.

In summary, we have proved that

$$\mathbb{E}\left[\widehat{L}_n - \min_{i=0,1} L_{i,n}\right] \geq \mathbb{E}\,\widehat{L}_n - n\left(\frac{1}{2} - \varepsilon\right)$$

$$= \sum_{t=1}^{n}\sum_{k=1}^{m}\mathbb{P}[K = k]\,\mathbb{P}_k[g_t(\mathbf{Z}) \neq Y_t] - n\left(\frac{1}{2} - \varepsilon\right)$$

$$= 2\varepsilon\sum_{t=1}^{n}\sum_{k=1}^{m}\mathbb{P}[K = k]\,\mathbb{P}_k[g_t(\mathbf{Z}) \neq \sigma]$$

$$\geq 2n\varepsilon \times 0.28 = 0.14\frac{n}{\sqrt{m}}$$

as desired. ∎

Now we extend Theorem 6.3 to the general case of $N > 2$ actions. The next result shows that, as suggested by the upper bounds of Theorems 6.1 and 6.2, the best achievable regret is proportional to the square root of the logarithm of the number of actions.

Theorem 6.4. *Assume that N is an integer power of 2. There exists a loss function ℓ such that for all sets of N actions and for all $n \geq m \geq 4(\sqrt{3} - 1)^2 \log_2 N$, the expected cumulative loss of any forecaster that asks for at most m labels while predicting a binary sequence of n outcomes satisfies the inequality*

$$\sup_{y^n \in \{0,1\}^n}\left(\mathbb{E}\,\widehat{L}_n - \min_{i=1,\ldots,N} L_{i,n}\right) \geq cn\sqrt{\frac{\log_2 N}{m}},$$

where $c = ((\sqrt{3} - 1)/8)e^{-\sqrt{3}/2} > 0.0384$.

Proof. The way to proceed is similar to Theorem 6.3, though the randomizing distribution of the outcomes and the losses needs to be chosen more carefully. The main idea is to consider a certain family of prediction problems defined by sequences of outcomes and loss functions and then show that for any forecaster there exists a prediction problem in the class such that the regret of the forecaster is at least as large as announced.

The family is parameterized by three sequences: the "side information" sequence $\mathbf{x} = (x_1, \ldots, x_n)$ with

$$x_1, \ldots, x_n \in \{1, 2, \ldots, \log_2 N\},$$

the binary vector $\boldsymbol{\sigma} = (\sigma_1 \ldots, \sigma_{\log_2 N}) \in \{0, 1\}^{\log_2 N}$, and the sequence $\mathbf{u}$ of real numbers $u_1, \ldots, u_n \in [0, 1]$. For any fixed value of these parameters, define the sequence of outcomes by

$$y_t = \begin{cases} 1 & \text{if } u_t \leq \frac{1}{2} + \varepsilon(2\sigma_{x_t} - 1) \\ 0 & \text{otherwise,} \end{cases}$$

where $\varepsilon > 0$ is a parameter whose value will be set later. The N actions correspond to the binary vectors $\mathbf{b} = (b_1 \ldots, b_{\log_2 N}) \in \{0, 1\}^{\log_2 N}$ such that the loss of action $\mathbf{b}$ at time t is $\ell(\mathbf{b}, y_t) = \mathbb{I}_{\{b_{x_t} \neq y_t\}}$. For any forecaster that asks for at most m labels, we establish a lower bound for the maximal regret within the family of problems by choosing the problem randomly and lower bounding the expected regret. To this end, we choose the parameters $\mathbf{x}$, $\boldsymbol{\sigma}$, and $\mathbf{u}$ randomly such that $X_1, \ldots, X_n$ are independent and uniformly distributed over $\{1, \ldots, \log_2 N\}$, the U_i are also i.i.d. uniformly distributed over $[0, 1]$, and the σ_i are independent symmetric Bernoulli random variables. Note that with this choice, given X_t and $\boldsymbol{\sigma}$, the conditional probability of $Y_t = 1$ is $1/2 + \varepsilon$ if $\sigma_{X_t} = 1$ and $1/2 - \varepsilon$ if $\sigma_{X_t} = 0$. Now we have

$$\sup_{\mathbf{x}, \boldsymbol{\sigma}, \mathbf{u}} \left(\mathbb{E} \widehat{L}_n - \min_{\mathbf{b}} L_{\mathbf{b}, n} \right) \geq \mathbb{E} \left(\widehat{L}_n - \min_{\mathbf{b}} L_{\mathbf{b}, n} \right),$$

where the expected value on the right-hand side is taken with respect to all randomizations introduced earlier, as well as the randomization the forecaster may use.

Clearly, for each fixed value of $\boldsymbol{\sigma}$,

$$\mathbb{E}_{\mathbf{X}, \mathbf{U}} \min_{\mathbf{b}} L_{\mathbf{b}, n} \leq \min_{\mathbf{b}} \mathbb{E}_{\mathbf{X}, \mathbf{U}} L_{\mathbf{b}, n} = n \left(\frac{1}{2} - \varepsilon \right),$$

where $\mathbb{E}_{\mathbf{X}, \mathbf{U}}$ denotes expectation with respect to $\mathbf{X}$ and $\mathbf{U}$ (i.e., conditioned on $\boldsymbol{\sigma}$). Thus, if I_t denotes the forecaster's decision at time t,

$$\mathbb{E} \left(\widehat{L}_n - \min_{\mathbf{b}} L_{\mathbf{b}, n} \right) \geq \sum_{t=1}^{n} \left(\mathbb{P}[I_t \neq Y_t] - \left(\frac{1}{2} - \varepsilon \right) \right).$$

By the same argument as in the proof of Theorem 6.3 it suffices to consider forecasters of the form $I_t = g_t(\mathbf{Z})$, where, as before, g_t is an arbitrary $\{0, 1\}$-valued function and $\mathbf{Z} = (Y_{T_1}, \ldots, Y_{T_K})$ is the vector of outcomes at the times in which the forecaster asked for labels. To derive a lower bound for

$$\sum_{t=1}^{n} \inf_{g_t} \left(\sum_{k=1}^{m} \mathbb{P}[K = k] \, \mathbb{P}_k[g_t(\mathbf{Z}) \neq Y_t] - \left(\frac{1}{2} - \varepsilon \right) \right)$$

$$\geq \sum_{t=1}^{n} \sum_{k=1}^{m} \mathbb{P}[K = k] \inf_{g_t} \left(\mathbb{P}_k[g_t(\mathbf{Z}) \neq Y_t] - \left(\frac{1}{2} - \varepsilon \right) \right),$$

note that for each t,

$$\inf_{g_t} \mathbb{P}_k[g_t(\mathbf{Z}) \neq Y_t] \geq \inf_{g'_t} \mathbb{P}_k[g'_t(\mathbf{Z}') \neq Y_t]$$

where $\mathbf{Z}' = (X_{T_1}, Y_{T_1}, \ldots, X_{T_K}, Y_{T_K}, X_t)$ is the vector of revealed labels augmented by the corresponding side information plus the actual side information X_t. Now g'_t can be any binary-valued function of $\mathbf{Z}'$.

Consider the classification problem of guessing Y_t from the pair $\mathbf{Z}'$, $\boldsymbol{\sigma}$ (see Section A.3 for the basic notions). The Bayes decision is clearly $g^*(\mathbf{Z}', \boldsymbol{\sigma}) = \sigma_{X_t}$ whose probability of error is $1/2 - \varepsilon$. Thus, by Lemma A.15,

$$\mathbb{P}_k[g'_t(\mathbf{Z}') \neq Y_t] - \left(\frac{1}{2} - \varepsilon \right) = (2\varepsilon) \mathbb{P}_k[g'_t(\mathbf{Z}') \neq \sigma_{X_t}],$$

where we used the fact that $\mathbb{P}_k[Y_t = 1 \mid \mathbf{Z}', \boldsymbol{\sigma}] = 1/2 + \varepsilon(2\sigma_{X_t} - 1)$. To bound $\mathbb{P}_k[g'_t(\mathbf{Z}') \neq \sigma_{X_t}]$ we use Lemmas A.14 and A.15. Clearly, this probability may be bounded from below by the Bayes probability of error $L^*(\mathbf{Z}', \sigma_{X_t})$ of guessing the value of σ_{X_t} from $\mathbf{Z}'$.

All we have to do is to find a suitable lower bound for

$$\mathbb{P}_k[g_t'(\mathbf{Z}') \neq \sigma_{X_t}] \geq L^*(\mathbf{Z}', \sigma_{X_t}) = \mathbb{E}_k \min\{\mathbb{P}_k[\sigma_{X_t} = 1 \mid \mathbf{Z}'], \mathbb{P}_k[\sigma_{X_t} = 0 \mid \mathbf{Z}']\}.$$

Observe that

$$\mathbb{P}_k[\sigma_{X_t} = 1 \mid \mathbf{Z}'] = \begin{cases} 1/2 & \text{if } X_t \neq X_{t_1}, \ldots, X_t \neq X_{t_k} \\ \mathbb{P}_k[\sigma_{X_t} = 1 \mid Y_{i_1}, \ldots, Y_{i_j}] & \text{otherwise,} \end{cases}$$

where $i_1, \ldots, i_j$ are those indices among $t_1, \ldots, t_k$ for which $X_{i_1} = \ldots = X_{i_j} = X_t$.
Using i to denote the value of X_t in $\mathbf{Z}'$, we compute

$$\mathbb{P}_k[\sigma_i = 1 \mid Y_{i_1} = y_1, \ldots, Y_{i_j} = y_j]$$

for $y_1, \ldots, y_j \in \{0, 1\}$. Denoting with j_0 and j_1 the numbers of 0's and 1's in $y_1, \ldots, y_j$, we see that

$$\mathbb{P}_k[\sigma_i = 1 \mid Y_{i_1} = y_1, \ldots, Y_{i_j} = y_j]$$
$$= \frac{(1 - 2\varepsilon)^{j_0}(1 + 2\varepsilon)^{j_1}}{(1 - 2\varepsilon)^{j_0}(1 + 2\varepsilon)^{j_1} + (1 + 2\varepsilon)^{j_0}(1 - 2\varepsilon)^{j_1}}.$$

Therefore, if $X_t = X_{i_1} = \ldots = X_{i_j} = i$, then

$$\min\{\mathbb{P}_k[\sigma_{X_t} = 1 \mid \mathbf{Z}'], \mathbb{P}_k[\sigma_{X_t} = 0 \mid \mathbf{Z}']\}$$
$$= \frac{\min\left\{(1 - 2\varepsilon)^{j_0}(1 + 2\varepsilon)^{j_1}, (1 + 2\varepsilon)^{j_0}(1 - 2\varepsilon)^{j_1}\right\}}{(1 - 2\varepsilon)^{j_0}(1 + 2\varepsilon)^{j_1} + (1 + 2\varepsilon)^{j_0}(1 - 2\varepsilon)^{j_1}}$$
$$= \frac{\min\left\{1, \left(\frac{1+2\varepsilon}{1-2\varepsilon}\right)^{j_0 - j_1}\right\}}{1 + \left(\frac{1+2\varepsilon}{1-2\varepsilon}\right)^{j_0 - j_1}}$$
$$= \frac{1}{1 + \left(\frac{1+2\varepsilon}{1-2\varepsilon}\right)^{|j_1 - j_0|}}.$$

In summary, denoting $a = (1 + 2\varepsilon)/(1 - 2\varepsilon)$, we have

$$L^*(\mathbf{Z}', \sigma_{X_t}) = \mathbb{E}_k \left[\frac{1}{1 + a^{\left|\sum_{l:X_{t_l} = X_t}(2Y_{t_l} - 1)\right|}} \right]$$
$$\geq \mathbb{E}_k \left[\frac{1}{2a^{\left|\sum_{l:X_{t_l} = X_t}(2Y_{t_l} - 1)\right|}} \right]$$
$$= \frac{1}{2} \sum_{i=1}^{\log_2 N} \frac{1}{\log_2 N} \mathbb{E}_k a^{-\left|\sum_{l:X_{t_l} = i}(2Y_{t_l} - 1)\right|}$$
$$= \frac{1}{2} a^{-\mathbb{E}_k\left|\sum_{l:X_{t_l} = 1}(2Y_{t_l} - 1)\right|}.$$

Next we bound $\mathbb{E}_k \left| \sum_{l:X_{t_l}=1}(2Y_{t_l}-1)\right|$. Clearly, if $B(j,q)$ denotes a binomial random variable with parameters j and q and $\mathbb{E}_{k,\sigma_1=y}$ denotes the $\mathbb{E}_k$ further conditioned on $\sigma_1 = y$,

$$
\mathbb{E}_k \left| \sum_{l:X_{t_l}=1}(2Y_{t_l}-1)\right| = \mathbb{P}[\sigma_1=0]\,\mathbb{E}_{k,\sigma_1=0} \left| \sum_{l:X_{t_l}=1}(2Y_{t_l}-1)\right|
$$

$$
+ \mathbb{P}[\sigma_1=1]\,\mathbb{E}_{k,\sigma_1=1} \left| \sum_{l:X_{t_l}=1}(2Y_{t_l}-1)\right|
$$

$$
= \mathbb{E}_{k,\sigma_1=0} \left| \sum_{l:X_{t_l}=1}(2Y_{t_l}-1)\right| \qquad \text{(by symmetry)}
$$

$$
= \sum_{j=0}^{k} \binom{k}{j} p^j (1-p)^{k-j}\, \mathbb{E}\left|2B(j,1/2-\varepsilon)-j\right|,
$$

where we write $p = 1/\log_2 N$. However, by straightforward calculation we see that

$$
\mathbb{E}\left|2B(j,1/2-\varepsilon)-j\right| \le \sqrt{\mathbb{E}[(2B(j,1/2-\varepsilon)-j)^2]}
$$

$$
= \sqrt{j(1-4\varepsilon^2)+4j^2\varepsilon^2}
$$

$$
\le 2j\varepsilon + \sqrt{j}.
$$

Therefore, applying Jensen's inequality, we get

$$
\sum_{j=0}^{k} \binom{k}{j} p^j (1-p)^{k-j}\, \mathbb{E}\left|2B(j,1/2-\varepsilon)-j\right| \le 2kp\varepsilon + \sqrt{kp}.
$$

Summarizing what we have obtained so far, we have

$$
\sup_{\mathbf{x},\sigma,\mathbf{u}} \left(\mathbb{E}\,\widehat{L}_n - \min_{\mathbf{b}} L_{\mathbf{b},n} \right) \ge \sum_{t=1}^{n}\sum_{k=1}^{m} \mathbb{P}[K=k](2\varepsilon) L^*(\mathbf{Z}',\sigma_{X_t})
$$

$$
\ge \sum_{t=1}^{n}\sum_{k=1}^{m} \mathbb{P}[K=k](2\varepsilon)\frac{1}{2} a^{-2k\varepsilon/\log_2 N - \sqrt{k/\log_2 N}}
$$

$$
\ge n\varepsilon a^{-2m\varepsilon/\log_2 N - \sqrt{m/\log_2 N}} \qquad \text{(because } k \le m\text{)}
$$

$$
\ge n\varepsilon e^{-(a-1)\left(2m\varepsilon/\log_2 N + \sqrt{m/\log_2 N}\right)}
$$

$$
\text{(using } \ln a \le a-1\text{)}
$$

$$
= n\varepsilon \exp\left(-\frac{8m\varepsilon^2}{(1-2\varepsilon)\log_2 N} - \frac{4\varepsilon}{1-2\varepsilon}\sqrt{\frac{m}{\log_2 N}} \right).
$$

We choose $\varepsilon = c\sqrt{\log_2 N/m}$, which is less than $1/4$ if $m > (4c)^2 \log_2 N$. With this choice the lower bound is at least $nc\sqrt{\log_2 N/m}\, e^{-16c^2-8c}$. This is maximized by choosing $c = (\sqrt{3}-1)/8$, which leads to the announced result. ∎

6.4 Partial Monitoring

In a wide and important class of prediction problems the forecaster does not know the losses he has suffered in the past and instead receives feedback often carrying quite limited information. Such situations have often been called prediction problems with *partial monitoring*.

Before describing the formal setup, consider the following dynamic pricing problem as a nontrivial example of a partial-monitoring problem. A vendor sells a product to a sequence of customers who he attends one by one. To each customer, the seller offers the product at a price he selects, say, from the set $\{1, \ldots, N\}$. The customer then decides whether to buy the product. No bargaining is possible and no other information is exchanged between buyer and seller. The goal of the seller is to achieve an income almost as large as if he knew the maximal price each customer is willing to pay for the product. Thus, if the price offered to the tth customer is I_t and the highest price this customer is willing to pay is $Y_t \in \{1, \ldots, N\}$, then the loss of the seller is

$$\ell(I_t, Y_t) = \frac{(Y_t - I_t)\mathbb{I}_{\{I_t \leq Y_t\}} + c\mathbb{I}_{\{I_t > Y_t\}}}{N},$$

where $0 \leq c \leq N$. Thus, if the product is bought (i.e., $I_t \leq Y_t$), then the loss of the seller is proportional to the difference between the best possible and the offered prices, and if the product is not bought, then the seller suffers a constant loss c/N. (The factor $1/N$ is merely here to assure that the loss is between 0 and 1.) In another version of the problem the constant c is replaced by Y_t. In either case, if the seller knew in advance the sequence of Y_t's then he could set a constant price $i \in \{1, \ldots, N\}$ that minimizes his overall loss. A question we investigate in this section is whether there exists a randomized algorithm for the seller such that his regret

$$\sum_{t=1}^{n} \ell(I_t, Y_t) - \min_{i=1,\ldots,N} \sum_{t=1}^{n} \ell(i, Y_t)$$

is guaranteed to be $o(n)$ regardless of the sequence $Y_1, Y_2, \ldots$ of highest customer prices. The difficulty in this problem is that the only information the seller (i.e., the forecaster) has access to is whether $I_t > Y_t$, but neither Y_t nor $\ell(I_t, Y_t)$ are revealed. (Note that if Y_t were revealed to the forecaster in each step, then we would be back to the full-information case studied in Section 4.2.)

We treat such limited-feedback (or *partial monitoring*) prediction problems in a more general framework, which we describe next. The dynamic pricing problem is a special case.

In the prediction problem with partial monitoring, we assume that the outcome space is finite with M elements. Without loss of generality, we assume that $\mathcal{Y} = \{1, \ldots, M\}$. Denote the matrix of losses by $\mathbf{L} = [\ell(i, j)]_{N \times M}$. (This matrix is assumed to be known by the forecaster.) If, at time t, the forecaster chooses an action $I_t \in \{1, \ldots, N\}$ and the outcome is $Y_t \in \mathcal{Y}$, then the forecaster suffers loss $\ell(I_t, Y_t)$. However, instead of the outcome Y_t, the forecaster only observes the feedback $h(I_t, Y_t)$, where h is a known *feedback function* that assigns, to each action/outcome pair in $\{1, \ldots, N\} \times \mathcal{Y}$, an element of a finite set $\mathcal{S} = \{s_1, \ldots, s_m\}$ of *signals*. The values of h are collected in a *feedback matrix* $\mathbf{H} = [h(i, j)]_{N \times M}$. Here we also allow a nonoblivious adversary; that is, the outcome Y_t may depend on the past actions $I_1, \ldots, I_{t-1}$ of the forecaster.

The partial monitoring prediction game is described as follows.

PREDICTION WITH PARTIAL MONITORING

Parameters: finite outcome space $\mathcal{Y} = \{1, \ldots, M\}$, number of actions N, loss function ℓ, feedback function h.

For each round $t = 1, 2 \ldots,$

   (1) the environment chooses the next outcome $Y_t \in \mathcal{Y}$ without revealing it;
   (2) the forecaster chooses an action $I_t \in \{1, \ldots, N\}$;
   (3) the forecaster incurs loss $\ell(I_t, Y_t)$ and each action i incurs loss $\ell(i, Y_t)$, where none of these values is revealed to the forecaster;
   (4) the feedback $h(I_t, Y_t)$ is revealed to the forecaster.

We note here that some authors consider a more general setup in which the feedback may be random. For the sake of clarity we stay with the simpler problem described above. Exercise 6.11 points out that most results shown below may be extended, in a straightforward way, to the case of random feedbacks.

It is an interesting and complex problem to investigate the possibilities of a predictor only supplied by the limited information of the feedback. For example, one may ask under what conditions it is possible to achieve Hannan consistency, that is, to guarantee that, asymptotically, the cumulative loss of the predictor is not larger than that of the best constant action, with probability 1. Naturally, this depends on the relationship between the loss and feedback functions. Note that the predictor is free to encode the values $h(i, j)$ of the feedback function by real numbers. The only restriction is that if $h(i, j) = h(i, j')$, then the corresponding real numbers should also coincide. To avoid ambiguities by trivial rescaling, we assume that $|h(i, j)| \leq 1$ for all pairs (i, j). Thus, in the sequel we assume that $\mathbf{H} = [h(i, j)]_{N \times M}$ is a matrix of real numbers between -1 and 1 and keep in mind that the predictor may replace this matrix by $\mathbf{H}_\phi = [\phi_i(h(i, j))]_{N \times M}$ for arbitrary functions $\phi_i : [-1, 1] \to [-1, 1]$, $i = 1, \ldots, N$. Note that the set $\mathcal{S}$ of signals may be chosen such that it has $m \leq M$ elements, though after numerical encoding the matrix may have as many as MN distinct elements.

Before introducing a general prediction strategy, we describe a few concrete examples.

Example **6.1** (***Multi-armed bandit problem***). In many prediction problems the forecaster, after taking an action, is able to measure his loss (or reward) but does not have access to what would have happened had he chosen another possible action. Such prediction problems have been known as *multi-armed bandit* problems. The name refers to a gambler who plays a pool of slot machines (called "one-armed bandits"). The gambler places his bet each time on a possibly different slot machine and his goal is to win almost as much as if he had known in advance which slot machine would return the maximal total reward. The multi-armed bandit problem is a special case of the partial monitoring problem. Here we may simply take $\mathbf{H} = \mathbf{L}$, that is, the feedback received by the forecaster is just his own loss. This problem has been widely studied both in a stochastic and a worst-case setting, and has several unique features, which we study separately in Sections 6.7, 6.8, and 6.9. ☐

Example 6.2 (Dynamic pricing). In the dynamic pricing problem described in the introduction of the section we may take $M = N$ and the loss matrix is

$$\mathbf{L} = [\ell(i, j)]_{N \times N} \quad \text{where} \quad \ell(i, j) = \frac{(j - i)\mathbb{I}_{\{i \le j\}} + c\mathbb{I}_{\{i > j\}}}{N}.$$

The information the forecaster (i.e., the vendor) receives is simply whether the predicted value I_t is greater than the outcome Y_t. Thus, the entries of the feedback matrix $\mathbf{H}$ may be taken to be $h(i, j) = \mathbb{I}_{\{i > j\}}$ or, after an appropriate re-encoding,

$$h(i, j) = a\mathbb{I}_{\{i \le j\}} + b\mathbb{I}_{\{i > j\}}, \qquad i, j = 1, \ldots, N$$

where a and b are constants chosen by the forecaster satisfying $a, b \in [-1, 1]$. □

Example 6.3 (Apple tasting). Consider the simple example in which $N = M = 2$ and the loss and feedback matrices are given by

$$\mathbf{L} = \begin{bmatrix} 1 & 0 \\ 0 & 1 \end{bmatrix} \quad \text{and} \quad \mathbf{H} = \begin{bmatrix} a & a \\ b & c \end{bmatrix}.$$

Thus, the predictor only receives feedback about the outcome Y_t when he chooses the second action. This example has been known as the *apple tasting problem*. (Imagine that apples are to be classified as "good for sale" or "rotten." An apple classified as "rotten" may be opened to check whether its classification was correct. On the other hand, since apples that have been checked cannot be put on sale, an apple classified "good for sale" is never checked.) □

Example 6.4 (Label efficient prediction). A variant of the label efficient prediction problem of Sections 6.2 and 6.3 may also be cast as a partial monitoring problem. Let $N = 3$, $M = 2$, and consider loss and feedback matrices of the form

$$\mathbf{L} = \begin{bmatrix} 1 & 1 \\ 0 & 1 \\ 1 & 0 \end{bmatrix} \quad \text{and} \quad \mathbf{H} = \begin{bmatrix} a & b \\ c & c \\ c & c \end{bmatrix}.$$

In this example the only times useful feedback is received are when the first action is played, in which case a maximal loss is incurred regardless of the outcome. Thus, just as in the problem of label efficient prediction, playing the "informative" action has to be limited; otherwise there is no hope for Hannan consistency. □

Remark 6.2 (Compound actions and dynamic strategies). In setting up the problem, for simplicity, we restricted our attention to forecasters whose aim is to predict as well as the best constant action. This is reflected in the definition of regret in which the cumulative loss of the forecaster is compared with $\min_{i=1,\ldots,N} \sum_{t=1}^{n} \ell(i, Y_t)$, the cumulative loss of the best constant action. However, just as in the full information case described in Sections 4.2 and 5.2, one may define the regret in terms of a class of compound actions (or dynamic strategies). Recall that a compound action is a sequence $\mathbf{i} = (i_1, \ldots, i_n)$ of actions $i_t \in \{1, \ldots, N\}$. Given a class $\mathcal{S}$ of compound actions, one may define the regret

$$\sum_{t=1}^{n} \ell(I_t, Y_t) - \min_{\mathbf{i} \in \mathcal{S}} \sum_{t=1}^{n} \ell(i_t, Y_t).$$

The forecasters defined for the partial monitoring problem introduced below can be easily generalized to handle this more general case; see, for example, Exercise 6.16.

6.5   A General Forecaster for Partial Monitoring

We now present a general prediction strategy that works in the partial monitoring setting provided the feedback matrix contains "enough information" about the loss matrix. The forecaster is a modification of the exponentially weighted average forecaster (see Section 4.2). The main modification is that the losses $\ell(i, Y_t)$ are now replaced by appropriate estimates. However, an estimate with the desired properties can only be constructed under some conditions on the loss and feedback matrices.

The crucial assumption is that there exists a matrix $\mathbf{K} = [k(i, j)]_{N \times N}$ such that $\mathbf{L} = \mathbf{K}\mathbf{H}$, that is,

$$\mathbf{H} \quad \text{and} \quad \begin{bmatrix} \mathbf{H} \\ \mathbf{L} \end{bmatrix}$$

have the same rank. In other words, we may write, for all $i \in \{1, \dots, N\}$ and $j \in \{1, \dots, M\}$,

$$\ell(i, j) = \sum_{l=1}^{N} k(i, l) h(l, j).$$

In this case one may define the estimated losses $\widetilde{\ell}$ by

$$\widetilde{\ell}(i, Y_t) = \frac{k(i, I_t) h(I_t, Y_t)}{p_{I_t, t}}, \qquad i = 1, \dots, N$$

and their sums as $\widetilde{L}_{i,n} = \widetilde{\ell}(i, Y_1) + \cdots + \widetilde{\ell}(i, Y_n)$. The forecaster for partial monitoring is then defined as follows.

A GENERAL FORECASTER FOR PARTIAL MONITORING

Parameters: matrix of losses $\mathbf{L}$, feedback matrix $\mathbf{H}$, matrix $\mathbf{K}$ such that $\mathbf{L} = \mathbf{K}\mathbf{H}$, real numbers $0 < \eta, \gamma < 1$.

Initialization: $\mathbf{w}_0 = (1, \dots, 1)$.

For each round $t = 1, 2, \dots$

(1) draw an action $I_t \in \{1, \dots, N\}$ according to the distribution

$$p_{i,t} = (1 - \gamma) \frac{w_{i,t-1}}{W_{t-1}} + \frac{\gamma}{N} \qquad i = 1, \dots, N\,;$$

(2) get feedback $h_t = h(I_t, Y_t)$ and compute $\widetilde{\ell}_{i,t} = k(i, I_t) h_t / p_{I_t, t}$ for all $i = 1, \dots, N$;

(3) compute $w_{i,t} = w_{i,t-1} e^{-\eta \widetilde{\ell}(i, Y_t)}$ for all $i = 1, \dots, N$.

As this forecaster is randomized, we carry out its analysis in the nonoblivious opponent model and thus write the outcomes as random variables Y_t.

Denoting by $\mathbb{E}_t$ the conditional expectation given $I_1, \ldots, I_{t-1}$ (i.e., the expectation with respect to the distribution $\mathbf{p}_t$ of the random variable I_t), observe that

$$\mathbb{E}_t \widetilde{\ell}(i, Y_t) = \sum_{j=1}^{N} p_{j,t} \frac{k(i, j) h(j, Y_t)}{p_{j,t}}$$

$$= \sum_{j=1}^{N} k(i, j) h(j, Y_t) = \ell(i, Y_t)$$

and therefore $\widetilde{\ell}(i, Y_t)$ is an unbiased estimate of the loss $\ell(i, Y_t)$.

The next result bounds the expected regret of the forecaster defined above. It serves as a first step of a more useful result, Theorem 6.6, which states that a similar bound also applies for the actual (random) regret with overwhelming probability. In this result the per-round regret $\frac{1}{n} \left(\widehat{L}_n - \min_{i=1,\ldots,N} L_{i,n} \right)$ decreases to 0 at a rate $n^{-1/3}$. This is significantly slower than the best rate $n^{-1/2}$ obtained in the "full information" case. In Section 6.6 we show that this rate cannot be improved in general. Thus, the price paid for having access only to some feedback except for the actual outcomes is the deterioration in the rate of convergence. However, Hannan consistency is still achievable whenever the conditions of the theorem are satisfied. (See also Theorem 6.6 for a significantly more precise statement.)

Theorem 6.5. *Consider a partial monitoring game* $(\mathbf{L}, \mathbf{H})$ *such that the loss and feedback matrices satisfy* $\mathbf{L} = \mathbf{K}\mathbf{H}$ *for some* $N \times N$ *matrix* $\mathbf{K}$, *with* $k^* = \max\{1, \max_{i,j} |k(i, j)|\}$. *Then the forecaster for partial monitoring, run with parameters*

$$\eta = \frac{1}{C} \left(\frac{\ln N}{Nn} \right)^{2/3} \qquad \text{and} \qquad \gamma = C \left(\frac{N^2 \ln N}{n} \right)^{1/3},$$

where $C = (k^* \sqrt{e - 2})^{2/3}$, *satisfies*

$$\mathbb{E}\left[\sum_{t=1}^{n} \ell(I_t, Y_t) \right] - \min_{i=1,\ldots,N} \mathbb{E}\left[\sum_{t=1}^{n} \ell(i, Y_t) \right] \leq 3 \left(k^* \sqrt{e - 2} \right)^{2/3} (Nn)^{2/3} (\ln N)^{1/3}$$

for all $n \geq (\ln N)/(Nk^* \sqrt{e - 2})$.

Proof.   The first steps of the proof are based on a simple modification of the standard argument of Theorem 2.2. On the one hand, for any $j = 1, \ldots, N$ we have

$$\ln \frac{W_n}{W_0} = \ln \left(\sum_{i=1}^{N} e^{-\eta \widetilde{L}_{i,n}} \right) - \ln N \geq -\eta \widetilde{L}_{j,n} - \ln N.$$

On the other hand, for each $t = 1, \ldots, n$,

$$\ln \frac{W_t}{W_{t-1}} = \ln \sum_{i=1}^{N} \frac{w_{i,t-1}}{W_{t-1}} e^{-\eta \widetilde{\ell}(i, Y_t)}$$

$$= \ln \sum_{i=1}^{N} \frac{p_{i,t} - \gamma/N}{1 - \gamma} e^{-\eta \widetilde{\ell}(i, Y_t)}$$

$$\leq \ln \sum_{i=1}^{N} \frac{p_{i,t} - \gamma/N}{1-\gamma} \left(1 - \eta\widetilde{\ell}(i,Y_t) + (e-2)\eta^2\,\widetilde{\ell}(i,Y_t)^2\right)$$

$$(\text{since } e^x \leq 1 + x + (e-2)x^2 \text{ whenever } x \leq 1)$$

$$\leq \ln\left(1 - \frac{\eta}{1-\gamma}\sum_{i=1}^{N}\widetilde{\ell}(i,Y_t)\left(p_{i,t} - \frac{\gamma}{N}\right) + \frac{(e-2)\eta^2}{1-\gamma}\sum_{i=1}^{N}\widetilde{\ell}(i,Y_t)^2 p_{i,t}\right)$$

$$\leq -\frac{\eta}{1-\gamma}\sum_{i=1}^{N}\widetilde{\ell}(i,Y_t)\left(p_{i,t} - \frac{\gamma}{N}\right) + \frac{(e-2)\eta^2}{1-\gamma}\sum_{i=1}^{N}\widetilde{\ell}(i,Y_t)^2 p_{i,t}.$$

Summing the inequality over $t = 1, \ldots, n$ and comparing the obtained upper and lower bounds for $\ln(W_n/W_0)$, we have

$$\sum_{t=1}^{n}\sum_{i=1}^{N}\widetilde{\ell}(i,Y_t)p_{i,t} - (1-\gamma)\widetilde{L}_{j,n}$$

$$\leq (1-\gamma)\frac{\ln N}{\eta} + \eta(1-\gamma)(e-2)\sum_{t=1}^{n}\sum_{i=1}^{N}\widetilde{\ell}(i,Y_t)^2\,p_{i,t} + \sum_{t=1}^{n}\sum_{i=1}^{N}\frac{\gamma}{N}\widetilde{\ell}_{i,t}$$

$$\leq \frac{\ln N}{\eta} + \eta(e-2)\sum_{t=1}^{n}\sum_{i=1}^{N}\widetilde{\ell}(i,Y_t)^2\,p_{i,t} + \frac{\gamma}{N}\sum_{i=1}^{N}\widetilde{L}_{i,n}. \qquad (6.2)$$

Note that we used the fact that $|\eta\widetilde{\ell}(i,Y_t)| \leq 1$ for all t and i. This condition is satisfied whenever $Nk^*\eta/\gamma \leq 1$, which holds for our choice of η, γ, and n. Note that the assumption on n guarantees that $\eta \leq 1$. Furthermore, since our choice of γ implies that for $\gamma > 1$ the bound stated in the theorem holds trivially, we also assume $\gamma \leq 1$.

Now, recalling that $\mathbb{E}_t\,\widetilde{\ell}(i,Y_t) = \ell(i,Y_t)$, we get, after some trivial upper bounding,

$$\mathbb{E}\left[\sum_{t=1}^{n}\ell(I_t,Y_t)\right] - \min_{j=1,\ldots,N}\mathbb{E}\,L_{j,n} \leq \frac{\ln N}{\eta} + \gamma n + \eta(e-2)\sum_{t=1}^{n}\sum_{i=1}^{N}\mathbb{E}\left[p_{i,t}\,\widetilde{\ell}(i,Y_t)^2\right],$$

where we used $L_{j,n} = \sum_{t=1}^{n}\ell(j,Y_t) \leq n$.

The proof is concluded by handling the squared terms as follows:

$$\mathbb{E}_t\left[\widetilde{\ell}(i,Y_t)^2\right] = \sum_{j=1}^{N}\frac{k(i,j)^2 h(j,Y_t)^2}{p_{j,t}} \leq \frac{N^2(k^*)^2}{\gamma}. \qquad (6.3)$$

Our choice of η and γ finally yields the statement. ∎

As promised, the next result shows that an upper bound of the order $n^{2/3}$ holds not only for the expected regret but also with a large probability. The extension is not at all immediate, because it requires a careful analysis of the estimated losses. This is done by appropriate tail estimates for sums of martingale differences. The main result of this section is the following theorem.

Theorem 6.6. *Consider a partial monitoring game* (**L**, **H**) *such that the loss and feedback matrices satisfy* $\mathbf{L} = \mathbf{K}\mathbf{H}$ *for some* $N \times N$ *matrix* **K**, *with* $k^* = \max\{1, \max_{i,j}|k(i,j)|\}$.

Let $\delta \in (0, 1)$. Then the forecaster for partial monitoring, run with parameters

$$\eta = \left(\frac{\ln N}{2Nnk^*}\right)^{2/3} \quad \text{and} \quad \gamma = \left(\frac{(k^*N)^2 \ln N}{4n}\right)^{1/3}$$

satisfies, for all

$$n \geq \frac{1}{k^*N}\left(\ln \frac{N+3}{\delta}\right)^{3/2}$$

and with probability at least $1 - \delta$,

$$\sum_{t=1}^{n} \ell(I_t, Y_t) - \min_{i=1,\ldots,N} \sum_{t=1}^{n} \ell(i, Y_t)$$

$$\leq 10 \left(Nnk^*\right)^{2/3} (\ln N)^{1/3} \sqrt{\ln \frac{2(N+3)}{\delta}}.$$

The starting point of the proof is inequality (6.2). We show that, with an overwhelming probability, the right-hand side is less than something of the order $n^{2/3}$ and that the left-hand side is close to the actual regret

$$\sum_{t=1}^{n} \ell(I_t, Y_t) - \min_{j=1,\ldots,N} L_{j,n}.$$

Our main tool is the martingale inequality in Lemma A.8. This inequality implies the following two lemmas. Recall the notation

$$\bar{\ell}(\mathbf{p}_t, Y_t) = \sum_{i=1}^{N} p_{i,t}\,\ell(I_t, Y_t) \quad \text{and} \quad \widetilde{\ell}(\mathbf{p}_t, Y_t) = \sum_{i=1}^{N} p_{i,t}\,\widetilde{\ell}(I_t, Y_t).$$

Lemma 6.3. *With probability at least $1 - \delta/(N + 3)$,*

$$\sum_{t=1}^{n} \bar{\ell}(\mathbf{p}_t, Y_t) \leq \sum_{t=1}^{n} \widetilde{\ell}(\mathbf{p}_t, Y_t) + 2k^*N\sqrt{\frac{n}{\gamma}\ln\frac{N+3}{\delta}}.$$

Proof. Define $X_t = \bar{\ell}(\mathbf{p}_t, Y_t) - \widetilde{\ell}(\mathbf{p}_t, Y_t)$. Clearly, $\mathbb{E}_t\,X_t = 0$ and the X_t's form a martingale difference sequence with respect to $I_1, I_2, \ldots$. Since

$$\mathbb{E}_t[X_t^2] = \sum_{i,j} p_{i,t}p_{j,t}\,\mathbb{E}_t\left[\widetilde{\ell}(i, Y_t)\widetilde{\ell}(j, Y_t)\right]$$

$$= \sum_{i,j} p_{i,t}p_{j,t}\sum_{m=1}^{N} p_{m,t}\frac{k(i, m)k(j, m)h(m, Y_t)^2}{p_{m,t}^2},$$

we have $\Sigma_n^2 = \sum_{t=1}^{n} \mathbb{E}_t[X_t^2] \leq n(k^*)^2N^2/\gamma$. Thus, the statement follows directly by Lemma A.8 and the assumption on n. ∎

Lemma 6.4. *For each fixed j, with probability at least* $1 - \delta/(N + 3)$,

$$\left| L_{j,n} - \widetilde{L}_{j,n} \right| \le 2k^* N \sqrt{\frac{n}{\gamma} \ln \frac{2(N + 3)}{\delta}}.$$

Proof. Just as in the previous lemma, use Lemma A.8 for the martingale difference sequence $\widetilde{\ell}(j, Y_t) - \ell(j, Y_t)$ to obtain the stated inequality. ∎

The next two lemmas are easy consequences of the Hoeffding–Azuma inequality. In particular, the following result is an immediate corollary of Lemma A.7.

Lemma 6.5. *With probability at least* $1 - \delta/(N + 3)$,

$$\sum_{t=1}^{n} \ell(I_t, Y_t) \le \sum_{t=1}^{n} \overline{\ell}(\mathbf{p}_t, Y_t) + \sqrt{\frac{n}{2} \ln \frac{N + 3}{\delta}}.$$

Lemma 6.6. *With probability at least* $1 - \delta/(N + 3)$,

$$\sum_{t=1}^{n} \sum_{i=1}^{N} \widetilde{\ell}(i, Y_t)^2 \, p_{i,t} \le \frac{(Nk^*)^2}{\gamma} n + \frac{(Nk^*)^2}{\gamma^2} \sqrt{\frac{n}{2} \ln \frac{N + 3}{\delta}}.$$

Proof. Let $X_t = \sum_{i=1}^{N} \widetilde{\ell}(i, Y_t)^2 \, p_{i,t}$. Since $0 \le X_t \le (Nk^*/\gamma)^2$, Lemma A.7 implies that

$$\mathbb{P}\left[\sum_{t=1}^{n} V_t > \left(\frac{Nk^*}{\gamma} \right)^2 \sqrt{\frac{n}{2} \ln \frac{N + 3}{\delta}} \right] \le \frac{\delta}{N + 3},$$

where $V_t = X_t - \mathbb{E}_t \, X_t$. The proof is now concluded by using $\mathbb{E}_t \, X_t \le (Nk^*)^2/\gamma$, as already proved in (6.3). ∎

The proof of the main result is now an easy combination of these lemmas.

Proof of Theorem 6.6. The condition $Nk^*\eta/\gamma \le 1$ is satisfied with the proposed choices of η and γ, thus (6.2) is still valid. By Lemmas 6.3, 6.4, 6.5, and 6.6, combined with the union-of-events bound, with probability at least $1 - \delta$ we have, simultaneously,

$$\sum_{t=1}^{n} \overline{\ell}(\mathbf{p}_t, Y_t) \le \sum_{t=1}^{n} \widetilde{\ell}(\mathbf{p}_t, Y_t) + 2k^* N \sqrt{\frac{n}{\gamma} \ln \frac{N + 3}{\delta}} \tag{6.4}$$

$$\left| L_{j,n} - \widetilde{L}_{j,n} \right| \le 2k^* N \sqrt{\frac{n}{\gamma} \ln \frac{2(N + 3)}{\delta}} \tag{6.5}$$

$$\sum_{t=1}^{n} \ell(I_t, Y_t) \le \sum_{t=1}^{n} \overline{\ell}(\mathbf{p}_t, Y_t) + \sqrt{\frac{n}{2} \ln \frac{N + 3}{\delta}} \tag{6.6}$$

and

$$\sum_{t=1}^{n}\sum_{i=1}^{N}\widetilde{\ell}(i, Y_t)^2 \, p_{i,t} < \frac{(Nk^*)^2}{\gamma}n + \frac{(Nk^*)^2}{\gamma^2}\sqrt{\frac{n}{2}\ln\frac{N+3}{\delta}}. \tag{6.7}$$

On this event, we can bound the regret as follows:

$$\sum_{t=1}^{n}\ell(I_t, Y_t) - \min_{j=1,\dots,N} L_{j,n}$$

$$\leq \sum_{t=1}^{n}\overline{\ell}(\mathbf{p}_t, Y_t) - \min_{j=1,\dots,N} L_{j,n} + \sqrt{\frac{n}{2}\ln\frac{N+3}{\delta}} \quad \text{(by (6.6))}$$

$$\leq \sum_{t=1}^{n}\widetilde{\ell}(\mathbf{p}_t, Y_t) - \min_{j=1,\dots,N} L_{j,n} + 2k^*N\sqrt{\frac{n}{\gamma}\ln\frac{N+3}{\delta}} + \sqrt{\frac{n}{2}\ln\frac{N+3}{\delta}} \quad \text{(by (6.4))}$$

$$\leq \sum_{t=1}^{n}\widetilde{\ell}(\mathbf{p}_t, Y_t) - \min_{j=1,\dots,N} \widetilde{L}_{j,n} + 4k^*N\sqrt{\frac{n}{\gamma}\ln\frac{2(N+3)}{\delta}} + \sqrt{\frac{n}{2}\ln\frac{N+3}{\delta}} \quad \text{(by (6.5))}$$

$$\leq \frac{\ln N}{\eta} + \eta(e-2)\sum_{t=1}^{n}\sum_{i=1}^{N}\widetilde{\ell}(i, Y_t)^2 \, p_{i,t} + n\gamma + 4k^*N\sqrt{\frac{n}{\gamma}\ln\frac{2(N+3)}{\delta}}$$

$$+ \sqrt{\frac{n}{2}\ln\frac{N+3}{\delta}} \quad \text{(by (6.2) and (6.5))}$$

$$\leq \frac{\ln N}{\eta} + \eta(e-2)\frac{(Nk^*)^2}{\gamma}n + \eta(e-2)\frac{(Nk^*)^2}{\gamma^2}\sqrt{\frac{n}{2}\ln\frac{N+3}{\delta}} + n\gamma$$

$$+ 4k^*N\sqrt{\frac{n}{\gamma}\ln\frac{2(N+3)}{\delta}} + \sqrt{\frac{n}{2}\ln\frac{N+3}{\delta}} \quad \text{(by (6.7))}.$$

Resubstituting the proposed values of γ and η, and overapproximating, gives the claimed result. ∎

Theorem 6.6 guarantees the existence of a forecasting strategy with a regret of order $n^{2/3}$ whenever the rank of the feedback matrix $\mathbf{H}$ is not smaller than the rank of the matrix $\begin{bmatrix}\mathbf{H}\\\mathbf{L}\end{bmatrix}$. (Note that Hannan consistency may be achieved under the same condition, see Exercise 6.5.) This condition is satisfied for a wide class of problems. As an illustration, we consider the examples described in Section 6.4.

Example 6.5 (Multi-armed bandit problem). Recall that in the case of the multi-armed bandit problem the condition of Theorem 6.6 is trivially satisfied because $\mathbf{H} = \mathbf{L}$. Indeed, one may take $\mathbf{K}$ to be the identity matrix so that $k^* = 1$. In a subsequent section we show that in this case significantly smaller regrets may be achieved than those guaranteed by Theorem 6.6 by a carefully designed prediction algorithm. □

Example **6.6** *(Dynamic pricing).* In the dynamic pricing problem, described in the introduction of this chapter, the feedback matrix is given by $h(i, j) = a\,\mathbb{I}_{\{i \le j\}} + b\,\mathbb{I}_{\{i > j\}}$ for some arbitrarily chosen values of a and b. By choosing, for example, $a = 1$ and $b = 0$, it is clear that **H** is an invertible matrix and therefore one may choose $\mathbf{K} = \mathbf{L} \cdot \mathbf{H}^{-1}$ and obtain a Hannan-consistent strategy with regret of order $n^{2/3}$. Thus, the seller has a way of selecting the prices I_t such that his loss is not much larger than what could have been achieved had he known the values Y_t of all customers and offered the best constant price. Note that with this choice of a and b the value of k^* equals 1 (i.e., does not depend on N). Therefore the upper bound for the regret in terms of n and N is of the order $(nN \log N)^{2/3}$. Note also that the defining expression of **K** does not assume any special form for the loss matrix **L**. Hence, whenever **H** is invertible, Hannan consistency is achieved no matter how the loss matrix is chosen. $\square$

Example **6.7** *(Apple tasting).* In the apple tasting problem described earlier one may choose the feedback values $a = b = 1$ and $c = 0$. This makes the feedback matrix invertible and, once again, Theorem 6.6 applies. $\square$

Example **6.8** *(Label efficient prediction).* Recall next the variant of the label efficient prediction problem in which the loss and feedback matrices are

$$\mathbf{L} = \begin{bmatrix} 1 & 1 \\ 0 & 1 \\ 1 & 0 \end{bmatrix} \quad \text{and} \quad \mathbf{H} = \begin{bmatrix} a & b \\ c & c \\ c & c \end{bmatrix}.$$

Here the rank of **L** equals 2, and so it suffices to encode the feedback matrix such that its rank equals 2. One possibility is to choose $a = 1/2$, $b = 1$, and $c = 1/4$. Then we have $\mathbf{L} = \mathbf{K}\mathbf{H}$ for

$$\mathbf{K} = \begin{bmatrix} 0 & 2 & 2 \\ 2 & -2 & -2 \\ -2 & 4 & 4 \end{bmatrix}.$$

This example of label efficient prediction reveals that the bound of Theorems 6.5 and 6.6 cannot be improved significantly in general. In particular, there exist partial monitoring games for which the conditions of the theorems hold, yet the regret is $\Omega(n^{2/3})$. This follows by a slight modification of the proof of Theorem 6.4 by noting that the lower bound obtained in the setting of label efficient prediction holds in the earlier example in the partial monitoring problem. More precisely, we have the following. $\square$

Theorem 6.7. *For any label efficient forecaster there exists a sequence of outcomes* $y_1, y_2, \ldots$ *such that, for all large enough n, the forecaster's expected regret satisfies*

$$\mathbb{E}\left[\sum_{t=1}^{n} \ell(I_t, y_t) - \min_{i=1,\ldots,N} \sum_{t=1}^{n} \ell(i, y_t) \right] \ge c n^{2/3}$$

where c is a universal constant.

The proof is left to the reader as an exercise.

Remark 6.3. Even though it is not possible to improve the dependence in n of the upper bounds of Theorems 6.5 and 6.6 in general, in some special cases a rate of $O(n^{-1/2})$ is achievable. A main example of this situation is the multi-armed bandit problem (see Section 6.8). Another instance is described in Exercise 6.7. Note also that the bound of Theorem 6.6 does not depend explicitly on the value of the cardinality M of the set of outcomes, but a dependence on M may be hidden in k^*. However, in some important special cases, such as the multi-armed bandit problem, this value is independent of M. In such cases the result extends easily to infinite sets $\mathcal{Y}$ of outcomes. In particular, the case when the loss matrix changes with time can be treated this way.

6.6   Hannan Consistency and Partial Monitoring

In this section we discuss conditions on the loss and feedback matrices under which it is possible to construct Hannan-consistent forecasting strategies. Theorem 6.6 (more precisely, Exercise 6.5) states that whenever there is an encoding of the values of the feedback such that the rank of the loss-feedback matrix $\begin{bmatrix} \mathbf{H} \\ \mathbf{L} \end{bmatrix}$ does not exceed that of the feedback matrix $\mathbf{H}$, then Hannan consistency is achievable.

This condition is basically sufficient and necessary for obtaining Hannan consistency if either $N = 2$ (i.e., the predictor has two actions to choose from) or $M = 2$ (i.e., the outcomes are binary). When $N = 2$ or $M = 2$, then, apart from trivial cases, Hannan consistency is impossible to achieve if $\mathbf{L}$ cannot be written as $\mathbf{K} \mathbf{H}$ for some encoding of the feedback matrix $\mathbf{H}$ and for some matrix $\mathbf{K}$ (for the precise statements, see Exercises 6.8 and 6.9).

In general, however, it is not true that the existence of a Hannan consistent predictor is guaranteed if and only if the loss matrix $\mathbf{L}$ can be expressed as $\mathbf{K} \mathbf{H}$. To see this, consider the following simple example.

Example 6.9. Let $N = M = 3$ and

$$\mathbf{L} = \begin{bmatrix} 0 & 1 & 1 \\ 1 & 0 & 1 \\ 1 & 1 & 0 \end{bmatrix} \quad \text{and} \quad \mathbf{H} = \begin{bmatrix} a & b & c \\ d & d & d \\ e & e & e \end{bmatrix}.$$

Clearly, for all choices of the numbers a, b, c, d, e, the rank of the feedback matrix is at most 2 and therefore there is no matrix $\mathbf{K}$ for which $\mathbf{L} = \mathbf{K} \mathbf{H}$. However, note that whenever the first action is played, the forecaster has full information about the outcome Y_t. Formally, an action $i \in \{1, \ldots, N\}$ is said to be *revealing* for a feedback matrix $\mathbf{H}$ if all entries in the ith row of $\mathbf{H}$ are different. We now prove the existence of a Hannan-consistent forecaster for all problems in which there exists a revealing action. $\square$

We start by introducing our forecasting strategy for partial monitoring games with revealing actions.

A FORECASTER FOR REVEALING ACTIONS

Parameters: $0 \le \varepsilon \le 1$ and $\eta > 0$. Action r is revealing.

Initialization: $\mathbf{w}_0 = (1, \ldots, 1)$.

For each round $t = 1, 2, \ldots$,

    (1) draw an action J_t from $\{1, \ldots, N\}$ according to the distribution $p_{i,t} = w_{i,t-1}/(w_{1,t-1} + \cdots + w_{N,t-1})$ for $i = 1, \ldots, N$;

    (2) draw a Bernoulli random variable Z_t such that $\mathbb{P}[Z_t = 1] = \varepsilon$;

    (3) if $Z_t = 1$, then play the revealing action, $I_t = r$, observe Y_t, and compute

$$w_{i,t} = w_{i,t-1} e^{-\eta\, \ell(i, Y_t)/\varepsilon} \qquad \text{for each } i = 1, \ldots, N;$$

    (4) otherwise, play $I_t = J_t$ and let $w_{i,t} = w_{i,t-1}$ for each $i = 1, \ldots, N$.

Theorem 6.8. *Consider a partial monitoring game* $(\mathbf{L}, \mathbf{H})$ *such that* $\mathbf{L}$ *has a revealing action. Let* $\delta \in (0, 1)$. *If the forecaster for revealing actions is run with parameters*

$$\varepsilon = \max\left\{0, \frac{m - \sqrt{2m \ln(4/\delta)}}{n}\right\} \qquad and \qquad \eta = \sqrt{\frac{2\varepsilon \ln N}{n}},$$

where $m = (4n)^{2/3}(\ln(4N/\delta))^{1/3}$, *then*

$$\frac{1}{n}\left(\sum_{t=1}^{n} \ell(I_t, Y_t) - \min_{i=1,\ldots,N} L_{1,n}\right) \le 8 n^{-1/3}\left(\ln \frac{4N}{\delta}\right)^{1/3}$$

holds with probability at least $1 - \delta$.

Proof. The proof is a straightforward adaptation of the proof of Theorem 6.2 for the label efficient forecaster. In particular, the forecaster for revealing actions essentially coincides with the label efficient forecaster in Section 6.2. Indeed, Theorem 6.2 ensures that, with probability at least $1 - \delta$, not more than m among the Z_t have value 1 and that the regret accumulated over those rounds with $Z_t = 0$ is bounded by $8n\sqrt{\frac{1}{m} \ln \frac{4N}{\delta}}$. Since each time a revealing action is chosen the loss suffered is at most 1, this in turn implies that

$$\sum_{t=1}^{n} \ell(I_t, Y_t) - \min_{j=1,\ldots,N} \sum_{t=1}^{n} \ell(j, Y_t) \le m + 8n\sqrt{\frac{\ln(4N/\delta)}{m}}.$$

Substituting the proposed value for the parameter m concludes the proof. ∎

Remark 6.4 (Dependence on the number of actions). Observe that, even when the condition of Theorem 6.6 is satisfied, the bound of Theorem 6.8 is considerably tighter. Indeed, even though the dependence on the time horizon n is identical in both bounds (of order $n^{-1/3}$), the bound of Theorem 6.8 depends on the number of actions N in a logarithmic way only. As an example, consider the case of the multi-armed bandit problem. Recall that here $\mathbf{H} = \mathbf{L}$ and there is a revealing action if and only if the loss matrix has a row whose elements are all different. In such a case Theorem 6.8 provides a bound of order $((\ln N)/n)^{1/3}$. On the other hand, there exist bandit problems for which, if $N \le n$, it is impossible to achieve a per-round regret smaller than $\frac{1}{20}\sqrt{N/n}$ (see Theorem 6.11). If N is large, the logarithmic dependence of Theorem 6.8 thus gives a considerable advantage.

Interestingly, even if $\mathbf{L}$ cannot be expressed as $\mathbf{K}\mathbf{H}$, the existence of a revealing action ensures that the general forecaster of Section 6.5 may be used to achieve a small regret. This may be done by first converting the problem into another partial monitoring problem for which the general forecaster can be used. The basic step of this conversion is to replace the pair $(\mathbf{L}, \mathbf{H})$ of $N \times M$ matrices by a pair $(\mathbf{L}', \mathbf{H}')$ of $mN \times M$ matrices where $m \leq M$ denotes the cardinality of the set $S = \{s_1, \ldots, s_m\}$ of signals (i.e., the number of distinct elements of the matrix $\mathbf{H}$). In the obtained prediction problem the forecaster chooses among mN actions at each time instance. The converted loss matrix $\mathbf{L}'$ is obtained simply by repeating each row of the original loss matrix m times. The new feedback matrix $\mathbf{H}'$ is binary and is defined by

$$H'(m(i - 1) + k, j) = \mathbb{I}_{\{h(i,j)=s_k\}}, \qquad i = 1, \ldots, N, \ k = 1, \ldots, m, \ j = 1, \ldots, M.$$

Note that this way we get rid of the inconvenient problem of how to encode, in a natural way, the feedback symbols. If the matrices

$$\mathbf{H}' \quad \text{and} \quad \begin{bmatrix} \mathbf{H}' \\ \mathbf{L}' \end{bmatrix}$$

have the same rank, then there exists a matrix $\mathbf{K}'$ such that $\mathbf{L}' = \mathbf{K}'\mathbf{H}'$ and the forecaster of Section 6.5 may be applied to obtain a forecaster that has an average regret of order $n^{-1/3}$ for the converted problem. However, it is easy to see that any forecaster A with such a bounded regret for the converted problem may be trivially transformed into a forecaster A' for the original problem with the same regret bound: A' simply takes an action i whenever A takes an action of the form $m(i - 1) + k$ for any $k = 1, \ldots, m$.

The conversion procedure guarantees Hannan consistency for a large class of partial monitoring problems. For example, if the original problem has a revealing action i, then $m = M$ and the $M \times M$ submatrix formed by the rows $M(i - 1) + 1, \ldots, Mi$ of $\mathbf{H}'$ is the identity matrix (up to some permutations over the rows) and therefore has full rank. Then obviously a matrix $\mathbf{K}'$ with the desired property exists and the procedure described above leads to a forecaster with an average regret of order $n^{-1/3}$.

This last statement may be generalized in a straightforward way to an even larger class of problems as follows.

Corollary 6.2 (Distinguishing actions). *Assume that the feedback matrix $\mathbf{H}$ is such that for each outcome $j = 1, \ldots, M$ there exists an action $i \in \{1, \ldots, N\}$ such that for all outcomes $j' \neq j$, $h(i, j) \neq h(i, j')$. Then the conversion procedure described above leads to a Hannan-consistent forecaster with an average regret of order $n^{-1/3}$.*

The rank of $\mathbf{H}'$ may be considered as a measure of the information provided by the feedback. The highest possible value is achieved by matrices $\mathbf{H}'$ with rank M. For such feedback matrices, Hannan-consistency may be achieved for all associated loss matrices $\mathbf{L}'$.

Even though the above conversion strategy applies to a large class of problems, the associated condition fails to characterize the set of pairs $(\mathbf{L}, \mathbf{H})$ for which a Hannan consistent forecaster exists. Indeed, Piccolboni and Schindelhauer [234] show a second simple conversion of the pair $(\mathbf{L}', \mathbf{H}')$ that can be applied in situations when there is no matrix $\mathbf{K}'$ with the property $\mathbf{L}' = \mathbf{K}' \mathbf{H}'$ (this second conversion basically deals with some actions that they define as "useless"). In these situations a Hannan-consistent procedure may be constructed on the basis of the forecaster of Section 6.5. On the other hand, Piccolboni and Schindelhauer also show that if the condition of Theorem 6.6 is not satisfied after the second step of conversion, then there exists an external randomization over the sequences of outcomes such that the sequence of expected regrets grows at least as n, where the expectations are understood with respect to the forecaster's auxiliary randomization and the external randomization. Thus, a proof by contradiction using the dominated-convergence theorem shows that Hannan consistency is impossible to achieve in these cases. This result, combined with Theorem 6.6, implies the following gap theorem.

Corollary 6.3. *Consider a partial monitoring game* $(\mathbf{L}, \mathbf{H})$. *If Hannan consistency can be achieved, then there exists a Hannan-consistent forecaster whose average regret vanishes at rate* $n^{-1/3}$.

Thus, whenever it is possible to force the average regret to converge to 0, a convergence rate of order $n^{-1/3}$ is also possible.

We close this section by pointing out a situation in which Hannan consistency is impossible to achieve.

Example 6.10. Consider a case with $N = M = 3$ and

$$
\mathbf{L} = \begin{bmatrix} 0 & 1 & 1 \\ 1 & 0 & 1 \\ 1 & 1 & 0 \end{bmatrix} \quad \text{and} \quad \mathbf{H} = \begin{bmatrix} a & b & b \\ a & b & b \\ a & b & b \end{bmatrix}.
$$

In this example, the second and third outcomes are indistinguishable for the forecaster. Obviously, Hannan consistency is impossible to achieve in this case. However, it is easy to construct a strategy for which

$$
\frac{1}{n} \left(\sum_{t=1}^{n} \ell(I_t, Y_t) - \min \left(L_{1,n}, \frac{L_{2,n} + L_{3,n}}{2} \right) \right) = o(1),
$$

with probability 1 (see Exercise 6.10 for a somewhat more general statement). □

6.7 Multi-armed Bandit Problems

This and the next two sections are dedicated to multi-armed bandit problems, which we define in Example 6.1 of Section 6.4. Recall that in this problem the forecaster, after making a prediction, learns his own loss $\ell(I_t, Y_t)$ but not the value of the outcome Y_t. Thus, the forecaster does not have access to the losses he would have suffered had he chosen a different action. The goal of the forecaster remains the same, which is to guarantee that his cumulative loss $\sum_{t=1}^{n} \ell(I_t, Y_t)$ is not much larger than the cumulative loss of the best action, $\min_{i=1,\dots,N} \sum_{t=1}^{n} \ell(i, Y_t)$.

In the classical formulation of multi-armed bandit problems (see, e.g., Robbins [245], Lai and Robbins [189]) it is assumed that, for each action i, the losses $\ell(i, y_1), \dots, \ell(i, y_n)$

are randomly and independently drawn according to a fixed but unknown distribution. In such a case, at the beginning of the game one may sample all arms to estimate the means of the loss distributions (this is called the *exploration* phase), and while the forecaster has a high level of confidence in the sharpness of the estimated values, one may keep choosing the action with the smallest estimated loss (the *exploitation* phase). Indeed, under mild conditions on the distribution, one may achieve that the per-round regret

$$\frac{1}{n}\sum_{t=1}^{n}\ell(I_t, y_t) - \frac{1}{n}\min_{i=1,\dots,N}\sum_{t=1}^{n}\ell(i, y_t)$$

converges to 0 with probability 1, and delicate tradeoff between exploitation and exploration may be achieved under additional assumptions (see the exercises).

Here we investigate the significantly more challenging problem when the outcomes Y_t are generated in the nonoblivious opponent model. This variant has been called the *nonstochastic* (or *adversarial*) multi-armed bandit problem. Thus, the problem we consider is the same as in Section 4.2, but now the forecaster's actions cannot depend on the past values of $\ell(i, Y_t)$ except when $i = I_t$.

As we have already observed in Example 6.1, the adversarial bandit problem is a special case of the prediction problem under partial monitoring defined in Section 6.4. In this special case the feedback matrix **H** equals the loss matrix **L**. Therefore, Theorems 6.5 and 6.6 apply because one may use the general forecaster for partial monitoring with **K** taken as the identity matrix. The forecaster that, according to these theorems, achieves a per-round regret of order $n^{-1/3}$ (and is, therefore, Hannan-consistent) takes, at time t, the action I_t drawn according to the distribution $\mathbf{p}_t$, defined by

$$p_{i,t} = (1-\gamma)\frac{e^{-\eta\tilde{L}_{i,t-1}}}{\sum_{k=1}^{N}e^{-\eta\tilde{L}_{k,t-1}}} + \frac{\gamma}{N},$$

where $\tilde{L}_{i,t} = \sum_{s=1}^{t}\tilde{\ell}(i, Y_t)$ is the estimated cumulative loss and

$$\tilde{\ell}(i, Y_t) = \begin{cases} \ell(i, Y_t)/p_{i,t} & \text{if } I_t = i \\ 0 & \text{otherwise} \end{cases}$$

is used to estimate the loss $\ell(i, Y_t)$ at time t for all $i = 1, \dots, N$. The parameters $\gamma, \eta \in (0, 1)$ may be set according to the values specified in Theorems 6.5 and 6.6 (with $k^* = 1$).

Interestingly, even though the bounds of order $n^{2/3}$ established in Theorems 6.5 and 6.6 are not improvable in general partial monitoring problems (see Theorem 6.7), in the special case of the multi-armed bandit problem, significantly better performance may be achieved by an appropriate modification of the forecaster described above. The details and the corresponding bound are shown in Section 6.8, and Section 6.9 establishes a matching lower bound.

We close this section by mentioning that the forecaster strategy defined above, which may be viewed as an extension of the exponentially weighted average predictor, may be generalized. In particular, just as in Section 4.2, we allow the use of potential functions other than the exponential. This way we obtain a large family of Hannan-consistent forecasting strategies for the adversarial multi-armed bandit problem.

Recall that weighted-average randomized strategies were defined such that at time t, the forecaster chooses action i randomly with probability

$$p_{i,t} = \frac{\nabla_i \Phi(\mathbf{R}_{t-1})}{\sum_{k=1}^{N} \nabla_k \Phi(\mathbf{R}_{t-1})} = \frac{\phi'(R_{i,t-1})}{\sum_{k=1}^{N} \phi'(R_{k,t-1})},$$

where Φ is an appropriate potential function defined in Section 4.2. In the bandit problem this strategy is not feasible because the regrets $R_{i,t-1} = \sum_{s=1}^{t-1} \left(\overline{\ell}(\mathbf{p}_s, Y_s) - \ell(i, Y_s) \right)$ are not available to the forecaster. The components $r_{i,t} = \overline{\ell}(\mathbf{p}_t, Y_t) - \ell(i, Y_t)$ of the regret vector $\mathbf{r}_t$ are substituted by the components $\widetilde{r}_{i,t} = \ell(I_t, Y_t) - \widetilde{\ell}(i, Y_t)$ of the *estimated regret* $\widetilde{\mathbf{r}}_t$. Finally, at time t an action I_t is chosen from the set $\{1, \ldots, N\}$ randomly according to the distribution $\mathbf{p}_t$, defined by

$$p_{i,t} = (1 - \gamma_t) \frac{\phi'(\widetilde{R}_{i,t-1})}{\sum_{k=1}^{N} \phi'(\widetilde{R}_{k,t-1})} + \frac{\gamma_t}{N},$$

where $\gamma_t \in (0, 1)$ is a nonincreasing sequence of constants that we typically choose to converge to 0 at a certain rate.

First of all note that the defined prediction strategy is feasible because at time t it only depends on the past losses $\ell(I_s, Y_s)$, $s = 1, \ldots, t - 1$. Note that the estimated regret $\widetilde{\mathbf{r}}_t$ is an "unbiased" estimate of the regret $\mathbf{r}_t$ in the sense that $\mathbb{E}\left[\widetilde{r}_{i,t} \mid I_1, \ldots, I_{t-1} \right] = r_{i,t}$.

Observe also that, apart from the necessary modification of the notion of regret, we have also introduced the constants γ_t whose role is to keep the probabilities $p_{i,t}$ far away from 0 for all i, which is necessary to make sure that a sufficient amount of time is spent for "exploration."

The next result states Hannan consistency of the strategy defined above under general conditions on the potential function.

Theorem 6.9. *Let*

$$\Phi(\mathbf{u}) = \psi \left(\sum_{i=1}^{N} \phi(u_i) \right)$$

be a potential function. Assume that

(i) $\sum_{t=1}^{n} 1/\gamma_t^2 = o(n^2 / \ln n)$;

(ii) *For all vectors* $\mathbf{v}_t = (v_{1,t}, \ldots, v_{n,t})$ *with* $|v_{i,t}| \leq N/\gamma_t$,

$$\lim_{n \to \infty} \frac{1}{\psi(\phi(n))} \sum_{t=1}^{n} C(\mathbf{v}_t) = 0,$$

where C is the function defined in Theorem 2.1;

(iii) *for all vectors* $\mathbf{u}_t = (u_{1,t}, \ldots, u_{n,t})$, *with* $u_{i,t} \leq t$,

$$\lim_{n \to \infty} \frac{1}{\psi(\phi(n))} \sum_{t=1}^{n} \gamma_t \sum_{i=1}^{N} \nabla_i \Phi(\mathbf{u}_t) = 0$$

(iv) *for all vectors* $\mathbf{u}_t = (u_{1,t}, \ldots, u_{n,t})$, *with* $u_{i,t} \leq t$,

$$\lim_{n \to \infty} \frac{\ln n}{\psi(\phi(n))} \sqrt{\sum_{t=1}^{n} \frac{1}{\gamma_t^2} \left(\sum_{i=1}^{N} \nabla_i \Phi(\mathbf{u}_t) \right)^2} = 0$$

Then the potential-based prediction strategy defined above satisfies

$$\lim_{n\to\infty}\frac{1}{n}\left(\sum_{t=1}^{n}\ell(I_t,Y_t)-\min_{i=1,\ldots,N}\sum_{t=1}^{n}\ell(i,Y_t)\right)=0,$$

with probability 1.

The proof is an appropriate extension of the proof of Theorem 2.1 and is left as a guided exercise (see Exercise 6.19). The theorem merely states Hannan consistency, but the rates of convergence that may be deduced from the proof are far from being optimal. To achieve the best rates the martingale inequalities used in the proof should be considerably refined, as is done in the next section. Two concrete examples follow.

Exponential Potentials

In the special case of exponential potentials of the form

$$\Phi_\eta(\mathbf{u})=\frac{1}{\eta}\ln\left(\sum_{i=1}^{N}e^{\eta u_i}\right),$$

the forecaster of Theorem 6.9 coincides with that described at the beginning of the section. Its Hannan consistency may be deduced from both Theorem 6.9 and Theorem 6.6.

Polynomial Potentials

Recall, from Chapter 2, the polynomial potentials of the form

$$\Phi_p(\mathbf{u})=\left(\sum_{i=1}^{N}(u_i)_+^p\right)^{2/p}=\|\mathbf{u}_+\|_p^2,$$

where $p\geq 2$. Here one may take $\phi(x)=x_+^p$ and $\psi(x)=x^{2/p}$. In this case the conditions of Theorem 6.9 may be checked easily. First note that $\psi(\phi(n))=n^2$. Recall from Section 2.1 that for any $\mathbf{u}\in R^N$, $C(\mathbf{u})\leq 2(p-1)\|\mathbf{u}\|_p^2$. Thus for condition (ii) of Theorem 6.9 to hold, it suffices that $\sum_{t=1}^{n}(1/\gamma_t^2)=o(n^2)$, which is implied by condition (i). To verify conditions (iii) and (iv) note that, for any $\mathbf{u}=(u_1,\ldots,u_N)\in R^N$,

$$\sum_{i=1}^{N}\nabla_i\Phi(\mathbf{u})=\frac{2\|\mathbf{u}_+\|_{p-1}^{p-1}}{\|\mathbf{u}_+\|_p^{p-2}}\leq\frac{2N^p\|\mathbf{u}_+\|_p^{p-1}}{\|\mathbf{u}_+\|_p^{p-2}}=2N^p\|\mathbf{u}_+\|_p,$$

where $\mathbf{u}_+=((u_1)_+,\ldots,(u_N)_+)$ and we applied Hölder's inequality. Thus, conditions (iii) and (iv) are satisfied whenever $(1/n^2)\sum_{t=1}^{n}t\,\gamma_t\to 0$ and $(\ln n/n^2)\sqrt{\sum_{t=1}^{n}t^2/\gamma_t^2}\to 0$, respectively. These two conditions, together with condition (i) requiring $(\ln n/n^2)\sum_{t=1}^{n}(1/\gamma_t^2)\to 0$, are sufficient to guarantee Hannan consistency of the potential-based strategy for any polynomial potential with $p\geq 2$. Taking, for example, $\gamma_t=t^a$, it is easy to check that all three conditions are satisfied for any $a\in(-1/2,0)$.

6.8   An Improved Bandit Strategy

In the previous sections we presented several forecasting strategies that guarantee Hannan-consistent prediction in the nonstochastic multi-armed bandit problem. The rates of convergence that may be obtained in a straightforward manner from Theorems 6.5 and 6.9 are, however, suboptimal. The purpose of this section is to introduce a slight modification in the forecaster of the previous section and achieve optimal rates of convergence.

We only consider exponential potentials and assume that the horizon (i.e., the total length n of the sequence to be predicted) is fixed and known in advance. The extension to unbounded or unknown horizon is, by now, a routine exercise.

Two modifications of the strategy described at the beginning of the previous section are necessary to achieve better rates of convergence. First of all, the modified strategy estimates *gains* instead of losses. For convenience, we introduce the notation $g(i, Y_t) = 1 - \ell(i, Y_t)$ and the estimated gains

$$\widetilde{g}(i, Y_t) = \begin{cases} g(i, Y_t)/p_{i,t} & \text{if } I_t = i \\ 0 & \text{otherwise,} \end{cases} \qquad i = 1, \dots, N.$$

Note that $\mathbb{E}[\widetilde{g}(i, Y_t) \mid I_1, \dots, I_{t-1}] = g(i, Y_t)$, and therefore $\widetilde{g}(i, Y_t)$ is an unbiased estimate of $g(i, Y_t)$ (different from $1 - \widetilde{\ell}(i, Y_t)$ used in the previous section). The reason for this modification is subtle. With the modified estimate the difference $g(i, t) - \widetilde{g}(i, t)$ is bounded by 1 from above, which is used in the martingale-type bound of Lemma 6.7 below.

The forecasting strategy is defined as follows.

A STRATEGY FOR THE MULTI-ARMED BANDIT PROBLEM

Parameters: Number of actions N, positive reals $\beta, \eta, \gamma \leq 1$.

Initialization: $w_{i,0} = 1$ and $p_{i,1} = 1/N$ for $i = 1, \dots, N$.

For each round $t = 1, 2 \dots$

  (1) select an action $I_t \in \{1, \dots, N\}$ according to the probability distribution $\mathbf{p}_t$;
  (2) calculate the estimated gains

$$g'(i, Y_t) = \widetilde{g}(i, Y_t) + \frac{\beta}{p_{i,t}} = \begin{cases} (g(i, Y_t) + \beta)/p_{i,t} & \text{if } I_t = i \\ \beta/p_{i,t} & \text{otherwise;} \end{cases}$$

  (3) update the weights $w_{i,t} = w_{i,t-1} e^{\eta g'(i, Y_t)}$;
  (4) calculate the updated probability distribution

$$p_{i,t+1} = (1 - \gamma)\frac{w_{i,t}}{W_t} + \frac{\gamma}{N}, \qquad i = 1, \dots, N.$$

Another modification is that instead of an unbiased estimate, a slightly larger quantity is used by the strategy. To this end, the strategy uses the quantities $g'(i, Y_t) = \widetilde{g}(i, Y_t) + \beta/p_{i,t}$, where β is a positive parameter whose value is to be determined later. Note that we give up the unbiasedness of the estimate to guarantee that the estimated cumulative gains are, with large probability, not much smaller than the actual (unknown) cumulative gains. Thus, the new estimate may be interpreted as an upper confidence bound on the gain.

The next theorem shows that, as a function of the number of rounds n, the regret is of the same order $O(\sqrt{n})$ of magnitude as in the "full information" case, that is, in the problem of randomized prediction with expert advice discussed in Section 4.2. The price one has to pay for not being able to measure the loss of the actions (except for the selected one) is in the dependence on the number N of actions. The bound derived in Theorem 6.10 is proportional to $\sqrt{N \ln N}$, as opposed to the "full information" bound, which only grows as $\sqrt{\ln N}$ with the number of actions. Thus, the bound is significantly better than that implied by Theorem 6.6, which only guarantees a bound of order $(nN)^{2/3}(\ln N)^{1/3}$. In Section 6.9 we show that the $\sqrt{nN \ln N}$ upper bound shown here is optimal up to a factor of order $\sqrt{\ln N}$. Thus, the per-round regret is about the order $\sqrt{\ln N/(n/N)}$, opposed to $\sqrt{(\ln N)/n}$ achieved in the full information case. This bound reflects the fact that the available information in the bandit problem is the Nth part of that of the original, full information case. This phenomenon is similar to the one we observed in the case of label efficient prediction, where the per-round regret was of the form $\sqrt{\ln N/m}$.

Theorem 6.10. *For any $\delta \in (0, 1)$ and for any $n \geq 8N \ln(N/\delta)$, if the forecaster for the multi-armed bandit problem is run with parameters*

$$\gamma \leq \frac{1}{2}, \qquad 0 < \eta \leq \frac{\gamma}{2N}, \qquad and \qquad \sqrt{\frac{1}{nN} \ln \frac{N}{\delta}} \leq \beta \leq 1$$

then, with probability at least $1 - \delta$, the regret satisfies

$$\widehat{L}_n - \min_{i=1,\dots,N} L_{i,n} \leq n\big(\gamma + \eta(1 + \beta)N\big) + \frac{\ln N}{\eta} + 2nN\beta.$$

In particular, choosing

$$\beta = \sqrt{\frac{1}{nN} \ln \frac{N}{\delta}}, \qquad \gamma = \frac{4N\beta}{3 + \beta}, \qquad and \qquad \eta = \frac{\gamma}{2N},$$

one has

$$\widehat{L}_n - \min_{i=1,\dots,N} L_{i,n} \leq \frac{11}{2}\sqrt{nN \ln(N/\delta)} + \frac{\ln N}{2}.$$

The condition on n ensures that $4N\beta/(3 + \beta) = \gamma$ is at most $1/2$ for the stated choice of β.

The analysis of Theorem 6.10 is similar, in spirit, to the proof of Theorem 6.6. The essential novelty necessary to obtain the refined bounds is a more careful bounding of the difference between the estimated and true cumulative losses of each action.

Introduce the notation

$$G'_{i,n} = \sum_{t=1}^{n} g'(i, Y_t) \qquad and \qquad G_{i,n} = \sum_{t=1}^{n} g(i, Y_t).$$

The following lemma is the key to the proof of Theorem 6.10.

Lemma 6.7. *Let $\delta \in (0, 1)$. For any $\beta \in \big[\sqrt{\ln(N/\delta)/(nN)}, 1\big]$ and $i \in \{1, \dots, N\}$, we have $\mathbb{P}\big[G_{i,n} > G'_{i,n} + \beta nN\big] \leq \delta/N$.*

Proof.

$$\mathbb{P}\big[G_{i,n} > G'_{i,n} + \beta nN\big] = \mathbb{P}\big[G_{i,n} - G'_{i,n} > \beta nN\big]$$
$$\le \mathbb{E}\big[\exp\big(\beta\,(G_{i,n} - G'_{i,n})\big)\big]\exp\big(-\beta^2 nN\big)$$
$$\text{(by Markov's inequality).}$$

Observe now that since $\beta \ge \sqrt{\ln(N/\delta)/(nN)}$, $\exp\big(-\beta^2 nN\big) \le \delta/N$, and therefore it suffices to prove that $\mathbb{E}\big[\exp\big(\beta\,(G_{i,n} - G'_{i,n})\big)\big] \le 1$. Introducing for $t = 1, \dots, n$ the random variable

$$Z_t = \exp\big(\beta(G_{i,t} - G'_{i,t})\big),$$

we clearly have

$$Z_t = \exp\left(\beta\left(g(i, Y_t) - \widetilde{g}(i, Y_t) - \frac{\beta}{p_{i,t}}\right)\right) Z_{t-1}.$$

Next, for $t = 2, \dots, n$, we bound $\mathbb{E}[Z_t \mid I_1, \dots, I_{t-1}] = \mathbb{E}_t\, Z_t$ as follows:

$$\mathbb{E}_t\, Z_t = Z_{t-1}\,\mathbb{E}_t\left[\exp\left(\beta\left(g(i, Y_t) - \widetilde{g}(i, Y_t) - \frac{\beta}{p_{i,t}}\right)\right)\right]$$
$$\le Z_{t-1}e^{-\beta^2/p_{i,t}}\,\mathbb{E}_t\left[1 + \beta\big(g(i, Y_t) - \widetilde{g}(i, Y_t)\big) + \beta^2\big(g(i, Y_t) - \widetilde{g}(i, Y_t)\big)^2\right]$$
$$\text{(since } \beta \le 1,\ g(i, Y_t) - \widetilde{g}(i, Y_t) \le 1 \text{ and } e^x \le 1 + x + x^2 \text{ for } x \le 1\text{)}$$
$$= Z_{t-1}e^{-\beta^2/p_{i,t}}\,\mathbb{E}_t\left[1 + \beta^2\big(g(i, Y_t) - \widetilde{g}(i, Y_t)\big)^2\right]$$
$$\text{(since } \mathbb{E}_t\big[g(i, Y_t) - \widetilde{g}(i, Y_t)\big] = 0\text{)}$$
$$\le Z_{t-1}e^{-\beta^2/p_{i,t}}\left(1 + \frac{\beta^2}{p_{i,t}}\right)$$
$$\text{(since } \mathbb{E}_t\big[(g(i, Y_t) - \widetilde{g}(i, Y_t))^2\big] \le \mathbb{E}_t\big[\widetilde{g}(i, Y_t)^2\big] \le 1/p_{i,t}\text{)}$$
$$\le Z_{t-1} \quad \text{(since } 1 + x \le e^x\text{)}.$$

Taking expected values of both sides of the inequality, we have $\mathbb{E}\, Z_t \le \mathbb{E}\, Z_{t-1}$. Because $\mathbb{E}\, Z_1 \le 1$, we obtain $\mathbb{E} Z_n \le 1$, as desired. ∎

Proof of Theorem 6.10. Let $W_t = \sum_{i=1}^{N} w_{i,t}$. Note first that

$$\ln\frac{W_n}{W_0} = \ln\left(\sum_{i=1}^{N} e^{\eta G'_{i,n}}\right) - \ln N$$
$$\ge \ln\left(\max_{i=1,\dots,N} e^{\eta G'_{i,n}}\right) - \ln N$$
$$= \eta \max_{i=1,\dots,N} G'_{i,n} - \ln N.$$

On the other hand, for each $t = 1, \ldots, n$, since $\beta \leq 1$ and $\eta \leq \gamma/(2N)$ imply that $\eta g'(i, Y_t) \leq 1$, we may write

$$\ln \frac{W_t}{W_{t-1}} = \ln \sum_{i=1}^{N} \frac{w_{i,t-1}}{W_{t-1}} e^{\eta g'(i,Y_t)}$$

$$= \ln \sum_{i=1}^{N} \frac{p_{i,t} - \gamma/N}{1 - \gamma} e^{\eta g'(i,Y_t)}$$

$$\leq \ln \sum_{i=1}^{N} \frac{p_{i,t} - \gamma/N}{1 - \gamma} \left(1 + \eta g'(i, Y_t) + \eta^2 g'(i, Y_t)^2\right)$$

(since $e^x \leq 1 + x + x^2$ for $x \leq 1$)

$$\leq \ln \left(1 + \frac{\eta}{1 - \gamma} \sum_{i=1}^{N} p_{i,t}\, g'(i, Y_t) + \frac{\eta^2}{1 - \gamma} \sum_{i=1}^{N} p_{i,t}\, g'(i, Y_t)^2\right)$$

(since $\sum_{i=1}^{N} (p_{i,t} - \gamma/N) = 1 - \gamma$)

$$\leq \frac{\eta}{1 - \gamma} \sum_{i=1}^{N} p_{i,t}\, g'(i, Y_t) + \frac{\eta^2}{1 - \gamma} \sum_{i=1}^{N} p_{i,t}\, g'(i, Y_t)^2$$

(since $\ln(1 + x) \leq x$ for all $x > -1$).

Observe now that, by the definition of $g'(i, Y_t)$,

$$\sum_{i=1}^{N} p_{i,t}\, g'(i, Y_t) = g(I_t, Y_t) + N\beta$$

and that

$$\sum_{i=1}^{N} p_{i,t}\, g'(i, Y_t)^2 = \sum_{i=1}^{N} p_{i,t}\, g'(i, Y_t) \left(\mathbb{I}_{\{I_t=i\}} \frac{g(i, Y_t)}{p_{i,t}} + \frac{\beta}{p_{i,t}}\right)$$

$$= g'(I_t, Y_t) g(I_t, Y_t) + \beta \sum_{i=1}^{N} g'(i, Y_t)$$

$$\leq (1 + \beta) \sum_{i=1}^{N} g'(i, Y_t).$$

Substituting into the upper bound, summing over $t = 1, \ldots, n$, and writing $\widehat{G}_n = \sum_{t=1}^{n} g(I_t, Y_t)$, we obtain

$$\ln \frac{W_n}{W_0} \leq \frac{\eta}{1 - \gamma} \widehat{G}_n + \frac{\eta}{1 - \gamma} nN\beta + \frac{\eta^2(1 + \beta)}{1 - \gamma} \sum_{i=1}^{N} G'_{i,n}.$$

Comparing the upper and lower bounds for $\ln(W_n/W_0)$ and rearranging,

$$\widehat{G}_n - (1 - \gamma) \max_{i=1,\ldots,N} G'_{i,n} \geq -\frac{(1 - \gamma)\ln N}{\eta} - nN\beta - \eta(1 + \beta) \sum_{i=1}^{N} G'_{i,n}$$

$$\geq -\frac{\ln N}{\eta} - nN\beta - \eta(1 + \beta)N \max_{i=1,\ldots,N} G'_{i,n};$$

that is,

$$\widehat{G}_n \geq \left(1 - \gamma - \eta(1+\beta)N\right) \max_{i=1,\ldots,N} G'_{i,n} - \frac{\ln N}{\eta} - nN\beta.$$

By Lemma 6.7 and the union-of-events bound, with probability at least $1 - \delta$,

$$\max_{i=1,\ldots,N} G'_{i,n} \geq \max_{i=1,\ldots,N} G_{i,n} - \beta nN$$

whenever $\sqrt{\ln(N/\delta)/(nN)} \leq \beta \leq 1$. Thus, with probability at least $1 - \delta$, we have

$$\widehat{G}_n \geq \left(1 - \gamma - \eta(1+\beta)N\right) \max_{i=1,\ldots,N} G_{i,n} - \frac{\ln N}{\eta} - nN\beta\left(2 - \gamma - \eta(1+\beta)N\right).$$

In terms of the losses $\widehat{L}_n = n - \widehat{G}_n$ and $L_{i,n} = n - G_{i,n}$, and noting that $1 - \gamma - \eta(1+\beta)N \geq 0$ by the choice of the parameters, the inequality is rewritten as

$$\begin{aligned}
\widehat{L}_n &\leq \left(1 - \gamma - \eta(1+\beta)N\right) \min_{i=1,\ldots,N} L_{i,n} + n\left(\gamma + \eta(1+\beta)N\right) + \frac{\ln N}{\eta} \\
&\quad + nN\beta\left(2 - \gamma - \eta(1+\beta)N\right) \\
&\leq \min_{i=1,\ldots,N} L_{i,n} + n\left(\gamma + \eta(1+\beta)N\right) + \frac{\ln N}{\eta} + 2nN\beta,
\end{aligned}$$

as desired. ∎

Remark 6.5 (Gains vs. losses). It is worth noting that there exists a fundamental asymmetry in the non-stochastic multi-armed bandit problem considered here. The fact that our randomized strategies sample with overwhelming probability the action with the currently best estimate makes, in a certain sense, the game with losses easier than the game with gains. The following simple argument explains why: with losses, if the loss of the action more often sampled starts to increase, its sampling probability drops quickly. With gains, if some action sampled with overwhelming probability becomes a bad action (yielding small gains), its sampling probability simply ceases to grow.

Remark 6.6 (A technical note). One may be tempted to try to generalize the argument of Theorem 6.10 to other problems of prediction under partial monitoring. By doing that, one quickly sees that the key property of the bandit problem, which allows to obtain the regret bound of order $\sqrt{n}$, is that the quadratic term $\sum_{i=1}^{N} p_{i,t} g'(i, Y_t)^2$ can be bounded by a random variable whose expected value is at most proportional to N. The corresponding term in the proof of Theorem 6.5, dealing with the general partial monitoring problem, could only be bounded by something of the order $N^2(k^*)^2/\gamma$, making the regret bound of order $n^{2/3}$ inevitable.

6.9 Lower Bounds for the Bandit Problem

Next we present a simple lower bound for the performance of any multi-armed bandit strategy. The main result of the section shows that the upper bound derived in the previous section cannot be improved by more than logarithmic factors. In particular, it is shown below that the regret of any prediction strategy (randomized or not) in the nonstochastic multi-armed bandit problem can be as large as $\Omega(\sqrt{nN})$. The dependence on time n is similar to the "full information" case in which the best obtainable bound is of order $\sqrt{n \ln N}$. The main message of the next theorem is that the multi-armed bandit problem is essentially more difficult than the simple randomized prediction problem of Section 4.2 in that the dependence on the number of actions (or experts) is much heavier. This is due to the fact that, because of the limited information available in bandit problems, an important part of the effort has to be devoted to exploration, that is, to the estimation of the cumulative losses of each action.

Theorem 6.11. *Let n, $N \geq 1$ be such that $n > N/(4 \ln(4/3))$, and assume that the cardinality $M = |\mathcal{Y}|$ of the outcome space is at least 2^N. There exists a loss function such that for any, possibly randomized, prediction strategy*

$$\sup_{y^n \in \mathcal{Y}^n} \left(\mathbb{E} \, \widehat{L}_n - \min_{i=1,\dots,N} L_{i,n} \right) \geq \sqrt{nN} \frac{\sqrt{2} - 1}{\sqrt{32 \ln(4/3)}}.$$

Proof. First we prove the theorem for deterministic strategies. The general case will follow by a simple argument. The main idea of the proof is to show that there exists a loss function and random choices of the outcomes y_t such that for any prediction strategy, the expected regret is large (here expectation is understood with respect to the random choice of the y_t). More precisely, we describe a probability distribution for the random choice of $\ell(i, y_t)$. It is easy to see that if $M \geq 2^N$, then there exists a loss function ℓ and a distribution for y_t such that the distribution of $\ell(i, y_t)$ is as described next. Let $\ell(i, y_t) = X_{i,t}, i = 1, \dots, N, t = 1, \dots, n$ be random variables whose joint distribution is defined as follows: let Z be uniformly distributed on $\{1, \dots, N\}$. For each i, given $Z = i$, $X_{j,1}, \dots, X_{j,n}$ are conditionally independent Bernoulli random variables with parameter $1/2$ if $j \neq i$ and with parameter $1/2 - \varepsilon$ if $j = i$, where the value of the positive parameter $\varepsilon < 1/4$ is specified below. Then obviously, for any (non-randomized) prediction strategy,

$$\sup_{y^n \in \mathcal{Y}^n} \left(\widehat{L}_n - \min_{i=1,\dots,N} L_{i,n} \right) \geq \mathbb{E} \left[\widehat{L}_n - \min_{i=1,\dots,N} L_{i,n} \right],$$

where the expectation on the right-hand side is now with respect to the random variables $X_{i,t}$. Thus, it suffices to bound, from below, the expected regret for the randomly chosen losses. First observe that

$$\mathbb{E} \left[\min_{i=1,\dots,N} L_{i,n} \right] = \sum_{j=1}^{N} \mathbb{P}[Z = j] \, \mathbb{E} \left[\min_{i=1,\dots,N} L_{i,n} \,\Big|\, Z = j \right]$$

$$\leq \frac{1}{N} \sum_{j=1}^{N} \min_{i=1,\dots,N} \mathbb{E} \left[L_{i,n} \,\big|\, Z = j \right]$$

$$= \frac{n}{2} - n\varepsilon.$$

The nontrivial part is to bound, from below, the expected loss $\mathbb{E} \, \widehat{L}_n$ of an arbitrary prediction strategy. To this end, fix a (deterministic) prediction strategy, and let I_t denote the action it chooses at time t. Clearly, I_t is determined by the losses $X_{I_1,1}, \dots, X_{I_{t-1},t-1}$. Also, let $T_j = \sum_{t=1}^{n} \mathbb{I}_{\{I_t = j\}}$ be the number of times action j is played by the strategy. Then, writing

$\mathbb{E}_i$ for $\mathbb{E}[\cdot \mid Z = i]$, we may write

$$\mathbb{E}\,\widehat{L}_n = \frac{1}{N}\sum_{i=1}^{N}\mathbb{E}_i\,\widehat{L}_n \quad \text{(by symmetry)}$$

$$= \frac{1}{N}\sum_{i=1}^{N}\mathbb{E}_i\sum_{t=1}^{n}\sum_{j=1}^{N}X_{j,t}\,\mathbb{I}_{\{I_t=j\}}$$

$$= \frac{1}{N}\sum_{i=1}^{N}\sum_{t=1}^{n}\sum_{j=1}^{N}\mathbb{E}_i\,\mathbb{E}_i\,[X_{j,t}\,\mathbb{I}_{\{I_t=j\}} \mid X_{I_1,1},\dots,X_{I_{t-1},t-1}]$$

$$= \frac{1}{N}\sum_{i=1}^{N}\sum_{t=1}^{n}\sum_{j=1}^{N}\mathbb{E}_i\,X_{j,t}\,\mathbb{E}_i\,\mathbb{I}_{\{I_t=j\}}$$

(since I_t is determined by $X_{I_1,1},\dots,X_{I_{t-1},t-1}$)

$$= \frac{n}{2} - \varepsilon\frac{1}{N}\sum_{i=1}^{N}\mathbb{E}_i\,T_i.$$

Hence,

$$\mathbb{E}\left[\widehat{L}_n - \min_{i=1,\dots,N}L_{i,n}\right] \geq \varepsilon\left(n - \frac{1}{N}\sum_{i=1}^{N}\mathbb{E}_i\,T_i\right)$$

and the proof reduces to bounding $\mathbb{E}_i\,T_i$ from above, that is, to showing that if ε is sufficiently small, the best action cannot be chosen too many times by any prediction strategy. We do this by comparing $\mathbb{E}_i\,T_i$ with the expected number of times action i is played by the same prediction strategy when the distribution of the losses of all actions are Bernoulli with parameter $1/2$. To this end, introduce the i.i.d. random variables $X'_{j,t}$ such that $\mathbb{P}[X'_{j,t} = 0] = \mathbb{P}[X'_{j,t} = 1] = 1/2$ and let T'_i be the number of times action i is played by the prediction strategy when $\ell(j, y_t) = X'_{j,t}$ for all j and t. Similarly, I'_t denotes the index of the action played at time t under the losses $X'_{j,t}$. Writing $\mathbb{P}_i$ for the conditional distribution $\mathbb{P}[\cdot \mid Z = i]$, introduce the probability distributions over the set of binary sequences $b^n = (b_1, \dots, b_n) \in \{0, 1\}^n$,

$$q(b^n) = \mathbb{P}_i\big[X_{I_1,1} = b_1, \dots, X_{I_n,n} = b_n\big]$$

and

$$q'(b^n) = \mathbb{P}_i\big[X'_{I'_1,1} = b_1, \dots, X'_{I'_n,n} = b_n\big].$$

Note that $q'(b^n) = 2^{-n}$ for all b^n. Observe that for any $b^n \in \{0, 1\}^n$,

$$\mathbb{E}_i\big[T_i \mid X_{I_1,1} = b_1, \dots, X_{I_n,n} = b_n\big] = \mathbb{E}\big[T'_i \mid X'_{I'_1,1} = b_1, \dots, X'_{I'_n,n} = b_n\big],$$

and therefore we may write

$$\mathbb{E}_i\,T_i - \mathbb{E}\,T'_i$$

$$= \sum_{b^n \in \{0,1\}^n} q(b^n)\,\mathbb{E}_i\big[T_i \mid X_{I_1,1} = b_1, \dots, X_{I_n,n} = b_n\big]$$

$$- \sum_{b^n \in \{0,1\}^n} q'(b^n)\,\mathbb{E}\big[T'_i \mid X'_{I'_1,1} = b_1, \dots, X'_{I'_n,n} = b_n\big]$$

$$= \sum_{b^n \in \{0,1\}^n} (q(b^n) - q'(b^n)) \mathbb{E}_i\big[T_i \mid X_{I_1,1} = b_1, \dots, X_{I_n,n} = b_n\big]$$

$$\leq \sum_{b^n \,:\, q(b^n) > q'(b^n)} (q(b^n) - q'(b^n)) \mathbb{E}_i\big[T_i \mid X_{I_1,1} = b_1, \dots, X_{I_n,n} = b_n\big]$$

$$\leq n \sum_{b^n \,:\, q(b^n) > q'(b^n)} (q(b^n) - q'(b^n))$$

$$\text{(since } \mathbb{E}_i\big[T_i \mid X_{I_1,1} = b_1, \dots, X_{I_n,n} = b_n\big] \leq n\text{).}$$

The expression on the right-hand side is n times the so-called *total variation* distance of the probability distributions q and q'. The total variation distance may be bounded conveniently by Pinsker's inequality (see Section A.2), which states that

$$\sum_{b^n \,:\, q(b^n) > q'(b^n)} (q(b^n) - q'(b^n)) \leq \sqrt{\frac{1}{2} D(q' \| q)},$$

where

$$D(q' \| q) = \sum_{b^n \in \{0,1\}^n} q'(b^n) \ln \frac{q'(b^n)}{q(b^n)}$$

is the Kullback–Leibler divergence of the distributions q' and q. Denoting

$$q_t(b_t \mid b^{t-1}) = \mathbb{P}_i\big[X_{I_t,t} = b_t \mid X_{I_1,1} = b_1, \dots, X_{I_{t-1},t-1} = b_{t-1}\big]$$

and

$$q'_t(b_t \mid b^{t-1}) = \mathbb{P}_i\big[X'_{I'_t,t} = b_t \mid X'_{I'_1,1} = b_1, \dots, X'_{I'_{t-1},t-1} = b_{t-1}\big]$$

by the chain rule for relative entropy (see Section A.2) we have

$$D(q' \| q) = \sum_{t=1}^{n} \frac{1}{2^{t-1}} \sum_{b^{t-1} \in \{0,1\}^{t-1}} D\big(q'_t(\cdot \mid b^{t-1}) \,\|\, q_t(\cdot \mid b^{t-1})\big)$$

$$= \sum_{t=1}^{n} \frac{1}{2^{t-1}} \left(\sum_{b^{t-1} \,:\, I_t \neq i} D\big(q'_t(\cdot \mid b^{t-1}) \,\|\, q_t(\cdot \mid b^{t-1})\big) \right.$$

$$\left. + \sum_{b^{t-1} \,:\, I_t = i} D\big(q'_t(\cdot \mid b^{t-1}) \,\|\, q_t(\cdot \mid b^{t-1})\big) \right)$$

$$\text{(since } b^{t-1} \text{ determines the value } I_t\text{).}$$

Clearly, if b^{t-1} is such that $I_t \neq i$, then $q'_t(\cdot \mid b^{t-1})$ and $q_t(\cdot \mid b^{t-1})$ both are symmetric Bernoulli distributions and $D\big(q'_t(\cdot \mid b^{t-1}) \,\|\, q_t(\cdot \mid b^{t-1})\big) = 0$. On the other hand, if b^{t-1} is such that $I_t = i$, then $q'_t(\cdot \mid b^{t-1})$ is a symmetric Bernoulli distribution and $q_t(\cdot \mid b^{t-1})$ is Bernoulli with parameter $1/2 - \varepsilon$. In this case

$$D\big(q'_t(\cdot \mid b^{t-1}) \,\|\, q_t(\cdot \mid b^{t-1})\big) = -\frac{1}{2} \ln(1 - 4\varepsilon^2) \leq 8 \ln(4/3)\varepsilon^2,$$

where we used the elementary inequality $-\ln(1-x) \leq 4\ln(4/3)x$ for $x \in [0, 1/4]$. We have thus obtained

$$D(q'\|q) \leq 8\ln(4/3)\varepsilon^2 \sum_{t=1}^{n} \frac{1}{2^{t-1}} \sum_{b^{t-1}} \mathbb{I}_{\{b^{t-1} : I_t=i\}}.$$

Summarizing, we have

$$\frac{1}{N}\sum_{i=1}^{N}\left(\mathbb{E}_i\, T_i - \frac{n}{N}\right) = \frac{1}{N}\sum_{i=1}^{N}\left(\mathbb{E}_i\, T_i - \mathbb{E}\, T_i'\right)$$

$$\leq \frac{1}{N}\sum_{i=1}^{N} n\sqrt{\frac{1}{2}8\ln(4/3)\varepsilon^2 \sum_{t=1}^{n}\frac{1}{2^{t-1}}\sum_{b^{t-1}}\mathbb{I}_{\{b^{t-1} : I_t=i\}}}$$

$$\leq n\sqrt{\frac{1}{N}\sum_{i=1}^{N}4\ln(4/3)\varepsilon^2 \sum_{t=1}^{n}\frac{1}{2^{t-1}}\sum_{b^{t-1}}\mathbb{I}_{\{b^{t-1} : I_t=i\}}}$$

$$\text{(by Jensen's inequality)}$$

$$= n\sqrt{4\ln(4/3)\varepsilon^2 \sum_{t=1}^{n}\frac{1}{N}\sum_{i=1}^{N}\frac{1}{2^{t-1}}\sum_{b^{t-1}}\mathbb{I}_{\{b^{t-1} : I_t=i\}}}$$

$$= n\varepsilon\sqrt{\frac{4\ln(4/3)n}{N}},$$

and therefore

$$\mathbb{E}\left[\widehat{L}_n - \min_{i=1,\dots,N} L_{i,n}\right] \geq \varepsilon\left(n\left(1 - \frac{1}{N}\right) - n^{3/2}\varepsilon\sqrt{\frac{4\ln(4/3)}{N}}\right).$$

Bounding $1/N \leq 1/2$ and choosing $\varepsilon = \sqrt{cN/n}$, with $c = 1/(8\ln(4/3))$ (which is guaranteed to be less than $1/4$ by the condition on n), we obtain

$$\mathbb{E}\left[\widehat{L}_n - \min_{i=1,\dots,N} L_{i,n}\right] \geq \sqrt{nN}\frac{\sqrt{2}-1}{\sqrt{32\ln(4/3)}}$$

as desired. This finishes the proof for deterministic strategies. To see that the result remains true for any randomized strategy, just note that any randomized strategy may be regarded as a randomized choice from a class of deterministic strategies. Since the inequality is true for any deterministic strategy, it must hold even if we average over all deterministic strategies according to the randomization. Then, by Fubini's theorem, we find that the expected value (with respect to the random choice of the losses) of $\mathbb{E}\,\widehat{L}_n - \min_{i=1,\dots,N} L_{i,n}$ is bounded from below by $\sqrt{nN}(\sqrt{2}-1)/\sqrt{32\ln(4/3)}$ (where in $\mathbb{E}\,\widehat{L}_n$ the expectation is meant only with respect to the randomization of the strategy). Thus, because the maximum is at least as large as the expected value, we conclude that

$$\sup_{y^n \in \mathcal{Y}^n}\left(\mathbb{E}\,\widehat{L}_n - \min_{i=1,\dots,N} L_{i,n}\right) \geq \sqrt{nN}\frac{\sqrt{2}-1}{\sqrt{32\ln(4/3)}}. \quad \blacksquare$$

6.10   How to Select the Best Action

So far we have described several regret-minimizing strategies that draw, at each step, an action according to a certain probability distribution over the possible actions. In this section we investigate a different scenario in which the randomized strategy performs a single draw from the set of possible actions and then is forced to use the drawn action at each subsequent step. However, before performing the draw, the strategy is allowed to observe the outcome of all actions for an arbitrary amount of time. The goal of the strategy is to pick as early as possible an action yielding a large total gain. (In this setup it is more convenient to work with gains rather than losses.)

As a motivating application consider an entrepreneur who wants to start manufacturing a certain product. The production line can be configured to manufacture one of N different products. As reconfiguring the line has a certain fixed cost, the entrepreneur wants to choose a product whose sales will yield a total profit of at least d. The decision is based on a market analysis reporting the temporal evolution of potential sales for each of the N products. At the end of this "surveillance phase," a single product is chosen to be manufactured. We cast this example in our game-theoretic setup by assigning gain $x_{i,t}$ to action i at time t if $x_{i,t}$ is the profit of the entrepreneur originating from the sales of product i in the tth time interval. If the t-th time interval falls in the surveillance phase, then $x_{i,t}$ is the profit the entrepreneur would have obtained had he chosen to manufacture product i at any time earlier than t (we make the simplifying assumption that each such potential profit is measured exactly in the surveillance phase).

In this analysis we only consider actions yielding binary gains; that is, $x_{i,t} \in \{0, 1\}$ for each $t = 1, 2 \ldots$ and $i = 1, \ldots, N$. We assume gains are generated in the oblivious opponent model, specifying the binary gain of each action $i = 1, \ldots, N$ at each time step $t = 1, 2, \ldots$ so that every action has a finite total gain. That is, for every i there exists n_i such that $x_{i,t} = 0$ for all $t > n_i$. Let $G_{i,t} = x_{i,1} + \cdots + x_{i,t}$, and let $G_i = G_{i,n_i}$ be the total gain of action i. We write G^* to denote $\max_i G_i$. Because we are restricted to the oblivious opponent model, we may think of a *gain assignment* $x_{i,t} \in \{0, 1\}$ for $t = 1, \ldots, n_i$ and $i = 1, \ldots, N$ being determined at the beginning of the game and identify the choice of the opponent with the choice of a specific gain assignment.

Given an arbitrary and unknown gain assignment, at each time $t = 1, 2, \ldots$ a selection strategy observes the tuple $(x_{1,t}, \ldots, x_{N,t})$ of action gains and decides whether to choose an action or not. If no action is chosen, then the next tuple is shown, otherwise, the game ends. Suppose the game ends at time step t when the strategy chooses action k. Then the total gain of the strategy is the remaining gain $G_k - G_{k,t}$ of action k (all gains up to time t are lost).

The question we investigate here is how large the best total gain G^* has to be such that some randomized selection algorithm guarantees (with large probability) a gain of at least d, where d is a fixed quantity. Obviously, G^* has to be at least d, and the larger G^* the "easier" it is to select an action with a large gain. On the other hand, it is clear intuitively that G^* has to be substantially larger than d. Just observe that any selection strategy has a gain of d with probability at most $1/N$ on some game assignment satisfying $G^* = d$. (Let $x_{i,t} = 1$ for all i and $t \leq d - 1$, and let $x_{i,d} = 0$ for all but one action i.) The main result of this section shows that there exists a strategy gaining d with a large probability on every gain assignment satisfying $G^* = \Omega(d \ln N)$. More precisely, we show that the following randomized selection strategy, for any given $d \geq 1$, gains at least d with probability at least $1 - \delta$ on any gain assignment such that $G^* = \Omega\left(\frac{d}{\delta} \ln \frac{N}{\delta}\right)$.

A RANDOMIZED STRATEGY TO SELECT THE BEST ACTION

Parameters: real numbers $a, b > 0$.

Initialization: $G_{i,0} = 0$ for $i = 1, \ldots, N$.

For each round $t = 1, 2, \ldots$

    (1) for each $j = 1, \ldots, N$ observe $x_{j,t}$ and compute $G_{j,t} = G_{j,t-1} + x_{j,t}$;
    (2) determine the subset $\mathcal{N}_t \subseteq \{1, \ldots, N\}$ of actions j such that $x_{j,t} = 1$;
    (3) for each $j \in \mathcal{N}_t$ draw a Bernoulli random variable $Z_j = Z_{j,G_{j,t}}$ such that $\mathbb{P}[Z_j] = \min\{1, \ e^{a\,G_{j,t}-b}\}$;
    (4) if $Z_1 = 0, \ldots, Z_N = 0$, then continue; otherwise output the smallest index $i \in \mathcal{N}_t$ such that $Z_i = 1$ and exit.

This bound cannot be significantly improved. In fact, we show that no selection strategy can gain more than d with probability at least $1 - \delta$ on all gain assignments satisfying $G^* = O\left(\frac{d}{\delta} \ln N\right)$. Our randomized selection strategy uses, for each action i, independent Bernoulli random variables $Z_{i,1}, Z_{i,2}, \ldots$ such that $Z_{i,k}$ has parameter

$$p(k) = \min\{1, \ e^{ak-b}\}$$

for $a, b > 0$ (to be specified later).

Theorem 6.12. *For all $d \geq 1$ and $0 < \delta < 1$, if the randomized strategy defined above is run with parameters $a = \delta/(6d)$ and $b = \ln(6dN/\delta)$, then, with probability at least $1 - \delta$, some action i with a remaining gain of at least d will be selected whenever the gain assignment is such that*

$$G^* \geq d\left(1 + \frac{6}{\delta} \ln\left(\frac{6N}{\delta} \ln \frac{3}{\delta}\right)\right).$$

Proof. Fix a gain assignment such that G^* satisfies the condition of the theorem. We work in the sample space generated by the independent random variables $Z_{i,s}$ for $i = 1, \ldots, N$ and $s \geq 1$. For each i and for each $s > n_i$ we set $Z_{i,s} = 0$ with probability 1 to simplify notation. Thus, $Z_{i,s}$ can only be equal to 1 if s equals $G_{i,t}$ for some t with $x_{i,t} = 1$. Hence the sample space may be taken to be $\Omega = \{0, 1\}^M$, where $M \leq NG^*$ is the total number of those $x_{i,t}$ that are equal to 1.

Say that an action i is *up* at time t if $x_{i,t} = 1$. Say that an action i is *marked* at time t if i is up at time t and $Z_{i,G_{i,t}} = 1$. Hence, the strategy selects action i at time t if i is marked at time t, no other action $j < i$ is marked at time t, and no action has been marked before time t.

Let $A \subset \Omega$ be the event such that $Z_{j,s} = 0$ for $j = 1, \ldots, N$ and $s = 1, \ldots, d$. Let $W_{i,t} \subset \Omega$ be the event such that (i) action i is the only action marked at time t and (ii) $Z_{j,s} = 0$ for all $j = 1, \ldots, N$ and all $d < s < G_{j,t}$. Note that $W_{i,t}$ and $W_{j,t}$ are disjoint for $i \neq j$ and $W_{i,t}$ is empty unless $G_i > d$. Let $W = \bigcup_{i,t} W_{i,t}$. Define the one-to-one mapping

μ with domain $A \cap W$ that, for each i and t, maps each elementary event $\omega \in A \cap W_{i,t}$ to the elementary event $\mu(\omega)$ such that (recall that $p(k) = \min\{1, e^{ak-b}\}$)

- if $p(G_{i,t} - d) \geq 1/2$, then, $\mu(\omega)$ is equal to ω except for the component of ω corresponding to $Z_{i,G_{i,t}-d}$, which is set to 1.
- if $p(G_{i,t} - d) < 1/2$, then $\mu(\omega)$ is equal to ω except for the component of $Z_{i,G_{i,t}}$, which is set to 0, and the component of $Z_{i,G_{i,t}-d}$, which is set to 1.

(Note that for all $\omega \in A \cap W_{i,t}$, $Z_{i,G_{i,t}} = 1$ and $Z_{i,G_{i,t}-d} = 0$ by definition.)

The realization of the event $\mu(A \cap W)$ implies that the strategy selects an action i at time s such that $G_i - G_{i,s} \geq d$ (we call this a *winning event*). In fact, $A \cap W_{i,t}$ implies that no action other than i is selected before time t. Hence, $Z_{i,G_{i,t}-d} = 1$ ensures that i is selected at time $s < t$ and $G_i - G_{i,s} \geq d$.

We now move on to lower bounding the probability of $\mu(A \cap W_{i,t})$ in terms of $\mathbb{P}[A \cap W_{i,t}]$. We distinguish three cases.

Case 1. If $p(G_{i,t} - d) = 1$, then $\mathbb{P}[\mu(A \cap W_{i,t})] > \mathbb{P}[A \cap W_{i,t}] = 0$.

Case 2. If $1/2 \leq p(G_{i,t} - d) < 1$, then

$$\mathbb{P}[\mu(A \cap W_{i,t})] = \frac{p(G_{i,t} - d)}{1 - p(G_{i,t} - d)} \mathbb{P}[A \cap W_{i,t}],$$

and using $1/2 \leq p(G_{i,t} - d) < 1$ together with $e^{-ad} > 0$,

$$\frac{p(G_{i,t} - d)}{1 - p(G_{i,t} - d)} = \frac{e^{-ad} e^{a G_{i,t} - b}}{1 - e^{-ad} e^{a G_{i,t} - b}} \geq \frac{e^{-ad}/2}{1 - e^{-ad}/2}.$$

Case 3. If $p(G_{i,t} - d) < 1/2$, then

$$\mathbb{P}[\mu(A \cap W_{i,t})] = \frac{p(G_{i,t} - d)}{1 - p(G_{i,t} - d)} \frac{1 - p(G_{i,t})}{p(G_{i,t})} \mathbb{P}[A \cap W_{i,t}].$$

Using $p(G_{i,t} - d) < 1/2$ and $e^{-ad} \leq 1$, we get

$$\frac{p(G_{i,t} - d)}{1 - p(G_{i,t} - d)} \frac{1 - p(G_{i,t})}{p(G_{i,t})} = e^{-ad} \frac{1 - p(G_{i,t})}{1 - e^{-ad} p(G_{i,t})} \geq \frac{e^{-ad}/2}{1 - e^{-ad}/2}.$$

Now, because

$$\frac{e^{-ad}/2}{1 - e^{-ad}/2} = \frac{e^{-ad}}{2 - e^{-ad}} \geq \frac{1 - ad}{1 + ad} \geq 1 - 2ad,$$

exploiting the independence of A and W we get

$$\mathbb{P}[\mu(A \cap W)] \geq (1 - 2ad)\mathbb{P}[A]\mathbb{P}[W].$$

We now proceed by lower bounding the probabilities of the events A and W. For A we get

$$\mathbb{P}[A] \geq \prod_{j=1}^{N} \left(1 - p(\min\{d, n_j\})\right)^{\min\{d,n_j\}}$$

$$\geq \prod_{j=1}^{N} \left(1 - e^{a\min\{d,n_j\}-b}\right)^{\min\{d,n_j\}}$$

$$\geq \left(1 - e^{ad-b}\right)^{dN}$$

$$\geq 1 - dN\, e^{ad-b}.$$

To lower bound $\mathbb{P}[W]$, first observe that $\mathbb{P}[W] \geq 1 - (1 - p(G^* - d))^d$. Indeed, the complement of W implies that no action is ever marked after it has been up for d times, and this in turn implies that even the action that gains G^* is not marked the last d times it has been up (here, without loss of generality, we implicitly assume that $G^* \geq 2d$). Furthermore,

$$1 - \left(1 - p(G^* - d)\right)^d = \begin{cases} 1 & \text{if } p(G^* - d) = 1 \\ 1 - \left(1 - e^{a(G^*-d)-b}\right)^d & \text{if } p(G^* - d) < 1. \end{cases}$$

Piecing all together, we obtain

$$\mathbb{P}\left[\mu(A \cap W)\right]$$

$$\geq (1 - 2ad)\left(1 - dN\, e^{ad-b}\right)\left(1 - \left(1 - e^{a(G^*-d)-b}\right)^d\right)$$

$$\geq 1 - 2ad - dN\, e^{ad-b} - \left(1 - e^{a(G^*-d)-b}\right)^d.$$

To complete the proof, note that the setting $a = \delta/(6d)$ implies $2ad = \delta/3$. Moreover, the setting $b = \ln(6dN/\delta)$ implies $dN\, e^{ad-b} \leq \delta/3$. Finally, using $1 - x \leq e^{-x}$ for all x, straightforward algebra yields $\left(1 - e^{a(G^*-d)-b}\right)^d \leq \delta/3$ whenever

$$G^* \geq d\left(1 + \frac{6}{\delta}\ln\left(\frac{6N}{\delta}\ln\frac{3}{\delta}\right)\right).$$

This concludes the proof. ∎

We now state and prove the lower bound.

Theorem 6.13. *Let $N \geq 2$, $d \geq 1$, and $0 < \delta < (\ln N)/(\ln N + 1)$. For any selection strategy there exists a gain assignment with*

$$G^* = \left\lfloor \frac{1-\delta}{\delta}\ln N \right\rfloor d$$

such that, with probability at least $1 - \delta$, the gain of the strategy is not more than d.

Proof. As in the proof of Theorem 6.11 in Section 6.9, we prove the lower bound with respect to a random gain assignment and a possibly deterministic selection strategy. Then we use Fubini's theorem to turn this into a lower bound with respect to a deterministic gain assignment and a randomized selection strategy. We begin by specifying a probability distribution over gain assignments. Each action i satisfies $x_{i,t} = 1$ for $t = 1, \ldots, T_i - 1$ and $x_{i,t} = 0$ for all $t \geq T_i$, where $T_1, \ldots, T_N$ are random variables specified as follows. Say that an action i is *alive* at time t if $t < T_i$ and *dead* otherwise. Immediately before each of the time steps $t = 1, 1 + d, 1 + 2d, \ldots$ a random subset of the currently alive actions is chosen and all actions in this subset become dead. The subset is chosen so that for each $k = 1, 2, \ldots$ there are exactly $N_k = \lceil N^{1-k/m} \rceil$ actions alive at time steps $1 + (k - 1)d, \ldots, kd$, where the integer m will be determined by the analysis. Eventually, during time steps $1 + (m - 1)d, \ldots, md$ only one action remains alive (as we have $N_m = 1$), and from $t = 1 + md$ onward all actions are dead. Note that $G^* = md$ with probability 1.

It is easy to see that the strategy maximizing the probability, with respect to the random generation of gains, of choosing an action that survives for more than d time steps should select (it does not matter whether deterministically or probabilistically) an action among those still alive in the interval $1 + (m - 2)d, \ldots, (m - 1)d$ when $N_{m-1} = \lceil N^{1/m} \rceil$ actions are still alive. Set

$$m = \left\lfloor \frac{1 - \delta}{\delta} \ln N \right\rfloor.$$

The assumption $\delta < (\ln N)/(\ln N + 1)$ guarantees that $m \geq 1$ (if $m = 1$, then the optimal strategy chooses a random action at the very beginning of the game). Because $N_m = 1$, the probability of picking the single action that survives after time $(m - 1)d$ is at most

$$
\begin{aligned}
N^{-1/m} &\leq N^{-\frac{\delta/(1-\delta)}{\ln N}} \\
&= e^{-\delta/(1-\delta)} \\
&\leq e^{\ln(1-\delta)} \qquad \text{(using } \ln(1 + x) \leq x \text{ for all } x > -1\text{)} \\
&\leq 1 - \delta.
\end{aligned}
$$

Following the argument in the proof of Theorem 6.11, we view a randomized selection strategy as a probability distribution over deterministic strategies and then apply Fubini's theorem. Formally, for any randomized selection strategy achieving a total gain of $\widehat{G}$,

$$\inf_{\mu} \mathbb{E}' \left[\mathbb{I}_{\{\widehat{G} > d\}} \right] \leq \mathbb{E}\, \mathbb{E}' \left[\mathbb{I}_{\{\widehat{G} > d\}} \right] = \mathbb{E}' \, \mathbb{E} \left[\mathbb{I}_{\{\widehat{G} > d\}} \right] \leq \sup_{S} \mathbb{E} \left[\mathbb{I}_{\{\widehat{G} > d\}} \right] \leq 1 - \delta,$$

where μ ranges over all gain assignments, $\mathbb{E}'$ is the expectation taken with respect to the selection strategy's internal randomization, $\mathbb{E}$ is the expectation taken with respect to the random choice of the gain assignment, and S ranges over all deterministic selection strategies. ∎

6.11 Bibliographic Remarks

The problem of label efficient prediction was introduced by Helmbold and Panizza [155] in the restricted setup when losses are binary valued and there exists an action with zero cumulative loss. The material of Sections 6.2 and 6.3 is due to Cesa-Bianchi, Lugosi, and Stoltz [55]. However, the proof of Theorem 6.4 is substantially different from the proof appearing in [55] and borrows ideas from analogous results from statistical learning theory (see Devroye and Lugosi [89] and also Devroye, Györfi, and Lugosi [88]).

The notion of partial monitoring originates in game theory and was considered, among others, by Mertens, Sorin, and Zamir [216], Rustichini [251], and Mannor and

Shimkin [208]. Weissman and Merhav [308] and Weissman, Merhav, and Somekh-Baruch [309] consider various prediction problems in which the forecaster only observes a noisy version of the true outcomes. These may be considered as special partial monitoring problems with random feedback (see Exercises 6.11 and 6.12).

Piccolboni and Schindelhauer [234] rediscovered partial monitoring as a sequential prediction problem. Later, Cesa-Bianchi, Lugosi, and Stoltz [56] extended the results in [234] and addressed the problem of optimal rates. See also Auer and Long [14] for an analysis of some special cases of partial monitoring in prediction problems.

The forecaster strategy studied in Section 6.5 was defined by Piccolboni and Schindelhauer [234], who showed that its expected regret has a sublinear growth. The optimal rate of convergence and pointwise behavior of this strategy, stated in Theorems 6.5 and 6.6, were established in [56]. Piccolboni and Schindelhauer [234] describe sufficient and necessary conditions under which Hannan consistency is achievable (see also [56]). Rustichini [251]) and Mannor and Shimkin [208] consider a more general setup in which the feedback is not necessarily a deterministic function of the outcome and the action chosen by the fore-caster, but it may be random with a distribution depending on the action/outcome pair. Rustichini establishes a general existence theorem for Hannan-consistent strategies in this more general framework, though he does not offer an explicit prediction strategy. Mannor and Shimkin also consider cases when Hannan consistency may not be achieved, give a partial solution, and point out important difficulties in such cases.

The apple tasting problem was considered by Helmbold, Littlestone, and Long [154] in the special case when one of the actions has zero cumulative loss.

Multi-armed bandit problems were originally considered in a stochastic setting (see Robbins [245] and Lai and Robbins [189]). Several variants of the basic problems have been studied, see, for example, Berry and Fristedt [26] and Gittins [129]. The nonstochastic bandit problem studied here was first considered by Baños [21] (see also Megiddo [212]). Hannan-consistent strategies were constructed by Foster and Vohra [106], Auer, Cesa-Bianchi, Freund, and Schapire [12], and Hart and Mas Colell [145, 147], see also Fudenberg and Levine [119]. Hannan consistency of the potential-based strategy analyzed in Section 6.7 was proved by Hart and Mas-Colell [147] in the special case of the quadratic potential. The algorithm analyzed by Auer, Cesa-Bianchi, Freund, and Schapire [12] uses the exponential potential and is a simple variant of the strategy of Section 6.7. The multi-armed bandit strategy of Section 6.8 and the corresponding performance bound is due to Auer et al. [12], see also [10] (though the result presented here is an improved version). Theorem 6.11 is due to Auer et al. [12], though the main change-of-measure idea already appears in Lai and Robbins [189]. For related lower bounds we refer to Auer, Cesa-Bianchi, and Fischer [11], and Kulkarni and Lugosi [188]. Extensions of the nonstochastic bandits to a scenario where the regret is measured with respect to sequences of actions, instead of single actions (extending to the bandit framework the results on tracking actions described in Chapter 5), have been considered in [12].

Our formulation and analysis of the problem of selecting the best action is based on the paper by Awerbuch, Azar, Fiat, and Leighton [18]. Considering a natural extension of the setup described here, in the same paper Awerbuch et al. show that with probability $1 - O(1/N)$ one can achieve a total gain of $d \ln N$ on any gain assignment satisfying $G^* \geq C\, d \ln N$ whenever the selection strategy is allowed to change the selected action at least $\log_C N$ times for all (sufficiently large) constants C. By slightly increasing the number of allowed changes, one can also drop the requirement (implicit in Theorem 6.12) that an estimate of D^* is preliminarily available to the selection strategy.

6.12 Exercises

6.1 Consider the "zero-error" problem described at the beginning of Section 2.4, that is, when $\mathcal{Y} = \mathcal{D} = \{0, 1\}$, $\ell(\widehat{p}, y) = |\widehat{p} - y| \in \{0, 1\}$ and $\min_{i=1,\dots,N} L_{i,n} = 0$. Consider a label efficient version of the "halving" algorithm described is Section 2.4, which asks for a label randomly similarly to the strategy of Section 6.2. Show that if the expected number of labels asked by the forecaster is m, the expected number of mistakes it makes is bounded by $(n/m) \log_2 N$ (Helmbold and Panizza [155].) Derive a corresponding mistake bound that holds with large probability.

6.2 *(Switching actions not too often)* Prove that in the oblivious opponent model, the lazy label efficient forecaster achieves the regret bound of Theorem 6.1 with the additional feature that with probability 1, the number of changes of an action (i.e., the number of steps where $I_t \neq I_{t+1}$) is at most the number of queried labels.

6.3 *(Continued)* Strengthen Theorem 6.2 in the same way.

6.4 Let $m < n$. Show that there exists a label efficient forecaster that, with probability at least $1 - \delta$, reveals at most m labels and has an excess loss bounded by

$$\widehat{L}_n - L_n^* \le c \left(\sqrt{\frac{n L_n^* \ln(4N/\delta)}{m}} + \frac{n \ln(4N/\delta)}{m} \right),$$

where $L_n^* = \min_{i=1,\dots,N} L_{i,n}$ and c is a constant. Note that this inequality refines Theorem 6.2 in the spirit of Corollary 2.4 and, in the special case of $L_n^* = 0$, matches the order of magnitude of the bound of Exercise 6.1 (Cesa-Bianchi, Lugosi, and Stoltz [55].)

6.5 Complete the details of Hannan-consistency under the assumptions of Theorem 6.6. The prediction algorithm of the theorem assumes that the total number n of rounds is known in advance, because both η and γ depend on n. Show that this assumption may be dropped and construct a Hannan-consistent procedure in which η and γ only depend on t. (Cesa-Bianchi, Lugosi, and Stoltz [56].)

6.6 Prove Theorem 6.7.

6.7 *(Fast rates in partial monitoring problems)* Consider the version of the dynamic pricing problem described in Section 6.4 in which the feedback matrix $\mathbf{H}$ is as before but the losses are given by $\ell(i, j) = |i - j|/N$. Construct a prediction strategy for which, with large probability,

$$\frac{1}{n} \left(\sum_{t=1}^{n} \ell(I_t, y_t) - \min_{i=1,\dots,N} \sum_{t=1}^{n} \ell(i, y_t) \right) = O\left(n^{-1/2} \right).$$

Hint: Observe that the feedback reveals the value of the "derivative" of the loss and use an algorithm based on the gradient of the loss, as described in Section 2.5.

6.8 *(Consistency in partial monitoring)* Consider the prediction problem with partial monitoring in the special case when the predictor has $N = 2$ actions. (Note that the number M of outcomes may be arbitrary.) Assume that the $2 \times M$ loss matrix $\mathbf{L}$ is such that none of the two actions dominates the other in the sense that it is not true that for some $i = 1, 2$ and $i' \neq i$, $\ell(i, j) \le \ell(i', j)$ for all $j = 1, \dots, M$. (If one of the actions dominates the other, Hannan consistency is trivial to achieve by playing always the dominating action.) Show that there exists a Hannan-consistent procedure if and only if the feedback is such that a feedback matrix $\mathbf{H}$ can be constructed such that $\mathbf{L} = \mathbf{K} \mathbf{H}$ for some 2×2 matrix $\mathbf{K}$. *Hint:* If $\mathbf{L} = \mathbf{K} \mathbf{H}$, then Theorem 6.6 guarantees Hannan consistency. It suffices to show that if for all possible encoding of the feedback by real numbers the rank of $\mathbf{H}$ is 1, then Hannan consistency cannot be achieved.

6.9 *(Continued)* Consider now the case when $M = 2$, that is, the outcomes are binary but N may be arbitrary. Assume again that there is no dominating action. Show that there exists a Hannan consistent procedure if and only if for some version of $\mathbf{H}$ we may write $\mathbf{L} = \mathbf{K}\mathbf{H}$ for some $N \times N$ matrix $\mathbf{K}$. *Hint:* If the rank of $\mathbf{L}$ is less than 2, then there is a dominating action, so that we may assume that the rank of $\mathbf{L}$ is 2. Next show that if for all versions of $\mathbf{H}$, the rank of $\mathbf{H}$ is at most 1, then all rows of $\mathbf{H}$ are constants and therefore there is no useful feedback.

6.10 Consider the partial monitoring prediction problem. Assume that $M = N$ and the loss matrix $\mathbf{L}$ is the identity matrix. Show that if some columns of the feedback matrix $\mathbf{H}$ are identical then Hannan consistency is impossible to achieve. Partition the set of possible outcomes $\{1, \ldots, M\}$ into k sets $S_1, \ldots, S_k$ such that in each set the columns of the feedback matrix $\mathbf{H}$ corresponding to the outcomes in the set are identical. Denote the cardinality of these sets by $M_1 = |S_1|, \ldots, M_k = |S_k|$. (Thus, $M_1 + \cdots + M_k = M$.) Form an $N \times k$ matrix $\mathbf{H}'$ whose columns are the different columns of the feedback matrix $\mathbf{H}$ such that the jth column of $\mathbf{H}'$ is the column of $\mathbf{H}$ corresponding to the outcomes in the set S_j, $j = 1, \ldots, k$. Let $\mathbf{L}'$ be the $N \times k$ matrix whose jth column is the average of the M_j columns of $\mathbf{L}$ corresponding to the outcomes in S_j, $j = 1, \ldots, k$. Show that if there exists an $N \times N$ matrix $\mathbf{K}$ with $\mathbf{L}' = \mathbf{K}\mathbf{H}'$, then there is randomized strategy such that

$$\frac{1}{n} \left(\sum_{t=1}^{n} \ell(I_t, y_t) - \min_{i=1,\ldots,N} \sum_{t=1}^{n} \sum_{j=1}^{k} \mathbb{I}_{\{y_t \in S_j\}} \frac{1}{M_j} \sum_{m=1}^{M_j} \ell(i, m) \right) = o(1),$$

with probability 1. (See Rustichini [251] for a more general result.)

6.11 *(Partial monitoring with random feedback)* Consider an extension of the prediction model under partial monitoring described in Section 6.4 such that the feedback may not be a simple function of the action and the outcome but rather a random variable. More precisely, denote by $\Delta(\mathcal{S})$ the set of all probability distributions over the set of signals $\mathcal{S}$. The signaling structure is formed by a collection of NM probability distributions $\mu_{(i,j)}$ over $\mathcal{S}$ for $i = 1, \ldots, N$ and $j = 1, \ldots, M$. At each round, the forecaster now observes a random variable $H(I_t, y_t)$, drawn independently from all the other random variables, with distribution $\mu_{(I_t, y_t)}$.

Denote by $E_{(i,j)}$ the expectation of $\mu_{(i,j)}$ and by $\mathbf{E}$ the $N \times M$ matrix formed by these elements. Show that if there exists a matrix $\mathbf{K}$ such that $\mathbf{L} = \mathbf{K}\mathbf{E}$, then a Hannan-consistent forecaster may be constructed. *Hint:* Consider the modification of the forecaster of Section 6.5 defined by the estimated losses

$$\tilde{\ell}(i, y_t) = \frac{k(i, I_t) H(I_t, y_t)}{p_{I_t, t}} \qquad i = 1, \ldots, N.$$

6.12 *(Noisy observation)* Consider the forecasting problem in which the outcome sequence is binary, that is, $\mathcal{Y} = \{0, 1\}$, expert i predicts according to the real number $f_{i,t} \in [0, 1]$ $(i = 1, \ldots, N)$, and the loss of expert i is measured by the absolute loss $\ell(f_{i,t}, y_t) = |f_{i,t} - y_t|$ (as in Chapter 8). Suppose that instead of observing the true outcomes y_t, the forecaster only has access to a "noisy" version $y_t \oplus B_t$, where $\oplus$ denotes the xor operation (i.e., addition modulo 2) and $B_1, \ldots, B_n$ are i.i.d. Bernoulli random variables with unknown parameter $0 < p < 1/2$. Show that the simple exponentially weighted average forecaster achieves an expected regret

$$\mathbb{E} \widehat{L}_n - \min_{i=1,\ldots,N} \mathbb{E} L_{i,n} \leq \frac{1}{1-2p} \sqrt{\frac{n}{2} \ln N}.$$

(See Weissman and Merhav [308] and Weissman, Merhav, and Somekh-Baruch [309] for various versions of the problem of noisy observations.)

6.13 *(Label efficient partial monitoring)* Consider the label efficient version of the partial monitoring problem in which, during the n rounds of the game, the forecaster can ask for feedback at most m times at periods of his choice. Assume that the loss and feedback matrices satisfy $\mathbf{L} = \mathbf{K}\,\mathbf{H}$ for some $N \times N$ matrix $K = [k_{i,j}]$, with $k^* = \max\{1, \max_{i,j} |k(i,j)|\}$. Construct a forecasting strategy whose expected regret satisfies

$$\mathbb{E}\,\widehat{L}_n - \min_{i=1,\dots,N} \mathbb{E}\,L_{i,n} \le cn\frac{(Nk^*)^{2/3}(\ln N)^{1/3}}{m^{1/3}},$$

where c is a constant. Derive a similar upper bound for the regret that holds with high probability.

6.14 *(Internal regret minimization under partial monitoring)* Consider a partial monitoring problem in which the loss and feedback matrices satisfy $\mathbf{L} = \mathbf{K}\,\mathbf{H}$ for some $N \times N$ matrix $\mathbf{K} = [k_{i,j}]$, with $k^* = \max\{1, \max_{i,j} |k(i,j)|\}$. Construct a forecasting strategy such that, with probability at least $1 - \delta$, the internal regret

$$\max_{i,j=1,\dots,N} \sum_{t=1}^{n} p_{i,t}\big(\ell(i, Y_t) - \ell(j, Y_t)\big)$$

is bounded by a constant times $\big((k^*)^2 N^5 \ln(N/\delta)n^2\big)^{1/3}$. (Cesa-Bianchi, Lugosi, and Stoltz [56].) *Hint:* Use the conversion described at the end of Section 4.4 and proceed similarly as in Section 6.5.

6.15 *(Internal regret minimization in the bandit setting)* Construct a forecasting strategy that achieves, in the setting of the bandit problem, an internal regret of order $\sqrt{nN \ln(N/\delta)}$. *Hint:* Combine the conversion used in the previous exercise with the techniques of Section 6.8.

6.16 *(Compound actions and partial monitoring)* Let S be a set of compound actions (i.e., sequences $\mathbf{i} = (i_1, \dots, i_n)$ of actions $i_t \in \{1, \dots, N\}$) of cardinality $|S| = M$. Consider a partial monitoring problem in which the loss and feedback matrices satisfy $\mathbf{L} = \mathbf{K}\,\mathbf{H}$ for some $N \times N$ matrix $\mathbf{K}$. Construct a forecaster strategy whose expected regret (with respect to the S) satisfies

$$\mathbb{E} \sum_{t=1}^{n} \ell(I_t, Y_t) - \min_{\mathbf{i} \in S} \mathbb{E} \sum_{t=1}^{n} \ell(i_t, Y_t) \le 3\left(k^*\sqrt{e-2}\right)^{2/3} (Nn)^{2/3}(\ln M)^{1/3}.$$

(Note that the dependence on the number of compound actions is only logarithmic!) Derive a corresponding bound that holds with high probability. *Hint:* Consider the forecaster that assigns a weight to every compound action $\mathbf{i} = (i_1, \dots, i_n) \in S$ updated by $w_{\mathbf{i},t} = w_{\mathbf{i},t-1}e^{-\eta\widetilde{\ell}(i_t, Y_t)}$ (where $\widetilde{\ell}$ is the estimated loss introduced in Section 6.5) and draws action i with probability

$$p_{i,t} = (1 - \gamma)\frac{\sum_{\mathbf{i}:i_t=i} w_{\mathbf{i},t}}{\sum_{\mathbf{i} \in S} w_{\mathbf{i},t}} + \frac{\gamma}{N}.$$

6.17 *(The stochastic multi-armed bandit problem)* Consider the multi-armed bandit problem under the assumption that for each $i \in \{1, \dots, N\}$, the losses $\ell(i, y_1), \ell(i, y_2), \dots$ form an independent, identically distributed sequence of random variables such that $\mathbb{E}\,|\ell(i, y_1)| < \infty$ for all i. Construct a nonrandomized prediction scheme which guarantees that

$$\frac{1}{n}\sum_{t=1}^{n} \ell(I_t, y_t) - \frac{1}{n}\min_{i=1,\dots,N} \sum_{t=1}^{n} \ell(i, y_t) \to 0,$$

with probability 1.

6.18 *(Continued)* Consider the setup of the previous example under the additional assumption that the losses $\ell(i, y_t)$ take their values in the interval $[0, 1]$. Consider the prediction rule that, at time t, chooses an action $i \in \{1, \dots, N\}$ by minimizing

$$\frac{\sum_{s=1}^{t-1} \mathbb{I}_{\{I_s=i\}}\ell(i, y_s)}{\sum_{s=1}^{t-1} \mathbb{I}_{\{I_s=i\}}} + \sqrt{\frac{2\ln t}{\sum_{s=1}^{t-1} \mathbb{I}_{\{I_s=i\}}}}.$$

Prove that the expected number of times any action i with

$$\mathbb{E}\,\ell(i, y_t) > \min_{j=1,\ldots,N} \mathbb{E}\,\ell(j, y_t)$$

is played is bounded by a constant times $\ln n$. (Auer, Cesa-Bianchi, and Fischer [11], see also Lai and Robbins [189] for related results).

6.19 Prove Theorem 6.9. *Hint:* First observe that it suffices to prove that $\max_{i=1,\ldots,N} \widetilde{R}_{i,n} = o(n)$ with probability 1. This follows from the fact that for any fixed i,

$$\frac{1}{n}\left(\sum_{t=1}^n \ell(I_t, y_t) - \sum_{t=1}^n \ell(i, y_t)\right) = \frac{R_{i,n}}{n} = \frac{\widetilde{R}_{i,n}}{n} + \frac{1}{n}\sum_{t=1}^n \left(r_{i,t} - \widetilde{r}_{i,t}\right),$$

and from the Hoeffding–Azuma inequality. Next bound $\max_{i=1,\ldots,N} \widetilde{R}_{i,n}$ by an appropriate modification of Theorem 2.1. The additional difficulty is that the Blackwell condition is not satisfied and the first-order term cannot be ignored. Use Taylor's theorem to bound $\Phi(\widetilde{\mathbf{R}}_t)$ in terms of $\Phi(\widetilde{\mathbf{R}}_{t-1})$ to get

$$\Phi(\widetilde{\mathbf{R}}_n)$$

$$\leq \Phi(0) + \sum_{t=1}^n \mathbb{E}\left[\nabla\Phi(\widetilde{\mathbf{R}}_{t-1})\cdot\widetilde{\mathbf{r}}_t \mid I_1,\ldots,I_{t-1}\right] + \frac{1}{2}\sum_{t=1}^n C(\widetilde{\mathbf{r}}_t)$$

$$+ \sum_{t=1}^n \left(\nabla\Phi(\widetilde{\mathbf{R}}_{t-1})\cdot\widetilde{\mathbf{r}}_t - \mathbb{E}\left[\nabla\Phi(\widetilde{\mathbf{R}}_{t-1})\cdot\widetilde{\mathbf{r}}_t \mid I_1,\ldots,I_{t-1}\right]\right). \qquad (6.8)$$

Because $\max_i \widetilde{R}_{i,n} \leq \phi^{-1}(\psi^{-1}(\Phi(\widetilde{\mathbf{R}}_n)))$, it suffices to show that the last three terms on the right-hand side are of smaller order than $\psi(\phi(n))$, almost surely.

To bound the first of the three terms, use the unbiasedness of the estimator $\widetilde{\mathbf{r}}_t$ to show

$$\mathbb{E}\left[\nabla\Phi(\widetilde{\mathbf{R}}_{t-1})\cdot\widetilde{\mathbf{r}}_t \mid I_1,\ldots,I_{t-1}\right] \leq \gamma_t \sum_{i=1}^N \nabla_i\Phi(\widetilde{\mathbf{R}}_{t-1}).$$

Because the components of the regret vector satisfy $\widetilde{R}_{i,t-1} \leq t - 1$, assumption (iii) guarantees that

$$\sum_{t=1}^n \mathbb{E}\left[\nabla\Phi(\widetilde{\mathbf{R}}_{t-1})\cdot\widetilde{\mathbf{r}}_t \mid I_1,\ldots,I_{t-1}\right] = o(\psi(\phi(n))).$$

To bound the last term on the right-hand side of (6.8), observe that

$$\nabla\Phi(\widetilde{\mathbf{R}}_{t-1})\cdot\widetilde{\mathbf{r}}_t \leq \max_i |\widetilde{r}_{i,t}| \sum_{j=1}^N \nabla_i\Phi(\widetilde{\mathbf{R}}_{t-1}) \leq \frac{N}{\gamma_t}\sum_{j=1}^N \nabla_i\Phi(\widetilde{\mathbf{R}}_{t-1})$$

and use the Hoeffding–Azuma inequality.

6.20 Consider the potential-based strategy for the multi-armed bandit problem of Section 6.7 with the time-varying exponential potential

$$\Phi_t(\mathbf{u}) = \frac{1}{\eta_t}\ln\left(\sum_{i=1}^N e^{\eta_t u_i}\right),$$

where $\eta_t > 0$ may depend on t. Combine the proof of Theorem 6.9 with the techniques of Section 2.3 to determine values of η_t and γ_t that lead to a Hannan-consistent strategy.

6.21 *(The tracking problem in the bandit setting)* Consider the problem of tracking the best expert studied in Section 5.2. Extend Theorem 5.2 by bounding the expected regret

$$\mathbb{E}\left[\sum_{t=1}^{n}\ell(I_t, Y_t) - \sum_{t=1}^{n}\ell(i_t, Y_t)\right]$$

for any action sequence $i_1, \ldots, i_n$ under the bandit assumption: after making each prediction, the forecaster learns his own loss $\ell(I_t, Y_t)$ but not the value of the outcome Y_t (Auer, Cesa-Bianchi, Freund, and Schapire [12]). *Hint:* To bound the expected regret, it is enough to consider the forecaster of Section 6.7, drawing action i at time t with probability

$$p_{i,t} = (1 - \gamma)\frac{e^{-\eta \tilde{L}_{i,t-1}}}{\sum_{k=1}^{N} e^{-\eta \tilde{L}_{k,t-1}}} + \frac{\gamma}{N}$$

where $\tilde{L}_{i,t} = \sum_{s=1}^{t}\tilde{\ell}(i, Y_t)$ and

$$\tilde{\ell}(i, Y_t) = \begin{cases} \ell(i, Y_t)/p_{i,t} & \text{if } I_t = i \\ 0 & \text{otherwise.} \end{cases}$$

To get the right dependence on the horizon n in the bound, analyze this forecaster using parts of the proof of Theorem 6.10 combined with the proof of Theorem 5.2.

6.22 In the setup described in Section 6.10, at each time step t before the time step where an action is drawn, the selection strategy observes the gains $x_{1,t}, \ldots, x_{N,t}$ of all the actions. Prove a "bandit" variant of Theorem 6.12 where the selection strategy may only observe the gain $x_{k,t}$ of a single action k, where the index k of the action to observe is specified by the strategy.

7

Prediction and Playing Games

7.1 Games and Equilibria

The prediction problems studied in previous chapters have been often represented as repeated games between a forecaster and the environment. Our use of a game-theoretic formalism is not accidental: there exists an intimate connection between sequential prediction and some fundamental problems belonging to the theory of learning in games. We devote this chapter to the exploration of some of these connections.

Rather than giving an exhaustive account of the area of learning in games, we only focus on "regret-based" learning procedures (i.e., situations in which the players of the game base their strategies only on regrets they have suffered in the past) and our fundamental concern is whether such procedures lead to equilibria. We also limit our attention to finite *strategic* or *normal form* games.

In this introductory section we present the basic definitions of the games we consider, describe some notions of equilibria, and introduce the model of playing repeated games that we investigate in the subsequent sections of this chapter.

K-Person Normal Form Games

A (finite) *K-person game* given in its strategic (or normal) form is defined as follows. Player k ($k = 1, \ldots, K$) has N_k possible *actions* (or *pure strategies*) to choose from, where N_k is a positive integer. If the action of each player $k = 1, \ldots, K$ is $i_k \in \{1, \ldots, N_k\}$ and we denote the K-tuple of all the players' actions by $\mathbf{i} = (i_1, \ldots, i_K) \in \bigotimes_{k=1}^{K} \{1, \ldots, N_k\}$, then the *loss* suffered by player k is $\ell^{(k)}(\mathbf{i})$, where $\ell^{(k)} : \bigotimes_{k=1}^{K} \{1, \ldots, N_k\} \to [0, 1]$ for each $k = 1, \ldots, K$ are given loss functions for all players. Note that, slightly deviating from the usual game-theoretic terminology, we consider losses as opposed to the more standard payoffs. The reader should keep in mind that the goal of each player is to *minimize* his loss, which is the same as maximizing payoffs if one defines payoffs as negative losses. We use this convention to harmonize notation with the rest of the book.

A *mixed strategy* for player k is a probability distribution $\mathbf{p}^{(k)} = (p_1^{(k)}, \ldots, p_{N_k}^{(k)})$ over the set $\{1, \ldots, N_k\}$ of actions. When mixed strategies are used, players randomize, that is, choose an action according to the distribution specified by the mixed strategy. Denote the action played by player k by $I^{(k)}$. Thus, $I^{(k)}$ is a random variable taking values in the set $\{1, \ldots, N_k\}$ and distributed according to $\mathbf{p}^{(k)}$. Let $\mathbf{I} = (I^{(1)}, \ldots, I^{(k)})$ denote the K-tuple of actions played by all players. If the random variables $I^{(1)}, \ldots, I^{(k)}$ are independent (i.e., the players randomize independently of each other), we denote their joint distribution by π. That is, π is the joint distribution over the set $\bigotimes_{k=1}^{K} \{1, \ldots, N_k\}$ of all possible K-tuples of actions obtained by the product of the mixed strategies $\mathbf{p}^{(1)}, \ldots, \mathbf{p}^{(K)}$. The product distribution π is called a *mixed strategy profile*. Thus, for all $\mathbf{i} = (i_1, \ldots, i_k) \in \bigotimes_{k=1}^{K} \{1, \ldots, N_k\}$,

$$\pi(\mathbf{i}) = \mathbb{P}[\mathbf{I} = \mathbf{i}] = p_{i_1}^{(1)} \times \cdots \times p_{i_K}^{(K)}.$$

The expected loss of player k is

$$\pi \ell^{(k)} \overset{\text{def}}{=} \mathbb{E}\, \ell^{(k)}(\mathbf{I})$$
$$= \sum_{\mathbf{i} \in \bigotimes_{k=1}^{K} \{1, \ldots, N_k\}} \pi(\mathbf{i})\, \ell^{(k)}(\mathbf{i})$$
$$= \sum_{i_1=1}^{N_1} \cdots \sum_{i_K=1}^{N_K} p_{i_1}^{(1)} \times \cdots \times p_{i_K}^{(K)}\, \ell^{(k)}(i_1, \ldots, i_K).$$

Nash Equilibrium

Perhaps the most important notion of game theory is that of a Nash equilibrium. A mixed strategy profile $\pi = \mathbf{p}^{(1)} \times \cdots \times \mathbf{p}^{(K)}$ is called a *Nash equilibrium* if for all $k = 1, \ldots, K$ and all mixed strategies $\mathbf{q}^{(k)}$, if $\pi'_k = \mathbf{p}^{(1)} \times \cdots \times \mathbf{q}^{(k)} \times \cdots \times \mathbf{p}^{(K)}$ denotes the mixed strategy profile obtained by replacing $\mathbf{p}^{(k)}$ by $\mathbf{q}^{(k)}$ and leaving all other players' mixed strategies unchanged, then

$$\pi \ell^{(k)} \le \pi'_k \ell^{(k)}.$$

This means that if π is a Nash equilibrium, then no player has an incentive of changing his mixed strategy if all other players do not change theirs (i.e., every player is happy). A celebrated result of Nash [222] shows that every finite game has at least one Nash equilibrium. (The proof is typically based on fixed-point theorems.) However, a game may have multiple Nash equilibria, and the set $\mathcal{N}$ of all Nash equilibria can have a quite complex structure.

Two-Person Zero-Sum Games

A simple but important special class of games is the class of two-person zero-sum games. These games are played by two players (i.e., $K = 2$) and the payoff functions are such that for each pair of actions $\mathbf{i} = (i_1, i_2)$, where $i_1 \in \{1, \ldots, N_1\}$ and $i_2 \in \{1, \ldots, N_2\}$, the losses of the two players satisfy

$$\ell^{(1)}(\mathbf{i}) = -\ell^{(2)}(\mathbf{i}).$$

Thus, in such games the objective of the second player (often called *column player*) is to maximize the loss of the first player (the *row player*). To simplify notation we will just write ℓ for $\ell^{(1)}$, replace N_1, N_2 by N and M, and write (i, j) instead of (i_1, i_2). Mixed strategies of the row and column players will be denoted by $\mathbf{p} = (p_1, \ldots, p_N)$ and $\mathbf{q} = (q_1, \ldots, q_M)$. It is immediate to see that the product distribution $\pi = \mathbf{p} \times \mathbf{q}$ is a Nash equilibrium if and only if for all $\mathbf{p}' = (p'_1, \ldots, p'_N)$ and $\mathbf{q}' = (q'_1, \ldots, q'_M)$,

$$\sum_{i=1}^{N} \sum_{j=1}^{M} p_i q'_j\, \ell(i, j) \le \sum_{i=1}^{N} \sum_{j=1}^{M} p_i q_j\, \ell(i, j) \le \sum_{i=1}^{N} \sum_{j=1}^{M} p'_i q_j\, \ell(i, j).$$

Introducing the simplifying notation

$$\overline{\ell}(\mathbf{p}, \mathbf{q}) = \sum_{i=1}^{N} \sum_{j=1}^{M} p_i \, q_j \, \ell(i, j)$$

the above is equivalent to

$$\max_{\mathbf{q}'} \overline{\ell}(\mathbf{p}, \mathbf{q}') = \overline{\ell}(\mathbf{p}, \mathbf{q}) = \min_{\mathbf{p}'} \overline{\ell}(\mathbf{p}', \mathbf{q}).$$

This obviously implies that

$$\max_{\mathbf{q}'} \overline{\ell}(\mathbf{p}, \mathbf{q}') \leq \max_{\mathbf{q}'} \min_{\mathbf{p}'} \overline{\ell}(\mathbf{p}', \mathbf{q}'),$$

and therefore the existence of a Nash equilibrium $\mathbf{p} \times \mathbf{q}$ implies that

$$\min_{\mathbf{p}'} \max_{\mathbf{q}'} \overline{\ell}(\mathbf{p}', \mathbf{q}') \leq \max_{\mathbf{q}'} \min_{\mathbf{p}'} \overline{\ell}(\mathbf{p}', \mathbf{q}').$$

On the other hand, clearly, for all $\mathbf{p}$ and $\mathbf{q}'$, $\overline{\ell}(\mathbf{p}, \mathbf{q}') \geq \min_{\mathbf{p}'} \overline{\ell}(\mathbf{p}', \mathbf{q}')$ and therefore for all $\mathbf{p}$, $\max_{\mathbf{q}'} \overline{\ell}(\mathbf{p}, \mathbf{q}') \geq \max_{\mathbf{q}'} \min_{\mathbf{p}'} \overline{\ell}(\mathbf{p}', \mathbf{q}')$, and in particular,

$$\min_{\mathbf{p}'} \max_{\mathbf{q}'} \overline{\ell}(\mathbf{p}', \mathbf{q}') \geq \max_{\mathbf{q}'} \min_{\mathbf{p}'} \overline{\ell}(\mathbf{p}', \mathbf{q}').$$

In summary, the existence of a Nash equilibrium implies that

$$\min_{\mathbf{p}'} \max_{\mathbf{q}'} \overline{\ell}(\mathbf{p}', \mathbf{q}') = \max_{\mathbf{q}'} \min_{\mathbf{p}'} \overline{\ell}(\mathbf{p}', \mathbf{q}').$$

The common value of the left-hand and right-hand sides is called the *value of the game* and will be denoted by V. This equation, known as *von Neumann's minimax theorem*, is one of the fundamental results of game theory. Here we derived it as a consequence of the existence of Nash equilibria (which, in turn, is based on fixed-point theorems), but significantly simpler proofs may be given. In Section 7.2 we offer an elementary "learning-theoretic" proof, based on the basic techniques introduced in Chapter 2, of a powerful minimax theorem that, in turn, implies von Neumann's minimax theorem for two-person zero-sum games.

It is also clear from the argument that any Nash equilibrium $\mathbf{p} \times \mathbf{q}$ achieves the value of the game in the sense that

$$\overline{\ell}(\mathbf{p}, \mathbf{q}) = V$$

and that any product distribution $\mathbf{p} \times \mathbf{q}$ with $\overline{\ell}(\mathbf{p}, \mathbf{q}) = V$ is a Nash equilibrium.

Correlated Equilibrium

An important generalization of the notion of Nash equilibrium, introduced by Aumann [16], is the notion of *correlated equilibrium*. A probability distribution P over the set $\bigotimes_{k=1}^{K}\{1, \ldots, N_k\}$ of all possible K-tuples of actions is called a *correlated equilibrium* if for all $k = 1, \ldots, K$,

$$\mathbb{E}\, \ell^{(k)}(\mathbf{I}) \leq \mathbb{E}\, \ell^{(k)}(\mathbf{I}^-, \widetilde{I}^{(k)}),$$

where the random variable $\mathbf{I} = (I^{(1)}, \ldots, I^{(k)})$ is distributed according to P and $(\mathbf{I}^-, \widetilde{I}^{(k)}) = (I^{(1)}, \ldots, I^{(k-1)}, \widetilde{I}^{(k)}, I^{(k+1)}, \ldots, I^{(K)})$, where $\widetilde{I}^{(k)}$ is an arbitrary $\{1, \ldots, N_k\}$-valued random variable that is a function of $I^{(k)}$.

   The distinguishing feature of the notion is that, unlike in the definition of Nash equilibria, the random variables $I^{(k)}$ do not need to be independent, or, in other words, P is not necessarily a product distribution (hence the name "correlated"). Indeed, if P is a product measure, a correlated equilibrium becomes a Nash equilibrium. The existence of a Nash equilibrium of any game thus assures that correlated equilibria always exist.

   A correlated equilibrium may be interpreted as follows. Before taking an action, each player receives a recommendation $I^{(k)}$ such that the $I^{(k)}$ are drawn randomly according to the joint distribution of P. The defining inequality expresses that, in an average sense, no player has an incentive to divert from the recommendation, provided that all other players follow theirs. Correlated equilibria model solutions of games in which the actions of players may be influenced by external signals.

   A simple equivalent description of a correlated equilibrium is given by the following lemma whose proof is left as an exercise.

Lemma 7.1. *A probability distribution P over the set of all K-tuples $\mathbf{i} = (i_1, \ldots, i_K)$ of actions is a correlated equilibrium if and only if, for every player $k \in \{1, \ldots, K\}$ and actions $j, j' \in \{1, \ldots, N_k\}$, we have*

$$\sum_{\mathbf{i}:\, i_k = j} P(\mathbf{i}) \left(\ell^{(k)}(\mathbf{i}) - \ell^{(k)}(\mathbf{i}^-, j') \right) \leq 0,$$

where $(\mathbf{i}^-, j') = (i_1, \ldots, i_{k-1}, j', i_{k+1}, \ldots, i_K)$.

Lemma 7.1 reveals that the set of all correlated equilibria is given by an intersection of closed halfspaces and therefore it is a closed and convex polyhedron. For example, any convex combination of Nash equilibria is a correlated equilibrium. (This can easily be seen by observing that the inequalities of Lemma 7.1 trivially hold if one takes P as any weighted mixture of Nash equilibria.) However, there may exist correlated equilibria outside of the convex hull of Nash equilibria (see Exercise 7.4). In general, the structure of the set of correlated equilibria is much simpler than that of Nash equilibria. In fact, the existence of correlated equilibria may be proven directly and without having to resort to fixed point theorems. We do this implicitly in Section 7.4. Also, as we show in Section 7.4, given a game, it is computationally very easy to find a correlated equilibrium. Computing a Nash equilibrium, on the other hand, appears to be a significantly harder problem.

Playing Repeated Games

The most natural application of the ideas of randomized prediction of Chapters 4 and 6 is in the theory of playing repeated games. In the model we investigate, a K-person game (the so-called *one-shot game*) is played repeatedly such that at each time instant $t = 1, 2, \ldots$ player k ($k = 1, \ldots, K$) selects a mixed strategy $\mathbf{p}_t^{(k)} = (p_{1,t}^{(k)}, \ldots, p_{N_k,t}^{(k)})$ over the set $\{1, \ldots, N_k\}$ of his actions and draws an action $I_t^{(k)}$ according to this distribution. We assume that the randomizations of the players are independent of each other and of past randomizations. After the actions are taken, player k suffers a loss $\ell^{(k)}(\mathbf{I}_t)$, where $\mathbf{I}_t = (I_t^{(1)}, \ldots, I_t^{(K)})$. Formally, at time t player k has access to $U_t^{(k)}$, where the $U_t^{(k)}$ are independent random variables uniformly distributed in $[0, 1]$, and chooses $I_t^{(k)}$ such that

$$I_t^{(k)} = i \quad \text{if and only if} \quad U_t^{(k)} \in \left[\sum_{j=1}^{i-1} p_{j,t}^{(k)}, \sum_{j=1}^{i} p_{j,t}^{(k)} \right)$$

so that

$$\mathbb{P}\left[I_t^{(k)} = i \mid \text{past plays} \right] = p_{i,t}^{(k)}, \qquad i = 1, \ldots, N_k.$$

In the basic setup we assume that after taking an action $I_t^{(k)}$ each player observes all other players' actions, that is, the whole K-tuple $\mathbf{I}_t = (I_t^{(1)}, \ldots, I_t^{(K)})$. This means that the mixed strategy $\mathbf{p}_t^{(k)}$ played at time t may depend on the sequence of random variables $\mathbf{I}_1, \ldots, \mathbf{I}_{t-1}$.

However, we will be concerned only with "uncoupled" ways of playing, that is, when each player knows his own loss (or payoff) function but not those of the other players. More specifically, we only consider *regret-based* procedures in which the mixed strategy chosen by every player depends, in some way, on his past losses. We focus our attention on whether such simple procedures can lead to some kind of equilibrium of the (one-shot) game. In Section 7.3 we consider the simplest situation, the case of two-person zero-sum games. We show that a simple application of the regret-minimization procedures of Section 4.2 leads to a solution of the game in a quite robust sense.

In Section 7.4 it is shown that if all players play to keep their internal regret small, then the joint empirical frequencies of play converge to the set of correlated equilibria. The same convergence may also be achieved if every player uses a well-calibrated forecasting strategy to predict the K-tuple of actions $\mathbf{I}_t$ and chooses an action that is a best reply to the forecasted distribution. This is shown in Section 7.6. A model for learning in games even more restrictive than uncoupledness is the model of an "unknown game." In this model the players cannot even observe the actions of the other players; the only information available to them is their own loss suffered after each round of the game. In Section 7.5 we point out that the forecasting techniques for the bandit problem discussed in Chapter 6 allow convergence of the empirical frequencies of play even in this setup of limited information.

In Sections 7.7 and 7.8 we sketch Blackwell's approachability theory. Blackwell considered two-person zero-sum games with vector-valued losses and proved a powerful generalization of von Neumann's minimax theorem, which is deeply connected with the regret-minimizing forecasting methods of Chapter 4.

Sections 7.9 and 7.10 discuss the possibility of reaching a Nash equilibrium in uncoupled repeated games. Simple learning dynamics, versions of a method called "regret testing," are introduced that guarantee that the joint plays approach a Nash equilibrium in some sense. The case of unknown games is also investigated.

In Section 7.11 we address an important criticism of the notion of Hannan consistency. In fact, the basic notions of regret compare the loss of the forecaster with that of the best constant action, but without taking into account that the behavior of the opponent may depend on the actions of the forecaster. In Section 7.11 we show that asymptotic regret minimization is possible even in the presence of opponents that react, although we need to impose certain restrictions on the behavior of the opponents.

Fictitious Play

We close this introductory section by discussing perhaps the most natural strategy for playing repeated games: *fictitious play*. Player k is said to use fictitious play if, at every time instant t, he chooses an action that is a best response to the empirical distribution of the opponents' play up to time $t - 1$. In other words, the player chooses $I_t^{(k)}$ to minimize the estimated loss

$$I_t^{(k)} = \operatorname*{argmin}_{i_k \in \{1, \ldots, N_k\}} \frac{1}{t - 1} \sum_{s=1}^{t-1} \ell^{(k)}(\mathbf{I}_s^-, i_k),$$

where $(\mathbf{I}_s^-, i_k) = (I_s^{(1)}, \ldots, i_k, \ldots, I_s^{(K)})$. The nontrivial behavior of this simple strategy is a good demonstration of the complexity of the problem of describing regret-based strategies that lead to equilibrium. As we already mentioned in Section 4.3, fictitious play is not Hannan consistent. This fact may invite one to conjecture that there is no hope to achieve equilibrium via fictitious play. It may come as a surprise that this is often not the case. First, Robinson [246] proved that if in repeated playing of a two-person zero-sum game at each step both players use fictitious play, then the product distribution formed by the frequencies of actions played by both players converges to the set of Nash equilibria. This result was extended by Miyasawa [218] to general two-person games in which each player has two actions (i.e., $N_k = 2$ for all $k = 1, 2$); see also [220] for more special cases in which fictitious play leads to Nash equilibria in the same sense. However, Shapley [265] showed that the result cannot be extended even for two-person non-zero-sum games. In fact, the empirical frequencies of play may not even converge to the set of correlated equilibria (see Exercise 7.2 for Shapley's game).

7.2 Minimax Theorems

As a first contact with game-theoretic applications of the prediction problems studied in earlier chapters, we derive a simple learning-style proof of a general minimax theorem that implies von Neumann's minimax theorem cited in the introduction of this chapter. In particular, we prove the following.

Theorem 7.1. *Let $f(x, y)$ denote a bounded real-valued function defined on $\mathcal{X} \times \mathcal{Y}$, where $\mathcal{X}$ and $\mathcal{Y}$ are convex sets and $\mathcal{X}$ is compact. Suppose that $f(\cdot, y)$ is convex and continuous for each fixed $y \in \mathcal{Y}$ and $f(x, \cdot)$ is concave for each fixed $x \in \mathcal{X}$. Then*

$$\inf_{x \in \mathcal{X}} \sup_{y \in \mathcal{Y}} f(x, y) = \sup_{y \in \mathcal{Y}} \inf_{x \in \mathcal{X}} f(x, y).$$

Proof. For any function f, one obviously has

$$\inf_{x \in \mathcal{X}} \sup_{y \in \mathcal{Y}} f(x, y) \geq \sup_{y \in \mathcal{Y}} \inf_{x \in \mathcal{X}} f(x, y).$$

(To see this, just note that for all $x' \in \mathcal{X}$ and $y \in \mathcal{Y}$, $f(x', y) \geq \inf_x f(x, y)$, so that for all $x' \in \mathcal{X}$, $\sup_y f(x', y) \geq \sup_y \inf_x f(x, y)$, which implies the statement.)

To prove the reverse inequality, without loss of generality, we may assume that $f(x, y) \in [0, 1]$ for each $(x, y) \in \mathcal{X} \times \mathcal{Y}$. Fix a small $\varepsilon > 0$ and a large positive integer n. By the compactness of $\mathcal{X}$ one may find a finite set of points $\{x^{(1)}, \ldots, x^{(N)}\} \subset \mathcal{X}$ such that each

$x \in \mathcal{X}$ is within distance ε of at least one of the $x^{(i)}$. We define the sequences $x_1, \ldots, x_n \in \mathcal{X}$ and $y_1, \ldots, y_n \in \mathcal{Y}$ recursively as follows. y_0 is chosen arbitrarily. For each $t = 1, \ldots, n$ let

$$x_t = \frac{\sum_{i=1}^{N} x^{(i)} e^{-\eta \sum_{s=0}^{t-1} f(x^{(i)}, y_s)}}{\sum_{j=1}^{N} e^{-\eta \sum_{s=0}^{t-1} f(x^{(j)}, y_s)}},$$

where $\eta = \sqrt{8 \ln N / n}$ and y_t is such that $f(x_t, y_t) \geq \sup_{y \in \mathcal{Y}} f(x_t, y) - 1/n$. Then, by the convexity of f in its first argument, we obtain (by Theorem 2.2) that

$$\frac{1}{n} \sum_{t=1}^{n} f(x_t, y_t) \leq \min_{i=1,\ldots,N} \frac{1}{n} \sum_{t=1}^{n} f(x^{(i)}, y_t) + \sqrt{\frac{\ln N}{2n}}. \tag{7.1}$$

Thus, we have

$$\inf_{x \in \mathcal{X}} \sup_{y \in \mathcal{Y}} f(x, y)$$

$$\leq \sup_{y \in \mathcal{Y}} f\left(\frac{1}{n} \sum_{t=1}^{n} x_t, y\right)$$

$$\leq \sup_{y \in \mathcal{Y}} \frac{1}{n} \sum_{t=1}^{n} f(x_t, y) \quad \text{(by convexity of } f(\cdot, y))$$

$$\leq \frac{1}{n} \sum_{t=1}^{n} \sup_{y \in \mathcal{Y}} f(x_t, y)$$

$$\leq \frac{1}{n} \sum_{t=1}^{n} f(x_t, y_t) + \frac{1}{n} \quad \text{(by definition of } y_t)$$

$$\leq \min_{i=1,\ldots,N} \frac{1}{n} \sum_{t=1}^{n} f(x^{(i)}, y_t) + \sqrt{\frac{\ln N}{2n}} + \frac{1}{n} \quad \text{(by inequality (7.1))}$$

$$\leq \min_{i=1,\ldots,N} f\left(x^{(i)}, \frac{1}{n} \sum_{t=1}^{n} y_t\right) + \sqrt{\frac{\ln N}{2n}} + \frac{1}{n} \quad \text{(by concavity of } f(x, \cdot))$$

$$\leq \sup_{y \in \mathcal{Y}} \min_{i=1,\ldots,N} f\left(x^{(i)}, y\right) + \sqrt{\frac{\ln N}{2n}} + \frac{1}{n}.$$

Thus, we have, for each n,

$$\inf_{x \in \mathcal{X}} \sup_{y \in \mathcal{Y}} f(x, y) \leq \sup_{y \in \mathcal{Y}} \min_{i=1,\ldots,N} f\left(x^{(i)}, y\right) + \sqrt{\frac{\ln N}{2n}} + \frac{1}{n},$$

so that, letting $n \to \infty$, we get

$$\inf_{x \in \mathcal{X}} \sup_{y \in \mathcal{Y}} f(x, y) \leq \sup_{y \in \mathcal{Y}} \min_{i=1,\ldots,N} f\left(x^{(i)}, y\right).$$

Letting $\varepsilon \to 0$ and using the continuity of f, we conclude that

$$\inf_{x \in \mathcal{X}} \sup_{y \in \mathcal{Y}} f(x, y) \leq \sup_{y \in \mathcal{Y}} \inf_{x \in \mathcal{X}} f(x, y),$$

as desired. ∎

Remark 7.1 *(von Neumann's minimax theorem).* Observe that Theorem 7.1 implies von Neumann's minimax theorem for two-person zero-sum games. To see this, just note that function $\bar{\ell}$ is bounded and linear in both of its arguments and the simplex of all mixed strategies $\mathbf{p}$ (and similarly $\mathbf{q}$) is a compact set. In this special case the infima and suprema are achieved.

7.3 Repeated Two-Player Zero-Sum Games

We start our investigation of regret-based strategies for repeated game playing from the simple case of two-person zero-sum games. Recall that in our model, at each round t, based on the past plays of both players, the row player chooses an action $I_t \in \{1, \ldots, N\}$ according to the mixed strategy $\mathbf{p}_t = (p_{1,t}, \ldots, p_{N,t})$ and the column player chooses an action $J_t = \{1, \ldots, M\}$ according to the mixed strategy $\mathbf{q}_t = (q_{1,t}, \ldots, q_{M,t})$. The distributions $\mathbf{p}_t$ and $\mathbf{q}_t$ may depend on the past plays of both. The row player's loss at time t is $\ell(I_t, J_t)$ and the column player's loss is $-\ell(I_t, J_t)$. At each time instant, after making the play, the row player observes the losses $\ell(i, J_t)$ he would have suffered had he played strategy $i, i = 1, \ldots, N$.

In view of studying the convergence to equilibrium in such games, we consider the problem of minimizing the cumulative loss the row player. If the row player knew the column player's actions $J_1, \ldots, J_n$ in advance, he would, at each time instant, choose his actions to satisfy $I_t = \operatorname{argmin}_{i=1,\ldots,N} \ell(i, J_t)$ invoking a total loss $\sum_{t=1}^{n} \min_{i=1,\ldots,N} \ell(i, J_t)$. Achieving a cumulative loss close to this minimum without knowing the column player's actions is, except for trivial cases, impossible (see Exercise 7.6), and so the row player has to put up with a less ambitious goal. A meaningful objective is to play almost as well as the best constant strategy. Thus, we consider the problem of minimizing the difference between the row player's cumulative loss and the cumulative loss of the best constant strategy, that is,

$$\sum_{t=1}^{n} \ell(I_t, J_t) - \min_{i=1,\ldots,N} \sum_{t=1}^{n} \ell(i, J_t).$$

By a simple application of regret-minimizing forecasters we show that simple strategies indeed exist such that this difference grows sublinearly (almost surely) no matter how the column player plays. This result is a simple consequence of the Hannan consistency results of Chapter 4.

It is natural to consider regret-minimizing strategies for both players. For example, we may assume that the players play according to Hannan consistent forecasting strategies. More precisely, assume that the row player chooses his actions I_t such that, regardless of what the column player does,

$$\limsup_{n \to \infty} \left(\frac{1}{n} \sum_{t=1}^{n} \ell(I_t, J_t) - \min_{i=1,\ldots,N} \frac{1}{n} \sum_{t=1}^{n} \ell(i, J_t) \right) \leq 0 \qquad \text{almost surely.}$$

Recall from Section 4 that several such Hannan-consistent procedures are available. For example, this may be achieved by the exponentially weighted average mixed strategy

$$p_{i,t} = \frac{\exp\left(-\eta \sum_{s=1}^{t-1} \ell(i, J_s)\right)}{\sum_{k=1}^{N} \exp\left(-\eta \sum_{s=1}^{t-1} \ell(k, J_s)\right)}, \qquad i = 1, \ldots, N,$$

where $\eta > 0$. For this particular forecaster we have, with probability at least $1 - \delta$,

$$\sum_{t=1}^{n} \ell(I_t, J_t) - \min_{i=1,\ldots,N} \sum_{t=1}^{n} \ell(i, J_t) \leq \frac{\ln N}{\eta} + \frac{n\eta}{8} + \sqrt{\frac{n}{2} \ln \frac{1}{\delta}}$$

(see Corollary 4.2).

Remark 7.2 (Nonoblivious opponent). It is important to point out that in the definition of regret, the cumulative loss $\sum_{t=1}^{n} \ell(i, J_t)$ associated with the "constant" action i corresponds to the sequence of plays $J_1, \ldots, J_n$ of the opponent. The plays of the opponent may depend on the forecaster's actions, which, in this case, are $I_1, \ldots, I_n$. Therefore, it is important to keep in mind that if the opponent is nonoblivious (recall the definition from Chapter 4), then $\sum_{t=1}^{n} \ell(i, J_t)$ is not the same as the cumulative loss the forecaster would have suffered had he played action $I_t = i$ for all t. This issue is investigated in detail in Section 7.11.

Remark 7.3 (Time-varying games). The inequality above may be extended, in a straight-forward way, to the case of time-varying games, that is, when the loss matrix is allowed to change with time as long as the entries $\ell_t(i, j)$ stay uniformly bounded, say, between 0 and 1. The loss matrix ℓ_t does not need to be known in advance by the row player. All we need to assume is that before making the play at time t, the column $\ell_{t-1}(\cdot, J_{t-1})$ of the loss matrix corresponding to the opponent's play in the previous round is revealed to the row player. In a more difficult version of the problem, only the suffered loss $\ell_{t-1}(I_{t-1}, J_{t-1})$ is observed by the row player before time t. These problems may be handled by the techniques of Section 6.7 (see also Section 7.5).

We now show the following remarkable fact: if the row player plays according to any Hannan consistent strategy, then his average loss cannot be much larger than the value of the game, regardless of the opponent's strategy. (Note that by von Neumann's minimax theorem this may also be achieved if the row player plays according to any minimax strategy; see Exercise 7.7.)

Recall that the *value* of the game characterized by the loss matrix ℓ is defined by

$$V = \max_{\mathbf{q}} \min_{\mathbf{p}} \overline{\ell}(\mathbf{p}, \mathbf{q}),$$

where the maximum is taken over all probability vectors $\mathbf{q} = (q_1, \ldots, q_M)$, the minimum is taken over all probability vectors $\mathbf{p} = (q_1, \ldots, p_N)$, and

$$\overline{\ell}(\mathbf{p}, \mathbf{q}) = \sum_{i=1}^{N} \sum_{j=1}^{M} p_i \, q_j \, \ell(i, j).$$

(Note that the maximum and the minimum are always achieved.) With some abuse of notation we also write

$$\bar{\ell}(\mathbf{p}, j) = \sum_{i=1}^{N} p_i \, \ell(i, j) \quad \text{and} \quad \bar{\ell}(i, \mathbf{q}) = \sum_{j=1}^{M} q_j \, \ell(i, j).$$

Theorem 7.2. *Assume that in a two-person zero-sum game the row player plays according to a Hannan-consistent strategy. Then*

$$\limsup_{n \to \infty} \frac{1}{n} \sum_{t=1}^{n} \ell(I_t, J_t) \leq V \qquad \text{almost surely.}$$

Proof. By the assumption of Hannan consistency, it suffices to show that

$$\min_{i=1,\dots,N} \frac{1}{n} \sum_{t=1}^{n} \ell(i, J_t) \leq V.$$

This may be seen easily as follows. First,

$$\min_{i=1,\dots,N} \frac{1}{n} \sum_{t=1}^{n} \ell(i, J_t) = \min_{\mathbf{p}} \frac{1}{n} \sum_{t=1}^{n} \bar{\ell}(\mathbf{p}, J_t)$$

since $\sum_{t=1}^{n} \bar{\ell}(\mathbf{p}, J_t)$ is linear in $\mathbf{p}$ and its minimum, over the simplex of probability vectors, is achieved in one of the corners. Then, letting $\widehat{q}_{j,n} = \frac{1}{n} \sum_{t=1}^{n} \mathbb{I}_{\{J_t = j\}}$ be the empirical probability of the row player's action being j,

$$\min_{\mathbf{p}} \frac{1}{n} \sum_{t=1}^{n} \bar{\ell}(\mathbf{p}, J_t) = \min_{\mathbf{p}} \sum_{j=1}^{M} \widehat{q}_{j,n} \bar{\ell}(\mathbf{p}, j)$$

$$= \min_{\mathbf{p}} \bar{\ell}(\mathbf{p}, \widehat{\mathbf{q}}_n) \quad (\text{where } \widehat{\mathbf{q}}_n = (\widehat{q}_{1,n}, \dots, \widehat{q}_{M,n}))$$

$$\leq \max_{\mathbf{q}} \min_{\mathbf{p}} \bar{\ell}(\mathbf{p}, \mathbf{q}) = V. \quad \blacksquare$$

Theorem 7.2 shows that, regardless of what the opponent plays, if the row player plays according to a Hannan-consistent strategy, then his cumulative loss is guaranteed to be asymptotically not more than the value V of the game. It follows by symmetry that if both players use the same strategy, then the cumulative loss of the row player converges to V.

Corollary 7.1. *Assume that in a two-person zero-sum game, both players play according to some Hannan consistent strategy. Then*

$$\lim_{n \to \infty} \frac{1}{n} \sum_{t=1}^{n} \ell(I_t, J_t) = V \qquad \text{almost surely.}$$

Proof. By Theorem 7.2

$$\limsup_{n \to \infty} \frac{1}{n} \sum_{t=1}^{n} \ell(I_t, J_t) \leq V \qquad \text{almost surely.}$$

The same theorem, applied to the column player, implies, using the fact that the column player's loss that is the negative of the row player's loss, that

$$\liminf_{n \to \infty} \frac{1}{n} \sum_{t=1}^{n} \ell(I_t, J_t) \ge \min_{\mathbf{p}} \max_{\mathbf{q}} \overline{\ell}(\mathbf{p}, \mathbf{q}) \qquad \text{almost surely.}$$

By von Neumann's minimax theorem, the latter quantity equals V. ∎

Remark 7.4 (Convergence to equilibria). If both players follow some Hannan consistent strategy, then it is also easy to see that the product distribution $\widehat{\mathbf{p}}_n \times \widehat{\mathbf{q}}_n$ formed by the (marginal) empirical distributions of play

$$\widehat{p}_{i,n} = \frac{1}{n} \sum_{t=1}^{n} \mathbb{I}_{\{I_t = i\}} \qquad \text{and} \qquad \widehat{q}_{j,n} = \frac{1}{n} \sum_{t=1}^{n} \mathbb{I}_{\{J_t = j\}}$$

of the two players converges, almost surely, to the set of Nash equilibria $\pi = \mathbf{p} \times \mathbf{q}$ of the game (see Exercise 7.11). However, it is important to note that this does not mean that the players' joint play is close to a Nash equilibrium in the long run. Indeed, one cannot conclude that the *joint empirical frequencies of play*

$$\widehat{P}_n(i, j) = \frac{1}{n} \sum_{t=1}^{n} \mathbb{I}_{\{I_t = i, J_t = j\}}$$

converge to the set of Nash equilibria. All one can say is that $\widehat{P}_n$ converges to the Hannan set of the game (defined later), which, even for zero-sum games, may include joint distributions that are not Nash equilibria (see Exercise 7.15).

7.4 Correlated Equilibrium and Internal Regret

In this section we consider repeated play of general K-person games. In the previous section we have shown the following fact: if both players of a two-person zero-sum game follow a Hannan-consistent strategy (i.e, play so that their external regret vanishes asymptotically), then in the long run equilibrium is achieved in the sense that the product of the marginal empirical frequencies of play converges to the set of Nash equilibria. It is natural to ask whether the joint empirical frequencies of play converge in any general K-person game. The answer is easily seen to be negative in general by the following argument. Assume that in a repeated K-person game each player follows a Hannan consistent strategy; that is, if the K-tuple of plays of all players at time t is $\mathbf{I}_t = (I_t^{(1)}, \ldots, I_t^{(K)})$, then for all $k = 1, \ldots, K$ the cumulative loss of player k satisfies

$$\limsup_{n \to \infty} \left(\frac{1}{n} \sum_{t=1}^{n} \ell^{(k)}(\mathbf{I}_t) - \frac{1}{n} \min_{i_k = 1, \ldots, N_k} \sum_{t=1}^{n} \ell^{(k)}(I_t^{(1)}, \ldots, i_k, \ldots, I_t^{(K)}) \right) \le 0$$

almost surely. Writing

$$\widehat{P}_n(\mathbf{i}) = \frac{1}{n} \sum_{t=1}^{n} \mathbb{I}_{\{\mathbf{I}_t = \mathbf{i}\}}, \qquad \mathbf{i} = (i_1, \ldots, i_K) \in \bigotimes_{k=1}^{K} \{1, \ldots, N_k\},$$

for the empirical joint distribution of play, the property of Hannan consistency may be rewritten as follows: for all $k = 1, \ldots, K$ and for all $j = 1, \ldots, N_k$,

$$\limsup_{n \to \infty} \left(\sum_{\mathbf{i}} \widehat{P}_n(\mathbf{i}) \ell^{(k)}(\mathbf{i}) - \sum_{\mathbf{i}} \widehat{P}_n(\mathbf{i}) \ell^{(k)}(\mathbf{i}^-, j) \right) \le 0$$

almost surely, where $(\mathbf{i}^-, j) = (i_1, \ldots, j, \ldots, i_K)$ denotes the K-tuple obtained when the kth component i_k of $\mathbf{i}$ is replaced by j. Writing the condition of Hannan consistency in this form reveals that if all players follow such a strategy, the empirical frequencies of play converge, almost surely, to the set $\mathcal{H}$ of joint distributions P over $\bigotimes_{k=1}^{K} \{1, \ldots, N_k\}$ defined by

$$\mathcal{H} = \left\{ P : \forall k = 1, \ldots, K, \forall j = 1, \ldots, N_k, \quad \sum_{\mathbf{i}} P(\mathbf{i}) \ell^{(k)}(\mathbf{i}) \le \sum_{\mathbf{i}} P(\mathbf{i}) \ell^{(k)}(\mathbf{i}^-, j) \right\}$$

(see Exercise 7.14). The set $\mathcal{H}$ is called the *Hannan set* of the game. Since $\mathcal{C}$ is an intersection of $\sum_{k=1}^{K} N_k$ halfspaces, it is a closed and convex subset of the simplex of all joint distributions. In other words, if all players play according to any strategy that asymptotically minimizes their external regret, the empirical frequencies of play converge to the set $\mathcal{H}$. Unfortunately, distributions in the Hannan set do not correspond to any natural equilibrium concept. In fact, by comparing the definition of $\mathcal{H}$ with the characterization of correlated equilibria given in Lemma 7.1, it is easy to see that $\mathcal{H}$ always contains the set $\mathcal{C}$ of correlated equilibria. Even though for some special games (such as games in which all players have two actions; see Exercise 7.18) $\mathcal{H} = \mathcal{C}$, in typical cases $\mathcal{C}$ is a proper subset of $\mathcal{H}$ (see Exercise 7.16). Thus, except for special cases, if players are merely required to play according to Hannan-consistent strategies (i.e., to minimize their external regret), there is no hope to achieve a correlated equilibrium, let alone a Nash equilibrium.

However, by requiring just a little bit more, convergence to correlated equilibria may be achieved. The main result of this section is that if each player plays according to a strategy minimizing *internal* regret as described in Section 4.4, the joint empirical frequencies of play converge to a correlated equilibrium.

More precisely, consider the model of playing repeated games described in Section 7.1. For each player k and pair of actions $j, j' \in \{1, \ldots, N_K\}$ define the *conditional instantaneous regret* at time t by

$$\widehat{r}^{(k)}_{(j,j'),t} = \mathbb{I}_{\{I_t^{(k)} = j\}} \left(\ell^{(k)}(\mathbf{I}_t) - \ell^{(k)}(\mathbf{I}_t^-, j') \right),$$

where $(\mathbf{I}_t^-, j') = (I_t^{(1)}, \ldots, I_t^{(k-1)}, j', I_t^{(k+1)}, \ldots, I_t^{(K)})$ is obtained by replacing the play of player k by action j'. Note that the expected value of the conditional instantaneous regret $\widehat{r}^{(k)}_{(j,j'),t}$, calculated with respect to the distribution $\mathbf{p}_t^{(k)}$ of $I_t^{(k)}$, is just the instantaneous internal regret of player k defined in Section 4.4. The conditional regret $\sum_{t=1}^{n} \widehat{r}^{(k)}_{(j,j'),t}$ expresses how much better player k could have done had he chosen action j' every time he played action j.

The next lemma shows that if each player plays such that his conditional regret remains small, then the empirical distribution of plays will be close to a correlated equilibrium.

Lemma 7.2. *Consider a K-person game and denote its set of correlated equilibria by $\mathcal{C}$. Assume that the game is played repeatedly so that for each player $k = 1, \ldots, K$ and pair* *of actions* $j, j' \in \{1, \ldots, N_k\}$ *the conditional regrets satisfy*

$$\limsup_{n \to \infty} \frac{1}{n} \sum_{t=1}^{n} \widehat{r}_{(j,j'),t}^{(k)} \leq 0.$$

Then the distance $\inf_{P \in \mathcal{C}} \sum_{\mathbf{i}} |P(\mathbf{i}) - \widehat{P}_n(\mathbf{i})|$ *between the empirical distribution of plays and the set of correlated equilibria converges to* 0.

Proof. Observe that the assumption on the conditional regrets may be rewritten as

$$\limsup_{n \to \infty} \sum_{\mathbf{i} : i_k = j} \widehat{P}_n(\mathbf{i}) \left(\ell^{(k)}(\mathbf{i}) - \ell^{(k)}(\mathbf{i}^-, j') \right) \leq 0,$$

where $(\mathbf{i}^-, j')$ is the same as $\mathbf{i}$ except that its kth component is replaced by j'. Assume that the sequence $\widehat{P}_n$ does not converge to $\mathcal{C}$. Then by the compactness of the set of all probability distributions there is a distribution $P^* \notin \mathcal{C}$ and a subsequence $\widehat{P}_{n_k}$ of empirical distributions such that $\lim_{k \to \infty} \widehat{P}_{n_k} = P^*$. But since P^* is not a correlated equilibrium, by Lemma 7.1 there exists a player $k \in \{1, \ldots, K\}$ and a pair of actions $j, j' \in \{1, \ldots, N_k\}$ such that

$$\sum_{\mathbf{i} : i_k = j} P^*(\mathbf{i}) \left(\ell^{(k)}(\mathbf{i}) - \ell^{(k)}(\mathbf{i}^-, j') \right) > 0,$$

which contradicts the assumption. ∎

Now it is easy to show that if all players play according to an internal-regret-minimizing strategy, such as that described in Section 4.4, a correlated equilibrium is reached asymptotically. More precisely, for each player $k = 1, \ldots, K$ define the components of the internal instantaneous regret vector by

$$r_{(j,j'),t}^{(k)} = p_{j,t}^{(k)} \left(\ell^{(k)}(\mathbf{I}_t) - \ell^{(k)}(\mathbf{I}_t^-, j') \right),$$

where $j, j' \in \{1, \ldots, N_k\}$ and $(\mathbf{I}_t^-, j')$ is as defined above. In Section 4.4 we saw that player k has a simple strategy $\mathbf{p}_t^{(k)}$ such that, regardless of the other players' actions, it is guaranteed that the internal regret satisfies

$$\max_{j,j'} \frac{1}{n} \sum_{t=1}^{n} r_{(j,j'),t}^{(k)} \leq c \sqrt{\frac{\ln N_k}{n}}$$

for a universal constant c. Now, clearly, $r_{(j,j'),t}^{(k)}$ is the conditional expectation of $\widehat{r}_{(j,j'),t}^{(k)}$ given the past and the other players' actions. Thus $r_{(j,j'),t}^{(k)} - \widehat{r}_{(j,j'),t}^{(k)}$ is a bounded martingale difference sequence for any fixed j, j'. Therefore, by the Hoeffding–Azuma inequality (Lemma A.7) and the Borel–Cantelli lemma, we have, for each $k \in \{1, \ldots, K\}$ and $j, j' \in \{1, \ldots, N_k\}$,

$$\lim_{n \to \infty} \frac{1}{n} \sum_{t=1}^{n} \left(\widehat{r}_{(j,j'),t}^{(k)} - r_{(j,j'),t}^{(k)} \right) = 0 \qquad \text{almost surely,}$$

which implies that for each k

$$\limsup_{n \to \infty} \max_{j,j'} \frac{1}{n} \sum_{t=1}^{n} \widehat{r}_{(j,j'),t}^{(k)} \leq 0 \qquad \text{almost surely.}$$

The following theorem summarizes what we have just proved.

Theorem 7.3. *Consider a K-person game and denote its set of correlated equilibria by C. Assume that a game is played repeatedly such that each player $k = 1, \ldots, K$ plays according to an internal-regret-minimizing strategy (such as the ones described in Section 4.4). Then the distance $\inf_{P \in C} \sum_i |P(\mathbf{i}) - \widehat{P}_n(\mathbf{i})|$ between the empirical distribution of plays and the set of correlated equilibria converges to 0 almost surely.*

Remark 7.5 (*Existence of correlated equilibria*). Observe that the theorem implicitly entails the existence of a correlated equilibrium of any game. Of course, this fact follows from the existence of Nash equilibria. However, unlike the proof of existence of Nash equilibria, the above argument avoids the use of fixed-point theorems.

Remark 7.6 (*Computation of correlated equilibria*). Given a K-person game, it is a complex and important problem to exhibit a computationally efficient procedure that finds a Nash equilibrium (or even better, the set of all Nash equilibria) of the game. As of today, no polynomial-time algorithm is known to approximate a Nash equilibrium. (The algorithm is required to be polynomial in the number of players and the number of actions of each player.) The difficulty of the problem may be understood by noting that even if every player in a K-person game has just two actions to choose from, there are 2^K possible action profiles $\mathbf{i} = (i_1, \ldots, i_K)$, and so describing the payoff functions already takes exponential time. Interesting polynomial-time algorithms for computing Nash equilibria are available for important special classes of games that have a compact representation, such as symmetric games, graphical games, and so forth. We refer the interested reader to Papadimitriou [230, 231], Kearns and Mansour [179], Papadimitriou and Roughgarden [232]. Here we point out that the regret-based procedures described in this section may also be used to efficiently approximate correlated equilibria in a natural computational model. For any $\varepsilon > 0$, a probability distribution P over the set of all K-tuples $\mathbf{i} = (i_1, \ldots, i_K)$ of actions is called an ε-*correlated equilibrium* if, for every player $k \in \{1, \ldots, K\}$ and actions $j, j' \in \{1, \ldots, N_k\}$,

$$\sum_{\mathbf{i}:\, i_k = j} P(\mathbf{i}) \left(\ell^{(k)}(\mathbf{i}) - \ell^{(k)}(\mathbf{i}^-, j') \right) \leq \varepsilon.$$

Clearly, ε-correlated equilibria approximate correlated equilibria in the sense that if C_ε denotes the set of all ε-correlated equilibria, then $\bigcap_{\varepsilon > 0} C_\varepsilon = C$. Assume that an oracle is available that outputs the values of the loss functions $\ell^{(k)}(\mathbf{i})$ for any action profile $\mathbf{i} = (i_1, \ldots, i_K)$. Then it is easy to define an algorithm that calls the oracle polynomially many times and outputs an ε-correlated equilibrium. One may simply simulate as if all players played an internal-regret-minimizing procedure and calculate the joint distribution $\widehat{P}_n$ of plays. By the results of Section 4.4, the Hoeffding–Azuma inequality and the union bound, with probability at least $1 - \delta$, for each $k = 1, \ldots, K$,

$$\sum_{\mathbf{i}:\, i_k = j} \widehat{P}_n(\mathbf{i}) \left(\ell^{(k)}(\mathbf{i}) - \ell^{(k)}(\mathbf{i}^-, j') \right) \leq 2\sqrt{\frac{\ln N_k}{n}} + \sqrt{\frac{\ln(K/\delta)}{2n}}.$$

Thus, with probability at least $1 - \delta$, $\widehat{P}_n$ is an ε-correlated equilibrium if

$$n \geq \max_{k=1,\ldots,K} \frac{16}{\varepsilon^2} \ln \frac{N_k K}{\delta}.$$

To compute all regrets necessary to run this algorithms, the oracle needs to be called not more than

$$\max_{k=1,\ldots,K} \frac{16 N_k K}{\varepsilon^2} \ln \frac{N_k K}{\delta}$$

times to find an ε-correlated equilibrium, with probability at least $1 - \delta$. Thus, computation of an ε-correlated equilibrium is surprisingly fast: it takes time proportional to $1/\varepsilon^2$ and is polynomial (in fact, barely superlinear) in terms of the number of actions and the number of players of the game.

7.5   Unknown Games: Game-Theoretic Bandits

In this section we mention the possibility of learning correlated equilibria in an even more restricted model than the uncoupled model studied so far in this chapter. We assume that the K players of a game play repeatedly, and at each time instance t, after taking an action $I_t^{(k)}$, the kth player observes his loss $\ell^{(k)}(\mathbf{I}_t)$ (where $\mathbf{I}_t = (I_t^{(1)}, \ldots, I_t^{(K)})$ is the joint action profile played by the K players) but does not know his entire loss function $\ell^{(k)}$ and cannot observe the other players' actions $\mathbf{I}_t^-$. In fact, player k may not even know the number of players participating in the game, let alone the number of actions the other players can choose from.

It may come as a surprise that, with such limited information, the players have a way of playing that guarantees that the game reaches an equilibrium in some sense. Here we point out that there is a strategy such that if all players play according to it, then the joint empirical frequencies of play converge to a correlated equilibrium. The issue of convergence to a Nash equilibrium is addressed in Section 7.10.

The fact that convergence of the empirical frequencies of play to a correlated equilibrium may be achieved follows directly from Theorem 7.3 and the fact that each player can guarantee a small internal regret even if he cannot observe the actions of the other players. Indeed, in order to achieve the desired convergence, each player's job now is to minimize his internal regret in the bandit problem described in Chapter 6. Exercise 6.15 shows that such internal-regret minimizing procedures exist and therefore, if all players follow such a strategy, the empirical frequencies of play will converge to the set of correlated equilibria of the game.

7.6   Calibration and Correlated Equilibrium

In Section 4.5 we described the connection between calibrated and internal-regret-minimizing forecasting strategies. According to the results of Section 7.4, internal-regret-minimizing forecasters may be used, in a straightforward way, to achieve correlated equilibrium in a certain sense. In the present section we close the circle and point out an interesting connection between calibration and correlated equilibria; that is, we show that if each player bases his decision on a calibrated forecaster in an appropriate way (where the calibrated forecasters used by the different players may be completely different), then the joint empirical frequencies of play converge to the set of correlated equilibria.

The strategy we assume the players follow is quite natural: on the basis of past experience, each player predicts the mixed strategy his opponents will use in the next round and selects an action that would minimize his loss if the opponents indeed played according to the predicted distribution. More precisely, each player forecasts the joint probability of each possible outcome of the next action of his opponents and then chooses a "best response" to the forecasted distribution. We saw in Section 4.5 that no matter how the opponents play, each player can construct a (randomized) well-calibrated forecast of the opponents' sequence of play. The main result of this section shows that the mild requirement that all players use well calibrated forecasters guarantees that the joint empirical frequencies of play converge to the set $\mathcal{C}$ of correlated equilibria.

To lighten the exposition, we present the results for $K = 2$ players, but the results trivially extend to the general case (left as exercise). So assume that the actions I_t and J_t selected by the two players at time t are determined as follows. Depending on the past sequence of plays, for each $j = 1, \ldots, M$ the row player determines a probability forecast $\widehat{q}_{j,t} \in [0, 1]$ of the next play J_t of the column player where we require that $\sum_{j=1}^{M} \widehat{q}_{j,t} = 1$. Denote the forecasted mixed strategy by $\widehat{\mathbf{q}}_t = (\widehat{q}_{1,t}, \ldots, \widehat{q}_{M,t})$ and write $\overline{J}_t = (\mathbb{I}_{\{J_t=1\}}, \ldots, \mathbb{I}_{\{J_t=M\}})$. We only require that the forecast be well calibrated. Recall from Section 4.5 that this means that for any $\varepsilon > 0$, the function

$$\rho_n(A) = \frac{\sum_{t=1}^{n} \overline{J}_t \, \mathbb{I}_{\{\widehat{\mathbf{q}}_t \in A\}}}{\sum_{t=1}^{n} \mathbb{I}_{\{\widehat{\mathbf{q}}_t \in A\}}}$$

defined for all subsets A of the probability simplex (defined to be 0 if $\sum_{t=1}^{n} \mathbb{I}_{\{\widehat{q}_{j,t} \in A\}} = 0$) satisfies, for all A and for all $\varepsilon > 0$,

$$\limsup_{n \to \infty} \left| \rho_n(A_\varepsilon) - \frac{\int_{A_\varepsilon} x \, dx}{\lambda(A_\varepsilon)} \right| < \varepsilon.$$

(where $A_\varepsilon = \{x : \exists y \in A \text{ such that } \|x - y\| < \varepsilon\}$ is the ε-blowup of A and λ stands for the uniform probability measure over the simplex.) Recall from Section 4.5 (more precisely Exercise 4.17) that regardless of what the sequence $J_1, J_2, \ldots$ is, the row player can determine a randomized, well-calibrated forecaster. We assume that the row player best responds to the forecasted probability distribution in the sense that

$$I_t = \operatorname*{argmin}_{i=1,\ldots,N} \overline{\ell}^{(1)}(i, \widehat{\mathbf{q}}_t) = \operatorname*{argmin}_{i=1,\ldots,N} \sum_{j=1}^{M} \widehat{q}_{j,t} \, \ell^{(1)}(i, j).$$

Ties may be broken by an arbitrary but constant rule. The tie-breaking rule is described by the sets

$$\widehat{B}_i = \left\{ \mathbf{q} : \text{row player plays action } i \text{ if } \widehat{\mathbf{q}}_t = \mathbf{q} \right\}, \qquad i = 1, \ldots, N.$$

Note that for each i, $\widehat{B}_i$ is contained in the closed and convex set B_i of $\mathbf{q}$'s to which i is a best reply defined by

$$B_i = \left\{ \mathbf{q} : \overline{\ell}^{(1)}(i, \mathbf{q}) = \min_{i'=1,\ldots,N} \overline{\ell}^{(1)}(i', \mathbf{q}) \right\}.$$

Assume also that the column player proceeds similarly, that is,

$$J_t = \operatorname*{argmin}_{j=1,\ldots,M} \overline{\ell}^{(2)}(\widehat{\mathbf{p}}_t, j) = \operatorname*{argmin}_{j=1,\ldots,M} \sum_{i=1}^{N} \widehat{p}_{i,t}\, \ell^{(2)}(i, j),$$

where for each i, the sequence $\widehat{p}_{i,t}$ ($t = 1, 2, \ldots$) is a well calibrated forecaster of $I_1, I_2, \ldots$.

Theorem 7.4. *Assume that in a two-person game both players play by best responding to a calibrated forecast of the opponent's sequence of plays, as described above. Then the joint empirical frequencies of play*

$$\widehat{P}_n(i, j) = \frac{1}{n} \sum_{t=1}^{n} \mathbb{I}_{\{I_t=i, J_t=j\}}$$

converge to the set $\mathcal{C}$ of correlated equilibria in the sense that

$$\inf_{P \in \mathcal{C}} \sum_{(i,j)} |P(i, j) - \widehat{P}_n(i, j)| \to 0 \qquad \text{almost surely.}$$

Proof. Consider the sequence of empirical distributions $\widehat{P}_n$. Since the simplex of all joint distributions over $\{1, \ldots, N\} \times \{1, \ldots, M\}$ is a compact set, every sequence has a convergent subsequence. Thus, it suffices to show that the limit of every convergent subsequence of $\widehat{P}_n$ is in $\mathcal{C}$. Let $\widehat{P}_{n_k}$ be such a convergent subsequence and denote its limit by P. We need to show that P is a correlated equilibrium.

Note that by Lemma 7.1, P is a correlated equilibrium if and only if for each $i \in \{1, \ldots, N\}$ the conditional distribution

$$\mathbf{q}(\cdot \mid i) = \big(q(1 \mid i), \ldots, q(M \mid i)\big) = \left(\frac{P(i, 1)}{\sum_{j'=1}^{M} P(i, j')}, \ldots, \frac{P(i, M)}{\sum_{j'=1}^{M} P(i, j')} \right)$$

is in the set B_i and the symmetric statement for the other player holds as well. Therefore, it suffices to show that, for each $i = 1, \ldots, N$, the distribution

$$\widehat{\mathbf{q}}_{n_k}(\cdot \mid i) = \left(\frac{\widehat{P}_{n_k}(i, 1)}{\sum_{j'=1}^{M} \widehat{P}_{n_k}(i, j')}, \ldots, \frac{\widehat{P}_{n_k}(i, M)}{\sum_{j'=1}^{M} \widehat{P}_{n_k}(i, j')} \right)$$

approaches the set B_i. By the definition of I_t, for each $j = 1, \ldots, M$

$$\widehat{P}_{n_k}(i, j) = \frac{1}{n_k} \sum_{s=1}^{k} \mathbb{I}_{\{\widehat{\mathbf{q}}_{n_s} \in \widehat{B}_i\}} \mathbb{I}_{\{J_{n_s}=j\}}$$

and therefore

$$\widehat{\mathbf{q}}_{n_k}(\cdot \mid i) = \frac{\sum_{s=1}^{k} \overline{J}_{n_s} \mathbb{I}_{\{\widehat{\mathbf{q}}_{n_s} \in \widehat{B}_i\}}}{\sum_{s=1}^{k} \mathbb{I}_{\{\widehat{\mathbf{q}}_{n_s} \in \widehat{B}_i\}}} = \rho_{n_k}(\widehat{B}_i).$$

Since $\widehat{P}_{n_k}$ is convergent, the limit

$$\overline{x} = \lim_{k \to \infty} \rho_{n_k}(\widehat{B}_i)$$

exists. We need to show that $\overline{x} \in B_i$. If $(\widehat{B}_i)_\varepsilon$ denotes the ε-blowup of $\widehat{B}_i$ then well-calibration of the forecaster $\widehat{\mathbf{q}}_t$ implies that, for all $\varepsilon > 0$,

$$\limsup_{k \to \infty} \left| \rho_{n_k}\big((\widehat{B}_i)_\varepsilon\big) - \frac{\int_{(\widehat{B}_i)_\varepsilon} x \, dx}{\lambda\big((\widehat{B}_i)_\varepsilon\big)} \right| < \varepsilon.$$

Define

$$\overline{x}' \stackrel{\text{def}}{=} \lim_{\varepsilon \to 0} \frac{\int_{(\widehat{B}_i)_\varepsilon} x \, dx}{\lambda\big((\widehat{B}_i)_\varepsilon\big)}.$$

(The limit exists by the continuity of measure.) Because for all n_k we have $\lim_{\varepsilon \to 0} \rho_{n_k}((\widehat{B}_i)_\varepsilon) = \rho_{n_k}(\widehat{B}_i)$, it is easy to see that $\overline{x} = \overline{x}'$. But since $\widehat{B}_i \subset B_i$ and B_i is convex, the vector $\int_{(\widehat{B}_i)_\varepsilon} x \, dx / \lambda((\widehat{B}_i)_\varepsilon)$ lies in the ε-blowup of B_i. Therefore we indeed have $\overline{x} = \overline{x}' \in B_i$, as desired. ∎

7.7   Blackwell's Approachability Theorem

We investigate a powerful generalization, introduced by Blackwell, of the problem of playing repeated two-player zero-sum games. Consider the situation of Section 7.3 with the only but essential difference that losses are vector valued. More precisely, the setup is described as follows. Just as before, at each time instance the row player selects an action $i \in \{1, \ldots, N\}$ and the column player selects an action $j \in \{1, \ldots, M\}$. However, the "loss" $\boldsymbol{\ell}(i, j)$ suffered by the row player is not a real number in $[0, 1]$ but may take values in a bounded subset of $\mathbb{R}^m$. (We use bold characters to emphasize that losses are vector valued.)

For the sake of concreteness we assume that all losses are in the euclidean unit ball, that is, the entries of the loss matrix $\boldsymbol{\ell}$ are such that $\|\boldsymbol{\ell}(i, j)\| \leq 1$.

In the simpler case of scalar losses, the purpose of the row player is to minimize his average loss regardless of the actions of the column player. Then von Neumann's minimax theorem (together with martingale convergence, e.g., the Hoeffding–Azuma inequality) asserts that no matter how the column player plays, the row player can always keep the normalized accumulated loss $\frac{1}{n} \sum_{t=1}^{n} \ell(I_t, J_t)$ in, or very close to, the set $(-\infty, V]$, but not in the set $(-\infty, V - \varepsilon]$ if $\varepsilon > 0$ (see Exercise 7.7). In the case of vector-valued losses the general question is to determine which subsets of $\mathbb{R}^m$ can the row player keep his average loss close to. To this end, following Blackwell [28], we introduce the notion of approachability: a subset S of the unit ball of $\mathbb{R}^m$ is *approachable* (by the row player) if the row player has a (randomized) strategy such that no matter how the column player plays,

$$\lim_{n \to \infty} d\left(\frac{1}{n} \sum_{t=1}^{n} \boldsymbol{\ell}(I_t, J_t), S \right) = 0 \qquad \text{almost surely,}$$

where $d(\mathbf{u}, S) = \inf_{\mathbf{v} \in S} \|\mathbf{u} - \mathbf{v}\|$ denotes the euclidean distance of $\mathbf{u}$ from the set S. Because any set is approachable if and only if its closure is approachable, it suffices to consider only closed sets.

Our purpose in this section is to characterize which convex sets are approachable. In the one-dimensional case the minimax theorem can be rephrased as follows: a closed interval

$(-\infty, c]$ is approachable if and only if $c \geq V$. In other words, $(-\infty, c]$ is approachable if and only if the row player has a mixed strategy $\mathbf{p}$ such that $\max_{j=1,\dots,M} \overline{\ell}(\mathbf{p}, j) \leq c$.

In the general vector-valued case it is easy to characterize approachability of halfspaces. Consider a halfspace defined by $H = \{\mathbf{u} : \mathbf{a} \cdot \mathbf{u} \leq c\}$, where $\|\mathbf{a}\| = 1$. If we define an auxiliary game with scalar losses $\ell(i, j) = \mathbf{a} \cdot \boldsymbol{\ell}(i, j)$, then clearly, H is approachable if and only if the set $(-\infty, c]$ is approachable in the auxiliary game. By the above-mentioned consequence of the minimax theorem, this happens if and only if $\max_{j=1,\dots,M} \overline{\ell}(\mathbf{p}, j) = \max_{j=1,\dots,M} \mathbf{a} \cdot \overline{\boldsymbol{\ell}}(\mathbf{p}, j) \leq c$. (Note that, just as earlier, $\overline{\boldsymbol{\ell}}(\mathbf{p}, j) = \sum_i p_i \, \boldsymbol{\ell}(i, j)$.) Thus, we have proved the following characterization of the approachability of closed halfspaces.

Lemma 7.3. *A halfspace $H = \{\mathbf{u} : \mathbf{a} \cdot \mathbf{u} \leq c\}$ is approachable if and only if there exists a probability vector $\mathbf{p} = (p_1, \dots, p_N)$ such that*

$$\max_{j=1,\dots,M} \mathbf{a} \cdot \overline{\boldsymbol{\ell}}(\mathbf{p}, j) \leq c.$$

The lemma states that the halfspace H is approachable by the row player in a repeated play of the game if and only if in the *one-shot game* the row player has a mixed strategy that keeps the expected loss in the halfspace H. This is a simple and natural fact. What is interesting and much less obvious is that to approach any convex set S, it suffices that the row player has a strategy for each hyperplane not intersecting S to keep the average loss on the same side of the hyperplane as the set S. This is *Blackwell's Approachability Theorem*. stated and proved next.

Theorem 7.5 (Blackwell's approachability theorem). *A closed convex set S is approachable if and only if every halfspace H containing S is approachable.*

It is important to point out that for approachability of S, *every* halfspace containing S must be approachable. Even if S can be written as an intersection of finitely many closed halfspaces, that is, $S = \bigcap_i H_i$, the fact that all H_i are approachable does not imply that S is approachable: see Exercise 7.21.

The proof of Theorem 7.5 is constructive and surprisingly simple. At every time instance, if the average loss is not in the set S, then the row player projects the average loss to S and uses the mixed strategy $\mathbf{p}$ corresponding to the halfspace containing S, defined by the hyperplane passing through the projected loss vector, and perpendicular to the direction of the projection. In the next section we generalize this "approaching" algorithm to obtain a whole family of strategies that guarantee that the average loss approaches S almost surely.

Introduce the notation $A_t = \frac{1}{t} \sum_{s=1}^{t} \boldsymbol{\ell}(I_s, J_s)$ for the average loss vector at time t and denote by $\pi_S(\mathbf{u}) = \mathrm{argmin}_{\mathbf{v} \in S} \|\mathbf{u} - \mathbf{v}\|$ the projection of $\mathbf{u} \in \mathbb{R}^m$ onto S. (Note that $\pi_S(\mathbf{u})$ exists and is unique if S is closed and convex.)

Proof. To prove the statement, note first that S is clearly not approachable if there exists a halfspace $H \supset S$ that is not approachable.

Thus, it remains to show that if all halfspaces H containing S are approachable, then S is approachable as well. To this end, assume that the row player's mixed strategy $\mathbf{p}_t$ at time $t = 1, 2, \dots$ is arbitrary if $A_{t-1} \in S$, and otherwise it is such that

$$\max_{j=1,\dots,M} \mathbf{a}_{t-1} \cdot \overline{\boldsymbol{\ell}}(\mathbf{p}_t, j) \leq c_{t-1},$$

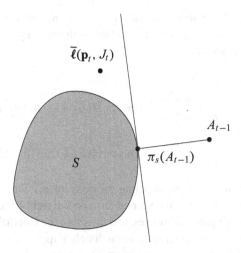

Figure 7.1. Approachability: the expected loss $\bar{\ell}(\mathbf{p}_t, J_t)$ is forced to stay on the same side of the hyperplane $\{\mathbf{u} : \mathbf{a}_{t-1} \cdot \mathbf{u} = c_{t-1}\}$ as the target set S, opposite to the current average loss A_{t-1}.

where

$$\mathbf{a}_{t-1} = \frac{A_{t-1} - \pi_S(A_{t-1})}{\|A_{t-1} - \pi_S(A_{t-1})\|} \qquad \text{and} \qquad c_{t-1} = \mathbf{a}_{t-1} \cdot \pi_S(A_{t-1}).$$

(Define A_0 as the zero vector.) Observe that the hyperplane $\{\mathbf{u} : \mathbf{a}_{t-1} \cdot \mathbf{u} = c_{t-1}\}$ contains $\pi_S(A_{t-1})$ and is perpendicular to the direction of projection of the average loss A_{t-1} to S. Since the halfspace $\{\mathbf{u} : \mathbf{a}_{t-1} \cdot \mathbf{u} \le c_{t-1}\}$ contains S, such a strategy $\mathbf{p}_t$ exists by assumption (see Figure 7.1). The defining inequality of $\mathbf{p}_t$ may be rewritten as

$$\max_{j=1,\dots,M} \mathbf{a}_{t-1} \cdot \big(\bar{\ell}(\mathbf{p}_t, j) - \pi_S(A_{t-1})\big) \le 0.$$

Since $A_t = \frac{t-1}{t} A_{t-1} + \frac{1}{t} \ell(I_t, J_t)$, we may write

$$
\begin{aligned}
d(A_t, S)^2 &= \|A_t - \pi_S(A_t)\|^2 \\
&\le \|A_t - \pi_S(A_{t-1})\|^2 \\
&= \left\| \frac{t-1}{t} A_{t-1} + \frac{\ell(I_t, J_t)}{t} - \pi_S(A_{t-1}) \right\|^2 \\
&= \left\| \frac{t-1}{t}\big(A_{t-1} - \pi_S(A_{t-1})\big) + \frac{\ell(I_t, J_t) - \pi_S(A_{t-1})}{t} \right\|^2 \\
&= \left(\frac{t-1}{t}\right)^2 \|A_{t-1} - \pi_S(A_{t-1})\|^2 + \frac{1}{t^2}\|\ell(I_t, J_t) - \pi_S(A_{t-1})\|^2 \\
&\quad + 2\frac{t-1}{t^2}\big(A_{t-1} - \pi_S(A_{t-1})\big) \cdot \big(\ell(I_t, J_t) - \pi_S(A_{t-1})\big).
\end{aligned}
$$

Using the assumption that all losses, as well as the set S, are in the unit ball, and therefore $\|\ell(I_t, J_t) - \pi_S(A_{t-1})\| \le 2$, and rearranging the obtained inequality, we get

$$
\begin{aligned}
t^2 \|A_t - \pi_S(A_t)\|^2 &- (t-1)^2 \|A_{t-1} - \pi_S(A_{t-1})\|^2 \\
&\le 4 + 2(t-1)\big(A_{t-1} - \pi_S(A_{t-1})\big) \cdot \big(\ell(I_t, J_t) - \pi_S(A_{t-1})\big).
\end{aligned}
$$

Summing both sides of the inequality for $t = 1, \ldots, n$, the left-hand side telescopes and becomes $n^2 \|A_n - \pi_S(A_n)\|^2$. Next, dividing both sides by n^2, and writing $K_{t-1} = \frac{t-1}{n} \|A_{t-1} - \pi_S(A_{t-1})\|$, we have

$$\|A_n - \pi_S(A_n)\|^2$$

$$\leq \frac{4}{n} + \frac{2}{n} \sum_{t=1}^{n} K_{t-1} \mathbf{a}_{t-1} \cdot \left(\boldsymbol{\ell}(I_t, J_t) - \pi_S(A_{t-1})\right)$$

$$\leq \frac{4}{n} + \frac{2}{n} \sum_{t=1}^{n} K_{t-1} \mathbf{a}_{t-1} \cdot \left(\boldsymbol{\ell}(I_t, J_t) - \overline{\boldsymbol{\ell}}(\mathbf{p}_t, J_t)\right),$$

where at the last step we used the defining property of $\mathbf{p}_t$. Since the random variable K_{t-1} is bounded between 0 and 2, the second term on the right-hand side is an average of bounded zero-mean martingale differences, and therefore the Hoeffding–Azuma inequality (together with the Borel–Cantelli lemma) immediately implies that $\|A_n - \pi_S(A_n)\|^2 \to 0$ almost surely, which is precisely what we wanted to prove. ∎

Remark 7.7 (Rates of convergence). The rate of convergence to 0 of the distance $\|A_n - \pi_S(A_n)\|$ that one immediately obtains from the proof is of order $n^{-1/4}$ (since the upper bound for the squared distance contains a sum of bounded martingale differences that, if bounded by the Hoeffding–Azuma inequality, gives a term that is $O_p(n^{-1/2})$). However, this bound can be improved substantially by a simple modification of the definition of the mixed strategy $\mathbf{p}_t$ used in the proof. Indeed, if instead of the average loss vector $A_t = \frac{1}{t} \sum_{s=1}^{t} \boldsymbol{\ell}(I_s, J_s)$ one uses the "expected" average loss $\overline{A}_t = \frac{1}{t} \sum_{s=1}^{t} \overline{\boldsymbol{\ell}}(\mathbf{p}_s, J_s)$, one easily obtains a bound for $\|A_n - \pi_S(A_n)\|$ that is of order $n^{-1/2}$; see Exercise 7.23.

Approachability and Regret Minimization

To demonstrate the power of Theorem 7.5 we show how it can be used to show the existence of Hannan consistent forecasters. Recall the problem of randomized prediction described in Section 4.1. In this case the goal of forecaster is to determine, at each round of play, a distribution $\mathbf{p}_t$ (i.e., a mixed strategy in the terminology of this chapter) so that regardless of what the outcomes Y_t (the opponents' play) are, the per-round regret

$$\frac{1}{n} \left(\sum_{t=1}^{n} \ell(I_t, Y_t) - \min_{i=1,\ldots,N} \sum_{t=1}^{n} \ell(i, Y_t) \right)$$

has a nonpositive limsup when each I_t is drawn randomly according to the distribution $\mathbf{p}_t$. Equivalently, the forecaster tries to keep the per-round regret vector $\frac{1}{n} \mathbf{R}_n$, of components $\frac{1}{n} R_{i,n} = \frac{1}{n} \sum_{t=1}^{n} (\ell(I_t, Y_t) - \ell(i, Y_t))$, close to the nonpositive orthant

$$S = \left\{ \mathbf{u} = (u_1, \ldots, u_N) : \forall i = 1, \ldots N, \ u_i \leq 0 \right\}.$$

Thus, the existence of a Hannan consistent forecaster is equivalent to the approachability of the orthant S in a two-player game in which the vector-valued losses of the row player are defined by $\boldsymbol{\ell}(i, j)$ whose kth component is

$$\ell^{(k)}(i, j) = \ell(i, j) - \ell(k, j).$$

(Note that with this choice the loss vectors fall in the ball, centered at the origin, of radius $2\sqrt{N}$. In the formulation of Theorem 7.5 we assumed that the loss vectors take their

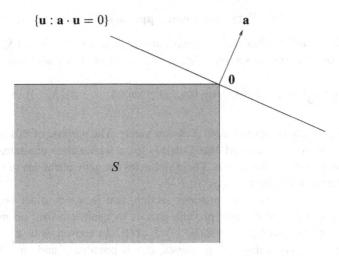

Figure 7.2. The normal vector **a** of any hyperplane corresponding to halfspaces containing the nonpositive orthant has nonnegative components.

values in the unit ball. The extension to the present case is a matter of trivial rescaling.) By Theorem 7.5 and Lemma 7.3, S is approachable if for every halfspace $\{\mathbf{u} : \mathbf{a} \cdot \mathbf{u} \le c\}$ containing S there exists a probability vector $\mathbf{p} = (p_1, \ldots, p_N)$ such that

$$\max_{j=1,\ldots,M} \mathbf{a} \cdot \overline{\boldsymbol{\ell}}(\mathbf{p}, j) \le c.$$

Clearly, it suffices to consider halfspaces of the form

$$\max_{j=1,\ldots,M} \mathbf{a} \cdot \overline{\boldsymbol{\ell}}(\mathbf{p}, j) \le 0,$$

where the normal vector $\mathbf{a} = (a_1, \ldots, a_N)$ is such that all its components are nonnegative (see Figure 7.2). This condition is equivalent to requiring that, for all $j = 1, \ldots, M$,

$$\sum_{k=1}^{N} a_k \, \overline{\ell}^{(k)}(\mathbf{p}, j) = \sum_{k=1}^{N} a_k \left(\overline{\ell}(\mathbf{p}, j) - \ell(k, j) \right) \le 0,$$

Choosing

$$\mathbf{p} = \frac{\mathbf{a}}{\sum_{k=1}^{N} a_k}$$

the inequality clearly holds for all j (with equality). Since **a** has only nonnegative components, **p** is indeed a valid mixed strategy. In summary, Blackwell's approachability theorem indeed implies the existence of a Hannan consistent forecasting strategy. Note that the constructive proof of Theorem 7.5 defines such a strategy. Observe that this strategy is just the weighted average forecaster of Section 4.2 when the quadratic potential is used. In the next section we describe a whole family of strategies that, when specialized to the forecasting problem discussed here, reduce to weighted average forecasters with more general potential functions. The approachability theorem may be (and has been) used to handle more general problems. For example, it is easy to see that it implies the existence of internal-regret-minimizing strategies (see Exercise 7.22).

7.8   Potential-based Approachability

The constructive proof of Blackwell's approachability theorem (Theorem 7.5) shows that if S is an approachable convex set, then for any strategy of the row player such that

$$\max_{j=1,\dots,M}\big(\mathbf{A}_{t-1} - \pi_S(\mathbf{A}_{t-1})\big) \cdot \overline{\ell}(\mathbf{p}_t, j) \le \sup_{\mathbf{x}\in S}\big(\mathbf{A}_{t-1} - \pi_S(\mathbf{A}_{t-1})\big) \cdot \mathbf{x}$$

the average loss $\mathbf{A}_n$ converges to the set S almost surely. The purpose of this section is to introduce, as proposed by Hart and Mas-Colell [146], a whole class of strategies for the row player that achieve the same goal. These strategies are generalizations of the strategy appearing in the proof of Theorem 7.5.

The setup is the same as in the previous section, that is, we consider vector-valued losses in the unit ball, and the row player's goal is to guarantee that, no matter what the opponent does, the average loss $\mathbf{A}_n = \frac{1}{n}\sum_{t=1}^{n}\ell(I_t, J_t)$ converges to a set S almost surely. Theorem 7.5 shows that if S is convex, this is possible if and only if all linear halfspaces containing S are approachable. Throughout this section we assume that S is closed, convex, and approachable, and we define strategies for the row player guaranteeing that $d(\mathbf{A}_n, S) \to 0$ with probability 1.

To define such a strategy, we introduce a nonnegative *potential function* $\Phi : \mathbb{R}^m \to \mathbb{R}$ whose role is to score the current situation of the average loss. A small value of $\Phi(\mathbf{A}_t)$ means that $\mathbf{A}_t$ is "close" to the target set S. All we assume about Φ is that it is convex, differentiable for all $\mathbf{x} \notin S$, and $\Phi(\mathbf{x}) = 0$ if and only if $\mathbf{x} \in S$. Note that such a potential always exists by convexity and closedness of S. One example is the function $\Phi(\mathbf{x}) = \inf_{\mathbf{y}\in S}\|\mathbf{x} - \mathbf{y}\|^2$.

The row player uses the potential function to determine, at time t, a mixed strategy $\mathbf{p}_t$ satisfying, whenever $\mathbf{A}_{t-1} \notin S$,

$$\max_{j=1,\dots,M}\mathbf{a}_{t-1} \cdot \overline{\ell}(\mathbf{p}_t, j) \le c_{t-1},$$

where

$$\mathbf{a}_{t-1} = \frac{\nabla\Phi(\mathbf{A}_{t-1})}{\|\nabla\Phi(\mathbf{A}_{t-1})\|} \qquad \text{and} \qquad c_{t-1} = \sup_{\mathbf{x}\in S}\mathbf{a}_{t-1} \cdot \mathbf{x}.$$

If $\mathbf{A}_{t-1} \in S$, the row player's action can be arbitrary. Observe that the existence of such a $\mathbf{p}_t$ is implied by the fact that S is convex and approachable and by Theorem 7.5. Geometrically, the hyperplane tangent to the level curve of the potential function Φ passing through $\mathbf{A}_{t-1}$ is shifted so that it intersects S but S falls entirely on one side of the shifted hyperplane. The distribution $\mathbf{p}_t$ is determined so that the expected loss $\overline{\ell}(\mathbf{p}_t, j)$ is forced to stay on the same side of the hyperplane as S (see Figure 7.3). Note also that, in the special case when $\Phi(\mathbf{x}) = \inf_{\mathbf{y}\in S}\|\mathbf{x} - \mathbf{y}\|^2$, this strategy is identical to Blackwell's strategy defined in the proof of Theorem 7.5, and therefore the potential-based strategy may be thought of as a generalization of Blackwell's strategy.

Remark 7.8 (Bregman projection). For any $\mathbf{x} \notin S$ we may define

$$\pi_S(\mathbf{x}) = \operatorname*{argmax}_{\mathbf{y}\in S} \nabla\Phi(\mathbf{x}) \cdot \mathbf{y}.$$

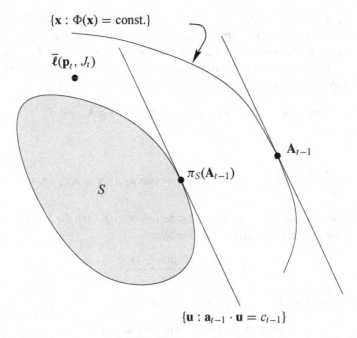

$\{\mathbf{x} : \Phi(\mathbf{x}) = \text{const.}\}$

$\overline{\ell}(\mathbf{p}_t, J_t)$

$\mathbf{A}_{t-1}$

$\pi_S(\mathbf{A}_{t-1})$

S

$\{\mathbf{u} : \mathbf{a}_{t-1} \cdot \mathbf{u} = c_{t-1}\}$

Figure 7.3. Potential-based approachability. The hyperplane $\{\mathbf{u} : \mathbf{a}_{t-1} \cdot \mathbf{u} = c_{t-1}\}$ is determined by shifting the hyperplane tangent to the level set $\{\mathbf{x} : \Phi(\mathbf{x}) = \text{const.}\}$ containing $\mathbf{A}_{t-1}$ to the Bregman projection $\pi_S(\mathbf{A}_{t-1})$. The expected loss $\overline{\ell}(\mathbf{p}_t, J_t)$ is guaranteed to stay on the same side of the shifted hyperplane as S.

It is easy to see that the conditions on Φ imply that the maximum exists and is unique. In fact, since $\Phi(\mathbf{y}) = 0$ for all $\mathbf{y} \in S$, $\pi_S(\mathbf{x})$ may be rewritten as

$$\pi_S(\mathbf{x}) = \left(\underset{\mathbf{y} \in S}{\text{argmin}} \ \Phi(\mathbf{y}) - \Phi(\mathbf{x}) - \nabla \Phi(\mathbf{x}) \cdot (\mathbf{y} - \mathbf{x}) \right) = \underset{\mathbf{y} \in S}{\text{argmin}} \ D_\Phi(\mathbf{y}, \mathbf{x}).$$

In other words, $\pi_S(\mathbf{x})$ is just the projection, under the Bregman divergence, of $\mathbf{x}$ onto the set S. (For the definition and basic properties of Bregman divergences and projections, see Section 11.2.)

This potential-based strategy has a very similar version with comparable properties. This version simply replaces $\mathbf{A}_{t-1}$ in the definition of the algorithm by $\overline{\mathbf{A}}_{t-1}$ where, for each $t = 1, 2, \ldots, \overline{\mathbf{A}}_t = \frac{1}{t} \sum_{s=1}^{t} \overline{\ell}(\mathbf{p}_s, J_s)$ is the "expected" average loss, see also Exercise 7.23. Recall that

$$\overline{\ell}(\mathbf{p}_s, J_s) = \sum_{i=1}^{N} p_{i,s} \, \ell(i, J_s) = \mathbb{E}\left[\ell(I_s, J_s) \mid I^{s-1}, J^s\right].$$

The main result of this section states that for any potential function, the row player's average loss approaches the target set S no matter how the opponent plays. The next theorem states this fact for the modified strategy (based on $\overline{\mathbf{A}}_{t-1}$). The analog statement for the strategy based on $\mathbf{A}_{t-1}$ may be proved similarly, and it is left as an exercise.

Theorem 7.6. *Let S be a closed, convex, and approachable subset of the unit ball in* $\mathbb{R}^m$, *and let* Φ *be a convex, twice differentiable potential function that vanishes in S and is positive outside of S. Denote the Hessian matrix of* Φ *at* $\mathbf{x} \in \mathbb{R}^m$ *by* $H(\mathbf{x})$ *and let* $B = \sup_{\mathbf{x}:\|\mathbf{x}\|\leq 1} \|H(\mathbf{x})\| < \infty$ *be the maximal norm of the Hessian in the unit ball. For each* $t = 1, 2, \ldots$ *let the potential-based strategy* $\mathbf{p}_t$ *be any strategy satisfying*

$$\max_{j=1,\ldots,M} \mathbf{a}_{t-1} \cdot \boldsymbol{\ell}(\mathbf{p}_t, j) \leq c_{t-1} \quad \text{if } \mathbf{A}_{t-1} \notin S \text{ if } \overline{\mathbf{A}}_{t-1} \notin S,$$

where

$$\mathbf{a}_{t-1} = \frac{\nabla\Phi(\overline{\mathbf{A}}_{t-1})}{\|\nabla\Phi(\overline{\mathbf{A}}_{t-1})\|} \quad \text{and} \quad c_{t-1} = \sup_{\mathbf{x}\in S} \mathbf{a}_{t-1} \cdot \mathbf{x} = \mathbf{a}_{t-1} \cdot \pi_S(\overline{\mathbf{A}}_{t-1}).$$

(If $\overline{\mathbf{A}}_{t-1} \in S$, *then the row player's action can be arbitrary.) Then for any strategy of the column player, the average "expected" loss satisfies*

$$\Phi(\overline{\mathbf{A}}_n) \leq \frac{2B(\ln n + 1)}{n}.$$

Also, for the average loss $\mathbf{A}_n = \frac{1}{n}\sum_{t=1}^{n} \boldsymbol{\ell}(I_t, J_t)$, *we have*

$$\lim_{n\to\infty} d(\mathbf{A}_n, S) = 0 \quad \text{with probability } 1.$$

Proof.   First note that for any $\mathbf{x} \notin S$ and $\mathbf{y} \in S$,

$$\nabla\Phi(\mathbf{x}) \cdot (\mathbf{y} - \mathbf{x}) \leq -\Phi(\mathbf{x}).$$

This follows simply from the fact that by convexity of Φ,

$$0 = \Phi(\mathbf{y}) \geq \Phi(\mathbf{x}) + \nabla\Phi(\mathbf{x}) \cdot (\mathbf{y} - \mathbf{x}).$$

The rest of the proof is based on a simple Taylor expansion of the potential $\Phi(\overline{\mathbf{A}}_t)$ around $\Phi(\overline{\mathbf{A}}_{t-1})$. Since $\overline{\mathbf{A}}_t = \overline{\mathbf{A}}_{t-1} + \frac{1}{t}\left(\boldsymbol{\ell}(\mathbf{p}_t, J_t) - \overline{\mathbf{A}}_{t-1}\right)$, we have

$$\Phi(\overline{\mathbf{A}}_t) = \Phi(\overline{\mathbf{A}}_{t-1}) + \frac{1}{t}\nabla\Phi(\overline{\mathbf{A}}_{t-1}) \cdot \left(\boldsymbol{\ell}(\mathbf{p}_t, J_t) - \overline{\mathbf{A}}_{t-1}\right)$$

$$+ \frac{1}{2t^2}\left(\boldsymbol{\ell}(\mathbf{p}_t, J_t) - \overline{\mathbf{A}}_{t-1}\right)^{\top} H(\boldsymbol{\xi})\left(\boldsymbol{\ell}(\mathbf{p}_t, J_t) - \overline{\mathbf{A}}_{t-1}\right)$$

(where $\boldsymbol{\xi}$ is a vector between $\overline{\mathbf{A}}_t$ and $\overline{\mathbf{A}}_{t-1}$)

$$\leq \Phi(\overline{\mathbf{A}}_{t-1}) + \frac{1}{t}\nabla\Phi(\overline{\mathbf{A}}_{t-1}) \cdot \left(\boldsymbol{\ell}(\mathbf{p}_t, J_t) - \overline{\mathbf{A}}_{t-1}\right)$$

$$+ \frac{1}{2t^2}\left\|\boldsymbol{\ell}(\mathbf{p}_t, J_t) - \overline{\mathbf{A}}_{t-1}\right\|^2 \sup_{\boldsymbol{\xi}:\|\boldsymbol{\xi}\|\leq 1} \|H(\boldsymbol{\xi})\|$$

(by the Cauchy–Schwarz inequality)

$$\leq \Phi(\overline{\mathbf{A}}_{t-1}) + \frac{1}{t}\nabla\Phi(\overline{\mathbf{A}}_{t-1}) \cdot \left(\pi_S(\overline{\mathbf{A}}_{t-1}) - \overline{\mathbf{A}}_{t-1}\right) + \frac{2B}{t^2}$$

(by the defining property of $\mathbf{p}_t$)

$$\leq \Phi(\overline{\mathbf{A}}_{t-1}) - \frac{1}{t}\Phi(\overline{\mathbf{A}}_{t-1}) + \frac{2B}{t^2}$$

(by the property noted at the beginning of the proof).

Multiplying both sides of the obtained inequality by t we get

$$t\Phi(\overline{\mathbf{A}}_t) \leq (t-1)\Phi(\overline{\mathbf{A}}_{t-1}) + \frac{2B}{t} \qquad \text{for all } t \geq 1.$$

Summing this inequality for $t = 1, \ldots, n$, we have

$$n\Phi(\overline{\mathbf{A}}_n) \leq \sum_{t=1}^{n} \frac{2B}{t},$$

which proves the first statement of the theorem. The almost sure convergence of $\mathbf{A}_n$ to S may now be obtained easily using the Hoeffding–Azuma inequality, just as in the proof of Theorem 7.5. ∎

7.9 Convergence to Nash Equilibria

We have seen in the previous sections that if all players follow simple strategies based on (internal) regret minimization, then the joint empirical frequencies of play approach the set of correlated equilibria at a remarkably fast rate. Here we investigate the considerably more difficult problem of achieving Nash equilibria.

Just as before, we only consider uncoupled strategies; that is, each player knows his own payoff function but not that of the rest of the players. In this section we assume *standard monitoring*; that is, after taking an action, all players observe the other players' moves. In other words, the participants of the game know *what* the others do, but they do not know *why* they do it. In the next section we treat the more difficult case in which the players only observe their own losses but not the actions the other players take.

Our main concern here is to describe strategies of play that guarantee that no matter what the underlying game is, the players end up playing a mixed strategy profile close to a Nash equilibrium. The difficulty is that players cannot optimize their play because of the assumption of uncoupledness. The problem becomes more pronounced in the case of an "unknown game" (i.e., when players only observe their own payoffs but know nothing about what the other participants of the game do), treated in the next section.

As mentioned in the introduction, in many cases, including two-person zero-sum games and K-person games in which every player has two actions (i.e., $N_k = 2$ for all k), simple fictitious play is sufficient to achieve convergence to a Nash equilibrium (in a certain weak sense). However, the case of general games is considerably more difficult.

To describe the first simple idea, assume that the game has a *pure action Nash equilibrium*, that is, a Nash equilibrium π concentrated on a single vector $\mathbf{i} = (i_1, \ldots, i_K)$ of actions. In this case it is easy to construct a randomized uncoupled strategy of repeated play such that if all players follow such a strategy, the joint strategy profiles converge to a Nash equilibrium almost surely. Perhaps the simplest such procedure is described as follows.

AN UNCOUPLED STRATEGY TO FIND PURE
NASH EQUILIBRIA

Strategy for player k.

For $t = 1, 2, \ldots$

    (1) if t is odd, choose an action $I_t^{(k)}$ randomly, according to the uniform distribution over $\{1, \ldots, N_k\}$;

    (2) if t is even, let

$$I_t^{(k)} = \begin{cases} 1 & \text{if } \ell^{(k)}(\mathbf{I}_{t-1}) \leq \min_{i_k=1,\ldots,N_k} \ell^{(k)}(\mathbf{I}_{t-1}^-, i_k) \\ 2 & \text{otherwise.} \end{cases}$$

    (3) If t is even and all players have played action 1, then repeat forever the action played in the last odd period.

In words, at each odd period the players choose an action randomly. At the next period they check if their action was a best response to the other players' actions and communicate it to the other players by playing action 1 or 2. If all players have best responded at some point (which they confirm by playing action 1 in the next round), then they repeat the same action forever. This strategy clearly realizes a random exhaustive search. Because the game is finite, eventually, almost surely, by pure chance, at some odd time period a pure action Nash equilibrium $\mathbf{i} = (i_1, \ldots, i_K)$ will be played (whose existence is guaranteed by assumption). The expected time it takes to find such an equilibrium is at most $2 \prod_{k=1}^{K} N_k$, a quantity exponentially large in the number K of players. By the definition of Nash equilibrium all players best respond at the time $\mathbf{i}$ is played and therefore stay with this choice forever.

Remark 7.9 (Exhaustive search). The algorithm shown above is a simple form of exhaustive search. In fact, all strategies that we describe here and in the next section are variants of the same principle. Of course, this also means that convergence is extremely slow in the sense that the whole space (exponentially large as a function of the number of players) needs to be explored. This is in sharp contrast to the internal-regret-minimizing strategies of Section 7.4 that guarantee rapid convergence to the set of correlated equilibria.

Remark 7.10 (Nonstationarity). The learning strategy described above may not be very appealing because of its nonstationarity. Exercise 7.25 describes a stationary strategy proposed by Hart and Mas-Colell [149] that also achieves almost sure convergence to a pure action Nash equilibrium whenever such an equilibrium exists.

Remark 7.11 (Multiple equilibria). The procedure always converges to a pure action Nash equilibrium. Of course, the game may have several Nash equilibria: some pure, others mixed. Some equilibria may be "better" than others, sometimes in quite a strong sense. However, the procedure does not make any distinction between different equilibria, and the one it finds is selected randomly, according to the uniform distribution over all pure action Nash equilibria.

Remark 7.12 (Two players). It is important to note that the case of $K = 2$ players is significantly simpler. In a two-player game (under a certain genericity assumption) it suffices to use a strategy that repeats the previous play if it was a best response and selects an action randomly otherwise (see Exercise 7.26). However, if the game is not generic or in the case of at least three players, this procedure may enter in a cycle and never converge (Exercise 7.27).

Next we show how the ideas described above may be extended to general games that may not have a pure action Nash equilibrium. The simplest version of this extension does not quite achieve a Nash equilibrium but approximates it. To make the statement precise, we introduce the notion of an ε-*Nash equilibrium*. Let $\varepsilon > 0$. A mixed strategy profile $\pi = \mathbf{p}^{(1)} \times \cdots \times \mathbf{p}^{(K)}$ is an ε-Nash equilibrium if for all $k = 1, \ldots, K$ and all mixed strategies $\mathbf{q}^{(k)}$,

$$\pi \ell^{(k)} \leq \pi'_k \ell^{(k)} + \varepsilon,$$

where $\pi'_k = \mathbf{p}^{(1)} \times \cdots \times \mathbf{q}^{(k)} \times \cdots \times \mathbf{p}^{(K)}$ denotes the mixed strategy profile obtained by replacing $\mathbf{p}^{(k)}$ by $\mathbf{q}^{(k)}$ and leaving all other players' mixed strategies unchanged. Thus, the definition of Nash equilibrium is modified simply by allowing some slack in the defining inequalities. Clearly, it suffices to check the inequalities for mixed strategies $\mathbf{q}^{(k)}$ concentrated on a single action i_k. The set of ε-Nash equilibria of a game is denoted by $\mathcal{N}_\varepsilon$.

The idea in extending the procedure discussed earlier for general games is that each player first selects a *mixed* strategy randomly and then checks whether it is an approximate best response to the others' mixed strategies. Clearly, this cannot be done in just one round of play because players cannot observe the mixed strategies of the others. But if the same mixed strategy is played during sufficiently many periods, then each player can simply test the hypothesis whether his choice is an approximate best response. This procedure is formalized as follows.

A REGRET-TESTING PROCEDURE TO FIND NASH EQUILIBRIA

Strategy for player k.

Parameters: Period length T, confidence parameter $\rho > 0$.

Initialization: Choose a mixed strategy $\pi_0^{(k)}$ randomly, according to the uniform distribution over the simplex $\mathcal{D}_k$ of probability distributions over $\{1, \ldots, N_k\}$;

For $t = 1, 2, \ldots$,

(1) if $t = mT + s$ for integers $m \geq 0$ and $1 \leq s \leq T - 1$, choose $I_t^{(k)}$ randomly according to the mixed strategy $\pi_m^{(k)}$;

(2) if $t = mT$ for an integer $m \geq 1$, then let

$$I_t^{(k)} = \begin{cases} 1 & \text{if } \frac{1}{T-1} \sum_{s=(m-1)T+1}^{mT-1} \ell^{(k)}(\mathbf{I}_s) \\ & \leq \min_{i_k=1,\ldots,N_k} \frac{1}{T-1} \sum_{s=(m-1)T+1}^{mT-1} \ell^{(k)}(\mathbf{I}_s^-, i_k) + \rho \\ 2 & \text{otherwise}; \end{cases}$$

(3) If $t = mT$ and all players have played action 1, then play the mixed strategy $\pi_{m-1}^{(k)}$ forever; otherwise, choose $\pi_m^{(k)}$ randomly, according to the uniform distribution over $\mathcal{D}_k$.

In this procedure every player tests, after each period of length T, whether he has been approximately best responding and sends a signal to the rest of the players at the end of the period. Once every player accepts the hypothesis of almost best response, the same mixed strategy profile is repeated forever. The next simple result summarizes the performance of this procedure.

Theorem 7.7. *Assume that every player of a game plays according to the regret-testing procedure described above that is run with parameters T and $\rho \le 1/2$ such that $(T - 1)\rho^2 \ge 2 \ln \sum_{k=1}^K N_k$. With probability 1, there is a mixed strategy profile $\pi = \mathbf{p}^{(1)} \times \cdots \times \mathbf{p}^{(K)}$ such that π is played for all sufficiently large m. The probability that π is not a 2ρ-Nash equilibrium is at most*

$$8T\rho^{2-d} \ln \left(T\rho^{2-d}\right) e^{-2(T-1)\rho^2},$$

where $d = \sum_{k=1}^K (N_k - 1)$ is the number of free parameters needed to specify any mixed strategy profile.

It is clear from the bound of the theorem that for an arbitrarily small value of ρ, if T is sufficiently large, the probability of not ending up in a 2ρ-Nash equilibrium can be made arbitrarily small. This probability decreases with T at a remarkably fast rate. Just note that if $T\rho^2$ is significantly larger than $d \ln d$, the probability may be further bounded by $e^{-T\rho^2}$. Thus, the size of the game plays a minor role in the bound of the probability. However, the time the procedure takes to reach the near-equilibrium state depends heavily on the size of the game. The estimates derived in the proof reveal that this stopping time is typically of order $T\rho^{-d}$, exponentially large in the number of players. However, convergence to ε-Nash equilibria cannot be achieved with this method for an arbitrarily small value of ε, because no matter how T and ρ are chosen, there is always a positive, though tiny, probability that all players accept a mixed strategy profile that is not an ε-Nash equilibrium. In the next section we describe a different procedure that may be converted into an almost surely convergent strategy.

Proof of Theorem 7.7. Let M denote the (random) index for which every player plays 1 at time MT. We need to prove that M is finite almost surely. Consider the process $\pi_0, \pi_1, \pi_2, \ldots$ of mixed strategy profiles found at times $0, T, 2T, \ldots$ by the players using the procedure. For convenience, assume that players keep drawing a new random mixed strategy π_m even if $m \ge M$ and the mixed strategy is not used anymore. In other words, $\pi_0, \pi_1, \pi_2, \ldots$ are independent random variables uniformly distributed over the $d = \sum_{k=1}^K (N_k - 1)$-dimensional set obtained by the product of the K simplices of the mixed strategies of the K players.

For any $\varepsilon \in (0, 1)$ we may write

$$\mathbb{P}[M \ge m_0] = \sum_{j=0}^{m_0-1} \mathbb{P}\big[\pi_m \in \mathcal{N}_\varepsilon \ j \text{ times}\big]$$

$$\times \mathbb{P}\big[\pi_m \text{ is rejected for every } m < m_0 \,\big|\, \pi_m \in \mathcal{N}_\varepsilon \ j \text{ times}\big].$$

We bound the terms on the right-hand side to derive the desired estimate for $\mathbb{P}[M \ge m_0]$.

First observe that since the game has at least one Nash equilibrium $\overline{\pi} = \overline{\mathbf{p}}^{(1)} \times \cdots \times \overline{\mathbf{p}}^{(K)}$, any mixed strategy profile $\widetilde{\pi} = \widetilde{\mathbf{p}}^{(1)} \times \cdots \times \widetilde{\mathbf{p}}^{(K)}$ such that

$$\max_{k=1,\ldots,K} \max_{i_k=1,\ldots,N_k} \left| \overline{p}^{(k)}(i_k) - \widetilde{p}^{(k)}(i_k) \right| \le \varepsilon$$

is an ε-Nash equilibrium. Thus, for every $m = 0, 1, \ldots$ we have

$$\mathbb{P}[\pi_m \in \mathcal{N}_\varepsilon] \ge \varepsilon^d.$$

This implies that

$$\mathbb{P}\big[\pi_m \in \mathcal{N}_\varepsilon\ j\ \text{times}\big] = \mathbb{P}\big[\pi_m \notin \mathcal{N}_\varepsilon\ m_0 - j\ \text{times}\big]$$

$$\le \binom{m_0}{j} \left(1 - \varepsilon^d\right)^{m_0 - j} \le m_0^j\, e^{-(m_0 - j)\varepsilon^d}.$$

To bound the other term in this expression of $\mathbb{P}[M \ge m_0]$, note that if $\pi_m \in \mathcal{N}_\varepsilon$ exactly j times for $m = 0, \ldots, m_0 - 1$, then $M \ge m_0$ implies that at least one player observes a regret at least ρ at all of these j periods. Note that at any given period m, if $\varepsilon > \rho$, by using the fact that the regret estimates are sums of $T - 1$ independent, identically distributed random variables, Hoeffding's inequality and the union-of-events bound imply that

$$\mathbb{P}\big[M \ne m \,\big|\, \pi_m \in \mathcal{N}_\varepsilon\big] \le \mathbb{P}\big[\exists k \le K : I_{mT}^{(k)} = 2 \,\big|\, \pi_m \in \mathcal{N}_\varepsilon\big]$$

$$\le \sum_{k=1}^{K} N_k e^{-2(T-1)(\varepsilon-\rho)^2}.$$

Therefore,

$$\mathbb{P}\big[\pi_m\ \text{is rejected for every}\ m < m_0 \,\big|\, \pi_m \in \mathcal{N}_\varepsilon\ j\ \text{times}\big]$$

$$\le \left(\sum_{k=1}^{K} N_k \right)^{j} e^{-2j(T-1)(\varepsilon-\rho)^2}.$$

Putting everything together, letting $\varepsilon = 2\rho$, using the assumption $(T-1)\rho^2 \ge 2\ln \sum_{k=1}^{K} N_k$, and fixing a $j_0 < m_0$, we have

$$\mathbb{P}[M \ge m_0] \le \sum_{j \le j_0} m_0^j\, e^{-(m_0-j)(2\rho)^d} + \sum_{j > j_0} \left(\sum_{k=1}^{K} N_k \right)^{j} e^{-j(T-1)\rho^2}$$

$$\le j_0 m_0^{j_0}\, e^{-(m_0-j_0)(2\rho)^d} + m_0\, e^{-j_0(T-1)\rho^2/2}.$$

Since we are free to choose j_0, we take $j_0 = \lfloor m_0\, \rho^{d-2}/(T \ln m_0) \rfloor$. To guarantee that $j_0 < m_0$ we assume that $m_0 \ge \rho^{-d} \left(2 \log \rho^{-d}\right)^2$. This implies that $m_0 > \rho^{-d}(\ln m_0)^2$, which in turn implies the desired condition $j_0 < m_0$. Thus, using this choice of m_0 and after some simplification, we get

$$\mathbb{P}[M \ge m_0] \le 2 e^{-m_0 \rho^d/(2 \ln m_0)}. \tag{7.2}$$

But then the Borel–Cantelli lemma implies that M is finite almost surely.

Now let π denote the mixed strategy profile that the process ends up repeating forever. (This random variable is well defined with probability 1 according to the fact that $M < \infty$ almost surely.) Then the probability that π is not a 2ρ-Nash equilibrium may be bounded by writing

$$\mathbb{P}\big[\pi \notin \mathcal{N}_{2\rho}\big] = \sum_{m=1}^{\infty} \mathbb{P}\big[M = m, \pi \notin \mathcal{N}_{2\rho}\big].$$

For $m \geq m_0$ (where the value of m_0 is determined later) we simply use the bound $\mathbb{P}[M = m, \pi \notin \mathcal{N}_{2\rho}] \leq \mathbb{P}[M = m]$. On the other hand, for any m, by Hoeffding's inequality,

$$\mathbb{P}\big[M = m, \pi \notin \mathcal{N}_{2\rho}\big] \leq \mathbb{P}\big[M = m \mid \pi \notin \mathcal{N}_{2\rho}\big] \leq e^{-2(T-1)\rho^2}.$$

Thus, for any m_0, we get

$$\mathbb{P}\big[\pi \notin \mathcal{N}_{2\rho}\big] \leq m_0 \, e^{-2(T-1)\rho^2} + \mathbb{P}[M \geq m_0].$$

Here we may use the estimate (7.2), which is valid for all $m_0 \geq \rho^{-d} \left(2 \log \rho^{-d}\right)^2$. A convenient choice is to take m_0 to be the greatest integer such that $m_0/(2 \ln m_0) \leq T\rho^{2-d}$. Then $m_0 \leq 4T\rho^{2-d} \ln \left(T\rho^{2-d}\right)$, and we obtain

$$\mathbb{P}\big[\pi \notin \mathcal{N}_{2\rho}\big] \leq 8T\rho^{2-d} \ln \left(T\rho^{2-d}\right) e^{-2(T-1)\rho^2}$$

as stated. ∎

7.10 Convergence in Unknown Games

The purpose of this section is to show that even in the much more restricted framework of "unknown" games described in Section 7.5, it is possible to achieve, asymptotically, an approximate Nash equilibrium. Recall that in this model, as the players play a game repeatedly, they not only do not know the other players' loss function but they do not even know their own, and the only information they receive is their loss suffered at each round of the game, after taking an action.

The basic idea of the strategy we investigate in this section is somewhat reminiscent of the regret-testing procedure described in the previous section. On a quick inspection of the procedure it is clear that the assumption of standard monitoring (i.e., that players are able to observe their opponents' actions) is used twice in the definition of the procedure. On the one hand, the players should be able to compute their estimated regret in each period of length T. On the other hand, they need to communicate to the others whether their estimated regret is smaller than a certain threshold or not. It turns out that it is easy to find a solution to the first problem, because players may easily and reliably estimate their regret even if they do not observe others' actions. This should not come as a surprise after having seen that regret minimization is possible in the bandit problem (see Sections 6.7, 6.8, and 7.5). In fact, the situation here is significantly simpler. However, the lack of ability of communication with the other players poses more serious problems because it is difficult to come up with a stopping rule as in the procedure shown in the previous section.

The solution is a procedure in which, just as before, time is divided into periods of length T, all players keep testing their regret in each period, and they stay with their previously chosen mixed strategy if they have had a satisfactorily small estimated regret. Otherwise they choose a new mixed strategy randomly, just like above. To make the ideas more transparent, first we ignore the issue of estimating regrets in the model of unknown game and assume that, after every period $(m-1)T + 1, \ldots, mT$, each player $k = 1, \ldots, K$ can compute the regrets

$$r_{m,i_k}^{(k)} = \frac{1}{T} \sum_{s=(m-1)T+1}^{mT} \ell^{(k)}(\mathbf{I}_s) - \frac{1}{T} \sum_{s=(m-1)T+1}^{mT} \ell^{(k)}(\mathbf{I}_s^-, i_k)$$

for all $i_k = 1, \ldots, N_k$. Now we may define a regret-testing procedure as follows.

EXPERIMENTAL REGRET TESTING

Strategy for player k.

Parameters: Period length T, confidence parameter $\rho > 0$, exploration parameter $\lambda > 0$.

Initialization: Choose a mixed strategy $\pi_0^{(k)}$ randomly, according to the uniform distribution over the simplex $\mathcal{D}_k$ of probability distributions over $\{1, \ldots, N_k\}$;

For $t = 1, 2, \ldots$

   (1) if $t = mT + s$ for integers $m \geq 0$ and $1 \leq s < T$, choose $I_t^{(k)}$ randomly according to the mixed strategy $\pi_m^{(k)}$;
   (2) if $t = mT$ for an integer $m \geq 1$, then
      • if

$$\max_{i_k = 1, \ldots, N_k} r_{m,i_k}^{(k)} > \rho$$

      then choose $\pi_m^{(k)}$ randomly according to the uniform distribution over $\mathcal{D}_k$;
      • otherwise, with probability $1 - \lambda$ let $\pi_m^{(k)} = \pi_{m-1}^{(k)}$, and with probability λ choose $\pi_m^{(k)}$ randomly according to the uniform distribution over $\mathcal{D}_k$.

The parameters ρ and T play a similar role to that played in the previous section. The introduction of the exploration parameter $\lambda > 0$ is technical; it is needed for the proofs given below but it is unclear whether the natural choice $\lambda = 0$ would give similar results. With $\lambda > 0$, even if a player has all regrets below the threshold ρ, the player will reserve a positive probability of exploration. A strictly positive value of λ guarantees that the sequence $\{\pi_m\}$ of mixed strategy profiles forms a rapidly mixing Markov process. In fact, the first basic lemma establishes this property. For convenience we denote the set $\prod_{k=1}^{K} \mathcal{D}_k$ of all mixed strategy profiles (i.e., product distributions) by Σ. Also, we introduce the notation $N = \sum_{k=1}^{K} N_k$.

Lemma 7.4. *The stochastic process $\{\pi_m\}$, $m = 0, 1, 2, \ldots$, defined by experimental regret testing with $0 < \lambda < 1$, is a homogeneous, recurrent, and irreducible Markov chain satisfying Doeblin's condition. In particular, for any measurable set $A \subset \Sigma$,*

$$P(\pi \to A) \geq \lambda^N \mu(A)$$

for every $\pi \in \Sigma$, where $P(\pi \to A) = \mathbb{P}[\pi_{m+1} \in A \mid \pi_m = \pi]$ denotes the transition probabilities of the Markov chain, μ denotes the uniform distribution on Σ, and m is any nonnegative integer.

Proof. To see that the process is a Markov chain, note that at each $m = 0, 1, 2, \ldots$, π_m depends only on π_{m-1} and the regrets $r_{m,i_k}^{(k)}$ ($i_k = 1, \ldots, N_k, k = 1, \ldots, K$). It is irreducible since at each $0, T, 2T, \ldots$, the probability of reaching some $\pi'_m \in A$ for any open set $A \subset \Sigma$ from any $\pi_{m-1} \in \Sigma$ is strictly positive when $\lambda > 0$, and it is recurrent since $\mathbb{E}\big[\sum_{m=0}^{\infty} \mathbb{I}_{\{\pi_m \in A\}} \,\big|\, \pi_0 \in A\big] = \infty$ for all $\pi_0 \in A$. Doeblin's condition follows simply from the presence of the exploration parameter λ in the definition of experimental regret testing. In particular, with probability λ^N every player chooses a mixed strategy randomly, and conditioned on this event the distribution of π_m is uniform. ∎

The lemma implies that $\{\pi_m\}$ is a rapidly mixing Markov chain. The behavior of such Markov processes is well understood (see, e.g., the monograph of Meyn and Tweedie [217] for an excellent coverage). The properties we use subsequently are summarized in the following corollary.

Corollary 7.2. *For $m = 0, 1, 2, \ldots$ let P_m denote the distribution of the mixed strategy profile $\pi_m = (\pi_m^{(1)}, \ldots, \pi_m^{(K)})$ chosen by the players at time mT, that is, $P_m(A) = \mathbb{P}[\pi_m \in A]$. Then there exists a unique probability distribution Q over Σ (the stationary distribution of the Markov process) such that*

$$\sup_A |P_m(A) - Q(A)| \le \big(1 - \lambda^N\big)^m,$$

where the supremum is taken over all measurable sets $A \subset \Sigma$ (see [217, Theorem 16.2.4]). Also, the ergodic theorem for Markov chains implies that

$$\lim_{M \to \infty} \frac{1}{M} \sum_{m=1}^{M} \pi_m = \int_\Sigma \pi \, dQ(\pi) \qquad \textit{almost surely.}$$

The main idea behind the regret-testing heuristics is that, after a not very long search period, by pure chance, the mixed strategy profile π_m will be an ε-Nash equilibrium, and then, since all players have a small expected regret, the process gets stuck with this value for a much longer time than the search period. The main technical result needed to justify such a statement is summarized in Lemma 7.5. This implies that if the parameters of the procedure are set appropriately, the length of the search period is negligible compared with the length of time the process spends in an ε-Nash equilibrium. The proof of Lemma 7.5 is quite technical and is beyond the scope of this book. See the bibliographic remarks for the appropriate pointers. In addition, the proof requires certain properties of the game that are not satisfied by all games. However, the necessary conditions hold for *almost all* games, in the sense that the Lebesgue measure of all those games that do not satisfy these conditions is 0. (Here we consider the representation of a game as the $K \prod_{k=1}^{K} N_k$-dimensional vector of all losses $\ell^{(k)}(\mathbf{i})$.) Let $\overline{\mathcal{N}}_\varepsilon = \Sigma \setminus \mathcal{N}_\varepsilon$ denote the complement of the set of ε-Nash equilibria.

Lemma 7.5. *For almost all K-person games there exist positive constants c_1, c_2 such that, for all sufficiently small $\rho > 0$, the K-step transition probabilities of experimental regret testing satisfy*

$$P^{(K)}\big(\overline{\mathcal{N}}_\rho \to \mathcal{N}_\rho\big) \ge c_1 \rho^{c_2},$$

where we use the notation $P^{(K)}(A \to B) = \mathbb{P}[\pi_{m+K} \in B \mid \pi_m \in A]$ *for the K-step transition probabilities.*

On the basis of this lemma, we can now state one of the basic properties of the experimental regret-testing procedure. The result states that, in the long run, the played mixed strategy profile is not an approximate Nash equilibrium at a tiny fraction of time.

Theorem 7.8. *Almost all games are such that there exists a positive number ε_0 and positive constants $c_1, \ldots, c_4$ such that for all $\varepsilon < \varepsilon_0$ if the experimental regret-testing procedure is used with parameters*

$$\rho \in (\varepsilon, \varepsilon + \varepsilon^{c_1}), \quad \lambda \le c_2 \varepsilon^{c_3}, \quad \text{and } T \ge -\frac{1}{2(\rho - \varepsilon)^2} \log \left(c_4 \varepsilon^{c_3} \right),$$

then for all $M \ge \log(\varepsilon/2)/\log(1 - \lambda^N)$,

$$P_M(\overline{\mathcal{N}}_\varepsilon) = \mathbb{P}[\sigma_{MT} \notin \mathcal{N}_\varepsilon] \le \varepsilon.$$

Proof.   First note that by Corollary 7.2,

$$P_M(\overline{\mathcal{N}}_\varepsilon) \le Q(\overline{\mathcal{N}}_\varepsilon) + (1 - \lambda^N)^M,$$

so that it suffices to bound the measure of $\overline{\mathcal{N}}_\varepsilon$ under the stationary probability Q. To this end, first observe that, by the defining property of the stationary distribution,

$$Q(\mathcal{N}_\rho) = Q(\overline{\mathcal{N}}_\rho)P^{(K)}(\overline{\mathcal{N}}_\rho \to \mathcal{N}_\rho) + Q(\mathcal{N}_\rho)P^{(K)}(\mathcal{N}_\rho \to \mathcal{N}_\rho).$$

Solving for $Q(\mathcal{N}_\rho)$ gives

$$Q(\mathcal{N}_\rho) = \frac{P^{(K)}(\overline{\mathcal{N}}_\rho \to \mathcal{N}_\rho)}{1 - P^{(K)}(\mathcal{N}_\rho \to \mathcal{N}_\rho) + P^{(K)}(\overline{\mathcal{N}}_\rho \to \mathcal{N}_\rho)}. \tag{7.3}$$

To derive a lower bound for the expression on the right-hand side, we write the elementary inequality

$$P^{(K)}(\overline{\mathcal{N}}_\rho \to \mathcal{N}_\rho) = \frac{Q(\mathcal{N}_\varepsilon)P^{(K)}(\mathcal{N}_\varepsilon \to \mathcal{N}_\rho)}{Q(\mathcal{N}_\rho)}$$

$$+ \frac{Q(\mathcal{N}_\rho \setminus \mathcal{N}_\varepsilon)P^{(K)}(\mathcal{N}_\rho \setminus \mathcal{N}_\varepsilon \to \mathcal{N}_\rho)}{Q(\mathcal{N}_\rho)}$$

$$\ge \frac{Q(\mathcal{N}_\varepsilon)P^{(K)}(\mathcal{N}_\varepsilon \to \mathcal{N}_\rho)}{Q(\mathcal{N}_\rho)}. \tag{7.4}$$

To bound $P^{(K)}(\mathcal{N}_\varepsilon \to \mathcal{N}_\rho)$, note that if $\pi_m \in \mathcal{N}_\varepsilon$, then the expected regret of all players is at most ε. Since the regret estimates $r_{m,i_k}^{(k)}$ are sums of T independent random variables taking values between 0 and 1 with mean at most ε, Hoeffding's inequality implies that

$$\mathbb{P}[r_{m,i_k}^{(k)} \ge \rho] \le e^{-2T(\rho-\varepsilon)^2}, \qquad i_k = 1, \ldots, N_k, \quad k = 1, \ldots, K.$$

Then the probability that there is at least one player k and a strategy $i_k \le N_k$ such that $r_{m,i_k}^{(k)} \ge \rho$ is bounded by $\sum_{k=1}^K N_k e^{-2T(\rho-\varepsilon)^2} = N e^{-2T(\rho-\varepsilon)^2}$. Thus, with probability at least

$(1 - \lambda)^K \left(1 - N e^{-2T(\rho - \varepsilon)^2}\right)$, all players keep playing the same mixed strategy, and therefore

$$P(\mathcal{N}_\varepsilon \to \mathcal{N}_\varepsilon) \geq (1 - \lambda)^K \left(1 - N e^{-2T(\rho - \varepsilon)^2}\right).$$

Consequently, since $\rho > \varepsilon$, we have $P^{(K)}(\mathcal{N}_\varepsilon \to \mathcal{N}_\rho) \geq P^{(K)}(\mathcal{N}_\varepsilon \to \mathcal{N}_\varepsilon)$ and hence

$$P^{(K)}(\mathcal{N}_\varepsilon \to \mathcal{N}_\rho) \geq P^{(K)}(\mathcal{N}_\varepsilon \to \mathcal{N}_\varepsilon) \geq P(\mathcal{N}_\varepsilon \to \mathcal{N}_\varepsilon)^K$$
$$\geq (1 - \lambda)^{K^2} \left(1 - N e^{-2T(\rho - \varepsilon)^2}\right)^K \geq 1 - K^2\lambda - NK e^{-2T(\rho - \varepsilon)^2}$$

(where we assumed that $\lambda \leq 1$ and $N e^{-2T(\rho - \varepsilon)^2} \leq 1$). Thus, using (7.4) and the obtained estimate, we have

$$P^{(K)}(\mathcal{N}_\rho \to \mathcal{N}_\rho) \geq \frac{Q(\mathcal{N}_\varepsilon)}{Q(\mathcal{N}_\rho)} \left(1 - K^2\lambda - NK e^{-2T(\rho - \varepsilon)^2}\right).$$

Next we need to show that, for proper choice of the parameters, $P^{(K)}(\overline{\mathcal{N}}_\rho \to \mathcal{N}_\rho)$ is sufficiently large. For almost all of K-person games, this follows from Lemma 7.5, which asserts that

$$P^{(K)}(\overline{\mathcal{N}}_\rho \to \mathcal{N}_\rho) \geq C_1 \rho^{C_2}$$

for some positive constants C_1 and C_2 that depend on the game. Hence, from (7.3) we obtain

$$Q(\mathcal{N}_\rho) \geq \frac{C_1 \rho^{C_2}}{1 - \left(1 - K^2\lambda - NK e^{-2T(\rho - \varepsilon)^2}\right)\frac{Q(\mathcal{N}_\varepsilon)}{Q(\mathcal{N}_\rho)} + C_1 \rho^{C_2}}.$$

It remains to estimate the measure $Q(\mathcal{N}_\varepsilon)/Q(\mathcal{N}_\rho)$. We need to show that the ratio is close to 1 whenever $\rho - \varepsilon \ll \varepsilon$. It turns out that one can show that, in fact, for almost every game there exists a constant C_5 such that

$$\frac{Q(\mathcal{N}_\varepsilon)}{Q(\mathcal{N}_\rho)} \geq 1 - \frac{C_3(\rho - \varepsilon)^{C_4}}{\rho^{C_5}},$$

where C_3 and C_4 are positive constants depending on the game. This inequality is not surprising, but the rigorous proof of this statement is somewhat technical and is skipped here. It may be found in [126]. Summarizing,

$$Q(\mathcal{N}_\varepsilon) \geq Q(\mathcal{N}_\rho) \left(1 - \frac{C_3(\rho - \varepsilon)^{C_4}}{\rho^{C_5}}\right)$$
$$\geq \left(1 - \frac{C_3(\rho - \varepsilon)^{C_4}}{\rho^{C_5}}\right)$$
$$\times \frac{C_1 \rho^{C_2}}{1 - \left(1 - K^2\lambda - NK e^{-2T(\rho - \varepsilon)^2}\right)\left(1 - \frac{C_3(\rho - \varepsilon)^{C_4}}{\rho^{C_5}}\right) + C_1 \rho^{C_2}}$$

for some positive constants $C_1, \ldots, C_5$. Choosing the parameters ρ, λ, T with appropriate constants $c_1, \ldots, c_4$, we have

$$Q(\overline{\mathcal{N}}_\varepsilon) \leq \varepsilon/2.$$

If M is so large that $(1 - \lambda^K)^M \leq \varepsilon/2$, we have $P_M(\overline{\mathcal{N}}_\varepsilon) \leq \varepsilon$, as desired. ∎

Theorem 7.8 states that if the parameters of the experimental regret-testing procedure are set in an appropriate way, the mixed strategy profiles will be in an approximate equilibrium most of the time. However, it is important to realize that the theorem does not claim convergence in any way. In fact, if the parameters T, ρ, and λ are kept fixed forever, the process will periodically abandon the set of ε-Nash equilibria and wander around for a long time before it gets stuck in a (possibly different) ε-Nash equilibrium. Then the process stays there for an even much longer time before leaving again. However, since the process $\{\pi_m\}$ forms an ergodic Markov chain, it is easy to deduce convergence of the empirical frequencies of play. Specifically, we show next that if all players play according to the experimental regret-testing procedure, then the joint empirical frequencies of play converge almost surely to a joint distribution $\overline{P}$ that is in the convex hull of ε-Nash equilibria. The precise statement is given in Theorem 7.9.

Recall that for each $t = 1, 2, \ldots$ we denote by $I_t^{(k)}$ the pure strategy played by the kth player. $I_t^{(k)}$ is drawn randomly according to the mixed strategy $\pi_m^{(k)}$ whenever $t \in \{mT + 1, \ldots, (m+1)T\}$. Consider the joint empirical distribution of plays $\widehat{P}_t$ defined by

$$\widehat{P}_t(\mathbf{i}) = \frac{1}{t} \sum_{s=1}^{t} \mathbb{I}_{\{\mathbf{I}_t = \mathbf{i}\}}, \qquad \mathbf{i} \in \prod_{k=1}^{K} \{1, \ldots, N_k\}.$$

Denote the convex hull of a set A by $\mathrm{co}(A)$.

Remark 7.13. Recall that Nash equilibria and ε-Nash equilibria π are mixed strategy profiles, that is, product distributions, and have been considered, up to this point, as elements of the set Σ of product distributions. However, a product distribution is a special joint distribution over the set $\prod_{k=1}^{K}\{1, \ldots, N_k\}$ of pure strategy profiles, and it is this "larger" space in which the convex hull of ε-Nash equilibria is defined. Thus, elements of the convex hull are typically not product distributions. (Recall that the convex hull of Nash equilibria is a subset of the set of correlated equilibria.)

Theorem 7.9. *For almost every game and for every sufficiently small $\varepsilon > 0$, there exists a choice of the parameters (T, ρ, λ) such that the following holds: there is a joint distribution $\overline{P}$ over the set of K-tuples $\mathbf{i} = (i_1, \ldots, i_K)$ of actions in the convex hull $\mathrm{co}(\mathcal{N}_\varepsilon)$ of the set of ε-Nash equilibria such that the joint empirical frequencies of play of experimental regret testing satisfy*

$$\lim_{t \to \infty} \widehat{P}_t \to \overline{P} \qquad \textit{almost surely.}$$

Proof. If $\pi = (\pi^{(1)} \times \cdots \times \pi^{(K)}) \in \Sigma$ is a product distribution, introduce notation

$$P(\pi, \mathbf{i}) = \prod_{k=1}^{K} \pi^{(k)}(i_k),$$

where $\mathbf{i} = (i_1, \ldots, i_K)$. In other words, $P(\pi, \cdot)$ is a joint distribution over the set of action profiles $\mathbf{i}$, induced by π.

First observe that, since at time t the vector $\mathbf{I}_t$ of actions is chosen according to the mixed strategy profile $\pi_{\lfloor t/T \rfloor}$, by martingale convergence, for every $\mathbf{i}$,

$$\widehat{P}_t(\mathbf{i}) - \frac{1}{t} \sum_{s=1}^{t} P(\pi_{\lfloor s/T \rfloor}, \mathbf{i}) \to 0 \qquad \text{almost surely,}$$

Therefore, it suffices to prove convergence of $\frac{1}{t} \sum_{s=1}^{t} P(\pi_{\lfloor s/T \rfloor}, \mathbf{i})$. Since $\pi_{\lfloor s/T \rfloor}$ is unchanged during periods of length T, we obviously have

$$\lim_{t \to \infty} \frac{1}{t} \sum_{\tau=1}^{t} P(\pi_{\lfloor t/T \rfloor}, \mathbf{i}) = \lim_{M \to \infty} \frac{1}{M} \sum_{m=1}^{M} P(\pi_m, \mathbf{i}).$$

By Corollary 7.2,

$$\lim_{M \to \infty} \frac{1}{M} \sum_{m=1}^{M} \pi_m = \overline{\pi} \qquad \text{almost surely,}$$

where $\overline{\pi} = \int_{\Sigma} \pi \, dQ(\pi)$. (Recall that Q is the unique stationary distribution of the Markov process.) This, in turn, implies by continuity of $P(\pi, \mathbf{i})$ in π that there exists a joint distribution $\overline{P}(\mathbf{i}) = \int_{\Sigma} P(\pi, \mathbf{i}) \, dQ(\pi)$ such that, for all $\mathbf{i}$,

$$\lim_{M \to \infty} \frac{1}{M} \sum_{m=1}^{M} P(\pi_m, \mathbf{i}) = \overline{P}(\mathbf{i}) \qquad \text{almost surely.}$$

It remains to show that $\overline{P} \in \text{co}(\mathcal{N}_\varepsilon)$.

Let $\varepsilon' < \varepsilon$ be a positive number such that the ε' blowup of $\text{co}(\mathcal{N}_{\varepsilon'})$ is contained in $\text{co}(\mathcal{N}_\varepsilon)$, that is,

$$\left\{ P \in \Sigma \ : \ \exists \, P' \in \text{co}(\mathcal{N}_{\varepsilon'}) \text{ such that } \| P - P' \|_1 < \varepsilon' \right\} \subset \text{co}(\mathcal{N}_\varepsilon).$$

Such an ε' always exists for almost all games by Exercise 7.28. In fact, one may choose $\varepsilon' = \varepsilon / c_3$ for a sufficiently large positive constant c_3 (whose value depends on the game).

Now choose the parameters (T, ρ, λ) such that $Q(\overline{\mathcal{N}}_{\varepsilon'}) < \varepsilon'$. Theorem 7.8 guarantees the existence of such a choice.

Clearly,

$$P(\overline{\pi}, \mathbf{i}) = \int_{\Sigma} P(\pi, \mathbf{i}) \, dQ(\pi) = \int_{\mathcal{N}_{\varepsilon'}} P(\pi, \mathbf{i}) \, dQ(\pi) + \int_{\overline{\mathcal{N}}_{\varepsilon'}} P(\pi, \mathbf{i}) \, dQ(\pi).$$

Since $\int_{\mathcal{N}_{\varepsilon'}} P(\pi) \, dQ(\pi) \in \text{co}(\mathcal{N}_{\varepsilon'})$, we find that the L_1 distance of $\overline{P}$ and $\text{co}(\mathcal{N}_{\varepsilon'})$ satisfies

$$d_1\left(\overline{P}, \text{co}(\mathcal{N}_{\varepsilon'}) \right) \leq \left\| \int_{\overline{\mathcal{N}}_{\varepsilon'}} P(\pi) \, dQ(\pi) \right\|_1 \leq \int_{\overline{\mathcal{N}}_{\varepsilon'}} dQ(\pi) = Q(\overline{\mathcal{N}}_{\varepsilon'}) < \varepsilon'.$$

By the choice of ε' we indeed have $\overline{P} \in \text{co}(\mathcal{N}_\varepsilon)$. $\blacksquare$

***Remark* 7.14 (*Convergence of the mixed strategy profiles*).** We only mention briefly that the experimental regret testing procedure can be extended to obtain an uncoupled strategy such that the mixed strategy profiles converge, with probability 1, to the set of Nash equilibria for almost all games. Note that we claim convergence not only of the empirical frequencies of plays but also of the actual mixed strategy profiles. Moreover, we claim convergence to $\mathcal{N}$ and to the convex hull $\text{co}(\mathcal{N}_\varepsilon)$ of all ε-Nash equilibria for a fixed ε. The basic idea is to "anneal" experimental regret testing such that first it is used with some parameters (T_1, ρ_1, λ_1) for a number M_1 of periods of length T_1 and then the parameters are changed to (T_2, ρ_2, λ_2) (by increasing T and decreasing ρ and λ properly) and experimental regret testing is used for a number $M_2 \gg M_1$ of periods (of length T_2), and so on. However, this is not sufficient to guarantee almost sure convergence, because at each change of parameters the process is reinitialized and therefore there is an infinite set of indices t such that σ_t is far away from any Nash equilibrium. A possible solution is based on "localizing" the search after each change of parameters such that each player limits its choice to a small neighborhood of the mixed strategy played right before the change of parameters (unless a player experiences a large regret in which case the search is extended again to the whole simplex). Another challenge one must face in designing a genuinely uncoupled procedure is that the values of the parameters of the procedure (i.e., T_ℓ, ρ_ℓ, λ_ℓ, and M_ℓ, $\ell = 1, 2, \ldots$) cannot depend on the parameters of the game, because by requiring uncoupledness we must assume that the players only know their payoff function but not those of the other players. We leave the details as an exercise.

Remark 7.15 (Nongeneric games). All results of this section up to this point hold for almost every game. The reason for this restriction is that our proofs require an assumption of genericity of the game. We do not know whether Theorems 7.8 and 7.9 extend to all games. However, by a simple trick one can modify experimental regret testing such that the results of these two theorems hold for all games. The idea is that before starting to play, each player slightly perturbes the values of his loss function and then plays as if his losses were the perturbed values. For example, define, for each player k and pure strategy profile $\mathbf{i}$,

$$\tilde{\ell}^{(k)}(\mathbf{i}) = \ell^{(k)}(\mathbf{i}) + Z_{i,s},$$

where the $Z_{i,s}$ are i.i.d. random variables uniformly distributed in the interval $[-\varepsilon, \varepsilon]$. Clearly, the perturbed game is generic with probability 1. Therefore, if all players play according to experimental regret testing but on the basis of the perturbed losses, then Theorems 7.8 and 7.9 are valid for this newly generated game. However, because for all k and $\mathbf{i}$ we have $\left|\tilde{\ell}^{(k)}(\mathbf{i}) - \ell^{(k)}(\mathbf{i})\right| < \varepsilon$, every ε-Nash equilibrium of the perturbed game is a 2ε-Nash equilibrium of the original game.

Finally, we show how experimental regret testing can be modified so that it can be played in the model of unknown games with similar performance guarantees. In order to adjust the procedure, recall that the only place in which the players look at the past is when they calculate the regrets

$$r_{m,i_k}^{(k)} = \frac{1}{T} \sum_{s=(m-1)T+1}^{mT} \ell^{(k)}(\mathbf{I}_s) - \frac{1}{T} \sum_{s=(m-1)T+1}^{mT} \ell^{(k)}(\mathbf{I}_s^-, i_k).$$

However, each player may estimate his regret in a simple way. Observe that the first term in the definition of $r_{m,i_k}^{(k)}$ is just the average loss player k over the mth period, which is available to the player, and does not need to be estimated. However, the second term is the average loss suffered by the player if he had chosen to play action i_k all the time during this period. This can be estimated by random sampling. The idea is that, at each time instant, player

k flips a biased coin and, if the outcome is head (the probability of which is very small), then instead of choosing an action according to the mixed strategy $\pi_m^{(k)}$ the player chooses one uniformly at random. At these time instants, the player collects sufficient information to estimate the regret with respect to each fixed action i_k.

To formalize this idea, consider a period between times $(m-1)T+1$ and mT. During this period, player k draws n_k samples for each $i_k = 1, \ldots, N_k$ actions, where $n_k \ll T$ is to be determined later. Formally, define the random variables $U_{k,s} \in \{0, 1, \ldots, N_k\}$, where, for s between $(m-1)T+1$, and mT, for each $i_k = 1, \ldots, N_k$, there are exactly n_k values of s such that $U_{k,s} = i_k$, and all such configurations are equally probable; for the remaining s, $U_{k,s} = 0$. (In other words, for each $i_k = 1, \ldots, N_k$, n_k values of s are chosen randomly, without replacement, such that these values are disjoint for different i_k's.) Then, at time s, player k draws an action $I_s^{(k)}$ as follows: conditionally on the past up to time $s-1$,

$$
I_s^{(k)} \begin{cases} \text{is distributed as } \pi_{m-1}^i & \text{if } U_{k,s} = 0 \\ \text{equals } i_k & \text{if } U_{k,s} = i_k. \end{cases}
$$

The regret $r_{m,i_k}^{(k)}$ may be estimated by

$$
\widehat{r}_{m,i_k}^{(k)} = \frac{1}{T - N_k n_k} \sum_{s=(m-1)T+1}^{mT} \ell^{(k)}(\mathbf{I}_s) \mathbb{I}_{\{U_{k,s}=0\}} - \frac{1}{n_k} \sum_{s=(m-1)T+1}^{mT} \ell^{(k)}(\mathbf{I}_s^-, i_k) \mathbb{I}_{\{U_{k,s}=i_k\}}
$$

$k = 1, \ldots, N_k$. The first term of the definition of $\widehat{r}_{m,i_k}^{(k)}$ is just the average of the losses of player k over those periods in which the player does not "experiment," that is, when $U_{k,s} = 0$. (Note that there are exactly $T - N_k n_k$ such periods.) Since $N_k n_k \ll T$, this average should be close to the first term in the definition of the average regret $r_{m,i_k}^{(k)}$. The second term is the average over those time periods in which player k experiments, and he plays action i_k (i.e., when $U_{k,s} = i_k$). This may be considered as an estimate, obtained by sampling without replacement, of the second term in the definition of $r_{m,i_k}^{(k)}$. Observe that $\widehat{r}_{m,i_k}^{(k)}$ only depends on the past payoffs experienced by player k, and therefore these estimates are feasible in the unknown game model.

In order to show that the estimated regrets work in this case, we only need to establish that the probability that the estimated regret exceeds ρ is small if the expected regret is not more than ε (whenever $\varepsilon < \rho$). This is done in the following lemma. It guarantees that if the experimental regret-testing procedure is run using the regret estimates described above, then results analogous to Theorems 7.8 and 7.9 may be obtained, in a straightforward way, in the unknown-game model.

Lemma 7.6. *Assume that in a certain period of length T, the expected regret $\mathbb{E}[r_{m,i_k}^{(k)} \mid \mathbf{I}_1, \ldots, \mathbf{I}_{mT}]$ of player k is at most ε. Then, for a sufficiently small ε, with the choice of parameters of Theorem 7.8,*

$$
\mathbb{P}[\widehat{r}_{m,i_k}^{(k)} \geq \rho] \leq cT^{-1/3} + \exp\left(-T^{1/3}(\rho - \varepsilon)^2\right).
$$

Proof. We show that, with large probability, $\widehat{r}_{m,i_k}^{(k)}$ is close to $r_{m,i_k}^{(k)}$. To this end, first we compare the first terms in the expression of both. Observe that at those periods s of time when none of the players experiments (i.e., when $U_{k,s} = 0$ for all $k = 1, \ldots, K$), the corresponding terms of both estimates are equal. Thus, by a simple algebra it is easy to see that the first terms differ by at most $\frac{2}{T}\sum_{k=1}^{K} N_k n_k$.

It remains to compare the second terms in the expressions of $\widehat{r}_{m,i_k}^{(k)}$ and $r_{m,i_k}^{(k)}$. Observe that if there is no time instant s for which $U_{k,s} = 1$ and $U_{k',s} = 1$ for some $k' \neq k$, then

$$\frac{1}{n_k}\sum_{s=t+1}^{t+T} \ell^{(k)}(\mathbf{I}_s^-, i_k)\mathbb{I}_{\{U_{k,s}=i_k\}}$$

is an unbiased estimate of

$$\frac{1}{T}\sum_{s=t+1}^{t+T} \ell^{(k)}(\mathbf{I}_s^-, i_k)$$

obtained by random sampling. The probability that no two players sample at the same time is at most

$$T K^2 \max_{k,k' \leq K} \frac{N_k n_k}{T}\frac{N_{k'} n_{k'}}{T},$$

where we used the union-of-events bound over all pairs of players and all T time instants. By Hoeffding's inequality for an average of a sample taken without replacement (see Lemma A.2), we have

$$\widehat{\mathbb{P}}\left[\left|\frac{1}{n_k}\sum_{s=t+1}^{t+T}\ell^{(k)}(\mathbf{I}_s^-, i_k)\mathbb{I}_{\{U_{k,s}=i_k\}} - \frac{1}{T}\sum_{s=t+1}^{t+T}\ell^{(k)}(\mathbf{I}_s^-, i_k)\right| > \alpha\right] \leq e^{-2n_k\alpha^2},$$

where $\widehat{\mathbb{P}}$ denotes the distribution induced by the random variables $U_{k,s}$. Putting everything together,

$$\mathbb{P}\left[\widehat{r}_{m,i_k}^{(k)} \geq \rho\right]$$

$$\leq T K^2 \max_{k,k' \leq K}\frac{N_k n_k}{T}\frac{N_{k'} n_{k'}}{T} + \exp\left(-2n_k\left(\rho - \varepsilon - 2\frac{\sum_{k=1}^{K} N_k n_k}{T}\right)^2\right).$$

Choosing $n_k \sim T^{1/3}$, the first term on the right-hand side is of order $T^{-1/3}$ and $\frac{1}{T}\sum_{k=1}^{K} N_k n_k = O(T^{-2/3})$ becomes negligible compared with $\rho - \varepsilon$. ∎

7.11 Playing Against Opponents That React

Regret-minimizing strategies, such as those discussed in Sections 4.2 and 4.3, set up the goal of predicting as well as the best constant strategy in hindsight, assuming that the actions of the opponents would have been the same had the forecaster been following that constant strategy. However, when a forecasting strategy is used to play a repeated game, the actions prescribed by the forecasting strategy may have an effect on the behavior of the opponents, and so measuring regret as the difference of the suffered cumulative loss and that of the best constant action in hindsight may be very misleading.

To simplify the setup of the problem, we consider playing a two-player game such that, at time t, the row player takes an action $I_t \in \{1, \ldots, N\}$ and the column player takes action $J_t \in \{1, \ldots, M\}$. The loss suffered by the row player at time t is $\ell(I_t, J_t)$. (The loss of the column player is immaterial in this section. Note also that since we are only concerned with the loss of the first player, there is no loss of generality in assuming that there are only two players, since otherwise J_t can represent the joint play of all other players.) In the language of Chapter 4, we consider the case of a nonoblivious opponent; that is, the actions of the column player (the opponent) may depend on the history $I_1, \ldots, I_{t-1}$ of past moves of the row player.

To illustrate why regret-minimizing strategies may fail miserably in such a scenario, consider the repeated play of a *prisoners' dilemma*, that is, a 2×2 game in which the loss matrix of the row player is given by

R\C	c	d
c	1/3	1
d	0	2/3

In the usual definition of the prisoners' dilemma, the column player has the same loss matrix as the row player. In this game both players can either cooperate ("c") or defect ("d"). Regardless of what the column player does, the row player is better off defecting (and the same goes for the column player). However, it is better for the players if they both cooperate than if they both defect.

Now assume that the game is played repeatedly and the row player plays according to a Hannan-consistent strategy; that is, the normalized cumulative loss $\frac{1}{n} \sum_{t=1}^{n} \ell(I_t, J_t)$ approaches $\min_{i=c,d} \frac{1}{n} \sum_{t=1}^{n} \ell(i, J_t)$. Clearly, the minimum is achieved by action "d" and therefore the row player will defect basically all the time. In a certain worst-case sense this may be the best one can hope for. However, in many realistic situations, depending on the behavior of the adversary, significantly smaller losses can be achieved. For example, the column player may be willing to try cooperation. Perhaps the simplest such strategy of the opponent is "tit for tat," in which the opponent repeats the row player's previous action. In such a case, by playing a Hannan consistent strategy, the row player's performance is much worse than what he could have achieved by following the expert "c" (which is the *worse* action in the sense of the notions of regret we have used so far).

The purpose of this section is to introduce forecasting strategies that avoid falling in traps similar to the one described above under certain assumptions on the opponent's behavior.

To this end, consider the scenario where, rather than requiring Hannan consistency, the goal of the forecaster is to achieve a cumulative loss (almost) as small as that of the best action, where the cumulative loss of each action is calculated by looking at what would have happened if *that action had been followed throughout the whole repeated game*.

It is obvious that a completely malicious adversary can make it impossible to estimate what would have happened if a certain action had been played all the time (unless that action *is* played all the time). But under certain natural assumptions on the behavior of the adversary, such an inference is possible. The assumptions under which our goal can be reached require a kind of "stationarity" and bounded memory of the opponent and are certainly satisfied for simple strategies such as tit for tat.

Remark 7.16 (Hannan consistent strategies are sometimes better). We have argued that in some cases it makes more sense to look for strategies that perform as well as the best action if that action had been played all the time rather than playing Hannan consistent strategies. The repeated prisoners' dilemma with the adversary playing tit for tat is a clear example. However, in some other cases Hannan consistent strategies may perform much better than the best action in this new sense. The following example describes such a situation: assume that the row player has $N = 2$ actions, and let n be even such that $n/2$ is odd. Assume that in the first $n/2$ time periods the losses of both actions are 1 in each period. After $n/2$ periods the adversary decides to assign losses $00\dots000$ ($n/2$ times) to the action that was played less times during the first $n/2$ rounds and $11\dots111$ to the other action. Clearly, a Hannan consistent strategy has a cumulative loss of about $n/2$ during the n periods of the game. On the other hand, if any of the two actions is played constantly, its cumulative loss is n.

The goal of this section is to design strategies that guarantee, under certain assumptions on the behavior of the column player, that the average loss $\frac{1}{n}\sum_{t=1}^{n}\ell(I_t, J_t)$ is not much larger than $\min_{i=1,\dots,N}\mu_{i,n}$, where $\mu_{i,n}$ is the average loss of a hypothetical player who plays the same action $I_t = i$ in each round of the game.

A key ingredient of the argument is a different way of measuring regret. The goal of the forecaster in this new setup is to achieve, during the n periods of play, an average loss almost as small as the average loss of the best action, where the average is computed over only those periods in which the action was chosen by the forecaster. To make the definition formal, denote by

$$\widehat{\mu}_t = \frac{1}{t}\sum_{s=1}^{t}\ell(I_s, J_s)$$

the averaged cumulative loss of the forecaster at time t and by

$$\mu_{i,t} = \frac{\sum_{s=1}^{t}\ell(I_s, J_s)\mathbb{I}_{\{I_s=i\}}}{\sum_{s=1}^{t}\mathbb{I}_{\{I_s=i\}}}$$

the averaged cumulative loss of action i, averaged over the time periods in which the action was played by the forecaster. If $\sum_{s=1}^{t}\mathbb{I}_{\{I_s=i\}} = 0$, let $\mu_{i,t}$ take the maximal value 1. At this point it may not be entirely clear how the averaged losses $\mu_{i,t}$ are related to the average loss of a player who plays the same action i all the time. However, shortly it will become clear that these quantities can be related under some assumptions of the behavior of the opponent and certain restrictions on the forecasting strategy.

The property that the forecaster needs to satisfy for our purposes is that, asymptotically, the average loss $\widehat{\mu}_n$ is not larger than the smallest asymptotic average loss $\mu_{i,t}$. More precisely, we need to construct a forecaster that achieves

$$\limsup_{n\to\infty}\widehat{\mu}_n \leq \min_{i=1,\dots,N}\limsup_{n\to\infty}\mu_{i,n}.$$

Surprisingly, there exists a *deterministic* forecaster that satisfies this asymptotic inequality regardless of the opponent's behavior. Here we describe such a strategy for the case of $N = 2$ actions. The simple extension to the general case of more than two actions is left as an exercise (Exercise 7.30). Consider the following simple deterministic forecaster.

DETERMINISTIC EXPLORATION–EXPLOITATION

For each round $t = 1, 2, \ldots$

   (1) (*Exploration*) if $t = k^2$ for an integer k, then set $I_t = 1$;
      if $t = k^2 + 1$ for an integer k, then set $I_t = 2$;
   (2) (*Exploitation*) otherwise, let $I_t = \operatorname{argmin}_{i=1,2} \mu_{i,t-1}$ (in case of a tie, break it, say, in favor of action 1).

This simple forecaster is a version of fictitious play, based on the averaged losses, in which the exploration step simply guarantees that every action is sampled infinitely often. There is nothing special about the time instances of the form $t = k^2, k^2 + 1$; any sparse infinite sequence would do the job. In fact, the original algorithm of de Farias and Megiddo [85] chooses the exploration steps randomly.

Observe, in passing, that this is a "bandit"-type predictor in the sense that it only needs to observe the losses of the played actions.

Theorem 7.10. *Regardless of the sequence of outcomes* $J_1, J_2, \ldots$ *the deterministic forecaster defined above satisfies*

$$\limsup_{n \to \infty} \widehat{\mu}_n \le \min_{i=1,2} \limsup_{n \to \infty} \mu_{i,n}.$$

Proof. For each $t = 1, 2, \ldots$, let $i_t^* = \operatorname{argmin}_{i=1,2} \mu_{i,t}$ and let $t_1, t_2, \ldots$ be the time instances such that $i_t^* \ne i_{t-1}^*$, that is, the "leader" is switched. If there is only a finite number of such t_k's, then, obviously,

$$\widehat{\mu}_n - \min_{i=1,2} \mu_{i,n} \to 0,$$

which implies the stated inequality. Thus, we may assume that there is an infinite number of switches and it suffices to show that whenever $T = \max\{t_k \,:\, t_k \le n\}$, then either

$$\widehat{\mu}_n - \min_{i=1,2} \mu_{i,T} \le \frac{\text{const.}}{T^{1/4}} \tag{7.5}$$

or

$$\widehat{\mu}_n - \min_{i=1,2} \mu_{i,n} \le \frac{\text{const.}}{T^{1/4}}, \tag{7.6}$$

which implies the statement.

First observe that, due to the exploration step, for any $t \ge 3$ and $i = 1, 2$,

$$\sum_{s=1}^{t} \mathbb{I}_{\{I_s = i\}} \ge \left\lfloor \sqrt{t-1} \right\rfloor \ge \sqrt{t}/2.$$

But then

$$|\mu_{1,T} - \mu_{2,T}| \le \frac{2}{\sqrt{T}}.$$

This inequality holds because by the boundedness of the loss, at time T, the averaged loss of action i can change by at most $1/\sum_{s=1}^{T} \mathbb{I}_{\{I_s = i\}} < 2/\sqrt{T}$, and the definition of the switch is that the one that was larger in the previous step becomes smaller, which is only possible if the averaged losses of the two actions were already $2/\sqrt{T}$ close to each other. But then the averaged loss of the forecaster at the time T (the last switch before time n) may be bounded by

$$\widehat{\mu}_T = \frac{1}{T}\left(\sum_{s=1}^{T}\ell(I_s, J_s)\mathbb{I}_{\{I_s=1\}} + \sum_{s=1}^{T}\ell(I_s, J_s)\mathbb{I}_{\{I_s=2\}}\right)$$

$$= \frac{1}{T}\left(\mu_{1,T}\sum_{s=1}^{T}\mathbb{I}_{\{I_s=1\}} + \mu_{2,T}\sum_{s=1}^{T}\mathbb{I}_{\{I_s=2\}}\right)$$

$$\leq \min_{i=1,2}\mu_{i,T} + \frac{2}{\sqrt{T}}.$$

Now assume that T is so large that $n - T \leq T^{3/4}$. Then clearly, $|\widehat{\mu}_n - \widehat{\mu}_T| \leq T^{3/4}/n \leq T^{-1/4}$ and (7.5) holds.

Thus, in the rest of the proof we assume that $n - T \geq T^{3/4}$. It remains to show that $\widehat{\mu}_n$ cannot be much larger than $\min_{i=1,2}\mu_{i,n}$. Introduce the notation

$$\delta = \widehat{\mu}_n - \min_{i=1,2}\mu_{i,T}.$$

Since

$$\widehat{\mu}_n = \frac{1}{n}\left(\sum_{t=1}^{T}\ell(I_t, J_t) + \sum_{t=T+1}^{n}\ell(I_t, J_t)\right)$$

$$\leq \frac{1}{n}\left(T\min_{i=1,2}\mu_{i,T} + 2\sqrt{T} + \sum_{t=T+1}^{n}\ell(I_t, J_t)\right)$$

we have

$$\sum_{t=T+1}^{n}\ell(I_t, J_t) \geq (n-T)\min_{i=1,2}\mu_{i,T} + \delta n - 2\sqrt{T}.$$

Since, apart from at most $\sqrt{n-T}$ exploration steps, the same action is played between times $T+1$ and n, we have

$$\min_{i=1,2}\mu_{i,n} \geq \frac{\mu_{i_n^*,T}\sum_{s=1}^{T}\mathbb{I}_{\{I_s=i_n^*\}} + \sum_{t=T+1}^{n}\ell(I_t, J_t) - \sqrt{n-T}}{\sum_{s=1}^{T}\mathbb{I}_{\{I_s=i_n^*\}} + (n-T)}$$

$$\geq \frac{\mu_{i_T^*,T}\sum_{s=1}^{T}\mathbb{I}_{\{I_s=i_n^*\}} + \sum_{t=T+1}^{n}\ell(I_t, J_t) - \sqrt{n-T}}{\sum_{s=1}^{T}\mathbb{I}_{\{I_s=i_n^*\}} + (n-T)}$$

$$\geq \frac{\mu_{i_T^*,T}\sum_{s=1}^{T}\mathbb{I}_{\{I_s=i_n^*\}} + (n-T)\min_{i=1,2}\mu_{i,T} + \delta n - 2\sqrt{T} - \sqrt{n-T}}{\sum_{s=1}^{T}\mathbb{I}_{\{I_s=i_n^*\}} + (n-T)}$$

$$= \frac{\mu_{i_T^*,T}\left(\sum_{s=1}^{T}\mathbb{I}_{\{I_s=i_n^*\}} + (n-T)\right) + \delta n - 2\sqrt{T} - \sqrt{n-T}}{\sum_{s=1}^{T}\mathbb{I}_{\{I_s=i_n^*\}} + (n-T)}$$

$$\geq \mu_{i_T^*,T} + \delta - 2\frac{\sqrt{T}}{n-T} - \frac{1}{\sqrt{n-T}}$$

$$\geq \mu_{i_T^*,T} + \delta - 3T^{-1/4}$$

$$= \widehat{\mu}_n - 3T^{-1/4},$$

where at the last inequality we used $n - T \geq T^{3/4}$. Thus, (7.6) holds in this case. ∎

There is one more ingredient we need in order to establish strategies of the desired behavior. As we have mentioned before, our aim is to design strategies that perform well if the behavior of the opponent is such that the row player can estimate, for each action, the average loss suffered by playing that action all the time. In order to do this, we modify the forecaster studied above such that whenever an action is chosen, it is played repeatedly sufficiently many times in a row so that the forecaster gets a good picture of the behavior of the opponent when that action is played. This modification is done trivially by simply repeating each action τ times, where the positive integer τ is a parameter of the strategy.

REPEATED DETERMINISTIC EXPLORATION–EXPLOITATION

Parameter: Number of repetitions τ.

For each round $t = 1, 2, \ldots$

(1) (*Exploration*) if $t = k^2\tau + s$ for integers k and $s = 0, 1, \ldots, \tau - 1$, then set $I_t = 1$;
if $t = (k^2 + 1)\tau + s$ for integers k and $s = 0, 1, \ldots, \tau - 1$, then set $I_t = 2$;
(2) (*Exploitation*) otherwise, let $I_t = \operatorname{argmin}_{i=1,2} \mu_{i,\tau\lfloor t/\tau\rfloor - 1}$ (in case of a tie, break it, say, in favor of action 1).

Theorem 7.10 (as well as Exercise 7.30) trivially extends to this case and the strategy defined above obviously satisfies

$$\limsup_{n\to\infty} \widehat{\mu}_n \le \min_{i=1,2} \limsup_{n\to\infty} \mu_{i,n}$$

regardless of the opponent's actions and the parameter τ.

Our main assumption on the opponent's behavior is that, for every action i, there exists a number $\overline{\mu}_i \in [0, 1]$ such that for any time instance t and past plays $I_1, \ldots, I_t$,

$$\frac{1}{\tau} \sum_{s=t+1}^{t+\tau} \ell(i, J_s) - \overline{\mu}_i \le \varepsilon_\tau,$$

where ε_τ is a sequence of nonnegative numbers converging to 0 as $\tau \to \infty$. (Here the average loss is computed by assuming that the row player's moves are $I_1, \ldots, I_t, i, i, \ldots, i$.) After de Farias and Megiddo [86], we call an opponent satisfying this condition *flexible*. Clearly, if the opponent is flexible, then for any action i the average loss of playing the action forever is at most $\overline{\mu}_i$. Moreover, the performance bound for the repeated deterministic exploration–exploitation immediately implies the following.

Corollary 7.3. *Assume that the row player plays according to the repeated deterministic exploration–exploitation strategy with parameter τ against a flexible opponent. Then the asymptotic average cumulative loss of the row player satisfies*

$$\limsup_{n\to\infty} \frac{1}{n} \sum_{t=1}^{n} \ell(I_t, J_t) \le \min_{i=1,\ldots,N} \overline{\mu}_i + \varepsilon_\tau.$$

The assumption of flexibility is satisfied in many cases when the opponent's long-term behavior against any fixed action can be estimated by playing the action repeatedly for a stretch of time of length τ. This is satisfied, for example, when the opponent is modeled by a finite automata. In the example of the opponent playing tit for tat in the prisoners' dilemma described at the beginning of this section, the opponent is clearly flexible with $\varepsilon_\tau = 1/\tau$. Note that in these cases one actually has

$$\left| \frac{1}{\tau} \sum_{s=t+1}^{t+\tau} \ell(i, J_s) - \overline{\mu}_i \right| \leq \varepsilon_\tau$$

(with $\overline{\mu}_1 = 1/3$ and $\overline{\mu}_2 = 2/3$); that is, the estimated average losses are actually close to the asymptotic performance of the corresponding action. However, for Corollary 7.3 it suffices to require the one-sided inequality.

Corollary 7.3 states the existence of a strategy of playing repeated games such that, against any flexible opponent, the average loss is at most that of the best action (calculated by assuming that the action is played constantly) plus the quantity ε_τ that can be made arbitrarily small by choosing the parameter τ of the algorithm sufficiently large. However, sequence ε_τ depends on the opponent and may not be known to the forecaster. Thus, it is desirable to find a forecaster whose average loss actually achieves $\min_{i=1,\dots,N} \overline{\mu}_i$ asymptotically. Such a method may now easily be constructed.

Corollary 7.4. *There exists a forecaster such that whenever the opponent is flexible,*

$$\limsup_{n \to \infty} \frac{1}{n} \sum_{t=1}^{n} \ell(I_t, J_t) \leq \min_{i=1,\dots,N} \overline{\mu}_i.$$

We leave the details as a routine exercise (Exercise 7.32).

Remark 7.17 (Randomized opponents). In some cases it may be meaningful to consider strategies for the adversary that use randomization. In such cases our definition of flexibility, which poses a deterministic condition on the opponent, is not realistic. However, the definition may be easily modified to accommodate a possibly randomized behavior. In fact, the original definition of de Farias and Megiddo [86] involves a probabilistic assumption.

7.12 Bibliographic Remarks

Playing and learning in repeated games is an important branch of game theory with an extensive literature. In this chapter we addressed only a tiny corner of this immense subject. The interested reader may consult the monographs of Fudenberg and Levine [119], Sorin [276], and Young [316]. Hart [144] gives an excellent survey of regret-based uncoupled learning dynamics.

von Neumann's minimax theorem is the classic result of game theory (see von Neumann and Morgenstern [296]), and most standard textbooks on game theory provide a proof. Various generalizations, including stronger versions of Theorem 7.1, are due to Fan [93] and Sion [271] (see also the references therein). The proof of Theorem 7.1 shown here is a generalization of ideas of Freund and Schapire [114], who prove von Neumann's minimax theorem using the strategy described in Exercise 7.9.

The notion and the proof of existence of Nash equilibria appears in the celebrated paper of Nash [222]. For the basic results on the Nash convergence of fictitious play, see Robinson [246], Miyasawa [218], Shapley [265], Monderer and Shapley [220]. Hofbauer and Sandholm [163] consider stochastic fictitious play, similar, in spirit, to the follow-the-perturbed-leader forecaster considered in Chapter 4, and prove its convergence for a class of games. See the references within [163] for various related results. Singh, Kearns, and Mansour [270] show that a simple dynamics based on gradient-descent yields average payoffs asymptotically equivalent of those of a Nash equilibrium in the special case of two-player games in which both players have two actions.

The notion of correlated equilibrium was first introduced by Aumann [16, 17]. A direct proof of the existence of correlated equilibria, using just von Neumann's minimax theorem (as opposed to the fixed point theorem needed to prove the existence of Nash equilibria) was given by Hart and Schmeidler [150]. The existence of adaptive procedures leading to a correlated equilibrium was shown by Foster and Vohra [105]; see also Fudenberg and Levine [118, 121] and Hart and Mas-Colell [145, 146]. Stoltz and Lugosi [278] generalize this to games with an infinite, but compact, set of actions. The connection of calibration and correlated equilibria, described in Section 7.6, was pointed out by Foster and Vohra [105]. Kakade and Foster [171] take these ideas further and show that if all players play according to a best response to a certain common, "almost deterministic," well-calibrated forecaster, then the joint empirical frequencies of play converge not only to the set of correlated equilibria but, in fact, to the convex hull of the set of Nash equilibria. Hart and Mas-Colell [145] introduce a strategy, the so-called regret matching, conceptually much simpler than the internal regret minimization procedures described in Section 4.4, which has the property that if all players follow this strategy, the joint empirical frequencies converge to the set of correlated equilibria; see also Cahn [44]. Kakade, Kearns, Langford, and Ortiz [172] consider efficient algorithms for computing correlated equilibria in graphical games. The result of Section 7.5 appears in Hart and Mas-Colell [147].

Blackwell's approachability theory dates back to [28], where Theorem 7.5 is proved. It was also Blackwell [29] who pointed out that the approachability theorem may be used to construct Hannan-consistent forecasting strategies. Various generalizations of this theorem may be found in Vielle [295] and Lehrer [193]. Fabian and Hannan [92] studied rates of convergence in an extended setting in which payoffs may be random and not necessarily bounded. The potential-based strategies of Section 7.8 were introduced by Hart and Mas-Colell [146] and Theorem 7.6 is due to them. In [146] the result is stated under a weaker assumption than convexity of the potential function.

The problem of learning Nash equilibria by uncoupled strategies has been pursued by Foster and Young [108, 109]. They introduce the idea of regret testing, which the procedures studied in Section 7.10 are based on. Their procedures guarantee that, asymptotically, the mixed strategy profiles are within distance ε of the set of Nash equilibria in a fraction of at least $1 - \varepsilon$ of time. On the negative side, Hart and Mas-Colell [148, 149] show that it is impossible to achieve convergence to Nash equilibrium for all games if one is restricted to use stationary strategies that have bounded memory. By "bounded memory" they mean that there is a finite integer T such that each player bases his play only on the last T rounds of play. On the other hand, for every $\varepsilon > 0$ they show a randomized bounded-memory stationary uncoupled procedure, different from those presented in Sections 7.9 and 7.10, for which the joint empirical frequencies of play converge almost surely to an ε-Nash equilibrium. Germano and Lugosi [126] modify the regret testing procedure of Foster and Young to achieve almost sure convergence to the set of ε-Nash equilibria for all games. The analysis of Section 7.10 is based on [126]. In particular, the proof of Lemma 7.5 is found in [126], though the somewhat simpler case of two players is shown in Foster and Young [109].

A closely related branch of literature that is not discussed in this chapter is based on learning rules that are based on players updating their beliefs using Bayes' rule. Kalai and Lehrer [176] show that if the priors "contain a grain of truth," the play converges to a Nash equilibrium of the game. See also Jordan [169, 170], Dekel, Fudenberg, and Levine [87], Fudenberg and Levine [117, 119], and Nachbar [221].

Kalai, Lehrer, and Smorodinsky [177] show that this type of learning is closely related to stronger notions of calibration and merging. See also Lehrer, and Smorodinsky [196], Sandroni and Smorodinsky [258].

The material presented in Section 7.11 is based on the work of de Farias and Megiddo [85, 86], though the analysis shown here is different. In particular, the forecaster of de Farias and Megiddo is randomized and conceptually simpler than the deterministic predictor used here.

7.13 Exercises

7.1 Show that the set of all Nash equilibria of a two-person zero-sum game is closed and convex.

7.2 *(Shapley's game)* Consider the two-person game described by the loss matrices of the two players ("R" and "C"), known as *Shapley's game*:

R\C	1	2	3
1	0	1	1
2	1	0	1
3	1	1	0

R\C	1	2	3
1	1	0	1
2	1	1	0
3	0	1	1

Show that if both players use fictitious play, the empirical frequencies of play do not converge to the set of correlated equilibria (Foster and Vohra [105]).

7.3 Prove Lemma 7.1.

7.4 Consider the two-person game given by the losses

R\C	1	2
1	1	5
2	0	7

R\C	1	2
1	1	0
2	5	7

Find all three Nash equilibria of the game. Show that the distribution given by $P(1, 1) = 1/3$, $P(1, 2) = 1/3$, $P(2, 1) = 1/3$, $P(2, 2) = 0$ is a correlated equilibrium that lies outside of the convex hull of the Nash equilibria. (Aumann [17]).

7.5 Show that a probability distribution P over $\bigotimes_{k=1}^{K} \{1, \ldots, N_k\}$ is a correlated equilibrium if and only if for all $k = 1, \ldots, K$,

$$\mathbb{E}\,\ell^{(k)}(\mathbf{I}) \leq \mathbb{E}\,\ell^{(k)}(\mathbf{I}^-, \widetilde{I}^{(k)}),$$

where $\mathbf{I} = (I^{(1)}, \ldots, I^{(k)})$ is distributed according to P and the random variable $\widetilde{I}^{(k)}$ is any function of $I^{(k)}$ and of a random variable U independent of $\mathbf{I}^-$.

7.6 Consider the repeated time-varying game described in Remark 7.3, with $N = M = 2$. Assume that there exist positive numbers ε, δ such that, for every sufficiently large n, at least for $n\delta$ time steps t between time 1 and n,

$$\max_{j=1,2} |\ell_t(1, j) - \ell_t(2, j)| > \varepsilon.$$

Show that then for any sequence of mixed strategies $\mathbf{p}_1, \mathbf{p}_2, \ldots$ of the row player, the column player can choose his mixed strategies $\mathbf{q}_1, \mathbf{q}_2, \ldots$ such that the row player's cumulative loss satisfies

$$\sum_{t=1}^{n} \ell_t(I_t, J_t) - \sum_{t=1}^{n} \min_{i=1,2} \ell_t(i, J_t) > \gamma n$$

for all sufficiently large n with probability 1, where γ is positive.

7.7 Assume that in a two-person zero-sum game, for all t, the row player plays according to the constant mixed strategy $\mathbf{p}_t = \mathbf{p}$, where $\mathbf{p}$ is any mixed strategy for which there exists a mixed strategy of the column player such that $\overline{\ell}(\mathbf{p}, \mathbf{q}) = V$. Show that

$$\limsup_{n \to \infty} \frac{1}{n} \sum_{t=1}^{n} \ell(I_t, J_t) \le V.$$

Show also that, for any $\varepsilon > 0$, the row player, regardless of how he plays, cannot guarantee that

$$\limsup_{n \to \infty} \frac{1}{n} \sum_{t=1}^{n} \ell(I_t, J_t) \le V - \varepsilon.$$

7.8 Consider a two-person zero-sum game and assume that the row player plays according to the exponentially weighted average mixed strategy

$$p_{i,t} = \frac{\exp\left(-\eta \sum_{s=1}^{t} \ell(i, J_s)\right)}{\sum_{k=1}^{N} \exp\left(-\eta \sum_{s=1}^{t} \ell(k, J_s)\right)}, \qquad i = 1, \ldots, N.$$

Show that, with probability at least $1 - \delta$, the average loss of the row player satisfies

$$\frac{1}{n} \sum_{t=1}^{n} \ell(I_t, J_t) \le V + \frac{\ln N}{n\eta} + \frac{\eta}{8} + \sqrt{\frac{2}{n} \ln \frac{2N}{\delta}}.$$

7.9 Freund and Schapire [113] investigate the weighted average forecaster in the simplified version of the setup of Section 7.3, in which the row player gets to see the distribution $\mathbf{q}_{t-1}$ chosen by the column player before making the play at time t. Then the following version of the weighted average strategy for the row player is feasible:

$$p_{i,t} = \frac{\exp\left(-\eta \sum_{s=1}^{t-1} \ell(i, \mathbf{q}_s)\right)}{\sum_{k=1}^{m} \exp\left(-\eta \sum_{s=1}^{t-1} \ell(k, \mathbf{q}_s)\right)}, \qquad i = 1, \ldots, N,$$

with $p_{i,1}$ set to $1/N$, where $\eta > 0$ is an appropriately chosen constant. Show that this strategy is an instance of the weighted average forecaster (see Section 4.2), which implies that

$$\sum_{t=1}^{n} \overline{\ell}(\mathbf{p}_t, \mathbf{q}_t) \le \min_{\mathbf{p}} \sum_{t=1}^{n} \overline{\ell}(\mathbf{p}, \mathbf{q}_t) + \frac{\ln N}{\eta} + \frac{n\eta}{8},$$

where

$$\overline{\ell}(\mathbf{p}_t, \mathbf{q}_t) = \sum_{i=1}^{N} \sum_{j=1}^{M} p_{i,t} \, q_{j,t} \, \ell(i, j).$$

Show that if I_t denotes the actual randomized play of the row player, then with an appropriately chosen $\eta = \eta_t$,

$$\lim_{n \to \infty} \frac{1}{n} \left(\sum_{t=1}^{n} \ell(I_t, \mathbf{q}_t) - \min_{i=1,\dots,N} \sum_{t=1}^{n} \ell(i, \mathbf{q}_t) \right) = 0 \qquad \text{almost surely}$$

(Freund and Schapire [113]).

7.10 Improve the bound of the previous exercise to

$$\sum_{t=1}^{n} \overline{\ell}(\mathbf{p}_t, \mathbf{q}_t) \leq \min_{\mathbf{p}} \left(\sum_{t=1}^{n} \overline{\ell}(\mathbf{p}, \mathbf{q}_t) - \frac{H(\mathbf{p})}{\eta} \right) + \frac{\ln N}{\eta} + \frac{n\eta}{8},$$

where $H(\mathbf{p}) = -\sum_{i=1}^{N} p_i \ln p_i$ denotes the entropy of the probability vector $\mathbf{p} = (p_1, \dots, p_N)$. *Hint:* Improve the crude bound $\frac{1}{\eta} \ln \left(\sum_i e^{\eta R_{i,n}} \right) \geq \max_i R_{i,n}$ to $\frac{1}{\eta} \ln \left(\sum_i e^{\eta R_{i,n}} \right) \geq \max_{\mathbf{p}} (\mathbf{R}_t \cdot \mathbf{p} + H(\mathbf{p})/\eta)$.

7.11 Consider repeated play in a two-person zero-sum game in which both players play such that

$$\lim_{n \to \infty} \frac{1}{n} \sum_{t=1}^{n} \ell(I_t, J_t) = V \qquad \text{almost surely.}$$

Show that the product distribution $\widehat{\mathbf{p}}_n \times \widehat{\mathbf{q}}_n$ with

$$\widehat{p}_{i,n} = \frac{1}{n} \sum_{t=1}^{n} \mathbb{I}_{\{I_t = i\}} \qquad \text{and} \qquad \widehat{q}_{j,n} = \frac{1}{n} \sum_{t=1}^{n} \mathbb{I}_{\{J_t = j\}}$$

converges, almost surely, to the set of Nash equilibria. *Hint:* Check the proof of Theorem 7.2.

7.12 Robinson [246] showed that if in repeated playing of a two-person zero-sum game both players play according to fictitious play (i.e., choose the best pure strategy against the average mixed strategy of their opponent), then the product of the marginal empirical frequencies of play converges to a solution of the game. Show, however, that fictitious play does not have the following robustness property similar to the exponentially weighted average strategy deduced in Theorem 7.2: if a player uses fictitious play but his opponent does not, then the player's normalized cumulative loss may be significantly larger than the value of the game.

7.13 *(Fictitious conditional regret minimization)* Consider a two-person game in which the loss matrix of both players is given by

1\2	1	2
1	0	1
2	1	0

Show that if both players play according to fictitious play (breaking ties randomly if necessary), then Nash equilibrium is achieved in a strong sense.

Consider now the "conditional" (or "internal") version of fictitious play in which both players $k = 1, 2$ select

$$I_t^{(k)} = \operatorname*{argmin}_{i_k \in \{1,2\}} \frac{1}{t-1} \sum_{s=1}^{t-1} \mathbb{I}_{\{I_s^{(k)} = I_{t-1}^{(k)}\}} \ell^{(k)}(\mathbf{I}_s^-, i_k).$$

Show that if the play starts with, say, $(1, 2)$, then both players will have maximal loss in every round of the game.

7.14 Show that if in a repeated play of a K-person game all players play according to some Hannan consistent strategy, then the joint empirical frequencies of play converge to the Hannan set of the game.

7.15 Consider the two-person zero-sum game given by the loss matrix

0	0	−1
0	0	1
1	−1	0

Show that the joint distribution

1/3	1/3	0
1/3	0	0
0	0	0

is a correlated equilibrium of the game. This example shows that even in zero-sum games the set of correlated equilibria may be strictly larger than the set of Nash equilibria (Forges [101]).

7.16 Describe a game for which $\mathcal{H} \setminus \mathcal{C} \neq \emptyset$, that is, the Hannan set contains some distributions that are not correlated equilibria.

7.17 Show that if $P \in \mathcal{H}$ is a product measure, then $P \in \mathcal{N}$. In other words, the product measures in the Hannan set are precisely the Nash equilibria.

7.18 Show that in a K-person game with $N_k = 2$, for all $k = 1, \ldots, K$ (i.e., each player has two actions to choose from), $\mathcal{H} = \mathcal{C}$.

7.19 Extend the procedure and the proof of Theorem 7.4 to the general case of K-person games.

7.20 Construct a game with two-dimensional vector-valued losses and a (nonconvex) set $S \subset \mathbb{R}^2$ such that all halfspaces containing S are approachable but S is not.

7.21 Construct a game with vector-valued losses and a closed and convex polytope such that if the polytope is written as a finite intersection of closed halfspaces, where the hyperplanes defining the halfspaces correspond to the faces of the polytope, then all these closed halfspaces are approachable but the polytope is not.

7.22 Use Theorem 7.5 to show that, in the setup of Section 7.4, each player has a strategy such that the limsup of the conditional regrets is nonpositive regardless of the other players' actions.

7.23 This exercise presents a strategy that achieves a significantly faster rate of convergence in Blackwell's approachability theorem than that obtained in the proof of the theorem in the text. Let S be a closed and convex set, and assume that all halfspaces H containing S are approachable. Define $\overline{A}_0 = \mathbf{0}$ and $\overline{A}_t = \frac{1}{t}\sum_{s=1}^{t} \ell(\mathbf{p}_s, J_s)$ for $t \geq 1$. Define the row player's mixed strategy $\mathbf{p}_t$ at time $t = 1, 2, \ldots$ as arbitrary if $\overline{A}_{t-1} \in S$ and by

$$\max_{j=1,\ldots,M} \overline{\mathbf{a}}_{t-1} \cdot \ell(\mathbf{p}_t, j) \leq \overline{c}_{t-1}$$

otherwise, where

$$\overline{\mathbf{a}}_{t-1} = \frac{\overline{A}_{t-1} - \pi_S(\overline{A}_{t-1})}{\|\overline{A}_{t-1} - \pi_S(\overline{A}_{t-1})\|} \quad \text{and} \quad \overline{c}_{t-1} = \overline{\mathbf{a}}_{t-1} \cdot \pi_S(\overline{A}_{t-1}).$$

Prove that there exists a universal constant C (independent of n and d) such that, with probability at least $1 - \delta$,

$$\|A_n - \pi_S(A_n)\| \leq \frac{2}{\sqrt{n}} + C\sqrt{\frac{\ln(1/\delta)}{n}}.$$

Hint: Proceed as in the proof of Theorem 7.5 to show that $\|\overline{A}_n - \pi_S(\overline{A}_n)\| \leq 2/\sqrt{n}$. To obtain a dimension-free constant when bounding $\|A_n - \overline{A}_n\|$, you will need an extension of the Hoeffding–Azuma inequality to vector-valued martingales; see, for example, Chen and White [58].

7.24 Consider the potential-based strategy, based on the average loss $\mathbf{A}_{t-1}$, described at the beginning of Section 7.8. Show that, under the same conditions on S and Φ as in Theorem 7.6, the average loss satisfies $\lim_{n\to\infty} d(\mathbf{A}_n, S) = 0$ with probability 1. *Hint:* Mimic the proof of Theorem 7.6.

7.25 (*A stationary strategy to find pure Nash equilibria*) Assume that a K-person game has a pure action Nash equilibrium and consider the following strategy for player k: If $t = 1, 2$, choose $I_t^{(k)}$ randomly. If $t > 2$, if all players have played the same action in the last two periods (i.e., $\mathbf{I}_{t-1} = \mathbf{I}_{t-2}$) and $I_{t-1}^{(k)}$ was a best response to $\mathbf{I}_{t-1}^{-}$, then repeat the same play, that is, define $I_t^{(k)} = I_{t-1}^{(k)}$. Otherwise, choose $I_t^{(k)}$ uniformly at random.

Prove that if all players play according to this strategy, then a pure action Nash equilibrium is eventually achieved, almost surely. (Hart and Mas-Colell [149].)

7.26 (*Generic two-player game with a pure Nash equilibrium*) Consider a two-player game with a pure action Nash equilibrium. Assume also that the player is *generic* in the sense that the best reply is always unique. Suppose at time t each player repeats the play of time $t - 1$ if it was a best response and selects an action randomly otherwise. Prove that a pure action Nash equilibrium is eventually achieved, almost surely [149]. *Hint:* The process $\mathbf{I}_1, \mathbf{I}_2, \ldots$ is a Markov chain with state space $\{1, \ldots, N_1\} \times \{1, \ldots, N_2\}$. Show that given any state $\mathbf{i} = (i_1, i_2)$, which is not a Nash equilibrium, the two-step transition probability satisfies

$$\mathbb{P}\big[\mathbf{I}_t \text{ is a Nash equilibrium} \,\big|\, \mathbf{I}_{t-2} = (i_1, i_2)\big] \geq c$$

for a constant $c > 0$.

7.27 (*A nongeneric game*) Consider a two-player game (played by "R" and "C") whose loss matrices are given by

R\C	1	2	3
1	0	1	0
2	1	0	0
3	1	1	0

R\C	1	2	3
1	1	0	1
2	0	1	1
3	0	0	0

Suppose both players play according to the strategy described in Exercise 7.26. Show that there is a positive probability that the unique pure Nash equilibrium is never achieved. (This example appears in Hart and Mas-Colell [149].)

7.28 Show that almost all games (with respect to the Lebesgue measure) are such that there exist constants $c_1, c_2 > 0$ such that for all sufficiently small $\varepsilon > 0$, the set $\mathcal{N}_\varepsilon$ of approximate Nash equilibria satisfies

$$D_\infty(\mathcal{N}, c_1\varepsilon) \subset \mathcal{N}_\varepsilon \subset D_\infty(\mathcal{N}, c_2\varepsilon),$$

where $D_\infty(\mathcal{N}, \varepsilon) = \{\pi \in \Sigma \,:\, \|\pi - \pi'\|_\infty \leq \varepsilon, \pi' \in \mathcal{N}\}$ is the L_∞ neighborhood of the set of Nash equilibria, of radius ε. (See, e.g., Germano and Lugosi [126].)

7.29 Use the procedure of experimental regret testing as a building block to design an uncoupled strategy such that if all players follow the strategy, the mixed strategy profiles converge almost surely to a Nash equilibrium of the game for almost all games. *Hint:* Follow the ideas described in Remark 7.14 and the Borel–Cantelli lemma. (Germano and Lugosi [126].)

7.30 Extend the forecasting strategy defined in Section 7.11 to the case of $N > 2$ actions such that, regardless of the sequence of outcomes,

$$\limsup_{n\to\infty} \widehat{\mu}_n \leq \min_{i=1,\ldots,N} \limsup_{n\to\infty} \mu_{i,n}.$$

Hint: Place the N actions in the leaves of a rooted binary tree and use the original algorithm recursively in every internal node of the tree. The strategy assigned to the root is the desired forecasting strategy.

7.31 Assume that both players follow the deterministic exploration–exploitation strategy while playing the prisoners' dilemma. Show that the players will end up cooperating. However, if their play is not synchronized (e.g., if the column player starts following the strategy at time $t = 3$), both players will defect most of the time.

7.32 Prove Corollary 7.4. *Hint:* Modify the repeated deterministic exploration–exploitation forecaster properly either by letting the parameter τ grow with time or by using an appropriate doubling trick.

8

Absolute Loss

8.1 Simulatable Experts

In this chapter we take a closer look at the sequential prediction problem of Chapter 2 in the special case when the outcome space is $\mathcal{Y} = \{0, 1\}$, the decision space is $\mathcal{D} = [0, 1]$, and the loss function is the "absolute loss" $\ell(\widehat{p}, y) = |\widehat{p} - y|$. We have already encountered this loss function in Chapter 3, where it was shown that, for general experts, the absolute loss is in some sense the "hardest" among all bounded convex losses. We now turn our attention to a different problem: the characterization of the minimax regret $V_n(\mathcal{F})$ for the absolute loss and for a *given* class $\mathcal{F}$ of *simulatable* experts (recall the definition of simulatable experts from Section 2.9).

In the entire chapter, an expert f means a sequence $f_1, f_2 \ldots$ of functions $f_t :$ $\{0, 1\}^{t-1} \to [0, 1]$, mapping sequences of past outcomes y^{t-1} into elements of the decision space. We use $\mathcal{F}$ to denote a class of (simulatable) experts f. Recall from Section 2.10 that a forecasting strategy P based on a class of simulatable experts is a sequence $\widehat{p}_1, \widehat{p}_2, \ldots$ of functions $\widehat{p}_t : \mathcal{Y}^{t-1} \to \mathcal{D}$ (to simplify notation, we often write $\widehat{p}_t$ instead of $\widehat{p}_t(y^{t-1})$). Recall also that the minimax regret $V_n(\mathcal{F})$ is defined for the absolute loss by

$$V_n(\mathcal{F}) = \inf_P \sup_{y^n \in \mathcal{Y}^n} \left(\widehat{L}(y^n) - \min_{f \in \mathcal{F}} L_f(y^n) \right),$$

where $\widehat{L}(y^n) = \sum_{t=1}^n |\widehat{p}_t(y^{t-1}) - y_t|$ is the cumulative absolute loss of the forecaster P and $L_f(y^n) = \sum_{t=1}^n |f_t(y^{t-1}) - y_t|$ denotes the cumulative absolute loss of expert f. The infimum is taken over all forecasters P. (In this chapter, and similarly in Chapter 9, we find it convenient to make the dependence of the cumulative loss on the outcome sequence explicit; this is why we write $\widehat{L}(y^n)$ for $\widehat{L}_n$.)

Clearly, if the cardinality of $\mathcal{F}$ is $|\mathcal{F}| = N$, then $V_n(\mathcal{F}) \leq V_n^{(N)}$, where $V_n^{(N)}$ is the minimax regret with N general experts defined in Section 2.10. As seen in Section 2.2, for all n and N, $V_n^{(N)} \leq \sqrt{(n/2) \ln N}$. Also, by the results of Section 3.7, $\sup_{n,N} V_n^{(N)} / \sqrt{n \ln N} \geq 1/\sqrt{2}$.

On the other hand, the behavior of $V_n(\mathcal{F})$ is significantly more complex as it depends on the structure of the class $\mathcal{F}$. To understand the phenomenon, just consider a class of $N = 2$ experts that always predict the same except for $t = n$, when one of the experts predicts 0 and the other one predicts 1. In this case, since the experts are simulatable, the forecaster may simply predict as both experts if $t < n$ and set $\widehat{p}_n = 1/2$. It is easy to see that this forecaster is minimax optimal, and therefore $V_n(\mathcal{F}) = 1/2$, which is significantly smaller than the worst-case bound $\sqrt{(n/2)\ln 2}$. In general, intuitively, $V_n(\mathcal{F})$ is small if the experts are "close" to each other in some sense and large if the experts are "spread out."

The primary goal of this chapter is to investigate what geometrical properties of $\mathcal{F}$ determine the size of $V_n(\mathcal{F})$. In Section 8.2 we describe a forecaster that is optimal in the minimax sense, that is, it achieves a worst-case regret equal to $V_n(\mathcal{F})$. The minimax optimal forecaster also suggests a way of calculating $V_n(\mathcal{F})$ for any given class of experts, and this calculation becomes especially simple in the case of *static* experts (see Section 2.9 for the definition of a static expert). In Section 8.3 the minimax regret $V_n(\mathcal{F})$ is characterized for static experts in terms of a so-called *Rademacher average*. Section 8.4 describes the possibly simplest nontrivial example that illustrates the use of this characterization. In Section 8.5 we derive general upper and lower bounds for classes of static experts in terms of the geometric structure of the class $\mathcal{F}$. Section 8.6 is devoted to general (not necessarily static) classes of simulatable experts. This case is somewhat more difficult to handle as there is no elegant characterization of the minimax regret. Nevertheless, using simple structural properties, we are able to derive matching upper and lower bounds for some interesting classes of experts, such as the class of linear forecasters or the class of Markov forecasters.

8.2   Optimal Algorithm for Simulatable Experts

The purpose of this section is to present, in the case of simulatable experts, a forecaster that is optimal in the sense that it minimizes, among all forecasters, the worst-case regret

$$\sup_{y^n \in \{0,1\}^n} \left(\widehat{L}(y^n) - \min_{f \in \mathcal{F}} L_f(y^n) \right);$$

that is,

$$\sup_{y^n \in \{0,1\}^n} \left(\widehat{L}(y^n) - \min_{f \in \mathcal{F}} L_f(y^n) \right) = V_n(\mathcal{F}),$$

where all losses – we recall it once more – are measured using the absolute loss.

Before describing the optimal forecaster, we note that, since the experts are simulatable, the forecaster may calculate the loss of each expert for any particular outcome sequence. In particular, for all $y^n \in \{0, 1\}^n$, the forecaster may compute $\inf_{f \in \mathcal{F}} L_f(y^n)$.

We determine the optimal forecaster "backwards," starting with $\widehat{p}_n$, and the prediction at time n. Assume that the first $n - 1$ outcomes y^{n-1} have been revealed and we want to determine, optimally, the prediction $\widehat{p}_n = \widehat{p}_n(y^{n-1})$. Since our goal is to minimize the worst-case regret, we need to determine $\widehat{p}_n$ to minimize

$$\max \left\{ \widehat{L}(y^{n-1}) + \ell(\widehat{p}_n, 0) - \inf_{f \in \mathcal{F}} L_f(y^{n-1}0), \right.$$

$$\left. \widehat{L}(y^{n-1}) + \ell(\widehat{p}_n, 1) - \inf_{f \in \mathcal{F}} L_f(y^{n-1}1) \right\},$$

where $y^{n-1}0$ denotes the string of n bits whose first $n - 1$ bits are y^{n-1} and the last bit is 0. Minimizing this quantity is equivalent to minimizing

$$\max\left\{\widehat{p}_n - \inf_{f \in \mathcal{F}} L_f(y^{n-1}0), \ 1 - \widehat{p}_n - \inf_{f \in \mathcal{F}} L_f(y^{n-1}1)\right\}.$$

Clearly, if we write $A_n(y^n) = -\inf_{f \in \mathcal{F}} L_f(y^n)$, then this is achieved by

$$\widehat{p}_n = \begin{cases} 0 & \text{if } A_n(y^{n-1}0) > A_n(y^{n-1}1) + 1 \\ 1 & \text{if } A_n(y^{n-1}0) + 1 < A_n(y^{n-1}1) \\ \dfrac{A_n(y^{n-1}1) - A_n(y^{n-1}0) + 1}{2} & \text{otherwise.} \end{cases}$$

A crucial observation is that this expression of $\widehat{p}_n$ does not depend on the previous predictions $\widehat{p}_1, \dots, \widehat{p}_{n-1}$. Define

$$A_{n-1}(y^{n-1}) \stackrel{\text{def}}{=} \min_{p_n \in [0,1]} \max\left\{p_n - \inf_{f \in \mathcal{F}} L_f(y^{n-1}0), \ 1 - p_n - \inf_{f \in \mathcal{F}} L_f(y^{n-1}1)\right\}.$$

This may be rewritten as

$$A_{n-1}(y^{n-1}) = \min_{p_n \in [0,1]} \max\left\{p_n + A_n(y^{n-1}0), \ 1 - p_n + A_n(y^{n-1}1)\right\}.$$

So far we have calculated the optimal prediction at the last time instance $\widehat{p}_n$. Next we determine optimally $\widehat{p}_{n-1}$, assuming that at time n the optimal prediction is used. Determining $\widehat{p}_{n-1}$ is clearly equivalent to minimizing

$$\max\left\{\widehat{L}(y^{n-2}) + \ell(\widehat{p}_{n-1}, 0) + A_{n-1}(y^{n-2}0), \\ \widehat{L}(y^{n-2}) + \ell(\widehat{p}_{n-1}, 1) + A_{n-1}(y^{n-2}1)\right\}$$

or, equivalently, to minimizing

$$\max\left\{\widehat{p}_{n-1} + A_{n-1}(y^{n-2}0), \ 1 - \widehat{p}_{n-1} + A_{n-1}(y^{n-2}1)\right\}.$$

The solution is, as before,

$$\widehat{p}_{n-1} = \begin{cases} 0 & \text{if } A_{n-1}(y^{n-2}0) > A_{n-1}(y^{n-2}1) + 1 \\ 1 & \text{if } A_{n-1}(y^{n-2}0) + 1 < A_{n-1}(y^{n-2}1) \\ \dfrac{A_{n-1}(y^{n-2}1) - A_{n-1}(y^{n-2}0) + 1}{2} & \text{otherwise.} \end{cases}$$

The procedure may be continued in the same way until we determine $\widehat{p}_1$.

Formally, given a class $\mathcal{F}$ of experts and a positive integer n, a forecaster whose worst-case regret equals $V_n(\mathcal{F})$ is determined by the following recursion.

MINIMAX OPTIMAL FORECASTER
FOR THE ABSOLUTE LOSS

Parameters: Class $\mathcal{F}$ of simulatable experts.

1. (Initialization) $A_n(y^n) = -\inf_{f \in \mathcal{F}} L_f(y^n)$.
2. (Recurrence) For $t = n, n-1, \ldots, 1$.

$$A_{t-1}(y^{t-1}) = \min_{p \in [0,1]} \max \left\{ p + A_t(y^{t-1}0), \ 1 - p + A_t(y^{t-1}1) \right\}$$

and

$$\widehat{p}_t = \begin{cases} 0 & \text{if } A_t(y^{t-1}0) \\ & \quad > A_t(y^{t-1}1) + 1 \\ 1 & \text{if } A_t(y^{t-1}0) + 1 \\ & \quad < A_t(y^{t-1}1) \\ \dfrac{A_t(y^{t-1}1) - A_t(y^{t-1}0) + 1}{2} & \text{otherwise.} \end{cases}$$

Note that the recurrence for A_t may also be written as

$$A_{t-1}(y^{t-1}) = \begin{cases} A_t(y^{t-1}0) & \text{if } A_t(y^{t-1}0) > A_t(y^{t-1}1) + 1 \\ A_t(y^{t-1}1) & \text{if } A_t(y^{t-1}0) + 1 < A_t(y^{t-1}1) \\ \dfrac{A_t(y^{t-1}1) + A_t(y^{t-1}0) + 1}{2} & \text{otherwise.} \end{cases} \tag{8.1}$$

The algorithm for calculating the optimal forecaster has an important by-product: the value A_0 of the quantity $A_{t-1}(y^{t-1})$ at the last step ($t = 1$) of the recurrence clearly gives

$$A_0 = \max_{y^n} \left\{ \sum_{t=1}^{n} \ell(\widehat{p}_t, y_t) + A_n(y^n) \right\} = V_n(\mathcal{F}).$$

Thus, the same algorithm also calculates the minimal worst-case regret. In the next section we will see some useful consequences of this fact.

8.3   Static Experts

In this section we focus our attention on static experts. Recall that an expert f is called static if for all $t = 1, 2, \ldots$ and $y^{t-1} \in \{0, 1\}^{t-1}$, $f_t(y^{t-1}) = f_t \in [0, 1]$. In other words, static experts' predictions do not depend on the past outcomes: they are fixed in advance. For example, the expert that always predicts 0 regardless of the past outcomes is static, but the expert whose prediction is the average of all previously seen outcomes is not static.

The following simple technical result has some surprising consequences. The simple inductive proof is left as an exercise.

Lemma 8.1. *Let $\mathcal{F}$ be an arbitrary class of static experts. Then for all $t = 1, \ldots, n$ and $y^{t-1} \in \{0, 1\}^{t-1}$,*

$$\left| A_t(y^{t-1}1) - A_t(y^{t-1}0) \right| \leq 1.$$

This lemma implies the following result.

Theorem 8.1. *If $\mathcal{F}$ is a class of static experts, then*

$$V_n(\mathcal{F}) = \frac{n}{2} - \frac{1}{2^n} \sum_{y^n \in \{0,1\}^n} \inf_{f \in \mathcal{F}} L_f(y^n).$$

Proof. Lemma 8.1 and (8.1) imply that for all $t = 1, \ldots, n$,

$$A_{t-1}(y^{t-1}) = \frac{A_t(y^{t-1}1) + A_t(y^{t-1}0) + 1}{2}.$$

Applying this equation recursively, we obtain

$$A_0 = \frac{1}{2^n} \sum_{y^n \in \{0,1\}^n} A_n(y^n) + \frac{n}{2}.$$

Recalling that $V_n(\mathcal{F}) = A_0$ and $A_n(y^n) = -\inf_{f \in \mathcal{F}} L_f(y^n)$, we conclude the proof. ∎

To understand better the behavior of the value $V_n(\mathcal{F})$, it is advantageous to reformulate the obtained expression. Recall that, because experts are static, each expert f is represented by a vector $(f_1, \ldots, f_n) \in [0, 1]^n$, where f_t is the prediction of expert f at time t. Since $\ell(f_t, y) = |f_t - y|$, $L_f(y^n) = \sum_{t=1}^{n} |f_t - y_t|$. Also, the average over all possible outcome sequences appearing in the expression of $V_n(\mathcal{F})$ may be treated as an expected value. To this end, introduce i.i.d. symmetric Bernoulli random variables $Y_1, \ldots, Y_n$ (i.e., $\mathbb{P}[Y_t = 0] = \mathbb{P}[Y_t = 1] = 1/2$). Then, by Theorem 8.1,

$$V_n(\mathcal{F}) = \frac{n}{2} - \mathbb{E}\left[\inf_{f \in \mathcal{F}} \sum_{t=1}^{n} |f_t - Y_t| \right]$$

$$= \mathbb{E}\left[\sup_{f \in \mathcal{F}} \sum_{t=1}^{n} \left(\frac{1}{2} - |f_t - Y_t| \right) \right]$$

$$= \mathbb{E}\left[\sup_{f \in \mathcal{F}} \sum_{t=1}^{n} \left(\frac{1}{2} - f_t \right) \sigma_t \right], \tag{8.2}$$

where $\sigma_t = 1 - 2Y_t$ are i.i.d. Rademacher random variables (i.e., with $\mathbb{P}[\sigma_t = 1] = \mathbb{P}[\sigma_t = -1] = 1/2$). Thus, $V_n(\mathcal{F})$ equals n times the Rademacher average

$$R_n(A) = \mathbb{E}\left[\sup_{\mathbf{a} \in A} \frac{1}{n} \sum_{i=1}^{n} \sigma_i a_i \right]$$

associated with the set A of vectors of the form

$$\mathbf{a} = (a_1, \ldots, a_n) = (1/2 - f_1, \ldots, 1/2 - f_n), \qquad f \in \mathcal{F}.$$

Rademacher averages are thoroughly studied objects in probability theory, and this will help us establish tight upper and lower bounds on $V_n(\mathcal{F})$ for various classes of static experts in Section 8.5. Some basic structural properties of Rademacher averages are summarized in Section A.1.8.

8.4   A Simple Example

We consider a simple example to illustrate the usage of the formula (8.2). In Section 8.5 we obtain general upper and lower bounds for $V_n(\mathcal{F})$ based on the same characterization in terms of Rademacher averages.

Consider the case when $\mathcal{F}$ is the class of all "constant" experts, that is, the class of all static experts, parameterized by $q \in [0, 1]$, of the form $f^q = (q, \ldots, q)$. Thus each expert predicts the same number throughout the n rounds. The first thing we notice is that the class $\mathcal{F}$ is the convex hull of the two "extreme" static experts $f^{(1)} \equiv 0$ and $f^{(2)} \equiv 1$. Since the Rademacher average of the convex hull of a set equals that of the set itself (see Section A.1.8 for the basic properties of Rademacher averages), the identity (8.2) implies that $V_n(\mathcal{F}) = V_n(\mathcal{F}_0)$, where $\mathcal{F}_0$ contains the two extreme experts. (One may also easily see that for any sequence y^n of outcomes the expert minimizing the cumulative loss $L_f(y^n)$ over the class $\mathcal{F}$ is one of the two extreme experts.) Thus, it suffices to find bounds for $V_n(\mathcal{F}_0)$. To this end recall that, by Theorem 2.2,

$$V_n(\mathcal{F}_0) \le V_n^{(2)} \le \sqrt{\frac{n \ln 2}{2}} \approx 0.5887 \sqrt{n}.$$

Next we contrast this bound with bounds obtained directly using (8.2). Since $f_t^{(1)} = 0$ and $f_t^{(2)} = 1$ for all t,

$$V_n(\mathcal{F}_0) = \frac{1}{2} \mathbb{E} \left[\max \left\{ \sum_{t=1}^{n} \sigma_t, \sum_{t=1}^{n} -\sigma_t \right\} \right] = \frac{1}{2} \mathbb{E} \left| \sum_{t=1}^{n} \sigma_t \right|.$$

Using the Cauchy–Schwarz inequality, we may easily bound this quantity from above as follows:

$$V_n(\mathcal{F}_0) = \frac{1}{2} \mathbb{E} \left| \sum_{t=1}^{n} \sigma_t \right| \le \frac{1}{2} \sqrt{\mathbb{E} \left(\sum_{t=1}^{n} \sigma_t \right)^2} = \frac{\sqrt{n}}{2}.$$

Observe that this bound has the same order of magnitude as the bound obtained by Theorem 2.2, but it has a slightly better constant.

We may obtain a similar lower bound as an easy consequence of Khinchine's inequality, which we recall here (see the Appendix for a proof).

Lemma 8.2 (Khinchine's inequality). *Let $a_1, \ldots, a_n$ be real numbers, and let $\sigma_1, \ldots, \sigma_n$ be i.i.d. Rademacher random variables. Then*

$$\mathbb{E} \left| \sum_{i=1}^{n} a_i \sigma_i \right| \ge \frac{1}{\sqrt{2}} \sqrt{\sum_{i=1}^{n} a_i^2}.$$

Applying Lemma 8.2 to our problem, we obtain the lower bound

$$V_n(\mathcal{F}_0) \ge \sqrt{\frac{n}{8}}.$$

Summarizing the upper and lower bounds, for every n we have

$$0.3535 \le \frac{V_n(\mathcal{F}_0)}{\sqrt{n}} \le 0.5.$$

For example, for $n = 100$ there exists a prediction strategy such that for any sequence $y_1, \ldots, y_{100}$ the total loss is not more than that of the best expert plus 5, but for any prediction strategy there exists a sequence $y_1, \ldots, y_{100}$ such that the regret is at least 3.5. The exact asymptotic value is also easy to calculate: $V_n(\mathcal{F}_0)/\sqrt{n} \to 1/\sqrt{2\pi} \approx 0.3989$ (see the exercises).

8.5 Bounds for Classes of Static Experts

In this section we use Theorem 8.1 and some results from the rich theory of empirical processes to obtain upper and lower bounds for $V_n(\mathcal{F})$ for general classes $\mathcal{F}$ of static experts.

Theorem 8.1 characterizes the minimax regret as the Rademacher average $R_n(A)$ of the set $A = \mathbf{1/2} - \mathcal{F}$, where $\mathbf{1/2} = (1/2, \ldots, 1/2)$, and the class $\mathcal{F}$ of static experts is now regarded as a subset of $\mathbb{R}^n$ (by associating, with each static expert f, the vector $(f_1, \ldots, f_n) \in [0, 1]^n$). There are various ways of bounding Rademacher averages. One is by using the structural properties summarized in Section A.1.8, another is in terms of the geometrical structure of the set A. To illustrate the first method, we consider the following example.

Example 8.1. Consider the class $\mathcal{F}$ of static experts $f = (f_1, \ldots, f_n)$ such that $f_t = (1 + \sigma(b_t))/2$ for any vector $\mathbf{b} = (b_1, \ldots, b_n)$ satisfying $\|\mathbf{b}\|^2 = \sum_{t=1}^n b_t^2 \le \lambda^2$ for a constant $\lambda > 0$ and

$$\sigma(x) = \frac{e^x - e^{-x}}{e^x + e^{-x}}$$

is the standard "sigmoid" function. In other words, $\mathcal{F}$ contains all experts obtained by "squashing" the elements of the unit ball of radius λ into the cube $[0, 1]^n$. Intuitively, the larger the λ, the more complex $\mathcal{F}$ is, which should be reflected in the value of $V_n(\mathcal{F})$. Next we derive an upper bound that reflects this behavior. By Theorem 8.1, $V_n(\mathcal{F}) = n R_n(A)$, where A is the set of vectors of the form $a = (a_1, \ldots, a_n)$, with $a_i = \sigma(b_i)/2$ with $\sum_i b_i^2 \le \lambda^2$. By the contraction principle (see Section A.1.8),

$$R_n(A) \le \frac{1}{2n} \mathbb{E}\left[\sup_{\mathbf{b}:\,\|\mathbf{b}\|\le\lambda} \sum_{i=1}^n \sigma_i b_i\right] = \frac{\lambda}{2n} \mathbb{E}\left[\sup_{\mathbf{b}:\,\|\mathbf{b}\|\le 1} \sum_{i=1}^n \sigma_i b_i\right],$$

where we used the fact that σ is Lipschitz with constant 1. Now by the Cauchy–Schwarz inequality, we have

$$\mathbb{E}\left[\sup_{\mathbf{b}:\,\|\mathbf{b}\|\le 1} \sum_{i=1}^n \sigma_i b_i\right] = \mathbb{E}\sqrt{\sum_{i=1}^n \sigma_i^2} = \sqrt{n}.$$

We have thus shown that $V_n(\mathcal{F}) \le \lambda \sqrt{n}/2$, and this bound may be shown to be essentially tight (see Exercise 8.11). $\square$

A way to capture the geometric structure of the class of experts $\mathcal{F}$ is to consider its *covering numbers*. The covering numbers suitable for our analysis are defined as follows. For any class $\mathcal{F}$ of static experts let $N_2(\mathcal{F}, r)$ be the minimum cardinality of a set $\mathcal{F}_r$ of static experts (possibly not all belonging to $\mathcal{F}$) such that for all $f \in \mathcal{F}$ there exists a $g \in \mathcal{F}_r$ such that

$$\sqrt{\sum_{t=1}^{n} (f_t - g_t)^2} \leq r.$$

The following bound shows how $V_n(\mathcal{F})$ may be bounded from above in terms of these covering numbers.

Theorem 8.2. *For any class $\mathcal{F}$ of static experts,*

$$V_n(\mathcal{F}) \leq 12 \int_0^{\sqrt{n}/2} \sqrt{\ln N_2(\mathcal{F}, r)} \, dr.$$

The result is a straightforward corollary of Theorem 8.1, Hoeffding's inequality (Lemma 2.2), and the following classical result of empirical process theory. To state the result in a general form, consider a family $\{T_f : f \in \mathcal{F}\}$ of zero mean random variables indexed by a metric space $(\mathcal{F}, \rho)$. Let $N_\rho(\mathcal{F}, r)$ denote the covering number of the metric space $\mathcal{F}$ with respect to the metric ρ. The family is called *subgaussian* in the metric ρ whenever

$$\mathbb{E}\left[e^{\lambda(T_f - T_g)}\right] \leq e^{\lambda^2 \rho(f,g)^2/2}$$

holds for any $f, g \in \mathcal{F}$ and $\lambda > 0$. The family is called *sample continuous* if for any sequence $f^{(1)}, f^{(2)}, \ldots \in \mathcal{F}$ converging to some $f \in \mathcal{F}$, we have $T_{f^{(n)}} - T_f \to 0$ almost surely. The proof of the following result is given in the Appendix.

Theorem 8.3. *If $\{T_f : f \in \mathcal{F}\}$ is subgaussian and sample continuous in the metric ρ, then*

$$\mathbb{E}\left[\sup_{f \in \mathcal{F}} T_f\right] \leq 12 \int_0^{D/2} \sqrt{\ln N_\rho(\mathcal{F}, \varepsilon)} \, d\varepsilon,$$

where D is the diameter of $\mathcal{F}$.

For completeness, and without proof, we mention a lower bound corresponding to Theorem 8.2. Once again, the inequality is a straightforward corollary of Theorem 8.1 and known lower bounds for the expected maximum of Rademacher averages.

Theorem 8.4. *Let $\mathcal{F}$ be an arbitrary class of static experts containing f and g such that $f_t = 0$ and $g_t = 1$ for all $t = 1, \ldots, n$. Then there exists a universal constant $K > 0$ such that*

$$V_n(\mathcal{F}) \geq K \sup_{r \geq 0} r \sqrt{\ln N_2(\mathcal{F}, r)}.$$

The bound of Theorem 8.4 is often of the same order of magnitude as that of Theorem 8.2. For examples we refer to the exercises.

The minimax regret $V_n(\mathcal{F})$ for static experts is expressed as the expected value of the supremum of a Rademacher process. Such expected values have been studied and well understood in empirical process theory. In fact, Theorems 8.3 and 8.4 are simple versions of classical general results (known as "Dudley's metric entropy bound" and "Sudakov's minoration") of empirical process theory. There exist more modern tools for establishing sharp bounds for expectations of maxima of random processes, such as "majorizing measures" and "generic chaining." In the bibliographic comments we point the interested reader to some of the references.

8.6 Bounds for General Classes

All bounds of the previous sections are based on Theorem 8.1, a characterization of $V_n(\mathcal{F})$ in terms of expected suprema of Rademacher processes. Unfortunately, no such tool is available in the general case when the experts in the class $\mathcal{F}$ are not static. This section discusses some techniques that may come to rescue.

We begin with a simple but very useful bound for expert classes that are subsets of "convex hulls" of just finitely many experts.

Theorem 8.5. *Assume that the class of experts $\mathcal{F}$ satisfies the following: there exist N experts $f^{(1)}, \ldots, f^{(N)}$ (not necessarily in $\mathcal{F}$) such that for all $f \in \mathcal{F}$ there exist convex coefficients $q_1, \ldots, q_N \geq 0$, with $\sum_{j=1}^{N} q_j = 1$, such that $f_t(y^{t-1}) = \sum_{j=1}^{N} q_j f_t^{(j)}(y^{t-1})$ for all $t = 1, \ldots, n$ and $y^{t-1} \in \{0, 1\}^{t-1}$. Then*

$$V_n(\mathcal{F}) \leq \sqrt{(n/2) \ln N}.$$

Proof. The key property is that for any bit sequence $y^n \in \{0, 1\}^n$ and expert $f = \sum_{j=1}^{N} q_j f^{(j)} \in \mathcal{F}$ there exists an expert among $f^{(1)}, \ldots, f^{(N)}$ whose loss on y^n is not larger than that of f. To see this, note that

$$
\begin{aligned}
L_f(y^n) &= \sum_{t=1}^{n} |f_t(y^{t-1}) - y_t| \\
&= \sum_{t=1}^{n} \left| \sum_{j=1}^{N} q_j f_t^{(j)}(y^{t-1}) - y_t \right| \\
&= \sum_{t=1}^{n} \sum_{j=1}^{N} q_j \left| f_t^{(j)}(y^{t-1}) - y_t \right| \\
&= \sum_{j=1}^{N} q_j \sum_{t=1}^{n} \left| f_t^{(j)}(y^{t-1}) - y_t \right| \\
&= \sum_{j=1}^{N} q_j L_{f^{(j)}}(y^n) \\
&\geq \min_{j=1,\ldots,N} L_{f^{(j)}}(y^n).
\end{aligned}
$$

Thus, for all $y^n \in \{0, 1\}^n$, $\inf_{f \in \mathcal{F}} L_f(y^n) \geq \min_{j=1,\ldots,N} L_{f^{(j)}}(y^n)$. This implies that if $\widehat{p}$ is the exponentially weighted average forecaster based on the finite class $f^{(1)}, \ldots, f^{(N)}$, then, by Theorem 2.2,

$$\widehat{L}(y^n) - \inf_{f \in \mathcal{F}} L_f(y^y) \le \widehat{L}(y^n) - \min_{j=1,\dots,N} L_{f^{(j)}}(y^n) \le \sqrt{\frac{n \ln N}{2}},$$

which completes the proof. ∎

We now review two basic examples.

Example 8.2 (Linear experts). As a first example, consider the class $\mathcal{L}_k$ of kth-order autoregressive linear experts, where $k \ge 2$ is a fixed positive integer. Because each prediction of an expert $f \in \mathcal{L}_k$ is determined by the last k bits observed, we add an arbitrary prefix $y_{-k+1}, \dots, y_0$ to the sequence y^n to be predicted. We use y_{1-k}^n to denote the resulting sequence of $n + k$ bits. The class $\mathcal{L}_k$ contains all experts f such that

$$f_t(y_{1-k}^{t-1}) = \sum_{i=1}^{k} q_i \, y_{t-i}$$

for some $q_1, \dots, q_k \ge 0$, with $\sum_{i=1}^{k} q_i = 1$. In other words, an expert in $\mathcal{L}_k$ predicts according to a convex combination of the k most recent outcomes in the sequence. Convexity of the coefficients q_i assures that $f_t(y_{1-k}^{t-1}) \in [0, 1]$. Accordingly, for such experts the value $V_n(\mathcal{F})$ is redefined by

$$V_n(\mathcal{F}) = \inf \max_{y_{1-k}^n \in \{0,1\}^{n+k}} \left(\widehat{L}(y_{1-k}^n) - \inf_{f \in \mathcal{F}} L_f(y_{1-k}^n) \right),$$

where

$$\widehat{L}(y_{1-k}^n) = \sum_{t=1}^{n} \left| \widehat{p}_t(y_{1-k}^{t-1}) - y_t \right|,$$

and $L_f(y_{1-k}^n)$ is defined similarly. □

Corollary 8.1. *For all positive integers n and $k \ge 2$,*

$$V_n(\mathcal{L}_k) \le \sqrt{\frac{n \ln k}{2}}.$$

Proof. The statement is a direct consequence of Theorem 8.5 if we observe that $\mathcal{L}_k$ is the convex hull of the k experts $f^{(1)}, \dots, f^{(k)}$ defined by $f_t^{(i)}(y^{t-1}) = y_{t-i}, i = 1, \dots, k$. ∎

Example 8.3 (Markov forecasters). For an arbitrary $k \ge 1$, we consider the class $\mathcal{M}_k$ of kth order Markov experts defined as follows. The class $\mathcal{M}_k$ is indexed by the set $[0, 1]^{2^k}$ so that the index of any $f \in \mathcal{M}_k$ is the vector $\alpha = (\alpha_0, \alpha_1, \dots, \alpha_{2^k-1})$, with $\alpha_s \in [0, 1]$ for $0 \le s < 2^k$. If f has index α, then $f_t(y_{-k+1}^{t-1}) = \alpha_s$ for all $1 \le t \le n$ and for all $y_{-k+1}^{t-1} \in \{0,1\}^{t+k-1}$, where s has binary expansion $y_{t-k}, \dots, y_{t-1}$. Because each prediction of a kth-order Markov expert is determined by the last k bits observed, we add a prefix $y_{-k+1}, \dots, y_0$ to the sequence to predict in the same way we did in the previous example for the autoregressive experts. Thus, the function f_t is now defined over the set $\{0, 1\}^{t+k-1}$. Once more, Theorem 8.5 immediately implies a bound for $V_n(\mathcal{M}_k)$. $\quad\square$

Corollary 8.2. *For any positive integers n and $k \geq 2$,*

$$V_n(\mathcal{M}_k) \leq \sqrt{\frac{2^k n \ln 2}{2}}.$$

Next we study how one can derive lower bounds for $V_n(\mathcal{F})$ for general classes of experts. Even though Theorem 8.1 cannot be generalized to arbitrary classes of experts, its analog remains true as an inequality.

Theorem 8.6. *For any class of experts $\mathcal{F}$,*

$$V_n(\mathcal{F}) \geq \mathbb{E}\left[\sup_{f \in \mathcal{F}} \sum_{t=1}^{n} \left(\frac{1}{2} - f_t(Y^{t-1})\right)(1 - 2Y_t)\right],$$

where $Y_1, \ldots, Y_n$ are independent Bernoulli $(1/2)$ random variables.

Proof. For any prediction strategy, if Y_t is a Bernoulli $(1/2)$ random variable, then $\mathbb{E}|\widehat{p}_t(y^{t-1}) - Y_t| = 1/2$ for each y^{t-1}. Hence,

$$\begin{aligned}
V_n(\mathcal{F}) &\geq \max_{y^n \in \{0,1\}^n} \left(\widehat{L}(y^n) - \inf_{f \in \mathcal{F}} L_f(y^n)\right) \\
&\geq \mathbb{E}\left[\widehat{L}(Y^n) - \inf_{f \in \mathcal{F}} L_f(Y^n)\right] \\
&= \frac{n}{2} - \mathbb{E}\left[\inf_{f \in \mathcal{F}} L_f(Y^n)\right] \\
&= \mathbb{E}\left[\sup_{f \in \mathcal{F}} \sum_{t=1}^{n} \left(\frac{1}{2} - f_t(Y^{t-1})\right)(1 - 2Y_t)\right]. \quad\blacksquare
\end{aligned}$$

We demonstrate how to use this inequality for the example of the class of linear forecasters described earlier. In fact, the following result shows that the bound of Corollary 8.3 is asymptotically optimal.

Corollary 8.3.

$$\liminf_{k \to \infty} \liminf_{n \to \infty} \frac{V_n(\mathcal{L}_k)}{\sqrt{n \ln k}} = \frac{1}{\sqrt{2}}.$$

Proof. We only sketch the proof, the details are left to the reader as an easy exercise. By Theorem 8.6, if we write $Z_t = 1 - 2Y_t$ for $t = -k + 1, \ldots, n$, then

$$V_n(\mathcal{L}_k) \geq \frac{1}{2}\mathbb{E}\left[\sup_{f \in \mathcal{L}_k} \sum_{t=1}^{n} (1 - 2f_t(Y^{t-1}))Z_t\right] \geq \frac{1}{2}\mathbb{E}\left[\max_{i=1,\ldots,k} \sum_{t=1}^{n} Z_t Z_{t-i}\right].$$

The proof is now similar to the proof of Theorem 3.7 with the exception that instead of the ordinary central limit theorem, we use a generalization of it to martingales.

Consider the k-vector $X_n = (X_{n,1}, \ldots, X_{n,k})$ of components

$$X_{n,i} \stackrel{\text{def}}{=} \frac{1}{\sqrt{n}} \sum_{t=1}^{n} Z_t Z_{t-i}, \qquad i = 1, \ldots, k.$$

By the *Cramér–Wold device* (see Lemma 13.11 in the Appendix) the sequence of vectors $\{X_n\}$ converges in distribution to a vector random variable $N = (N_1, \ldots, N_k)$ if and only if $\sum_{i=1}^{k} a_i X_{n,i}$ converges in distribution to $\sum_{i=1}^{k} a_i N_i$ for all possible choices of the coefficients $a_1, \ldots, a_k$. Thus consider

$$\sum_{i=1}^{k} a_i X_{n,i} = \frac{1}{\sqrt{n}} \sum_{t=1}^{n} Z_t \sum_{i=1}^{k} a_i Z_{t-i}.$$

It is easy to see that the sequence of random variables $\sqrt{n}\, X_{n,i}$, $n = 1, 2, \ldots$, forms a martingale with respect to the sequence of σ-algebras $\mathcal{G}_t$ generated by $Z_{-k+1}, \ldots, Z_t$. Furthermore, by the martingale central limit theorem (see, e.g., Hall and Heyde [140, Theorem 3.2]), $\sum_{i=1}^{k} a_i X_{n,i}$ converges in distribution, as $n \to \infty$, to a zero-mean normal random variable with variance $\sum_{i=1}^{k} a_i^2$. Then, by the Cramér–Wold device, as $n \to \infty$, the vector X_n converges in distribution to $N = (N_1, \ldots, N_k)$, where $N_1, \ldots, N_k$ are independent standard normal random variables. The rest of the proof is identical to that of Lemma 13.11 in the Appendix, except that Hoeffding's inequality needs to be replaced by its analog for bounded martingale differences (see Theorem A.7). ∎

8.7 Bibliographic Remarks

The forecaster presented in Section 8.2 appears in Chung [60], which also gives an optimal algorithm for nonsimulatable experts (see the exercises). See Chung [61] for many related results. The form of Khinchine's inequality cited here is due to Szarek [281]. The proof given in the Appendix is due to Littlewood [204]. The example described in Section 8.4 was first studied in detail by Cover [68], and then generalized substantially by Feder, Merhav, and Gutman [95].

Theorem 8.3 is a simple version of Dudley's metric entropy bound [91]. Theorem 8.4 follows from a result of Sudakov [280]; see Ledoux and Talagrand [192]. Understanding the behavior of the expected maximum of random processes, such as the Rademacher process characterizing the minimax regret for classes of static experts, has been an active topic of probability theory, and the first important results go back to Kolmogorov. Some of the key contributions are due to Fernique [97, 98], Pisier [235], and Talagrand [287]. We recommend that the interested reader consult the recent beautiful book of Talagrand [288] for the latest advances.

The Markov experts appearing in Section 8.6 were first considered by Feder, Merhav, and Gutman [95]. See also Cesa-Bianchi and Lugosi [51], where the lower bounds of Section 8.6 appear. We refer to [51] for more information on upper and lower bounds for general classes of experts.

8.8 Exercises

8.1 Calculate $V_n^{(1)}$, $V_1^{(2)}$, $V_2^{(2)}$, and $V_3^{(2)}$. Calculate $V_1(\mathcal{F})$, $V_2(\mathcal{F})$, and $V_3(\mathcal{F})$ when $\mathcal{F}$ contains two experts $f_{1,t} = 0$ and $f_{2,t} = 1$ for all t.

8.2 Prove or disprove

$$\sup_{\mathcal{F} : |\mathcal{F}| = N} V_n(\mathcal{F}) = V_n^{(N)}.$$

8.3 Prove Lemma 8.1. *Hint:* Proceed with a backward induction, starting with $t = n$. Visualizing the possible sequences of outcomes in a rooted binary tree may help.

8.4 Use Lemma 8.1 to show that if $\mathcal{F}$ is a class of static experts, then the optimal forecaster of Section 8.3 may be written as

$$\widehat{p}_t(y^{t-1}) = \frac{1}{2} + \mathbb{E}\left[\frac{\inf_{f \in \mathcal{F}} L_f(y^{t-1}0Y^{n-t}) - \inf_{f \in \mathcal{F}} L_f(y^{t-1}1Y^{n-t})}{2}\right],$$

where $Y_1, \ldots, Y_n$ are i.i.d. Bernoulli $(1/2)$ random variables (Chung [60]).

8.5 Give an appropriate modification of the optimal prediction algorithm of Section 8.2 for the case of general "non-simulatable" experts; that is, give a prediction algorithm that achieves the worst-case regret $V_n^{(N)}$. (See Cesa-Bianchi, Freund, Haussler, Helmbold, Schapire, and Warmuth [48] and Chung [60].) *Warning:* This exercise requires work.

8.6 Show that Lemma 8.1 and Theorem 8.1 are not necessarily true if the experts in $\mathcal{F}$ are not static.

8.7 Show that for the class of experts discussed in Section 8.4

$$\lim_{n \to \infty} \frac{V_n(\mathcal{F})}{\sqrt{n}} = \frac{1}{\sqrt{2\pi}}.$$

8.8 Consider the simple class of experts described in Section 8.4. Feder, Merhav, and Gutman [95] proposed the following forecaster. Let p_t denote the fraction of times outcome 1 appeared in the sequence $y_1, \ldots, y_{t-1}$. Then the forecaster is defined by $\widehat{p}_t = \psi_t(p_t)$, where for $x \in [0, 1]$,

$$\psi_t(x) = \begin{cases} 0 & \text{if } x < 1/2 - \varepsilon_t \\ 1 & \text{if } x > 1/2 + \varepsilon_t \\ 1/2 + (x - 1/2)/(2\varepsilon_t) & \text{otherwise} \end{cases}$$

and $\varepsilon_t > 0$ is some positive number. Show that if $\varepsilon_t = 1/(2\sqrt{t+2})$, then for all $n > 1$ and $y^n \in \{0, 1\}^n$,

$$\widehat{L}(y^n) - \min_{i=1,2} L_i(y^n) \le \sqrt{n+1} + \frac{1}{2}.$$

(See [95].) *Hint:* Show first that among all sequences containing $n_1 < n/2$ 1's the forecaster performs worst for the sequence which starts alternating 0's and 1's n_1 times and ends with $n - 2n_1$ 0's.

8.9 After reading the previous exercise you may wonder whether the simpler forecaster defined by

$$\psi'(x) = \begin{cases} 0 & \text{if } x < 1/2 \\ 1 & \text{if } x > 1/2 \\ 1/2 & \text{if } x = 1/2 \end{cases}$$

also does the job. Show that this is not true. More precisely, show that there exists a sequence y^n such that $\widehat{L}(y^n) - \min_{i=1,2} L_i(y^n) \approx n/4$ for large n. (See [95].)

8.10 Let $\mathcal{F}$ be the class of all static experts of the form $f_t = p$ regardless of t. The class contains all such experts with $p \in [0, 1]$. Estimate the covering numbers $N_2(\mathcal{F}, r)$ and compare the upper and lower bounds of Theorems 8.2 and 8.4 for this case.

8.11 Use Theorem 8.4 to show that the upper bound derived for $V_n(\mathcal{F})$ in Example 8.1 is tight up to a constant.

8.12 Consider the class $\mathcal{F}$ of all static experts that predict in a monotonic way; that is, for each $f \in \mathcal{F}$, either $f_t \le f_{t+1}$ for all $t \ge 1$ or $f_t \ge f_{t+1}$ for all $t \ge 1$. Apply Theorem 8.2 to conclude that

$$V_n(\mathcal{F}) = O\left(\sqrt{n \log n}\right).$$

What do you obtain using Theorem 8.4? Can you apply Theorem 8.5 in this case?

8.13 Construct a forecaster such that for *all* $k = 1, 2, \ldots$ and all sequences $y_1, y_2, \ldots$,

$$\limsup_{n \to \infty} \frac{1}{n} \left(\widehat{L}(y^n) - \inf_{f \in \mathcal{M}_k} L_f(y^n) \right) = 0.$$

In other words, the forecaster predicts asymptotically as well as any Markov forecaster of any order. (The existence of such a forecaster was shown by Feder, Merhav, and Gutman [95].) *Hint:* For an easy construction use the doubling trick.

8.14 Show that

$$\liminf_{k \to \infty} \liminf_{n \to \infty} \frac{V_n(\mathcal{M}_k)}{\sqrt{2^k n \ln 2}} = \frac{1}{\sqrt{2}}.$$

Hint: Mimic the proof of Corollary 8.3.

9

Logarithmic Loss

9.1 Sequential Probability Assignment

This chapter is entirely devoted to the investigation of a special loss function, the *logarithmic* loss, sometimes also called *self-information* loss. The reason for this distinguished attention is that this loss function has a meaningful interpretation in various sequential decision problems, including repeated gambling and data compression. These problems are briefly described later. Sequential prediction aimed at minimizing logarithmic loss is also intimately related to maximizing benefits by repeated investment in the stock market. This application is studied in Chapter 10.

Now we describe the setup for the whole chapter. Let $m > 1$ be a fixed positive integer and let the outcome space be $\mathcal{Y} = \{1, 2, \ldots, m\}$. The decision space is the probability simplex

$$\mathcal{D} = \left\{ \mathbf{p} = (p(1), \ldots, p(m)) : \sum_{j=1}^{m} p(j) = 1, \ p(j) \geq 0, j = 1, \ldots, m \right\} \subset \mathbb{R}^m.$$

A vector $\mathbf{p} \in \mathcal{D}$ is often interpreted as a probability distribution over the set $\mathcal{Y}$. Indeed, in some cases, the forecaster is required to assign a probability to each possible outcome, representing the forecaster's belief. For example, weather forecasts often take the form "the possibility of rain is 40%."

In the entire chapter we consider the model of *simulatable* experts introduced in Section 2.9. Thus, an expert f is a sequence $(\mathbf{f}_1, \mathbf{f}_2, \ldots)$ of functions $\mathbf{f}_t : \mathcal{Y}^{t-1} \to \mathcal{D}$, so that after having seen the past outcomes y^{t-1}, expert f outputs the probability vector $\mathbf{f}_t(\cdot \mid y^{t-1}) \in \mathcal{D}$. (If $t = 1$, $\mathbf{f}_1 = (f_1(1), \ldots, f_1(m))$ is simply an element of $\mathcal{D}$.) For the components of this vector we write

$$f_t(1 \mid y^{t-1}), \ldots, f_t(m \mid y^{t-1}).$$

This notation emphasizes the analogy between an expert and a probability distribution. Indeed, the jth component of the vector $f_t(j \mid y^{t-1})$ may be interpreted as the *conditional* probability f assigns to the jth element of $\mathcal{Y}$ given the past y^{t-1}.

Similarly, at each time instant the forecaster chooses a probability vector

$$\widehat{\mathbf{p}}_t(\cdot \mid y^{t-1}) = \left(\widehat{p}_t(1 \mid y^{t-1}), \ldots, \widehat{p}_t(m \mid y^{t-1}) \right).$$

Once again, using the analogy with probability distributions, we may introduce, for all $n \geq 1$ and $y^n \in \mathcal{Y}^n$, the notation

$$f_n(y^n) = \prod_{t=1}^{n} f_t(y_t \mid y^{t-1}), \qquad \widehat{p}_n(y^n) = \prod_{t=1}^{n} \widehat{p}_t(y_t \mid y^{t-1}).$$

Observe that

$$\sum_{y^n \in \mathcal{Y}^n} f_n(y^n) = \sum_{y^n \in \mathcal{Y}^n} \widehat{p}_n(y^n) = 1$$

and therefore expert f, as well as the forecaster, define probability distributions over the set of all sequences of length n. Conversely, any probability distribution $\widehat{p}_n(y^n)$ over the set $\mathcal{Y}^n$ defines a forecaster by the induced conditional distributions

$$\widehat{p}_t(y_t \mid y^{t-1}) = \frac{\widehat{p}_t(y^t)}{\widehat{p}_{t-1}(y^{t-1})},$$

where $\widehat{p}_t(y^t) = \sum_{y_{t+1}^n \in \mathcal{Y}^{n-t}} \widehat{p}_n(y^n)$.

The loss function we consider throughout this chapter is defined by

$$\ell(\mathbf{p}, y) = \sum_{j=1}^{m} \mathbb{I}_{\{y=j\}} \ln \frac{1}{p(j)} = \ln \frac{1}{p(y)}, \qquad y \in \mathcal{Y}, \mathbf{p} \in \mathcal{D}.$$

It is clear from the definition of the loss function that the goal of the forecaster is to assign a large probability to the outcomes in the sequence. For an outcome sequence $y_1, \ldots, y_n$ the cumulative loss of expert f and the forecaster are, respectively,

$$L_f(y^n) = \sum_{t=1}^{n} \ln \frac{1}{f_t(y_t \mid y^{t-1})} \quad \text{and} \quad \widehat{L}(y^n) = \sum_{t=1}^{n} \ln \frac{1}{\widehat{p}_t(y_t \mid y^{t-1})}.$$

The cumulative loss of an expert f may also be written as $L_f(y^n) = -\ln f_n(y^n)$. (Similarly, $\widehat{L}(y^n) = -\ln \widehat{p}_n(y^n)$.) In other words, the cumulative loss is just the negative log likelihood assigned to the outcome sequence by the expert f. Given a class $\mathcal{F}$ of experts, the difference between the cumulative loss of the forecaster and that of the best expert, that is, the regret, may now be written as

$$\widehat{L}(y^n) - \inf_{f \in \mathcal{F}} L_f(y^n) = \sum_{t=1}^{n} \ln \frac{1}{\widehat{p}_t(y_t \mid y^{t-1})} - \inf_{f \in \mathcal{F}} \sum_{t=1}^{n} \ln \frac{1}{f_t(y_t \mid y^{t-1})}$$

$$= \sup_{f \in \mathcal{F}} \ln \frac{f_n(y^n)}{\widehat{p}_n(y^n)}.$$

The regret may be interpreted as the logarithm of the ratio of the total probabilities that are sequentially assigned to the outcome sequence by the forecaster and the experts.

Remark 9.1 (*Infinite alphabets*). We restrict the discussion to the case when the outcome space is a finite set. Note, however, that most results can be extended easily to the more general case when $\mathcal{Y}$ is a measurable space. In such cases the decision space becomes the set of all densities over $\mathcal{Y}$ with respect to some fixed common dominating measure, and the loss is the negative logarithm of the density evaluated at the outcome.

We begin the study of prediction under the logarithmic loss by considering *mixture forecasters*, the most natural predictors for this case. In Section 9.3 we briefly describe two applications, gambling and sequential data compression, in which the logarithmic loss function appears in a natural way. These applications have served as a main motivation for the large body of work done on prediction using this loss function. A special property of the logarithmic loss is that the minimax optimal predictor can be explicitly determined for any class $\mathcal{F}$ of experts. This is done in Section 9.4. In Sections 9.6 and 9.7 we discuss, in detail, the special case when $\mathcal{F}$ contains all *constant predictors*. Two versions of mixture forecasters are described and it is shown that their performance approximates that of the minimax optimal predictor. Section 9.8 describes another phenomenon specific to the logarithmic loss. We obtain lower bounds conceptually stronger than minimax lower bounds for some special yet important classes of experts. In Section 9.9 we extend the setup by allowing side information taking values in a finite set. In Section 9.10 a general upper bound for the minimax regret is derived in terms of the geometrical structure of the class of experts. The examples of Section 9.11 show how this general result can be applied to various special cases.

9.2   Mixture Forecasters

Recall from Section 3.3 that the logarithmic loss function is exp-concave for $\eta \le 1$ and Theorem 3.2 applies. Thus, if the class $\mathcal{F}$ of experts is finite and $|\mathcal{F}| = N$, then the exponentially weighted average forecaster with parameter $\eta = 1$ satisfies

$$\widehat{L}(y^n) - \inf_{f \in \mathcal{F}} L_f(y^n) \le \ln N$$

or, equivalently,

$$\widehat{p}_n(y^n) \ge \frac{1}{N} \sup_{f \in \mathcal{F}} f_n(y^n).$$

It is worth noting that the exponentially weighted average forecaster has an interesting interpretation in this special case. Observe that the definition

$$\widehat{p}_t(y_t \mid y^{t-1}) = \frac{\sum_{f \in \mathcal{F}} f_t(y_t \mid y^{t-1}) e^{-\eta L_f(y^{t-1})}}{\sum_{f \in \mathcal{F}} e^{-\eta L_f(y^{t-1})}}$$

of the exponentially weighted average forecaster, with parameter $\eta = 1$, reduces to

$$\widehat{p}_t(y_t \mid y^{t-1}) = \frac{\sum_{f \in \mathcal{F}} f_t(y_t \mid y^{t-1}) f_{t-1}(y^{t-1})}{\sum_{f \in \mathcal{F}} f_{t-1}(y^{t-1})} = \frac{\sum_{f \in \mathcal{F}} f_t(y^t)}{\sum_{f \in \mathcal{F}} f_{t-1}(y^{t-1})}.$$

Thus, the total probability the forecaster assigns to a sequence y^n is just

$$\widehat{p}_n(y^n) = \prod_{t=1}^{n} \frac{\sum_{f \in \mathcal{F}} f_t(y^t)}{\sum_{f \in \mathcal{F}} f_{t-1}(y^{t-1})} = \frac{\sum_{f \in \mathcal{F}} f_n(y^n)}{N}$$

(recall that $f(y^0)$ is defined to be equal to 1). In other words, the probability distribution the exponentially weighted average forecaster $\widehat{p}$ defines over the set $\mathcal{Y}^n$ of all strings of length n is just the uniform *mixture* of the distributions defined by the experts. This is why we sometimes call the exponentially weighted average forecaster *mixture forecaster*.

Interestingly, for the logarithmic loss, with $\eta = 1$, the mixture forecaster coincides with the greedy forecaster, and it is also an aggregating forecaster, as we show in Sections 3.4 and 3.5.

Recalling that the aggregating forecaster may be generalized for a countable number of experts, we may consider the following extension. Let $f^{(1)}, f^{(2)}, \ldots$ be the experts of a countable family $\mathcal{F}$. To define the mixture forecaster, we assign a nonnegative number $\pi_i \geq 0$ to each expert $f^{(i)} \in \mathcal{F}$ such that $\sum_{i=1}^{\infty} \pi_i = 1$. Then the aggregating forecaster becomes

$$
\widehat{p}_t(y_t \mid y^{t-1}) = \frac{\sum_{i=1}^{\infty} \pi_i f_t^{(i)}(y_t \mid y^{t-1}) f_{t-1}^{(i)}(y^{t-1})}{\sum_{j=1}^{\infty} \pi_j f_{t-1}^{(j)}(y^{t-1})}
$$

$$
= \frac{\sum_{i=1}^{\infty} \pi_i f_t^{(i)}(y_t \mid y^{t-1}) e^{-\eta L_{f^{(i)}}(y^{t-1})}}{\sum_{j=1}^{\infty} \pi_j e^{-\eta L_{f^{(j)}}(y^{t-1})}}.
$$

Now it is obvious that the joint probability the forecaster $\widehat{p}$ assigns to each sequence y^n is

$$
\widehat{p}_n(y^n) = \sum_{i=1}^{\infty} \pi_i f^{(i)}(y^n).
$$

Note that $\widehat{p}$ indeed defines a valid probability distribution over $\mathcal{Y}^n$. Using the trivial bound $\widehat{p}_n(y^n) = \sum_{i=1}^{\infty} \pi_i f^{(i)}(y^n) \geq \pi_k f^{(k)}(y^n)$ for all k, we obtain, for all $y^n \in \mathcal{Y}^n$,

$$
\widehat{L}(y^n) \leq \inf_{i=1,2,\ldots} \left(L_{f^{(i)}}(y^n) + \ln \frac{1}{\pi_i} \right).
$$

This inequality is a special case of the "oracle inequality" derived in Section 3.5.

Because of their analogy with mixture estimators emerging in bayesian statistics, the mixture forecaster is sometimes called *bayesian mixture* or *bayesian model averaging*, and the "initial" weights π_i *prior probabilities*. Because our setup is not bayesian, we avoid this terminology.

Later in this chapter we extend the idea of a mixture forecaster to certain uncountably infinite classes of experts (see also Section 3.3).

9.3 Gambling and Data Compression

Imagine that we gamble in a horse race in which m horses run repeatedly many times. In the tth race we bet our entire fortune on the m horses according to proportions $\widehat{p}_t(1), \ldots, \widehat{p}_t(m)$, where the $\widehat{p}_t(j)$ are nonnegative numbers with $\sum_{j=1}^{m} \widehat{p}_t(j) = 1$. If horse j wins the tth race, we multiply our money bet on this horse by a factor of $o_t(j)$ and we lose it otherwise. The *odds* $o_t(j)$ are arbitrary positive numbers. In other words, if y_t denotes the index of the winning horse of the tth race, after the tth race we multiply our capital by a factor of

$$
\sum_{j=1}^{m} \mathbb{I}_{\{y_t=j\}} \widehat{p}_t(j) o_t(j) = \widehat{p}_t(y_t) o_t(y_t).
$$

To make it explicit that the proportions $\widehat{p}_t(j)$ according to which we bet may depend on the results of previous races, we write $\widehat{p}_t(j \mid y^{t-1})$. If we start with an initial capital of C

units, our capital after n races is

$$C \prod_{t=1}^{n} \widehat{p}_t(y_t \mid y^{t-1}) o_t(y_t).$$

Now assume that before each race we ask the advice of a class of experts and our goal is to win almost as much as the best of these experts. If expert f divides his capital in the tth race according to proportions $f_t(j \mid y^{t-1})$, $j = 1, \ldots, m$, and starts with the same initial capital C, then his capital after n races becomes

$$C \prod_{t=1}^{n} f_t(y_t \mid y^{t-1}) o_t(y_t).$$

The ratio between the best expert's money and ours is thus

$$\frac{\sup_{f \in \mathcal{F}} C \prod_{t=1}^{n} f_t(y_t \mid y^{t-1}) o_t(y_t)}{C \prod_{t=1}^{n} \widehat{p}_t(y_t \mid y^{t-1}) o_t(y_t)} = \sup_{f \in \mathcal{F}} \frac{f_n(y^n)}{\widehat{p}_n(y^n)}$$

independently of the odds. The logarithm of this quantity is just the difference of the cumulative logarithmic loss of the forecaster $\widehat{p}$ and that of the best expert described in the previous section. In Chapter 10 we discuss in great detail a model of gambling (i.e., sequential investment) that is more general than the one described here. We will see that sequential probability assignment under the logarithmic loss function is the key in the more general model as well.

Another important motivation for the study of the logarithmic loss function has its roots in information theory, more concretely in lossless source coding. Instead of describing the sequential data compression problem in detail, we briefly mention that it is well known that any probability distribution f_n over the set $\mathcal{Y}^n$ defines a *code* (the so-called *Shannon–Fano code*), which assigns, to each string $y^n \in \mathcal{Y}^n$, a *codeword*, that is, a string of bits of length $\Lambda_n(y^n) = \lceil -\log_2 f_n(y^n) \rceil$. Conversely, any code with codeword lengths $\Lambda_n(y^n)$, satisfying a natural condition (i.e., unique decodability), defines a probability distribution by $f_n(y^n) = 2^{-\Lambda_n(y^n)} / \sum_{x^n \in \mathcal{Y}^n} 2^{-\Lambda_n(x^n)}$. Given a class of codes, or equivalently, a class $\mathcal{F}$ of experts, the best compression of a string y^n is achieved by the code that minimizes the length $\lceil -\log_2 f_n(y^n) \rceil$, which is approximately equivalent to minimizing the logarithmic cumulative loss $L_f(y^n)$. Now assume that the symbols of the string y^n are revealed one by one and the goal is to compress it almost as well as the best code in the class. It turns out that for any forecaster $\widehat{p}_n$ (i.e., sequential probability assignment) it is possible to construct, sequentially, a codeword of length about $-\log_2 \widehat{p}_n(y^n)$ using a method called *arithmetic coding*. The regret

$$-\log_2 \widehat{p}_n(y^n) - \inf_{f \in \mathcal{F}} \left(-\log_2 f_n(y^n) \right) = \frac{1}{\ln 2} \left(\widehat{L}(y^n) - \inf_{f \in \mathcal{F}} L_f(y^n) \right)$$

is often called the *(pointwise) redundancy* of the code with respect to the class of codes $\mathcal{F}$. In this respect, the problem of sequential lossless data compression is equivalent to sequential prediction under the logarithmic loss.

9.4   The Minimax Optimal Forecaster

In this section we investigate the *minimax regret*, defined in Section 2.10 for the logarithmic loss. An important distinguishing feature of the logarithmic loss function is that the minimax optimal forecaster can be determined explicitly. This fact facilitates the investigation of the minimax regret, which, in turn, serves as a standard to which the performance of any forecaster should be compared. Recall that for a given class $\mathcal{F}$ of experts, and integer $n > 0$, the minimax regret is defined by

$$V_n(\mathcal{F}) = \inf_{\hat{p}} \sup_{y^n \in \mathcal{Y}^n} \left(\widehat{L}(y^n) - \inf_{f \in \mathcal{F}} L_f(y^n) \right) = \inf_{\hat{p}} \sup_{y^n \in \mathcal{Y}^n} \ln \frac{\sup_{f \in \mathcal{F}} f_n(y^n)}{\widehat{p}_n(y^n)}.$$

If for a given forecaster $\widehat{p}$ we define the worst-case regret by

$$V_n(\widehat{p}, \mathcal{F}) = \sup_{y^n \in \mathcal{Y}^n} \left(\widehat{L}(y^n) - \inf_{f \in \mathcal{F}} L_f(y^n) \right),$$

then $V_n(\mathcal{F}) = \inf_{\hat{p}} V_n(\widehat{p}, \mathcal{F})$. Interestingly, in the case of the logarithmic loss it is possible to identify explicitly the unique forecaster achieving the minimax regret. Theorem 9.1 shows that the forecaster p^* defined by the *normalized maximum likelihood* probability distribution

$$p_n^*(y^n) = \frac{\sup_{f \in \mathcal{F}} f_n(y^n)}{\sum_{x^n \in \mathcal{Y}^n} \sup_{f \in \mathcal{F}} f_n(x^n)}$$

has this property. Note that p_n^* is indeed a probability distribution over the set $\mathcal{Y}^n$, and recall that this probability distribution defines a forecaster by the corresponding conditional probabilities $p_t^*(y_t \mid y^{t-1})$.

Theorem 9.1. *For any class $\mathcal{F}$ of experts and integer $n > 0$, the normalized maximum likelihood forecaster p^* is the unique forecaster such that*

$$\sup_{y^n \in \mathcal{Y}^n} \left(\widehat{L}(y^n) - \inf_{f \in \mathcal{F}} L_f(y^n) \right) = V_n(\mathcal{F}).$$

Moreover, p^* is an equalizer; that is, for all $y^n \in \mathcal{Y}^n$,

$$\ln \frac{\sup_{f \in \mathcal{F}} f_n(y^n)}{p_n^*(y^n)} = \ln \sum_{x^n \in \mathcal{Y}^n} \sup_{f \in \mathcal{F}} f_n(x^n) = V_n(\mathcal{F}).$$

Proof.   First we show the second part of the statement. Note that by the definition of p^*, its cumulative loss satisfies

$$\widehat{L}(y^n) - \inf_{f \in \mathcal{F}} L_f(y^n) = \ln \frac{\sup_{f \in \mathcal{F}} f_n(y^n)}{p_n^*(y^n)}$$

$$= \ln \sum_{x^n \in \mathcal{Y}^n} \sup_{f \in \mathcal{F}} f_n(x^n),$$

which is independent of y^n, so p^* is indeed an equalizer.

To show that p^* is minimax optimal, let $p \neq p^*$ be an arbitrary forecaster. Then since $\sum_{y^n \in \mathcal{Y}^n} p_n(y^n) = \sum_{y^n \in \mathcal{Y}^n} p_n^*(y^n) = 1$, for some $y^n \in \mathcal{Y}^n$ we must have $p_n(y^n) < p_n^*(y^n)$. But then, for this y^n,

$$\ln \frac{\sup_{f \in \mathcal{F}} f_n(y^n)}{p_n(y^n)} > \ln \frac{\sup_{f \in \mathcal{F}} f_n(y^n)}{p_n^*(y^n)} = \text{const.} = V_n(p^*, \mathcal{F})$$

by the equalizer property. Hence,

$$V_n(p, \mathcal{F}) = \sup_{y^n \in \mathcal{Y}^n} \ln \frac{\sup_{f \in \mathcal{F}} f_n(y^n)}{p_n(y^n)} > V_n(p^*, \mathcal{F}),$$

which proves the theorem. ∎

In Section 2.10 we show that, under general conditions satisfied here, the maximin regret

$$U_n(\mathcal{F}) = \sup_q \inf_{\hat{p}} \sum_{y^n \in \mathcal{Y}^n} q(y^n) \ln \frac{\sup_{f \in \mathcal{F}} f_n(y^n)}{\hat{p}_n(y^n)}$$

equals the minimax regret $V_n(\mathcal{F})$. It is evident that the normalized maximum likelihood forecaster p^* achieves the maximin regret as well, in the sense that for any probability distribution q over $\mathcal{Y}^n$,

$$U_n(\mathcal{F}) = \sup_q \sum_{y^n \in \mathcal{Y}^n} q(y^n) \ln \frac{\sup_{f \in \mathcal{F}} f_n(y^n)}{p_n^*(y^n)}.$$

Even though we have been able to determine the minimax optimal forecaster explicitly, note that the practical implementation of the forecaster may be problematic. First of all, we determined the forecaster via the joint probabilities it assigns to all strings of length n, and calculation of the actual predictions $p_t^*(y_t \mid y^{t-1})$ involves sums of exponentially many terms.

It is important to point out that previous knowledge of the total length n of the sequence to be predicted is necessary to determine the minimax optimal forecaster p^*. Indeed, it is easy to see that if the minimax optimal forecaster is determined for a certain horizon n, then the forecaster is not the extension of the minimax optimal forecaster for horizon $n - 1$, even for nicely structured classes of experts. (See Exercise 9.4.)

Theorem 9.1 not only describes the minimax optimal forecaster but also gives a useful formula for the minimax regret $V_n(\mathcal{F})$, which we study in detail in the subsequent sections.

9.5 Examples

Next we work out a few simple examples to understand better the behavior of the minimax regret $V_n(\mathcal{F})$.

Finite Classes

To start with the simplest possible case, consider a finite class of experts with $|\mathcal{F}| = N$. Then clearly,

$$
\begin{aligned}
V_n(\mathcal{F}) &= \ln \sum_{y^n \in \mathcal{Y}^n} \sup_{f \in \mathcal{F}} f_n(y^n) \\
&\leq \ln \sum_{y^n \in \mathcal{Y}^n} \sum_{f \in \mathcal{F}} f(y^n) \\
&= \ln \sum_{f \in \mathcal{F}} \sum_{y^n \in \mathcal{Y}^n} f(y^n) \\
&= \ln N.
\end{aligned}
$$

Of course, we already know this. In fact, the mixture forecaster described in Section 9.1 achieves the same bound. In Exercise 9.3 we point out that this upper bound cannot be improved in the sense that there exist classes of N experts such that the minimax regret equals $\ln N$. With the notation introduced in Section 2.10, $V_n^{(N)} = \ln N$ (if $n \geq \log_2 N$).

The mixture forecaster has obvious computational advantages over the normalized maximum likelihood forecaster and does not suffer from the "horizon-dependence" of the latter mentioned earlier. These bounds suggest that one does not lose much by using the simple uniform mixture forecaster instead of the optimal but horizon-dependent forecaster. We will see later that this fact remains true in more general settings, even for certain infinite classes of experts. However, as it is pointed out in Exercise 9.7, even if $\mathcal{F}$ is finite, in some cases $V_n(\mathcal{F})$ may be significantly smaller than the worst-case loss achievable by any mixture forecaster.

Constant Experts

Next we consider the class $\mathcal{F}$ of all experts such that $f_t(j \mid y^{t-1}) = f(j)$ (with $f(j) \geq 0$, $\sum_{j=1}^{m} f(j) = 1$) for each $f \in \mathcal{F}$ and independently of t and y^{t-1}. In other words, $\mathcal{F}$ contains all forecasters f_n so that the associated probability distribution over $\mathcal{Y}^n$ is a product distribution with identical components. Here we only consider the case when $m = 2$. This simplifies the notation and the calculations while all the main ideas remain present. Generalization to $m > 2$ is straightforward, and we leave the calculations as exercises.

If $m = 2$, (i.e., $\mathcal{Y} = \{1, 2\}$ and $\mathcal{D} = \{(q, 1 - q) \in \mathbb{R}^2 : q \in [0, 1]\}$), each expert in $\mathcal{F}$ may be identified with a number $q \in [0, 1]$ representing $q = f(1)$. Thus, this expert predicts, at each time t, according to the vector $(q, 1 - q) \in \mathcal{D}$, regardless of t and the past outcomes $y_1, \ldots, y_{t-1}$. We call this class the class of *constant experts*. Next we determine the asymptotic value of the minimax regret $V_n(\mathcal{F})$ for this class.

Theorem 9.2. *The minimax regret $V_n(\mathcal{F})$ of the class $\mathcal{F}$ of all constant experts over the alphabet $\mathcal{Y} = \{1, 2\}$ defined above satisfies*

$$
V_n(\mathcal{F}) = \frac{1}{2} \ln n + \frac{1}{2} \ln \frac{\pi}{2} + \varepsilon_n,
$$

where $\varepsilon_n \to 0$ as $n \to \infty$.

Proof. Recall that by Theorem 9.1,

$$V_n(\mathcal{F}) = \ln \sum_{y^n \in \mathcal{Y}^n} \sup_{f \in \mathcal{F}} f_n(y^n).$$

Now assume that the number of 1's in the sequence $y^n \in \{1, 2\}^n$ is n_1 and the number of 2's is $n_2 = n - n_1$. Then for the expert f that predicts according to $(q, 1 - q)$, we have $f_n(y^n) = q^{n_1}(1 - q)^{n_2}$.

Then it is easy to see, for example, by differentiating the logarithm of the above expression, that this is maximized for $q = n_1/n$, and therefore

$$V_n(\mathcal{F}) = \ln \sum_{y^n \in \mathcal{Y}^n} \left(\frac{n_1}{n}\right)^{n_1} \left(\frac{n_2}{n}\right)^{n_2}.$$

Since there are $\binom{n}{n_1}$ sequences containing exactly n_1 1's, we have

$$V_n(\mathcal{F}) = \ln \sum_{n_1=1}^{n-1} \binom{n}{n_1} \left(\frac{n_1}{n}\right)^{n_1} \left(\frac{n_2}{n}\right)^{n_2}.$$

We show the proof of the upper bound $V_n(\mathcal{F}) \le \frac{1}{2}\ln n + \frac{1}{2}\ln \frac{\pi}{2} + o(1)$, whereas the similar proof of the lower bound is left as an exercise. Recall Stirling's formula

$$\sqrt{2\pi n}\left(\frac{n}{e}\right)^n e^{1/(12n)} \le n! \le \sqrt{2\pi n}\left(\frac{n}{e}\right)^n e^{1/(12n+1)}$$

(see, e.g., Feller [96]). Using this to approximate the binomial coefficients, each term of the sum may be bounded as

$$\binom{n}{n_1} \left(\frac{n_1}{n}\right)^{n_1} \left(\frac{n_2}{n}\right)^{n_2} \le \frac{1}{\sqrt{2\pi}} \sqrt{\frac{n}{n_1 n_2}} e^{1/(12n+1)}.$$

Thus,

$$V_n(\mathcal{F}) \le \ln\left(\sqrt{\frac{n}{2\pi}} e^{1/(12n+1)} \sum_{n_1=1}^{n-1} \frac{1}{\sqrt{n_1 n_2}}\right).$$

Writing the last sum in the expression as

$$\sum_{n_1=1}^{n-1} \frac{1}{\sqrt{n_1 n_2}} = \sum_{n_1=1}^{n-1} \frac{1}{n} \frac{1}{\sqrt{\frac{n_1}{n}\left(1 - \frac{n_1}{n}\right)}},$$

we notice that it is just a Riemann approximation of the integral

$$\int_0^1 \frac{1}{\sqrt{x(1-x)}}\, dx = \pi$$

(see the exercises). This implies that $\lim_{n\to\infty} \sum_{n_1=1}^{n-1} 1/\sqrt{n_1 n_2} = \pi$, and so

$$V_n(\mathcal{F}) \le \ln\left((1 + o(1))\sqrt{\frac{n\pi}{2}}\right)$$

as desired. ∎

Remark 9.2. *(m-ary alphabet).* In the general case, when $m \geq 2$ is a positive integer, Theorem 9.2 becomes

$$V_n(\mathcal{F}) = \frac{m-1}{2} \ln \frac{n}{2\pi} + \ln \frac{\Gamma(1/2)^m}{\Gamma(m/2)} + o(1),$$

where Γ denotes the Gamma function (see Exercise 9.8). The fact that the minimax regret grows as a constant times $\ln n$, the constant being the half of the number of "free parameters," is a general phenomenon. In Section 9.9 we discuss the class of *Markov experts*, a generalization of the class of constant experts discussed here, that also obeys this formula. We study $V_n(\mathcal{F})$ in a much more general setting in Section 9.10. In particular, Corollary 9.1 in Section 9.11 establishes a result showing that, under general conditions, $V_n(\mathcal{F})$ behaves like $\frac{k}{2} \ln n$, where k is the "dimension" of class $\mathcal{F}$.

9.6   The Laplace Mixture

The purpose of this section is to introduce the idea of mixture forecasters discussed in Section 9.2 to certain uncountably infinite classes of experts. In Section 3.3 we have already extended the exponentially weighted average forecaster over the convex hull of a finite set of experts for general exp-concave loss functions. Special properties of the logarithmic loss allow us to derive sharp bounds and to bring the mixture forecaster into a particularly simple form.

For simplicity we show the idea for the class of all constant experts introduced in Section 9.5. Once again, we gain simplicity by considering only the case of $m = 2$. That is, the outcome space is $\mathcal{Y} = \{1, 2\}$ and $\mathcal{D} = \{(q, 1-q) \in \mathbb{R}^2 : q \in [0, 1]\}$, so that each expert in $\mathcal{F}$ predicts, at each time t, according to the vector $(q, 1-q) \in \mathcal{D}$ regardless of t and the past outcomes $y_1, \ldots, y_{t-1}$. Theorem 9.2 shows that $V_n(\mathcal{F}) \approx \frac{1}{2} \ln n + \frac{1}{2} \ln \frac{\pi}{2}$.

In Section 9.5 we pointed out that, for finite classes of experts, the exponentially weighted average forecaster assigns, to each sequence y^n, the average of the probabilities assigned by each expert; that is, $\widehat{p}_n(y^n) = \frac{1}{N} \sum_{i=1}^{N} f_n^{(i)}(y^n)$.

This idea may be generalized in a natural way to the class of constant experts. As before, let n_1 and n_2 denote the number of 1's and 2's in a sequence y^n. Then the probability assigned to such a sequence by any expert in the class has the form $q^{n_1}(1-q)^{n_2}$. The *Laplace mixture* of these experts is defined as the forecaster that assigns, to any $y^n \in \{1, 2\}^n$, the average of all these probabilities according to the uniform distribution over the class $\mathcal{F}$; that is,

$$\widehat{p}_n(y^n) = \int_0^1 q^{n_1}(1-q)^{n_2} dq.$$

After calculating this integral, it will be easy to understand the behavior of the forecaster.

Lemma 9.1.

$$\int_0^1 q^{n_1}(1-q)^{n_2} dq = \frac{1}{(n+1)\binom{n}{n_1}}.$$

Proof. We may prove the equality by a backward induction with respect to n_1. If $n_1 = n$, we clearly have $\int_0^1 q^n \mathrm{d}q = 1/(n+1)$. On the other hand, assuming

$$\int_0^1 q^{n_1+1}(1-q)^{n_2-1}\mathrm{d}q = \frac{1}{(n+1)\binom{n}{n_1+1}}$$

and integrating by parts, we obtain

$$\int_0^1 q^{n_1}(1-q)^{n_2}\mathrm{d}q = \frac{n-n_1}{n_1+1} \int_0^1 q^{n_1+1}(1-q)^{n_2-1}\mathrm{d}q$$

$$= \frac{n-n_1}{n_1+1} \times \frac{1}{(n+1)\binom{n}{n_1+1}}$$

$$= \frac{1}{(n+1)\binom{n}{n_1}}. \quad\blacksquare$$

The first thing we observe is that the actual predictions of the Laplace mixture forecaster can be calculated very easily and have a natural interpretation. Assume that the number of 1's and 2's in the past outcome sequence y^{t-1} are t_1 and t_2. Then the probability the Laplace forecaster assigns to the next outcome being 1 is, by Lemma 9.1,

$$\widehat{p}_t(1 \mid y^{t-1}) = \frac{\widehat{p}_t(y^{t-1}1)}{\widehat{p}_{t-1}(y^{t-1})} = \frac{\frac{1}{(t+1)\binom{t}{t_1+1}}}{\frac{1}{t\binom{t-1}{t_1}}} = \frac{t_1+1}{t+1}.$$

Similarly, $\widehat{p}_t(2 \mid y^{t-1}) = (t_2+1)/(t+1)$. We may interpret $\widehat{p}_t(1 \mid y^{t-1})$ as a slight modification of the relative frequency $t_1/(t-1)$. In fact, the Laplace forecaster may be interpreted as a "smoothed" version of the empirical frequencies. By smoothing, one prevents infinite losses that may occur if $t_1 = 0$ or $t_2 = 0$. All we need to analyze the cumulative loss of the Laplace mixture is a simple property of binomial coefficients.

Lemma 9.2. *For all $1 \le k \le n$,*

$$\binom{n}{k} \le \frac{1}{\left(\frac{k}{n}\right)^k \left(\frac{n-k}{n}\right)^{n-k}}.$$

Proof. If the random variables $Y_1, \ldots, Y_n$ are drawn i.i.d. according to the distribution $\mathbb{P}[Y_i = 1] = 1 - \mathbb{P}[Y_i = 2] = k/n$, then the probability that exactly k of them equals 1 is $\binom{n}{k}\left(\frac{k}{n}\right)^k \left(\frac{n-k}{n}\right)^{n-k}$ and therefore this last expression cannot be larger than 1. $\quad\blacksquare$

Theorem 9.3. *The regret of the Laplace mixture forecaster satisfies*

$$\sup_{y^n \in \{1,2\}^n} \left(\widehat{L}(y^n) - \inf_{f \in \mathcal{F}} L_f(y^n) \right) = \ln(n+1).$$

Proof. Let n_1 and n_2 denote the number of 1's and 2's in the sequence y^n. We have already observed in the proof of Theorem 9.2 that

$$\sup_{q \in [0,1]} q^{n_1}(1-q)^{n_2} = \left(\frac{n_1}{n}\right)^{n_1} \left(\frac{n_2}{n}\right)^{n_2}.$$

Thus, the regret of the forecaster for such a sequence is

$$
\widehat{L}(y^n) - \inf_{f \in \mathcal{F}} L_f(y^n) = \ln \frac{\sup_{q \in [0,1]} q^{n_1}(1-q)^{n_2}}{\int_0^1 q^{n_1}(1-q)^{n_2}\,dq}
$$

$$
= \ln \frac{\left(\frac{n_1}{n}\right)^{n_1}\left(\frac{n_2}{n}\right)^{n_2}}{\frac{1}{(n+1)\binom{n}{n_1}}} \qquad \text{(by Lemma 9.1)}
$$

$$
\leq \ln(n+1) \qquad \text{(by Lemma 9.2).}
$$

Equality is achieved for the sequence $y^n = (1, 1, \ldots, 1)$. ∎

Thus, the extremely simple Laplace mixture forecaster achieves an excess cumulative loss that is of the same order of magnitude as that of the minimax optimal forecaster, though the leading constant is 1 instead of $1/2$. In the next section we show that a slight modification of the forecaster achieves this optimal leading constant as well.

***Remark* 9.3.** Theorem 9.3 can be extended, in a straightforward way, to the general case of alphabet size $m \geq 2$. In this case,

$$
\sup_{y^n \in \mathcal{Y}^n} \left(\widehat{L}(y^n) - \inf_{f \in \mathcal{F}} L_f(y^n) \right) = \ln \binom{n+m-1}{m-1} \leq (m-1)\ln(n+1)
$$

(see Exercise 9.10).

9.7   A Refined Mixture Forecaster

With a small modification of the Laplace forecaster, we may obtain a mixture forecaster that achieves a worst-case regret comparable to that of the minimax optimal normalized maximum likelihood forecaster. The proof of Theorem 9.3 reveals that the Laplace mixture achieves the largest regret for sequences containing either very few 1's or very few 0's. Because the optimal forecaster is an equalizer (recall Theorem 9.1), a good forecaster should attempt to achieve a nearly equal regret for all sequences. This may be done by modifying the mixture so that it gives a slightly larger weight to those experts that predict well on these critical sequences. The idea, first suggested by Krichevsky and Trofimov, is to use, instead of the uniform weighting distribution, the Beta $(1/2, 1/2)$ density $1/\left(\pi\sqrt{q(1-q)}\right)$. (See Section A.1.9 for some basic properties of the Beta family of densities.) Thus, we define the Krichevsky–Trofimov mixture forecaster by

$$
\widehat{p}_n(y^n) = \int_0^1 \frac{q^{n_1}(1-q)^{n_2}}{\pi\sqrt{q(1-q)}}\,dq,
$$

where we use the notation of the previous section. It is easy to see, by a recursive argument similar to the one seen in the proof of Lemma 9.1, that the predictions of the Krichevsky–Trofimov mixture may be calculated by

$$
\widehat{p}_t(1 \mid y^{t-1}) = \frac{t_1 + 1/2}{t},
$$

a formula very similar to that obtained in the case of the Laplace forecaster.

The performance of the forecaster is easily bounded once the following lemma is established.

Lemma 9.3. *For all $q \in [0, 1]$,*

$$\int_0^1 \frac{q^{n_1}(1-q)^{n_2}}{\pi\sqrt{q(1-q)}} \, dq \geq \frac{1}{2\sqrt{n}} \left(\frac{n_1}{n}\right)^{n_1} \left(\frac{n_2}{n}\right)^{n_2}.$$

The proof is left as an exercise. On the basis of this lemma we immediately derive the following performance bound.

Theorem 9.4. *The regret of the Krichevsky–Trofimov mixture forecaster satisfies*

$$\sup_{y^n \in \{1,2\}^n} \left(\widehat{L}(y^n) - \inf_{f \in \mathcal{F}} L_f(y^n)\right) \leq \frac{1}{2}\ln n + \ln 2.$$

Proof.

$$
\begin{aligned}
\widehat{L}(y^n) - \inf_{f \in \mathcal{F}} L_f(y^n) &= \ln \frac{\sup_{q \in [0,1]} q^{n_1}(1-q)^{n_2}}{\displaystyle\int_0^1 \frac{q^{n_1}(1-q)^{n_2}}{\pi\sqrt{q(1-q)}}\, dq} \\[2mm]
&= \ln \frac{\left(\dfrac{n_1}{n}\right)^{n_1}\left(\dfrac{n_2}{n}\right)^{n_2}}{\displaystyle\int_0^1 \frac{q^{n_1}(1-q)^{n_2}}{\pi\sqrt{q(1-q)}}\, dq} \\[2mm]
&\leq \ln\left(2\sqrt{n}\right) \qquad \text{(by Lemma 9.3)}
\end{aligned}
$$

as desired. ∎

Remark 9.4. The Krichevsky–Trofimov mixture estimate may be generalized to the class of all constant experts when the outcome space is $\mathcal{Y} = \{1, \ldots, m\}$, where $m \geq 2$ is an arbitrary integer. In this case the mixture is calculated with respect to the so-called Dirichlet$(1/2, \cdots, 1/2)$ density

$$\phi(\mathbf{p}) = \frac{\Gamma(m/2)}{\Gamma(1/2)^m} \prod_{j=1}^{m} \frac{1}{\sqrt{p(j)}}$$

over the probability simplex $\mathcal{D}$, containing all vectors $\mathbf{p} = \big(p(1), \ldots, p(m)\big) \in \mathbb{R}^m$ with nonnegative components and adding up to 1. As for the bound of Theorem 9.4, one may show that the worst-case regret of the obtained forecaster

$$\widehat{p}_n(y^n) = \int_{\mathcal{D}} \prod_{j=1}^{m} p(j)^{n_j} \phi(\mathbf{p}) \, d\mathbf{p}$$

(where $n_1, \ldots, n_m$ denote the number of occurrences of each symbol in the string y^n) is upper bounded by

$$\frac{m-1}{2}\ln n + \ln \frac{\Gamma(1/2)^m}{\Gamma(m/2)} + \frac{m-1}{2}\ln 2 + o(1).$$

This upper bound exceeds the minimax regret by just a constant $\frac{m-1}{2} \ln 2$. Moreover, the forecaster may easily be calculated by the simple formula

$$\widehat{p}_t(i \mid y^{t-1}) = \frac{t_i + 1/2}{t - 1 + m/2}, \qquad i = 1, \ldots, m,$$

where t_i denotes the number of occurrences of i in y^{t-1}.

To understand the behavior of the Krichevsky–Trofimov forecaster, we derive a lower bound for its regret that holds for *every* sequence y^n of outcomes. The following result shows that this mixture forecaster is indeed an approximate equalizer, since no matter what the sequence y^n is, its regret differs from $\frac{1}{2} \ln n$ by at most a constant. (Recall that the minimax optimal forecaster is an exact equalizer.)

Theorem 9.5. *For all outcome sequences $y^n \in \{0, 1\}^n$, the regret of the Krichevsky–Trofimov mixture forecaster satisfies*

$$\widehat{L}(y^n) - \inf_{f \in \mathcal{F}} L_f(y^n) = \frac{1}{2} \ln n + \Theta(1).$$

Proof. Fix an outcome sequence y^n. As before, let n_1 and n_2 denote the number of occurrences of 1's and 2's in y^n. It suffices to derive a lower bound for the ratio of $\max_{q \in [0,1]} q^{n_1}(1-q)^{n_2} = (n_1/n)^{n_1}(n_2/n)^{n_2}$ and the Krichevsky–Trofimov mixture probability $\widehat{p}_n(y^n)$. To this end, observe that this probability may be expressed in terms of the gamma function as

$$\widehat{p}_n(y^n) = \frac{\Gamma\left(n_1 + \frac{1}{2}\right) \Gamma\left(n_2 + \frac{1}{2}\right)}{\pi \, n!}$$

(see Section A.1.9). Thus,

$$\widehat{L}(y^n) - \inf_{f \in \mathcal{F}} L_f(y^n) - \frac{1}{2} \ln n = \ln \frac{\pi \, n! \, n_1^{n_1} n_2^{n_2}}{\Gamma\left(n_1 + \frac{1}{2}\right) \Gamma\left(n_2 + \frac{1}{2}\right) n^n \sqrt{n}}.$$

In order to investigate this quantity, introduce the function

$$F(n_1, n_2) = \frac{\pi \, (n_1 + n_2)! \, n_1^{n_1} n_2^{n_2}}{\Gamma\left(n_1 + \frac{1}{2}\right) \Gamma\left(n_2 + \frac{1}{2}\right) (n_1 + n_2)^{n_1 + n_2} \sqrt{n_1 + n_2}} \qquad (9.1)$$

defined for all pairs of positive integers n_1, n_2. A straightforward calculation, left as an exercise, shows that F is decreasing in both of its arguments. Hence, $F(n_1, n_2) \geq F(n, n)$, and therefore

$$\widehat{L}(y^n) - \inf_{f \in \mathcal{F}} L_f(y^n) - \frac{1}{2} \ln n \geq \ln \frac{\pi \, (2n)! \, n^{2n}}{\Gamma\left(n + \frac{1}{2}\right)^2 (2n)^{2n} \sqrt{2n}}.$$

Using Stirling's approximation $\Gamma(x) = \sqrt{2\pi} \, (x/e)^x / \sqrt{x}(1 + o(1))$ as $x \to \infty$, it is easy to see that the right-hand side converges to a positive constant as $n \to \infty$. ∎

9.8 Lower Bounds for Most Sequences

In Section 9.4 we determined the minimax regret $V_n(\mathcal{F})$ exactly for any arbitrary class $\mathcal{F}$ of experts. The definition of $V_n(\mathcal{F})$ implies that for any forecaster $\widehat{p}_n$ there exists a sequence $y^n \in \mathcal{Y}^n$ such that the regret $\widehat{L}(y^n) - \inf_{f \in \mathcal{F}} L_f(y^n)$ is at least as large as $V_n(\mathcal{F})$. In this section we point out that in some cases one may obtain much stronger lower bounds. In fact, we show that for some classes $\mathcal{F}$, no matter what the forecaster $\widehat{p}_n$ is, the regret cannot be much smaller than $V_n(\mathcal{F})$ for "most" sequences of outcomes y^n. This indicates that the minimax value is achieved not only for an exceptional unfortunate sequence of outcomes, but in fact for "most" of them. (Of course, since the minimax optimal forecaster is an equalizer, we already knew this for p_n^*. The result shown in this section indicates that all forecasters share this property.) What we mean by "most" will be made clear later. We just note here that the word "most" does not directly refer to cardinality.

In this section, just like in the previous ones, we focus on the special case of binary alphabet $\mathcal{Y} = \{1, 2\}$ and the class $\mathcal{F}$ of constant experts. This is the simplest case for which the basic ideas may be seen in a transparent way. The result obtained for this simple class may be generalized to more complex cases such as constant experts over an m-ary alphabet, Markov experts, and classes of experts based on finite state machines. Some of these cases are left to the reader as exercises.

Thus, the class we consider $\mathcal{F}$ contains all probability distributions on $\{1, 2\}^n$ that assign, to any sequence $y^n \in \{1, 2\}^n$, probability $q^j (1 - q)^{n-j}$, where j is the number of 1's in the sequence and $q \in [0, 1]$ is the parameter determining the expert. Recall that for such a sequence the best expert assigns probability

$$\max_{q \in [0,1]} q^j (1 - q)^{n-j} = \left(\frac{j}{n}\right)^j \left(\frac{n-j}{n}\right)^{n-j}$$

and therefore $\inf_{f \in \mathcal{F}} L_f(y^n) = -j \ln \frac{j}{n} - (n - j) \ln \frac{n-j}{n}$.

Next we formulate the result. To this end, we partition the set $\{1, 2\}^n$ into $n + 1$ classes of *types* according to the number of 1's contained in the sequence. To this purpose, define the sets

$$T_j = \left\{ y^n \in \{1, 2\}^n \ : \ \text{the number of 1's in } y^n \text{ is exactly } j \right\}, \qquad j = 0, 1, \dots, n.$$

In Theorem 9.6 think of δ_n as a small positive number, and $\varepsilon_n \ll \delta_n$ even smaller but still not too small. For example, one may consider $\delta_n \sim 1/\ln\ln n$ and $\varepsilon_n \sim 1/\ln n$ or $\delta_n \sim 1/\sqrt{\ln\ln n}$ and $\varepsilon_n \sim 1/\ln\ln n$ to get a meaningful result.

Theorem 9.6. *Consider the class $\mathcal{F}$ of constant experts over the binary alphabet $\mathcal{Y} = \{1, 2\}$. Let ε_n be a positive number, and consider an arbitrary forecaster $\widehat{p}_n$. Define the set*

$$A = \left\{ y^n \in \{1, 2\}^n \ : \ \widehat{L}(y^n) \leq \inf_{f \in \mathcal{F}} L_f(y^n) + \frac{1}{2} \ln n - \ln \frac{C}{\varepsilon_n} \right\},$$

where $C = \sqrt{\pi}\, e^{1/6} / \sqrt{2} \approx 1.4806$. Then, for any $\delta_n > 0$,

$$\left| \left\{ j \ : \ \frac{|A \cap T_j|}{|T_j|} > \delta_n \right\} \right| \leq \frac{n \varepsilon_n}{\delta_n}.$$

If ε_n is small, the set A contains all sequences for which the regret of the forecaster $\widehat{p}_n$ is significantly smaller than the minimax value $V_n(\mathcal{F}) \approx \frac{1}{2} \ln n$ (see Theorem 9.2).

Theorem 9.6 states that if $\varepsilon_n \ll \delta_n$, the vast majority of types T_j are such that the proportion of sequences in T_j falling in A is smaller than δ_n.

Remark 9.5. The interpretation we have given to Theorem 9.6 is that for any forecaster, the regret cannot be significantly smaller than the minimax value for "most" sequences. What the theorem really means is that for the majority of classes T_j the subset of sequences of T_j for which the regret is small is tiny. However, the theorem does not imply that there exist few sequences in $\{1, 2\}^n$ for which the regret is small. Just note that a relatively small number of classes of types (say, those with j between $n/2 - 10\sqrt{n}$ and $n/2 + 10\sqrt{n}$) contain the vast majority of sequences. Indeed, the forecaster that assigns the uniform probability 2^{-n} to all sequences will work reasonably well for a huge number of sequences. This example shows that the notion of "most" considered in Theorem 9.6 may be more adequate than just counting sequences.

Proof.   First observe that the logarithm of the cardinality of each class T_j may be bounded, using Stirling's formula, by

$$\ln |T_j| = \ln \binom{n}{j}$$

$$\geq \ln \left(\frac{n}{j}\right)^j \left(\frac{n}{n-j}\right)^{n-j} + \ln \frac{\sqrt{n}}{\sqrt{2\pi\, j(n-j)}\, e^{1/6}}$$

$$\geq \ln \left(\frac{n}{j}\right)^j \left(\frac{n}{n-j}\right)^{n-j} - \frac{1}{2}\ln n - \ln C,$$

where at the last step we used the inequality $\sqrt{j(n-j)} \leq n/2$. Therefore, for any sequence $y^n \in T_j$, we have

$$\inf_{f \in \mathcal{F}} L_f(y^n) \leq \ln |T_j| + \frac{1}{2}\ln n + \ln C.$$

This implies that if $y^n \in A \cap T_j$, then

$$\widehat{L}(y^n) \leq \ln |T_j| + \ln n - \ln \frac{1}{\varepsilon_n}$$

or, in other words,

$$\widehat{p}_n(y^n) \geq \frac{1}{|T_j| n \varepsilon_n}.$$

To finish the proof, note that

$$\left|\left\{ j : \frac{|A \cap T_j|}{|T_j|} > \delta_n \right\}\right| \leq \frac{1}{\delta_n} \sum_{j=0}^{n} \frac{|A \cap T_j|}{|T_j|}$$

$$= \frac{1}{\delta_n} \sum_{y^n \in A} \frac{1}{|T(y^n)|}$$

$$\text{(where } T(y^n) \text{ denotes the set } T_j \text{ containing } y^n\text{)}$$

$$\leq \frac{n\varepsilon_n}{\delta_n} \sum_{y^n \in A} \widehat{p}_n(y^n)$$

$$\leq \frac{n\varepsilon_n}{\delta_n}. \quad \blacksquare$$

9.9   Prediction with Side Information

The purpose of this section is to extend the framework of prediction when the forecaster has access to certain "side information." At each time instant, before making a prediction, a side information symbol is revealed to the forecaster. In our setup this side information is completely arbitrary, it may contain any external information and it may even depend on the sequence to be predicted. In this section we restrict our attention to the case when side information comes from a finite set. In Chapter 11 we develop a general framework of prediction with side information when the side information is a finite-dimensional vector, and the class of experts contains linear functions of the side information. The formal setup is the following.

We consider prediction of sequences taking values in a finite alphabet $\mathcal{Y} = \{1, \ldots, m\}$. Let K be a positive integer, and let $\mathcal{G}_1, \ldots, \mathcal{G}_K$ be "base" classes of static forecasters. (We assume the static property to lighten notation, the definitions and the results that follow can be generalized easily.) The class $\mathcal{G}_j$ contains forecasters of the form

$$g^{(j)}(y^n) = \prod_{t=1}^{n} g_t^{(j)}(y_t),$$

where for each $t = 1, \ldots, n$ the vector $\left(g_t^{(j)}(1), \ldots, g_t^{(j)}(m)\right)$ is an element of the probability simplex $\mathcal{D}$ in $\mathbb{R}^m$. At each time t, a side information symbol $z_t \in \mathcal{Z} = \{1, \ldots, K\}$ becomes available to the forecaster. The class $\mathcal{F}$ of forecasters against which our predictor competes contains all forecasters f of the form

$$f_t(y \mid y^{t-1}, z_t) = f_t(y \mid z_t) = g_{\bar{t}_{z_t}}^{(z_t)}(y),$$

where for each j, $\bar{t}_j$ is the length of the sequence of times $s < t$ such that $z_s = j$. In other words, each f ignores the past and uses the side information symbol z_t to pick a class $\mathcal{G}_{z_t}$. In this class a forecaster is determined on the basis of the subsequence of the past defined by the time instances when the side information coincided with the actual side information z_t. Note that in some sense f is static, but z_t may depend in an arbitrary manner on the sequence of past (or even future) outcomes.

The loss of $f \in \mathcal{F}$ for a given sequence of outcomes $y^n \in \mathcal{Y}^n$ and side information $z^n \in \mathcal{Z}^n$ is

$$-\sum_{t=1}^{n} \ln f_t(y_t \mid y^{t-1}, z_t) = -\sum_{t=1}^{n} \ln g_{\bar{t}_{z_t}}^{(z_t)}(y_t).$$

Our goal is to define forecasters $\widehat{p}_t$ whose cumulative loss

$$-\sum_{t=1}^{n} \ln \widehat{p}_t(y_t \mid y^{t-1}, z_t)$$

is close to that of the best expert $\inf_{f \in \mathcal{F}} -\sum_{t=1}^{n} \ln f_t(y_t \mid y^{t-1}, z_t)$ for all outcome sequences $y^n \in \mathcal{Y}^n$ and side-information sequences $z^n \in \mathcal{Z}^n$. Assume that for each static expert class $\mathcal{G}_j$ we have a forecaster $q^{(j)}$ with worst-case regret

$$V_n(q^{(j)}, \mathcal{G}_j) = \sup_{y^n \in \mathcal{Y}^n} \sup_{g^{(j)} \in \mathcal{G}_j} \sum_{t=1}^{n} \ln \frac{g_t^{(j)}(y_t)}{q_t^{(j)}(y_t \mid y^{t-1})}.$$

On the basis of these "elementary" forecasters, we may define, in a natural way, the following forecaster p with side information

$$p_t(y \mid y^{t-1}, z_t) = q_{\bar{t}_{z_t}}^{(z_t)}(y \mid \overline{y}_{z_t}^t),$$

where for each j, $\overline{y}_j^t$ denotes the sequence of y_s's ($s < t$) such that $z_s = j$. In other words, the forecaster p looks back at the past sequence $y_1, \ldots, y_{t-1}$ and considers only those time instants at which the side-information symbol agreed with the current symbol z_t. The prediction of p is just that of $q^{(z_t)}$ based on these past symbols. The performance of p may be bounded easily as follows.

Theorem 9.7. *For any outcome sequence $y^n \in \mathcal{Y}^n$ and side information sequence $z^n \in \mathcal{Z}^n$, the regret of forecaster p with respect to all forecasters in class $\mathcal{F}$ satisfies*

$$\sup_{f \in \mathcal{F}} \sum_{t=1}^{n} \ln \frac{f_t(y_t \mid y^{t-1}, z_t)}{p_t(y_t \mid y^{t-1}, \overline{y}_{z_t}^t)} \leq \sum_{j=1}^{K} V_{\overline{n}_j}(q^{(j)}, \mathcal{G}_j),$$

where $\overline{n}_j = \sum_{t=1}^{n} \mathbb{I}_{\{z_t = j\}}$ is the number of occurrences of symbol j in the side-information sequence.

Proof.

$$\sup_{f \in \mathcal{F}} \sum_{t=1}^{n} \ln \frac{f_t(y_t \mid y^{t-1}, z_t)}{p_t(y_t \mid y^{t-1}, z_t)}$$

$$= \sup_{f \in \mathcal{F}} \sum_{t=1}^{n} \ln \frac{g_{\bar{t}_{z_t}}^{(z_t)}(y_t)}{q_{\bar{t}_{z_t}}^{(z_t)}(y_t \mid \overline{y}_{z_t}^t)} \qquad \text{(by definition of } p\text{)}$$

$$= \sup_{f \in \mathcal{F}} \sum_{j=1}^{K} \left(\sum_{t=1}^{n} \mathbb{I}_{\{z_t = j\}} \ln \frac{g_{\bar{t}_j}^{(j)}(y_t)}{q_{\bar{t}_j}^{(j)}(y_t \mid \overline{y}_j^t)} \right)$$

$$= \sum_{j=1}^{K} \sup_{g^{(j)} \in \mathcal{G}_j} \sum_{t=1}^{n} \mathbb{I}_{\{z_t = j\}} \ln \frac{g_{\bar{t}_j}^{(j)}(y_t)}{q_{\bar{t}_j}^{(j)}(y_t \mid \overline{y}_j^t)}$$

(because the expression within the parentheses depends only on $g^{(j)}$)

$$\leq \sum_{j=1}^{K} V_{\overline{n}_j}(q^{(j)}, \mathcal{G}_j). \qquad \blacksquare$$

The next simple example sheds some light on the power of this simple result.

Example 9.1 (Markov forecasters). Let $k \geq 1$ and consider the class $\mathcal{M}_k$ of all kth order stationary Markov experts defined over the binary alphabet $\mathcal{Y} = \{1, 2\}$. More precisely, $\mathcal{M}_k$ contains all forecasters f for which the prediction at time t is a function of the last k outcomes $(y_{t-k}, \ldots, y_{t-1})$ (independent of t and outcomes y_s for $s < t - k$). In other words, for a Markov forecaster one may write $f_t(y \mid y^{t-1}) = f_t(y \mid y_{t-k}^{t-1})$. Such forecasters are also considered in Section 8.6 for different loss functions. As each prediction of a kth order Markov expert is determined by the last k bits observed, we add a prefix $y_{-k+1}, \ldots, y_0$ to the sequence to predict in the same way as we did in Section 8.6.

To obtain an upper bound for the minimax regret $V_n(\mathcal{M}_k)$, we may use Theorem 9.7 in a simple way. The side information z_t is now defined as $(y_{t-k}, \dots, y_{t-1})$, that is, z_t takes one of $K = 2^k$ values. If we define $\mathcal{G}_1 = \cdots = \mathcal{G}_K$ as the class $\mathcal{G}$ of all constant experts over the alphabet $\mathcal{Y} = \{1, 2\}$ defined in the previous sections, then it is easy to see that class $\mathcal{F}$ of all forecasters using the side information $(y_{t-k}, \dots, y_{t-1})$ is just class $\mathcal{M}_k$. Let $q^{(1)} = \cdots = q^{(k)}$ be the Krichevsky–Trofimov forecaster for class $\mathcal{G}$, and define the forecaster f as in Theorem 9.7. Then, according to Theorem 9.7, for any sequence of outcomes y_{-k+1}^n the loss of f may be bounded as

$$\widehat{L}(y^n) - \inf_{f \in \mathcal{M}_k} L_f(y^n) \le \sum_{j=1}^{2^k} V_{\bar{n}_j}(\mathcal{G}).$$

According to Theorem 9.4,

$$V_n(\mathcal{G}) \le \frac{1}{2} \ln n + \ln 2.$$

Using this bound, we obtain

$$\widehat{L}(y^n) - \inf_{f \in \mathcal{M}_k} L_f(y^n) \le \sum_{j=1}^{2^k} \frac{1}{2} \ln \bar{n}_j + 2^k \ln 2$$

$$\le \frac{1}{2} \ln \left(\frac{1}{2^k} \sum_{j=1}^{2^k} \bar{n}_j \right)^{2^k} + 2^k \ln 2$$

$$= \frac{2^k}{2} \ln \frac{n}{2^k} + 2^k \ln 2,$$

where we used the arithmetic–geometric mean inequality.

The upper bound obtained this way can be shown to be quite sharp. Indeed, the minimax regret $V_n(\mathcal{M}_k)$ may be seen to behave like $2^{k-1} \ln(n/2^k)$ (see Exercise 9.13). $\qquad\square$

9.10 A General Upper Bound

Next we investigate the minimax regret $V_n(\mathcal{F})$ for general classes of experts. We derive a general bound that shows how the "size" of the class $\mathcal{F}$ affects the cumulative regret.

To any class $\mathcal{F}$ of experts, we associate the metric d defined as

$$d(f, g) = \sqrt{\sum_{t=1}^n \sup_{y^t} \left(\ln f(y_t \mid y^{t-1}) - \ln g(y_t \mid y^{t-1}) \right)^2}.$$

Denote by $N(\mathcal{F}, \varepsilon)$ the ε-covering number of $\mathcal{F}$ under the metric d. Recall that for any $\varepsilon > 0$, the ε-covering number is the cardinality of the smallest subset $\mathcal{F}' \subset \mathcal{F}$ such that for all $f \in \mathcal{F}$ there exists a $g \in \mathcal{F}'$ such that $d(f, g) \le \varepsilon$. The main result of this section is the following upper bound.

Theorem 9.8. *For any class $\mathcal{F}$ of experts,*

$$V_n(\mathcal{F}) \le \inf_{\varepsilon > 0} \left(\ln N(\mathcal{F}, \varepsilon) + 24 \int_0^\varepsilon \sqrt{\ln N(\mathcal{F}, \delta)}\, d\delta \right).$$

Note that if $\mathcal{F}$ is a finite class, then the right-hand side converges to $\ln |\mathcal{F}|$ as $\varepsilon \to 0$, and therefore we recover our earlier general bound. However, even for finite classes, the right-hand side may be significantly smaller than $\ln |\mathcal{F}|$. Also, this result allows us to derive upper bounds for very general classes of experts.

As a first step in the proof of Theorem 9.8, we obtain a weak bound for $V_n(\mathcal{F})$. This will be later refined to prove the stronger bound of Theorem 9.8.

Lemma 9.4. *For any class $\mathcal{F}$ of experts,*

$$V_n(\mathcal{F}) \le 24 \int_0^{D/2} \sqrt{\ln N(\mathcal{F}, \varepsilon)}\, d\varepsilon,$$

where $D = \sup_{f,g \in \mathcal{F}} d(f, g)$ is the diameter of $\mathcal{F}$.

Proof. Recall that, by the equalizer property of the normalized maximum likelihood forecaster p^* established in Theorem 9.1, for all $y^n \in \mathcal{Y}^n$, $V_n(\mathcal{F}) = \sup_{f \in \mathcal{F}} \ln \frac{f_n(y^n)}{p_n^*(y^n)}$. Because the right-hand side is a constant function of y^n, we may take any weighted average of it without changing its value. The trick is to weight the average according to the probability distribution defined by p^*. Thus, we may write

$$V_n(\mathcal{F}) = \sum_{y^n \in \mathcal{Y}^n} \left(\sup_{f \in \mathcal{F}} \ln \frac{f_n(y^n)}{p_n^*(y^n)} \right) p_n^*(y^n).$$

If we introduce a vector $Y^n = (Y_1, \ldots, Y_n)$ of random variables distributed according to p_n^*, we obtain

$$
\begin{aligned}
V_n(\mathcal{F}) &= \mathbb{E}\left[\sup_{f \in \mathcal{F}} \ln \frac{f_n(Y^n)}{p_n^*(Y^n)} \right] \\
&= \mathbb{E}\left[\sup_{f \in \mathcal{F}} \sum_{t=1}^n \ln \frac{f_t(Y_t \mid Y^{t-1})}{p_t^*(Y_t \mid Y^{t-1})} \right] \\
&\le \mathbb{E}\left[\sup_{f \in \mathcal{F}} \sum_{t=1}^n \left(\ln \frac{f(Y_t \mid Y^{t-1})}{p^*(Y_t \mid Y^{t-1})} - \mathbb{E}\left[\ln \frac{f(Y_t \mid Y^{t-1})}{p^*(Y_t \mid Y^{t-1})} \,\Big|\, Y^{t-1} \right] \right) \right],
\end{aligned}
$$

where the last step follows from the nonnegativity of the Kullback–Leibler divergence of the conditional densities, that is, from the fact that

$$\mathbb{E}\left[\ln \frac{p^*(Y_t \mid Y^{t-1} = y^{t-1})}{f(Y_t \mid Y^{t-1} = y^{t-1})} \right] \ge 0$$

(see Section A.2). Now, for each $f \in \mathcal{F}$ let

$$T_f(y^n) = \frac{1}{2} \sum_{t=1}^n \left(\ln \frac{f(y_t \mid y^{t-1})}{p^*(y_t \mid y^{t-1})} - \mathbb{E}\left[\ln \frac{f(Y_t \mid Y^{t-1})}{p^*(Y_t \mid Y^{t-1})} \,\Big|\, Y^{t-1} \right] \right)$$

so we have $V_n(\mathcal{F}) \le 2\, \mathbb{E}\left[\sup_{f \in \mathcal{F}} T_f \right]$, where we write $T_f = T_f(Y^n)$.

To obtain a suitable upper bound for this quantity, we apply Theorem 8.3. To do this, we need to show that the process $\{T_f : f \in \mathcal{F}\}$ is indeed a subgaussian family under the metric d. (Sample continuity of the process is obvious.) To this end, note that for any $f, g \in \mathcal{F}$,

$$T_f(y^n) - T_g(y^n) = \sum_{t=1}^{n} Z_t(y^t),$$

where

$$Z_t(y^t) = \frac{1}{2}\left(\ln\frac{f(y_t \mid y^{t-1})}{g(y_t \mid y^{t-1})} - \mathbb{E}\left[\ln\frac{f(Y_t \mid Y^{t-1} = y^{t-1})}{g(Y_t \mid Y^{t-1} = y^{t-1})}\right]\right).$$

Now it is easy to see that $T_f - T_g = T_f(Y^n) - T_g(Y^n)$ is a sum of bounded martingale differences with respect to the sequence $Y_1, Y_2, \ldots, Y_n$; that is, each term Z_t has zero conditional mean and range bounded by $2d_t(f, g)$. Then Lemma A.6 implies that, for all $\lambda > 0$,

$$\mathbb{E}\left[e^{\lambda(T_f - T_g)}\right] \le \exp\left(\frac{\lambda^2}{2}d(f, g)^2\right).$$

Thus, the family $\{T_f : f \in \mathcal{F}\}$ is indeed subgaussian. Hence, using $V_n(\mathcal{F}) \le 2\mathbb{E}\left[\sup_{f \in \mathcal{F}} T_f\right]$ and applying Theorem 8.3 we obtain the statement of the lemma. ∎

Proof of Theorem 9.8. To prove the main inequality, we partition $\mathcal{F}$ into small subclasses and calculate the minimax forecaster for each subclass. Lemma 9.4 is then applied in each subclass. Finally, the optimal forecasters for these subclasses are combined by a simple finite mixture.

Fix an arbitrary $\varepsilon > 0$ and let $\mathcal{G} = \{g_1, \ldots, g_N\}$ be an ε-covering of $\mathcal{F}$ of minimal size $N = N(\mathcal{F}, \varepsilon)$. Determine the subsets $\mathcal{F}_1, \ldots, \mathcal{F}_N$ of $\mathcal{F}$ by

$$\mathcal{F}_i = \{f \in \mathcal{F} : d(f, g_i) \le d(f, g_j) \text{ for all } j = 1, \ldots, N\};$$

that is, $\mathcal{F}_i$ contains all experts that are closest to g_i in the covering. Clearly, the union of $\mathcal{F}_1, \ldots, \mathcal{F}_N$ is $\mathcal{F}$. For each $i = 1, \ldots, N$, let $g^{(i)}$ denote the normalized maximum likelihood forecaster for $\mathcal{F}_i$

$$g_n^{(i)}(y^n) = \frac{\sup_{f \in \mathcal{F}_i} f_n(y^n)}{\sum_{x^n \in \mathcal{Y}^n} \sup_{f \in \mathcal{F}_i} f_n(x^n)}.$$

Now let the forecaster p_ε be the uniform mixture of "experts" $g^{(1)}, \ldots, g^{(N)}$. Clearly, $V_n(\mathcal{F}) \le \inf_{\varepsilon > 0} V_n(p_\varepsilon, \mathcal{F})$. Thus, all we have to do is to bound the regret of p_ε. To this end, fix any $y^n \in \mathcal{Y}^n$ and let $k = k(y^n)$ be the index of the subset $\mathcal{F}_k$ containing the best expert for sequence y^n; that is,

$$\ln\sup_{f \in \mathcal{F}} f(y^n) = \ln\sup_{f \in \mathcal{F}_k} f(y^n).$$

Then

$$\ln \frac{\sup_{f \in \mathcal{F}} f(y^n)}{p_\varepsilon(y^n)} = \ln \frac{g^{(k)}(y^n)}{p_\varepsilon(y^n)} + \ln \frac{\sup_{\mathcal{F}_k} f(y^n)}{g^{(k)}(y^n)}.$$

On the one hand, by the upper bound for the loss of the mixture forecaster,

$$\sup_{y^n} \ln \frac{g^{(k)}(y^n)}{p_\varepsilon(y^n)} \le \ln N.$$

On the other hand,

$$\sup_{y^n} \ln \frac{\sup_{\mathcal{F}_k} f(y^n)}{g^{(k)}(y^n)} \le \max_{i=1,\dots,N} \sup_{y^n} \ln \frac{\sup_{\mathcal{F}_i} f(y^n)}{g^{(i)}(y^n)} = \max_{i=1,\dots,N} V_n(\mathcal{F}_i).$$

Hence, we get

$$V_n(p_\varepsilon, \mathcal{F}) \le \ln N + \max_{i=1,\dots,N} V_n(\mathcal{F}_i).$$

Now note that the diameter of each element of partition $\mathcal{F}_1, \dots, \mathcal{F}_N$ is at most 2ε. Hence, applying Lemma 9.4 to each $\mathcal{F}_i$, we find that

$$V_n(p_\varepsilon, \mathcal{F}) \le \ln N + \max_{i=1,\dots,N} 24 \int_0^\varepsilon \sqrt{\ln N(\mathcal{F}_i, \delta)} \, d\delta,$$

$$\le \ln N(\mathcal{F}, \varepsilon) + 24 \int_0^\varepsilon \sqrt{\ln N(\mathcal{F}, \delta)} \, d\delta,$$

which concludes the proof. ∎

Theorem 9.8 requires the existence of finite coverings of $\mathcal{F}$ in the metric d. But since the definition of d involves the logarithm of the experts' predictions, this is only possible if all $f_i(j \mid y^{t-1})$ are bounded away from 0. If the class of experts $\mathcal{F}$ does not satisfy this property, one may appeal to the following simple property. For simplicity, we state the lemma for the binary-alphabet case $m = 2$. Its extension to $m > 2$ is obvious.

Lemma 9.5. *Let $m = 2$, and let $\mathcal{F}$ be a class of experts. Define the class $\mathcal{F}^{(\delta)}$ as the set of all experts $f^{(\delta)}$ of the form*

$$f_t^{(\delta)}(1 \mid y^{t-1}) = \tau_\delta\big(f_t(1 \mid y^{t-1})\big),$$

where

$$\tau_\delta(x) = \begin{cases} \delta & \text{if } x < \delta \\ x & \text{if } x \in [\delta, 1 - \delta] \\ 1 - \delta & \text{if } x > 1 - \delta \end{cases}$$

for some fixed $0 < \delta < 1/2$. Then $V_n(\mathcal{F}) \le V_n(\mathcal{F}^{(\delta)}) + 2n\delta$.

Thus, to obtain bounds for $V_n(\mathcal{F})$, we may first calculate a bound for the truncated class $\mathcal{F}^{(\delta)}$ using Theorem 9.8 and then choose δ to optimize the right-hand side of the inequality of Lemma 9.5. The bound of the lemma is convenient but quite crude, and the resulting bounds are not always optimal.

Proof. Simply observe that for any sequence y^n, and any $f \in \mathcal{F}$,

$$\ln f_n(y^n)$$

$$= \sum_{t=1}^{n} \ln f_t(y_t \mid y^{t-1})$$

$$\leq \sum_{t:\, f_t^{(\delta)}(y_t|y^{t-1})<1-\delta} \ln f_t^{(\delta)}(y_t \mid y^{t-1}) + \sum_{t:\, f_t^{(\delta)}(y_t|y^{t-1})=1-\delta} \ln 1$$

$$\leq \sum_{t:\, f_t^{(\delta)}(y_t|y^{t-1})<1-\delta} \ln f_t^{(\delta)}(y_t \mid y^{t-1}) \sum_{t:\, f_t^{(\delta)}(y_t|y^{t-1})=1-\delta} \left(\ln(1-\delta) + 2\delta\right)$$

(since $\ln 1 \leq \ln(1-\delta) + \delta/(1-\delta)$ by concavity, and using $0 < \delta < 1/2$)

$$\leq \sum_{t=1}^{n} \left(\ln f_t^{(\delta)}(y_t \mid y^{t-1}) + 2\delta\right)$$

$$= \ln f_n^{(\delta)}(y^n) + 2n\delta.$$

Thus, for any forecaster $\widehat{p}$,

$$\widehat{L}(y^n) - \inf_{f \in \mathcal{F}} L_f(y^n) = -\ln \widehat{p}_n(y^n) + \sup_{f \in \mathcal{F}} \ln f_n(y^n)$$

$$\leq -\ln \widehat{p}_n(y^n) + \sup_{f^{(\delta)} \in \mathcal{F}^{(\delta)}} \ln f_n^{(\delta)}(y^n) + 2n\delta$$

$$= \widehat{L}(y^n) - \inf_{f^{(\delta)} \in \mathcal{F}^{(\delta)}} L_{f^{(\delta)}}(y^n) + 2n\delta. \qquad \blacksquare$$

9.11 Further Examples

Parametric Classes

Consider first classes $\mathcal{F}$ such that there exist positive constants k and c satisfying, for all $\varepsilon > 0$,

$$\ln N(\mathcal{F}, \varepsilon) \leq k \ln \frac{c\sqrt{n}}{\varepsilon}.$$

This is the case for most "parametric" classes, that is, classes that can be parameterized by a bounded subset of $\mathbb{R}^k$ in some "smooth" way provided that all experts' predictions are bounded away from 0.

Corollary 9.1. *Assume that the covering numbers of the class $\mathcal{F}$ satisfy the inequality above. Then*

$$V_n(\mathcal{F}) \leq \frac{k}{2} \ln n + o(\ln n).$$

The main term $\frac{k}{2} \ln n$ is the same as the one we have seen in the case of the class of all constant and Markov experts. In those cases we could derive much sharper expressions for $V_n(\mathcal{F})$ even without requiring that the experts' predictions be bounded away from 0. On the other hand, this corollary allows us to handle, in a simple way, much more complicated classes of experts. An example is provided in Exercise 9.18.

Proof of Corollary 9.1. Substituting the condition on covering numbers in the upper bound of Theorem 9.8, the first term of the expression is bounded by $\frac{k}{2}\ln n + k\ln c - k\ln\varepsilon$. Then the second term may be bounded as follows:

$$24\int_0^\varepsilon \sqrt{\ln N(\mathcal{F},\delta)}\,d\delta \le 48c\sqrt{kn}\int_{a_n}^\infty x^2 e^{-x^2}\,dx$$

$$\text{(by substituting } x = \sqrt{\ln(c\sqrt{n}/\delta)}$$
$$\text{and writing } a_n = \sqrt{\ln(c\sqrt{n}/\varepsilon)})$$

$$= 48c\sqrt{kn}\left[\frac{a_n}{2c\sqrt{n}/\varepsilon} + \frac{1}{2}\int_{a_n}^\infty e^{-x^2}\,dx\right]$$
$$\text{(by integrating by parts)}$$

$$\le 48c\sqrt{kn}\left[\frac{a_n}{2c\sqrt{n}/\varepsilon} + \frac{1}{2a_n c\sqrt{n}/\varepsilon}\right]$$
$$\text{(by using the gaussian tail estimate}$$
$$\int_t^\infty e^{-x^2}\,dx \le e^{-t^2}/(2t))$$

$$\le 48\sqrt{k}a_n\varepsilon \quad \text{(whenever } e\varepsilon \le c\sqrt{n})$$

$$\le 48\sqrt{2}\varepsilon\sqrt{k\ln(c\sqrt{n})} \quad \text{(whenever } \varepsilon \ge 1/(c\sqrt{n}).)$$

The obtained upper bound is minimized for

$$\varepsilon = \frac{1}{48\sqrt{2}}\sqrt{\frac{k}{\ln(c\sqrt{n})}}.$$

So, for every n so large that

$$c\sqrt{n} \ge 48\sqrt{2}\sqrt{\frac{\ln(c\sqrt{n})}{k}},$$

we have

$$V_n(\mathcal{F}) \le \frac{k}{2}\ln n + \frac{k}{2}\ln\frac{\ln(c\sqrt{n})}{k} + k\ln c + 6k,$$

which proves the statement. ∎

Nonparametric Classes

Theorem 9.8 may also be used to handle much larger, "nonparametric" classes. In such cases the minimax regret $V_n(\mathcal{F})$ may be of a significantly larger order of magnitude than the logarithmic bounds characteristic of parametric classes. We work out one simple example here.

Let $\mathcal{Y} = \{1, 2\}$ be a binary alphabet, and consider the class $\mathcal{F}^{(\delta)}$ of all experts f such that $f(1 \mid y^{t-1}) = f_t(1) \in [\delta, 1-\delta]$, where $\delta \in (0, 1/2)$ is some fixed constant, and for each $t = 2, 3, \ldots, n$, $f_t(1) \ge f_{t-1}(1)$. (The case when $\delta = 0$ may be treated by Lemma 9.5.) In other words, $\mathcal{F}^{(\delta)}$ contains all static experts that assign a probability to outcome 1 in a monotonically increasing manner. To estimate the covering numbers of $\mathcal{F}^{(\delta)}$, consider the finite subclass $\mathcal{G}$ of $\mathcal{F}^{(\delta)}$ containing only those monotone experts g that take values of the form $g_t(1) = \delta + (i/k)(1 - 2\delta)$, $i = 0, \ldots, k$, where k is a positive integer to be specified later. It is easy to see that $|\mathcal{G}| = \binom{n+k}{k} \le (2n)^k$ if $k \le n$, and $|\mathcal{G}| \le 2^k$ otherwise. On the other hand, for any $f \in \mathcal{F}^{(\delta)}$, if g is the expert in $\mathcal{G}$ closest to f, then for each $t \leq n$,

$$
\max_{y \in \{1,2\}} |\ln f_t(y) - \ln g_t(y)| \leq \frac{1}{\delta} \max_{y \in \{1,2\}} |f_t(y) - g_t(y)|
$$
$$
= \frac{1}{\delta} |f_t(1) - g_t(1)|
$$
$$
\leq \frac{1}{\delta k}.
$$

Thus, $d(f, g) \leq \sqrt{n}/(\delta k)$. By taking $k = \sqrt{n}/(\delta \varepsilon)$, it follows that the covering number of $\mathcal{F}^{(\delta)}$ is bounded as

$$
N(\mathcal{F}^{(\delta)}, \varepsilon) \leq \begin{cases} (2n)^{\sqrt{n}/(\delta \varepsilon)} & \text{if } \varepsilon \geq \frac{1}{\delta \sqrt{n}} \\ 2^{\sqrt{n}/(\delta \varepsilon)} & \text{otherwise.} \end{cases}
$$

Substituting this bound into Theorem 9.8, it is a matter of straightforward calculation to obtain

$$
V_n(\mathcal{F}^{(\delta)}) = O\left(n^{1/3} \delta^{-2/3} \ln^{2/3} n\right).
$$

Note that the radius optimizing the bound of Theorem 9.8 is $\varepsilon \approx n^{1/6} \delta^{-1/3} \ln^{1/3} n$. Finally, by Lemma 9.5, if $\mathcal{F}$ is the class of all monotonically predicting experts, without restricting predictions in $[\delta, 1 - \delta]$, then by Lemma 9.5, $V_n(\mathcal{F}) \leq V_n(\mathcal{F}^{(\delta)}) + 2n\delta$. By optimizing the value of δ in the upper bound obtained, we get $V_n(\mathcal{F}) = O\left(n^{3/5} \ln^{2/5} n\right)$.

9.12 Bibliographic Remarks

The literature about predicting "individual sequences" under the logarithmic loss function has been intimately tied with a closely related "probabilistic" setup in which one assumes that the sequence of outcomes is generated randomly by one of the distributions in the class of experts. Even though in this chapter we do not consider the probabilistic setup at all, often one cannot separate the literature on the two problems, sometimes commonly known as the problem of *universal prediction*. The related literature is huge, and here we only mention a small selection of references. A survey summarizing a large body of the literature on prediction under the logarithmic loss is offered by Merhav and Feder [214]. The tight connection of sequential probability assignment and universal (lossless) source coding goes back to Kolmogorov [185] and Solomonoff [274, 275]. Fitingof [99, 100] and Davisson [79] were also among the pioneers of the field.

The connection of sequential probability assignment and data compression with arithmetic coding was first revealed by Rissanen [236] and Rissanen and Langdon [243]. One of the most successful sequential coding methods, also applicable to prediction, is the Lempel–Ziv algorithm (see [197, 319] and also Feder, Merhav, and Gutman [95]).

The equivalence of sequential gambling and forecasting under the logarithmic loss function was noted by Kelly [180]; see also Cover [69] and Feder [94].

De Santis, Markowski, and Wegman [260] consider the logarithmic loss in the context of online learning. Theorem 9.1 is due to Shtarkov [267] just like Theorem 9.2; see also Freund [111], Xie and Barron [312]. The Laplace mixture forecaster was introduced, in the context of universal coding, by Davisson [79], and also investigated by Rissanen [239]. The refined mixture forecaster presented in Section 9.7 was suggested by Krichevsky and

Trofimov [186]. Lemma 9.3 appears in Willems, Shtarkov, and Tjalkens [311]. It is shown in Xie and Barron [312] and Freund [111] that the Krichevsky–Trofimov mixture, in fact, achieves a regret $\frac{1}{2} \ln n + \frac{1}{2} \ln \frac{\pi}{2} + o(1)$. This is optimal even in the additive constant for all sequences except for those containing very few 1's or 2's. Xie and Barron [312] refine the mixture further so that it achieves a worst-case cumulative regret of $\frac{1}{2} \ln n + \frac{1}{2} \ln \frac{\pi}{2} + o(1)$, matching the performance of the minimax optimal forecaster. Xie and Barron [312] also derive the analog of all these results in the general case $m \geq 2$. Theorem 9.5 also appears in [312], where the case of m-ary alphabet is also treated and the asymptotic constant is determined. Szpankowski [282] develops analytical tools to determine $V_n(\mathcal{F})$ to arbitrary precision for the class of constant experts; see also Drmota and Szpankowski [90].

The material of Section 9.6 is based on the work of Weinberger, Merhav, and Feder [307], who prove a similar result in a significantly more general setup. In [307] an analog lower bound is shown for classes of experts defined by a finite-state machine with a strongly connected state transition graph. The work of Weinberger, Merhav, and Feder was inspired by a similar result of Rissanen [238] in the model of probabilistic prediction.

Lower bounds for the minimax regret under general metric entropy assumptions may be obtained by noting that lower bounds for the probabilistic counterpart work in the setup of individual sequences as well. We mention the important work of Haussler and Opper [152].

Theorem 9.8 is due to Cesa-Bianchi and Lugosi [53], who improve an earlier result of Opper and Haussler [228] for classes of static experts. A general expression for the minimax regret, not described in this chapter, for certain regular parametric classes has been derived by Rissanen [242]. More specifically, Rissanen considers classes $\mathcal{F}$ of experts $f_{n,\theta}$ parameterized by an open and bounded set of parameters $\Theta \subset \mathbb{R}^k$. It is shown in [242] that under certain regularity assumptions,

$$V_n(\mathcal{F}) = \frac{k}{2} \ln \frac{n}{2\pi} + \ln \int_{\Theta} \sqrt{\det(I(\theta))} \, d\theta + o(1),$$

where the $k \times k$ matrix $I(\theta)$ is the so-called *Fisher information matrix*, whose entry in position (i, j) is defined by

$$-\frac{1}{n} \sum_{y^n} f_{n,\theta}(y^n) \frac{\partial^2 \ln f_{n,\theta}(y^n)}{\partial \theta_i \partial \theta_j},$$

where θ_i is the ith component of vector θ. Yamanishi [313] generalizes Rissanen's results to a wider class of loss functions. The expressions of the minimax regret for the class of Markov experts were determined by Rissanen [242] and Jacquet and Szpankowski [168].

Finally, we mention that the problem of prediction under the logarithmic loss has applications in the study of the general principle of *minimum description length* (MDL), first proposed by Rissanen [237, 238, 241]. For quite exhaustive surveys see Barron, Rissanen, Yu [22], Grünwald [134], and Hansen and Yu [143].

9.13 Exercises

9.1 Let $\mathcal{F}$ be the class of all experts such that for each $f \in \mathcal{F}$, $f_t(j \mid y^{t-1}) = f(j)$ (with $f(j) \geq 0$, $\sum_{j=1}^{m} f(j) = 1$) independently of t and y^{t-1}. For a particular sequence $y^n \in \mathcal{Y}^n$, determine the best expert and its cumulative loss.

9.2 Assume that you want to bet in the horse race only once and that you know that the jth horse wins with probability p_j and the odds are $o_1, \ldots, o_m$. How would you distribute your money to maximize your expected winnings? Contrast your result with the setup described in Section 9.3, where the optimal betting strategy is independent of the odds.

9.3 Show that there exists a class $\mathcal{F}$ of experts with cardinality $|\mathcal{F}| = N$ such that for all $n \geq \log_2 N$, $V_n(\mathcal{F}) \geq \ln N$. This exercise shows that the bound $\ln N$ achieved by the uniform mixture forecaster is not improvable for some classes.

9.4 Consider class $\mathcal{F}$ of all constant experts. Show that the normalized maximum likelihood forecaster p_n^* is horizon dependent in the sense that if p_t' denotes the normalized maximum likelihood forecaster for some $t < n$ (i.e., p_t' achieves the minimax regret $V_t(\mathcal{F})$), then it is not true that

$$\sum_{y_{t+1}^n \in \mathcal{Y}^{n-t}} p_n^*(y^n) = p_t'(y^t).$$

9.5 Let $\mathcal{F}$ be a class of experts and let q and $\widehat{p}$ be arbitrary forecasters (i.e., probability distributions over $\mathcal{Y}^n$). Show that

$$\sum_{y^n \in \mathcal{Y}^n} q(y^n) \ln \frac{\sup_{f \in \mathcal{F}} f_n(y^n)}{\widehat{p}_n(y^n)} \geq \sum_{y^n \in \mathcal{Y}^n} q(y^n) \ln \frac{\sup_{f \in \mathcal{F}} f_n(y^n)}{q(y^n)}$$

and that

$$\sum_{y^n \in \mathcal{Y}^n} q(y^n) \ln \frac{\sup_{f \in \mathcal{F}} f_n(y^n)}{q(y^n)} = V_n(\mathcal{F}) - D(q \| p_n^*),$$

where p_n^* is the normalized maximum likelihood forecaster and D denotes Kullback–Leibler divergence.

9.6 Show that

$$\int_0^1 \frac{1}{\sqrt{x(1-x)}} dx = \pi.$$

Hint: Substitute x by $\sin^2 \alpha$.

9.7 Show that for every $n > 1$ there exists a class $\mathcal{F}_n$ of two static experts such that if $\widehat{p}$ denotes the exponentially weighted average (or mixture) forecaster, then

$$\frac{V_n(\widehat{p}, \mathcal{F}_n)}{V_n(\mathcal{F}_n)} \geq c\sqrt{n}$$

for some universal constant c (see Cesa-Bianchi and Lugosi [53]). *Hint:* Let $\mathcal{Y} = \{0, 1\}$ and let $\mathcal{F}_n$ contain the two experts f, g defined by $f(1 \mid y^{t-1}) = \frac{1}{2}$ and $g(1 \mid y^{t-1}) = \frac{1}{2} + \frac{1}{2n}$. Show, on the one hand, that $V_n(\mathcal{F}_n) \leq c_1 n^{-1/2}$ and on the other hand that $V_n(\widehat{p}, \mathcal{F}_n) \geq c_2$ for appropriate constants c_1, c_2.

9.8 Extend Theorem 9.2 to the case when the outcome space is $\mathcal{Y} = \{1, \ldots, m\}$. More precisely, show that the minimax regret of the class of constant experts is

$$V_n(\mathcal{F}) = \frac{m-1}{2} \ln \frac{n}{2\pi} + \ln \frac{\Gamma(1/2)^m}{\Gamma(m/2)} + o(1) = \frac{m-1}{2} \ln \frac{ne}{m} + o(1)$$

(Xie and Barron [312]).

9.9 Complete the proof of Theorem 9.2 by showing that $V_n(\mathcal{F}) \geq \frac{1}{2} \ln n + \frac{1}{2} \ln \frac{\pi}{2} + o(1)$. *Hint:* The proof goes the same way as that of the upper bound, but to get the right constant you need to be a bit careful when n_1/n or n_2/n is small.

9.10 Define the Laplace forecaster for the class of all constant experts over the alphabet $\mathcal{Y} = \{1, 2, \ldots, m\}$ for $m > 2$. Extend the arguments of Section 9.6 to this general case. In particular, show that the worst-case cumulative regret of the uniformly weighted mixture forecaster satisfies

$$\sup_{y^n \in \mathcal{Y}^n} \left(\widehat{L}(y^n) - \inf_{f \in \mathcal{F}} L_f(y^n) \right) = \ln \binom{n + m - 1}{m - 1} \leq (m - 1) \ln(n + 1).$$

9.11 Prove Lemma 9.3. *Hint:* Show that the ratio of the two sides decreases if we replace n by $n + 1$ (and also increase either n_1 or n_2 by 1) and thus achieves its minimum when $n = 1$. *Warning:* This requires some work.

9.12 Show that the function defined by (9.1) is decreasing in both of its variables. *Hint:* Proceed by induction.

9.13 Show that the minimax regret $V_n(\mathcal{M}_k)$ of the class of all kth-order Markov experts over a binary alphabet $\mathcal{Y} = \{1, 2\}$ satisfies

$$V_n(\mathcal{M}_k) = \frac{2^k}{2} \ln \frac{n}{2^k} + O(1)$$

(Rissanen [242].)

9.14 Generalize Theorem 9.6 to the case when $\mathcal{Y} = \{1, \ldots, m\}$, with $m > 2$, and $\mathcal{F}$ is the class of all constant experts.

9.15 Generalize Theorem 9.6 to the case when $\mathcal{Y} = \{1, 2\}$ and $\mathcal{F} = \mathcal{M}_k$ is the class of all kth-order Markov experts. *Hint:* You may need to redefine classes T_j as classes of "Markov types" adequately. Counting the cardinality of these classes is not as trivial as in the case of constant experts. (See Weinberger, Merhav, and Feder [307] for a more general result.)

9.16 (*Double mixture for markov experts*) Assume that $\mathcal{Y} = \{1, 2\}$. Construct a forecaster $\widehat{p}$ such that for any $k = 1, 2, \ldots$ and any kth-order Markov expert $f \in \mathcal{M}_k$,

$$\sup_{y^n \in \mathcal{Y}^n} \left(\widehat{L}(y^n) - L_f(y^n) \right) \leq \frac{2^k}{2} \ln \frac{n}{2^k} + \alpha_{k,n},$$

where for each k, $\limsup_{n \to \infty} \alpha_{k,n} \leq \beta_k < \infty$. *Hint:* For each k consider the forecaster described in Example 9.1. Then combine them by the countable mixture described in Section 9.2 (see also Ryabko [252, 253]).

9.17 (*Predicting as well as the best finite-state machine*) Consider $\mathcal{Y} = \{1, 2\}$. A k-*state finite-state machine* forecaster is defined as a triple (S, F, G) where S is a finite set of k elements, $F : S \to [0, 1]$ is the *output function*, and $G : \mathcal{Y} \times S \to S$ is the *next-state function*. For a sequence of outcomes $y_1, y_2, \ldots$, the finite-state forecaster produces a prediction given by the recursions

$$s_t = G(s_{t-1}, y_{t-1}) \qquad \text{and} \qquad f_t(1 \mid y^{t-1}) = F(s_t)$$

for $t = 2, 3, \ldots$ while $f_1(1) = F(s_1)$ for an initial state $s_1 \in S$. Construct a forecaster that predicts almost as well as any finite-state machine forecaster in the sense that

$$\sup_{y^n \in \mathcal{Y}^n} \left(\widehat{L}(y^n) - L_f(y^n) \right) = O(\ln n)$$

for every finite-state machine forecaster f. *Hint:* Use the previous exercise. (See also Feder, Merhav, and Gutman [95].)

9.18 (*Experts with fading memory*) Let $\mathcal{Y} = \{0, 1\}$ and consider the one-parameter class $\mathcal{F}$ of distributions on $\{0, 1\}^n$ containing all experts $f^{(a)}$, with $a \in [0, 1]$, where each $f^{(a)}$ is defined by its conditionals as $f_1^{(a)}(1) = 1/2$, $f_2^{(a)}(1 \mid y_1) = y_1$, and

$$f_t^{(a)}(1 \mid y^{t-1}) = \frac{1}{t-1} \sum_{s=1}^{t-1} y_s \left(1 + \frac{a(2s - t)}{t - 2}\right)$$

for all $y^{t-1} \in \{0, 1\}^{t-1}$ and for all $t > 2$. Show that

$$V_n(\mathcal{F}) = O(\ln n).$$

Hint: First show using Theorem 9.8 that $V_n(\mathcal{F}^{(\delta)}) \le \frac{1}{2} \ln n + \frac{1}{2} \ln \ln \frac{\sqrt{n}}{\delta} + \ln \frac{1}{\delta} + O(1)$ and then use Lemma 9.5.

10

Sequential Investment

10.1 Portfolio Selection

This chapter is devoted to the application of the ideas described in Chapter 9 to the problem of sequential investment. Imagine a market of m assets (stocks) in which, in each trading period (day), the price of a stock may vary in an arbitrary way. An investor operates on this market for n days with the goal of maximizing his final wealth. At the beginning of each day, on the basis of the past behavior of the market, the investor redistributes his current wealth among the m assets. Following the approach developed in the previous chapters, we avoid any statistical assumptions about the nature of the stock market, and evaluate the investor's wealth relative to the performance achieved by the best strategy in a class of reference investment strategies (the "experts").

In the idealized stock market we assume that there are no transaction costs and the amount of each stock that can be bought at any trading period is only limited by the investor's wealth at that time. Similarly, the investor can sell any quantity of the stocks he possesses at any time at the actual market price.

The model may be formalized as follows. A *market vector* $\mathbf{x} = (x_1, \ldots, x_m)$ for m assets is a vector of nonnegative real numbers representing price relatives for a given trading period. In other words, the quantity $x_i \geq 0$ denotes the ratio of closing to opening price of the ith asset for that period. Hence, an initial wealth invested in the m assets according to fractions $Q_1, \ldots, Q_m$ multiplies by a factor of $\sum_{i=1}^{m} x_i Q_i$ at the end of the period. The market behavior during n trading periods is represented by a sequence of market vectors $\mathbf{x}^n = (\mathbf{x}_1, \ldots, \mathbf{x}_n)$. The jth component of $\mathbf{x}_t$, denoted by $x_{j,t}$, is the factor by which the wealth invested in asset j increases in the tth period.

As in Chapter 9, we denote the probability simplex in $\mathbb{R}^m$ by $\mathcal{D}$. An *investment strategy* Q for n trading periods is a sequence $\mathbf{Q}_1, \ldots, \mathbf{Q}_n$ of vector-valued functions $\mathbf{Q}_t : \mathbb{R}_+^{t-1} \to \mathcal{D}$, where the ith component $Q_{i,t}(\mathbf{x}^{t-1})$ of the vector $\mathbf{Q}_t(\mathbf{x}^{t-1})$ denotes the fraction of the current wealth invested in the ith asset at the beginning of the tth period on the basis of the past market behavior $\mathbf{x}^{t-1}$. We use

$$S_n(Q, \mathbf{x}^n) = \prod_{t=1}^{n} \left(\sum_{i=1}^{m} x_{i,t}\, Q_{i,t}(\mathbf{x}^{t-1}) \right)$$

to denote the *wealth factor* of strategy Q after n trading periods. The fact that $\mathbf{Q}_t$ has nonnegative components summing to 1 expresses the condition that short sales and buying on margin are excluded.

Example* 10.1 *(Buy-and-hold strategies). The simplest investment strategies are the so called *buy-and-hold* strategies. An investor following such a strategy simply distributes his initial wealth among m assets according to some distribution $\mathbf{Q}_1 \in \mathcal{D}$ before the first trading period and does not trade anymore. The wealth factor of such a strategy, after n periods, is simply

$$S_n(Q, \mathbf{x}^n) = \sum_{j=1}^{m} Q_{j,1} \prod_{t=1}^{n} x_{j,t}.$$

Clearly, this wealth factor is at most as large as the gain $\max_{j=1,\dots,m} \prod_{t=1}^{n} x_{j,t}$ of the best stock over the same investment period and achieves this maximal wealth if $\mathbf{Q}_1$ concentrates on this best stock. □

Example* 10.2 *(Constantly rebalanced portfolios). Another simple and important class of investment strategies is the class of *constantly rebalanced portfolios*. Such a strategy B is parameterized by a probability vector $\mathbf{B} = (B_1, \dots, B_m) \in \mathcal{D}$ and simply $\mathbf{Q}_t(\mathbf{x}^{t-1}) = \mathbf{B}$ regardless of t and the past market behavior $\mathbf{x}^{t-1}$. Thus, an investor following such a strategy rebalances, at every trading period, his current wealth according to the distribution $\mathbf{B}$ by investing a proportion B_1 of this wealth in the first stock, a proportion B_2 in the second stock, and so on. Observe that, as opposed to buy-and-hold strategies, an investor using a constantly rebalanced portfolio $\mathbf{B}$ is engaged in active trading in each period. The wealth factor achieved after n trading periods is

$$S_n(\mathbf{B}, \mathbf{x}^n) = \prod_{t=1}^{n} \left(\sum_{i=1}^{m} x_{i,t} B_i \right).$$

To understand the power of constantly rebalanced strategies, consider a simple market of $m = 2$ stocks such that the sequence of market vectors is $\left(1, \frac{1}{2}\right), (1, 2), \left(1, \frac{1}{2}\right), (1, 2), \dots$. Thus, the first stock maintains its value stable while the second stock is more volatile: on even days it doubles its price, whereas on odd days it loses half of its value. Clearly, on a long run, none of the two stocks (and therefore no buy-and-hold strategy) yields any gain. On the other hand, the investment strategy that rebalances every day uniformly (i.e., with $\mathbf{B} = \left(\frac{1}{2}, \frac{1}{2}\right)$) achieves an exponentially increasing wealth at a rate $(9/8)^{n/2}$. The importance of constantly rebalanced portfolios is largely due to the fact that if the market vectors $\mathbf{x}_t$ are realizations of an i.i.d. process and the number n of investment periods is large, then the best possible investment strategy, in a quite strong sense, is a constantly rebalanced portfolio (see Cover and Thomas [74] for a nice summary). □

As for the other models of prediction considered in this book, the performance of any investment strategy is measured by comparing it to the best in a fixed class of strategies. To formalize this notion, we introduce the worst-case logarithmic wealth ratio in the next section. In Section 10.3 the main result of this chapter is presented, which points out a certain equivalence between the problem of sequential investment and prediction under the logarithmic loss studied in Chapter 9. This equivalence permits one to determine the limits of any investment strategy as well as to design strategies with near optimal performance guarantees. In particular, in Section 10.4 a strategy called "universal portfolio" is introduced that is shown to be an analog of the mixture forecasters of Chapter 9. The so-called EG investment strategy is presented in Section 10.5 whose aim is to relieve the computational burden of the universal portfolio. In Section 10.6 we allow the investor to take certain side information into account and develop investment strategies in this extended framework.

10.2   The Minimax Wealth Ratio

The investor's objective is to achieve a wealth comparable to the best of a certain class of investment strategies regardless of the market behavior. Thus, given a class $\mathcal{Q}$ of investment strategies, we define the *worst-case logarithmic wealth ratio* of strategy P by

$$W_n(P, \mathcal{Q}) = \sup_{\mathbf{x}^n} \sup_{Q \in \mathcal{Q}} \ln \frac{S_n(Q, \mathbf{x}^n)}{S_n(P, \mathbf{x}^n)}.$$

Clearly, the investor's goal is to choose a strategy P for which $W_n(P, \mathcal{Q})$ is as small as possible. $W_n(P, \mathcal{Q}) = o(n)$ means that the investment strategy P achieves the same exponent of growth as the best reference strategy in class $\mathcal{Q}$ for all possible market behaviors. The *minimax logarithmic wealth ratio* is just the best possible worst-case logarithmic wealth ratio achievable by any investment strategy P:

$$W_n(\mathcal{Q}) = \inf_P W_n(P, \mathcal{Q}).$$

Example 10.3 (Finite classes). Assume that the investor competes against a finite class $\mathcal{Q} = \{Q^{(1)}, \dots, Q^{(N)}\}$ of investment strategies. A very simple strategy P divides the initial wealth in N equal parts and invests each part according to the "experts" $Q^{(i)}$. Then the total wealth of the strategy is

$$S_n(P, \mathbf{x}^n) = \frac{1}{N} \sum_{i=1}^{N} S_n(Q^{(i)}, \mathbf{x}^n)$$

and the worst-case logarithmic wealth ratio is bounded as

$$W_n(P, \mathcal{Q}) = \sup_{\mathbf{x}^n} \ln \frac{\max_{i=1,\dots,N} S_n(Q^{(i)}, \mathbf{x}^n)}{\frac{1}{N} \sum_{j=1}^{N} S_n(Q^{(j)}, \mathbf{x}^n)}$$

$$\leq \sup_{\mathbf{x}^n} \ln \frac{\max_{i=1,\dots,N} S_n(Q^{(i)}, \mathbf{x}^n)}{\frac{1}{N} \max_{j=1,\dots,N} S_n(Q^{(j)}, \mathbf{x}^n)}$$

$$= \ln N. \quad \Box$$

10.3   Prediction and Investment

In this section we point out an intimate connection between the sequential investment problem and the problem of prediction under the logarithmic loss studied in Chapter 9.

The first thing we observe is that any investment strategy Q over m assets may be used to define a forecaster that predicts the elements $y_t \in \mathcal{Y} = \{1, \dots, m\}$ of a sequence $y^n \in \mathcal{Y}^n$ with probability vectors $\widehat{\mathbf{p}}_t \in \mathcal{D}$. To do this, we simply restrict our attention to those market vectors $\mathbf{x}$ that have a single component that is equal to 1 and all other components equal to 0. Such vectors are called *Kelly market vectors*. Observe that a Kelly market is just like the horse race described in Section 9.3, with the only restriction that all odds are supposed to be equal to 1. If $\mathbf{x}_1, \ldots, \mathbf{x}_n$ are Kelly market vectors and we denote the index of the only nonzero component of each vector $\mathbf{x}_t$ by y_t, then we may define forecaster f by

$$f_t(y \mid y^{t-1}) = Q_{y,t}(\mathbf{x}^{t-1}).$$

We say that the forecaster f is *induced* by the investment strategy Q. With some abuse of notation we write $S_n(Q, y^n)$ for $S_n(Q, \mathbf{x}^n)$ when $\mathbf{x}^n$ is a sequence of Kelly vectors determined by the sequence y^n of indices. Clearly, $S_n(Q, y^n) = f_n(y^n)$ if f is the forecaster induced by Q.

To relate the regret in forecasting to the logarithmic wealth ratio, we use the logarithmic loss $\ell(\widehat{\mathbf{p}}_t, y_t) = -\ln \widehat{p}_t(y_t \mid y^{t-1})$. Then the regret against a reference forecaster f is

$$\widehat{L}_n - L_{f,n} = \ln \frac{f_n(y^n)}{\widehat{p}_n(y^n)} = \ln \frac{Q(y^n)}{P(y^n)},$$

where Q and P are the investment strategies induced by f and $\widehat{p}$ (see Section 9.1).

Now it is obvious that the investment problem is at least as difficult as the corresponding prediction problem.

Lemma 10.1. *Let Q be a class of investment strategies, and let $\mathcal{F}$ denote the class of forecasters induced by the strategies in Q. Then the minimax regret*

$$V_n(\mathcal{F}) = \inf_{P_n} \sup_{y^n} \sup_{f \in \mathcal{F}} \ln \frac{f_n(y^n)}{p_n(y^n)}$$

satisfies $W_n(Q) \geq V_n(\mathcal{F})$.

Proof. Let P be any investment strategy and let p be its induced forecaster. Then

$$\sup_{\mathbf{x}^n} \sup_{Q \in Q} \ln \frac{S_n(Q, \mathbf{x}^n)}{S_n(P, \mathbf{x}^n)} \geq \max_{y^n \in \mathcal{Y}^n} \sup_{Q \in Q} \ln \frac{S_n(Q, y^n)}{S_n(P, y^n)}$$

$$= \max_{y^n \in \mathcal{Y}^n} \sup_{f \in \mathcal{F}} \ln \frac{f_n(y^n)}{p_n(y^n)}$$

$$= V_n(p, \mathcal{F}) \geq V_n(\mathcal{F}). \qquad \blacksquare$$

Surprisingly, as it turns out, the investment problem is not genuinely more difficult than that of prediction. In what follows, we show that in many interesting cases the two problems are, in fact, equivalent in a minimax sense.

Given a prediction strategy p, we define an investment strategy P as follows:

$$P_{j,t}(\mathbf{x}^{t-1}) = \frac{\sum_{y^{t-1} \in \mathcal{Y}^{t-1}} p_t(j \mid y^{t-1}) p_{t-1}(y^{t-1}) \left(\prod_{s=1}^{t-1} x_{y_s, s} \right)}{\sum_{y^{t-1} \in \mathcal{Y}^{t-1}} p_{t-1}(y^{t-1}) \left(\prod_{s=1}^{t-1} x_{y_s, s} \right)}.$$

Note that the factors $\prod_{t=1}^{n} x_{y_t, t}$ may be viewed as the return of the "extremal" investment strategy that, on each trading period t, invests everything on the y_tth asset. Clearly, the obtained investment strategy induces p, and so we will say that p and P induce each other.

The following result is the key in relating the minimax wealth ratio to the minimax regret of forecasters.

Theorem 10.1. *Let P be an investment strategy induced by a forecaster p, and let Q be an arbitrary class of investment strategies. Then for any market sequence $\mathbf{x}^n$,*

$$\sup_{Q \in \mathcal{Q}} \ln \frac{S_n(Q, \mathbf{x}^n)}{S_n(P, \mathbf{x}^n)} \leq \max_{y^n \in \mathcal{Y}^n} \sup_{Q \in \mathcal{Q}} \ln \frac{\prod_{t=1}^n Q_{y_t, t}(\mathbf{x}^{t-1})}{p_n(y^n)}.$$

The proof of the theorem uses the following two simple lemmas. The first is an elementary inequality, whose proof is left as an exercise.

Lemma 10.2. *Let $a_1, \ldots, a_n, b_1, \ldots, b_n$ be nonnegative numbers. Then*

$$\frac{\sum_{i=1}^n a_i}{\sum_{i=1}^n b_i} \leq \max_{j=1,\ldots,n} \frac{a_j}{b_j},$$

where we define $0/0 = 0$.

Lemma 10.3. *The wealth factor achieved by an investment strategy Q may be written as*

$$S_n(Q, \mathbf{x}^n) = \sum_{y^n \in \mathcal{Y}^n} \left(\prod_{t=1}^n x_{y_t, t} \right) \left(\prod_{t=1}^n Q_{y_t, t}(\mathbf{x}^{t-1}) \right).$$

If the investment strategy P is induced by a forecaster p_n, then

$$S_n(P, \mathbf{x}^n) = \sum_{y^n \in \mathcal{Y}^n} \left(\prod_{t=1}^n x_{y_t, t} \right) p_n(y^n).$$

Proof. First, we expand the product in the definition of $S_n(Q, \mathbf{x}^n)$:

$$S_n(Q, \mathbf{x}^n) = \prod_{t=1}^n \left(\sum_{j=1}^m x_{j,t} \, Q_{j,t}(\mathbf{x}^{t-1}) \right)$$

$$= \sum_{y^n \in \mathcal{Y}^n} \left(\prod_{t=1}^n x_{y_t, t} \, Q_{y_t, t}(\mathbf{x}^{t-1}) \right)$$

$$= \sum_{y^n \in \mathcal{Y}^n} \left(\prod_{t=1}^n x_{y_t, t} \right) \left(\prod_{t=1}^n Q_{y_t, t}(\mathbf{x}^{t-1}) \right).$$

On the other hand, if an investment strategy is induced by a forecaster p, then

$$S_n(P, \mathbf{x}^n) = \prod_{t=1}^n \left(\sum_{j=1}^m x_{j,t} P_{j,t}(\mathbf{x}^{t-1}) \right)$$

$$= \prod_{t=1}^n \frac{\sum_{j=1}^m \sum_{y^{t-1} \in \mathcal{Y}^{t-1}} p_t(y^{t-1} j) x_{j,t} \left(\prod_{s=1}^{t-1} x_{y_s, s} \right)}{\sum_{y^{t-1} \in \mathcal{Y}^{t-1}} p_{t-1}(y^{t-1}) \left(\prod_{s=1}^{t-1} x_{y_s, s} \right)}$$

$$= \prod_{t=1}^{n} \frac{\sum_{y^t \in \mathcal{Y}^t} \left(\prod_{s=1}^{t} x_{y_s,s} \right) p_t(y^t)}{\sum_{y^{t-1} \in \mathcal{Y}^{t-1}} \left(\prod_{s=1}^{t-1} x_{y_s,s} \right) p_{t-1}(y^{t-1})}$$

$$= \sum_{y^n \in \mathcal{Y}^n} \left(\prod_{t=1}^{n} x_{y_t,t} \right) p_n(y^n),$$

where in the last equality we set $\sum_{y^{t-1} \in \mathcal{Y}^{t-1}} \left(\prod_{s=1}^{t-1} x_{y_s,s} \right) p_{t-1}(y^{t-1}) = 1$ for $t = 1$. ∎

Proof of Theorem 10.1. Fix any market sequence $\mathbf{x}^n$ and choose any reference strategy $Q' \in \mathcal{Q}$. To simplify notation, we write $S_n(y^n, \mathbf{x}^n) = \prod_{t=1}^{n} x_{y_t,t}$. Then using the expressions derived above for $S_n(Q', \mathbf{x}^n)$ and $S_n(P, \mathbf{x}^n)$, we have

$$\frac{S_n(Q', \mathbf{x}^n)}{S_n(P, \mathbf{x}^n)} = \frac{\sum_{y^n \in \mathcal{Y}^n} S_n(y^n, \mathbf{x}^n) \left(\prod_{t=1}^{n} Q'_{y_t,t}(\mathbf{x}^{t-1}) \right)}{\sum_{y^n \in \mathcal{Y}^n} S_n(y^n, \mathbf{x}^n) p_n(y^n)}$$

$$\leq \max_{y^n : S_n(y^n,\mathbf{x}^n)>0} \frac{S_n(y^n, \mathbf{x}^n) \prod_{t=1}^{n} Q'_{y_t,t}(\mathbf{x}^{t-1})}{S_n(y^n, \mathbf{x}^n) p_n(y^n)}$$

(by Lemma 10.2)

$$= \max_{y^n \in \mathcal{Y}^n} \frac{\prod_{t=1}^{n} Q'_{y_t,t}(\mathbf{x}^{t-1})}{p_n(y^n)}$$

$$\leq \max_{y^n \in \mathcal{Y}^n} \sup_{Q \in \mathcal{Q}} \frac{\prod_{t=1}^{n} Q_{y_t,t}(\mathbf{x}^{t-1})}{p_n(y^n)}. \qquad \blacksquare$$

An important and immediate corollary of Theorem 10.1 is that the minimax logarithmic wealth ratio $W_n(\mathcal{Q})$ of any class $\mathcal{Q}$ of static strategies equals the minimax regret associated with the class of the induced forecasters. To make this statement precise, we introduce the notion of static investment strategies, similar to the notion of static experts in prediction problems. A *static* investment strategy Q satisfies $\mathbf{Q}_t(\mathbf{x}^{t-1}) = \mathbf{Q}_t \in \mathcal{D}$ for each $t = 1, \ldots, n$. Thus, the allocation of wealth $\mathbf{Q}_t$ for each trading period does not depend on the past market behavior.

Theorem 10.2. *Let $\mathcal{Q}$ be a class of static investment strategies, and let $\mathcal{F}$ denote the class of forecasters induced by strategies in $\mathcal{Q}$. Then*

$$W_n(\mathcal{Q}) = V_n(\mathcal{F}).$$

Furthermore, the minimax optimal investment strategy is defined by

$$P^*_{j,t}(\mathbf{x}^{t-1}) = \frac{\sum_{y^{t-1} \in \mathcal{Y}^{t-1}} p^*_t(j \mid y^{t-1}) p^*_{t-1}(y^{t-1}) \left(\prod_{s=1}^{t-1} x_{y_s,s} \right)}{\sum_{y^{t-1} \in \mathcal{Y}^{t-1}} p^*_{t-1}(y^{t-1}) \left(\prod_{s=1}^{t-1} x_{y_s,s} \right)},$$

where p^* is the normalized maximum likelihood forecaster

$$p^*_n(y^n) = \frac{\sup_{Q \in \mathcal{Q}} \prod_{t=1}^{n} Q_{y_t,t}}{\sum_{y^n \in \mathcal{Y}^n} \sup_{Q \in \mathcal{Q}} \prod_{t=1}^{n} Q_{y_t,t}}.$$

Proof. By Lemma 10.1 we have $W_n(\mathcal{Q}) \geq V_n(\mathcal{F})$; so it suffices to prove that $W_n(\mathcal{Q}) \leq V_n(\mathcal{F})$. Recall from Theorem 9.1 that the normalized maximum likelihood forecaster p^* is minimax optimal for the class $\mathcal{F}$; that is,

$$\max_{y^n \in \mathcal{Y}^n} \ln \sup_{Q \in \mathcal{Q}} \frac{\prod_{t=1}^n Q_{y_t,t}}{p_n^*(y^n)} = V_n(\mathcal{F}).$$

Now let P^* be the investment strategy induced by the minimax forecaster p^* for $\mathcal{Q}$. By Theorem 10.1 we get

$$W_n(\mathcal{Q}) \leq \sup_{x^n} \sup_{Q \in \mathcal{Q}} \ln \frac{S_n(Q, x^n)}{S_n(P^*, x^n)} \leq \max_{y^n \in \mathcal{Y}^n} \sup_{Q \in \mathcal{Q}} \ln \frac{\prod_{t=1}^n Q_{y_t,t}}{p_n^*(y^n)} = V_n(\mathcal{F}).$$

The fact that the worst-case wealth ratio $\sup_{x^n} \sup_{Q \in \mathcal{Q}} S_n(Q, x^n)/S_n(P^*, x^n)$ achieved by the strategy P^* equals $W_n(\mathcal{Q})$ follows by the inequality above and the fact that $V_n(\mathcal{F}) \leq W_n(\mathcal{Q})$. ∎

Example 10.4 (*Constantly rebalanced portfolios*). Consider now the class $\mathcal{Q}$ of all constantly rebalanced portfolios. It is obvious that the strategies of this class induce the "constant" forecasters studied in Sections 9.5, 9.6, and 9.7. Thus, combining Theorem 10.2 with the remark following Theorem 9.2, we obtain the following expression for the behavior of the minimax logarithmic wealth ratio:

$$W_n(\mathcal{Q}) = \frac{m-1}{2} \ln n + \ln \frac{\Gamma(1/2)^m}{\Gamma(m/2)} + o(1).$$

This result shows that the wealth $S_n(P^*, \mathcal{Q})$ of the minimax optimal investment strategy given by Theorem 10.2 comes within a factor of $n^{(m-1)/2}$ of the best possible constantly rebalanced portfolio, regardless of the market behavior. Since, typically, $\sup_{Q \in \mathcal{Q}} S_n(Q, x^n)$ increases exponentially with n, this factor becomes negligible on the long run. □

10.4 Universal Portfolios

Just as in the case of the prediction problem of Chapter 9, the minimax optimal solution for the investment problem is not feasible in practice. In this section we introduce computationally more attractive methods, close in spirit to the mixture forecasters of Sections 9.6 and 9.7.

For simplicity and for its importance, in this section we restrict our attention to class $\mathcal{Q}$ of all constantly rebalanced portfolios. Recall that each strategy Q in this class is determined by a vector $\mathbf{B} = (B_1, \ldots, B_m)$ in the probability simplex $\mathcal{D}$ in $\mathbb{R}^m$. In order to compete with the best strategy in $\mathcal{Q}$, we introduce the *universal portfolio* strategy P by

$$P_{j,t}(\mathbf{x}^{t-1}) = \frac{\int_{\mathcal{D}} B_j \, S_{t-1}(\mathbf{B}, \mathbf{x}^{t-1}) \mu(\mathbf{B}) \, d\mathbf{B}}{\int_{\mathcal{D}} S_{t-1}(\mathbf{B}, \mathbf{x}^{t-1}) \mu(\mathbf{B}) \, d\mathbf{B}}, \qquad j = 1, \ldots, m, \quad t = 1, \ldots, n,$$

where μ is a density function on $\mathcal{D}$. In the simplest case μ is just the uniform density, though we will see that it may be advantageous to consider nonuniform densities such as the Dirichlet$(1/2, \ldots, 1/2)$ density. In any case, the universal portfolio is a weighted average of the strategies in $\mathcal{Q}$, weighted by their past performance. We will see in the proof of Theorem 10.3 below that the universal portfolio is nothing but the investment strategy induced by the mixture forecaster (the Laplace mixture in case of uniform μ and the Krichevsky–Trofimov mixture if μ is the Dirichlet$(1/2, \ldots, 1/2)$ density).

The wealth achieved by the universal portfolio is just the average of the wealths achieved by the individual strategies in the class. This may be easily seen by observing that

$$
\begin{aligned}
S_n(P, \mathbf{x}^n) &= \prod_{t=1}^{n} \sum_{j=1}^{m} P_{j,t}(\mathbf{x}^{t-1}) x_{j,t} \\
&= \prod_{t=1}^{n} \frac{\int_{\mathcal{D}} \sum_{j=1}^{m} x_{j,t} B_j \, S_{t-1}(\mathbf{B}, \mathbf{x}^{t-1}) \mu(\mathbf{B}) \, d\mathbf{B}}{\int_{\mathcal{D}} S_{t-1}(\mathbf{B}, \mathbf{x}^{t-1}) \mu(\mathbf{B}) \, d\mathbf{B}} \\
&= \prod_{t=1}^{n} \frac{\int_{\mathcal{D}} S_t(\mathbf{B}, \mathbf{x}^t) \mu(\mathbf{B}) \, d\mathbf{B}}{\int_{\mathcal{D}} S_{t-1}(\mathbf{B}, \mathbf{x}^{t-1}) \mu(\mathbf{B}) \, d\mathbf{B}} \\
&= \int_{\mathcal{D}} S_n(\mathbf{B}, \mathbf{x}^n) \mu(\mathbf{B}) \, d\mathbf{B}
\end{aligned}
$$

because the product is telescoping and $S_0 \equiv 1$. This last expression offers an intuitive explanation of what the universal portfolio does: by approximating the integral by a Riemann sum, we have

$$
S_n(P, \mathbf{x}^n) \approx \sum_i Q_i \, S_n(\mathbf{B}_i, \mathbf{x}^n),
$$

where, given the elements Δ_i of a fine finite partition of the simplex $\mathcal{D}$, we assume that $\mathbf{B}_i \in \Delta_i$ and $Q_i = \int_{\Delta_i} \mu(\mathbf{B}) d\mathbf{B}$. The right-hand side is the capital accumulated by a strategy that distributes its initial capital among the constantly rebalanced investment strategies $\mathbf{B}_i$ according to the proportions Q_i and lets these strategies work with their initial share. In other words, the universal portfolio performs a kind of buy-and-hold over all constantly rebalanced portfolios.

This simple observation is the key in establishing performance bounds for the universal portfolio.

Theorem 10.3. *If μ is the uniform density on the probability simplex $\mathcal{D}$ in $\mathbb{R}^m$, then the wealth achieved by the universal portfolio satisfies*

$$
\sup_{\mathbf{x}^n} \sup_{\mathbf{B} \in \mathcal{D}} \ln \frac{S_n(\mathbf{B}, \mathbf{x}^n)}{S_n(P, \mathbf{x}^n)} \le (m-1) \ln(n+1).
$$

If the universal portfolio is defined using the Dirichlet $(1/2, \ldots, 1/2)$ density μ, then

$$
\sup_{\mathbf{x}^n} \sup_{\mathbf{B} \in \mathcal{D}} \ln \frac{S_n(\mathbf{B}, \mathbf{x}^n)}{S_n(P, \mathbf{x}^n)} \le \frac{m-1}{2} \ln n + \ln \frac{\Gamma(1/2)^m}{\Gamma(m/2)} + \frac{m-1}{2} \ln 2 + o(1).
$$

The second statement shows that the logarithmic worst-case wealth ratio of the universal portfolio based on the Dirichlet $(1/2, \ldots, 1/2)$ density comes within a constant of the minimax optimal investment strategy.

Proof. First recall that each constantly rebalanced portfolio strategy indexed by $\mathbf{B}$ is induced by the "constant" forecaster $p^{\mathbf{B}}$, which assigns probability

$$
p_n^{\mathbf{B}}(y^n) = B_1^{n_1} \cdots B_m^{n_m}
$$

to each sequence y^n in which the number of occurrences of symbol j is n_j ($j = 1, \ldots, m$). By Lemma 10.3, the wealth achieved by such a strategy is

$$S_n(\mathbf{B}, \mathbf{x}^n) = \sum_{y^n} \left(\prod_{t=1}^{n} x_{y_t,t} \right) p_n^{\mathbf{B}}(y^n).$$

Using the fact that the wealth achieved by the universal portfolio is just the average of the wealths achieved by the strategies in $\mathcal{Q}$, we have

$$S_n(P, \mathbf{x}^n) = \int_{\mathcal{D}} S_n(\mathbf{B}, \mathbf{x}^n) \mu(\mathbf{B}) \, d\mathbf{B}$$

$$= \sum_{y^n} \left(\prod_{t=1}^{n} x_{y_t,t} \right) \int_{\mathcal{D}} p_n^{\mathbf{B}}(y^n) \mu(\mathbf{B}) \, d\mathbf{B}.$$

The last expression shows that the universal portfolio P is induced by the mixture forecaster

$$p_n(y^n) = \int_{\mathcal{D}} p_n^{\mathbf{B}}(y^n) \mu(\mathbf{B}) \, d\mathbf{B}.$$

(Simply note that by Lemma 10.3 the wealth achieved by the strategy induced by the mixture forecaster is the same as the wealth achieved by the universal portfolio; hence the two strategies must coincide.)

By Theorem 10.1,

$$\sup_{\mathbf{x}^n} \sup_{\mathbf{B} \in \mathcal{D}} \ln \frac{S_n(\mathbf{B}, \mathbf{x}^n)}{S_n(P, \mathbf{x}^n)} \leq \max_{y^n \in \mathcal{Y}^n} \sup_{\mathbf{B} \in \mathcal{D}} \ln \frac{p_n^{\mathbf{B}}(y^n)}{p_n(y^n)}.$$

In other words, the worst-case logarithmic wealth factor achieved by the universal portfolio is bounded by the worst-case logarithmic regret of the mixture forecaster. But we have already studied this latter quantity. In particular, if μ is the uniform density, then p_n is just the Laplace forecaster whose performance is bounded by Theorem 9.3 (for $m = 2$) and by Exercise 9.10 (for $m \geq 2$), yielding the first half of the theorem.

The second statement is obtained by noting that if the universal portfolio is defined on the basis of the Dirichlet($1/2, \ldots, 1/2$) density, then p_n is the Krichevsky–Trofimov forecaster whose loss is bounded in Section 9.7. ∎

10.5   The EG Investment Strategy

The worst-case performance of the universal portfolio is basically unimprovable, but it has some practical disadvantages. Just note that the definition of the universal portfolio involves integration over an m-dimensional simplex. Even for moderate values of m, the exponential computational cost may become prohibitive. In this section we describe a simple strategy P whose computational cost is linear in m, a dramatic improvement. Unfortunately, the performance guarantees of this version are inferior to those established in Theorem 10.3 for the universal portfolio.

This strategy, called the EG *investment strategy*, invests at time t using the vector $\mathbf{P}_t = (P_{1,t}, \ldots, P_{m,t})$ where $\mathbf{P}_1 = (1/m, \ldots, 1/m)$ and

$$P_{i,t} = \frac{P_{i,t-1} \exp\big(\eta(x_{i,t-1}/\mathbf{P}_{t-1} \cdot \mathbf{x}_{t-1})\big)}{\sum_{j=1}^{m} P_{j,t-1} \exp\big(\eta(x_{j,t-1}/\mathbf{P}_{t-1} \cdot \mathbf{x}_{t-1})\big)}, \qquad i = 1, \ldots, m, \quad t = 2, 3, \ldots.$$

This weight assignment is a special case of the gradient-based forecaster for linear regression introduced in Section 11.4:

$$P_{i,t} = \frac{P_{i,t-1} \exp\big(\eta \nabla \ell_{t-1}(\mathbf{P}_{t-1})_i\big)}{\sum_{j=1}^{m} P_{j,t-1} \exp\big(\eta \nabla \ell_{t-1}(\mathbf{P}_{t-1})_j\big)}$$

when the loss functions is set as $\ell_{t-1}(\mathbf{P}_{t-1}) = -\ln \mathbf{P}_{t-1} \cdot \mathbf{x}_{t-1}$.

Note that with this loss function, $\widehat{L}_n = -\ln S(P, \mathbf{x}^n)$, where $\widehat{L}_n$ is the cumulative loss of the gradient-based forecaster, and $L_n(\mathbf{B}) = -\ln S(\mathbf{B}, \mathbf{x}^n)$, where $L_n(\mathbf{B})$ is the cumulative loss of the forecaster with fixed coefficients $\mathbf{B}$. Hence, by adapting the proof of Theorem 11.3, which shows a bound on the regret of the gradient-based forecaster, we can bound the worst-case logarithmic wealth ratio of the EG investment strategy. On the other hand, the following simple and direct analysis provides slightly better constants.

Theorem 10.4. *Assume that the price relatives $x_{i,t}$ all fall between two positive constants $c < C$. Then the worst-case logarithmic wealth ratio of the EG investment strategy with $\eta = (c/C)\sqrt{(8 \ln m)/n}$ is bounded by*

$$\frac{\ln m}{\eta} + \frac{n\eta}{8} \frac{C^2}{c^2} = \frac{C}{c}\sqrt{\frac{n}{2} \ln m}.$$

Proof. The worst-case logarithmic wealth ratio is

$$\max_{\mathbf{x}^n} \max_{\mathbf{B} \in \mathcal{D}} \ln \frac{\prod_{t=1}^{n} \mathbf{B} \cdot \mathbf{x}_t}{\prod_{t=1}^{n} \mathbf{P}_t \cdot \mathbf{x}_t},$$

where the first maximum is taken over market sequences satisfying the boundedness assumption. By using the elementary inequality $\ln(1 + u) \le u$, we obtain

$$\ln \frac{\prod_{t=1}^{n} \mathbf{B} \cdot \mathbf{x}_t}{\prod_{t=1}^{n} \mathbf{P}_t \cdot \mathbf{x}_t} = \sum_{t=1}^{n} \ln\left(1 + \frac{(\mathbf{B} - \mathbf{P}_t) \cdot \mathbf{x}_t}{\mathbf{P}_t \cdot \mathbf{x}_t}\right)$$

$$\le \sum_{t=1}^{n} \sum_{i=1}^{m} \frac{(B_i - P_{i,t}) x_{i,t}}{\mathbf{P}_t \cdot \mathbf{x}_t}$$

$$= \sum_{t=1}^{n} \left(\sum_{j=1}^{m} B_j \frac{x_{j,t}}{\mathbf{P}_t \cdot \mathbf{x}_t} - \sum_{i=1}^{m} P_{i,t} \frac{x_{i,t}}{\mathbf{P}_t \cdot \mathbf{x}_t}\right).$$

Introducing the notation

$$\ell'_{i,t} = \frac{C}{c} - \frac{x_{i,t}}{\mathbf{P}_t \cdot \mathbf{x}_t}$$

and noting that, under the boundedness assumption $0 < c \le x_{i,t} \le C$, $\ell'_{i,t} \in [0, C/c]$, we may rewrite the wealth ratio above as

$$\ln \frac{\prod_{t=1}^{n} \mathbf{B} \cdot \mathbf{x}_t}{\prod_{t=1}^{n} \mathbf{P}_t \cdot \mathbf{x}_t} \le \sum_{t=1}^{n} \sum_{i=1}^{m} P_{i,t} \ell'_{i,t} - \sum_{t=1}^{n} \sum_{i=1}^{m} B_i \ell'_{i,t}.$$

Because this expression is a linear function of $\mathbf{B}$, it achieves its maximum in one of the corners of the simplex $\mathcal{D}$, and therefore

$$\max_{\mathbf{B} \in \mathcal{D}} \ln \frac{\prod_{t=1}^{n} \mathbf{B} \cdot \mathbf{x}_t}{\prod_{t=1}^{n} \mathbf{P}_t \cdot \mathbf{x}_t} \le \sum_{t=1}^{n} \sum_{i=1}^{m} \ell'_{i,t} P_{i,t} - \min_{j=1,\ldots,m} \sum_{t=1}^{n} \ell'_{j,t}.$$

Now note that

$$P_{i,t} = \frac{w_{i,t-1}}{W_{t-1}} = \frac{\exp\left(\eta \sum_{s=1}^{t-1}(x_{i,s}/\mathbf{P}_s \cdot \mathbf{x}_s)\right)}{\sum_{j=1}^{m} \exp\left(\eta \sum_{s=1}^{t-1}(x_{j,s}/\mathbf{P}_s \cdot \mathbf{x}_s)\right)} = \frac{\exp\left(-\eta \sum_{s=1}^{t-1} \ell'_{i,s}\right)}{\sum_{j=1}^{m} \exp\left(-\eta \sum_{s=1}^{t-1} \ell'_{j,s}\right)}.$$

Hence, $\mathbf{P}_1, \mathbf{P}_2, \ldots$ are the predictions of the exponentially weighted average forecaster applied to a linear loss function with range $[0, C/c]$. The regret

$$\sum_{t=1}^{n} \sum_{i=1}^{m} \ell'_{i,t} P_{i,t} - \min_{j=1,\ldots,m} \sum_{t=1}^{n} \ell'_{j,t}$$

can thus be bounded using Theorem 2.2 applied to scaled losses (see Section 2.6). (Note that this theorem also applies when, as in this case, the losses at time t depend on the forecaster's prediction $\mathbf{P}_t \cdot \mathbf{x}_t$). ∎

The knowledge of constants c and C can be avoided using exponential forecasters with time-varying potentials like the one described in Section 2.8.

***Remark* 10.1.** A linear upper bound on the worst-case logarithmic wealth ratio is inevitably suboptimal. Indeed, the linear upper bound

$$\sum_{j=1}^{m} B_j \left(\sum_{t=1}^{n} \left(\sum_{i=1}^{m} P_{i,t} \ell_{i,t} \right) - \ell_{j,t} \right) = \sum_{j=1}^{m} B_j \sum_{i=1}^{m} \left(\sum_{t=1}^{n} P_{i,t} \left(\ell_{i,t} - \ell_{j,t} \right) \right)$$

is maximized for a constantly rebalanced portfolio $\mathbf{B}$ lying in a corner of the simplex $\mathcal{D}$, whereas the logarithmic wealth ratio $\ln \prod_{t=1}^{n} (\mathbf{B} \cdot \mathbf{x}_t / \mathbf{P}_t \cdot \mathbf{x}_t)$ is concave in $\mathbf{B}$, and therefore it is possibly maximized in the interior of the simplex. Thus, no algorithm trying to minimize the linear upper bound on the worst-case logarithmic wealth ratio can be minimax optimal. Note also that the bound obtained for the worst-case logarithmic wealth ratio of the EG strategy grows as $\sqrt{n}$, whereas that of the universal portfolio has only a logarithmic growth.

The following simple example shows that the bound of the order of $\sqrt{n}$ cannot be improved for the EG strategy. Consider a market with two assets and market vectors $\mathbf{x}_t = (1, 1/2)$ for all t. Then, for every wealth allocation $\mathbf{P}_t$, $1/2 \le \mathbf{P}_t \cdot \mathbf{x}_t \le 1$. The best constantly rebalanced portfolio is clearly $(1, 0)$, and the worst-case logarithmic wealth ratio is

$$\sum_{t=1}^{n} \ln \frac{1}{1 - P_{2,t}/2} \ge \sum_{t=1}^{n} P_{2,t}/2.$$

In the case of the EG strategy, we may lower bound $P_{2,t}$ by

$$
\begin{aligned}
P_{2,t} &= \frac{\exp\left(\eta \sum_{s=1}^{t-1} \frac{1}{2\mathbf{P}_s \cdot \mathbf{x}_s}\right)}{\exp\left(\eta \sum_{s=1}^{t-1} \frac{1}{\mathbf{P}_s \cdot \mathbf{x}_s}\right) + \exp\left(\eta \sum_{s=1}^{t-1} \frac{1}{2\mathbf{P}_s \cdot \mathbf{x}_s}\right)} \\
&= \frac{\exp\left(-\eta \sum_{s=1}^{t-1} \frac{1}{2\mathbf{P}_s \cdot \mathbf{x}_s}\right)}{1 + \exp\left(-\eta \sum_{s=1}^{t-1} \frac{1}{2\mathbf{P}_s \cdot \mathbf{x}_s}\right)} \\
&\geq \frac{\exp\left(-\eta(t-1)\right)}{2}.
\end{aligned}
$$

Thus, the logarithmic wealth ratio of the EG algorithm is bounded from below by

$$
\sum_{t=1}^{n} \frac{\exp\left(-\eta(t-1)\right)}{4} = \frac{1}{4} \times \frac{1 - e^{-\eta n}}{1 - e^{-\eta}} \approx \frac{1}{4\eta},
$$

where the last approximation holds for large values of n. Since η is proportional to $1/\sqrt{n}$, the worst-case logarithmic wealth ratio is proportional to $\sqrt{n}$, a value significantly larger than the logarithmic growth obtained for the universal portfolio.

10.6 Investment with Side Information

The investment strategies considered up to this point determine their portfolio as a function of the past market behavior and the investment strategies in the comparison class. However, sometimes an investor may want to incorporate external information in constructing a portfolio. For example, the price of oil may have an effect on stock prices, and one may not want to ignore them even if oil is not traded on the market. Such arguments lead us to incorporating the notion of *side information*. We do this similarly as in Section 9.9.

Suppose that, at trading period t, before determining a portfolio, the investor observes the side information z_t, which we assume to take values in a set $\mathcal{Z}$ of finite cardinality. For simplicity, and without loss of generality, we take $\mathcal{Z} = \{1, \ldots, K\}$. The portfolio chosen by the forecaster at time t may now depend on the side information z_t. Formally, an *investment strategy with side information Q* is a sequence of functions $\mathbf{Q}_t : \mathbb{R}_+^{t-1} \times \mathcal{Z} \to \mathcal{D}$, $t = 1, \ldots, n$. At time t, on observing the side information z_t, the strategy uses the portfolio $\mathbf{Q}_t(\mathbf{x}^{t-1}, z_t)$. Starting with a unit capital, the accumulated wealth after n trading periods becomes

$$
S_n(Q, \mathbf{x}^n, z^n) = \prod_{t=1}^{n} \mathbf{x}_t \cdot \mathbf{Q}_t(\mathbf{x}^{t-1}, z_t).
$$

Our goal is to design investment strategies that compete with the best in a given reference class of investment strategies with side information. For simplicity, we consider reference classes built from static classes of investment strategies. More precisely, let $\mathcal{Q}_1, \ldots, \mathcal{Q}_K$ be "base" classes of *static* investment strategies and let $Q^{(1)} \in \mathcal{Q}_1, \ldots, Q^{(K)} \in \mathcal{Q}_K$ be arbitrary strategies. The class of investment strategies with side information we consider are such that

$$
\mathbf{Q}_t(\mathbf{x}^{t-1}, z_t) = \mathbf{Q}_{\overline{n}_{z_t}}^{z_t},
$$

where $\mathbf{Q}_t^j \in \mathcal{D}$ is the portfolio of an investment strategy $Q^{(j)} \in \mathcal{Q}_j$ at the tth time period and $\bar{n}_j$ is the length of the sequence of those time instances $s < t$ when $z_s = j$ ($j = 1, \ldots, K$). In other words, a strategy in the comparison class assigns a static strategy $Q^{(j)}$ to any $j = 1, \ldots, K$ and uses this strategy whenever the side information equals j. This formulation is the investment analogue of the problem of prediction with side information described in Section 9.9.

In analogy with the forecasting strategies introduced in Section 9.9, we may consider the following investment strategy: let $\mathcal{G}_1, \ldots, \mathcal{G}_K$ denote the classes of (static) forecasters induced by the classes of investment strategies $\mathcal{Q}_1, \ldots, \mathcal{Q}_K$, respectively. Let $q_n^{(1)}, \ldots, q_n^{(K)}$ be forecasters with worst-case cumulative regrets (with respect to the corresponding reference classes)

$$V_n(q_n^{(j)}, \mathcal{G}_j) = \sup_{y^n \in \mathcal{Y}^n} \sup_{g^{(j)} \in \mathcal{G}_j} \sum_{t=1}^{n} \ln \frac{g_t^{(j)}(y_t)}{q_t^{(j)}(y_t \mid y^{t-1})}.$$

On the basis of this, one may define the forecaster with side information in Section 9.9:

$$p_t(y \mid y^{t-1}, z_t) = q_{\bar{n}_{z_t}}^{(z_t)}(y \mid \bar{y}_{z_t}^t).$$

This forecaster now induces the investment strategy with side-information $\mathbf{P}_t(\mathbf{x}^{t-1}, z_t)$ defined by its components

$$P_{j,t}(\mathbf{x}^{t-1}, z_t) = \frac{\sum_{y^{t-1} \in \mathcal{Y}^{t-1}} p_s(j \mid y^{s-1}, z_s) \prod_{s=1}^{t-1} \left(x_{y_s,s} \, p_s(y_s \mid y^{s-1}, z_s) \right)}{\sum_{y^{t-1} \in \mathcal{Y}^{t-1}} \prod_{s=1}^{t-1} \left(x_{y_s,s} \, p_s(y_s \mid y^{s-1}, z_s) \right)}.$$

The following result is a straightforward combination of Theorems 9.7 and 10.1. The proof is left as an exercise.

Theorem 10.5. *For any side-information sequence $z_1, \ldots, z_n$, the investment strategy defined above has a worst-case logarithmic wealth ratio bounded by*

$$\sup_{\mathbf{x}^n} \sup_{Q \in \mathcal{Q}} \ln \frac{S_n(Q, \mathbf{x}^n, z^n)}{S_n(P, \mathbf{x}^n, z^n)} \leq \sum_{j=1}^{K} V_{\bar{n}_j}(q_n^{(j)}, \mathcal{G}_j).$$

If the base classes $\mathbf{Q}_1, \ldots, \mathbf{Q}_K$ all equal to the class of all constantly rebalanced portfolios and the forecasters $q^{(j)}$ are mixture forecasters, then it is easy to see that the forecaster of Theorem 10.5 takes the simple form

$$P_{j,t}(\mathbf{x}^{t-1}, z_t) = \frac{\int_{\mathcal{D}} B_j \, S_{\bar{n}_{z_t}}(\mathbf{B}, \bar{\mathbf{x}}_{z_t}^{t-1}) \mu(\mathbf{B}) \, d\mathbf{B}}{\int_{\mathcal{D}} S_{\bar{n}_{z_t}}(\mathbf{B}, \bar{\mathbf{x}}_{z_t}^{t-1}) \mu(\mathbf{B}) \, d\mathbf{B}}, \qquad j = 1, \ldots, m, \quad t = 1, \ldots, n,$$

where μ is a density function on $\mathcal{D}$ and $\bar{\mathbf{x}}_j^{t-1}$ is the subsequence of the past market sequence $\mathbf{x}^{t-1}$ determined by those time instances $s < t$ when $z_s = j$. Thus, the strategy defined above simply selects the subsequence of the past corresponding to the times when the side information was the same as the actual value of side information z_t and calculates a universal portfolio over that subsequence. Theorem 10.5, combined with Theorem 10.3, implies the following.

Corollary 10.1. *Assume that the universal portfolio with side information defined above is calculated on the basis of the Dirichlet* $(1/2, \ldots, 1/2)$ *density* μ. *Let* $\mathcal{Q}$ *denote the class of investment strategies with side information such that the base classes* $\mathcal{Q}_1, \ldots, \mathcal{Q}_K$ *all coincide with the class of constantly rebalanced portfolios. Then, for any side information sequence, the worst-case logarithmic wealth ratio with respect to class* $\mathcal{Q}$ *satisfies*

$$\sup_{\mathbf{x}^n} \sup_{Q \in \mathcal{Q}} \ln \frac{S_n(Q, \mathbf{x}^n, z^n)}{S_n(P, \mathbf{x}^n, z^n)}$$
$$\leq \frac{K(m-1)}{2} \ln \frac{n}{K} + K \ln \frac{\Gamma(1/2)^m}{\Gamma(m/2)} + \frac{K(m-1)}{2} \ln 2 + o(1).$$

10.7 Bibliographic Remarks

The theory of portfolio selection was initiated by the influential work of Markowitz [209], who introduced a statistical theory of investment. Kelly [180] considered a quite different approach, closer to the spirit of this chapter, for horse race markets of the type described in Section 9.3, and assumed an independent, identically distributed sequence of market vectors. Breiman [41] extended Kelly's framework to general markets with i.i.d. returns. The assumption of independence was substantially relaxed by Algoet and Cover [6], who considered stationary and ergodic markets; see also Algoet [4,5], Walk and Yakowitz [304], Györfi and Schäfer [136], and Györfi, Lugosi, and Udina [135] for various results under such general assumptions.

The problem of sequential investment of arbitrary markets was first considered by Cover and Gluss [71], who used Blackwell's approachability (see Section 7.7) to construct an investment strategy that performs almost as well as the best constantly rebalanced portfolio if the market vectors take their values from a given finite set. The universal portfolio strategy, discussed in Section 10.4, was introduced and analyzed in a pioneering work of Cover [70]. The minimax value $W_n(\mathcal{Q})$ for the class of all constantly rebalanced portfolios was found by Ordentlich and Cover [229]. The bound for the universal portfolios over the class of constantly rebalanced portfolios was obtained by Cover and Ordentlich [72]. The general results of Theorems 10.1 and 9.2 were given in Cesa-Bianchi and Lugosi [52]. The EG investments strategy was introduced and analyzed by Hembold, Schapire, Singer, and Warmuth [158]. Theorem 10.4 is due to them (though the proof presented here is taken from Stoltz and Lugosi [279]).

The model of investment with side information described in Section 10.6 was introduced by Cover and Ordentlich [72], and Corollary 10.1 is theirs. Györfi, Lugosi, and Udina [135] choose the side information by nonparameteric methods and construct investment strategies with universal guarantees for stationary and ergodic markets.

Singer [269] considers the problem of "tracking the best portfolio" and uses the techniques described in Section 5.2 to construct investment strategies that perform almost as well as the best investment strategy, in hindsight, which is allowed to switch between portfolios a limited number of times.

Kalai and Vempala [175] develop efficient algorithms for approximate calculation of the universal portfolio.

Vovk and Watkins [303] describe various versions of the universal portfolio, considering, among others, the possibility of "short sales," that is, when the portfolio vectors may have negative components (see also Cover and Ordentlich [73]).

Cross and Barron [78] extend the universal portfolio to general smoothly parameterized classes of investment strategies and also extend the problem of sequential investment to continuous time.

One important aspect of sequential trading that we have ignored throughout the chapter is transaction costs. Including transaction costs in the model is a complex problem that has been considered from various different points of view. We just mention the work of Blum and Kalai [33], Iyengar and Cover [167], Iyengar [166], and Merhav, Ordentlich, Seroussi, and Weinberger [215].

Borodin, El-Yaniv, and Gogan [37] propose ad hoc investment strategies with very convincing empirical performance.

Stoltz and Lugosi [279] introduce and study the notion of internal regret (see Section 4.4) in the framework of sequential investment.

10.8 Exercises

10.1 Show that for any constantly rebalanced portfolio strategy $\mathbf{B}$, the achieved wealth $S_n(\mathbf{B}, \mathbf{x}^n)$ is invariant under permutations of the sequence $\mathbf{x}_1, \dots, \mathbf{x}_n$.

10.2 Show that the wealth $S_n(P, \mathbf{x}^n)$ achieved by the universal portfolio P is invariant under permutations of the sequence $\mathbf{x}_1, \dots, \mathbf{x}_n$. Show that the same is true for the minimax optimal investment strategy P^* (with respect to the class of constantly rebalanced portfolios).

10.3 *(Universal portfolio exceeds value line index)* Let P be the universal portfolio strategy based on the uniform density μ. Show that the wealth achieved by P is at least as large as the geometric mean of the wealth achieved by the individual stocks, that is,

$$S_n(P, \mathbf{x}^n) \geq \left(\prod_{j=1}^{m} \prod_{t=1}^{n} x_{j,t} \right)^{1/m}$$

(Cover [70].) *Hint:* Use Jensen's inequality twice.

10.4 Let $\mathcal{F}$ be a finite class of forecasters. Show that the investment strategy induced by the mixture forecaster over this class is just the strategy described in the first example of Section 10.2 based on the class $\mathcal{Q}$ of investment strategies induced by members of $\mathcal{F}$.

10.5 Prove Lemma 10.2.

10.6 Consider the following randomized approximation of the universal portfolio. Observe that an interpretation of the identity $S_n(P, \mathbf{x}^n) = \int_{\mathcal{D}} S_n(\mathbf{B}, \mathbf{x}^n)\mu(\mathbf{B})d\mathbf{B}$ is that the wealth achieved by the universal portfolio is the expected value, with respect to the density μ, of the wealth of all constantly rebalanced strategies. This expectation may be approximated by randomly choosing N vectors $\mathbf{B}_1, \dots, \mathbf{B}_N$ according to the density μ and distributing the initial wealth uniformly among them just as in the example of Section 10.2. Investigate the relationship of the wealth achieved by this randomized strategy and that of the universal portfolio. What value of N do you suggest? (Blum and Kalai [33].)

10.7 Consider a market of $m > 2$ assets and class $\mathcal{Q}$ of all investment strategies that rebalance between two assets. More precisely, $\mathcal{Q}$ is the class of all constantly rebalanced portfolios such that the probability vector $\mathbf{B} \in \mathcal{D}$ characterizing the strategy has at most two nonzero components. Determine tight bounds for the minimax logarithmic wealth ratio $W_n(\mathcal{Q})$. Define and analyze a universal portfolio for this class.

10.8 *(Universal portfolio for smoothly parameterized classes)* Let $\mathcal{Q}$ be a class of static investment strategies that is, each $Q \in \mathcal{Q}$ is given by a sequence $\mathbf{B}_1, \ldots, \mathbf{B}_n$ of portfolio vectors (i.e., $\mathbf{B}_t \in \mathcal{D}$). Assume that the strategies in $\mathcal{Q}$ are parameterized by a set of vectors $\Theta \subset \mathbb{R}^d$, that is, $\mathbf{Q} \equiv \{Q_\theta = (\mathbf{B}_{\theta,1}, \ldots, \mathbf{B}_{\theta,n}) : \theta \in \Theta\}$. Assume that Θ is a convex, compact set with nonempty interior, and the parameterization is smooth in the sense that

$$\left\| \mathbf{B}_{\theta,t} - \mathbf{B}_{\theta',t} \right\| \le c \left\| \theta - \theta' \right\|$$

for all $\theta, \theta' \in \Theta$ and $t = 1, \ldots, n$, where $c > 0$ is a constant. Let μ be a bounded density on Θ and define the generalized universal portfolio by

$$P_{j,t}(\mathbf{x}^{t-1}) = \frac{\int_\Theta B_{\theta,t}^j S_{t-1}(Q_\theta, \mathbf{x}^{t-1})\mu(\theta)\, d\theta}{\int_\Theta S_{t-1}(Q_\theta, \mathbf{x}^{t-1})\mu(\theta)\, d\theta}, \qquad j = 1, \ldots, m, \quad t = 1, \ldots, n,$$

where $B_{\theta,t}^j$ denotes the $j$the component of the portfolio vector $\mathbf{B}_{\theta,t}$. Show that if the price relatives $x_{i,t}$ fall between $1/C$ and C for some constant $C > 1$, then the worst-case logarithmic wealth ratio satisfies

$$\sup_{\mathbf{x}^n} \sup_{\theta \in \Theta} \ln \frac{S_n(Q_\theta, \mathbf{x}^n)}{S_n(P, \mathbf{x}^n)} = O\left(d \ln n\right).$$

(Cross and Barron [78]).

10.9 *(Switching portfolios)* Define class $\mathcal{Q}$ of investment strategies that can switch buy-and-hold strategies at most k times during n trading periods. More precisely, any strategy in $Q \in \mathcal{Q}$ is characterized by a sequence $i_1, \ldots, i_n \in \{1, \ldots, m\}$ of indices of assets with $\mathrm{size}(i_1, \ldots, i_n) \le k$ (where size denotes the number of switches in the sequence; see the definition in Section 5.2) such that, at time t, Q invests all its capital in asset i_t. Construct an efficiently computable investment strategy P whose worst-case logarithmic wealth ratio satisfies

$$\sup_{\mathbf{x}^n} \sup_{Q \in \mathcal{Q}} \ln \frac{S_n(Q, \mathbf{x}^n)}{S_n(P, \mathbf{x}^n)} \le (k+1) \ln m + k \ln \frac{n}{k}.$$

(Singer [269]). *Hint:* Combine Theorem 10.1 with the techniques in Section 5.2.

10.10 *(Switching constantly rebalanced portfolios)* Consider now class $\mathcal{Q}$ of investment strategies that can switch constantly rebalanced portfolios at most k times. Thus, a strategy in $Q \in \mathcal{Q}$ is defined by a sequence of portfolio vectors $\mathbf{B}_1, \ldots, \mathbf{B}_n$ such that the number of times $t = 1, \ldots, n - 1$ with $\mathbf{B}_t \ne \mathbf{B}_{t+1}$ is bounded by k. Construct an efficiently computable investment strategy P whose logarithmic wealth ratio satisfies

$$\sup_{Q \in \mathcal{Q}} \ln \frac{S_n(Q, \mathbf{x}^n)}{S_n(P, \mathbf{x}^n)} \le \frac{C}{c} \sqrt{\frac{n}{2} \left((k+1) \ln m + (n-1) H \left(\frac{k}{n-1} \right) \right)}$$

whenever the price relatives $x_{i,t}$ fall between the constants $c < C$. *Hint:* Combine the EG investment strategy with the algorithm for tracking the best expert of Section 5.2.

10.11 *(Internal regret for sequential investment)* Given any investment strategy Q, one may define its *internal regret* (in analogy to the internal regret of forecasting strategies; see Section 4.4), for any $i, j \in \{1, \ldots, m\}$, by

$$R_{(i,j),n} = \sum_{t=1}^{n} \ln \frac{\mathbf{Q}_t^{i \to j} \cdot \mathbf{x}_t}{\mathbf{Q}_t \cdot \mathbf{x}_t},$$

where the modified portfolio $\mathbf{Q}_t^{i \to j}$ is defined such that its ith component equals 0, its jth component equals $Q_{j,t} + Q_{i,t}$, and all other components are equal to those of $\mathbf{Q}_t$. Construct an investment strategy such that if the price relatives are bounded between two constants c and C, then $\max_{i,j} R_{(i,j),n} = O(n^{1/2})$ and, at the same time, the logarithmic wealth ratio with respect to the class of all constantly rebalanced portfolios is also bounded by $O(n^{1/2})$ (Stoltz and Lugosi [279]). *Hint:* First establish a linear upper bound as in Section 10.4 and then use an internal regret minimizing forecaster from Section 4.4.

10.12 Prove Theorem 10.5 and Corollary 10.1.

11

Linear Pattern Recognition

11.1 Prediction with Side Information

We extend the protocol of prediction with expert advice by assuming that some *side information*, represented by a real vector $\mathbf{x}_t \in \mathbb{R}^d$, is observed at the beginning of each prediction round t. In this extended protocol we study experts and forecasters whose predictions are based on linear functions of the side information.

Let the decision space $\mathcal{D}$ and the outcome space $\mathcal{Y}$ be a common subset of the real line $\mathbb{R}$. *Linear experts* are experts indexed by vectors $\mathbf{u} \in \mathbb{R}^d$. In the sequel we identify experts with this corresponding parameter, thus referring to a vector $\mathbf{u}$ as a linear expert. The prediction $f_{\mathbf{u},t}$ of a linear expert $\mathbf{u}$ at time t is a linear function of the side information: $f_{\mathbf{u},t} = \mathbf{u} \cdot \mathbf{x}_t$. Likewise, the prediction $\widehat{p}_t$ of the *linear forecaster* at time t is $\widehat{p}_t = \mathbf{w}_{t-1} \cdot \mathbf{x}_t$, where the weight vector $\mathbf{w}_{t-1}$ is typically updated making use of the side information $\mathbf{x}_t$.

This prediction protocol can be naturally related to a sequential model of pattern recognition: by viewing the components of the side-information vector as features of an underlying data element, we can use linear forecasters to solve pattern classification or regression problems, as described in Section 11.3 and subsequent sections.

As usual, we define the regret of a forecaster with respect to expert $\mathbf{u} \in \mathbb{R}^d$ by

$$R_n(\mathbf{u}) = \widehat{L}_n - L_n(\mathbf{u}) = \sum_{t=1}^{n} \Big(\ell(\widehat{p}_t, y_t) - \ell(\mathbf{u} \cdot \mathbf{x}_t, y_t) \Big),$$

where ℓ is a fixed loss function.

In some applications we slightly depart from the linear prediction model by considering forecasters and experts that, given the side information $\mathbf{x}$, predict with $\sigma(\mathbf{u} \cdot \mathbf{x})$, where $\sigma : \mathbb{R} \to \mathbb{R}$ is a nonlinear *transfer function*. This transfer function, if chosen in conjunction with a specific loss function, makes the proof of regret bounds easier.

In this chapter we derive bounds on the regret of forecasters using weights of the form $\mathbf{w} = \nabla\Phi$, where Φ is a potential function. Unlike in the case of the weighted average forecasters using the advice of finitely many experts, we do not define potentials over the regret space (which is now a space of functions indexed by $\mathbb{R}^d$). Rather, we generalize the approach of defining potentials over the gradient of the loss presented in Section 2.5 for the exponential potential. To carry out this generalization we need some tools from convex analysis that are described in the next section. In Section 11.3 we introduce the gradient-based linear forecaster and prove a general bound for its regret. This bound is specialized to the polynomial and exponential potentials in Section 11.4, where we analyze the gradient-based forecaster using a nonlinear transfer function to control the norm of the loss gradient.

Section 11.5 introduces the projected forecaster, a gradient-based forecaster whose weights are kept in a given convex and closed region by means of repeated projections. This forecaster, when used with a polynomial potential, enjoys some remarkable properties. In particular, we show that projected forecasters are able to "track" the best linear expert and to dynamically tune their learning rate in a nearly optimal way.

In the rest of the chapter we explore potentials that change over time. The regret bounds that we obtain for the square loss grow logarithmically with time, providing an exponential improvement on the bounds obtained using static potentials. In Section 11.9 we show that these bounds cannot be improved any further. Finally, in Section 11.10 we obtain similar improved regret bounds for the logarithmic loss. However, the forecaster that achieves such logarithmic regret bounds is different, because it is based on a mixture of experts, similar, in spirit, to the mixture forecasters studied in Chapter 9.

11.2 Bregman Divergences

In this section we make a digression to introduce Bregman divergences, a notion that plays a key role in the analysis of linear forecasters.

Bregman divergences are a natural way of defining a notion of "distance" on the basis of an arbitrary convex function. To ensure that these divergences enjoy certain useful properties, the convex functions must obey some restrictions.

We call *Legendre* any function $F : \mathcal{A} \to \mathbb{R}$ such that

1. $\mathcal{A} \subseteq \mathbb{R}^d$ is nonempty and its interior $\text{int}(\mathcal{A})$ is convex;
2. F is strictly convex with continuous first partial derivatives throughout $\text{int}(\mathcal{A})$;
3. if $\mathbf{x}_1, \mathbf{x}_2, \ldots \in \mathcal{A}$ is a sequence converging to a boundary point of $\mathcal{A}$, then $\|\nabla F(\mathbf{x}_n)\| \to \infty$ as $n \to \infty$.

The *Bregman divergence* induced by a Legendre function $F : \mathcal{A} \to \mathbb{R}$ is the nonnegative function $D_F : \mathcal{A} \times \text{int}(\mathcal{A}) \to \mathbb{R}$ defined by

$$D_F(\mathbf{u}, \mathbf{v}) = F(\mathbf{u}) - F(\mathbf{v}) - (\mathbf{u} - \mathbf{v}) \cdot \nabla F(\mathbf{v}).$$

Hence, the Bregman divergence from $\mathbf{u}$ to $\mathbf{v}$ is simply the difference between $F(\mathbf{u})$ and its linear approximation via the first-order Taylor expansion of F around $\mathbf{v}$. Due to the convexity of F, this difference is always nonnegative. Clearly, if $\mathbf{u} = \mathbf{v}$, $D_F(\mathbf{u}, \mathbf{v}) = 0$. Note also that the divergence is not symmetric in the arguments $\mathbf{u}$ and $\mathbf{v}$, so we will speak of $D_F(\mathbf{u}, \mathbf{v})$ as the divergence from $\mathbf{u}$ to $\mathbf{v}$.

Example **11.1.** The half of the squared euclidean distance $\frac{1}{2} \|\mathbf{u} - \mathbf{v}\|^2$ is the (symmetric) Bregman divergence induced by the half of the squared euclidean norm $F(\mathbf{x}) = \frac{1}{2} \|\mathbf{x}\|^2$. In this example we may take $\mathcal{A} = \mathbb{R}^d$. □

Example **11.2.** The unnormalized Kullback–Leibler divergence

$$D_F(\mathbf{p}, \mathbf{q}) = \sum_{i=1}^{d} p_i \ln \frac{p_i}{q_i} + \sum_{i=1}^{d} (q_i - p_i)$$

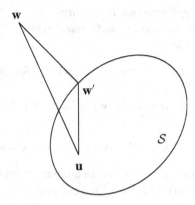

Figure 11.1. This figure illustrates the generalized pythagorean inequality for squared euclidean distances. The law of cosines states that $\|\mathbf{u} - \mathbf{w}\|^2$ is equal to $\|\mathbf{u} - \mathbf{w}'\|^2 + \|\mathbf{w}' - \mathbf{w}\|^2 - 2\|\mathbf{u} - \mathbf{w}'\|\,\|\mathbf{w}' - \mathbf{w}\|\cos\theta$, where θ is the angle at vertex $\mathbf{w}'$ of the triangle. If $\mathbf{w}'$ is the closest point to $\mathbf{w}$ in the convex set S, then $\cos\theta \leq 0$, implying that $\|\mathbf{u} - \mathbf{w}\|^2 \geq \|\mathbf{u} - \mathbf{w}'\|^2 + \|\mathbf{w}' - \mathbf{w}\|^2$.

is the Bregman divergence induced by the unnormalized negative entropy

$$F(\mathbf{p}) = \sum_{i=1}^{d} p_i \ln p_i - \sum_{i=1}^{d} p_i$$

defined on $\mathcal{A} = (0, \infty)^d$. $\quad\Box$

The following result, whose proof is left as an easy exercise, shows a basic relationship between the divergences of three arbitrary points. This relationship is used several times in subsequent sections.

Lemma 11.1. *Let $F : \mathcal{A} \to \mathbb{R}$ be Legendre. Then, for all $\mathbf{u} \in \mathcal{A}$ and all $\mathbf{v}, \mathbf{w} \in \text{int}(\mathcal{A})$,*

$$D_F(\mathbf{u}, \mathbf{v}) + D_F(\mathbf{v}, \mathbf{w}) = D_F(\mathbf{u}, \mathbf{w}) + (\mathbf{u} - \mathbf{v})\big(\nabla F(\mathbf{w}) - \nabla F(\mathbf{v})\big).$$

We now investigate the properties of projections based on Bregman divergences. Let $F : \mathcal{A} \to \mathbb{R}$ be a Legendre function and let $S \subset \mathbb{R}^d$ be a closed convex set with $S \cap \mathcal{A} \neq \emptyset$. The Bregman projection of $\mathbf{w} \in \text{int}(\mathcal{A})$ onto S is

$$\underset{\mathbf{u} \in S \cap \mathcal{A}}{\text{argmin}}\, D_F(\mathbf{u}, \mathbf{w}).$$

The following lemma, whose proof is based on standard calculus, ensures existence and uniqueness of projections.

Lemma 11.2. *For all Legendre functions $F : \mathcal{A} \to \mathbb{R}$, for all closed convex sets $S \subset \mathbb{R}^d$ such that $\mathcal{A} \cap S \neq \emptyset$, and for all $\mathbf{w} \in \text{int}(\mathcal{A})$, the Bregman projection of $\mathbf{w}$ onto S exists and is unique.*

With respect to projections, all Bregman divergences behave similarly to the squared euclidean distance, as shown by the next result (see Figure 11.1).

Lemma 11.3 (Generalized pythagorean inequality). *Let F be a Legendre function. For all $\mathbf{w} \in \text{int}(\mathcal{A})$ and for all convex and closed sets $\mathcal{S} \subseteq \mathbb{R}^d$ with $\mathcal{S} \cap A \neq \emptyset$, if $\mathbf{w}' = \arg\min_{\mathbf{v} \in \mathcal{S} \cap \mathcal{A}} D_F(\mathbf{v}, \mathbf{w})$ then*

$$D_F(\mathbf{u}, \mathbf{w}) \geq D_F(\mathbf{u}, \mathbf{w}') + D_F(\mathbf{w}', \mathbf{w}) \qquad \text{for all } \mathbf{u} \in \mathcal{S}.$$

Proof. Define the function $G(\mathbf{x}) = D_F(\mathbf{x}, \mathbf{w}) - D_F(\mathbf{x}, \mathbf{w}')$. Expanding the divergences and simplifying, we note that

$$G(\mathbf{x}) = -F(\mathbf{w}) - (\mathbf{x} - \mathbf{w})\nabla F(\mathbf{w}) + F(\mathbf{w}') + (\mathbf{x} - \mathbf{w}')\nabla F(\mathbf{w}').$$

Thus G is linear. Let $\mathbf{x}_\alpha = \alpha \mathbf{u} + (1 - \alpha)\mathbf{w}'$ be an arbitrary point on the line joining $\mathbf{u}$ and $\mathbf{w}'$. By linearity, $G(\mathbf{x}_\alpha) = \alpha G(\mathbf{u}) + (1 - \alpha)G(\mathbf{w}')$ and thus

$$\begin{aligned} D_F(\mathbf{x}_\alpha, \mathbf{w}) &- D_F(\mathbf{x}_\alpha, \mathbf{w}') \\ &= \alpha\big(D_F(\mathbf{u}, \mathbf{w}) - D_F(\mathbf{u}, \mathbf{w}')\big) + (1 - \alpha)D_F(\mathbf{w}', \mathbf{w}). \end{aligned}$$

For $\alpha > 0$, this leads to

$$\begin{aligned} D_F(\mathbf{u}, \mathbf{w}) &- D_F(\mathbf{u}, \mathbf{w}') - D_F(\mathbf{w}', \mathbf{w}) \\ &= \frac{D_F(\mathbf{x}_\alpha, \mathbf{w}) - D_F(\mathbf{x}_\alpha, \mathbf{w}') - D_F(\mathbf{w}', \mathbf{w})}{\alpha} \geq \frac{-D_F(\mathbf{x}_\alpha, \mathbf{w}')}{\alpha}, \end{aligned}$$

where we used $D_F(\mathbf{x}_\alpha, \mathbf{w}) \geq D_F(\mathbf{w}', \mathbf{w})$. This last inequality is true since $\mathbf{w}'$ is the point in $\mathcal{S}$ with smallest divergence to $\mathbf{w}$ and $\mathbf{x}_\alpha \in \mathcal{S}$ since $\mathbf{u} \in \mathcal{S}$ and $\mathcal{S}$ is convex by hypothesis. Let $D(\mathbf{x}) = D_F(\mathbf{x}, \mathbf{w}')$. To prove the theorem it is then enough to prove that $D(\mathbf{x}_\alpha)/\alpha = 0$ for some $\alpha > 0$. Indeed,

$$\lim_{\alpha \to 0^+} \frac{D(\mathbf{x}_\alpha)}{\alpha} = \lim_{\alpha \to 0^+} \frac{D(\mathbf{w}' + \alpha(\mathbf{u} - \mathbf{w}')) - D(\mathbf{w}')}{\alpha}.$$

The last limit is the directional derivative $D'_{\mathbf{u} - \mathbf{w}'}(\mathbf{w}')$ of D in the direction $\mathbf{u} - \mathbf{w}'$ evaluated at $\mathbf{w}'$ (the directional derivative exists in $\text{int}(\mathcal{A})$ because of the second condition in the definition of Legendre functions; moreover, if $\mathbf{w} \in \text{int}(\mathcal{A})$, then the third condition guarantees that $\mathbf{w}'$ does not belong to the boundary of $\mathcal{A}$). Now, exploiting a well-known relationship between the directional derivative of a function and its gradient, we find that

$$D'_{\mathbf{u} - \mathbf{w}'}(\mathbf{w}') = (\mathbf{u} - \mathbf{w}) \cdot \nabla D(\mathbf{w}').$$

Since D is differentiable and nonnegative and $D(\mathbf{w}') = 0$, we have $\nabla D(\mathbf{w}') = 0$. This completes the proof. ∎

Note that Lemma 11.3 holds with equality whenever $\mathcal{S}$ is a hyperplane (see Exercise 11.2).

To derive some additional key properties of Bregman divergences, we need a few basic notions about convex duality. Let $F : \mathcal{A} \to \mathbb{R}$ be Legendre. Then its *Legendre dual* (or Legendre conjugate) is the function F^* defined by

$$F^*(\mathbf{u}) = \sup_{\mathbf{v} \in \mathcal{A}}\big(\mathbf{u} \cdot \mathbf{v} - F(\mathbf{v})\big).$$

The conditions defining Legendre functions guarantee that whenever F is Legendre, then $F^* : \mathcal{A}^* \to \mathbb{R}$ is also Legendre and such that $\mathcal{A}^*$ is the range of the mapping

$\nabla F : \text{int}(\mathcal{A}) \to \mathbb{R}^d$. Moreover, the Legendre dual F^{**} of F^* equals F (see, e.g., Section 26 in Rockafellar [247]). The following simple identity relates a pair of Legendre duals.

Lemma 11.4. *For all Legendre functions* F, $F(\mathbf{u}) + F^*(\mathbf{u}') = \mathbf{u} \cdot \mathbf{u}'$ *if and only if* $\mathbf{u}' = \nabla F(\mathbf{u})$.

Proof. By definition of Legendre duality, $F^*(\mathbf{u}')$ is the supremum of the concave function $G(\mathbf{x}) = \mathbf{u}' \cdot \mathbf{x} - F(\mathbf{x})$. If this supremum is attained at $\mathbf{u} \in \mathbb{R}^d$, then $\nabla G(\mathbf{u}) = 0$, which is to say $\mathbf{u}' = \nabla F(\mathbf{u})$. On the other hand, if $\mathbf{u}' = \nabla F(\mathbf{u})$, then $\mathbf{u}$ is a maximizer of $G(\mathbf{x})$, and therefore $F^*(\mathbf{u}') = \mathbf{u} \cdot \mathbf{u}' - F(\mathbf{u})$. ∎

The following lemma shows that gradients of a pair of dual Legendre functions are inverses of each other.

Lemma 11.5. *For all Legendre functions* F, $\nabla F^* = (\nabla F)^{-1}$.

Proof. Using Lemma 11.4 twice,

$$\mathbf{u}' = \nabla F(\mathbf{u}) \quad \text{if and only if} \quad F(\mathbf{u}) + F^*(\mathbf{u}') = \mathbf{u} \cdot \mathbf{u}'$$
$$\mathbf{u} = \nabla F^*(\mathbf{u}') \quad \text{if and only if} \quad F^*(\mathbf{u}') + F^{**}(\mathbf{u}) = \mathbf{u} \cdot \mathbf{u}'.$$

Because $F^{**} = F$, the lemma is proved. ∎

Example 11.3. The Legendre dual of the half of the squared p-norm $\frac{1}{2}\|\mathbf{u}\|_p^2$, $p \geq 2$, is the half of the squared q-norm $\frac{1}{2}\|\mathbf{u}\|_q^2$, where p and q are conjugate exponents; that is, $1/p + 1/q = 1$. The euclidean norm $\frac{1}{2}\|\mathbf{u}\|^2$ is the only self-dual norm (it is the dual of itself). The squared p-norms are Legendre, and therefore the gradients of their duals are inverses of each other,

$$\left(\nabla \tfrac{1}{2}\|\mathbf{u}\|_p^2\right)_i = \frac{\text{sgn}(u_i)\,|u_i|^{p-1}}{\|\mathbf{u}\|_p^{p-2}} \quad \text{and} \quad \left(\nabla \tfrac{1}{2}\|\mathbf{u}\|_p^2\right)^{-1} = \nabla \tfrac{1}{2}\|\mathbf{u}\|_q^2 ,$$

where, as before, $1/p + 1/q = 1$. □

Example 11.4. The function $F(\mathbf{u}) = e^{u_1} + \cdots + e^{u_d}$ has gradient $\nabla F(\mathbf{u})_i = e^{u_i}$ whose inverse is $\nabla F^*(\mathbf{v})_i = \ln v_i$, $v_i > 0$. Hence, the Legendre dual of F is

$$F^*(\mathbf{v}) = \sum_{i=1}^{d} v_i(\ln v_i - 1).$$

Note that if $\mathbf{v}$ lies on the probability simplex in $\mathbb{R}^d$ and $H(\mathbf{v})$ is the entropy of $\mathbf{v}$, then $F^*(\mathbf{v}) = -(H(\mathbf{v}) + 1)$. □

Example 11.5. The hyperbolic cosine potential

$$F(\mathbf{u}) = \frac{1}{2} \sum_{i=1}^{d} \left(e^{u_i} + e^{-u_i}\right)$$

has gradient with components equal to the hyperbolic sine $\nabla F(\mathbf{u})_i = \sinh(u_i) = \frac{1}{2}(e^{u_i} - e^{-u_i})$. Therefore, the inverse gradient is the hyperbolic arcsine, $\nabla F^*(\mathbf{v})_i = \operatorname{arcsinh}(v_i) = \ln(\sqrt{v_i^2 + 1} + v_i)$, whose integral gives us the dual of F

$$F^*(\mathbf{v}) = \sum_{i=1}^{d} \left(v_i \operatorname{arcsinh}(v_i) - \sqrt{v_i^2 + 1} \right). \quad \square$$

We close this section by mentioning an additional property that relates a divergence based on F to that based on its Legendre dual F^*.

Proposition 11.1. *Let $F : \mathcal{A} \to \mathbb{R}$ be a Legendre function. For all $\mathbf{u}, \mathbf{v} \in \operatorname{int}(\mathcal{A})$, if $\mathbf{u}' = \nabla F(\mathbf{u})$ and $\mathbf{v}' = \nabla F(\mathbf{v})$, then $D_F(\mathbf{u}, \mathbf{v}) = D_{F^*}(\mathbf{v}', \mathbf{u}')$.*

Proof. We have

$$
\begin{aligned}
D_F(\mathbf{u}, \mathbf{v}) &= F(\mathbf{u}) - F(\mathbf{v}) - (\mathbf{u} - \mathbf{v}) \cdot \nabla F(\mathbf{v}) \\
&= F(\mathbf{u}) - F(\mathbf{v}) - (\mathbf{u} - \mathbf{v}) \cdot \mathbf{v}' \\
&= \mathbf{u}' \cdot \mathbf{u} - F^*(\mathbf{u}') - \mathbf{v}' \cdot \mathbf{v} + F^*(\mathbf{v}') - (\mathbf{u} - \mathbf{v}) \cdot \mathbf{v}' \\
&\quad \text{(using Lemma 11.4)} \\
&= \mathbf{u}' \cdot \mathbf{u} - F^*(\mathbf{u}') + F^*(\mathbf{v}') - \mathbf{u} \cdot \mathbf{v}' \\
&= F^*(\mathbf{v}') - F^*(\mathbf{u}') - (\mathbf{v}' - \mathbf{u}') \cdot \mathbf{u} \\
&= F^*(\mathbf{v}') - F^*(\mathbf{u}') - (\mathbf{v}' - \mathbf{u}') \cdot \nabla F^*(\mathbf{u}') \\
&\quad \text{(using } \mathbf{u}' = \nabla F(\mathbf{u}) \text{ and Lemma 11.5)} \\
&= D_{F^*}(\mathbf{v}', \mathbf{u}').
\end{aligned}
$$

This concludes the proof. ∎

11.3 Potential-Based Gradient Descent

Now we return to the main topic of this chapter introduced in Section 11.1, that is, to the design and analysis of forecasters that use the side-information vector $\mathbf{x}_t$ and compete with linear experts, or, in other words, with reference forecasters whose prediction takes the form $f_{\mathbf{u},t} = \mathbf{u} \cdot \mathbf{x}_t$ for some fixed vector $\mathbf{u} \in \mathbb{R}^d$. In this and the four subsequent sections we focus our attention on linear forecasters whose prediction, at time t, takes the form $\widehat{p}_t = \mathbf{w}_{t-1} \cdot \mathbf{x}_t$. The weight vector $\mathbf{w}_t$ used in the next round of prediction is determined as a function of the current weight $\mathbf{w}_{t-1}$, the side information $\mathbf{x}_t$, and the outcome y_t. The forecasters studied in these sections differ in the way the weight vectors are updated. We start by describing a family of forecasters that update their weights by performing a kind of gradient descent based on an appropriately defined potential function.

To motivate the gradient descent forecasters defined below, we compare them first to the potential-based forecasters introduced in Chapter 2 in a different setup. Recall that in Chapter 2 we define weighted average forecasters using potential functions in order to control the dependence of the weights on the regret. More precisely, we define weights at time t by $\mathbf{w}_{t-1} = \nabla \Phi(\mathbf{R}_{t-1})$, where $\mathbf{R}_{t-1}$ is the cumulative regret up to time $t - 1$. The convexity of the loss function, through which the regret is defined, entails (via Lemma 2.1) an invariant that we call the Blackwell condition: $\mathbf{w}_{t-1} \cdot \mathbf{r}_t \leq 0$. This invariant, together with Taylor's theorem, is the main tool used in Theorem 2.1.

If Φ is a Legendre function, then Lemma 11.5 provides the dual relations $\mathbf{w}_t = \nabla\Phi(\mathbf{R}_t)$ and $\mathbf{R}_t = \nabla\Phi^*(\mathbf{w}_t)$. As Φ and Φ^* are Legendre duals, we may call *primal weights* the regrets $\mathbf{R}_t$ and *dual weights* the weights $\mathbf{w}_t$, where $\nabla\Phi$ maps the primal weights to the dual weights and $\nabla\Phi^*$ performs the inverse mapping. Introducing the notation $\boldsymbol{\theta}_t = \mathbf{R}_t$ to stress the fact that we now view regrets as parameters, we see that $\boldsymbol{\theta}_t$ satisfies the recursion

$$\boldsymbol{\theta}_t = \boldsymbol{\theta}_{t-1} + \mathbf{r}_t \qquad \text{(primal regret update).}$$

Via the identities $\boldsymbol{\theta}_t = \mathbf{R}_t = \nabla\Phi^*(\mathbf{w}_t)$, the primal regret update can be also rewritten in the equivalent dual form

$$\nabla\Phi^*(\mathbf{w}_t) = \nabla\Phi^*(\mathbf{w}_{t-1}) + \mathbf{r}_t \qquad \text{(dual regret update).}$$

To appreciate the power of this dual interpretation for the regret-based update, consider the following argument. The direct application of the potential-based forecaster to the class of linear experts requires a quantization (discretization) of the linear coefficient domain $\mathbb{R}^d$ in order to obtain a finite approximation of the set of experts. Performing this quantization in, say, a bounded region $[-W, W]^d$ of $\mathbb{R}^d$ results in a number of experts of the order of $(W/\varepsilon)^d$, where ε is the quantization scale. This inconvenient exponential dependence on the dimension d can be avoided altogether by replacing the regret minimization approach of Chapter 2 with a different loss minimization method. This method, which we call *sequential gradient descent*, is applicable to linear forecasters generating predictions of the form $\widehat{p}_t = \boldsymbol{\theta}_{t-1} \cdot \mathbf{x}_t$ and uses the weight update rule

$$\boldsymbol{\theta}_t = \boldsymbol{\theta}_{t-1} - \lambda \nabla\ell_t(\boldsymbol{\theta}_{t-1}) \qquad \text{(primal gradient update),}$$

where $\boldsymbol{\theta}_t \in \mathbb{R}^d$, $\lambda > 0$ is an arbitrary scaling factor, and we set $\ell_t(\boldsymbol{\theta}_{t-1}) = \ell(\boldsymbol{\theta}_{t-1} \cdot \mathbf{x}_t, y_t)$. With this method we replace *regret minimization* taking place in $\mathbb{R}^N$ (where $N = \mathbb{R}^d$ in this case) with *gradient minimization* taking place in $\mathbb{R}^d$. Note also that, due to the convexity of the loss functions $\ell(\cdot, y)$, minimizing the gradient implies minimizing the loss.

In full analogy with the regret minimization approach, we may now introduce a potential Φ, the associated dual weights $\mathbf{w}_t = \nabla\Phi(\boldsymbol{\theta}_t)$, and the forecaster

$$\widehat{p}_t = \mathbf{w}_{t-1} \cdot \mathbf{x}_t \qquad \text{(gradient-based linear forecaster)}$$

whose weights $\mathbf{w}_{t-1}$ are updated using the rule

$$\nabla\Phi^*(\mathbf{w}_t) = \nabla\Phi^*(\mathbf{w}_{t-1}) - \lambda\nabla\ell_t(\mathbf{w}_{t-1}) \qquad \text{(dual gradient update).}$$

By rewriting the dual gradient update as

$$\boldsymbol{\theta}_t = \boldsymbol{\theta}_{t-1} - \lambda\nabla\ell_t(\mathbf{w}_{t-1})$$

we see that this update corresponds to performing a gradient descent step on the weights $\boldsymbol{\theta}_t$, which are the image of $\mathbf{w}_t$ according to the bijection $\nabla\Phi^*$, using $\nabla\ell_t(\mathbf{w}_{t-1})$ rather than $\nabla\ell_t(\boldsymbol{\theta}_{t-1})$ (see Figure 11.2).

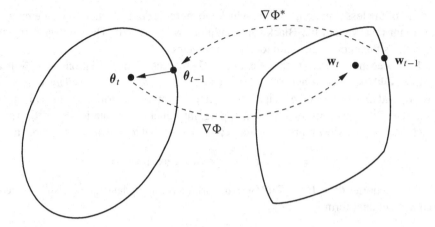

Figure 11.2. An illustration of the dual gradient update. A weight $\mathbf{w}_{t-1} \in \mathbb{R}^2$ is updated as follows: first, $\mathbf{w}_{t-1}$ is mapped to the corresponding primal weight $\boldsymbol{\theta}_{t-1}$ via the bijection $\nabla\Phi^*$. Then a gradient descent step is taken obtaining the updated primal weight $\boldsymbol{\theta}_t$. Finally, $\boldsymbol{\theta}_t$ is mapped to the dual weight $\mathbf{w}_t$ via the inverse mapping $\nabla\Phi$. The curve on the left-hand side shows a surface of constant loss. The curve on the right-hand side is the image of this surface according to the mapping $\nabla\Phi$, where Φ is the polynomial potential with degree $p = 2.6$.

Since $\nabla\Phi$ is the inverse of $\nabla\Phi^*$, it is easy to express explicitly the update in terms of $\mathbf{w}_t$:

$$\mathbf{w}_t = \nabla\Phi\Big(\nabla\Phi^*(\mathbf{w}_{t-1}) - \lambda\nabla\ell_t(\mathbf{w}_{t-1})\Big).$$

A different intuition on the gradient-based linear forecaster is gained by observing that $\mathbf{w}_t$ may be viewed as an approximate solution to

$$\min_{\mathbf{u}\in\mathbb{R}^d}\Big[D_{\Phi^*}(\mathbf{u}, \mathbf{w}_{t-1}) + \lambda\ell_t(\mathbf{u})\Big].$$

In other words, $\mathbf{w}_t$ expresses a tradeoff between the distance from the old weight $\mathbf{w}_{t-1}$ (measured by the Bregman divergence induced by the dual potential Φ^*) and the loss suffered by $\mathbf{w}_t$ if the last observed pair $(\mathbf{x}_t, y_t)$ appeared again at the next time step. To terminate the discussion on $\mathbf{w}_t$, note that $\mathbf{w}_t$ is in fact characterized as a solution to the following convex minimization problem:

$$\min_{\mathbf{u}\in\mathbb{R}^d}\Big[D_{\Phi^*}(\mathbf{u}, \mathbf{w}_{t-1}) + \lambda\Big(\ell_t(\mathbf{w}_{t-1}) + (\mathbf{u} - \mathbf{w}_{t-1})\nabla\ell_t(\mathbf{w}_{t-1})\Big)\Big].$$

This second minimization problem is an approximated version of the first one because the term $\ell_t(\mathbf{w}_{t-1}) + (\mathbf{u} - \mathbf{w}_{t-1})\nabla\ell_t(\mathbf{w}_{t-1})$ is the first-order Taylor approximation of $\ell_t(\mathbf{u})$ around $\mathbf{w}_{t-1}$.

We call *regular loss function* any convex, differentiable, nonnegative function $\ell : \mathbb{R} \times \mathbb{R} \to \mathbb{R}$ such that, for any fixed $\mathbf{x}_t \in \mathbb{R}^d$ and $y_t \in \mathbb{R}$, the function $\ell_t(\mathbf{w}) = \ell(\mathbf{w} \cdot \mathbf{x}_t, y_t)$ is differentiable. The next result shows a general bound on the regret of the gradient-based linear forecaster.

Theorem 11.1. *Let ℓ be a regular loss function. If the gradient-based linear forecaster is run with a Legendre potential Φ, then, for all $\mathbf{u} \in \mathbb{R}^d$, the regret $R_n(\mathbf{u}) = \widehat{L}_n - L_n(\mathbf{u})$*

satisfies

$$R_n(\mathbf{u}) \le \frac{1}{\lambda} D_{\Phi^*}(\mathbf{u}, \mathbf{w}_0) + \frac{1}{\lambda} \sum_{t=1}^{n} D_{\Phi^*}(\mathbf{w}_{t-1}, \mathbf{w}_t).$$

Proof. Consider any linear forecaster using fixed weights $\mathbf{u} \in \mathbb{R}^d$. Then

$$\ell_t(\mathbf{w}_{t-1}) \le \ell_t(\mathbf{u}) - (\mathbf{u} - \mathbf{w}_{t-1}) \cdot \nabla\ell_t(\mathbf{w}_{t-1})$$

(by Taylor's theorem and using convexity of ℓ)

$$= \ell_t(\mathbf{u}) + \frac{1}{\lambda}(\mathbf{u} - \mathbf{w}_{t-1}) \cdot \left(\nabla\Phi^*(\mathbf{w}_t) - \nabla\Phi^*(\mathbf{w}_{t-1})\right)$$

(by definition of the dual gradient update)

$$= \ell_t(\mathbf{u}) + \frac{1}{\lambda}\left(D_{\Phi^*}(\mathbf{u}, \mathbf{w}_{t-1}) - D_{\Phi^*}(\mathbf{u}, \mathbf{w}_t) + D_{\Phi^*}(\mathbf{w}_{t-1}, \mathbf{w}_t)\right)$$

(by Lemma 11.1).

Summing over t and using the nonnegativity of Bregman divergences to drop the term $-D_{\Phi^*}(\mathbf{u}, \mathbf{w}_n)$ completes the proof. ∎

At a first glance, the bound of Theorem 11.1 may give the impression that the larger the λ, the smaller the regret is. However, a large value of λ may make the weight vectors $\mathbf{w}_t$ change rapidly with time, causing an increase in the divergences in the second term. In the concrete examples that follow, we will see that the learning rate λ needs to be tuned carefully to obtain optimal performance.

It is interesting to compare the bound of Theorem 11.1 (for $\lambda = 1$) with the bound of Theorem 2.1. Rewriting both bounds in primal weight form, we obtain, setting $\mathbf{w}_0 = \nabla\Phi(\mathbf{0})$,

$$\Phi(\mathbf{R}_n) \le \Phi(\mathbf{0}) + \sum_{t=1}^{n} D_\Phi(\boldsymbol{\theta}_t, \boldsymbol{\theta}_{t-1})$$

$$R_n(\mathbf{u}) \le D_\Phi\left(\mathbf{0}, \nabla\Phi^*(\mathbf{u})\right) + \sum_{t=1}^{n} D_\Phi\left(\boldsymbol{\theta}'_t, \boldsymbol{\theta}'_{t-1}\right),$$

where the $\boldsymbol{\theta}_t$ are updated using the primal regret update (as in Theorem 2.1) and the $\boldsymbol{\theta}'_t$ are updated using the primal gradient update (as in Theorem 11.1). Note that, in both cases, the terms in the sum on the right-hand side are the divergences from the old primal weight to the new primal weight. However, whereas the first bound applies to a set of N arbitrary experts, the second bound applies to the set of all (continuously many) linear experts.

11.4 The Transfer Function

To add flexibility to the gradient-based linear forecaster, and to make its analysis easier, we constrain its predictions $\widehat{p}_t = \mathbf{w}_{t-1} \cdot \mathbf{x}_t$ by introducing a differentiable and nondecreasing *transfer function* $\sigma : \mathbb{R} \to \mathbb{R}$ and letting $\widehat{p}_t = \sigma(\mathbf{w}_{t-1} \cdot \mathbf{x}_t)$. Similarly, we redefine the predictions of expert $\mathbf{u}$ as $\sigma(\mathbf{u} \cdot \mathbf{x}_t)$. and let $\ell_t^\sigma(\mathbf{w}_{t-1}) = \ell\left(\sigma(\mathbf{w}_{t-1} \cdot \mathbf{x}_t), y_t\right)$. The forecaster predicting with a transfer function, which we simply call *gradient-based forecaster*, is sketched in the following:

THE GRADIENT-BASED FORECASTER

Parameters: learning rate $\lambda > 0$, transfer function σ.

Initialization: $\mathbf{w}_0 = \nabla \Phi(\mathbf{0})$.

For each round $t = 1, 2, \ldots$

    (1) observe $\mathbf{x}_t$ and predict $\widehat{p}_t = \sigma(\mathbf{w}_{t-1} \cdot \mathbf{x}_t)$;
    (2) get $y_t \in \mathbb{R}$ and incur loss $\ell_t^\sigma(\mathbf{w}_{t-1}) = \ell(\widehat{p}_t, y_t)$;
    (3) let $\mathbf{w}_t = \nabla \Phi\big(\nabla \Phi^*(\mathbf{w}_{t-1}) - \lambda \nabla \ell_t^\sigma(\mathbf{w}_{t-1})\big)$.

The regret of the gradient-based forecaster with respect to a linear expert $\mathbf{u}$ takes the form

$$R_n^\sigma(\mathbf{u}) = \sum_{t=1}^n \Big(\ell_t^\sigma(\mathbf{w}_{t-1}) - \ell_t^\sigma(\mathbf{u})\Big).$$

Note that, for fairness, the loss of the forecaster $\widehat{p}_t = \sigma(\mathbf{w}_{t-1} \cdot \mathbf{x}_t)$ is compared with the loss of the "transferred" linear expert $\sigma(\mathbf{u} \cdot \mathbf{x}_t)$. Instances of the gradient-based forecaster obtained by considering specific potentials correspond to well-known pattern recognition algorithms. For example, the Widrow–Hoff rule [310] $\mathbf{w}_t = \mathbf{w}_{t-1} - \lambda(\mathbf{w}_{t-1} \cdot \mathbf{x}_t - y_t)$ is equivalent to the gradient-based forecaster using the quadratic potential (i.e., the polynomial potential with $p = 2$), the square loss, and the identity transfer function $\sigma(p) = p$. The EG algorithm of Kivinen and Warmuth [181] corresponds to the forecaster using the exponential potential. Regret bounds for these concrete potentials are derived later in this section.

To apply Theorem 11.1 with transfer functions, we have to make sure that the loss $\ell(\sigma(\mathbf{w} \cdot \mathbf{x}), y)$ is a convex function of $\mathbf{w}$ for all y. Because $\mathbf{w} \cdot \mathbf{x}$ is linear, it suffices to guarantee that $\ell(\sigma(v), y)$ is convex in v. We call *nice pair* any pair (σ, ℓ) such that $\ell(\sigma(\cdot), y)$ is convex for all fixed y. Trivially, any regular loss function forms a nice pair with the identity transfer function. Less trivial examples are as follows.

***Example* 11.6.** The hyperbolic tangent $\sigma(v) = (e^v - e^{-v})/(e^v + e^{-v}) \in [-1, 1]$ and the entropic loss

$$\ell(p, y) = \frac{1+y}{2} \ln \frac{1+y}{1+p} + \frac{1-y}{2} \ln \frac{1-y}{1-p}$$

form a nice pair. $\quad\square$

***Example* 11.7.** The logistic transfer function $\sigma(v) = (1 + e^{-v})^{-1} \in [0, 1]$ and the Hellinger loss $\ell(p, y) = (\sqrt{p} - \sqrt{y})^2 + (\sqrt{1-p} - \sqrt{1-y})^2$ form a nice pair. $\quad\square$

To avoid imposing artificial conditions on the sequence of outcomes and side information, we focus on nice pairs (σ, ℓ) satisfying the additional condition

$$\left(\frac{\mathrm{d}\ell(\sigma(v), y)}{\mathrm{d}v}\right)^2 \le \alpha \, \ell(\sigma(v), y) \qquad \text{for some } \alpha > 0.$$

We call such pairs α-*subquadratic*. The nice pair of Example 11.6 is 2-subquadratic and the nice pair of Example 11.7 is 1/4-subquadratic. The nice pair formed by the identity transfer function and the square loss $\ell(p, y) = \frac{1}{2}(p - y)^2$ is 1-subquadratic. (To analyze the gradient-based forecaster, it is more convenient to work with this definition of square loss equal to half of the square loss used in previous chapters.) We now illustrate the regret bounds that we can obtain through the use of α-subquadratic nice pairs. Let $R_n^\sigma(\mathbf{u}) = \widehat{L}_n^\sigma - L_n^\sigma(\mathbf{u})$, where

$$\widehat{L}_n^\sigma = \sum_{t=1}^n \ell\big(\sigma(\mathbf{w}_{t-1} \cdot \mathbf{x}_t), y_t\big) \qquad \text{and} \qquad L_n^\sigma(\mathbf{u}) = \sum_{t=1}^n \ell\big(\sigma(\mathbf{u} \cdot \mathbf{x}_t), y_t\big).$$

Polynomial Potential

The polynomial potential $\|\mathbf{u}_+\|_p^2$ defined in Chapter 2 is not Legendre because, owing to the $(\cdot)_+$ operator, it is not strictly convex outside of the positive orthant. To make this potential Legendre, we may redefine it as $\Phi_p(\mathbf{u}) = \frac{1}{2}\|\mathbf{u}\|_p^2$, where we also introduced an additional scaling factor of 1/2 so as to have $\Phi_p^*(\mathbf{u}) = \Phi_q(\mathbf{u}) = \frac{1}{2}\|\mathbf{u}\|_q^2$ (see Example 11.3). It is easy to check that all the regret bounds we proved in Chapter 2 for the polynomial potential still hold for the Legendre polynomial potential.

***Theorem* 11.2.** *For any α-subquadratic nice pair (σ, ℓ), if the gradient-based forecaster using the Legendre polynomial potential Φ_p is run with learning rate $\lambda = 2\varepsilon/\big((p - 1)\alpha X_p^2\big)$ on a sequence $(\mathbf{x}_1, y_1), (\mathbf{x}_2, y_2)\ldots \in \mathbb{R}^d \times \mathbb{R}$, where $0 < \varepsilon < 1$, then for all $\mathbf{u} \in \mathbb{R}^d$ and for all $n \geq 1$ such that $\max_{t=1,\ldots,n} \|\mathbf{x}_t\|_p \leq X_p$,*

$$\widehat{L}_n^\sigma \leq \frac{L_n^\sigma(\mathbf{u})}{1 - \varepsilon} + \frac{\|\mathbf{u}\|_q^2}{\varepsilon(1 - \varepsilon)} \times \frac{(p - 1)\alpha X_p^2}{4},$$

where q is the conjugate exponent of p.

Proof. We apply Theorem 11.1 to the Legendre potential $\Phi_p(\mathbf{u})$ and to the convex loss $\ell_t^\sigma(\cdot)$ and obtain

$$R_n^\sigma(\mathbf{u}) \leq \frac{1}{\lambda} D_{\Phi_q}(\mathbf{u}, \mathbf{w}_0) + \frac{1}{\lambda} \sum_{t=1}^n D_{\Phi_q}(\mathbf{w}_{t-1}, \mathbf{w}_t).$$

Since the initial primal weight $\boldsymbol{\theta}_0$ is $\mathbf{0}$, $\mathbf{w}_0 = \nabla \Phi_p(\mathbf{0}) = \mathbf{0}$ and $\Phi_q(\mathbf{w}_0) = 0$. This implies $D_{\Phi_q}(\mathbf{u}, \mathbf{w}_0) = \Phi_q(\mathbf{u})$. As for the other terms, we simply observe that, by Proposition 11.1, $D_{\Phi_q}(\mathbf{w}_{t-1}, \mathbf{w}_t) = D_{\Phi_p}(\boldsymbol{\theta}_t, \boldsymbol{\theta}_{t-1})$, where $\boldsymbol{\theta}_t = \nabla \Phi_q(\mathbf{w}_t)$ and $\boldsymbol{\theta}_t = \boldsymbol{\theta}_{t-1} - \lambda \nabla \ell_t^\sigma(\mathbf{w}_{t-1})$. We can then adapt the proof of Corollary 2.1 replacing N by d and $\mathbf{r}_t$ by $-\lambda \nabla \ell_t^\sigma(\mathbf{w}_{t-1})$ and adjusting for the scaling factor 1/2. This yields

$$R_n^\sigma(\mathbf{u}) \leq \frac{\Phi_q(\mathbf{u})}{\lambda} + \frac{1}{\lambda} \sum_{t=1}^n D_{\Phi_q}(\mathbf{w}_{t-1}, \mathbf{w}_t)$$

$$\leq \frac{\Phi_q(\mathbf{u})}{\lambda} + (p - 1)\frac{\lambda}{2} \sum_{t=1}^n \big\|\nabla \ell_t^\sigma(\mathbf{w}_{t-1})\big\|_p^2$$

$$\leq \frac{\Phi_q(\mathbf{u})}{\lambda} + (p - 1)\frac{\lambda}{2} \sum_{t=1}^n \left(\frac{d\ell(\sigma(v_t), y_t)}{dv_t}\bigg|_{v_t = \mathbf{w}_{t-1} \cdot \mathbf{x}_t}\right)^2 \|\mathbf{x}_t\|_p^2$$

$$\leq \frac{\Phi_q(\mathbf{u})}{\lambda} + (p-1)\frac{\lambda}{2} \sum_{t=1}^{n} \alpha \, \ell_t^\sigma(\mathbf{w}_{t-1}) \, \|\mathbf{x}_t\|_p^2$$

(as (σ, ℓ) is α-subquadratic)

$$\leq \frac{\Phi_q(\mathbf{u})}{\lambda} + (p-1)\frac{\alpha \lambda}{2} X_p^2 \, \widehat{L}_n^\sigma.$$

Note that $R_n^\sigma(\mathbf{u}) = \widehat{L}_n^\sigma - L_n^\sigma(\mathbf{u})$. Rearranging terms, substituting our choice of λ, and using the equality $\frac{1}{2}\Phi_q(\mathbf{u}) = \|\mathbf{u}\|_q^2$ yields the result. ∎

Choosing, say, $\varepsilon = 1/2$, the bound of Theorem 11.2 guarantees that the cumulative loss of the gradient-based forecaster is not larger than twice the loss of any linear expert plus a constant depending on the expert. If ε is chosen to be a smaller constant, the factor of 2 in front of $L_n^\sigma(\mathbf{u})$ may be decreased to any value greater than 1, at the price of increasing the constant terms. One may be tempted to choose the value of the tuning parameter ε so as to minimize the obtained upper bound. However, this tuned ε would have to depend on the preliminary knowledge of $L_n^\sigma(\mathbf{u})$. Since the bound holds for all $\mathbf{u}$, and $\mathbf{u}$ is arbitrary, such optimization is not feasible. In Section 11.5 we introduce a so-called self-confident forecaster that dynamically tunes the value of the learning rate λ to achieve a bound of the order $\sqrt{L_n^\sigma(\mathbf{u})}$ for all $\mathbf{u}$ for which $\Phi_q(\mathbf{u})$ is bounded by a constant. Note that this bound behaves as if λ had been optimized in the bound of Theorem 11.2 separately for each $\mathbf{u}$ in the set considered.

Exponential Potential

As for the polynomial potential, the exponential potential defined as

$$\frac{1}{\eta} \ln \sum_{i=1}^{d} e^{\eta \, u_i}$$

is not Legendre (in particular, the gradient is constant along the line $u_1 = u_2 = \cdots = u_d$, and therefore the potential is not strictly convex). We thus introduce the Legendre exponential potential $\Phi(\mathbf{u}) = e^{u_1} + \cdots + e^{u_d}$ (the parameter η, used for the exponential potential in Chapter 2, is redundant here). Recalling Example 11.4, $\nabla \Phi^*(\mathbf{w})_i = \ln w_i$. For this potential, the dual gradient update $\mathbf{w}_t = \nabla \Phi\big(\nabla \Phi^*(\mathbf{w}_{t-1}) - \lambda \, \nabla \ell_t(\mathbf{w}_{t-1})\big)$ can thus be written as

$$w_{i,t} = \exp\big(\ln w_{i,t-1} - \lambda \nabla \ell_t(\mathbf{w}_{t-1})_i\big) = w_{i,t-1} \, e^{-\lambda \nabla \ell_t(\mathbf{w}_{t-1})_i} \qquad \text{for } i = 1, \dots, d.$$

Adding normalization, which we need for the analysis of the regret, results in the final weight update rule

$$w_{i,t} = \frac{w_{i,t-1} e^{-\lambda \nabla \ell_t(\mathbf{w}_{t-1})_i}}{\sum_{j=1}^{d} w_{j,t-1} e^{-\lambda \nabla \ell_t(\mathbf{w}_{t-1})_j}}.$$

This normalization corresponds to a Bregman projection of the original weight onto the probability simplex in $\mathbb{R}^d$, where the projection is taken according to the Legendre dual

$$\Phi^*(\mathbf{u}) = \sum_{i=1}^{d} u_i (\ln u_i - 1)$$

(see Exercise 11.4). A thorough analysis of gradient-based forecasters with projected weights is carried out in Section 11.5.

The gradient-based forecaster using the Legendre exponential potential with projected weights is sometimes called the EG (exponentiated gradient) algorithm. Although we used the Legendre version of the exponential potential to be able to define EG as a gradient-based forecaster, it turns out that the original potential is better suited to prove a regret bound. For this reason, we slightly change the proof of Theorem 11.1 and use the standard exponential potential. Finally, because the EG forecaster uses normalized weights, we also restrict our expert class to those $\mathbf{u}$ that belong to the probability simplex in $\mathbb{R}^d$.

Theorem 11.3. *For any α-subquadratic nice pair (σ, ℓ), if the EG forecaster is run with learning rate $\lambda = 2\varepsilon/(\alpha X_\infty^2)$ on a sequence $(\mathbf{x}_1, y_1), (\mathbf{x}_2, y_2) \ldots \in \mathbb{R}^d \times \mathbb{R}$, where $0 < \varepsilon < 1$, then for all $\mathbf{u} \in \mathbb{R}^d$ in the probability simplex and for all $n \geq 1$ such that $\max_{t=1,\ldots,n} \|\mathbf{x}_t\|_\infty \leq X_\infty$,*

$$\widehat{L}_n^\sigma \leq \frac{L_n^\sigma(\mathbf{u})}{1 - \varepsilon} + \frac{\alpha X_\infty^2 \ln d}{2\varepsilon(1 - \varepsilon)}.$$

Proof. Recall the (non-Legendre) exponential potential, with $\eta = 1$,

$$\Phi(\mathbf{u}) = \ln \sum_{i=1}^d e^{u_i}.$$

We now go through the proof of Theorem 11.1 using the relative entropy

$$D(\mathbf{u}\|\mathbf{v}) = \sum_{i=1}^d u_i \ln \frac{u_i}{v_i}.$$

(see Section A.2) in place of the divergence $D_{\Phi^*}(\mathbf{u}, \mathbf{v})$. Example 11.2 tells us that the relative entropy is the Bregman divergence for the unnormalized negative entropy potential

$$\Phi(\mathbf{u}) = \sum_{i=1}^d u_i \ln u_i - \sum_{i=1}^d u_i, \qquad \mathbf{u} \in (0, \infty)^d,$$

in the special case when both $\mathbf{u}$ and $\mathbf{v}$ belong to the probability simplex in $\mathbb{R}^d$.

Let $w'_{i,t} = w_{i,t-1} e^{-\lambda \nabla \ell_t(\mathbf{w}_{t-1})_i}$ and let $\mathbf{w}_t$ be $\mathbf{w}'_t$ normalized. Just as in Theorem 11.1, we begin the analysis by applying Taylor's theorem to ℓ:

$$\ell_t^\sigma(\mathbf{w}_{t-1}) - \ell_t^\sigma(\mathbf{u}) \leq -(\mathbf{u} - \mathbf{w}_{t-1}) \cdot \nabla \ell_t^\sigma(\mathbf{w}_{t-1}).$$

Introducing the abbreviation $\mathbf{z} = \lambda \nabla \ell_t^\sigma(\mathbf{w}_{t-1})$ and the new vector $\mathbf{v}$ with components $v_i = \mathbf{w}_{t-1} \cdot \mathbf{z} - z_i$, we proceed as follows:

$$-(\mathbf{u} - \mathbf{w}_{t-1}) \cdot \mathbf{z}$$

$$= -\mathbf{u} \cdot \mathbf{z} + \mathbf{w}_{t-1} \cdot \mathbf{z} - \ln \left(\sum_{i=1}^d w_{i,t-1} e^{v_i} \right) + \ln \left(\sum_{i=1}^d w_{i,t-1} e^{v_i} \right)$$

$$= -\mathbf{u} \cdot \mathbf{z} - \ln \left(\sum_{i=1}^d w_{i,t-1} e^{-z_i} \right) + \ln \left(\sum_{i=1}^d w_{i,t-1} e^{v_i} \right)$$

$$= \sum_{j=1}^{d} u_j \ln e^{-z_j} - \ln\left(\sum_{i=1}^{d} w_{i,t-1} e^{-z_i}\right) + \ln\left(\sum_{i=1}^{d} w_{i,t-1} e^{v_i}\right)$$

$$= \sum_{j=1}^{d} u_j \ln\left(\frac{1}{w_{j,t-1}} \frac{w_{j,t-1} e^{-z_j}}{\sum_{i=1}^{d} w_{i,t-1} e^{-z_i}}\right) + \ln\left(\sum_{i=1}^{d} w_{i,t-1} e^{v_i}\right)$$

$$= \sum_{j=1}^{d} u_j \ln \frac{w_{j,t}}{w_{j,t-1}} + \ln\left(\sum_{i=1}^{d} w_{i,t-1} e^{v_i}\right)$$

$$= D(\mathbf{u}\|\mathbf{w}_{t-1}) - D(\mathbf{u}\|\mathbf{w}_t) + \ln\left(\sum_{i=1}^{d} w_{i,t-1} e^{v_i}\right).$$

Note that, as in Theorem 11.1, we have obtained a telescoping sum. However, unlike Theorem 11.1, the third term is not a relative entropy.

On the other hand, bounding this extra term is not difficult. Since $\mathbf{w}_{t-1}$ belongs to the simplex, we may view $v_1, \ldots, v_d$ as the range of a zero-mean random variable V distributed according to $\mathbf{w}_{t-1}$. To this end, let

$$C_t = \left.\frac{d\ell(\sigma(v), y_t)}{dv}\right|_{v=\mathbf{w}_{t-1}\cdot\mathbf{x}_t} \|\mathbf{x}_t\|_\infty$$

so that $z_i \in [-\lambda C_t, \lambda C_t]$. Applying Hoeffding's inequality (Lemma A.1) to V then yields

$$\ln\left(\sum_{i=1}^{d} w_{i,t-1} e^{v_i}\right) \le \frac{\lambda^2 C_t^2}{2}.$$

Summing over $t = 1, \ldots, n$ gives

$$\sum_{t=1}^{n}\left(\ell_t^\sigma(\mathbf{w}_{t-1}) - \ell_t^\sigma(\mathbf{u})\right) \le \frac{D(\mathbf{u}\|\mathbf{w}_0)}{\lambda} + \frac{\lambda}{2}\sum_{t=1}^{n} C_t^2,$$

where the negative term $-D(\mathbf{u}\|\mathbf{w}_n)$ has been discarded. Using the assumption that (σ, ℓ) is α-subquadratic, we have $C_t^2 \le \alpha \ell_t^\sigma(\mathbf{w}_{t-1}) X_\infty^2$. Moreover, $\boldsymbol{\theta}_0 = \mathbf{0}$ implies that, after normalization, $\mathbf{w}_0 = (1/d, \ldots, 1/d)$. This gives $D(\mathbf{u}\|\mathbf{w}_0) \le \ln d$ (see Examples 11.2 and 11.4). Substituting these values in the above inequality we get

$$R_n^\sigma(\mathbf{u}) \le \frac{\ln d}{\lambda} + \frac{\alpha\lambda}{2} X_\infty^2 \widehat{L}_n^\sigma.$$

Note that this inequality has the same form as the corresponding inequality at the end of the proof of Theorem 11.2. Substituting our choice of λ and rearranging yields the desired result. ∎

Note that, as for the analysis in Chapter 2, we can obtain a bound equivalent to that of Theorem 11.3 by using Theorem 11.2 with the polynomial potential tuned to $p = 2 \ln d$.

The exponential potential has the additional limitation of using only positive weights. As explained in Grove, Littlestone, and Schuurmans [133], this limitation can be actually overcome by feeding to the forecaster modified side-information vectors $\mathbf{x}_t' \in \mathbb{R}^{2d}$, where

$$\mathbf{x}_t' = (-x_{1,t}, x_{1,t}, -x_{2,t}, x_{2,t}, \ldots, -x_{d,t}, x_{d,t})$$

and $\mathbf{x}_t = (x_{1,t}, \ldots, x_{d,t})$ is the original unmodified vector. Note that running the gradient-based linear forecaster with exponential potential on these modified vectors amounts to running the same forecaster with the hyperbolic cosine potential (see Example 11.5) on the original sequence of side information vectors.

We close this section by comparing the results obtained so far for the gradient-based forecaster. Note that the bounds of Theorem 11.2 (for the polynomial potential) and Theorem 11.3 (for the exponential potential) are different just because they use different pairs of dual norms. To allow a fair comparison between these bounds, fix some linear expert $\mathbf{u}$ and consider a slight extension of Theorem 11.3 in which we scale the simplex such that each $\mathbf{w}_t$ is projected enough to contain the chosen $\mathbf{u}$. Then the bound for the exponential potential takes the form

$$\frac{L_n^\sigma(\mathbf{u})}{1 - \varepsilon} + \frac{\alpha}{2\varepsilon(1 - \varepsilon)} \times (\ln d) \, \|\mathbf{u}\|_1^2 \, X_\infty^2,$$

where $X_\infty = \max_t \|\mathbf{x}_t\|_\infty$. The bound of Theorem 11.2 for the polynomial potential is very similar:

$$\frac{L_n^\sigma(\mathbf{u})}{1 - \varepsilon} + \frac{\alpha}{2\varepsilon(1 - \varepsilon)} \times \frac{p - 1}{2} \|\mathbf{u}\|_q^2 \, X_p^2,$$

where $X_p = \max_t \|\mathbf{x}_t\|_p$ and (p, q) are conjugate exponents. Note that the two bounds differ only because the sizes of $\mathbf{u}$ and $\mathbf{x}_t$ are measured using different pairs of dual norms (1 is the conjugate exponent of ∞). For $p \approx 2 \ln d$ the bound for the polynomial potential becomes essentially equivalent to the one for the exponential potential. To analyze the other extreme, $p = 2$ (the spherical potential), note that, using $\|\mathbf{v}\|_\infty \le \|\mathbf{v}\|_2 \le \|\mathbf{v}\|_1$ for all $\mathbf{v} \in \mathbb{R}^d$, it is easy to construct sequences such that one of the two potentials gives a regret bound substantially smaller than the other. For instance, consider a sequence $(\mathbf{x}_1, y_1), (\mathbf{x}_2, y_2) \ldots$ where, for all t, $\mathbf{x}_t \in \{-1, 1\}^d$ and $y_t = \mathbf{u}^\top \cdot \mathbf{x}_t$ for $\mathbf{u} = (1, 0, \ldots, 0)$. Then $\|\mathbf{u}\|_2^2 X_2^2 = d$ and $\|\mathbf{u}\|_1^2 X_\infty^2 = 1$. Hence, the exponential potential has a considerable advantage when a sequence of "dense" side information $\mathbf{x}_t$ can be well predicted by some "sparse" expert $\mathbf{u}$. In the symmetric situation (sparse side information and dense experts) the spherical potential is better. As shown by the arguments of Kivinen and Warmuth [181], these discrepancies turn out to be real properties of the algorithms, and not mere artifacts of the proofs.

11.5 Forecasters Using Bregman Projections

In this section we introduce a modified gradient-based linear forecaster, which always chooses its weights from a given convex set. This is done by following each gradient-based update by a projection onto the convex set, where the projection is based on the Bregman divergence defined by the forecaster's potential (Theorem 11.3 is a first example of this technique). Using this simple trick, we are able to extend some of the results proven in the previous sections.

In essence, projection is used to guarantee that the forecaster's weights are kept in a region where they enjoy certain useful properties. For example, in one of the applications of projected forecasters shown later, confining the weights in a convex region S of small diameter allows to effectively "track" the best linear forecaster as it moves around in the same region S. This is reminiscent of the "weight sharing" technique of Section 5.2, where, in order to track the best expert, the forecaster's weights were kept close to the uniform distribution.

Let $S \subseteq \mathbb{R}^d$ be a convex and closed set and define the forecaster based on the update

$$\mathbf{w}_t = \mathcal{P}_{\Phi^*}(\mathbf{w}'_t, S) \qquad \text{(projected gradient-based linear update)},$$

where $\mathbf{w}'_t = \nabla\Phi\big(\nabla\Phi^*(\mathbf{w}_{t-1}) - \lambda\nabla\ell_t(\mathbf{w}_{t-1})\big)$ is the standard dual gradient update, used here as an intermediate step, and $\mathcal{P}_{\Phi^*}(\mathbf{v}, S)$ denotes the Bregman projection $\text{argmin}_{\mathbf{u} \in S} D_{\Phi^*}(\mathbf{u}, \mathbf{v})$ of $\mathbf{v}$ onto S (if $\mathbf{v} \in S$, then we set $\mathcal{P}_{\Phi^*}(\mathbf{v}, S) = \mathbf{v}$). We now show two interesting applications of the projected forecaster.

Tracking Linear Experts

All results shown so far in this chapter have a common feature: even though the bounds hold for wide classes of data sequences, the forecaster's regret is always measured against the best *fixed* linear expert. In this section we show that the projected gradient-based linear forecaster has a good regret against any linear expert that is allowed to change its weight at each time step in a controlled fashion. More precisely, the regret of the projected forecaster is shown to scale with a measure of the overall amount of changes the expert undergoes.

Given a transfer function σ and an arbitrary sequence of experts $\langle \mathbf{u}_t \rangle = \mathbf{u}_0, \mathbf{u}_1, \ldots \in \mathbb{R}^d$, define the *tracking regret* by

$$R_n^\sigma(\langle\mathbf{u}_t\rangle) = \widehat{L}_n^\sigma - L_n^\sigma(\langle\mathbf{u}_t\rangle) = \sum_{t=1}^n \ell_t^\sigma(\mathbf{w}_{t-1}) - \sum_{t=1}^n \ell_t^\sigma(\mathbf{u}_{t-1}).$$

Theorem 11.4. *Fix any α-subquadratic nice pair (σ, ℓ). Let $1/p + 1/q = 1$, $U_q > 0$, and $\varepsilon \in (0, 1)$ be parameters. If the projected gradient-based forecaster based on the Legendre polynomial potential Φ_p is run with $S = \{\mathbf{w} \in \mathbb{R}^d : \Phi_q(\mathbf{w}) \le U_q\}$ and learning rate $\lambda = 2\varepsilon/\big((p-1)\alpha X_p^2\big)$ on a sequence $(\mathbf{x}_1, y_1), (\mathbf{x}_2, y_2)\ldots$ in $\mathbb{R}^d \times \mathbb{R}$, then for all sequences $\langle\mathbf{u}_t\rangle = \mathbf{u}_0, \mathbf{u}_1\ldots \in S$ and for all $n \ge 1$ such that $\max_{t=1,\ldots,n} \|\mathbf{x}_t\|_p \le X_p$,*

$$\widehat{L}_n^\sigma \le \frac{L_n^\sigma(\langle\mathbf{u}_t\rangle)}{1-\varepsilon} + \frac{(p-1)\alpha X_p^2}{2\varepsilon(1-\varepsilon)}\left(\sqrt{2\,U_q}\sum_{t=1}^n \|\mathbf{u}_{t-1} - \mathbf{u}_t\|_q + \frac{\|\mathbf{u}_n\|_q^2}{2}\right).$$

Observe that the smaller the parameter U_q, the smaller the second term becomes in the upper bound. On the other hand, with a small value of U_q, the set S shrinks and the loss of the forecaster is compared to sequences $\langle\mathbf{u}_t\rangle$ taking values in a reduced set.

Note that when $\mathbf{u}_0 = \mathbf{u}_1 = \cdots = \mathbf{u}_n$, the regret bound reduces to the bound proven in Theorem 11.2 for the regret against a fixed linear expert. The term

$$\sum_{t=1}^n \|\mathbf{u}_{t-1} - \mathbf{u}_t\|_q$$

can thus be viewed as a measure of "complexity" for the sequence $\langle\mathbf{u}_t\rangle$.

Before proving Theorem 11.4 we need a technical lemma stating that the polynomial potential of a vector is invariant with respect to the invertible mapping $\nabla\Phi_p$.

Lemma 11.6. *Let Φ_p be the Legendre polynomial potential. For all $\boldsymbol{\theta} \in \mathbb{R}^d$, $\Phi_p(\boldsymbol{\theta}) = \Phi_q(\nabla\Phi_p(\boldsymbol{\theta}))$.*

Proof.   Let $\mathbf{w} = \nabla\Phi_p(\boldsymbol{\theta})$. By Lemma 11.4, $\Phi_p(\boldsymbol{\theta}) + \Phi_q(\mathbf{w}) = \boldsymbol{\theta} \cdot \mathbf{w}$. By Hölder's inequality, $\boldsymbol{\theta} \cdot \mathbf{w} \le 2\sqrt{\Phi_p(\boldsymbol{\theta})\Phi_q(\mathbf{w})}$. Hence,

$$\left(\sqrt{\Phi_p(\boldsymbol{\theta})} - \sqrt{\Phi_q(\mathbf{w})}\right)^2 \le 0,$$

which implies $\Phi_p(\boldsymbol{\theta}) = \Phi_q(\mathbf{w})$.   ∎

We are now ready to prove the theorem bounding the tracking regret of the projected gradient-based forecaster.

Proof of Theorem 11.4.   From the proof of Theorem 11.1 we get

$$\ell_t^\sigma(\mathbf{w}_{t-1}) - \ell_t^\sigma(\mathbf{u}_{t-1})$$
$$\le \frac{1}{\lambda}\left(D_{\Phi_q}(\mathbf{u}_{t-1}, \mathbf{w}_{t-1}) - D_{\Phi_q}(\mathbf{u}_{t-1}, \mathbf{w}_t') + D_{\Phi_q}(\mathbf{w}_{t-1}, \mathbf{w}_t')\right)$$
$$\le \frac{1}{\lambda}\left(D_{\Phi_q}(\mathbf{u}_{t-1}, \mathbf{w}_{t-1}) - D_{\Phi_q}(\mathbf{u}_{t-1}, \mathbf{w}_t) + D_{\Phi_q}(\mathbf{w}_{t-1}, \mathbf{w}_t')\right),$$

where in the second step we used the fact that, since $\mathbf{u}_{t-1} \in S$, by the generalized pythagorean inequality Lemma 11.3,

$$D_{\Phi_q}(\mathbf{u}_{t-1}, \mathbf{w}_t') \ge D_{\Phi_q}(\mathbf{u}_{t-1}, \mathbf{w}_t) + D_{\Phi_q}(\mathbf{w}_t', \mathbf{w}_t)$$
$$\ge D_{\Phi_q}(\mathbf{u}_{t-1}, \mathbf{w}_t).$$

With the purpose of obtaining a telescoping sum, we add and subtract $D_{\Phi_q}(\mathbf{u}_{t-1}, \mathbf{w}_t) - D_{\Phi_q}(\mathbf{u}_t, \mathbf{w}_t)$ in the last formula, obtaining

$$\ell_t^\sigma(\mathbf{w}_{t-1}) - \ell_t^\sigma(\mathbf{u}_{t-1})$$
$$\le \frac{1}{\lambda}\Big(D_{\Phi_q}(\mathbf{u}_{t-1}, \mathbf{w}_{t-1}) - D_{\Phi_q}(\mathbf{u}_t, \mathbf{w}_t)$$
$$- D_{\Phi_q}(\mathbf{u}_{t-1}, \mathbf{w}_t) + D_{\Phi_q}(\mathbf{u}_t, \mathbf{w}_t) + D_{\Phi_q}(\mathbf{w}_{t-1}, \mathbf{w}_t')\Big).$$

We analyze the five terms on the right-hand side as we sum for $t = 1, \ldots, n$. The first two terms telescope; hence – as in the proof of Theorem 11.2 – we get

$$\sum_{t=1}^{n}\left(D_{\Phi_q}(\mathbf{u}_{t-1}, \mathbf{w}_{t-1}) - D_{\Phi_q}(\mathbf{u}_t, \mathbf{w}_t)\right) \le \Phi_q(\mathbf{u}_0).$$

Using the definition of Bregman divergence, the third and fourth terms can be rewritten as

$$-D_{\Phi_q}(\mathbf{u}_{t-1}, \mathbf{w}_t) + D_{\Phi_q}(\mathbf{u}_t, \mathbf{w}_t)$$
$$= \Phi_q(\mathbf{u}_t) - \Phi_q(\mathbf{u}_{t-1}) + (\mathbf{u}_{t-1} - \mathbf{u}_t) \cdot \nabla\Phi_q(\mathbf{w}_t).$$

Note that the sum of $\Phi_q(\mathbf{u}_t) - \Phi_q(\mathbf{u}_{t-1})$ telescopes. Moreover, letting $\theta_t = \nabla \Phi_q(\mathbf{w}_t)$,

$$(\mathbf{u}_{t-1} - \mathbf{u}_t) \cdot \nabla \Phi_q(\mathbf{w}_t) = (\mathbf{u}_{t-1} - \mathbf{u}_t) \cdot \theta_t$$

$$\leq 2\sqrt{\Phi_q(\mathbf{u}_{t-1} - \mathbf{u}_t)\Phi_p(\theta_t)} \qquad \text{(by Hölder's inequality)}$$

$$= 2\sqrt{\Phi_q(\mathbf{u}_{t-1} - \mathbf{u}_t)\Phi_q(\mathbf{w}_t)} \qquad \text{(by Lemma 11.6)}$$

$$\leq \|\mathbf{u}_{t-1} - \mathbf{u}_t\|_q \sqrt{2 U_q} \qquad \text{(since } \mathbf{w}_t \in S\text{)}.$$

Hence,

$$-\sum_{t=1}^{n} \left(D_{\Phi_q}(\mathbf{u}_{t-1}, \mathbf{w}_t) + D_{\Phi_q}(\mathbf{u}_t, \mathbf{w}_t) \right)$$

$$\leq \Phi_q(\mathbf{u}_n) - \Phi_q(\mathbf{u}_0) + \sqrt{2 U_q} \sum_{t=1}^{n} \|\mathbf{u}_{t-1} - \mathbf{u}_t\|_q .$$

Finally, we bound the fifth term using the techniques described in the proof of Theorem 11.2:

$$\sum_{t=1}^{n} D_{\Phi_q}\left(\mathbf{w}_{t-1}, \mathbf{w}'_t\right) \leq (p-1)\frac{\alpha \lambda^2}{2} X_p^2 \widehat{L}_n^\sigma .$$

Hence, piecing everything together,

$$\sum_{t=1}^{n} \left(\ell_t^\sigma(\mathbf{w}_{t-1}) - \ell_t^\sigma(\mathbf{u}_{t-1}) \right)$$

$$\leq \frac{\Phi_q(\mathbf{u}_0) + \Phi_q(\mathbf{u}_n) - \Phi_q(\mathbf{u}_0)}{\lambda}$$

$$+ \frac{\sqrt{2 U_q}}{\lambda} \sum_{t=1}^{n} \|\mathbf{u}_{t-1} - \mathbf{u}_t\|_q + (p-1)\frac{\alpha \lambda}{2} X_p^2 \widehat{L}_n^\sigma$$

$$= \frac{\Phi_q(\mathbf{u}_n)}{\lambda} + \frac{\sqrt{2 U_q}}{\lambda} \sum_{t=1}^{n} \|\mathbf{u}_{t-1} - \mathbf{u}_t\|_q + (p-1)\frac{\alpha \lambda}{2} X_p^2 \widehat{L}_n^\sigma .$$

Rearranging, substituting our choice of λ, and using the equality $\Phi_q(\mathbf{u}_n) = \frac{1}{2} \|\mathbf{u}_n\|_q^2$ yields the desired result. ∎

Self-Confident Linear Forecasters

The results of Section 11.4 leave open the problem of finding a forecaster with a regret growing sublinearly in $L_n^\sigma(\mathbf{u})$. If one limited the possible values of $\mathbf{u}$ to a bounded subset, then by choosing the learning rate λ as a function of n (assuming that the total number of rounds n is known in advance), one could optimize the bound for the maximal regret and obtain a bound that grows at a rate of $\sqrt{n}$. However, ideally, the regret bound should scale as $\sqrt{L_n^\sigma(\mathbf{u})}$ for each $\mathbf{u}$. Next, we show that, using a time-varying learning rate, the regret of the projected forecaster is bounded by a quantity of the order of $\sqrt{L_n^\sigma(\mathbf{u})}$ uniformly over time and for all $\mathbf{u}$ in a region of bounded potential.

SELF-CONFIDENT GRADIENT-BASED FORECASTER

Parameters: α-subquadratic nice pair (σ, ℓ), reals $p \geq 2$, $U_q > 0$, convex set $\mathcal{S} = \{\mathbf{u} \in \mathbb{R}^d : \Phi_q(\mathbf{u}) \leq U_q\}$, where $1/p + 1/q = 1$.

Initialization: $\mathbf{w}_0 = \nabla\Phi_q(\mathbf{0})$.

For each round $t = 1, 2, \ldots$

(1) observe $\mathbf{x}_t$ and predict $\widehat{p}_t = \sigma(\mathbf{w}_{t-1} \cdot \mathbf{x}_t)$;
(2) get $y_t \in \mathbb{R}$ and incur loss $\ell_t^\sigma(\mathbf{w}_{t-1}) = \ell(\widehat{p}_t, y_t)$;
(3) let $\mathbf{w}_t' = \nabla\Phi_p\big(\nabla\Phi_q(\mathbf{w}_{t-1}) - \lambda_t \nabla\ell_t^\sigma(\mathbf{w}_{t-1})\big)$, where

$$\lambda_t = \frac{\beta_t}{(p-1)\alpha X_{p,t}^2}, \qquad X_{p,t} = \max_{s=1,\ldots,t} \|\mathbf{x}_s\|_p, \qquad \beta_t = \sqrt{\frac{k_t}{k_t + \widehat{L}_t^\sigma}}$$

$$k_t = (p-1)\alpha X_{p,t}^2 U_q, \qquad \widehat{L}_t^\sigma = \sum_{s=1}^{t} \ell_s^\sigma(\mathbf{w}_{s-1});$$

(4) let $\mathbf{w}_t = \mathcal{P}_{\Phi_q}(\mathbf{w}_t', \mathcal{S})$.

A similar result is achieved in Section 2.3 of Chapter 2 by tuning the exponentially weighted average forecaster at time t with the loss of the best expert up to time t. Here, however, there are infinitely many experts, and the problem of tracking the cumulative loss of the best expert could easily become impractical. Hence, we use the trick of tuning the forecaster at time $t + 1$ using his own loss $\widehat{L}_t^\sigma$. Since replacing the best expert's loss with the forecaster's loss is justified only if the forecaster is doing almost as well as the currently best expert in predicting the sequence, we call this the "self-confident" gradient-based forecaster. The next result shows that the forecaster's self-confidence is indeed justified.

Theorem 11.5. *Fix any α-subquadratic nice pair (σ, ℓ). If the self-confident gradient-based forecaster is run on a sequence $(\mathbf{x}_1, y_1), (\mathbf{x}_2, y_2) \ldots \in \mathbb{R}^d \times \mathbb{R}$, then for all $\mathbf{u} \in \mathbb{R}^d$ such that $\Phi_q(\mathbf{u}) \leq U_q$ and for all $n \geq 1$,*

$$R_n^\sigma(\mathbf{u}) \leq 5\sqrt{(p-1)\alpha X_p^2 U_q L_n^\sigma(\mathbf{u})} + 30(p-1)\alpha X_p^2 U_q,$$

where $X_p = \max_{t=1,\ldots,n} \|\mathbf{x}_t\|_p$.

Note that the self-confident forecaster assumes a bound $2U_q$ on the norm $\|\mathbf{u}\|_q$ of the linear experts $\mathbf{u}$ against which the regret is measured. The gradient-based forecaster of Section 11.4, instead, assumes a bound X_p on the largest norm $\|\mathbf{x}_t\|_p$ of the side-information sequence $\mathbf{x}_1, \ldots, \mathbf{x}_n$. Since $\mathbf{u} \cdot \mathbf{x}_t \leq \|\mathbf{u}\|_q \|\mathbf{x}_t\|_p$, the two assumptions impose similar constraints on the experts.

Before proceeding to the proof of Theorem 11.5, we give two lemmas. The first states that the divergence of vectors with bounded polynomial potential is bounded. This simple fact is crucial in the proof of the theorem. Note that the same lemma is not true for the exponential potential, and this is the main reason why we analyze the self-confident predictor for the polynomial potential only.

Lemma 11.7. *For all* $\mathbf{u}, \mathbf{v} \in \mathbb{R}^d$ *such that* $\Phi_q(\mathbf{u}) \leq U_q$ *and* $\Phi_q(\mathbf{v}) \leq U_q$, $D_{\Phi_q}(\mathbf{u}, \mathbf{v}) \leq 4 U_q$.

Proof. First of all, note that the Bregman divergence based on the polynomial potential can be rewritten as

$$D_{\Phi_q}(\mathbf{u}, \mathbf{v}) = \Phi_q(\mathbf{u}) + \Phi_q(\mathbf{v}) - \mathbf{u} \cdot \nabla \Phi_q(\mathbf{w}).$$

This implies the following:

$$
\begin{aligned}
D_{\Phi_q}&(\mathbf{u}, \mathbf{v}) \\
&\leq \Phi_q(\mathbf{u}) + \Phi_q(\mathbf{v}) + |\mathbf{u} \cdot \nabla \Phi_q(\mathbf{w})| \\
&\leq \Phi_q(\mathbf{u}) + \Phi_q(\mathbf{v}) + 2\sqrt{\Phi_q(\mathbf{u})\Phi_p\left(\nabla \Phi_q(\mathbf{w})\right)} \quad \text{(by Hölder's inequality)} \\
&= \Phi_q(\mathbf{u}) + \Phi_q(\mathbf{v}) + 2\sqrt{\Phi_q(\mathbf{u})\Phi_q(\mathbf{w})} \quad \text{(by Lemma 11.6)} \\
&\leq 4 U_q
\end{aligned}
$$

and the proof is concluded. ∎

The proof of the next lemma is left as exercise.

Lemma 11.8. *Let* $a, \ell_1, \ldots, \ell_n$ *be nonnegative real numbers. Then*

$$\sum_{t=1}^{n} \frac{\ell_t}{\sqrt{a + \sum_{s=1}^{t} \ell_s}} \leq 2 \left(\sqrt{a + \sum_{t=1}^{n} \ell_t} - \sqrt{a} \right).$$

Proof of Theorem 11.5. Proceeding as in the proof of Theorem 11.4, we get

$$
\begin{aligned}
\ell_t^\sigma&(\mathbf{w}_{t-1}) - \ell_t^\sigma(\mathbf{u}) \\
&\leq \frac{1}{\lambda_t}\left(D_{\Phi_q}(\mathbf{u}, \mathbf{w}_{t-1}) - D_{\Phi_q}(\mathbf{u}, \mathbf{w}_t) + D_{\Phi_q}\left(\mathbf{w}_{t-1}, \mathbf{w}_t'\right) \right).
\end{aligned}
$$

Now, by our choice of λ_t,

$$
\begin{aligned}
\frac{1}{\lambda_t}&\left(D_{\Phi_q}(\mathbf{u}, \mathbf{w}_{t-1}) - D_{\Phi_q}(\mathbf{u}, \mathbf{w}_t) + D_{\Phi_q}\left(\mathbf{w}_{t-1}, \mathbf{w}_t'\right) \right) \\
&= (p-1)\alpha \left(\frac{X_{p,t}^2}{\beta_t} D_{\Phi_q}(\mathbf{u}, \mathbf{w}_{t-1}) - \frac{X_{p,t}^2}{\beta_t} D_{\Phi_q}(\mathbf{u}, \mathbf{w}_t) \right) + \frac{1}{\lambda_t} D_{\Phi_q}\left(\mathbf{w}_{t-1}, \mathbf{w}_t'\right) \\
&= (p-1)\alpha \left(\frac{X_{p,t}^2}{\beta_t} D_{\Phi_q}(\mathbf{u}, \mathbf{w}_{t-1}) - \frac{X_{p,t+1}^2}{\beta_{t+1}} D_{\Phi_q}(\mathbf{u}, \mathbf{w}_t) \right. \\
&\quad \left. + D_{\Phi_q}(\mathbf{u}, \mathbf{w}_t) \left(\frac{X_{t+1}^2}{\beta_{t+1}} - \frac{X_{p,t}^2}{\beta_t} \right) \right) + \frac{1}{\lambda_t} D_{\Phi_q}\left(\mathbf{w}_{t-1}, \mathbf{w}_t'\right) \\
&\leq (p-1)\alpha \left(\frac{X_{p,t}^2}{\beta_t} D_{\Phi_q}(\mathbf{u}, \mathbf{w}_{t-1}) - \frac{X_{p,t+1}^2}{\beta_{t+1}} D_{\Phi_q}(\mathbf{u}, \mathbf{w}_t) \right. \\
&\quad \left. + 4 U_q \left(\frac{X_{p,t+1}^2}{\beta_{t+1}} - \frac{X_{p,t}^2}{\beta_t} \right) \right) + \frac{1}{\lambda_t} D_{\Phi_q}\left(\mathbf{w}_t, \mathbf{w}_t'\right),
\end{aligned}
$$

where we used Lemma 11.7 in the last step. To bound the last term, we again apply techniques from the proof of Theorem 11.2:

$$\frac{1}{\lambda_t} D_{\Phi_q}(\mathbf{w}_{t-1}, \mathbf{w}'_t) \le (p-1)\frac{\alpha\,\lambda_t}{2} X_{p,t}^2\,\ell_t^\sigma(\mathbf{w}_{t-1}) \le \frac{\beta_t}{2}\,\ell_t^\sigma(\mathbf{w}_{t-1}).$$

We now sum over $t = 1, \ldots, n$. Note that the quantity $X_{p,n+1}^2/\beta_{n+1}$ is a free parameter here, and we conveniently set $\beta_{n+1} = \beta_n$ and $X_{p,n+1} = X_{p,n}$. This yields

$$\sum_{t=1}^{n}\left(\ell_t^\sigma(\mathbf{w}_{t-1}) - \ell_t^\sigma(\mathbf{u})\right)$$

$$\le (p-1)\alpha\left(\frac{X_{p,1}^2}{\beta_1} D_{\Phi_q}(\mathbf{u}, \mathbf{w}_0) + 4\,U_q\left(\frac{X_{p,n+1}^2}{\beta_{n+1}} - \frac{X_{p,1}^2}{\beta_1}\right)\right) + \frac{1}{2}\sum_{t=1}^{n}\beta_t\ell_t^\sigma(\mathbf{w}_{t-1})$$

$$\le 4(p-1)\alpha\,U_q\,\frac{X_p^2}{\beta_n} + \frac{1}{2}\sum_{t=1}^{n}\beta_t\ell_t^\sigma(\mathbf{w}_{t-1}),$$

where we again applied Lemma 11.7 to the term $D_{\Phi_q}(\mathbf{u}, \mathbf{w}_0)$. Recalling that $k_t = (p-1)\alpha\,X_{p,t}^2\,U_q$, we can rewrite the above as

$$\sum_{t=1}^{n}\left(\ell_t^\sigma(\mathbf{w}_{t-1}) - \ell_t^\sigma(\mathbf{u})\right) \le 4\sqrt{k_n(k_n + \widehat{L}_n^\sigma)} + \frac{1}{2}\sum_{t=1}^{n}\beta_t\ell_t^\sigma(\mathbf{w}_{t-1})$$

$$\le 4\sqrt{k_n(k_n + \widehat{L}_n^\sigma)} + \frac{1}{2}\sqrt{k_n}\sum_{t=1}^{n}\frac{\ell_t^\sigma(\mathbf{w}_{t-1})}{\sqrt{k_n + \widehat{L}_t^\sigma}},$$

where we used

$$\beta_t = \sqrt{\frac{k_t}{k_t + \widehat{L}_t^\sigma}} \le \sqrt{\frac{k_n}{k_n + \widehat{L}_t^\sigma}}.$$

Applying Lemma 11.8, we then immediately get

$$\widehat{L}_n^\sigma - L_n^\sigma(\mathbf{u}) \le 4\sqrt{k_n(k_n + \widehat{L}_n^\sigma)} + \sqrt{k_n(k_n + \widehat{L}_n^\sigma)} = 5\sqrt{k_n(k_n + \widehat{L}_n^\sigma)}.$$

Solving for $\widehat{L}_n^\sigma$ and overapproximating gives the desired result. ∎

Projected gradient-based forecasters can be used with the exponential potential. However, the convex set S onto which weights are projected should not be taken as the probability simplex in $\mathbb{R}^d$, which is the most natural choice for this potential (see, e.g., Theorem 11.3). The region of the simplex where one or more of the weight components are close to 0 would blow up either the dual of the exponential potential (preventing the tracking analysis of Theorem 11.4) or the Bregman divergence (preventing the self-confident analysis of Theorem 11.5). A simple trick to fix this problem is to intersect the simplex with the hypercube $[\beta/d, 1]^d$, where $0 < \beta < 1$ is a free parameter. This amounts to imposing a lower bound on each weight component (see Exercise 11.10).

11.6   Time-Varying Potentials

Consider again the gradient-based forecasters introduced in Section 11.3 (without the use of any transfer function). To motivate such forecasters, we observed that the dual weight $\mathbf{w}_t$ is a solution to the convex minimization problem

$$\min_{\mathbf{u}\in\mathbb{R}^d}\Big[D_{\Phi^*}(\mathbf{u},\mathbf{w}_{t-1}) + \lambda\Big(\ell_t(\mathbf{w}_{t-1}) + (\mathbf{u}-\mathbf{w}_{t-1})\nabla\ell_t(\mathbf{w}_{t-1})\Big)\Big],$$

where the term $\ell_t(\mathbf{w}_{t-1}) + (\mathbf{u}-\mathbf{w}_{t-1})\nabla\ell_t(\mathbf{w}_{t-1})$ is the first-order Taylor approximation of $\ell_t(\mathbf{u})$ around $\mathbf{w}_{t-1}$. As mentioned in Exercise 11.3, an alternative (and more natural) definition of $\mathbf{w}_t$ would look like

$$\mathbf{w}_t = \operatorname*{argmin}_{\mathbf{u}\in\mathbb{R}^d}\Big[D_{\Phi^*}(\mathbf{u},\mathbf{w}_{t-1}) + \lambda\,\ell_t(\mathbf{u})\Big].$$

An interesting closed-form solution for $\mathbf{w}_t$ in this expression is obtained for a potential that evolves with time, where the evolution depends on the loss. In particular, let Φ be an arbitrary Legendre potential and Φ^* its dual potential. Define the recurrence

$$\begin{cases} \Phi_0^* = \Phi^* \\ \Phi_t^* = \Phi_{t-1}^* + \ell_t \end{cases} \qquad \text{(time-varying potential)}.$$

Here, as usual, $\ell_t(\mathbf{w}) = \ell(\mathbf{w}\cdot\mathbf{x}_t, y_t)$ is the convex function induced by the loss at time t and, conventionally, we let ℓ_0 be the zero function. If the potentials in the sequence $\Phi_0^*, \Phi_1^*, \dots$ are all Legendre, then for all $t \geq 1$, the associated forecaster is defined by

$$\mathbf{w}_t = \operatorname*{argmin}_{\mathbf{u}\in\mathbb{R}^d}\Big[D_{\Phi_{t-1}^*}(\mathbf{u},\mathbf{w}_{t-1}) + \ell_t(\mathbf{u})\Big], \qquad t = 1, 2, \dots,$$

where $\mathbf{w}_0 = \mathbf{0}$. (Note that, for simplicity, here we take $\lambda = 1$ because the learning parameter is not exploited below.) This can also be rewritten as

$$\mathbf{w}_t = \operatorname*{argmin}_{\mathbf{u}\in\mathbb{R}^d}\Big[D_{\Phi_{t-1}^*}(\mathbf{u},\mathbf{w}_{t-1}) + \Phi_t^*(\mathbf{u}) - \Phi_{t-1}^*(\mathbf{u})\Big].$$

By setting to 0 the gradient of the expression in brackets, one finds that the solution $\mathbf{w}_t$ is defined by $\nabla\Phi_t^*(\mathbf{w}_t) = \nabla\Phi_{t-1}^*(\mathbf{w}_{t-1})$. Solving for $\mathbf{w}_t$ one then gets $\mathbf{w}_t = \nabla\Phi_t\big(\nabla\Phi_{t-1}^*(\mathbf{w}_{t-1})\big)$. Note that, due to $\nabla\Phi_t^*(\mathbf{w}_t) = \nabla\Phi_{t-1}^*(\mathbf{w}_{t-1})$, the above solution can also be written as $\mathbf{w}_t = \nabla\Phi_t(\boldsymbol{\theta}_0)$, where $\boldsymbol{\theta}_0 = \nabla\Phi^*(\mathbf{0})$ is a base primal weight. This shows that, in contrast to the fixed potential case, no explicit update is carried out, and the potential evolution is entirely responsible for the weight dynamics. The following two diagrams below illustrate the evolution of primal and dual weights in the case of fixed (left-hand side) and time-varying (right-hand side) potential.

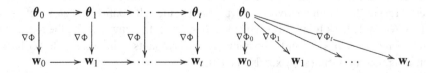

Remark 11.1. If $\nabla\Phi^*(\mathbf{0}) = \mathbf{0}$, then $\nabla\Phi_t^*(\mathbf{w}_t) = \mathbf{0}$ for all $t \geq 0$ and one can equivalently define $\mathbf{w}_t$ by

$$\mathbf{w}_t = \underset{\mathbf{u}\in\mathbb{R}^d}{\operatorname{argmin}} \, \Phi_t^*(\mathbf{u}),$$

where, we recall, Φ_t^* is convex for all t (see also Exercise 11.13 for additional remarks on this alternative formulation).

Remark 11.2. Note that expanding the Bregman divergence term in the above definition of gradient-based linear forecaster, and performing an obvious simplification, yields

$$\mathbf{w}_t = \underset{\mathbf{u}\in\mathbb{R}^d}{\operatorname{argmin}}\left[\Phi_t^*(\mathbf{u}) - \Phi_{t-1}^*(\mathbf{w}_{t-1}) + (\mathbf{u} - \mathbf{w}_{t-1})\nabla\Phi_{t-1}^*(\mathbf{w}_{t-1})\right].$$

The term in brackets is the difference between $\Phi_t^*(\mathbf{u})$ and the linear approximation of Φ_{t-1}^* around $\mathbf{w}_{t-1}$, which again looks like a divergence.

The gradient-based forecaster using the time-varying potential defined above is sketched in the following.

GRADIENT-BASED FORECASTER WITH TIME-VARYING POTENTIAL

Initialization: $\mathbf{w}_0 = \mathbf{0}$ and $\Phi_0^* = \Phi^*$.

For each round $t = 1, 2, \ldots$

    (1) observe $\mathbf{x}_t$ and predict $\widehat{p}_t = \mathbf{w}_{t-1} \cdot \mathbf{x}_t$;
    (2) get $y_t \in \mathbb{R}$ and incur loss $\ell_t(\mathbf{w}_{t-1}) = \ell(\widehat{p}_t, y_t)$;
    (3) let $\mathbf{w}_t = \nabla\Phi_t\left(\nabla\Phi_{t-1}^*(\mathbf{w}_{t-1})\right)$.

Theorem 11.6. *Fix a regular loss function ℓ. If the gradient-based linear forecaster is run with a time-varying Legendre potential Φ such that $\nabla\Phi^*(\mathbf{0}) = \mathbf{0}$, then, for all $\mathbf{u} \in \mathbb{R}^d$,*

$$R_n(\mathbf{u}) = D_{\Phi_0^*}(\mathbf{u}, \mathbf{w}_0) - D_{\Phi_n^*}(\mathbf{u}, \mathbf{w}_n) + \sum_{t=1}^{n} D_{\Phi_t^*}(\mathbf{w}_{t-1}, \mathbf{w}_t).$$

Proof. Choose any $\mathbf{u} \in \mathbb{R}^d$. Using $\nabla\Phi_t^*(\mathbf{w}_t) = \mathbf{0}$ for all $t \geq 0$ (see Remark 11.1), one immediately gets $D_{\Phi_t^*}(\mathbf{u}, \mathbf{w}_t) = \Phi_t^*(\mathbf{u}) - \Phi_t^*(\mathbf{w}_t)$ for all $\mathbf{u} \in \mathbb{R}^d$. Since $\Phi_t^*(\mathbf{u}) = \Phi_{t-1}^*(\mathbf{u}) + \ell_t(\mathbf{u})$, we get $\ell_t(\mathbf{u}) = D_{\Phi_t^*}(\mathbf{u}, \mathbf{w}_t) + \Phi_t^*(\mathbf{w}_t) - \Phi_{t-1}^*(\mathbf{u})$ and $\ell_t(\mathbf{w}_{t-1}) = D_{\Phi_t^*}(\mathbf{w}_{t-1}, \mathbf{w}_t) + \Phi_t^*(\mathbf{w}_t) - \Phi_{t-1}^*(\mathbf{w}_{t-1})$. This yields

$$\ell_t(\mathbf{w}_{t-1}) - \ell_{t-1}(\mathbf{u})$$
$$= D_{\Phi_t^*}(\mathbf{w}_{t-1}, \mathbf{w}_t) - \Phi_{t-1}^*(\mathbf{w}_{t-1}) - D_{\Phi_t^*}(\mathbf{u}, \mathbf{w}_t) + \Phi_{t-1}^*(\mathbf{u})$$
$$= D_{\Phi_t^*}(\mathbf{w}_{t-1}, \mathbf{w}_t) - D_{\Phi_t^*}(\mathbf{u}, \mathbf{w}_t) + D_{\Phi_{t-1}^*}(\mathbf{u}, \mathbf{w}_{t-1}).$$

Summing over t gives the desired result. ∎

Note that Theorem 11.6 provides an exact characterization (there are no inequalities!) of the regret in terms of Bregman divergences. In Section 11.7 we show the elliptic potential, a concrete example of time-varying potential. Using Theorem 11.6 we derive a bound on the cumulative regret of the gradient-based forecaster using the elliptic potential.

11.7　The Elliptic Potential

We now show an application of the time-varying potential based on the polynomial potential (with $p = 2$) and the square loss. To this end, we introduce some additional notation.

A vector $\mathbf{u}$ is always understood as a column vector. Let $(\cdot)^\top$ be the transpose operator. Then $\mathbf{u}^\top$ is a row vector, $A^\top$ is the transpose of matrix A, and $\mathbf{u}^\top \mathbf{v}$ is the inner product between vectors $\mathbf{u}$ and $\mathbf{v}$ (which we also denote with $\mathbf{u} \cdot \mathbf{v}$). Likewise, we define the outer product $\mathbf{u}\mathbf{v}^\top$ yielding the square matrix whose element in row i and column j is $u_i v_j$.

Let the $d \times d$ matrix M be symmetric, positive definite and of rank d. Let $\mathbf{v} \in \mathbb{R}^d$ and $c \in \mathbb{R}$ be arbitrary. The triple $(M, \mathbf{v}, c)$ defines the potential

$$\Phi(\mathbf{u}) = \frac{1}{2}\mathbf{u}^\top M\mathbf{u} + \mathbf{u}^\top \mathbf{v} + c \qquad \text{(the elliptic potential)}.$$

Note that because M is positive definite, $M^{1/2}$ exists, and therefore we can also write $\Phi(\mathbf{u}) = \frac{1}{2}\left\| M^{1/2}\mathbf{u} \right\|^2 + \mathbf{u}^\top \mathbf{v} + c$. The elliptic potential is easily seen to be Legendre with $\nabla \Phi(\mathbf{u}) = M\mathbf{u} + \mathbf{v}$. Since M is full rank, M^{-1} exists and $\nabla \Phi^*(\mathbf{u}) = M^{-1}(\mathbf{u} - \mathbf{v})$. Hence,

$$\Phi^*(\mathbf{u}) = \frac{1}{2}\left\| M^{-1/2}(\mathbf{u} - \mathbf{v}) \right\|^2 = \frac{1}{2}\left\| M^{-1/2}\mathbf{u} \right\|^2 - \mathbf{u}^\top M^{-1}\mathbf{v} + \frac{1}{2}\left\| M^{-1/2}\mathbf{v} \right\|^2,$$

which shows that the dual potential of an elliptic potential is also elliptic.

Elliptic potentials enjoy the following property.

Lemma 11.9. *Let Φ be an elliptic potential defined by the triple $(M, \mathbf{v}, c)$. Then, for all $\mathbf{u}, \mathbf{w} \in \mathbb{R}^d$,*

$$D_\Phi(\mathbf{u}, \mathbf{w}) = \frac{1}{2}\left\| M^{1/2}(\mathbf{u} - \mathbf{w}) \right\|^2.$$

The proof is left as an exercise.

We now show that the time-varying potential obtained from the polynomial potential $\Phi(\mathbf{u}) = \frac{1}{2}\|\mathbf{u}\|^2$ and the square loss $\ell(\widehat{p}, y) = \frac{1}{2}(\widehat{p} - y)^2$ is an elliptic potential. First note that $\Phi = \Phi^*$, due to the self-duality of the 2-norm. Rewrite $\Phi^*(\mathbf{u})$ as $\frac{1}{2}\mathbf{u}^\top I \mathbf{u}$, where I is the $d \times d$ identity matrix, and let $\Phi_0^* = \Phi^*$. Then, following the definition of time-varying potential,

$$\Phi_1^*(\mathbf{u}) = \Phi_0^*(\mathbf{u}) + \ell_1(\mathbf{u})$$
$$= \frac{1}{2}\mathbf{u}^\top I \mathbf{u} + \left(\mathbf{u}^\top \mathbf{x}_1 - y_1\right)^2$$
$$= \frac{1}{2}\mathbf{u}^\top I \mathbf{u} + \frac{1}{2}\mathbf{u}^\top \mathbf{x}_1 \mathbf{x}_1^\top \mathbf{u} - y_1\mathbf{u}^\top \mathbf{x}_1 + \frac{y_1^2}{2}$$
$$= \frac{1}{2}\mathbf{u}^\top \left(I + \mathbf{x}_1 \mathbf{x}_1^\top \right)\mathbf{u} - y_1\mathbf{u}^\top \mathbf{x}_1 + \frac{y_1^2}{2}.$$

Iterating this argument, we obtain the *time-varying elliptic potential*

$$\Phi_t^*(\mathbf{u}) = \frac{1}{2}\mathbf{u}^\top \left(I + \sum_{s=1}^t \mathbf{x}_s\,\mathbf{x}_s^\top \right)\mathbf{u} - \mathbf{u}^\top \sum_{s=1}^t y_s\,\mathbf{x}_s + \frac{1}{2}\sum_{s=1}^t y_s^2.$$

We now take a look at the update rule $\mathbf{w}_t = \nabla\Phi_t \left(\nabla\Phi_{t-1}^*(\mathbf{w}_{t-1}) \right)$ when Φ_t is the time-varying elliptic potential. Introduce

$$A_t = \left(I + \sum_{s=1}^t \mathbf{x}_s\,\mathbf{x}_s^\top \right) \qquad \text{for all } t = 0, 1, 2, \dots$$

Using the definition of Φ_t^*, we can easily compute the gradient

$$\nabla\Phi_t^*(\mathbf{u}) = A_t\,\mathbf{u} - \sum_{s=1}^t y_s\,\mathbf{x}_s.$$

Before proceeding with the argument, we need to check that Φ_t^* is Legendre. Since Φ_t^* is defined on $\mathbb{R}^d$, and $\nabla\Phi_t^*$ computed above is continuous, we only need to verify that Φ_t^* is strictly convex. To see this, note that A_t is the Hessian matrix of Φ_t^*. Furthermore, A_t is positive definite for all $t = 0, 1, \dots$ because

$$\mathbf{v}^\top A_t\,\mathbf{v} = \|\mathbf{v}\|^2 + \sum_{s=1}^d \left(\mathbf{x}_s^\top \mathbf{v} \right)^2 \geq 0$$

for any $\mathbf{v} \in \mathbb{R}^d$, and $\mathbf{v}^\top A_t\,\mathbf{v} = 0$ if and only if $\mathbf{v} = \mathbf{0}$. This implies that Φ_t^* is strictly convex. Since Φ_t^* is Legendre, Lemma 11.5 applies, and we can invert $\nabla\Phi_t^*$ to obtain

$$\nabla\Phi_t(\mathbf{u}) = A_t^{-1} \left(\mathbf{u} + \sum_{s=1}^t y_s\,\mathbf{x}_s \right).$$

This last equation immediately yields a closed-form expression for $\mathbf{w}_t$:

$$\mathbf{w}_t = \nabla\Phi_t(\mathbf{0}) = A_t^{-1} \sum_{s=1}^t y_s\,\mathbf{x}_s.$$

In this form, $\mathbf{w}_t$ can be recognized as the solution of

$$\operatorname*{argmin}_{\mathbf{u}\in\mathbb{R}^d} \left[\frac{1}{2}\|\mathbf{u}\|^2 + \frac{1}{2}\sum_{s=1}^t (\mathbf{u}^\top\mathbf{x}_s - y_s)^2 \right] = \operatorname*{argmin}_{\mathbf{u}\in\mathbb{R}^d} \Phi_t^*(\mathbf{u}),$$

which defines the well-known *ridge regression* estimator of Hoerl and Kennard [162]. As noted in Remark 11.1, of Section 11.6, this alternative nonrecursive definition of $\mathbf{w}_t$ is possible under any time-varying potential. However, notwithstanding this equivalence, it is the recursive definition of $\mathbf{w}_t$ that makes it easy to prove regret bounds as witnessed by Theorem 11.6.

After this short digression, we now return to the analysis of the regret. Applying the above formulas to $\mathbf{w}_t = \nabla\Phi_t \left(\nabla\Phi_{t-1}^*(\mathbf{w}_{t-1}) \right)$, and using a little algebra, we obtain $\mathbf{w}_t = A_t^{-1}\left(A_{t-1}\,\mathbf{w}_{t-1} + y_t\,\mathbf{x}_t \right)$. We now state (proof left as exercise) a more explicit form for the update rule. In the rest of this chapter, we abbreviate the name of the gradient-based forecaster using the time-varying elliptic potential with the more concise "ridge regression forecaster."

The next lemma, used in the analysis of ridge regression, shows that the weight update rule of this forecaster can be written as an instance of the Widrow-Hoff rule (mentioned in Section 11.4) using a real matrix (instead of a scalar) as learning rate.

Lemma 11.10. *The weights generated by the ridge regression forecaster satisfy, for each $t \geq 1$,*

$$\mathbf{w}_t = \mathbf{w}_{t-1} - A_t^{-1} \left(\mathbf{w}_{t-1}^\top \mathbf{x}_t - y_t \right) \mathbf{x}_t.$$

Before proving the main result of this section, we need a further technical lemma.

Lemma 11.11. *Let B be an arbitrary $n \times n$ full-rank matrix, let $\mathbf{x}$ an arbitrary vector, and let $A = B + \mathbf{x}\mathbf{x}^\top$. Then*

$$\mathbf{x}^\top A^{-1} \mathbf{x} = 1 - \frac{\det(B)}{\det(A)}.$$

Proof. If $\mathbf{x} = (0, \ldots, 0)$, then the theorem holds trivially. Otherwise, we write

$$B = A - \mathbf{x}\mathbf{x}^\top = A \left(I - A^{-1}\mathbf{x}\mathbf{x}^\top \right).$$

Hence, computing the determinant of the leftmost and rigthmost matrices,

$$\det(B) = \det(A) \det \left(I - A^{-1}\mathbf{x}\mathbf{x}^\top \right).$$

The right-hand side of this equation can be transformed as follows:

$$
\begin{aligned}
&\det(A) \det \left(I - A^{-1}\mathbf{x}\mathbf{x}^\top \right) \\
&= \det(A) \det \left(A^{1/2} \right) \det \left(I - A^{-1}\mathbf{x}\mathbf{x}^\top \right) \det \left(A^{-1/2} \right) \\
&= \det(A) \det \left(I - A^{-1/2}\mathbf{x}\mathbf{x}^\top A^{-1/2} \right).
\end{aligned}
$$

Hence, we are left to show that $\det \left(I - A^{-1/2}\mathbf{x}\mathbf{x}^\top A^{-1/2} \right) = 1 - \mathbf{x}^\top A^{-1} \mathbf{x}$. Letting $\mathbf{z} = A^{-1/2}\mathbf{x}$, this can be rewritten as $\det(I - \mathbf{z}\mathbf{z}^\top) = 1 - \mathbf{z}^\top \mathbf{z}$. It is easy to see that $\mathbf{z}$ is an eigenvector of $I - \mathbf{z}\mathbf{z}^\top$ with eigenvalue $\lambda_1 = 1 - \mathbf{z}^\top \mathbf{z}$. Moreover, the remaining $d - 1$ eigenvectors $\mathbf{u}_2, \ldots, \mathbf{u}_d$ of $I - \mathbf{z}\mathbf{z}^\top$ form an orthogonal basis of the subspace of $\mathbb{R}^d$ orthogonal to $\mathbf{z}$, and the corresponding eigenvalues $\lambda_2 \ldots, \lambda_d$ are all equal to 1. Hence,

$$\det(I - \mathbf{z}\mathbf{z}^\top) = \prod_{i=1}^d \lambda_i = 1 - \mathbf{z}^\top \mathbf{z},$$

which concludes the proof. ∎

We are now ready to prove a bound on the regret for the square loss of the ridge regression forecaster.

Theorem 11.7. *If the ridge regression forecaster is run on a sequence $(\mathbf{x}_1, y_1), (\mathbf{x}_2, y_2) \ldots \in \mathbb{R}^d \times \mathbb{R}$, then, for all $\mathbf{u} \in \mathbb{R}^d$ and for all $n \geq 1$, the regret $R_n(\mathbf{u})$ defined in terms of the square loss satisfies*

$$R_n(\mathbf{u}) \leq \frac{1}{2} \|\mathbf{u}\|^2 + \left(\sum_{i=1}^d \ln(1 + \lambda_i) \right) \max_{t=1,\ldots,n} \ell_t(\mathbf{w}_{t-1}),$$

where $\lambda_1, \ldots, \lambda_d$ are the eigenvalues of the matrix $\mathbf{x}_1 \mathbf{x}_1^\top + \cdots + \mathbf{x}_n \mathbf{x}_n^\top$.

Proof. Note that $\nabla \Phi_0^*(\mathbf{0}) = \nabla \frac{1}{2} \|\mathbf{0}\|^2 = \mathbf{0}$. Hence, Theorem 11.6 can be applied. Using the nonnegativity of Bregman divergences, we get

$$R_n(\mathbf{u}) \leq D_{\Phi_0^*}(\mathbf{u}, \mathbf{w}_0) + \sum_{t=1}^{n} D_{\Phi_t^*}(\mathbf{w}_{t-1}, \mathbf{w}_t),$$

where $D_{\Phi_0^*}(\mathbf{u}, \mathbf{w}_0) = \frac{1}{2} \|\mathbf{u}\|^2$ because $\mathbf{w}_0 = \mathbf{0}$.

Using Lemmas 11.9 and 11.10, we can write

$$
\begin{aligned}
D_{\Phi_t^*}(\mathbf{w}_{t-1}, \mathbf{w}_t) &= \frac{1}{2}(\mathbf{w}_{t-1} - \mathbf{w}_t)^\top A_t (\mathbf{w}_{t-1} - \mathbf{w}_t) \\
&= \frac{1}{2}(\mathbf{w}_{t-1} - \mathbf{w}_t)^\top \left(\mathbf{w}_{t-1}^\top \mathbf{x}_t - y_t \right) \mathbf{x}_t \\
&= \frac{1}{2} \left(\mathbf{w}_{t-1}^\top \mathbf{x}_t - y_t \right)^2 \mathbf{x}_t^\top A_t^{-1} \mathbf{x}_t \\
&= \ell_t(\mathbf{w}_{t-1}) \, \mathbf{x}_t^\top A_t^{-1} \mathbf{x}_t .
\end{aligned}
$$

Applying Lemma 11.11, we get

$$
\begin{aligned}
\sum_{t=1}^{n} \mathbf{x}_t^\top A_t^{-1} \mathbf{x}_t &= \sum_{t=1}^{n} \left(1 - \frac{\det(A_{t-1})}{\det(A_t)} \right) \\
&\leq \sum_{t=1}^{n} \ln \frac{\det(A_t)}{\det(A_{t-1})} \qquad \text{(because } 1 - x \leq -\ln x \text{ for all } x > 0) \\
&= \ln \frac{\det(A_n)}{\det(A_0)} \\
&= \sum_{i=1}^{d} \ln(1 + \lambda_i),
\end{aligned}
$$

where the last equality holds because $\det(A_0) = \det(I) = 1$ and because $\det(A_n) = (1 + \lambda_1) \times \cdots \times (1 + \lambda_d)$, where $\lambda_1, \ldots, \lambda_d$ are the eigenvalues of the $d \times d$ matrix $A_n - I = \mathbf{x}_1 \mathbf{x}_1^\top + \cdots + \mathbf{x}_n \mathbf{x}_n^\top$. Hence,

$$\sum_{t=1}^{n} \ell_t(\mathbf{w}_{t-1}) \, \mathbf{x}_t^\top A_t^{-1} \mathbf{x}_t \leq \left(\sum_{i=1}^{d} \ln(1 + \lambda_i) \right) \max_{t=1,\ldots,n} \ell_t(\mathbf{w}_{t-1})$$

this concludes the proof. ∎

Theorem 11.7 is somewhat disappointing because we do not know how to control the term $\max_t \ell_t(\mathbf{w}_{t-1})$. If this term were bounded by a constant (which is certainly the case if the pairs $(\mathbf{x}_t, y_t)$ come from a bounded subset of $\mathbb{R}^d \times \mathbb{R}$), then the regret would be bounded by $O(\ln n)$, an exponential improvement over the forecasters using fixed potentials! To see this, choose X such that $\|\mathbf{x}_t\| \leq X$ for all $t = 1, \ldots, n$. A basic algebraic fact states that $A_n - I$ has the same nonzero eigenvalues as the matrix G with entries $G_{i,j} = \mathbf{x}_i^\top \mathbf{x}_j$ (G is called the

Gram matrix of the points $\mathbf{x}_1, \ldots, \mathbf{x}_n$). Therefore $\lambda_1 + \cdots + \lambda_d = \mathbf{x}_1^\top \mathbf{x}_1 + \cdots + \mathbf{x}_n^\top \mathbf{x}_n \leq n X^2$. The quantity $(1 + \lambda_1) \times \ldots \times (1 + \lambda_d)$, under the constraint $\lambda_1 + \cdots + \lambda_d \leq n X^2$, is maximized when $\lambda_i = n X^2 / d$ for each i. This gives

$$\sum_{i=1}^{d} \ln(1 + \lambda_i) \leq d \ln \left(1 + \frac{n X^2}{d} \right).$$

11.8   A Nonlinear Forecaster

In this section we show a variant of the ridge regression forecaster achieving a logarithmic regret bound with an improved leading constant. In Section 11.9 we show that this constant is optimal.

We start from the nonrecursive definition, given in Section 11.7, of the gradient-based forecaster using the time-varying elliptic potential (i.e., the ridge regression forecaster)

$$\mathbf{w}_{t-1} = \operatorname*{argmin}_{\mathbf{u} \in \mathbb{R}^d} \left[\frac{1}{2} \|\mathbf{u}\|^2 + \frac{1}{2} \sum_{s=1}^{t-1} (\mathbf{u}^\top \mathbf{x}_s - y_s)^2 \right] = \operatorname*{argmin}_{\mathbf{u} \in \mathbb{R}^d} \Phi_{t-1}^*(\mathbf{u}).$$

We now introduce the Vovk–Azoury–Warmuth forecaster, introduced by Vovk [300], as an extension to linear experts of his aggregating forecaster (see Sections 3.5 and 11.10), and also studied by Azoury and Warmuth [20] as a special case of a different algorithm. The Vovk–Azoury–Warmuth forecaster predicts at time t with $\widehat{\mathbf{w}}_t^\top \mathbf{x}_t$, where

$$\widehat{\mathbf{w}}_t = \operatorname*{argmin}_{\mathbf{u} \in \mathbb{R}^d} \left[\frac{1}{2} \|\mathbf{u}\|^2 + \frac{1}{2} \sum_{s=1}^{t-1} (\mathbf{u}^\top \mathbf{x}_s - y_s)^2 + \frac{1}{2} (\mathbf{u}^\top \mathbf{x}_t)^2 \right].$$

Note that now the weight $\widehat{\mathbf{w}}_t$ used to predict $\mathbf{x}_t$ has index t rather than $t - 1$. We use this, along with the "hat" notation, to stress the fact that now $\widehat{\mathbf{w}}_t$ does depend on $\mathbf{x}_t$. Note that this makes the Vovk–Azoury–Warmuth forecaster nonlinear.

Comparing this choice of $\widehat{\mathbf{w}}_t$ with the corresponding choice of $\mathbf{w}_{t-1}$ for the gradient-based forecaster, one can note that we simply added the term $\frac{1}{2}(\mathbf{u}^\top \mathbf{x}_t)^2$. This additional term can be viewed as the loss $\frac{1}{2}(\mathbf{u}^\top \mathbf{x}_t - y_t)^2$, where the outcome y_t, unavailable when $\widehat{\mathbf{w}}_t$ is computed, has been "estimated" by 0.

As we did in Section 11.7, it is easy to derive an explicit form for this new $\widehat{\mathbf{w}}_t$ also:

$$\widehat{\mathbf{w}}_t = A_t^{-1} \sum_{s=1}^{t-1} y_s \mathbf{x}_s.$$

We now prove a logarithmic bound on the regret for the square loss of the Vovk–Azoury–Warmuth forecaster. Though its proof heavily relies on the techniques developed for proving Theorems 11.6 and 11.7, it is not clear how to derive the bound directly as a corollary of those results. On the other hand, the same regret bound can be obtained (see the proof in Azoury and Warmuth [20]) using the gradient-based linear forecaster with a modified time-varying potential, and then adapting the proof of Theorem 11.6 in Section 11.6. We do not follow that route in order to keep the proof as simple as possible.

Theorem 11.8. *If the Vovk–Azoury–Warmuth forecaster is run on a sequence* $(\mathbf{x}_1, y_1), (\mathbf{x}_2, y_2), \ldots \in \mathbb{R}^d \times \mathbb{R}$, *then, for all* $\mathbf{u} \in \mathbb{R}^d$ *and for all* $n \geq 1$,

$$R_n(\mathbf{u}) \leq \frac{1}{2} \|\mathbf{u}\|^2 + \frac{Y^2}{2} \left(\sum_{i=1}^d \ln(1 + \lambda_i) \right)$$

$$\leq \frac{1}{2} \|\mathbf{u}\|^2 + \frac{dY^2}{2} \ln \left(1 + \frac{n X^2}{d} \right),$$

where $X = \max_{t=1,\ldots,n} \|\mathbf{x}_t\|$, $Y = \max_{t=1,\ldots,n} |y_t|$, *and* $\lambda_1, \ldots, \lambda_d$ *are the eigenvalues of the matrix* $\mathbf{x}_1 \mathbf{x}_1^\top + \cdots + \mathbf{x}_n \mathbf{x}_n^\top$.

Proof. For convenience, we introduce the shorthand

$$\mathbf{a}_t = \sum_{s=1}^t y_t \mathbf{x}_t.$$

In what follows, we use $\widehat{\mathbf{w}}_t = A_t^{-1} \mathbf{a}_{t-1}$ to denote the weight, at time t, of the Vovk–Azoury–Warmuth forecaster, and $\mathbf{w}_{t-1} = A_{t-1}^{-1} \mathbf{a}_{t-1}$ to denote the weight, at time t, of the ridge regression forecaster. A key step in the proof is the observation that, for all $\mathbf{u} \in \mathbb{R}^d$,

$$L_n(\mathbf{u}) \geq \inf_{\mathbf{v} \in \mathbb{R}^d} \Phi_n^*(\mathbf{v}) - \frac{1}{2} \|\mathbf{u}\|^2 = \Phi_n^*(\mathbf{w}_n) - \frac{1}{2} \|\mathbf{u}\|^2,$$

where we recall that $L_n(\mathbf{u}) = \ell_1(\mathbf{u}) + \cdots + \ell_n(\mathbf{u})$. Hence, the loss of an arbitrary linear expert is simply bounded by the potential of the weight of the ridge regression forecaster. This can be exploited as follows:

$$R_n(\mathbf{u}) = \widehat{L}_n - L_n(\mathbf{u})$$

$$\leq \widehat{L}_n + \frac{1}{2} \|\mathbf{u}\|^2 - \Phi_n^*(\mathbf{w}_n)$$

$$= \sum_{t=1}^n \left(\ell_t(\widehat{\mathbf{w}}_t) + \Phi_{t-1}^*(\mathbf{w}_{t-1}) - \Phi_t^*(\mathbf{w}_t) \right)$$

$$= \sum_{t=1}^n \left(\ell_t(\widehat{\mathbf{w}}_t) - \ell_t(\mathbf{w}_{t-1}) \right) + \sum_{t=1}^n D_{\Phi_t^*}(\mathbf{w}_{t-1}, \mathbf{w}_t),$$

where in the last step we used the equality

$$\ell_t(\mathbf{w}_{t-1}) = D_{\Phi_t^*}(\mathbf{w}_{t-1}, \mathbf{w}_t) + \Phi_t^*(\mathbf{w}_t) - \Phi_{t-1}^*(\mathbf{w}_{t-1})$$

established at the beginning of the proof of Theorem 11.6. Note that we upper bounded the regret $R_n(\mathbf{u})$ with the difference

$$\sum_{t=1}^n \left(\ell_t(\widehat{\mathbf{w}}_t) - \ell_t(\mathbf{w}_{t-1}) \right)$$

between the Vovk–Azoury–Warmuth forecaster and the ridge regression forecaster plus a sum of divergence terms.

Now, the identities $A_t - A_{t-1} = \mathbf{x}_t\,\mathbf{x}_t^\top$, $A_{t-1}^{-1} - A_t^{-1} = A_{t-1}^{-1}\mathbf{x}_t\,\mathbf{x}_t^\top A_t^{-1}$ and $A_{t-1}^{-1} - A_t^{-1} = A_t^{-1}\mathbf{x}_t\,\mathbf{x}_t^\top A_{t-1}^{-1}$ together imply that

$$A_{t-1}^{-1} - A_t^{-1} - A_t^{-1}\mathbf{x}_t\,\mathbf{x}_t^\top A_t^{-1} = \left(\mathbf{x}_t^\top A_{t-1}^{-1}\mathbf{x}_t\right) A_t^{-1}\mathbf{x}_t\,\mathbf{x}_t^\top A_t^{-1}.$$

Using this and the definition of the time-varying elliptic potential (see Section 11.7),

$$\Phi_t^*(\mathbf{w}_t) = \frac{1}{2}\mathbf{w}_t^\top A_t\mathbf{w}_t - \mathbf{w}_t^\top\mathbf{a}_t + \frac{1}{2}\sum_{s=1}^{t}y_s^2,$$

we prove that

$$\ell_t(\widehat{\mathbf{w}}_t) - \ell_t(\mathbf{w}_{t-1}) + D_{\Phi_t^*}(\mathbf{w}_{t-1}, \mathbf{w}_t)$$
$$= \frac{y_t^2}{2}\mathbf{x}_t^\top A_t^{-1}\mathbf{x}_t - \frac{1}{2}\left(\mathbf{x}_t^\top A_{t-1}^{-1}\mathbf{x}_t\right)(\mathbf{w}_{t-1}^\top\mathbf{x}_t)^2 \le \frac{y_t^2}{2}\mathbf{x}_t^\top A_t^{-1}\mathbf{x}_t,$$

where the term dropped in the last step is negative (recall that A_t is positive definite implying that A_t^{-1} also is positive definite). Using Lemma 11.11 then gives the desired result. ∎

As a final remark, note that, using the Sherman–Morrison formula,

$$A_t^{-1} = A_{t-1}^{-1} - \frac{\left(A_{t-1}^{-1}\mathbf{x}_t\right)\left(A_{t-1}^{-1}\mathbf{x}_t\right)^\top}{1 + \mathbf{x}_t^\top A_{t-1}^{-1}\mathbf{x}_t}.$$

The $d \times d$ matrix A_t^{-1}, where $A_t = A_{t-1} + \mathbf{x}_t\,\mathbf{x}_t^\top$, can be computed from A_{t-1}^{-1} in time $\Theta(d^2)$. This is much better than $\Theta(d^3)$ required by a direct inversion of A_t. Hence, both the ridge regression update and the Vovk–Azoury–Warmuth update can be computed in time $\Theta(d^2)$. In contrast, the time needed to compute the forecasters based on fixed potentials is only $\Theta(d)$.

11.9 Lower Bounds

We now prove that the Vovk–Azoury–Warmuth forecaster is optimal in the sense that its leading constant cannot be decreased.

Theorem 11.9. *Let ℓ be the square loss $\ell(p, y) = \frac{1}{2}(p - y)^2$. For all $d \ge 1$, for all $Y > 0$, for all $\varepsilon > 0$, and for any forecaster, there exists a sequence $(\mathbf{x}_1, y_1), (\mathbf{x}_2, y_2), \ldots \in \mathbb{R}^d \times [-Y, Y]$, with $\|\mathbf{x}_t\| = 1$ for $t = 1, 2, \ldots$, such that*

$$\liminf_{n\to\infty} \frac{\widehat{L}_n - \inf_{\mathbf{u}\in\mathbb{R}^d}\left(L_n(\mathbf{u}) + \|\mathbf{u}\|^2\right)}{\ln n} \ge (d - \varepsilon)\frac{Y^2}{2}.$$

Proof.   We only prove the theorem in the case $d = 1$; the easy generalization to an arbitrary $d \ge 1$ is left as exercise. Without loss of generality, set $Y = 1/2$ (the bound can be rescaled to any range). Let $x_t = 1$ for $t = 1, 2, \ldots$, so that all losses are of the form $\frac{1}{2}(w - y)^2$. Since this value does not change if the same constant is added to w and y, without loss of generality we may assume that $y_t \in \{0, 1\}$ for all t (instead of $y_t \in \{-1/2, 1/2\}$, as suggested by the assumption $Y = 1/2$).

Let $L(F, y^n)$ be the cumulative square loss of forecaster F on the sequence $(1, y_1), \ldots, (1, y_n)$ and let $L(u, y^n)$ be the cumulative square loss of expert u on the same sequence. Then

$$\inf_F \max_{y^n} \left(L(F, y^n) - \inf_u \left(L(u, y^n) + u^2 \right) \right)$$

$$\geq \inf_F \mathbb{E} \left[L(F, Y_1, \ldots, Y_n) - \inf_u \left(L(u, Y_1, \ldots, Y_n) + u^2 \right) \right],$$

where the expectation is taken with respect to a probability distribution on $\{0, 1\}^n$ defined as follows: first, $Z \in [0, 1]$ is drawn from the Beta distribution with parameters (a, a), where $a > 1$ is specified later. Then each Y_t is drawn independently from a Bernoulli distribution of parameter Z. It is easy to show that the forecaster F achieving the infimum of $\mathbb{E} L(F, Y_1, \ldots, Y_n)$ predicts at time $t + 1$ by minimizing the expected loss on the next outcome Y_{t+1} conditioned on the realizations of the previous outcomes $Y_1, \ldots, Y_t$. The prediction $\widehat{p}_{t+1}$ minimizing the expected square loss on Y_{t+1} is simply the expected value of Y_{t+1} conditioned on the number of times $S_t = Y_1 + \cdots + Y_t$ the outcome 1 showed up in the past. Using simple properties of the Beta distribution (see Section A.1.9), we find that the conditional density $f_Z(p \mid S_t = k)$ of Z, given the event $S_t = k$, equals

$$f_Z(p \mid S_t = k) = \frac{p^{a+k-1}(1 - p)^{a+t-k-1}}{B(a + k, a + t - k)},$$

where $B(x, y) = \Gamma(x)\Gamma(y)/\Gamma(x + y)$ is the Beta function. Therefore,

$$\widehat{p}_{t+1} = \mathbb{E}\left[Y_{t+1} \mid S_t = k\right] = \int_0^1 \mathbb{E}\left[Y_{t+1} \mid Z = p\right] f_Z(p \mid S_t = k)\,\mathrm{d}p$$

$$= \int_0^1 p \frac{p^{a+k-1}(1 - p)^{a+t-k-1}}{B(a + k, a + t - k)}\,\mathrm{d}p$$

$$= \frac{k + a}{t + 2a}.$$

Let $\mathbb{E}_p$ be the conditional expectation $\mathbb{E}[\cdot \mid Z = p]$. Then,

$$\mathbb{E}_p\left[(\widehat{p}_{t+1} - Y_{t+1})^2\right] = \mathbb{E}_p\left[(\widehat{p}_{t+1} - p)^2\right] + \mathbb{E}_p\left[(Y_{t+1} - p)^2\right]$$

$$= \mathbb{E}_p\left[\left(\frac{S_t + a}{t + 2a} - p\right)^2\right] + p(1 - p)$$

$$= \mathbb{E}_p\left[\left(\frac{S_t + a}{t + 2a} - \frac{pt + a}{t + 2a}\right)^2\right] + \left(p - \frac{pt + a}{t + 2a}\right)^2 + p(1 - p)$$

$$(\text{since } \mathbb{E}_p S_t = pt)$$

$$= \mathbb{E}_p \frac{S_t - pt}{t + 2a} + \left(\frac{2ap - a}{t + 2a}\right)^2 + p(1 - p)$$

$$= \frac{tp(1 - p)}{(t + 2a)^2} + \left(\frac{2ap - a}{t + 2a}\right)^2 + p(1 - p).$$

Hence, recalling that $a > 1$, the expected cumulative loss of the optimal forecaster F is computed as

$$\mathbb{E} \, L(F, Y_1, \ldots, Y_n) = \frac{1}{2} \mathbb{E} \, [Z(1-Z)] \sum_{t=0}^{n-1} \frac{t}{(t+2a)^2}$$

$$+ \frac{1}{2} \mathbb{E} \, [(2aZ - a)^2] \sum_{t=0}^{n-1} \frac{1}{(t+2a)^2}$$

$$+ \frac{1}{2} \sum_{t=0}^{n-1} \mathbb{E} \, [Z(1-Z)]$$

$$\geq \frac{1}{2} \mathbb{E} \, [Z(1-Z)] \int_1^{n-1} \frac{t}{(t+2a)^2} \, dt$$

$$+ \frac{a^2}{2} \left(\frac{1}{4a^2} + \int_0^{n-1} \frac{dt}{(t+2a)^2} \right)$$

$$+ \frac{1}{2} \sum_{t=0}^{n-1} \mathbb{E} \, [Z(1-Z)] .$$

We now lower bound the three terms on the right-hand side. The integral in the first term equals

$$\ln \frac{n-1+2a}{1+2a} - \frac{2a(n-2)}{(1+2a)(n-1+2a)} = \ln \frac{n-1+2a}{1+2a} + \Theta(1),$$

where, here and in what follows, $\Theta(1)$ is understood for a constant and $n \to \infty$. As the entire second term is $\Theta(1)$, using $\mathbb{E}[Z(1-Z)] = a/(4a+2)$, we get

$$\mathbb{E} \, L(F, Y_1, \ldots, Y_n) \geq \frac{a}{4(2a+1)} \ln \frac{n-1+2a}{1+2a} + \frac{an}{4(2a+1)} + \Theta(1).$$

Now we compute the cumulative loss of the best expert. Recalling that $S_n = Y_1 + \cdots + Y_n$, we have

$$\mathbb{E}_p \left[\inf_u \sum_{t=1}^n (u - Y_t)^2 \right] = \mathbb{E}_p \left[\sum_{t=1}^n (S_n/n - Y_t)^2 \right]$$

$$= \sum_{t=1}^n \mathbb{E}_p \, Y_t^2 - \frac{2}{n} \mathbb{E}_p \left[\sum_{t=1}^n Y_t S_n \right] + n \mathbb{E}_p \left[\left(\frac{S_n}{n} \right)^2 \right]$$

$$= \sum_{t=1}^n \mathbb{E}_p \, Y_t^2 - \frac{2}{n} \mathbb{E}_p \left[\left(\sum_{t=1}^n Y_t \right)^2 \right] + \frac{1}{n} \mathbb{E}_p \, S_n^2.$$

Hence, recalling that the variance of any random variable X is $\mathbb{E} \, X^2 - (\mathbb{E} \, X)^2$, and that the variance of the Binomial random variable S_n is $np(1-p)$, we get

$$\mathbb{E}_p \left[\inf_u \sum_{t=1}^n (u - Y_t)^2 \right]$$

$$= np - \frac{2}{n} \left(np(1-p) + (np)^2 \right) + \frac{1}{n} \left(np(1-p) + (np)^2 \right)$$

$$= np(1-p) - p(1-p).$$

Integrating over p yields

$$\mathbb{E}\left[\inf_u \sum_{t=1}^n (u - Y_t)^2\right] = \frac{an}{2(2a+1)} - p(1-p).$$

Therefore, as $0 \le u \le 1$,

$$\mathbb{E}\left[L(F, Y_1, \ldots, Y_n) - \inf_u \left(L(u, Y_1, \ldots, Y_n) + u^2\right)\right]$$

$$= \frac{a}{4(2a+1)} \ln \frac{n-1+2a}{1+2a} + \frac{an}{4(2a+1)} - \frac{an}{4(2a+1)} + \Theta(1)$$

$$= \left(1 - \frac{1}{2a+1}\right) \frac{1}{8} \ln \frac{n-1+2a}{1+2a} + \Theta(1).$$

We conclude the proof by observing that the factor multiplying $\ln n$ can be made arbitrarily close to 1 by choosing a large enough. ∎

11.10 Mixture Forecasters

We have seen that in the case of linear experts, regret bounds growing logarithmically with time are obtainable for the squared loss function. The purpose of this section is to show that by a natural extension of the mixture forecasters introduced in Chapter 9, one may obtain a class of algorithms that achieve logarithmic regret bounds under general conditions for the logarithmic loss function.

We start by describing a general framework for linear prediction under the logarithmic loss function. The basic setup is reminiscent of sequential probability assignment introduced in Chapter 9. The model is extended to allow side information and experts that depend on "squashed" linear functions of the side-information vector. To harmonize notation with Chapter 9, consider the following model. At each time instance t, before making a prediction, the forecaster observes the side-information vector $\mathbf{x}_t$ such that $\|\mathbf{x}_t\| \le 1$. The forecaster, based on the side-information vector and the past, assigns a nonnegative number $\widehat{p}_t(y, \mathbf{x}_t)$ to each element y of the outcome space $\mathcal{Y}$. Note that, as opposed to the rest of the section, we do not require that $\mathcal{Y}$ be a subset of the real line. The function $\widehat{p}_t(\cdot, \mathbf{x}_t)$ is sometimes interpreted as a "density" over $\mathcal{Y}$, though $\mathcal{Y}$ does not even need to be a measurable space. The loss at time t of the forecaster is defined by the logarithmic loss $-\ln \widehat{p}_t(y_t, \mathbf{x}_t)$, and the corresponding cumulative loss is

$$\widehat{L}_n = -\ln \prod_{t=1}^n \widehat{p}_t(y_t, \mathbf{x}_t).$$

Just as in earlier sections in this chapter, each expert is indexed by a vector $\mathbf{u} \in \mathbb{R}^d$, and its prediction depends on the inner product of $\mathbf{u}$ and the side-information vector through a transfer function. Here the transfer function $\sigma : \mathcal{Y} \times \mathbb{R} \to \mathbb{R}$ is nonnegative, and the prediction of expert $\mathbf{u}$, on observing the side information $\mathbf{x}_t$, is the "density" $\sigma(\cdot, \mathbf{u} \cdot \mathbf{x}_t)$. The cumulative loss of expert $\mathbf{u}$ is thus

$$L_n(\mathbf{u}) = -\ln \prod_{t=1}^n \sigma(y_t, \mathbf{u} \cdot \mathbf{x}_t).$$

In this section we consider *mixture forecasters* of the form

$$\widehat{p}_t(y, \mathbf{x}_t) = \int \sigma(y, \mathbf{u} \cdot \mathbf{x}_t) q_t(\mathbf{u}) \, d\mathbf{u},$$

where q_t is a density function (i.e., a nonnegative function with integral 1) over $\mathbb{R}^d$ defined, for $t = 1, 2, \ldots$, by

$$q_t(\mathbf{u}) = \frac{q_0(\mathbf{u}) e^{-L_{t-1}(\mathbf{u})}}{\int q_0(\mathbf{v}) e^{-L_{t-1}(\mathbf{v})} \, d\mathbf{v}} = \frac{q_0(\mathbf{u}) \prod_{s=1}^{t-1} \sigma(y_s, \mathbf{u} \cdot \mathbf{x}_s)}{\int q_0(\mathbf{v}) \prod_{s=1}^{t-1} \sigma(y_s, \mathbf{v} \cdot \mathbf{x}_s) \, d\mathbf{v}},$$

where q_0 denotes a fixed initial density. Thus, $\widehat{p}_t$ is the prediction of the exponentially weighted average forecaster run with initial weights given by the "prior" density q_0.

Example 11.8 (*Square loss*). Assume now that $\mathcal{Y}$ is a subset of the real line. By considering the "gaussian" transfer function

$$\sigma(y, \mathbf{u} \cdot \mathbf{x}) = \frac{1}{\sqrt{2\pi}} e^{-(\mathbf{u} \cdot \mathbf{x} - y)^2 / 2}$$

the logarithmic loss of expert $\mathbf{u}$ becomes $\ln \sqrt{2\pi} + \frac{1}{2}(\mathbf{u} \cdot \mathbf{x}_t - y_t)^2$, which is basically the square loss studied in earlier sections. However, the logarithmic loss of the mixture forecaster $\widehat{p}_t(y_t, \mathbf{x}_t)$ does not always correspond to the squared loss of any vector-valued forecaster $\mathbf{w}_t$. If the initial density q_0 is the multivariate gaussian density with identity covariance matrix, then it is possible to modify the mixture predictor such that it becomes equivalent to the Vovk–Azoury–Warmuth forecaster (see Exercise 11.18). □

The main result of this section is the following general performance bound.

Theorem 11.10. *Assume that the transfer function σ is such that, for each fixed $y \in \mathcal{Y}$, the function $F_y(z) = -\ln \sigma(y, z)$, defined for $z \in \mathbb{R}$, is twice continuously differentiable, and there exists a constant c such that $|F_y''(z)| \leq c$ for all $z \in \mathbb{R}$. Let $\mathbf{u} \in \mathbb{R}^d$, $\varepsilon > 0$, and let $q_{\mathbf{u}}^\varepsilon$ be any density over $\mathbb{R}^d$ with mean $\int \mathbf{v} q_{\mathbf{u}}^\varepsilon(\mathbf{v}) \, d\mathbf{v} = \mathbf{u}$ and covariance matrix $\varepsilon^2 I$. Then the regret of the mixture forecaster defined above, with respect to expert $\mathbf{u}$, is bounded as*

$$\widehat{L}_n - L_n(\mathbf{u}) \leq \frac{nc\varepsilon^2}{2} + D(q_{\mathbf{u}}^\varepsilon \| q_0),$$

where

$$D(q_{\mathbf{u}}^\varepsilon \| q_0) = \int q_{\mathbf{u}}^\varepsilon(\mathbf{v}) \ln \frac{q_{\mathbf{u}}^\varepsilon(\mathbf{v})}{q_0(\mathbf{v})} \, d\mathbf{v}$$

is the Kullback–Leibler divergence between $q_{\mathbf{u}}^\varepsilon$ and the initial density q_0.

Proof. Fix $\mathbf{u} \in \mathbb{R}^d$, and let $q_{\mathbf{u}}^\varepsilon$ be any density with mean $\mathbf{u}$ and covariance matrix $\varepsilon^2 I$. In the first step of the proof we relate the cumulative loss $\widehat{L}_n$ to the averaged cumulative loss

$$L_n(q_{\mathbf{u}}^\varepsilon) \stackrel{\text{def}}{=} \int L_n(\mathbf{v}) q_{\mathbf{u}}^\varepsilon(\mathbf{v}) \, d\mathbf{v}.$$

First observe that by Taylor's theorem and the condition on the transfer function, for any $y \in \mathcal{Y}$ and $z, z_0 \in \mathbb{R}$,

$$F_y(z) \le F_y(z_0) + F_y'(z_0)(z - z_0) + \frac{c}{2}(z - z_0)^2.$$

Next we apply this inequality for $z = \mathbf{V} \cdot \mathbf{x}_t$ and $z_0 = \mathbb{E}[\mathbf{V}] \cdot \mathbf{x}_t$, where $\mathbf{V}$ is a random variable distributed according to the density $q_{\mathbf{u}}^\varepsilon$. Noting that $z_0 = \mathbf{u} \cdot \mathbf{x}_t$, and taking expected values on both sides, we have

$$\mathbb{E}\, F_y(\mathbf{V} \cdot \mathbf{x}_t) \le F_y(\mathbf{u} \cdot \mathbf{x}_t) + \frac{c}{2}\varepsilon^2,$$

where we used the fact that $\mathrm{var}(\mathbf{x} \cdot \mathbf{V}) = \sum_{i=1}^d \mathrm{var}(V_i) x_i^2 = \varepsilon^2 \sum_{i=1}^d x_i^2 \le \varepsilon^2$. Observing that

$$\sum_{t=1}^n F_{y_t}(\mathbf{u} \cdot \mathbf{x}_t) = L_n(\mathbf{u}) \qquad \text{and} \qquad \sum_{t=1}^n \mathbb{E}\, F_{y_t}(\mathbf{V} \cdot \mathbf{x}_t) = L_n(q_{\mathbf{u}}^\varepsilon)$$

we obtain

$$L_n(q_{\mathbf{u}}^\varepsilon) \le L_n(\mathbf{u}) + \frac{nc\varepsilon^2}{2}.$$

To finish the proof, it remains to compare $\widehat{L}_n$ with $L_n(q_{\mathbf{u}}^\varepsilon)$. By definition of the mixture forecaster,

$$
\begin{aligned}
\widehat{L}_n - L_n(q_{\mathbf{u}}^\varepsilon) &= -\ln \prod_{t=1}^n \widehat{p}_t(y_t, \mathbf{x}_t) + \int q_{\mathbf{u}}^\varepsilon(\mathbf{v}) \ln \prod_{t=1}^n \sigma(y_t, \mathbf{v} \cdot \mathbf{x}_t)\, d\mathbf{v} \\
&= \int q_{\mathbf{u}}^\varepsilon(\mathbf{v}) \ln \frac{\prod_{t=1}^n \sigma(y_t, \mathbf{v} \cdot \mathbf{x}_t)}{\prod_{t=1}^n \widehat{p}_t(y_t, \mathbf{x}_t)}\, d\mathbf{v} \\
&= \int q_{\mathbf{u}}^\varepsilon(\mathbf{v}) \ln \frac{\prod_{t=1}^n \sigma(y_t, \mathbf{v} \cdot \mathbf{x}_t)}{\int q_0(\mathbf{w}) \prod_{t=1}^n \sigma(y_t, \mathbf{w} \cdot \mathbf{x}_t)\, d\mathbf{w}}\, d\mathbf{v} \\
&= \int q_{\mathbf{u}}^\varepsilon(\mathbf{v}) \ln \frac{q_n(\mathbf{v})}{q_0(\mathbf{v})}\, d\mathbf{v} \qquad \text{(by definition of } q_n) \\
&= \int q_{\mathbf{u}}^\varepsilon(\mathbf{v}) \ln \frac{q_{\mathbf{u}}^\varepsilon(\mathbf{v})}{q_0(\mathbf{v})}\, d\mathbf{v} - \int q_{\mathbf{u}}^\varepsilon(\mathbf{v}) \ln \frac{q_{\mathbf{u}}^\varepsilon(\mathbf{v})}{q_n(\mathbf{v})}\, d\mathbf{v} \\
&= D(q_{\mathbf{u}}^\varepsilon \| q_0) - D(q_{\mathbf{u}}^\varepsilon \| q_n) \\
&\le D(q_{\mathbf{u}}^\varepsilon \| q_0),
\end{aligned}
$$

where at the last step we used the nonnegativity of the Kullback–Leibler divergence (see Section A.2). This concludes the proof of the theorem. ∎

***Remark* 11.3.** The boundedness condition of the second derivative of the logarithm of the transfer function is satisfied in several natural applications. For example, for the gaussian transfer function $\sigma(y, z) = (1/\sqrt{2\pi})e^{-(z-y)^2/2}$, we have $F_y''(z) = 1$ for all $y, z \in \mathbb{R}$. Another popular transfer function is the one used in logistic regression. In this case $\mathcal{Y} = \{-1, 1\}$, and σ is defined by $\sigma(y, \mathbf{u} \cdot \mathbf{x}) = 1/(1 + e^{-y\mathbf{u}\cdot\mathbf{x}})$. It is easy to see that $|F_y''(z)| \le 1$ for both $y = -1, 1$.

Note that the definition of the mixture forecaster does not depend on the choice of $q_{\mathbf{u}}^{\varepsilon}$, so that we are free to choose this density to minimize the obtained upper bound. Minimization the Kullback–Leibler divergence given the variance constraint is a complex variational problem, in general. However, useful upper bounds can easily be derived in various special cases. Next we work out a specific example in which the variational problem can be solved easily and $q_{\mathbf{u}}^{\varepsilon}$ can be chosen optimally. See the exercises for other examples.

Corollary 11.1. *Assume that the mixture forecaster is used with the gaussian initial density* $q_0(\mathbf{u}) = (2\pi)^{-d/2} e^{-\|\mathbf{u}\|^2/2}$. *If the transfer function satisfies the conditions of Theorem 11.10, then for any* $\mathbf{u} \in \mathbb{R}^d$,

$$\widehat{L}_n - L_n(\mathbf{u}) \leq \frac{\|\mathbf{u}\|^2}{2} + \frac{d}{2} \ln\left(1 + \frac{nc}{d}\right).$$

Proof. The Kullback–Leibler divergence between q_0 and any density $q_{\mathbf{u}}^{\varepsilon}$ with mean $\mathbf{u}$ and covariance matrix $\varepsilon^2 I$ equals

$$D(q_{\mathbf{u}}^{\varepsilon} \| q_0) = \int q_{\mathbf{u}}^{\varepsilon}(\mathbf{v}) \ln q_{\mathbf{u}}^{\varepsilon}(\mathbf{v}) \, d\mathbf{v} - \int q_{\mathbf{u}}^{\varepsilon}(\mathbf{v}) \ln q_0(\mathbf{v}) \, d\mathbf{v}$$

$$= \int q_{\mathbf{u}}^{\varepsilon}(\mathbf{v}) \ln q_{\mathbf{u}}^{\varepsilon}(\mathbf{v}) \, d\mathbf{v} - \int q_{\mathbf{u}}^{\varepsilon}(\mathbf{v}) \ln \frac{1}{(2\pi)^{d/2}} \, d\mathbf{v} + \int q_{\mathbf{u}}^{\varepsilon}(\mathbf{v}) \frac{\|\mathbf{v}\|^2}{2} \, d\mathbf{v}$$

$$= \int q_{\mathbf{u}}^{\varepsilon}(\mathbf{v}) \ln q_{\mathbf{u}}^{\varepsilon}(\mathbf{v}) \, d\mathbf{v} + \frac{d}{2} \ln(2\pi) + \frac{\|\mathbf{u}\|^2}{2} + \frac{d\varepsilon^2}{2}.$$

The first term on the right-hand side is just the negative of the differential entropy of the density $q_{\mathbf{u}}^{\varepsilon}(\mathbf{v})$. It is easy to see (Exercise 11.19) that among all densities with a given covariance matrix, the differential entropy is maximized for the gaussian density. Therefore, the best choice for $q_{\mathbf{u}}^{\varepsilon}(\mathbf{v})$ is the multivariate normal density with mean $\mathbf{u}$ and covariance matrix $\varepsilon^2 I$. With this choice,

$$\int q_{\mathbf{u}}^{\varepsilon}(\mathbf{v}) \ln q_{\mathbf{u}}^{\varepsilon}(\mathbf{v}) \, d\mathbf{v} = -\frac{d}{2} \ln(2\pi e \varepsilon^2)$$

and the statement follows by choosing ε to minimize the obtained bound. ∎

11.11 Bibliographic Remarks

Sequential gradient descent can be viewed as an application of the well-known stochastic gradient descent procedure of Tsypkin [291] (see Bottou and Murata [39] for a survey) to a deterministic (rather than stochastic) data sequence. The gradient-based linear fore-caster was introduced with the name *general additive regression algorithm* by Warmuth and Jagota [305] (see also Kivinen and Warmuth [183]) for regression problems, and independently with the name *quasi-additive classification algorithm* by Grove, Littlestone, and Schuurmans [133] for classification problems. Potentials in pattern recognition have been introduced to describe, in a single unified framework, seemingly different algorithms such as the Widrow–Hoff rule [310] (weights updated additively) and the exponentiated gradient (EG) of Kivinen and Warmuth [181] (weights updated multiplicatively). The frame-work of potential functions enables one to view both algorithms as instances of a single algorithm, the gradient-based linear forecaster, whose weights are updated as in the dual gradient update. In particular, the Widrow–Hoff rule corresponds to the gradient-based linear forecaster applied to square loss and using the quadratic potential (Legendre polynomial potential with $p = 2$), while the EG algorithm corresponds to the forecaster of Theorem 11.3. As it has been observed by Grove, Littlestone, and Schuurmans [133], the polynomial potential provides a parameterized interpolation between genuinely additive algorithms and multiplicative algorithms. Earlier individual sequence analyses of additive and multiplicative algorithms for linear experts appear in Foster [103], Littlestone, Long, and Warmuth [202], Cesa-Bianchi, Long, and Warmuth [50], and Bylander [43]. For an extensive discussion on the advantages of using polynomial vs. exponential potentials in regression problems, see Kivinen and Warmuth [181].

Gordon [131] develops an analysis of regret for more general problems than regression based on a generalized notion of Bregman divergence.

The interpretation of the gradient-based update in terms of iterated minimization of a convex functional was suggested by Helmbold, Schapire, Singer, and Warmuth [157]. However, the connection with convex optimization is far from being accidental. An analog of the dual gradient update rule was introduced by Nemirovski and Yudin [223] under the name of *mirror descent algorithm* for the iterative solution of nonsmooth convex optimization problems. The description of this algorithm in the framework of Bregman divergences is due to Beck and Teboulle [24], who also propose a version of the algorithm based on the exponential potential. In the context of convex optimization, the iterated minimization of the functional

$$\min_{\mathbf{u} \in \mathbb{R}^d} \left[D_{\Phi^*}(\mathbf{u}, \mathbf{w}_{t-1}) + \lambda \ell_t(\mathbf{u}) \right]$$

(which we used to motivate the dual gradient update) corresponds to the well-known proximal point algorithm (see, e.g., Martinet [210] and Rockafellar [248]). A version of the proximal point algorithm based on the exponential potential was proposed by Tseng and Bertsekas [290].

Theorem 11.1 is due to Warmuth and Jagota [305]. The use of transfer functions in this context was pioneered by Helmbold, Kivinen, and Warmuth [153]. The good properties of subquadratic pairs of transfer and loss functions were observed by Cesa-Bianchi [46]. A different approach, based on the notion "matching loss functions," uses Bregman divergences to build nice pairs of transfer and loss functions and was investigated in Haussler, Kivinen, and Warmuth [153]. In spite of its elegance, the matching-loss approach is not discussed here because it does not fit very well with the proof techniques used in this chapter.

The projected gradient-based forecaster of Section 11.5 has been introduced by Herbster and Warmuth [160]. They prove Theorem 11.4 about tracking linear experts. The self-confident forecaster has been introduced by Auer, Cesa-Bianchi, and Gentile [13], who also prove Theorem 11.5.

The time varying potential for gradient-based forecasters of Section 11.6 was introduced and studied by Azoury and Warmuth [20], who also proved Theorem 11.6. The forecaster based on the elliptic potential, also analyzed in [20], corresponds to the well-known ridge regression algorithm (see Hoerl and Kennard [162]). An early analysis of the least-squares forecaster in the case where $y_t = \mathbf{u}^\top \mathbf{x}_t + \varepsilon_t$, where $\mathbf{u} \in \mathbb{R}^d$ is an unknown target vector and ε_t are i.i.d. random variables with finite variance, is due to Lai, Robbins, and Wei [190]. Lemma 11.11 is due to Lai and Wei [191]. Theorem 11.7 is proven by Vovk in [300]. A different proof of the same result is shown by Azoury and Warmuth in [20]. The proof presented here uses ideas from Forster [102] and [20].

The derivation and analysis of the nonlinear forecaster in Section 11.8 is taken from Azoury and Warmuth [20], who introduced it as the "forward algorithm." In [300], Vovk derives exactly the same forecaster generalizing to continuously many experts the aggregating forecaster described in Section 3.5, where the initial weights assigned to the linear experts are gaussian. Using different (and somewhat more complex techniques) Vovk also proves the same bound as the one proven in Theorem 11.8. The first logarithmic regret bound for the square loss with linear experts is due to Foster [103], who analyzes a variant of the ridge regression forecaster in the more specific setup where outcomes are binary, the side-information elements $\mathbf{x}_t$ belong to $[0, 1]^d$, and the linear experts $\mathbf{u}$ belong to the probability simplex in $\mathbb{R}^d$. The lower bound in Section 11.9 on prediction with linear experts and square loss is due to Vovk [300] (see also Singer, Kozat, and Feder [268] for a stronger result).

Mixture forecasters in the spirit of Section 11.10 were considered by Vovk [299, 300]. Vovk's aggregating forecaster is, in fact, a mixture forecaster and the Vovk–Azoury–Warmuth forecaster is obtained via a generalization of the aggregating forecaster. Theorem 11.10 was proved by Kakade and Ng [173]. A logarithmic regret bound may also be derived by a variation on a result of Yamanishi [314], who proved a general logarithmic bound for all mixable losses and for general parametric classes of experts using the aggregating forecaster. However, the resulting forecaster is not computationally efficient. It is worth pointing out that the mixture forecasters in Section 11.10 are formally equivalent to predictive bayesian mixtures. In fact, if q_0 is the prior density, the mixture predictors are obtained by bayesian updating. Such predictors have been thoroughly studied in the bayesian literature under the assumption that the sequence of outcomes is generated by one of the models (see, e.g., Clarke and Barron [62, 63]). The choice of prior has been studied in the individual sequence framework by Clarke and Dawid [64].

11.12   Exercises

11.1 Prove Lemma 11.1.

11.2 Prove that Lemma 11.3 holds with equality whenever S is a hyperplane.

11.3 Consider the modified gradient-based linear forecaster whose weight $\mathbf{w}_t$ at time t is the solution of the equation

$$\mathbf{w}_t = \underset{\mathbf{u} \in \mathbb{R}^d}{\operatorname{argmin}} \Big[D_{\Phi^*}(\mathbf{u}, \mathbf{w}_{t-1}) + \lambda \, \ell_t(\mathbf{u}) \Big].$$

Note that this amounts to not taking the linear approximation of $\ell_t(\mathbf{u})$ around $\mathbf{w}_{t-1}$, as done in the original characterization of the gradient-based linear forecaster expressed as solution of a convex optimization problem.

Prove that a solution to this equation always exists and then adapt the proof of Theorem 11.1 to prove a bound on the regret of the modified forecaster.

11.4 Prove that the weight update rule

$$w_{i,t} = \frac{w_{i,t-1} e^{-\lambda \nabla \ell_t(\mathbf{w}_{t-1})_i}}{\sum_{j=1}^d w_{j,t-1} e^{-\lambda \nabla \ell_t(\mathbf{w}_{t-1})_j}}$$

corresponds to a Bregman projection of $w_{i,t} = w_{i,t-1}\, e^{-\lambda \nabla \ell_t(\mathbf{w}_{t-1})_i}$, $i = 1, \ldots, d$, onto the probability simplex in $\mathbb{R}^d$, where the projection is taken according to the Legendre dual

$$\Phi^*(\mathbf{u}) = \sum_{i=1}^{d} u_i (\ln u_i - 1)$$

of the potential $\Phi(\mathbf{u}) = e^{u_1} + \cdots + e^{u_d}$.

11.5 Consider the Legendre polynomial potential Φ_p. Show that if the loss function is the square loss $\ell(p, y) = \frac{1}{2}(p - y)^2$, then for all $\mathbf{w}, \mathbf{u} \in \mathbf{R}^d$, for all $y \in \mathbb{R}$, and for all $c > 0$,

$$\frac{1}{1+c} \ell(\mathbf{w} \cdot \mathbf{x}, y) - \ell(\mathbf{u} \cdot \mathbf{x}) \le \frac{(p-1)\,\|\mathbf{x}\|_p^2}{c} \left(D_{\Phi_q}(\mathbf{u}, \mathbf{w}) - D_{\Phi_q}(\mathbf{u}, \mathbf{w}') \right),$$

where $\mathbf{w}' = \Phi_p\big(\Phi_q(\mathbf{w}) - \lambda \nabla \ell(\mathbf{w})\big)$ is the dual gradient update, and $\eta = c/((1+c)(p-1)\,\|\mathbf{x}\|_p^2)$ (Kivinen and Warmuth [181], Gentile [124].) *Warning:* This exercise is difficult.

11.6 *(Continued)* Use the inequality stated in Exercise 11.5 to derive a bound on the square loss regret $R_n(\mathbf{u})$ for the gradient-based linear forecaster using the identity function as transfer function. Find a value of c that yields a regret bound for the square loss slightly better than that of Theorem 11.2.

11.7 Derive a regret bound for the gradient-based forecaster using the absolute loss $\ell(\widehat{p}, y) = |\widehat{p} - y|$. Note that this loss is not regular as it is not differentiable at $\widehat{p} = y$ (Cesa-Bianchi [46], Long [205].)

11.8 Prove a regret bound for the projected gradient-based linear forecaster using the hyperbolic cosine potential.

11.9 Prove Lemma 11.8. *Hint:* Set $\ell_0 = a$ and prove, for each $t = 1, \ldots, n$, the inequality

$$\frac{\ell_t}{2\sum_{s=0}^{t} \ell_s} \le \sqrt{\sum_{s=0}^{t} \ell_s} - \sqrt{\sum_{s=0}^{t-1} \ell_s}.$$

11.10 Prove an analogue of Theorem 11.4 using the Legendre exponential potential and projecting the weights to the convex set obtained by intersecting the probability simplex in $\mathbb{R}^d$ with the hypercube $[\beta/d, 1]^d$, where β is a free parameter (Herbster and Warmuth [160]).

11.11 Prove Lemma 11.9.

11.12 Show that

1. the nice pair of Example 11.6 is 2-subquadratic,
2. the nice pair of Example 11.7 is 1/4-subquadratic.

11.13 Consider the alternative definition of gradient-based forecaster using the time-varying potential

$$\mathbf{w}_t = \underset{\mathbf{u} \in \mathbb{R}^d}{\operatorname{argmin}} \, \Phi_t^*(\mathbf{u}),$$

where

$$\Phi_t^*(\mathbf{u}) = D_{\Phi^*}(\mathbf{u}, \mathbf{w}_0) + \sum_{s=1}^{t} \ell_s(\mathbf{u})$$

for some initial weight $\mathbf{w}_0$ and Legendre potential $\Phi = \Phi_0$. Using this forecaster, show a more general version of Theorem 11.6 proving the same bound without the requirement $\nabla \Phi_t^*(\mathbf{w}_t) = \mathbf{0}$ for all $t \ge 0$ (Azoury and Warmuth [20]).

11.14 Prove Lemma 11.10.

11.15 *(Follow the best expert)* Consider the online linear prediction problem with the square loss $\ell(\mathbf{w}_t \cdot \mathbf{x}_t, y) = (\mathbf{w}_t \cdot \mathbf{x}_t - y)^2$. Consider the follow-the-best-expert (or least-squares) forecaster with weights

$$\mathbf{w}_t = \underset{\mathbf{u} \in \mathbb{R}^d}{\operatorname{argmin}} \sum_{s=1}^{t} (\mathbf{u} \cdot \mathbf{x}_s - y_s)^2.$$

Show that

$$\mathbf{w}_t = \left(\sum_{s=1}^{t} \mathbf{x}_s \mathbf{x}_s^\top \right)^{-1} \sum_{s=1}^{t} y_s \mathbf{x}_s$$

whenever $\mathbf{x}_1 \mathbf{x}_1^\top + \cdots + \mathbf{x}_t \mathbf{x}_t^\top$ is invertible. Use the analysis in Section 3.2 to derive logarithmic regret bounds for this forecaster when $y_t \in [-1, 1]$. What conditions do you need for the $\mathbf{x}_t$?

11.16 Provide a proof of Theorem 11.9 in the general case $d \geq 1$.

11.17 By adapting the proof of Theorem 11.9, show a lower bound for the relative entropy loss in the univariate case $d = 1$. (Yamanishi [314].)

11.18 Consider the mixture forecaster $\widehat{p}_t(\cdot, \mathbf{x}_t)$ of Section 11.10 with the gaussian transfer function. Assume that the gaussian initial density $q_0(\mathbf{u}) = (2\pi)^{-d/2} e^{-\|\mathbf{u}\|^2/2}$ is used. Assume that $\mathcal{Y} = [-1, 1]$. Show that the forecaster $\mathbf{w}_t$ defined by

$$\mathbf{w}_t = \frac{\widehat{p}_t(-1, \mathbf{x}_t) - \widehat{p}_t(1, \mathbf{x}_t)}{4}$$

is just the Vovk–Azoury–Warmuth forecaster (Vovk [300]).

11.19 Show that for any multivariate density q on $\mathbb{R}^d$ with zero mean $\int \mathbf{u} q(\mathbf{u}) \, d\mathbf{u} = \mathbf{0}$ and covariance matrix K, the differential entropy $h(q) = -\int q(\mathbf{u}) \ln q(\mathbf{u}) \, d\mathbf{u}$ satisfies

$$h(q) \leq \frac{d}{2} \ln(2\pi e) + \frac{1}{2} \ln \det(K)$$

and equality is achieved by the multivariate normal density with covariance matrix K (see, e.g., Cover and Thomas [74]).

11.20 Consider the mixture predictor in Section 11.10 and choose the initial density q_0 to be uniform in a cube $[-B, B]^d$. Show that for any vector $\mathbf{u}$ with $\|\mathbf{u}\|_\infty \leq B - (3d/nc)^{1/2}$, the regret satisfies

$$\widehat{L}_n - L_n(\mathbf{u}) \leq \frac{d}{2} \ln \frac{enc}{3d} + d \ln B.$$

Hint: Choose the auxiliary density $q_{\mathbf{u}}^\varepsilon$ to be uniform on a cube centered at $\mathbf{u}$.

12

Linear Classification

12.1 The Zero–One Loss

An important special case of linear prediction with side information (Chapter 11) is the problem of binary pattern classification, where the decision space $\mathcal{D}$ and the outcome space $\mathcal{Y}$ are both equal to $\{-1, 1\}$. To predict an outcome $y_t \in \{-1, 1\}$, given the side information $\mathbf{x}_t \in \mathbb{R}^d$, the forecaster uses the linear classification $\widehat{y}_t = \mathrm{sgn}(\mathbf{w}_{t-1} \cdot \mathbf{x}_t)$, where $\mathbf{w}_{t-1}$ is a weight vector and $\mathrm{sgn}(\cdot)$ is the sign function. In the entire chapter we use the terminology and notation introduced in Chapter 11.

A natural loss function in the framework of classification is the *zero–one loss* $\ell(\widehat{y}, y) = \mathbb{I}_{\{\widehat{y} \neq y\}}$ counting the number of classification mistakes $\widehat{y} \neq y$. Since this loss function is not convex, we cannot analyze forecasters in this model using the machinery developed in Chapter 11. A possibility, which we investigate in Chapter 4 for arbitrary losses, is to allow the forecaster to randomize his predictions. As the expected zero–one loss is equivalent to the absolute loss $\frac{1}{2}|y - p|$, where $y \in \{-1, 1\}$ and $p \in [-1, +1]$, we see that randomization provides a convex variant of the original problem, which we can study using the techniques of Chapter 11. In this chapter we show that, even in the case of deterministic predictions, meaningful zero–one loss bounds can be derived by twisting the analysis for convex losses.

Let $\widehat{p}$ be a real-valued prediction used to determine the forecast $\widehat{y}$ by $\widehat{y} = \mathrm{sgn}(\widehat{p})$, and then consider a regular (and thus convex) loss function ℓ such that $\mathbb{I}_{\{\widehat{y} \neq y\}} \leq \ell(\widehat{p}, y)$ for all $\widehat{p} \in \mathbb{R}$ and $y \in \{-1, 1\}$. Now take any forecaster for linear experts, such as one of the gradient-based forecasters in Chapter 11. The techniques developed in Chapter 11 allow one to derive bounds for the regret $\widehat{L}_n - L_n(\mathbf{u})$, where

$$\widehat{L}_n = \sum_{t=1}^n \ell(\widehat{p}_t, y_t) \quad \text{and} \quad L_n(\mathbf{u}) = \sum_{t=1}^n \ell(\mathbf{u} \cdot \mathbf{x}_t, y_t).$$

Since $\mathbb{I}_{\{\widehat{y} \neq y\}} \leq \ell(\widehat{p}, y)$, we immediately obtain a bound on the "regret"

$$\sum_{t=1}^n \mathbb{I}_{\{\widehat{y}_t \neq y_t\}} - L_n(\mathbf{u})$$

of the forecaster using classifications of the form $\widehat{y}_t = \mathrm{sgn}(\widehat{p}_t)$. Note that this notion of regret evaluates the performance of the linear reference predictor $\mathbf{u}$ with a loss function

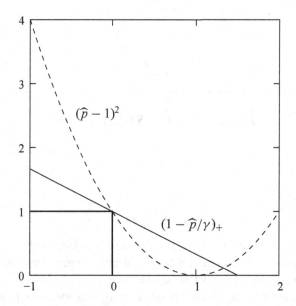

Figure 12.1. A plot of the square loss $\ell(\widehat{p}, y) = (\widehat{p} - y)^2$ for $y = 1$. This loss upper bounds the zero–one loss. The "normalized" hinge loss $(1 - y\widehat{p}/\gamma)_+$ is another convex upper bound on the zero–one loss (see Section 12.2). The plot shows $(1 - \widehat{p}/\gamma)_+$ for $\gamma = 3/2$.

larger than the one used to evaluate the forecaster $\widehat{y}$. This discrepancy is inherent to our analysis, which is largely based on convexity arguments.

An example of the results we can obtain using such an argument is the following. Consider the square loss $\ell(\widehat{p}, y) = (\widehat{p} - y)^2$. This loss is regular and upper bounds the zero–one loss (see Figure 12.1). If we predict each binary outcome y_t using $\widehat{y}_t = \mathrm{sgn}(\widehat{p}_t)$, where $\widehat{p}_t$ is the Vovk–Azoury–Warmuth forecaster (see Section 11.8), then Theorem 11.8 immediately implies the bound

$$\sum_{t=1}^{n} \mathbb{I}_{\{\widehat{y}_t \neq y_t\}} \leq \sum_{t=1}^{n} (\mathbf{u} \cdot \mathbf{x}_t - y_t)^2 + \|\mathbf{u}\|^2 + \sum_{i=1}^{d} \ln(1 + \lambda_i),$$

where $\lambda_1, \dots, \lambda_d$ are the eigenvalues of the matrix $\mathbf{x}_1 \mathbf{x}_1^\top + \cdots + \mathbf{x}_n \mathbf{x}_n^\top$. This bound holds for any sequence $(\mathbf{x}_1, y_1), (\mathbf{x}_2, y_2), \dots \in \mathbb{R}^d \times \{-1, 1\}$ and for all $\mathbf{u} \in \mathbb{R}^d$.

In the next sections we illustrate a more sophisticated "variational" approach to the analysis of forecasters for linear classification. This approach is based on the idea of finding a parametric family of functions that upper bound the zero–one loss and then expressing the regret using the best of these functions to evaluate the performance of the reference forecaster.

The rest of this chapter is organized as follows. In Section 12.2 we introduce the hinge loss, which we use to derive mistake bounds for forecasters based on various potentials. In Section 12.3 we show that by modifying the forecaster based on the quadratic potential, we can obtain, after a finite number of weight updates, a maximum margin linear separator for any linearly separable data sequence. In Section 12.4 we extend the label efficient setup to linear classification and prove label efficient mistake bounds for several forecasters. Finally,

Section 12.5 shows that some of the linear forecasters analyzed here can perform nonlinear classification, with a moderate computational overhead, by implicitly embedding the side information into a suitably chosen Hilbert space.

12.2 The Hinge Loss

In general, the convex upper bound on the zero–one loss yielding the tightest approximation of the overall mistake count depends on the whole unknown sequence of side information and outcome pairs $(\mathbf{x}_t, y_t)$, $t = 1, 2, \ldots$. In this section we introduce the hinge loss, a parameterized approximation to the zero–one loss, and we show simple forecasters that achieve a mistake bound that strikes an optimal tradeoff for the value of the parameter.

Following a consolidated terminology in learning theory, we call *instance* any side information $\mathbf{x}$, and *example* any pair $(\mathbf{x}, y)$, where y is the label associated with $\mathbf{x}$.

The *hinge loss*, with hinge at $\gamma > 0$, is defined by

$$\ell_\gamma(p, y) = (\gamma - py)_+ \qquad \text{(the hinge loss),}$$

where $p \in \mathbb{R}$, $y \in \{-1, 1\}$, and $(x)_+$ denotes the positive part of x. Note that $\ell_\gamma(p, y)$ is convex in p and ℓ_γ/γ is an upper bound on the zero–one loss (see Figure 12.1). Equipped with this notion of loss, we derive bounds on the regret

$$\sum_{t=1}^{n} \mathbb{I}_{\{\widehat{y}_t \neq y_t\}} - \inf_{\gamma > 0} \frac{1}{\gamma} \sum_{t=1}^{n} \ell_\gamma(\mathbf{u} \cdot \mathbf{x}_t, y_t)$$

that hold for an arbitrarily chosen $\mathbf{u} \in \mathbb{R}^d$.

We develop forecasters for classification that adopt a *conservative* updating policy. This means that the current weight vector $\mathbf{w}_{t-1}$ is updated only when $\widehat{y}_t \neq y_t$. So, the prediction of a conservative forecaster at time t only depends on the past examples $(\mathbf{x}_s, y_s)$, for $s < t$ such that $\widehat{y}_s \neq y_s$. The philosophy behind this conservative policy is that there is no reason to change the weight vector if it has worked well at the last time instance. We focus on conservative gradient-based forecasters whose update is based on the hinge loss. Recall from Section 11.3 that the gradient-based linear forecaster computes predictions $\widehat{p}_t = \mathbf{w}_{t-1} \cdot \mathbf{x}_t$, where the weights $\mathbf{w}_{t-1}$ are updated using the dual gradient update

$$\nabla \Phi^*(\mathbf{w}_t) = \nabla \Phi^*(\mathbf{w}_{t-1}) - \lambda \nabla \ell_{\gamma,t}(\mathbf{w}_{t-1}),$$

where $\nabla \ell_{\gamma,t}(\mathbf{w}) = \nabla \ell_\gamma(\mathbf{w} \cdot \mathbf{x}_t, y_t)$. Technically, $\ell_\gamma(p, y)$ is not differentiable at $p = \gamma/y$. However, since our algorithms are conservative, the derivative of $\ell_\gamma(\cdot, y)$ is computed only when p and y have different signs. Thus, we may set $\nabla \ell_{\gamma,t}(\mathbf{w}) = -y_t \mathbf{x}_t \mathbb{I}_{\{\widehat{y}_t \neq y_t\}}$, where $\widehat{y} = \text{sgn}(\mathbf{w} \cdot \mathbf{x}_t)$.

The conservative gradient-based forecaster for classifications is spelled out, for a Legendre potential Φ, here. For the definition of a Legendre potential function Φ and its dual Φ^* see Section 11.2.

THE CONSERVATIVE FORECASTER
FOR LINEAR CLASSIFICATION

Parameters: learning rate $\lambda > 0$, Legendre potential Φ.

Initialization: $\mathbf{w}_0 = \nabla \Phi(\mathbf{0})$.

For each round $t = 1, 2, \ldots$

    (1) observe $\mathbf{x}_t$, set $\widehat{p}_t = \mathbf{w}_{t-1} \cdot \mathbf{x}_t$, and predict $\widehat{y}_t = \mathrm{sgn}(\widehat{p}_t)$;

    (2) get $y_t \in \{-1, 1\}$;

    (3) if $\widehat{y}_t \neq y_t$, then let $\mathbf{w}_t = \nabla \Phi\big(\nabla \Phi^*(\mathbf{w}_{t-1}) + \lambda y_t \mathbf{x}_t\big)$;

        else let $\mathbf{w}_t = \mathbf{w}_{t-1}$.

A direct application of the results from Chapter 11 would not serve to prove regret bounds where γ is set optimally. We take a different route that can be followed in the case of any gradient-based forecaster using the hinge loss with a conservative updating policy. A basic inequality for such forecasters, shown in the proof of Theorem 11.1 using Taylor's theorem, is

$$\lambda\big(\ell_{\gamma,t}(\mathbf{w}_{t-1}) - \ell_{\gamma,t}(\mathbf{u})\big) \leq \lambda(\mathbf{u} - \mathbf{w}_{t-1}) \cdot \big(-\nabla \ell_{\gamma,t}(\mathbf{w}_{t-1})\big)$$
$$= D_{\Phi^*}(\mathbf{u}, \mathbf{w}_{t-1}) - D_{\Phi^*}(\mathbf{u}, \mathbf{w}_t) + D_{\Phi^*}(\mathbf{w}_{t-1}, \mathbf{w}_t)$$

for any $\mathbf{u} \in \mathbb{R}^d$ and any Legendre potential Φ. Now observe that, at any step t such that $\mathrm{sgn}(\widehat{p}_t) \neq y_t$, the hinge loss $\ell_{\gamma,t}(\mathbf{u}) = (\gamma - y_t \mathbf{u} \cdot \mathbf{x}_t)_+$ obeys the inequality

$$\gamma - \ell_{\gamma,t}(\mathbf{u}) = \gamma - (\gamma - y_t \mathbf{u} \cdot \mathbf{x}_t)_+ \leq y_t \mathbf{u} \cdot \mathbf{x}_t = \mathbf{u} \cdot \big(-\nabla \ell_{\gamma,t}(\mathbf{w}_{t-1})\big).$$

Therefore,

$$\lambda\big(\gamma - \ell_{\gamma,t}(\mathbf{u})\big)\mathbb{I}_{\{\widehat{y}_t \neq y_t\}} \leq \lambda \mathbf{u} \cdot \big(-\nabla \ell_{\gamma,t}(\mathbf{w}_{t-1})\big)$$
$$\leq \lambda(\mathbf{u} - \mathbf{w}_{t-1}) \cdot \big(-\nabla \ell_{\gamma,t}(\mathbf{w}_{t-1})\big)$$
$$= D_{\Phi^*}(\mathbf{u}, \mathbf{w}_{t-1}) - D_{\Phi^*}(\mathbf{u}, \mathbf{w}_t) + D_{\Phi^*}(\mathbf{w}_{t-1}, \mathbf{w}_t).$$

To understand the second inequality note that $\nabla \ell_{\gamma,t} \neq 0$ only when $\mathrm{sgn}(\widehat{p}_t) \neq y_t$ and, in this case, $\mathbf{w}_{t-1} \cdot \nabla \ell_{\gamma,t}(\mathbf{w}_{t-1}) = -y_t \mathbf{w}_{t-1} \cdot \mathbf{x}_t > 0$. The equality holds when $\nabla \ell_{\gamma,t} = 0$ because, in that case, $\mathbf{w}_{t-1} = \mathbf{w}_t$.

The advantage of this approach is seen as follows: if we multiply both sides of

$$\lambda\big(\gamma - \ell_{\gamma,t}(\mathbf{u})\big)\mathbb{I}_{\{\widehat{y}_t \neq y_t\}} \leq \lambda \mathbf{u} \cdot \big(-\nabla \ell_{\gamma,t}(\mathbf{w}_{t-1})\big)$$

by an arbitrary extra parameter $\alpha > 0$, and proceed as above, we obtain the new inequality

$$\alpha\lambda\big(\gamma - \ell_{\gamma,t}(\mathbf{u})\big)\mathbb{I}_{\{\widehat{y}_t \neq y_t\}} \leq D_{\Phi^*}(\alpha\mathbf{u}, \mathbf{w}_{t-1}) - D_{\Phi^*}(\alpha\mathbf{u}, \mathbf{w}_t) + D_{\Phi^*}(\mathbf{w}_{t-1}, \mathbf{w}_t).$$

Note that on the right-hand side $\mathbf{u}$ is now scaled by α. Summing for $t = 1, \ldots, n$ and using some simple algebraic manipulation, we obtain

$$\sum_{t=1}^{n} \big(\alpha\lambda\gamma - D_{\Phi^*}(\mathbf{w}_{t-1}, \mathbf{w}_t)\big)\mathbb{I}_{\{\widehat{y}_t \neq y_t\}} \leq \alpha\lambda L_{\gamma,n}(\mathbf{u}) + D_{\Phi^*}(\alpha\mathbf{u}, \mathbf{w}_0). \qquad (12.1)$$

This is our basic inequality for the hinge loss, and we now apply it to different potential functions.

Polynomial Potential and the Perceptron

Consider first the conservative forecaster for classification based on the Legendre polynomial potential $\Phi_p(\mathbf{u}) = \frac{1}{2} \|\mathbf{u}\|_p^2$, where $p \geq 2$. The conservative update rule for this forecaster can be written as

$$\mathbf{w}_t = \nabla \Phi_p\big(\nabla \Phi_q(\mathbf{w}_{t-1}) + \lambda y_t \mathbf{x}_t \, \mathbb{I}_{\{\hat{y}_t \neq y_t\}}\big).$$

It turns out that for the polynomial potential linear classification is, in some sense, easier than the linear pattern recognition problem of Chapter 11. In particular, a constant learning rate ($\lambda = 1$) is sufficient to obtain a good bound for the number of mistakes. Unfortunately, as we see, this is not the case for the exponential potential, which still needs a careful choice of the learning rate.

Theorem 12.1. *If the conservative forecaster using the Legendre polynomial potential Φ_p is run on a sequence $(\mathbf{x}_1, y_1), (\mathbf{x}_2, y_2) \ldots \in \mathbb{R}^d \times \{-1, 1\}$ with learning rate $\lambda = 1$, then for all $n \geq 1$, for all $\mathbf{u} \in \mathbb{R}^d$, and for all $\gamma > 0$,*

$$\sum_{t=1}^n \mathbb{I}_{\{\hat{y}_t \neq y_t\}}$$

$$\leq \frac{L_{\gamma,n}(\mathbf{u})}{\gamma} + (p-1)\left(\frac{X_p}{\gamma} \|\mathbf{u}\|_q\right)^2 + \sqrt{(p-1)\left(\frac{X_p}{\gamma} \|\mathbf{u}\|_q\right)^2 \frac{L_{\gamma,n}(\mathbf{u})}{\gamma}},$$

where $X_p = \max_{t=1,\ldots,n} \|\mathbf{x}_t\|_p$ and $q = p/(p-1)$ is the conjugate exponent of p.

Note that this bound holds simultaneously for all $\mathbf{u} \in \mathbb{R}^d$ and for all $\gamma > 0$. Hence, in particular, it holds for the best possible γ for each linear classifier $\mathbf{u}$. Note also that this bound has the same general form as of the bound stated in Theorem 11.2 in which λ is set optimally for each choice of γ and $\mathbf{u}$. So, linear classification does not require the self-confident tuning techniques that we used in Section 11.5.

Proof. We start from inequality (12.1). Following the proof of Theorem 11.2, for any t with $\hat{y}_t \neq y_t$, we upper bound $D_{\Phi^*}(\mathbf{w}_{t-1}, \mathbf{w}_t)$ as follows

$$D_{\Phi^*}(\mathbf{w}_{t-1}, \mathbf{w}_t) \leq \frac{p-1}{2} \big\| \nabla \ell_{y,t}(\mathbf{w}_{t-1}) \big\|_p^2 \leq \frac{p-1}{2} X_p^2.$$

Now apply this bound to (12.1) for $\mathbf{u} \in \mathbb{R}^d$ arbitrary and with $\lambda = 1$. This yields

$$\sum_{t=1}^n \left(\alpha \gamma - \frac{p-1}{2} X_p^2\right) \mathbb{I}_{\{\hat{y}_t \neq y_t\}} \leq \alpha L_{\gamma,n}(\mathbf{u}) + \frac{\|\mathbf{u}\|_q^2}{2} \alpha^2,$$

where we used the equality $D_{\Phi^*}(\alpha \mathbf{u}, \mathbf{w}_0) = \alpha^2 \frac{1}{2} \|\mathbf{u}\|_q^2$.

Setting $\alpha = \big(2\varepsilon + (p-1)X_p^2\big)/(2\gamma)$ for $\varepsilon > 0$ (to be determined later), and dividing by $\varepsilon > 0$, gives

$$\sum_{t=1}^n \mathbb{I}_{\{\hat{y}_t \neq y_t\}} \leq \frac{L_{\gamma,n}(\mathbf{u})}{\gamma} + \frac{(p-1)X_p^2}{2\varepsilon} \frac{L_{\gamma,n}(\mathbf{u})}{\gamma} + \frac{\big(2\varepsilon + (p-1)X_p^2\big)^2}{4\varepsilon\gamma^2} \frac{\|\mathbf{u}\|_q^2}{2}.$$

To minimize the bound, set

$$\varepsilon = \frac{X_p}{\|\mathbf{u}\|_q} \sqrt{(p-1)\gamma L_{\gamma,n}(\mathbf{u}) + \left(\frac{p-1}{2} X_p \|\mathbf{u}\|_q\right)^2}.$$

With an easy algebraic manipulation we then get

$$\sum_{t=1}^{n} \mathbb{I}_{\{\hat{y}_t \neq y_t\}} \leq \frac{L_{\gamma,n}(\mathbf{u})}{\gamma} + \frac{p-1}{2} \left(\frac{X_p}{\gamma} \|\mathbf{u}\|_q\right)^2$$

$$+ \frac{X_p \|\mathbf{u}\|_q}{\gamma} \sqrt{(p-1)\frac{L_{\gamma,n}(\mathbf{u})}{\gamma} + \left(\frac{(p-1)X_p \|\mathbf{u}\|_q}{2\gamma}\right)^2}.$$

Using $\sqrt{a+b} \leq \sqrt{a} + \sqrt{b}$ for all $a, b > 0$ we get the inequality stated in the theorem. Since $\mathbf{u}$ and $\gamma > 0$ were arbitrary, the proof is concluded. ∎

The forecaster of Theorem 12.1 is also known as the *p-norm Perceptron* algorithm. For $p = 2$, this reduces to the classical *Perceptron algorithm*, whose weight updating rule is simply $\mathbf{w}_t = \mathbf{w}_{t-1} + y_t \mathbf{x}_t \mathbb{I}_{\{\hat{y}_t \neq y_t\}}$. Note also that, for $p = 2$ and $L_{\gamma,n}(\mathbf{u}) = 0$, the bound of Theorem 12.1 reduces to

$$\sum_{t=1}^{n} \mathbb{I}_{\{\hat{y}_t \neq y_t\}} \leq \left(\frac{\max\limits_{t=1,\dots,n} \|\mathbf{x}_t\| \|\mathbf{u}\|}{\gamma}\right)^2.$$

In this special case, the result is equivalent to the *Perceptron convergence theorem* (see Section 12.6). More precisely, $L_{\gamma,n}(\mathbf{u}) = 0$ implies that the sequence $(\mathbf{x}_1, y_1), \dots, (\mathbf{x}_n, y_n)$ is linearly separated by the hyperplane $\mathbf{u}$ with margin at least γ. The *margin* of the linearly separable data sequence with respect to the separating hyperplane $\mathbf{u}$ is defined by $\min_t y_t \mathbf{u} \cdot \mathbf{x}_t / \|\mathbf{u}\|$. The Perceptron convergence theorem states that the number of mistakes (or, equivalently, updates) performed by the Perceptron algorithm on any linearly separable sequence is at most the squared ratio of (1) the radius of the smallest origin-centered euclidean ball enclosing all instances and (2) the margin γ of any separating hyperplane $\mathbf{u}$ (see Figure 12.2).

The dynamic tuning $\lambda_t = 1/\|\mathbf{x}_t\|$ is known to improve the empirical performance of the Perceptron algorithm. Indeed, we can easily extend the analysis of Theorem 12.1 (see Exercise 12.1) and prove a bound that, in the case of linearly separable sequences, can be stated as

$$\sum_{t=1}^{n} \mathbb{I}_{\{\hat{y}_t \neq y_t\}} \leq \left(\max_{t=1,\dots,n} \frac{\|\mathbf{x}_t\| \|\mathbf{u}\|}{y_t \mathbf{u} \cdot \mathbf{x}_t}\right)^2,$$

where $\mathbf{u}$ is any linear separator. The improvement is clear when we rewrite the bound for the Perceptron with static tuning $\lambda = 1$ as

$$\sum_{t=1}^{n} \mathbb{I}_{\{\hat{y}_t \neq y_t\}} \leq \left(\frac{\max\limits_{t=1,\dots,n} \|\mathbf{x}_t\| \|\mathbf{u}\|}{\min\limits_{t=1\dots,n} (y_t \mathbf{u} \cdot \mathbf{x}_t)}\right)^2.$$

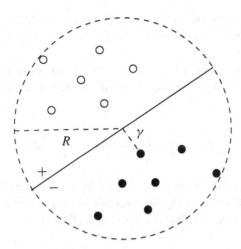

Figure 12.2. The instances $\mathbf{x}_t \in \mathbb{R}^2$ of a linearly separable sequence $(\mathbf{x}_1, y_1), \ldots, (\mathbf{x}_n, y_n)$. Empty circles denote instances $\mathbf{x}_t$ with label $y_t = 1$ and filled circles denote instances with label $y_t = -1$. A separating hyperplane, passing through the origin, with margin γ is drawn. The Perceptron convergence theorem states that, on this sequence, the Perceptron algorithm will make at most $(R/\gamma)^2$ mistakes or, equivalently, perform at most $(R/\gamma)^2$ updates.

Exponential Potential and Winnow

We proceed by considering the conservative linear forecaster based on the Legendre exponential potential $\Phi(\mathbf{u}) = e^{u_1} + \cdots + e^{u_d}$. Unlike the analysis of the polynomial potential, here the choice of the learning rate makes a difference. Indeed, our result does not address the issue of tuning λ, and the regret bound we prove retains the same general form as the bound proven in Theorem 11.3 for the linear pattern recognition problem.

Theorem 12.2. *Assume the conservative forecaster using the Legendre exponential potential* $\Phi(\mathbf{u}) = e^{u_1} + \cdots + e^{u_d}$ *with normalized weights is run with learning rate* $\lambda = (2\gamma\varepsilon)/X_\infty^2$, *where* $0 < \varepsilon < 1$, *on a sequence* $(\mathbf{x}_1, y_1), (\mathbf{x}_2, y_2) \ldots \in \mathbb{R}^d \times \{-1, 1\}$. *Then for all* $n \geq 1$ *such that* $X_\infty \geq \max_{t=1,\ldots,n} \|\mathbf{x}_t\|_\infty$ *and for all* $\mathbf{u} \in \mathbb{R}^d$ *in the probability simplex,*

$$\sum_{t=1}^{n} \mathbb{I}_{\{\hat{y}_t \neq y_t\}} \leq \frac{1}{1-\varepsilon} \frac{L_{\gamma,n}(\mathbf{u})}{\gamma} + \left(\frac{X_\infty}{\gamma}\right)^2 \frac{\ln d}{2\varepsilon(1-\varepsilon)}.$$

Proof. Following the proof of Theorem 11.3, we upper bound $D_{\Phi^*}(\mathbf{w}_{t-1}, \mathbf{w}_t)$ as follows:

$$D_{\Phi^*}(\mathbf{w}_{t-1}, \mathbf{w}_t) \leq D_{\Phi^*}\left(\mathbf{w}_{t-1}, \mathbf{w}_t'\right) \leq \frac{\lambda^2}{2} X_\infty^2,$$

where $w_{i,t}' = w_{i,t-1} e^{-\lambda \nabla \ell_t(\mathbf{w}_t)_i}$ and $\mathbf{w}_t$ is $\mathbf{w}_t'$ normalized (as in the proof of Theorem 11.3, we applied the generalized pythagorean inequality, Lemma 11.3, in the second step of this derivation). Now apply this bound to (12.1) for $\alpha = 1$ and for any $\mathbf{u} \in \mathbb{R}^d$ in the probability simplex. This yields

$$\sum_{t=1}^{n} \left(\lambda \gamma - \frac{\lambda^2}{2} X_\infty^2\right) \mathbb{I}_{\{\hat{y}_t \neq y_t\}} \leq \lambda L_{\gamma,n}(\mathbf{u}) + \ln d,$$

where we used the inequality $D_{\Phi^*}(\mathbf{u}, \mathbf{w}_0) \leq \ln d$ for $\mathbf{w}_0 = (1/d, \ldots, 1/d)$. Dividing both sides by $\lambda\gamma > 0$ and substituting our choice of λ yields the desired bound. ∎

The forecaster used in Theorem 12.2 is a "zero-threshold" variant of the *Winnow algorithm*. In the linearly separable case, the bound of Theorem 12.2, with $\varepsilon = 1/2$, reduces to

$$\sum_{t=1}^{n} \mathbb{I}_{\{\hat{y}_t \neq y_t\}} \leq 2 \left(\frac{\max\limits_{t=1,\ldots,n} \|\mathbf{x}_t\|_\infty}{\gamma} \right)^2 \ln d,$$

where γ is the margin of the hyperplane defined by $\mathbf{u}$. A comparison with the corresponding bound for the Perceptron algorithm reveals an interplay between polynomial and exponential potential analogous to that discussed in Section 11.4.

The Second-Order Perceptron

We close this section by showing an analysis of the conservative classifier based on the Vovk–Azoury–Warmuth forecaster (see the discussion at the end of Section 12.2). Following the terminology introduced by Cesa-Bianchi, Conconi, and Gentile [47], we call this classifier *second-order Perceptron*. At each time step $t = 1, 2, \ldots$ the second-order Perceptron predicts with $\hat{y}_t = \text{sgn}(\widehat{\mathbf{w}}_t^\top \mathbf{x}_t)$, where

$$\widehat{\mathbf{w}}_t = A_t^{-1} \sum_{s=1}^{t-1} y_s \mathbf{x}_s \, \mathbb{I}_{\{\hat{y}_s \neq y_s\}} \quad \text{and} \quad A_t = \left(aI + \sum_{s=1}^{t-1} \mathbf{x}_s \mathbf{x}_s^\top \, \mathbb{I}_{\{\hat{y}_s \neq y_s\}} + \mathbf{x}_t \mathbf{x}_t^\top \right)$$

(following the notation introduced in Chapter 11, we use $\widehat{\mathbf{w}}_t$ instead of $\widehat{\mathbf{w}}_{t-1}$ to denote the weight vector of this forecaster at time t). Note that we have introduced a parameter $a > 0$ multiplying the identity matrix I. Even though this parameter is not used in the analysis of the second-order Perceptron, it becomes convenient when we compare the behavior of this algorithm with that of the standard Perceptron.

Rather than using the inequality (12.1), we follow the arguments developed in Section 11.8 for the analysis of the Vovk-Azoury-Warmuth forecaster.

Theorem 12.3. *If the second-order Perceptron (the conservative Vovk-Azoury-Warmuth forecaster) is run on a sequence* $(\mathbf{x}_1, y_1), (\mathbf{x}_2, y_2) \ldots \in \mathbb{R}^d \times \{-1, 1\}$, *then for all* $n \geq 1$, *for all* $\mathbf{u} \in \mathbb{R}^d$, *and for all* $\gamma > 0$,

$$\sum_{t=1}^{n} \mathbb{I}_{\{\hat{y}_t \neq y_t\}} \leq \frac{L_{\gamma,n}(\mathbf{u})}{\gamma} + \frac{1}{\gamma} \sqrt{\left(a \|\mathbf{u}\|^2 + \mathbf{u}^\top A_n \mathbf{u} \right) \sum_{i=1}^{d} \ln\left(1 + \frac{\lambda_i}{a}\right)},$$

where $\lambda_1, \ldots, \lambda_d$ *are the eigenvalues of the matrix*

$$A_n = \sum_{t=1}^{n} \mathbf{x}_t \mathbf{x}_t^\top \, \mathbb{I}_{\{\hat{y}_t \neq y_t\}}.$$

The bound stated by Theorem 12.3 is not in closed form as the terms $\mathbb{I}_{\{\hat{y}_t \neq y_t\}}$ appear on both sides. We could obtain a closed form by replacing A_n with the matrix $\mathbf{x}_1 \mathbf{x}_1^\top + \cdots + \mathbf{x}_n \mathbf{x}_n^\top$ including all instances. Note that this substitution can only increase the eigenvalues

$\lambda_1, \ldots, \lambda_d$. However, the closed-form bound is probably too weak to reveal the improvements brought about by the second-order Perceptron analysis with respect to the classical Perceptron (see the end of this subsection for a detailed comparison of the two bounds in a special case).

Proof of Theorem 12.3. We follow the notation of Section 11.8 with the necessary adjustments because we have introduced the new parameter a and we are considering conservative forecasters. So, in particular, define

$$\Phi_t^*(\mathbf{u}) = \left[\frac{a}{2} \|\mathbf{u}\|^2 + \frac{1}{2} \sum_{s=1}^{t-1} (\mathbf{u}^\top \mathbf{x}_s - y_s)^2 \, \mathbb{I}_{\{\hat{y}_s \neq y_s\}} \right].$$

This potential is connected to $\hat{\mathbf{w}}_t$ by the following relation (see the proof of Theorem 11.8):

$$\frac{1}{2}\left(\hat{\mathbf{w}}_t^\top \mathbf{x}_t - y_t\right)^2 \mathbb{I}_{\{\hat{y}_t \neq y_t\}} = \inf_{\mathbf{v}} \Phi_{t+1}^*(\mathbf{v}) - \inf_{\mathbf{v}} \Phi_t^*(\mathbf{v}) + \frac{1}{2}\mathbf{x}_t^\top A_t^{-1}\mathbf{x}_t \, \mathbb{I}_{\{\hat{y}_t \neq y_t\}}$$
$$- \frac{1}{2}\left(\mathbf{x}_t^\top A_{t-1}^{-1}\mathbf{x}_t\right)\left(\hat{\mathbf{w}}_t^\top \mathbf{x}_t\right)^2 \mathbb{I}_{\{\hat{y}_t \neq y_t\}},$$

where, if $\hat{y}_t = y_t$, the equality holds because $\inf_{\mathbf{v}} \Phi_{t+1}^*(\mathbf{v}) = \inf_{\mathbf{v}} \Phi_t^*(\mathbf{v})$. We drop the last term, which is negative because A_{t-1} is positive definite, and sum over $t = 1, \ldots, n$, obtaining, for any $\mathbf{u} \in \mathbb{R}^d$,

$$\frac{1}{2} \sum_{t=1}^n \left(\hat{\mathbf{w}}_t^\top \mathbf{x}_t - y_t\right)^2 \mathbb{I}_{\{\hat{y}_t \neq y_t\}}$$

$$\leq \inf_{\mathbf{v}} \Phi_{n+1}^*(\mathbf{v}) - \inf_{\mathbf{v}} \Phi_1^*(\mathbf{v}) + \frac{1}{2} \sum_{t=1}^n \mathbf{x}_t^\top A_t^{-1}\mathbf{x}_t \, \mathbb{I}_{\{\hat{y}_t \neq y_t\}}$$

$$\leq \Phi_{n+1}^*(\mathbf{u}) + \frac{1}{2} \sum_{t=1}^n \mathbf{x}_t^\top A_t^{-1}\mathbf{x}_t \, \mathbb{I}_{\{\hat{y}_t \neq y_t\}}$$

$$= \frac{a}{2} \|\mathbf{u}\|^2 + \frac{1}{2} \sum_{t=1}^n (\mathbf{u}^\top \mathbf{x}_t - y_t)^2 \, \mathbb{I}_{\{\hat{y}_t \neq y_t\}} + \frac{1}{2} \sum_{t=1}^n \mathbf{x}_t^\top A_t^{-1}\mathbf{x}_t \, \mathbb{I}_{\{\hat{y}_t \neq y_t\}},$$

where we used $\inf_{\mathbf{v}} \Phi_1^*(\mathbf{v}) = 0$. Expanding the squares and performing trivial simplifications, we get to the following inequality:

$$\frac{1}{2} \sum_{t=1}^n \left(\left(\hat{\mathbf{w}}_t^\top \mathbf{x}_t\right)^2 - 2 y_t \hat{\mathbf{w}}_t^\top \mathbf{x}_t\right) \mathbb{I}_{\{\hat{y}_t \neq y_t\}} \leq \frac{1}{2} \left[a \|\mathbf{u}\|^2 + \sum_{t=1}^n (\mathbf{u}^\top \mathbf{x}_t)^2 \, \mathbb{I}_{\{\hat{y}_t \neq y_t\}} \right]$$
$$- \sum_{t=1}^n y_t \mathbf{u}^\top \mathbf{x}_t \, \mathbb{I}_{\{\hat{y}_t \neq y_t\}} + \frac{1}{2} \sum_{t=1}^n \mathbf{x}_t^\top A_t^{-1}\mathbf{x}_t \, \mathbb{I}_{\{\hat{y}_t \neq y_t\}}.$$

Note that the left-hand side of this inequality is a sum of positive terms, because $-2 y_t \hat{\mathbf{w}}_t^\top \mathbf{x}_t \geq 0$ whenever $\hat{y}_t \neq y_t$. In addition, we can write

$$\frac{1}{2} \left[a \|\mathbf{u}\|^2 + \sum_{t=1}^n (\mathbf{u}^\top \mathbf{x}_t)^2 \, \mathbb{I}_{\{\hat{y}_t \neq y_t\}} \right] = \frac{1}{2} \mathbf{u}^\top \left(I + \sum_{t=1}^n \mathbf{x}_t \mathbf{x}_t^\top \, \mathbb{I}_{\{\hat{y}_t \neq y_t\}} \right) \mathbf{u} = \frac{1}{2} \mathbf{u}^\top A_n \mathbf{u}$$

and, using Lemma 11.11,

$$\frac{1}{2}\sum_{t=1}^{n} \mathbf{x}_t^\top A_t^{-1} \mathbf{x}_t \, \mathbb{I}_{\{\hat{y}_t \neq y_t\}} \leq \frac{1}{2}\sum_{i=1}^{d} \ln\left(1 + \frac{\lambda_i}{a}\right).$$

This allows us to write the simpler form

$$0 \leq \frac{1}{2}\mathbf{u}^\top (aI + A_n)\mathbf{u} - \sum_{t=1}^{n} y_t \mathbf{u}^\top \mathbf{x}_t \, \mathbb{I}_{\{\hat{y}_t \neq y_t\}} + \frac{1}{2}\sum_{i=1}^{d} \ln\left(1 + \frac{\lambda_i}{a}\right).$$

Since $\mathbf{u}$ was chosen arbitrarily, this inequality also holds when $\mathbf{u}$ is replaced by $\alpha\mathbf{u}$, where $\alpha > 0$ is a free parameter. Performing this substitution, we end up with

$$0 \leq \frac{\alpha^2}{2}\mathbf{u}^\top (I + A_n)\mathbf{u} - \alpha\sum_{t=1}^{n} y_t \mathbf{u}^\top \mathbf{x}_t \, \mathbb{I}_{\{\hat{y}_t \neq y_t\}} + \frac{1}{2}\sum_{i=1}^{d} \ln\left(1 + \frac{\lambda_i}{a}\right).$$

To introduce hinge loss terms, observe that $-y_t \mathbf{u}^\top \mathbf{x}_t \leq \ell_{\gamma,t}(\mathbf{u}) - \gamma$ for all $\gamma > 0$. Substituting this into the above inequality, rearranging, and dividing both sides by $\alpha\gamma > 0$ yields

$$\sum_{t=1}^{n} \mathbb{I}_{\{\hat{y}_t \neq y_t\}} \leq \frac{L_{\gamma,n}(\mathbf{u})}{\gamma} + \frac{\alpha}{2\gamma}\mathbf{u}^\top (I + A_n)\mathbf{u} + \frac{1}{2\alpha\gamma}\sum_{i=1}^{d} \ln\left(1 + \frac{\lambda_i}{a}\right).$$

Substituting the choice

$$\alpha = \sqrt{\frac{\sum_{i=1}^{d} \ln(1 + \lambda_i/a)}{\mathbf{u}^\top (I + A_n)\mathbf{u}}}$$

implies the claimed bound. ∎

We now compare the bound of Theorem 12.3 with the corresponding bound for the Perceptron algorithm (Theorem 12.1 with $p = 2$).

Consider the simple case of a sequence $(\mathbf{x}_1, y_1), \ldots, (\mathbf{x}_n, y_n)$ where $\|\mathbf{x}_t\| = 1$ for all t and such that there exists some $\mathbf{u} \in \mathbb{R}^d$, with $\|\mathbf{u}\| = 1$, satisfying $y_t\, \mathbf{u}^\top \mathbf{x}_t \geq \gamma > 0$ for all $t = 1, \ldots, n$. For this linearly separable sequence, the bound of Theorem 12.3 may be then written as

$$\sum_{t=1}^{n} \mathbb{I}_{\{\hat{y}_t \neq y_t\}} \leq \frac{1}{\gamma}\sqrt{\left(a + \mathbf{u}^\top A_n \mathbf{u}\right)\sum_{i=1}^{d} \ln\left(1 + \frac{\lambda_i}{a}\right)}. \tag{12.2}$$

Recall that this bound is not in closed form as A_n (and its eigenvalues) depend on the mistake terms $\mathbb{I}_{\{\hat{y}_t \neq y_t\}}$. Then let m be the largest cardinality of a subset $\mathcal{M} \subseteq \{1, \ldots, n\}$ such that (12.2) is still satisfied when a mistake is made on each $t \in \mathcal{M}$. Moreover, let $m' = 1/\gamma^2$, where $1/\gamma^2$ is the Perceptron bound specialized to the case $\|\mathbf{u}\| = 1$ and $\|\mathbf{x}_t\| = 1$ for all t. We want to investigate conditions on the sequence guaranteeing that $m < m'$. To do that, we represent m' as the unique positive solution of

$$m' = \frac{\sqrt{m'}}{\gamma}.$$

Thus $m < m'$ whenever

$$\left(a + \mathbf{u}^\top A_n \mathbf{u}\right) \sum_{i=1}^{d} \ln\left(1 + \frac{\lambda_i}{a}\right) < m. \tag{12.3}$$

Now note that, since $\|\mathbf{u}\| = 1$ and $\|\mathbf{x}_t\| = 1$,

$$\mathbf{u}^\top A_n \mathbf{u} = \sum_{t=1}^{n} (\mathbf{u}^\top \mathbf{x}_t)^2 \, \mathbb{I}_{\{\hat{y}_t \neq y_t\}} < m.$$

Using $(\mathbf{u}^\top \mathbf{x}_t)^2 = (y_t \mathbf{u}^\top \mathbf{x}_t)^2 \geq \gamma^2$, we conclude $\gamma^2 m \leq \mathbf{u}^\top A_n \mathbf{u} \leq m$ for all $\mathbf{u} \in \mathbb{R}^d$. Hence, we may write $\mathbf{u}^\top A_n \mathbf{u} = \alpha m$ for some $\gamma^2 \leq \alpha \leq 1$. Since $\|\mathbf{x}_t\| = 1$ also implies $\lambda_1 + \cdots + \lambda_d = m$, we may set $\lambda_i = \alpha_i m$, where the coefficients $\alpha_1, \ldots, \alpha_d \geq 0$ are such that $\alpha_1 + \cdots + \alpha_d = 1$. Performing these substitutions in (12.3) we obtain

$$(a + \alpha m) \sum_{i=1}^{d} \ln\left(1 + \frac{\alpha_i m}{a}\right) < m. \tag{12.4}$$

If $\alpha m = \mathbf{u}^\top A_n \mathbf{u}$ is small compared with the large eigenvalues of A_n, then there exist choices of a that satisfy (12.4) (see Exercise 12.5).

This discussion suggests that the linearly separable sequences on which the second-order Perceptron has an advantage over the classical Perceptron are those where linear separators $\mathbf{u}$ tend to be nearly orthogonal to the eigenvectors of A_n with large eigenvalues. In such sequences, a large share of instances $\mathbf{x}_t$ must thus have the property that $y_t \mathbf{u}^\top \mathbf{x}_t$ is close to the minimum value γ.

As a final remark note that the bounds of Theorems 12.1 and 12.3 are invariant to simultaneous rescalings of γ and $\|\mathbf{u}\|$ that do not change the ratio $\|\mathbf{u}\|/\gamma$ (in Theorem 12.1 this ratio should take the form $\|\mathbf{u}\|_q/\gamma$). This is what we expect, because the loss $L_{\gamma,n}(\mathbf{u})/\gamma$ exhibits the same kind of invariance. Hence, we do not lose any generality if these results are stated with γ set to 1.

12.3 Maximum Margin Classifiers

In this section we study the scenario in which a forecaster is repeatedly run on the same sequence of examples. More specifically, we say that a forecaster is *cyclically run* on a "base sequence" $(\mathbf{x}_1, y_1), \ldots, (\mathbf{x}_n, y_n) \in \mathbb{R}^d \times \{-1, 1\}$ if it is run on the sequence $(\mathbf{x}'_1, y'_1), (\mathbf{x}'_2, y'_2), \ldots,$ where $(\mathbf{x}'_{kn+t}, y'_{kn+t}) = (\mathbf{x}_t, y_t)$ for all $k \geq 0$ and $t = 1, \ldots, n$.

If the base sequence is linearly separable, then the mistake bound for a conservative forecaster tells us how many updates are performed at most before the forecaster's current classifier converge to a linear separator of the base sequence. For example, the Perceptron convergence theorem (see Section 12.2) states that at most $\left(\max_t \|\mathbf{x}_t\|/\gamma\right)^2$ updates are needed to find a linear separator for any sequence linearly separable with margin $\gamma > 0$. However, the results of Section 12.2 do not provide information on the margin of the separator found by the forecaster.

The question addressed here is whether we can modify the forecasters of Section 12.2 so that the classifier obtained after the last update has a margin close to the largest margin achievable by any linear separator of the sequence.

Assume that the sequence $(\mathbf{x}_1, y_1), (\mathbf{x}_2, y_2), \ldots \in \mathbb{R}^d \times \{-1, 1\}$ is linearly separable by $\mathbf{u} \in \mathbb{R}^d$ such that $\|\mathbf{x}_t\| = 1$ for all t. We now show that the following algorithm, a simple modification of the Perceptron, when cyclically run on a sequence with margin γ, finds a linear separator with margin $(1 - \alpha)\gamma$ after at most $1/(\alpha\gamma)^2$ updates, where α is an input parameter. Following the terminology of Gentile [123], we call this modified Perceptron ALMA (approximate large margin algorithm).

THE ALMA FORECASTER

Parameter: $\alpha \in (0, 1]$.

Initialization: $\mathbf{w}_0 = (0, \ldots, 0)$, $k = 1$.

For each round $t = 1, 2, \ldots$

    (1) $\gamma_t = \left(\sqrt{8/k}\right)/\alpha$;
    (2) observe $\mathbf{x}_t$, set $\widehat{p}_t = \mathbf{w}_{t-1} \cdot \mathbf{x}_t$, and predict with $\widehat{y}_t = \mathrm{sgn}(\widehat{p}_t)$;
    (2) get label $y_t \in \{-1, 1\}$;
    (3) if $y_t \mathbf{w}_{t-1} \cdot \mathbf{x}_t \leq (1 - \alpha)\gamma_t$, then
        (3.1) $\eta_t = \sqrt{2/k}$ and $\mathbf{w}'_t = \mathbf{w}_{t-1} + \eta_t y_t \mathbf{x}_t$;
        (3.2) $\mathbf{w}_t = \mathbf{w}'_t / \|\mathbf{w}'_t\|$;
        (3.3) $k \leftarrow k + 1$;
    (4) else, let $\mathbf{w}_t = \mathbf{w}_{t-1}$.

Theorem 12.4. *Suppose the* ALMA *forecaster is cyclically run on a sequence* $(\mathbf{x}_1, y_1), \ldots, (\mathbf{x}_n, y_n) \in \mathbb{R}^d \times \{-1, 1\}$ *with* $\|\mathbf{x}_t\| = 1$ *for all t, linearly separable by* $\mathbf{u} \in \mathbb{R}^d$ *with margin* $\gamma > 0$. *Let m be the number of updates performed by* ALMA *on this sequence. Then the number of mistakes* $m = \sum_{t=1}^{\infty} \mathbb{I}_{\{\widehat{y}_t \neq y_t\}}$ *is finite and satisfies*

$$m \leq \frac{2}{\gamma^2}\left(\frac{2}{\alpha} - 1\right)^2 + \frac{8}{\alpha} - 4.$$

Furthermore, let s be the time step when the last update occurs. Then the weight $\mathbf{w}_s$ *computed by* ALMA *at time s is a linear separator of the sequence achieving margin* $(1 - \alpha)\gamma$.

Proof. For any $t = 1, 2, \ldots$, let $N_t = \|\mathbf{w}'_t\|$, and $\gamma_t(\mathbf{u}) = y_t \mathbf{u} \cdot \mathbf{x}_t$. We first find an upper bound on m by studying the quantity $\mathbf{u} \cdot \mathbf{w}_s$. Choose any round t such that $y_t \mathbf{w}_{t-1} \cdot \mathbf{x}_t \leq (1 - \alpha)\gamma_t$. Then

$$\mathbf{u} \cdot \mathbf{w}_t = \frac{\mathbf{u} \cdot \mathbf{w}_{t-1} + \eta_t y_t \mathbf{u} \cdot \mathbf{x}_t}{N_t} \geq \frac{\mathbf{u} \cdot \mathbf{w}_{t-1} + \eta_t \gamma}{N_t}$$

and

$$
\begin{aligned}
N_t^2 &= \|\mathbf{w}'_t\|^2 \\
&= \|\mathbf{w}_{t-1} + \eta_t y_t \mathbf{x}_t\|^2 \\
&= 1 + \eta_t^2 + 2\eta_t y_t \mathbf{w}_{t-1} \cdot \mathbf{x}_t \\
&\leq 1 + \eta_t^2 + 2(1 - \alpha)\eta_t \gamma_t.
\end{aligned}
$$

The inequality holds because an update at time t implies that $y_t \, \mathbf{w}_{t-1} \cdot \mathbf{x}_t \leq (1 - \alpha)\gamma_t$. Substituting the values of η_t and γ_t in the last expression, we obtain $N_t^2 \leq 1 + 2A/k_t$, where $A = 4/\alpha - 3$ and k_t is the number of updates performed after the first t time steps.

Now we bound m by analyzing $\mathbf{u} \cdot \mathbf{w}_s$ through the recursion

$$
\begin{aligned}
\mathbf{u} \cdot \mathbf{w}_s &\geq \frac{\mathbf{u} \cdot \mathbf{w}_{s-1} + \eta_s \gamma}{\sqrt{1 + 2A/m}} \\
&= \frac{\mathbf{u} \cdot \mathbf{w}_{s-1}}{\sqrt{1 + 2A/m}} + \frac{\gamma}{\sqrt{m/2 + A}}.
\end{aligned}
$$

Solving this recursion, while keeping in mind that $\mathbf{w}_0 = \mathbf{0}$ and $\mathbf{u} \cdot \mathbf{w}_t = \mathbf{u} \cdot \mathbf{w}_{t-1}$ if no update takes place at time t, we obtain

$$
\mathbf{u} \cdot \mathbf{w}_s \geq \sum_{k=1}^{m} \frac{\gamma}{\sqrt{k/2 + A}} \prod_{j=k+1}^{m} \frac{1}{\sqrt{1 + 2A/j}},
$$

where for $k = m$ the product has value 1. Now,

$$
\begin{aligned}
-\ln \prod_{j=k+1}^{m} \frac{1}{\sqrt{1 + 2A/j}} &= \frac{1}{2} \sum_{j=k+1}^{m} \ln\left(1 + \frac{2A}{j}\right) \\
&\leq \frac{1}{2} \sum_{j=k+1}^{m} \frac{2A}{j} \qquad \text{(since } \ln(1 + x) \leq x \text{ for all } x \geq -1\text{)} \\
&\leq A \int_{j=k}^{m} \frac{dx}{x} \\
&= A \ln \frac{m}{k}.
\end{aligned}
$$

Therefore,

$$
\prod_{j=k+1}^{m} \frac{1}{\sqrt{1 + 2A/k}} \geq \left(\frac{k}{m}\right)^{A}.
$$

Now, since $\mathbf{u} \cdot \mathbf{w}_s \leq 1$, we obtain

$$
\begin{aligned}
1 &\geq \gamma \sum_{k=1}^{m} \frac{(k/m)^A}{\sqrt{k/2 + A}} \\
&\geq \gamma \sum_{k=1}^{m} \frac{(k/m)^A}{\sqrt{m/2 + A}} \\
&\geq \frac{\gamma}{m^A \sqrt{m/2 + A}} \int_0^m k^A \, dk \\
&= \frac{\gamma}{A + 1} \frac{m}{\sqrt{m/2 + A}}.
\end{aligned}
$$

Solving for m yields

$$m \leq \frac{(A+1)^2}{4\gamma^2} + \sqrt{\frac{(A+1)^4}{16\gamma^4} + \frac{(A+1)^2 A}{\gamma^2}}$$

$$\leq \frac{(A+1)^2}{4\gamma^2} + \frac{(A+1)^{3/2}}{\gamma}\sqrt{\frac{A+1}{16\gamma^2} + 1}$$

$$\leq \frac{(A+1)^2}{4\gamma^2} + \frac{(A+1)^2}{4\gamma^2} + 2(A+1),$$

where we used the inequality $\sqrt{x+1} \leq \sqrt{x} + 1/(2\sqrt{x})$ for $x > 0$ in the last step. Substituting our choice of A yields the desired result.

To show that $\mathbf{w}_s$ is a linear separator with margin $(1-\alpha)\gamma$, note that

$$\gamma_s = \frac{1}{\alpha}\sqrt{\frac{8}{m}}$$

$$\geq \frac{1}{\alpha}\sqrt{\frac{8}{\frac{(A+1)^2}{2\gamma^2} + 2(A+1)}}$$

$$\geq \frac{1}{\alpha}\sqrt{\frac{\gamma}{\frac{(A+1)^2}{16} + \frac{A+1}{4}}} \qquad \text{(since } 0 \leq \gamma \leq 1\text{)}$$

$$= \frac{\gamma}{\sqrt{1 - \alpha^2/4}}$$

$$\geq \gamma.$$

Since the last update occurs at time n, this means that $y_t \mathbf{w}_s \cdot \mathbf{x}_t > (1-\alpha)\gamma$ for all $t > s$. ∎

12.4   Label Efficient Classifiers

In Section 6.2 we looked at prediction in a "label efficient" scenario where the forecaster has limited access to the sequence of outcomes $y_1, y_2, \ldots$. Using an independent random process for selecting the outcomes to observe, we have been able to control the regret of the weighted average forecasters when an a priori bound is imposed on the overall number of outcomes that may be observed.

In this section we cast label efficient prediction in the model of linear classification with side information: after generating the prediction $\widehat{y}_t = \mathrm{sgn}(\widehat{p}_t)$ for the next label y_t given the side information $\mathbf{x}_t$, the forecaster uses randomization to decide whether to query y_t or not. If y_t is not queried, its value remains unknown to the forecaster, and the current classifier is not updated. It is important to remark that, as in Section 6.2, in this model also the forecaster is evaluated by counting prediction mistakes on those time steps when the true labels y_t remained unknown.

We study selective sampling algorithms that use a simple randomized rule to decide whether to query the label of the current instance. This rule prescribes that the label should be obtained with probability $c/(c + |\widehat{p}_t|)$, where $\widehat{p}_t$ is the margin achieved by the current linear classifier on the instance, and $c > 0$ is a parameter of the algorithm acting as a scaling factor on $\widehat{p}_t$. Note that a label is sampled with a small probability whenever the margin is large.

Unlike the approach described in Section 6.2, this rule provides no control on the number of queried labels. In fact, this number is a random variable depending, through the margin $\widehat{p}_t$, on the interaction between the algorithm and the data sequence on which the algorithm is run. Owing to the complex nature of this interaction, the analysis fails to characterize the behavior of this random variable in terms of simple quantities related to the data sequence. However, the analysis does reveal an interesting phenomenon. In all of the label efficient algorithms we analyzed, a proper choice of the scaling factor c in the randomized rule yields the same mistake bound as that achieved by the original forecaster before the introduction of the label efficient mechanism. Hence, in some sense, the randomization uses the margin information to select those labels that can be ignored without increasing (in expectation) the overall number of mistakes.

To provide some intuition on how the randomized selection rule works, consider the standard Perceptron algorithm run on a sequence $(\mathbf{x}_1, y_1), \ldots, (\mathbf{x}_n, y_n) \in \mathbb{R}^d \times \{-1, 1\}$, where we assume $\|\mathbf{x}_t\| = 1$ for $t = 1, \ldots, n$. For the sake of simplicity, assume that this sequence is linearly separated by a hyperplane $\mathbf{u} \in \mathbb{R}^d$. Recall that $\widehat{p}_t = \mathbf{w}_{t-1} \cdot \mathbf{x}_t$. A basic inequality controlling the hinge loss in this case (see Section 12.2, and also the proof of Theorem 12.5 below) is

$$(1 - y_t \widehat{p}_t)_+ \le \frac{1}{2} \left(\|\mathbf{u} - \mathbf{w}_{t-1}\|^2 - \|\mathbf{u} - \mathbf{w}_t\|^2 + 1 \right).$$

Now, if $y_t \widehat{p}_t \le 0$ and $|\widehat{p}_t|$ is large, then the hinge loss $(1 - y_t \widehat{p}_t)_+$ is also large. This in turn implies that the difference $\|\mathbf{u} - \mathbf{w}_{t-1}\|^2 - \|\mathbf{u} - \mathbf{w}_t\|^2$ must be big. This means that $\|\mathbf{u} - \mathbf{w}_{t-1}\|^2$ drops as $\mathbf{w}_{t-1}$ is updated to $\mathbf{w}_t$. So, whenever the Perceptron makes a classification mistake with a large margin value $|\widehat{p}_t|$, the weight $\mathbf{w}_{t-1}$ is moved by a significant amount toward the linear separator $\mathbf{u}$. In this respect, mistakes with large margin bear a bigger progress than mistakes with margin close to 0. On the other hand, the standard Perceptron algorithm does not take into account the information brought by $|\widehat{p}_t|$. The basic idea underlying the label efficient method is a way to incorporate this information into the prediction by using the size of $|\widehat{p}_t|$ to trade off a potential progress with a spared label.

We now formally define and analyze a label efficient version of the Perceptron algorithm. Similar arguments can be developed to prove analogous bounds for other conservative gradient-based forecasters analyzed in this chapter (see the exercises).

As our forecasters are randomized, we adopt the terminology introduced in Chapter 4. The forecaster has access to a sequence $U_1, U_2, \ldots$ of i.i.d. random variables uniformly distributed in $[0, 1]$. The decision of querying the outcome at time t is defined by the value of a Bernoulli random variable Z_t of parameter q_t (where q_t is determined by $U_1, \ldots, U_{t-1}$ and by the specific selection rule used by the forecaster). To obtain a realization of Z_t, the forecaster assigns $Z_t = 1$ if and only if $U_t \in [0, q_t)$. The sequence of outcomes is represented by the random variables $Y_1, Y_2, \ldots$, where each Y_t is measurable with respect to the σ-algebra generated by $U_1, \ldots, U_{t-1}$. This implies that Y_t is determined before the value of Z_t is drawn. Our results hold also when instances $\mathbf{x}_t$ are measurable functions of $U_1, \ldots, U_{t-1}$. However, to keep the notation simple, we derive our results in the special case of arbitrary and fixed instance sequences.

THE LABEL EFFICIENT PERCEPTRON ALGORITHM

Parameter: $c > 0$.

Initialization: $\mathbf{w}_0 = (0, \ldots, 0)$.

For each round $t = 1, 2, \ldots$

    (1) observe $\mathbf{x}_t$, set $\widehat{p}_t = \mathbf{w}_{t-1} \cdot \mathbf{x}_t$, and predict with $\widehat{y}_t = \mathrm{sgn}(\widehat{p}_t)$;

    (2) draw a Bernoulli random variable $Z_t \in \{0, 1\}$ of parameter $c/(c + |\widehat{p}_t|)$;

    (3) if $Z_t = 1$, then query label $Y_t \in \{-1, 1\}$, and let $\mathbf{w}_t = \mathbf{w}_{t-1} + Y_t \mathbf{x}_t \, \mathbb{I}_{\{\widehat{y}_t \neq Y_t\}}$;

    (4) if $Z_t = 0$, then $\mathbf{w}_t = \mathbf{w}_{t-1}$.

Theorem 12.5. *If the label efficient Perceptron algorithm is run on a sequence* $(\mathbf{x}_1, Y_1), (\mathbf{x}_2, Y_2) \ldots \in \mathbb{R}^d \times \{-1, 1\}$, *then for all* $n \geq 1$, *for all* $\mathbf{u} \in \mathbb{R}^d$, *and for all* $\gamma > 0$, *the expected number of mistakes satisfies*

$$\mathbb{E}\left[\sum_{t=1}^n \mathbb{I}_{\{\widehat{y}_t \neq Y_t\}}\right] \leq \frac{L_{\gamma,n}(\mathbf{u})}{\gamma} + \frac{X^2}{2c} \frac{L_{\gamma,n}(\mathbf{u})}{\gamma} + \frac{\|\mathbf{u}\|^2 (2c + X^2)^2}{8c\gamma^2},$$

where $X = \max_{t=1,\ldots,n} \|\mathbf{x}_t\|$.

Note that by choosing

$$c = \frac{X}{\|\mathbf{u}\|} \sqrt{\gamma L_{\gamma,n}(\mathbf{u}) + \left(\frac{X \|\mathbf{u}\|}{2}\right)^2}$$

one recovers (in expectation) the bound shown by Theorem 12.1 (in the special case $p = 2$). However, as c is an input parameter of the algorithm, this setting implies that, at the beginning of the prediction process, the algorithm needs some information on the sequence of examples. In addition, unlike the bound of Theorem 12.1 that holds simultaneously for all γ and $\mathbf{u}$, this refined bound can only be obtained for fixed choices of these quantities.

Proof of Theorem 12.5. Introduce the Bernoulli random variable $M_t = \mathbb{I}_{\{\widehat{y}_t \neq Y_t\}}$. We start from the chain of inequalities

$$\begin{aligned}
\gamma - \ell_{\gamma,t}(\mathbf{u}) &\leq \mathbf{u} \cdot \left(-\nabla \ell_{\gamma,t}(\mathbf{w}_{t-1})\right) \\
&\leq (\mathbf{u} - \mathbf{w}_{t-1}) \cdot \left(-\nabla \ell_{\gamma,t}(\mathbf{w}_{t-1})\right) \\
&= D_{\Phi^*}(\mathbf{u}, \mathbf{w}_{t-1}) - D_{\Phi^*}(\mathbf{u}, \mathbf{w}_t) + D_{\Phi^*}(\mathbf{w}_{t-1}, \mathbf{w}_t),
\end{aligned}$$

which we used for the derivation of (12.1) in Section 12.2. This holds for any conservative gradient-based forecaster on any time step t such that $M_t = 1$.

Just like the Perceptron, the label efficient Perceptron uses the quadratic potential $\Phi(\mathbf{v}) = \Phi^*(\mathbf{v}) = \frac{1}{2} \|\mathbf{v}\|^2$, and thus $D_{\Phi^*}(\mathbf{u}, \mathbf{v}) = \frac{1}{2} \|\mathbf{u} - \mathbf{v}\|^2$. Consider now a time step t where the label efficient Perceptron queries a label and makes a mistake. Then $Z_t = 1$, $M_t = 1$, and $-\nabla \ell_{\gamma,t}(\mathbf{w}_{t-1}) = Y_t \mathbf{x}_t$. Hence, we may rewrite this chain of inequalities as follows:

$$
\begin{aligned}
\gamma &- \ell_{\gamma,t}(\mathbf{u}) \\
&\leq Y_t \mathbf{u} \cdot \mathbf{x}_t \\
&= Y_t (\mathbf{u} - \mathbf{w}_{t-1} + \mathbf{w}_{t-1}) \cdot \mathbf{x}_t \\
&= Y_t \mathbf{w}_{t-1} \cdot \mathbf{x}_t + \frac{1}{2} \|\mathbf{u} - \mathbf{w}_{t-1}\|^2 - \frac{1}{2} \|\mathbf{u} - \mathbf{w}_t\|^2 + \frac{1}{2} \|\mathbf{w}_{t-1} - \mathbf{w}_t\|^2 .
\end{aligned}
$$

Note that this time we obtained a stronger inequality by adding and subtracting the negative term $Y_t \mathbf{w}_{t-1} \cdot \mathbf{x}_t = Y_t \widehat{p}_t$. The additional term provided by this more careful analysis is the key to obtain the final result.

Using $Y_t \widehat{p}_t \leq 0$ and replacing $\mathbf{u}$ with $\alpha \mathbf{u}$ for $\alpha > 0$, we obtain the inequality

$$
\begin{aligned}
(\alpha \gamma + |\widehat{p}_t|) M_t Z_t \\
\leq \alpha \ell_{\gamma,t}(\mathbf{u}) + \frac{1}{2} \|\alpha \mathbf{u} - \mathbf{w}_{t-1}\|^2 - \frac{1}{2} \|\alpha \mathbf{u} - \mathbf{w}_t\|^2 + \frac{1}{2} \|\mathbf{w}_{t-1} - \mathbf{w}_t\|^2
\end{aligned}
$$

that holds for all time steps t. Indeed, if $M_t Z_t = 0$ the inequality still holds because $\alpha \ell_{\gamma,t}(\mathbf{u}) \geq 0$ and $\mathbf{w}_{t-1} = \mathbf{w}_t$. Summing for $t = 1, \ldots, n$, we get

$$
\sum_{t=1}^{n} (\alpha \gamma + |\widehat{p}_t|) M_t Z_t \leq \alpha L_{\gamma,n}(\mathbf{u}) + \frac{\alpha^2}{2} \|\mathbf{u}\|^2 + \frac{1}{2} \sum_{t=1}^{n} \|\mathbf{w}_{t-1} - \mathbf{w}_t\|^2 ,
$$

where $\alpha^2 \|\mathbf{u}\| = \|\alpha \mathbf{u} - \mathbf{w}_0\|$ and we dropped $- \|\alpha \mathbf{u} - \mathbf{w}_n\|^2 /2$. Finally, since $M_t Z_t = 0$ implies $\|\mathbf{w}_{t-1} - \mathbf{w}_t\| = 0$, using $\|\mathbf{w}_{t-1} - \mathbf{w}_t\|^2 \leq X^2$ we get

$$
\sum_{t=1}^{n} \left(\alpha \gamma + |\widehat{p}_t| - \frac{X^2}{2} \right) M_t Z_t \leq \alpha L_{\gamma,n}(\mathbf{u}) + \frac{\alpha^2}{2} \|\mathbf{u}\|^2 .
$$

Now choose $\alpha = (c + X^2/2)/\gamma$ for some $c > 0$ to be determined. The above inequality then becomes

$$
\sum_{t=1}^{n} (c + |\widehat{p}_t|) M_t Z_t \leq \frac{c L_{\gamma,n}(\mathbf{u})}{\gamma} + \frac{X^2}{2} \frac{L_{\gamma,n}(\mathbf{u})}{\gamma} + \frac{\|\mathbf{u}\|^2 (2c + X^2)^2}{8\gamma^2} .
$$

We now take expectations on both sides. Note that, by definition of the algorithm, $\mathbb{E}_t Z_t = c/(c + |\widehat{p}_t|)$, where we use $\mathbb{E}_t$ to indicate conditional expectation given $U_1, \ldots, U_{t-1}$. Also, M_t and $\widehat{p}_t$ are measurable with respect to the σ-algebra generated by $U_1, \ldots, U_{t-1}$. Thus we get

$$
\mathbb{E} \left[\sum_{t=1}^{n} (c + |\widehat{p}_t|) M_t Z_t \right] = \mathbb{E} \left[\sum_{t=1}^{n} (c + |\widehat{p}_t|) M_t \, \mathbb{E}_t Z_t \right] = \mathbb{E} \left[\sum_{t=1}^{n} c M_t \right].
$$

Dividing both sides by c, we arrive at the claimed inequality

$$
\mathbb{E} \left[\sum_{t=1}^{n} M_t \right] \leq \frac{L_{\gamma,n}(\mathbf{u})}{\gamma} + \frac{X^2}{2c} \frac{L_{\gamma,n}(\mathbf{u})}{\gamma} + \frac{\|\mathbf{u}\|^2 (2c + X^2)^2}{8c\gamma^2} . \quad \blacksquare
$$

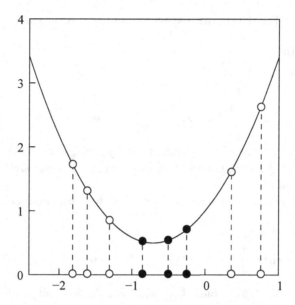

Figure 12.3. A set of labeled instances $x_t \in \mathbb{R}$ is shown on the abscissa as empty circles (label -1) and filled circles (label $+1$). This set is not linearly separable in $\mathbb{R}$. However, by mapping each $x_t \in \mathbb{R}$ via $\phi(x) = (x, 1 + x\sqrt{2} + x^2)$ we obtain a linearly separable set in $\mathbb{R}^2$. The coefficient $\sqrt{2}$ is chosen so that inner products $\phi(x)\phi(x')$ between mapped instances can be computed using the polynomial kernel function $K(x, x') = (1 + xx')^2$.

12.5 Kernel-Based Classifiers

Kernel functions are an elegant way of turning a linear forecaster into a nonlinear one with a reasonable computational cost. As a motivating example, consider the following simple reduction from quadratic classifiers in $\mathbb{R}^2$ to linear classifiers in $\mathbb{R}^6$. In $\mathbb{R}^2$, a quadratic classifier $f : \mathbb{R}^2 \rightarrow \{-1, 1\}$ is defined by

$$f(x_1, x_2) = \text{sgn}\big(p(x_1, x_2)\big),$$

where $p(x_1, x_2) = w_0 + w_1 x_1 + w_2 x_2 + w_3 x_1 x_2 + w_4 x_1^2 + w_5 x_2^2$ is any second-degree polynomial in the variables x_1 and x_2. The *decision surface* of f is the set of points $(x_1, x_2) \in \mathbb{R}^2$ satisfying the equation $p(x_1, x_2) = 0$. The decision surface of a linear classifier is a hyperplane, whereas for quadratic classifiers the decision surface is a conic (the family of curves to which ellipses, parabolas and hyperbolas belong). To learn a quadratic classifier with a linear forecaster, it is enough to observe that $p(x_1, x_2)$ of the above form can be written as $\mathbf{w} \cdot \mathbf{x'}$ for $\mathbf{w} = (w_0, w_1, \ldots, w_5)$ and $\mathbf{x'} = \big(1, x_1, x_2, x_1 x_2, x_1^2, x_2^2\big)$. Thus, we can transform each instance $\mathbf{x}_t = (x_{1,t}, x_{2,t})$ via the mapping

$$\phi(x_{1,t}, x_{2,t}) = \big(1, x_{1,t}, x_{2,t}, x_{1,t} x_{2,t}, x_{1,t}^2, x_{2,t}^2\big) = \mathbf{x'_t}$$

and then run the linear forecaster on the transformed instances $\mathbf{x'_t} \in \mathbb{R}^6$ instead of the original instances $\mathbf{x}_t \in \mathbb{R}^2$ (see Figure 12.3 for a 1-dimensional illustration). The vector $\mathbf{x'_t}$ is often called a *feature vector*, and in the example considered, $\mathbb{R}^6$ plays the role of the *feature space*.

This simple trick can be easily generalized to learn any kth-degree polynomial decision surface in $\mathbb{R}^d$. However, the computational cost of implementing the mapping ϕ, even for k moderately large, is too high. In fact, $\binom{d+k}{k}$ coefficients are needed to represent a kth-degree polynomial surface in $\mathbb{R}^d$, implying that we have to run our linear forecaster on instances of dimension exponentially large in k.

Computational problems nearly disappear if the classification of $\mathbf{x}_t$, at an arbitrary time t, can be computed using only inner products between instances. For example, the classifier computed by the Perceptron algorithm at time t can be written in the form

$$f(\mathbf{x}) = \mathrm{sgn}\left(\sum_i \alpha_i y_{t_i} \mathbf{x}_{t_i} \cdot \mathbf{x}\right),$$

where $\alpha_i \in \mathbb{R}$ and the sum ranges over a subset of the instance sequence $\mathbf{x}_1, \ldots, \mathbf{x}_{t-1}$. Now suppose the Perceptron is run on the transformed instances $\mathbf{x}'_t = \phi(\mathbf{x}_t)$, where we have rewritten the ϕ of our initial example as $\phi(x_1, x_2) = \left(1, x_1\sqrt{2}, x_2\sqrt{2}, x_1x_2\sqrt{2}, x_1^2, x_2^2\right)$. Note that the introduction of the scaling coefficients $\sqrt{2}$ makes no difference for the learning problem faced by the forecaster. Then, as $\phi(\mathbf{x}_t) \cdot \phi(\mathbf{x}) = (1 + \mathbf{x}_t \cdot \mathbf{x})^2$, we can avoid the computation of any $\phi(\mathbf{x}_t)$. Indeed,

$$f(\mathbf{x}) = \mathrm{sgn}\left(\sum_i \alpha_i y_{t_i} \phi(\mathbf{x}_{t_i}) \cdot \phi(\mathbf{x})\right) = \mathrm{sgn}\left(\sum_i \alpha_i y_{t_i} (1 + \mathbf{x}_{t_i} \cdot \mathbf{x})^2\right).$$

In general, if ϕ maps $\mathbf{x} \in \mathbb{R}^d$ to $\phi(\mathbf{x}) = \mathbf{x}'$ whose components are all the monomials of a kth-degree polynomial in the variables $\mathbf{x}$ (with suitable scaling coefficients), then $\phi(\mathbf{x}_t) \cdot \phi(\mathbf{x}) = (1 + \mathbf{x}_t \cdot \mathbf{x})^k$. Hence, the forecaster can learn a polynomial classifier without ever explicitly computing the coefficients of the polynomial curve.

Note that saying that a forecaster manipulates the transformed instances $\phi(\mathbf{x})$ using only inner products implies that the computation performed by the forecaster is invariant to transformations that map the instance sequence $(\mathbf{x}_1, \mathbf{x}_2, \ldots)$ to $(A\mathbf{x}_1, A\mathbf{x}_2, \ldots)$, where A performs a change between two orthonormal bases. To see this, note that $(A\mathbf{u})^\top (A\mathbf{v}) = \mathbf{u}^\top A^\top A\mathbf{v} = \mathbf{u}^\top \mathbf{v}$. Such forecasters are sometimes called *rotationally invariant*. Unfortunately, not all gradient-based forecasters for classification are rotationally invariant. In particular, among the linear forecasters studied in this chapter, only the Perceptron and the second-order Perceptron have this property (see Exercise 12.12).

In view of extending this approach to surfaces that go beyond polynomials, we investigate the conditions guaranteeing that a symmetric function $K : \mathbb{R}^d \times \mathbb{R}^d \to \mathbb{R}$ has the property $K(\mathbf{u}, \mathbf{v}) = \langle \phi(\mathbf{u}), \phi(\mathbf{v}) \rangle$ for all $\mathbf{u}, \mathbf{v} \in \mathbb{R}^d$ and for some ϕ mapping $\mathbb{R}^d$ to a Hilbert space (we use $\langle \cdot, \cdot \rangle$ to denote the inner product in this space). We call *kernel* any such function K. Note that we changed the range of ϕ from a finite-dimensional euclidean space to a Hilbert space. In this space, our transformed instances $\phi(\mathbf{x})$ are vectors with possibly an infinite number of components. This allows, for example, to learn a certain class of infinite-degree polynomial decision curves. For reasons that are made clear in the proof of the following result, the Hilbert space $\mathcal{H}$ associated to a kernel function is called *reproducing kernel Hilbert space*.

It turns out that a simple characterization of kernels exists.

Theorem 12.6. *A symmetric function* $K : \mathbb{R}^d \times \mathbb{R}^d \to \mathbb{R}$ *is a kernel if and only if for all* $n \in \mathbb{N}$ *and for all* $\mathbf{x}_1, \ldots, \mathbf{x}_n \in \mathbb{R}^d$ *the* $n \times n$ *matrix* $\mathbf{K}$ *with elements* $K(\mathbf{x}_i, \mathbf{x}_j)$ *is positive semidefinite.*

Proof. Assume first that $K : \mathbb{R}^d \times \mathbb{R}^d \to \mathbb{R}$ is such that $K(\mathbf{u}, \mathbf{v}) = \langle \phi(\mathbf{u}), \phi(\mathbf{v}) \rangle$. Fix any positive integer $n \in \mathbb{N}$, choose $\mathbf{x}_1, \ldots, \mathbf{x}_n \in \mathbb{R}^d$ arbitrarily, and let $\mathbf{K}$ be the associated matrix. Then, for all $\mathbf{u} \in \mathbb{R}^d$,

$$
\begin{aligned}
\mathbf{u}^\top \mathbf{K} \mathbf{u} &= \sum_{i,j=1}^n K(\mathbf{x}_i, \mathbf{x}_j) u_i u_j \\
&= \sum_{i,j=1}^n \langle \phi(\mathbf{x}_i), \phi(\mathbf{x}_j) \rangle u_i u_j \\
&= \left\langle \left(\sum_{i=1}^n \phi(\mathbf{x}_i) u_i \right), \left(\sum_{j=1}^n \phi(\mathbf{x}_j) u_j \right) \right\rangle \\
&= \left\| \sum_{i=1}^n \phi(\mathbf{x}_i) u_i \right\|^2 \geq 0.
\end{aligned}
$$

Hence $\mathbf{K}$ is positive semidefinite.

Assume now $K : \mathbb{R}^d \times \mathbb{R}^d \to \mathbb{R}$ is such that, for any choice of $\mathbf{x}_1, \ldots, \mathbf{x}_n \in \mathbb{R}^d$, the resulting kernel matrix is positive semidefinite. Introduce the linear space $\mathcal{V}$ of functions $f : \mathbb{R}^d \to \mathbb{R}$ defined by

$$
f(\cdot) = \sum_{i=1}^n \alpha_i K(\mathbf{u}_i, \cdot), \qquad \text{where} \quad n \in \mathbb{N},\ \alpha_i \in \mathbb{R},\ i = 1, \ldots, n,
$$

where we set $\alpha(f + g)(\mathbf{x}) = \alpha f(\mathbf{x}) + \alpha g(\mathbf{x})$ for any $\alpha \in \mathbb{R}$ and $\mathbf{u} \in \mathbb{R}^d$. We now make $\mathcal{V}$ an inner product space. Introduce the operator $\langle \cdot, \cdot \rangle$ such that, for any two $f, g \in \mathcal{V}$ defined by

$$
f(\cdot) = \sum_{i=1}^m \alpha_i K(\mathbf{u}_i, \cdot) \qquad \text{and} \qquad g(\cdot) = \sum_{j=1}^n \beta_j K(\mathbf{v}_j, \cdot),
$$

we have

$$
\langle f, g \rangle = \sum_{i=1}^m \sum_{j=1}^n \alpha_i \beta_j K(\mathbf{u}_i, \mathbf{v}_j).
$$

Clearly, $\langle \cdot, \cdot \rangle$ defined in this way is real valued, symmetric, and bilinear. In addition, for all $f \in \mathcal{V}$,

$$
\langle f, f \rangle = \sum_{i=1}^m \sum_{j=1}^n \alpha_i \alpha_j K(\mathbf{u}_i, \mathbf{u}_j) = \boldsymbol{\alpha}^\top \mathbf{K} \boldsymbol{\alpha} \geq 0
$$

because $\mathbf{K}$ is positive semidefinite by assumption. Thus, to verify that $\langle \cdot, \cdot \rangle$ is indeed an inner product on $\mathcal{V}$, we just have to show that $\langle f, f \rangle = 0$ implies $f \equiv 0$. To see this, first note that

$$\langle f, K(\mathbf{x}, \cdot) \rangle = \sum_{i=1}^{m} \alpha_i K(\mathbf{x}, \mathbf{u}_i) = f(\mathbf{x}) \qquad \text{(reproducing property)},$$

where the first equality follows from the definition of $\langle \cdot, \cdot \rangle$ by taking $g(\cdot) = K(\mathbf{x}, \cdot)$. Hence, $f(\mathbf{x})^2 = \langle f, K(\mathbf{x}, \cdot) \rangle^2 \leq \langle f, f \rangle K(\mathbf{x}, \mathbf{x})$ by the Cauchy–Schwarz inequality, and this yields the desired implication. Thus $\mathcal{V}$ endowed with $\langle \cdot, \cdot \rangle$ is an inner product space.

To make $\mathcal{V}$ into a complete Hilbert space, we introduce in $\mathcal{V}$ a norm defined by $\|f - g\| = \sqrt{\langle f - g, f - g \rangle}$.

By Lemma 12.1, all Cauchy sequences in $\mathcal{V}$ have a pointwise limit. Let $\mathcal{H}$ be the set obtained by adding to $\mathcal{V}$ all the functions g that are pointwise limits of Cauchy sequences with respect to this norm. For any $f, g \in \mathcal{H}$, define

$$\langle f, g \rangle_{\mathcal{H}} = \lim_{n,m \to \infty} \langle f_m, g_n \rangle \qquad \text{and} \qquad \|f\|_{\mathcal{H}} = \lim_{m \to \infty} \|f_m\|,$$

where $f_1, f_2, \ldots$ and $g_1, g_2, \ldots$ are Cauchy sequences in $\mathcal{V}$ with pointwise limits f and g, respectively. It is easy to check that $\langle \cdot, \cdot \rangle_{\mathcal{H}}$ is well defined (i.e., independent of the choice of the sequences f_m and g_n converging pointwise to f and g) and that it is an inner product in $\mathcal{H}$. It is also easy to see that $\mathcal{H}$ is a complete space (with respect to $\|\cdot\|_{\mathcal{H}}$) in which $\mathcal{V}$ is dense. Hence $\mathcal{H}$ is an Hilbert space.

To conclude the proof, we define the mapping $\phi : \mathbb{R}^d \to \mathcal{H}$ by $\phi(\mathbf{x}) = K(\mathbf{x}, \cdot)$. Then, the reproducing property ensures that $K(\mathbf{u}, \mathbf{v}) = \langle \phi(\mathbf{u}), \phi(\mathbf{v}) \rangle$. ∎

Note that the identity $\phi(\mathbf{x}) = K(\mathbf{x}, \cdot)$ provides a representation of the mapping ϕ directly in terms of the kernel function K.

Remark 12.1. In the proof of Theorem 12.6 we obtain the same characterization when $\mathbb{R}^d$ is replaced with an arbitrary set S. Hence, kernels may be more generally defined as functions $K : S \times S \to \mathbb{R}$ where no assumptions are imposed on S (e.g., S can be a set of combinatorial structures such as sequences, trees, or graphs). Since any kernel K defines a metric d in $\mathcal{H}$ by

$$d(s, s') = \|\phi(s) - \phi(s')\| = \sqrt{K(s, s) + K(s', s') - 2K(s, s')},$$

we may view a kernel as a way to embed an arbitrary set of objects in a metric space.

We now state and prove Lemma 12.1, which we used in the proof of Theorem 12.6.

Lemma 12.1. *For any sequence $(f_1, f_2, \ldots)$ of elements of $\mathcal{V}$, if*

$$\lim_{n \to \infty} \sup_{m > n} \|f_m - f_n\| = 0$$

(i.e., the sequence is a Cauchy sequence), then $g = \lim_{n \to \infty} f_n$, defined by $g(\mathbf{x}) = \lim_{n \to \infty} f_n(\mathbf{x})$ for all $\mathbf{x} \in \mathbb{R}^d$, exists.

Proof. Fix $\mathbf{x}$ and consider the sequence $(f_1(\mathbf{x}), f_2(\mathbf{x}), \ldots)$. Note that

$$|f_m(\mathbf{x}) - f_n(\mathbf{x})| = \sqrt{\langle f_m - f_n, K(\mathbf{x}, \cdot) \rangle} \leq \|f_m - f_n\| \sqrt{K(\mathbf{x}, \mathbf{x})},$$

where we used the reproducing property in the first step and the Cauchy–Schwarz inequality. Thus, because $(f_1, f_2, \ldots)$ is a Cauchy sequence $\big(f_1(\mathbf{x}), f_2(\mathbf{x}), \ldots\big)$ also is a Cauchy sequence. By the Cauchy criterion, every such sequence on the reals has a limit. ∎

Kernels of the form $K(\mathbf{u}, \mathbf{v}) = (1 + \mathbf{u} \cdot \mathbf{v})^k$ for $k \in \mathbb{N}$ are appropriately called *polynomial kernels*. A closely related kernel is the homogeneous polynomial kernel $K(\mathbf{u}, \mathbf{v}) = (\mathbf{u} \cdot \mathbf{v})^k$. An infinite-dimensional extension of the homogeneous polynomial kernel is the *exponential kernel* $K(\mathbf{u}, \mathbf{v}) = \exp(\mathbf{u} \cdot \mathbf{v}/\sigma^2)$ for $\sigma > 0$. The Taylor expansion

$$\exp(\mathbf{u} \cdot \mathbf{v}) = \sum_{k=0}^{\infty} \frac{(\mathbf{u} \cdot \mathbf{v})^k}{k!}$$

reveals that exponential kernels are linear combinations of infinitely many homogeneous polynomial kernels, where the coefficients of the polynomials decrease exponentially with the degree. By enforcing $\|\phi(\mathbf{x})\| = 1$ or, equivalently, $K(\mathbf{x}, \mathbf{x}) = 1$, the exponential kernel is transformed as follows:

$$\frac{K(\mathbf{u}, \mathbf{v})}{\sqrt{K(\mathbf{u}, \mathbf{u})K(\mathbf{v}, \mathbf{v})}} = \frac{\exp(\mathbf{u} \cdot \mathbf{v}/\sigma^2)}{\sqrt{\exp(\mathbf{u} \cdot \mathbf{u}/\sigma^2)\exp(\mathbf{v} \cdot \mathbf{v}/\sigma^2)}} = \exp\big(-\|\mathbf{u} - \mathbf{v}\|^2 /2\sigma^2\big).$$

This is the *gaussian kernel*, widely used in pattern classification. The classifier constructed by the Perceptron algorithm run with a gaussian kernel corresponds to a weighted mixture of spherical gaussians with equal variance and centered on a subset of the previously seen instances. Linear classifiers in the feature space defined by gaussian kernels have often been called *radial basis function (RBF) networks*.

Mistake Bounds and Computational Issues
The mistake bounds shown in Section 12.2 extend naturally to kernels. Consider, for instance, the second-order Perceptron run with a generic kernel function K in a reproducing kernel Hilbert space $\mathcal{H}$. Pick any sequence $(\mathbf{x}_1, y_1), \ldots, (\mathbf{x}_n, y_n) \in \mathbb{R}^d \times \{-1, 1\}$ and let the cumulative hinge loss of any function $f \in \mathcal{H}$ on this sequence be defined by

$$L_{\gamma,n}(f) = \sum_{t=1}^{n}\big(\gamma - y_t\, f(\mathbf{x}_t)\big)_+.$$

Then the number of mistakes made by the second-order Perceptron is bounded as

$$\sum_{t=1}^{n} \mathbb{I}_{\{\hat{y}_t \neq y_t\}} \leq \inf_{\gamma>0,\, f\in\mathcal{H}\,:\, \|f\|=1} \left(\frac{L_{\gamma,n}(f)}{\gamma} + \frac{1}{\gamma}\sqrt{\left(1 + \sum_{t=1}^{n} f(\mathbf{x}_t)^2\right) \sum_{i=1}^{n} \ln(1 + \lambda_i)} \right),$$

where the numbers λ_i are the eigenvalues of the kernel matrix with entries $K(\mathbf{x}_i, \mathbf{x}_j)$ for $i, j = 1, \ldots, n$.

Note that if a linear kernel $K(\mathbf{x}_i, \mathbf{x}_j) = \mathbf{x}_i^\top \mathbf{x}_j$ is used, so that $f(\mathbf{x}) = \mathbf{u}^\top \mathbf{x}$ for some $\mathbf{u} \in \mathbb{R}^d$, then the mistake bound of Theorem 12.3 (for the choice $\|\mathbf{u}\| = 1$) is recovered exactly. To see this let $\Lambda = \mathbf{x}_1 \mathbf{x}_1^\top + \cdots + \mathbf{x}_n \mathbf{x}_n^\top$ and observe that

$$\mathbf{u}^\top \Lambda \mathbf{u} = \sum_{t=1}^{n} (\mathbf{u}^\top \mathbf{x}_t)^2.$$

Also, the nonzero eigenvalues of the matrix Λ coincide with the nonzero eigenvalues of the kernel matrix.

We close this section by noting that the kernel-based version of the Perceptron uses space $\Theta(m)$ to store a linear classifier and time $\Theta(m)$ to update it, where m is the number of mistakes made so far. The second-order Perceptron, instead, uses space $\Theta(m^2)$ for storing and time $\Theta(m^2)$ for updating (this can be shown via simple linear algebraic identities about the update of inverse matrices). Thus, kernel-based forecasters have space and time requirements that grow with the number of mistakes. An interesting thread of research is the design of principled techniques allowing to trade off a reduction of space requirements with a moderate increase in the number of mistakes. The label efficient analysis in Section 12.4 is an example of this approach.

12.6 Bibliographic Remarks

Perceptrons, introduced by Rosenblatt [249] as an attempt to model "the capability of higher organisms for perceptual recognition, generalization, recall, and thinking," are among the earliest examples of learning algorithms. Versions of the Perceptron convergence theorem were proved by Rosenblatt [250], Block [31], and Novikoff [225]. p-Norm Perceptrons were introduced and analyzed in the linearly separable case by Grove, Littlestone, and Schuurmans [133], as a special case of their quasi-additive classification algorithm (see also Warmuth and Jagota [305] and Kivinen and Warmuth [183]). Generalization of this analysis to sequences that are not linearly separable was proposed by Freund and Schapire [114], Gentile and Warmuth [125], and Gentile [124]. Perceptrons with dynamic tuning were considered by Graepel, Herbrich, and Williamson [132].

The Winnow algorithm was introduced by Littlestone [200] as an alternative to Percep-tron. Just as the Perceptron algorithm is the counterpart for classification of the Widrow–Hoff rule used in regression, the version of Winnow presented here is the classification version of the exponentiated gradient algorithm of Kivinen and Warmuth (see the biblio-graphic remarks in Chapter 11). Recalling the discussion at the end of Section 11.4, we may conclude that Winnow should perform better than Perceptron on data sequences that have dense instance vectors and are well approximated by sparse linear experts. In fact, Winnow was originally proposed for boolean side information, $\mathbf{x}_t \in \{0, 1\}^d$, and for an expert class properly contained in the class of linear experts: the class of all monotone k-literal disjunction experts. Each such expert is defined by a subset of at most k coordi-nates, and its prediction on $\mathbf{x}_t \in \{0, 1\}^d$ is 1 if and only if these k coordinates have value 1 in $\mathbf{x}_t$. As shown by Littlestone [200], if the data sequence is perfectly classified by some k-literal disjunction expert, then Winnow makes at most $O(k \ln d)$ mistakes. On the other hand, Kivinen, Warmuth, and Auer [184] show that there are boolean data sequences of the same type on which the Perceptron algorithm makes $\Omega(kd)$ mistakes. For extensions and applications of the p-norm Perceptron to classification of k-literal disjunctions, see also Auer and Warmuth [15], Gentile [124], Littlestone [201].

The second-order Perceptron was introduced by Cesa-Bianchi, Conconi, and Gen-tile [47], who also studied variants using the pseudoinverse of $\mathbf{x}_1 \mathbf{x}_1^\top + \cdots + \mathbf{x}_t \mathbf{x}_t^\top$ rather than the inverse of $I + \mathbf{x}_1 \mathbf{x}_1^\top + \cdots + \mathbf{x}_t \mathbf{x}_t^\top$.

Forecasting strategies converging to a separating hyperplane with maximum margin have been proposed by several authors. A remarkable example is the Adatron of Anlauf and Biehl [8]. However, finite-time convergence results for approximate maximum margin hyperplanes, such as the analysis of ALMA in Section 12.3, have been proposed only recently. Such results include the relaxed maximum margin online algorithm of Li and Long [199] and the margin infused relaxed algorithm of Crammer and Singer [75]. The ALMA algorithm and Theorem 12.4 are due to Gentile [123]. Support vector machines (SVMs), an effective classification technique originally introduced by Vapnik and Lerner [294] (under a different name), find the maximum margin hyperplane at once by solving an optimization problem defined over the entire sequence of examples. In their modern form, SVMs were introduced by Boser, Guyon, and Vapnik [38] and Cortes and Vapnik [67]. See the monographs Cristianini and Shawe-Taylor [76], Schölkopf and Smola [262], and Vapnik [292] for extensive accounts on the theory of SVMs.

The label efficient forecasters presented in Section 12.4 were introduced and analyzed by Cesa-Bianchi, Gentile, and Zaniboni [49]. However, similar techniques aimed at saving labels have been extensively studied in pattern recognition. See, for instance, the pioneering paper of Cohn, Atlas, and Ladner [66], the query by committee algorithm of Freund, Seung, Shamir, and Tishby [116], and the more recent approaches of Campbell, Cristianini, and Smola [45], Tong and Koller [289], and Bordes, Ertekin, Weston, and Bottou [35].

The study of reproducing kernel Hilbert spaces was developed by Aronszajn [9] in the 1940's. The use of kernels has been introduced in learning since 1964 with the influential work of Aizerman, Braverman, and Rozonoer [1–3] and Bashkirov, Braverman, and Muchnik [23] (see also Specht [277]).

However, it took almost 30 years before the potentialities of kernels began to be fully understood with the paper of Boser, Guyon, and Vapnik [38]. The books of Schölkopf and Smola [262] and Cristianini and Shawe-Taylor [77] are two excellent monographs on learning with kernels. The proof of Theorem 12.6 is taken from Saitoh [255]. Kernel perceptrons were considered by Freund and Schapire [114]. The kernel second-order Perceptron is due to Cesa-Bianchi, Conconi, and Gentile [47].

12.7   Exercises

12.1 *(Perceptron with time-varying learning rate)* Extend Theorem 12.1 to prove that the Perceptron (i.e., the p-norm Perceptron with $p = 2$) with learning rate $\lambda_t = 1/\|\mathbf{x}_t\|$ achieves, on any sequence $(\mathbf{x}_1, y_1), (\mathbf{x}_2, y_2) \ldots \in \mathbb{R}^d \times \{-1, 1\}$, and for all $\gamma > 0$ and $\mathbf{u} \in \mathbb{R}^d$, the bound

$$\sum_{t=1}^{n} \mathbb{I}_{\{\hat{y}_t \neq y_t\}} \leq \frac{\widehat{L}_{\gamma,n}(\mathbf{u})}{\gamma} + \left(\frac{\|\mathbf{u}\|}{\gamma}\right)^2 + \sqrt{\left(\frac{\|\mathbf{u}\|}{\gamma}\right)^2 \frac{\widehat{L}_{\gamma,n}(\mathbf{u})}{\gamma}},$$

where $\widehat{L}_{\gamma,n}(\mathbf{u}) = \sum_{t=1}^{n} \left(\gamma - y_t \mathbf{u} \cdot \mathbf{x}_t / \|\mathbf{x}\|\right)_+$ is the normalized cumulative hinge loss.

12.2 *(p-Norm perceptron for the absolute loss)* By adapting the self-confident linear forecaster with polynomial potential introduced in Section 11.5, derive a forecaster for the absolute loss $\ell(p, y) = \frac{1}{2}|p - y|$, where $p \in [-1, +1]$ and $y \in \{-1, 1\}$. Prove a bound on the absolute loss of this forecaster in terms of the hinge loss $L_{\gamma,n}(\mathbf{u})$ of the best linear forecaster $\mathbf{u}$ with q-norm bounded by a known constant. Set the hinge γ to 1 (Auer, Cesa-Bianchi, and Gentile [13]). *Warning:* This exercise is difficult.

12.3 *(Learning r-of-k threshold functions)* An r-of-k threshold functions is a function $f :$ $\{0, 1\}^d \to \{-1, 1\}$ specified by k relevant attributes indexed by $i_1, \ldots, i_k \in \{1, \ldots, d\}$. On any $\mathbf{x} \in \{0, 1\}^d$, $f(\mathbf{x}) = 1$ if and only if $x_{i_1} + \cdots + x_{i_k} \geq r$. Given a sequence

$(\mathbf{x}_1, y_1), \ldots, (\mathbf{x}_n, y_n) \in \{0, 1\}^d \times \{-1, 1\}$, the attribute error A_f on the sequence is $a_{f,1} + \cdots + a_{f,n}$, where $a_{f,t}$ is the minimum number of components of $\mathbf{x}_t$ that have to be changed to ensure that $f(\mathbf{x}_t) = y_t$.

Prove a mistake bound for the p-norm Perceptron on sequences over $\{0, 1\}^d \times \{-1, 1\}$ such that the number of mistakes is bounded in terms of the attribute error A_f of an arbitrary r-of-k threshold function f. Investigate what happens to the bound when p is set to $2 \ln(d + 1)$ (see Gentile [124]).

12.4 *(Parameterized second-order Perceptron)* Consider the parameterized second-order fore-caster defined using

$$A_t = aI + \sum_{s=1}^{t-1} \mathbf{x}_s \mathbf{x}_s^\top,$$

where $a > 0$ is a free parameter. Hence, the parameterless second-order Perceptron corresponds to the setting $a = 1$. Prove an analog of Theorem 12.3 for this variant. Investigate different choices of the parameter a. What happens to the mistake bound for $a \to \infty$?

12.5 *(Second-order vs. classical Perceptron)* Show that there exists a choice of a such that inequality (12.4) is satisfied when $\alpha < 1/(2k)$, where k is the number of nonzero eigenvalues of A_n (Cesa-Bianchi, Conconi, and Gentile [47]).

12.6 *(Proofs via the Blackwell condition)* Consider the conservative classifiers introduced in Section 12.2. Observe that the weight vectors used by these classifiers can be equivalently defined using $\mathbf{w}_t = \nabla \Phi(\mathbf{R}_t)$, where $\mathbf{R}_t$ is the cumulative "regret"

$$\mathbf{R}_t = \sum_{s=1}^t \mathbf{r}_s = -\sum_{s=1}^t \nabla \ell_{\gamma,s}(\mathbf{w}_{s-1})$$

and $\ell_{\gamma,s}(\mathbf{w}_{s-1})$ is the hinge loss $(\gamma - y_s \, \mathbf{w}_{s-1} \cdot \mathbf{x}_s)_+$. Verify that the Blackwell condition

$$\sup_{y_t \in \{-1, 1\}} \mathbf{r}_t \cdot \nabla \Phi(\mathbf{R}_{t-1}) \le 0$$

holds for this definition of regret. Then use Corollary 2.1 to derive the same mistake bound shown in Theorem 12.1. *Hint:* Use Corollary 2.1 to upper bound $\Phi_p(\mathbf{R}_n)$ in terms of $\sum_{t=1}^n \mathbb{I}_{\{\widehat{y}_t \ne y_t\}}$, and then use Hölder's inequality to show the lower bound

$$\|\mathbf{R}_n\|_p \ge \gamma \sum_{t=1}^n \mathbb{I}_{\{\widehat{y}_t \ne y_t\}} - \sum_{t=1}^n \ell_{\gamma,t}(\mathbf{u})$$

for $\mathbf{u} \in \mathbb{R}^d$ arbitrary (Cesa-Bianchi and Lugosi [54]).

12.7 *(ALMA on arbitrary sequences)* Suppose ALMA is run on an arbitrary sequence $(\mathbf{x}_1, y_1), \ldots,$ $(\mathbf{x}_n, y_n), \ldots \in \mathbb{R}^d \times \{-1, 1\}$. Prove a bound on the number of updates of the form

$$m \le \frac{L_\gamma(\mathbf{u})}{\gamma} + \frac{c_1}{\gamma^2} + \frac{c_2}{\gamma} \sqrt{\frac{L_\gamma(\mathbf{u})}{\gamma}}$$

for any $\mathbf{u} \in \mathbb{R}^d$ with $\|\mathbf{u}\| = 1$ and for any $\gamma > 0$. *Note:* The bound does not depend on α, but you might have to change the constants in the definition of γ_t and η_t in order to prove it (Gentile [123]).

12.8 *(p-Norm ALMA)* Prove a version of Theorem 12.4 using a modified p-norm Perceptron (Gentile [123]).

12.9 *(Label efficient Winnow)* Adapt the proof of Theorem 12.2 to show that the label efficient version of Winnow, querying label Y_t with probability $c/(c + |\widehat{p}_t|)$, and run with parame-ters $\eta = 2\alpha\gamma/X_\infty^2$ and $c = (1 - \alpha)\gamma$ for some $0 < \alpha < 1$, achieves an expected number of mistakes satisfying

$$\mathbb{E}\left[\sum_{t=1}^{n} M_t\right] \le \frac{1}{1-\alpha}\frac{L_{\gamma,n}(\mathbf{u})}{\gamma} + \left(\frac{X_\infty}{\gamma}\right)^2 \frac{\ln d}{2\alpha(1-\alpha)}$$

for all $\mathbf{u} \in \mathbb{R}^d$ in the probability simplex (Cesa-Bianchi, Lugosi, and Stoltz [55] and Cesa-Bianchi, Gentile, and Zaniboni [49]).

12.10 *(Label efficient second order Perceptron)* Adapt the proof of Theorem 12.3 to show that the label efficient version of the second-order Perceptron, querying label Y_t with probability $c/(c + |\widehat{p}_t|)$, achieves an expected number of mistakes satisfying

$$\mathbb{E}\left[\sum_{t=1}^{n} M_t\right] \le \frac{L_{\gamma,n}(\mathbf{u})}{\gamma} + \frac{c}{2\gamma^2}\left(\|\mathbf{u}\|^2 + \mathbf{u}^\top \Lambda_n \mathbf{u}\right) + \frac{1}{2c}\sum_{i=1}^{d} \ln(1+\lambda_i)$$

for any choice $c > 0$ of the input parameter and for all $\mathbf{u} \in \mathbb{R}^d$ and $\gamma > 0$.

12.11 Show by induction that a kth-degree surface in $\mathbb{R}^d$ is specified by $\binom{d+k}{k}$ coefficients.

12.12 *(Second-order Perceptron in dual variables)* Show that the second-order Perceptron classification at time t can be computed using only inner product operations between instances $\mathbf{x}_1, \dots, \mathbf{x}_t$.

12.13 *(All subsets kernel)* Find an easily computable kernel for the mapping $\phi : \mathbb{R}^d \to \mathbb{R}^{2^d}$ defined by $\phi(\mathbf{x}) = (x'_A)_A$, where $x'_A = \prod_{i \in A} x_i$ and A ranges over all subsets of $\{1, \dots, d\}$ (Takimoto and Warmuth [286]).

12.14 *(ANOVA kernel)* Consider the mapping ϕ such that, for any $\mathbf{x} \in \mathbb{R}^d$, $\phi(\mathbf{x}) = (x'_A)_A$, where $x'_A = \prod_{i \in A} x_i$ and A ranges over all subsets of $\{1, \dots, d\}$ of size at most k for some fixed $k = 1, \dots, d$. Direct computation of $\phi(\mathbf{u}) \cdot \phi(\mathbf{v})$ takes time order of d^k. Use dynamic programming to show that the same computation can be performed in time $O(kd)$ (Watkins [306]).

Appendix

In this appendix we collect some of the technical tools used in the book and not proved in the main text. Most of the results reproduced here are quite standard; they are here to make the book as self-contained as possible. Here we take a minimalist approach and stick to the simplest possible versions that are necessary to follow the material in the main text. This appendix should not be taken as an attempt to an exhaustive survey. The cited references merely intend to point to the original source of the results.

A.1 Inequalities from Probability Theory

A.1.1 Hoeffding's Inequality

First we offer a proof of Lemma 2.2, which states the following:

Lemma A.1. *Let X be a random variable with $a \leq X \leq b$. Then for any $s \in \mathbb{R}$,*

$$\ln \mathbb{E}\left[e^{sX}\right] \leq s\,\mathbb{E}\,X + \frac{s^2(b-a)^2}{8}.$$

Proof. Since $\ln \mathbb{E}\left[e^{sX}\right] \leq s\,\mathbb{E}\,X + \ln \mathbb{E}\left[e^{s(X-\mathbb{E}X)}\right]$, it suffices to show that for any random variable X with $\mathbb{E}\,X = 0$, $a \leq X \leq b$,

$$\mathbb{E}\left[e^{sX}\right] \leq e^{s^2(b-a)^2/8}.$$

Note that by convexity of the exponential function,

$$e^{sx} \leq \frac{x-a}{b-a}e^{sb} + \frac{b-x}{b-a}e^{sa} \qquad \text{for } a \leq x \leq b.$$

Exploiting $\mathbb{E}\,X = 0$, and introducing the notation $p = -a/(b-a)$, we get

$$
\begin{aligned}
\mathbb{E}e^{sX} &\leq \frac{b}{b-a}e^{sa} - \frac{a}{b-a}e^{sb} \\
&= \left(1 - p + pe^{s(b-a)}\right)e^{-ps(b-a)} \\
&\stackrel{\text{def}}{=} e^{\phi(u)},
\end{aligned}
$$

where $u = s(b - a)$, and $\phi(u) = -pu + \log(1 - p + pe^u)$. But by straightforward calculation it is easy to see that the derivative of ϕ is

$$\phi'(u) = -p + \frac{p}{p + (1-p)e^{-u}}$$

and therefore $\phi(0) = \phi'(0) = 0$. Moreover,

$$\phi''(u) = \frac{p(1-p)e^{-u}}{(p + (1-p)e^{-u})^2} \le \frac{1}{4}.$$

Thus, by Taylor's theorem,

$$\phi(u) = \phi(0) + u\phi'(0) + \frac{u^2}{2}\phi''(\theta) \le \frac{u^2}{8} = \frac{s^2(b-a)^2}{8}$$

for some $\theta \in [0, u]$. ∎

Lemma A.1 was originally proven to derive the following result, also known as *Hoeffding's inequality*.

Corollary A.1. *Let $X_1, \dots, X_n$ be independent real-valued random variables such that for each $i = 1, \dots, n$ there exist some $a_i \le b_i$ such that $\mathbb{P}[a_i \le X_i \le b_i] = 1$. Then for every $\varepsilon > 0$,*

$$\mathbb{P}\left[\sum_{i=1}^n X_i - \mathbb{E}\sum_{i=1}^n X_i > \varepsilon\right] \le \exp\left(-\frac{2\varepsilon^2}{\sum_{i=1}^n (b_i - a_i)^2}\right)$$

and

$$\mathbb{P}\left[\sum_{i=1}^n X_i - \mathbb{E}\sum_{i=1}^n X_i < -\varepsilon\right] \le \exp\left(-\frac{2\varepsilon^2}{\sum_{i=1}^n (b_i - a_i)^2}\right).$$

Proof. The proof is based on a clever application of Markov's inequality, often referred to as *Chernoff's technique*: for any $s > 0$,

$$\mathbb{P}\left[\sum_{i=1}^n (X_i - \mathbb{E}X_i) > t\right] \le \frac{\mathbb{E}\left[\exp\left(s\sum_{i=1}^n (X_i - \mathbb{E}X_i)\right)\right]}{\exp(st)}$$

$$= \frac{\prod_{i=1}^n \mathbb{E}\left[\exp\left(s(X_i - \mathbb{E}X_i)\right)\right]}{\exp(st)},$$

where we used independence of the variables X_i. Bound the numerator using Lemma A.1 and minimize the obtained bound in s to get the first inequality. The second is obtained by symmetry. ∎

We close this section by a version of Corollary A.1, also due to Hoeffding [161], for the case when sampling is done without replacement.

Lemma A.2. *Let the set A consist of N numbers $a_1, \ldots, a_N$. Let $Z_1, \ldots, Z_n$ denote a random sample taken without replacement from A, where $n \leq N$. Denote*

$$m = \frac{1}{N} \sum_{i=1}^{N} a_i \quad and \quad c - \max_{i,j \leq N} |a_i - a_j|.$$

Then for any $\varepsilon > 0$ we have

$$\mathbb{P}\left[\left|\frac{1}{n} \sum_{i=1}^{n} Z_i - m\right| \geq \varepsilon\right] \leq 2e^{-2n\varepsilon^2/c^2}.$$

For more inequalities of this type, see Hoeffding [161] and Serfling [264].

A.1.2 Bernstein's Inequality

Next we present inequalities that, in certain situations, give tighter bounds than Hoeffding's inequality. The first result is a simple "poissonian" inequality.

Lemma A.3. *Let X be a random variable taking values in $[0, 1]$. Then, for any $s \in \mathbb{R}$,*

$$\ln \mathbb{E}\left[e^{sX}\right] \leq \left(e^s - 1\right) \mathbb{E} X.$$

Proof. As in the proof of Hoeffding's inequality, we exploit the convexity of e^{sx} by observing that for any $x \in [0, 1]$, $e^{sx} \leq xe^s + (1 - x)$. Thus,

$$\mathbb{E}\left[e^{sX}\right] \leq \mathbb{E} Xe^s + 1 - \mathbb{E} X.$$

By the elementary inequality $1 + x \leq e^x$ we have $\mathbb{E} Xe^s + 1 - \mathbb{E} X \leq e^{(e^s-1)\mathbb{E} X}$, as desired. ∎

The next inequality is a version of Bernstein's inequality [25]; see also Freedman [110], Neveu [224].

Lemma A.4. *Let X be a zero-mean random variable taking values in $(-\infty, 1]$ with variance $\mathbb{E} X^2 = \sigma^2$. Then, for any $\eta > 0$,*

$$\ln \mathbb{E}\, e^{\eta X} \leq \sigma^2 \left(e^\eta - 1 - \eta\right).$$

Proof. The key observation is that the function $(e^x - x - 1)/x^2$ is nondecreasing for all $x \in \mathbb{R}$. But then, since $X \leq 1$,

$$e^{\eta X} - \eta X - 1 \leq X^2(e^\eta - \eta - 1).$$

Taking expected values on both sides, taking logarithms, and using $\ln(1 + x) \leq x$, we obtain the stated result. ∎

A simple consequence of Lemma A.4 is the following inequality.

Lemma A.5. *Let X be a random variable taking values in $[0, 1]$. Let $\sigma = \sqrt{\mathbb{E} X^2 - (\mathbb{E} X)^2}$. Then for any $\eta > 0$,*

$$\ln \mathbb{E}\left[e^{-\eta(X-\mathbb{E} X)}\right] \leq \sigma^2 \left(e^\eta - 1 - \eta\right) \leq \mathbb{E} X(1 - \mathbb{E} X)(e^\eta - 1 - \eta).$$

Proof. The first inequality is a direct consequence of Lemma A.4. The second inequality follows by noting that, since $X \in [0, 1]$,

$$\sigma^2 = \mathbb{E} X^2 - (\mathbb{E} X)^2 \le \mathbb{E} X - (\mathbb{E} X)^2 = \mathbb{E} X(1 - \mathbb{E} X). \quad \blacksquare$$

Using Lemma A.4 together with Chernoff's technique as in the proof of Corollary A.1, it now is easy to deduce the following result.

Corollary A.2 (Bennett's inequality). *Let $X_1, \ldots, X_n$ be independent real-valued random variables with zero mean, and assume that $X_i \le 1$ with probability 1. Let*

$$\sigma^2 = \frac{1}{n} \sum_{i=1}^{n} \mathbb{E} X_i^2.$$

Then for any $t > 0$,

$$\mathbb{P} \left[\sum_{i=1}^{n} X_i > t \right] \le \exp \left(-n\sigma^2 h \left(\frac{t}{n\sigma^2} \right) \right),$$

where $h(u) = (1 + u) \log(1 + u) - u$ for $u \ge 0$.

The message of this inequality is perhaps best seen if we do some further bounding. Applying the elementary inequality $h(u) \ge u^2/(2 + 2u/3)$, $u \ge 0$ (which may be seen by comparing the derivatives of both sides), we obtain a classical inequality of Bernstein [25].

Corollary A.3 (Bernstein's inequality). *Under the conditions of the previous theorem, for any $\varepsilon > 0$,*

$$\mathbb{P} \left[\frac{1}{n} \sum_{i=1}^{n} X_i > \varepsilon \right] \le \exp \left(-\frac{n\varepsilon^2}{2\sigma^2 + 2\varepsilon/3} \right).$$

A.1.3 Hoeffding–Azuma Inequality and Related Results

The following extension of Hoeffding's inequality to bounded martingale difference sequences is simple and useful.

A sequence of random variables $V_1, V_2, \ldots$ is a *martingale difference sequence* with respect to the sequence of random variables $X_1, X_2, \ldots$ if, for every $i > 0$, V_i is a function of $X_1, \ldots, X_i$, and

$$\mathbb{E}[V_{i+1} \mid X_1, \ldots, X_i] = 0 \qquad \text{with probability 1.}$$

Lemma A.6. *Let $V_1, V_2, \ldots$ be a martingale difference sequence with respect to some sequence $X_1, X_2, \ldots$ such that $V_i \in [A_i, A_i + c_i]$ for some random variable A_i, measurable with respect to $X_1, \ldots, X_{i-1}$, and a positive constant c_i. If $S_k = \sum_{i=1}^{k} V_i$, then for any $s > 0$,*

$$\mathbb{E} \left[e^{sS_n} \right] \le e^{(s^2/8) \sum_{i=1}^{n} c_i^2}.$$

Proof.

$$\mathbb{E}\left[e^{s S_n}\right] = \mathbb{E}\left[e^{s S_{n-1}}\mathbb{E}\left[e^{s V_n} \mid X_1, \dots, X_{n-1}\right]\right]$$
$$\le \mathbb{E}\left[e^{s S_{n-1}} e^{s^2 c_n^2/8}\right]$$
$$= e^{s^2 c_n^2/8}\mathbb{E}\left[e^{s S_{n-1}}\right],$$

where we applied Lemma A.1. The desired inequality is obtained by iterating the argument. ∎

Just as in the case of Corollary A.1, we obtain the following corollary.

Lemma A.7. *Let* $V_1, V_2, \dots$ *be a martingale difference sequence with respect to some sequence* $X_1, X_2, \dots$ *such that* $V_i \in [A_i, A_i + c_i]$ *for some random variable* A_i, *measurable with respect to* $X_1, \dots, X_{i-1}$ *and a positive constant* c_i. *If* $S_n = \sum_{i=1}^n V_i$, *then for any* $t > 0$,

$$\mathbb{P}\left[S_n > t\right] \le \exp\left(\frac{-2t^2}{\sum_{i=1}^n c_i^2}\right)$$

and

$$\mathbb{P}\left[S_n < -t\right] \le \exp\left(\frac{-2t^2}{\sum_{i=1}^n c_i^2}\right).$$

In fact, as noted in [161], the following "maximal" version of Lemma A.7 also holds:

$$\mathbb{P}\left[\max_{i \le n} S_i > t\right] \le \exp\left(\frac{-2t^2}{\sum_{i=1}^n c_i^2}\right).$$

We also need the following "Bernstein-like" improvement that takes variance information into account (see Freedman [110]). The proof, which we omit, is an extension of the independent case just shown.

Lemma A.8 (Bernstein's inequality for martingales). *Let* $X_1, \dots, X_n$ *be a bounded martingale difference sequence with respect to the filtration* $\mathcal{F} = (\mathcal{F}_i)_{1 \le i \le n}$ *and with* $|X_i| \le K$. *Let*

$$S_i = \sum_{j=1}^i X_j$$

be the associated martingale. Denote the sum of the conditional variances by

$$\Sigma_n^2 = \sum_{t=1}^n \mathbb{E}\left[X_t^2 \mid \mathcal{F}_{t-1}\right].$$

Then for all constants $t, v > 0$,

$$\mathbb{P}\left[\max_{i=1,\dots,n} S_i > t \text{ and } \Sigma_n^2 \le v\right] \le \exp\left(-\frac{t^2}{2(v + Kt/3)}\right),$$

and therefore,

$$\mathbb{P}\left[\max_{i=1,\ldots,n} S_i > \sqrt{2vt} + (\sqrt{2}/3)Kt \text{ and } \Sigma_n^2 \leq v\right] \leq e^{-t}.$$

A.1.4 Khinchine's Inequality
Recall Lemma 8.2:

Lemma A.9. *Let $a_1, \ldots, a_n$ be real numbers, and let $\sigma_1, \ldots, \sigma_n$ be i.i.d. sign variables with $\mathbb{P}[\sigma_1 = 1] = \mathbb{P}[\sigma_1 = -1] = 1/2$. Then*

$$\mathbb{E}\left|\sum_{i=1}^n a_i\sigma_i\right| \geq \frac{1}{\sqrt{2}}\sqrt{\sum_{i=1}^n a_i^2}.$$

Here we give a short and elegant proof (with a suboptimal constant $1/\sqrt{3}$ instead of $1/\sqrt{2}$) due to Littlewood [204]. First note that for any random variable X with finite fourth moment,

$$\mathbb{E}|X| \geq \frac{\left(\mathbb{E}X^2\right)^{3/2}}{\left(\mathbb{E}X^4\right)^{1/2}}.$$

Indeed, by Hölder's inequality,

$$\mathbb{E}X^2 = \mathbb{E}\left[|X|^{4/3}|X|^{2/3}\right] \leq \left(\mathbb{E}X^4\right)^{1/3}\left(\mathbb{E}|X|\right)^{2/3}.$$

Applying this inequality for $X = \sum_{i=1}^n a_i\sigma_i$ gives

$$\mathbb{E}\left|\sum_{i=1}^n a_i\sigma_i\right| \geq \frac{\left(\sum_{i=1}^n a_i^2\right)^{3/2}}{\sqrt{\sum_{i=1}^n a_i^4 + 3\sum_{i\neq j}a_i^2 a_j^2}} \geq \frac{1}{\sqrt{3}}\sqrt{\sum_{i=1}^n a_i^2},$$

where we used $\sum_{i=1}^n a_i^4 + 3\sum_{i\neq j}a_i^2 a_j^2 \leq 3\left(\sum_{i=1}^n a_i^2\right)^2$.

A.1.5 Slud's Inequality
Here we recall, without proof, an inequality due to Slud [272] between binomial tails and their approximating normals.

Lemma A.10. *Let B be a binomial (n, p) random variable with $p \leq 1/2$. Then for $n(1 - p) \geq k \geq np$,*

$$\mathbb{P}[B \geq k] \geq \mathbb{P}\left[N \geq \frac{k - np}{\sqrt{np(1 - p)}}\right],$$

where N is a standard normal random variable.

A.1.6 A Simple Limit Theorem

Lemma A.11. *Let $\{Z_{i,t}\}$ be i.i.d. Rademacher random variables $(i = 1, \ldots, N; t = 1, 2, \ldots)$ with distribution $\mathbb{P}[Z_{i,t} = -1] = \mathbb{P}[Z_{i,t} = 1] = 1/2$, and let $G_1, \ldots, G_N$ be* *independent standard normal random variables. Then*

$$\lim_{n \to \infty} \mathbb{E}\left[\max_{i=1,\dots,N} \frac{1}{\sqrt{n}} \sum_{t=1}^{n} Z_{i,t}\right] = \mathbb{E}\left[\max_{i=1,\dots,N} G_i\right].$$

Proof. Define the N-vector $X_n = (X_{n,1}, \dots, X_{n,N})$ of components

$$X_{n,i} \stackrel{\text{def}}{=} \frac{1}{\sqrt{n}} \sum_{t=1}^{n} Z_{i,t}, \qquad i = 1, \dots, N.$$

By the "Cramér–Wold device" (see, e.g., Billingsley [27, p. 48]), the sequence of vectors $\{X_n\}$ converges in distribution to a vector random variable $G = (G_1, \dots, G_N)$ if and only if $\sum_{i=1}^{N} a_i X_{n,i}$ converges in distribution to $\sum_{i=1}^{N} a_i G_i$ for all possible choices of the coefficients $a_1, \dots, a_N$. Now clearly, $\sum_{i=1}^{N} a_i X_{n,i}$ converges in distribution, as $n \to \infty$, to a zero-mean normal random variable with variance $\sum_{i=1}^{N} a_i^2$. Then, by the Cramér–Wold device, as $n \to \infty$ the vector X_n converges in distribution to $G = (G_1, \dots, G_k)$, where $G_1, \dots, G_k$ are independent standard normal random variables.

Convergence in distribution is equivalent to the fact that for any bounded continuous function $\psi : \mathbb{R}^N \to \mathbb{R}$,

$$\lim_{n \to \infty} \mathbb{E}[\psi(X_{n,1}, \dots, X_{n,N})] = \mathbb{E}[\psi(G_1, \dots, G_N)]. \tag{A.1}$$

Consider, in particular, the function $\psi(x_1, \dots, x_N) = \phi_L(\max_i x_i)$, where $L > 0$, and ϕ_L is the "thresholding" function

$$\phi_L(x) = \begin{cases} -L & \text{if } x < -L, \\ x & \text{if } |x| \le L, \\ L & \text{if } x > L. \end{cases}$$

Clearly, ϕ_L is bounded and continuous. Hence, by (A.1), we conclude that

$$\lim_{n \to \infty} \mathbb{E}\left[\phi_L\left(\max_{i=1,\dots,N} X_{n,i}\right)\right] = \mathbb{E}\left[\phi_L\left(\max_{i=1,\dots,N} G_i\right)\right].$$

Now note that for any $L > 0$,

$$\mathbb{E}\left[\max_{i=1,\dots,N} X_{n,i}\right] \ge \mathbb{E}\left[\phi_L\left(\max_{i=1,\dots,N} X_{n,i}\right)\right]$$
$$+ \mathbb{E}\left[\left(L + \max_{i=1,\dots,N} X_{n,i}\right) \mathbb{I}_{\{\max_{i=1,\dots,N} X_{n,i} < -L\}}\right],$$

where

$$\left|\mathbb{E}\left[\left(L + \max_{i=1,\dots,N} X_{n,i}\right) \mathbb{I}_{\{\max_{i=1,\dots,N} X_{n,i} < -L\}}\right]\right|$$
$$\le \mathbb{E}\left[\left(\left|\max_{i=1,\dots,N} X_{n,i}\right| - L\right) \mathbb{I}_{\{|\max_{i=1,\dots,N} X_{n,i}| - L > 0\}}\right]$$
$$= \int_0^\infty \mathbb{P}\left[\left|\max_{1,\dots,N} X_{n,i}\right| > L + u\right] du$$
$$= \int_L^\infty \mathbb{P}\left[\left|\max_{1,\dots,N} X_{n,i}\right| > u\right] du$$

$$\leq \int_L^\infty N \max_{i=1,\ldots,N} \mathbb{P}\big[\,|X_{n,i}| > u\,\big]\,\mathrm{d}u$$

$$\leq 2N \int_L^\infty e^{-u^2/2}\,\mathrm{d}u$$

(by Hoeffding's inequality; see Corollary A.1)

$$\leq 2N \int_L^\infty \left(1 + \frac{1}{u^2}\right) e^{-u^2/2}\,\mathrm{d}u$$

$$= \frac{2N}{L} e^{-L^2/2}.$$

Therefore, we have, for any $L > 0$,

$$\liminf_{n\to\infty} \mathbb{E}\left[\max_{i=1,\ldots,N} X_{n,i}\right] \geq \mathbb{E}\left[\phi_L\left(\max_{i=1,\ldots,N} G_i\right)\right] - \frac{2N}{L} e^{-L^2/2}.$$

Letting $L \to \infty$ on the right-hand side, and using the dominated convergence theorem, we see that

$$\liminf_{n\to\infty} \mathbb{E}\left[\max_{1,\ldots,N} X_{n,i}\right] \geq \mathbb{E}\left[\max_{1,\ldots,N} G_i\right].$$

The proof that

$$\limsup_{n\to\infty} \mathbb{E}\left[\max_{i=1,\ldots,N} X_{n,i}\right] \leq \mathbb{E}\left[\max_{i=1,\ldots,N} G_i\right]$$

is similar. ∎

For a proof of the next result see, for example, Galambos [122].

Lemma A.12. *Let* $G_1,\ldots,G_N$ *be independent standard normal random variables. Then*

$$\lim_{N\to\infty} \frac{\mathbb{E}\big[\max_{i=1,\ldots,N} G_i\big]}{\sqrt{2\ln N}} = 1.$$

The following lemma is a related nonasymptotic inequality for maxima of subgaussian random variables.

Lemma A.13. *Let* $\sigma > 0$, *and let* $X_1,\ldots,X_N$ *be real-valued random variables such that for all* $\lambda > 0$ *and* $1 \leq i \leq N$, $\mathbb{E}\big[e^{\lambda X_i}\big] \leq e^{\lambda^2\sigma^2/2}$. *Then*

$$\mathbb{E}\left[\max_{i=1,\ldots,N} X_i\right] \leq \sigma\sqrt{2\ln N}.$$

Proof. By Jensen's inequality, for all $\lambda > 0$,

$$e^{\lambda\,\mathbb{E}[\max_{i=1,\ldots,N} X_i]} \leq \mathbb{E}\big[e^{\lambda\max_{i=1,\ldots,N} X_i}\big] = \mathbb{E}\left[\max_{i=1,\ldots,N} e^{\lambda X_i}\right]$$

$$\leq \sum_{i=1}^N \mathbb{E}\big[e^{\lambda X_i}\big] \leq N e^{\lambda^2\sigma^2/2}.$$

Thus,

$$\mathbb{E}\left[\max_{i=1,\dots,N} X_i\right] \leq \frac{\ln N}{\lambda} + \frac{\lambda\sigma^2}{2}$$

and taking $\lambda = \sqrt{2\ln N/\sigma^2}$ yields the result. ∎

A.1.7 Proof of Theorem 8.3

The technique of the proof, called "chaining," is due to Dudley [91].

For each $k = 0, 1, 2, \dots$, let $\mathcal{F}^{(k)}$ be a minimal cover of $\mathcal{F}$ of radius $D2^{-k}$. Note that $|\mathcal{F}^{(k)}| = N_\rho(\mathcal{F}, D2^{-k})$. Denote the unique element of $\mathcal{F}^{(0)}$ by f_0.

Let Ω be the common domain where the random variables T_f, $f \in \mathcal{F}$ are defined. Pick $\omega \in \Omega$ and let $f^* \in \mathcal{F}$ be such that $\sup_{f \in \mathcal{F}} T_f(\omega) = T_{f^*}(\omega)$. (Here we implicitly assume that such an element exists. The modification of the proof for the general case is straightforward.)

For each $k \geq 0$, let f_k^* denote an element of $\mathcal{F}^{(k)}$ whose distance to f^* is minimal. Clearly, $\rho(f^*, f_k^*) \leq D2^{-k}$, and therefore, by the triangle inequality, for each $k \geq 1$,

$$\rho(f_{k-1}^*, f_k^*) \leq \rho(f^*, f_k^*) + \rho(f^*, f_{k-1}^*) \leq 3D2^{-k}. \tag{A.2}$$

Clearly, $\lim_{k\to\infty} f_k^* = f^*$, and so by the sample continuity of the process,

$$\sup_f T_f(\omega) = T_{f^*}(\omega) = T_{f_0}(\omega) + \sum_{k=1}^{\infty} \left(T_{f_k^*}(\omega) - T_{f_{k-1}^*}(\omega)\right).$$

Therefore

$$\mathbb{E}\left[\sup_f T_f\right] \leq \sum_{k=1}^{\infty} \mathbb{E}\left[\max_{f,g} \left(T_f - T_g\right)\right],$$

where the max is taken over all pairs $(f, g) \in \mathcal{F}^{(k)} \times \mathcal{F}^{(k-1)}$ such that $\rho(f, g) \leq 3D2^{-k}$.

Noting that there are at most $N_\rho(\mathcal{F}, D2^{-k})^2$ of these pairs, and recalling that $\{T_f : f \in \mathcal{F}\}$ is subgaussian in the metric ρ, we can apply Lemma A.13 using (A.2). Thus, for each $k \geq 1$,

$$\mathbb{E}\left[\max_{f,g} \left(T_f - T_g\right)\right] \leq 3D2^{-k}\sqrt{2\ln N_\rho(\mathcal{F}, D2^{-k})^2}.$$

Summing over k, we obtain

$$\mathbb{E}\left[\sup_f T_f\right] \leq \sum_{k=1}^{\infty} 3D2^{-k}\sqrt{2\ln N_\rho(\mathcal{F}, D2^{-k})^2}$$

$$= 12\sum_{k=1}^{\infty} D2^{-(k+1)}\sqrt{\ln N_\rho(\mathcal{F}, D2^{-k})}$$

$$\leq 12\int_0^{D/2} \sqrt{\ln N_\rho(\mathcal{F}, \varepsilon)}\, d\varepsilon,$$

as desired. ∎

A.1.8 Rademacher Averages

Let $A \in \mathbb{R}^n$ be a bounded set of vectors $\mathbf{a} = (a_1, \ldots, a_n)$, and introduce the quantity

$$R_n(A) = \mathbb{E}\left[\sup_{\mathbf{a} \in A} \frac{1}{n} \sum_{i=1}^n \sigma_i a_i\right],$$

where $\sigma_1, \ldots, \sigma_n$ are independent random variables with $\mathbb{P}[\sigma_i = 1] = \mathbb{P}[\sigma_i = -1] = 1/2$. $R_n(A)$ is called the *Rademacher average* associated with A. $R_n(A)$ measures, in a sense, the richness of set A.

Next we recall some of the simple structural properties of Rademacher averages. Observe that if A is symmetric in the sense that $\mathbf{a} \in A$ implies $-\mathbf{a} \in A$, then

$$R_n(A) = \mathbb{E}\left[\sup_{\mathbf{a} \in A} \frac{1}{n} \left|\sum_{i=1}^n \sigma_i a_i\right|\right].$$

Let A, B be bounded symmetric subsets of $\mathbb{R}^n$ and let $c \in \mathbb{R}$ be a constant. Then the following subadditivity properties are obvious from the definition:

$$R_n(A \cup B) \le R_n(A) + R_n(B),$$
$$R_n(c \cdot A) = |c| R_n(A),$$
$$R_n(A \oplus B) \le R_n(A) + R_n(B),$$

where $c \cdot A = \{c\mathbf{a} : \mathbf{a} \in A\}$ and $A \oplus B = \{\mathbf{a} + \mathbf{b} : \mathbf{a} \in A, \mathbf{b} \in B\}$. It follows from Hoeffding's inequality (Lemma A.1) and Lemma A.13 that if $A = \{\mathbf{a}^{(1)}, \ldots, \mathbf{a}^{(N)}\} \subset \mathbb{R}^n$ is a finite set, then

$$R_n(A) \le \max_{j=1,\ldots,N} \|\mathbf{a}^{(j)}\| \frac{\sqrt{2 \log N}}{n}. \tag{A.3}$$

Finally, we mention two important properties of Rademacher averages. The first is that if $\text{absconv}(A) = \left\{\sum_{j=1}^N c_j \mathbf{a}^{(j)} : N \in \mathbb{N}, \sum_{j=1}^N |c_j| \le 1, \mathbf{a}^{(j)} \in A\right\}$ is the absolute convex hull of A, then

$$R_n(A) = R_n\big(\text{absconv}(A)\big),$$

as is easily seen from the definition. The second is known as the *contraction principle*: let $\phi : \mathbb{R} \to \mathbb{R}$ be a function with $\phi(0) = 0$ and Lipschitz constant L_ϕ. Defining $\phi \circ A$ as the set of vectors of form $(\phi(a_1), \ldots, \phi(a_n)) \in \mathbb{R}^n$ with $\mathbf{a} \in A$, we have

$$R_n(\phi \circ A) \le L_\phi R_n(A).$$

(see Ledoux and Talagrand [192]). Often it is useful to derive further upper bounds on Rademacher averages. As an illustration we consider the case when A is a subset of $\{-1, 1\}^n$. Obviously, $|A| \le 2^n$. By inequality (A.3), the Rademacher average is bounded in terms of the logarithm of the cardinality of A. This logarithm may be upper bounded in terms of a combinatorial quantity, called the VC *dimension*. If $A \subset \{-1, 1\}^n$, then the VC dimension of A is the size V of the largest set of indices $\{i_1, \ldots, i_V\} \subset \{1, \ldots, n\}$ such that for each binary V-vector $\mathbf{b} = (b_1, \ldots, b_V) \in \{-1, 1\}^V$ there exists an $\mathbf{a} = (a_1, \ldots, a_n) \in A$ such that $(a_{i_1}, \ldots, a_{i_V}) = \mathbf{b}$. The key inequality establishing a relationship between shatter coefficients and VC dimension is known as *Sauer's lemma* (proved independently by Sauer [261], Shelah [266], and Vapnik and Chervonenkis [293]) which states that the cardinality of any set $A \subset \{-1, 1\}^n$ may be upper bounded as

$$|A| \leq \sum_{i=0}^{V} \binom{n}{i} \leq (n+1)^V,$$

where V is the VC dimension of A. In particular, for any $A \subset \{-1, 1\}^n$,

$$R_n(A) \leq \frac{\sqrt{2V \log(n+1)}}{n}.$$

This bound is a version of what has been known as the *Vapnik–Chervonenkis inequality*. By a somewhat refined analysis (based on *chaining*, very much in the spirit of the proof of Theorem 8.3), the logarithmic factor can be removed, and this results in a bound of the form

$$R_n(A) \leq C \sqrt{\frac{V}{n}}$$

for a universal constant C (Dudley [91]; see also Lugosi [206]).

A.1.9 The Beta Distribution

A random variable X taking values in $[0, 1]$ is said to have the Beta distribution with parameters $a, b > 0$ if its density function is given by

$$f(x) = \frac{x^{a-1}(1-x)^{b-1}}{B(a, b)}$$

where $B(a, b) = \Gamma(a)\Gamma(b)/\Gamma(a, b)$ is the so-called *Beta function*. Here $\Gamma(a) = \int_0^\infty x^{a-1} e^{-x} \, dx$ denotes Euler's *Gamma function*.

Let X have Beta distribution (a, b) and consider a random variable B such that, given $X = x$, the conditional distribution of B is binomial with parameters n and x. Then the marginal distribution of B is calculated, for $k = 0, 1, \ldots, n$, by

$$\begin{aligned}
\mathbb{P}[B = k] &= \int_0^1 \mathbb{P}[B = k \mid X = x] \frac{x^{a-1}(1-x)^{b-1}}{B(a, b)} \, dx \\
&= \binom{n}{k} \int_0^1 \frac{x^{k+a-1}(1-x)^{n-k+b-1}}{B(a, b)} \, dx \\
&= \binom{n}{k} \frac{B(k+a, n-k+b)}{B(a, b)}.
\end{aligned}$$

Now it is easy to determine the conditional density of X given $B = k$:

$$\begin{aligned}
f(x \mid B = k) &= \frac{f(x)\mathbb{P}[B = k \mid X = x]}{\mathbb{P}[B = k]} \\
&= \frac{x^{a-1}(1-x)^{b-1} \binom{n}{k} x^k (1-x)^{n-k}}{\binom{n}{k} B(k+a, n-k+b)} \\
&= \frac{x^{k+a-1}(1-x)^{n-k+b-1}}{B(k+a, n-k+b)}.
\end{aligned}$$

This is recognized as a Beta distribution with parameters $k + a$ and $n - k + b$.

A.2 Basic Information Theory

In this section we summarize some basic properties of the entropy of a discrete-valued random variable. For an excellent introductory book on information theory we refer to Cover and Thomas [74].

Let X be a random variable taking values in the countable set $\mathcal{X}$ with distribution $\mathbb{P}[X = x] = p(x)$, $x \in \mathcal{X}$. The *entropy* of X is defined by

$$H(X) = \mathbb{E}\big[-\log p(X)\big] = -\sum_{x \in \mathcal{X}} p(x) \log p(x)$$

(where log denotes natural logarithm and $0 \log 0 = 0$). If X, Y is a pair of discrete random variables taking values in $\mathcal{X} \times \mathcal{Y}$, then the *joint entropy* $H(X, Y)$ of X and Y is defined as the entropy of the pair (X, Y). The *conditional entropy* $H(X \mid Y)$ is defined as

$$H(X \mid Y) = H(X, Y) - H(Y).$$

If we write $p(x, y) = \mathbb{P}[X = x, Y = y]$ and $p(x \mid y) = \mathbb{P}[X = x \mid Y = y]$, then

$$H(X \mid Y) = -\sum_{x \in \mathcal{X}, y \in \mathcal{Y}} p(x, y) \log p(x \mid y),$$

from which we see that $H(X \mid Y) \geq 0$. It is also easy to see that the defining identity of the conditional entropy remains true conditionally, that is, for any three (discrete) random variables X, Y, Z:

$$H(X, Y \mid Z) = H(Y \mid Z) + H(X \mid Y, Z).$$

(Just add $H(Z)$ to both sides and use the definition of the conditional entropy.) A repeated application of this yields the *chain rule for entropy*: for arbitrary discrete random variables $X_1, \ldots, X_n$,

$$H(X_1, \ldots, X_n)$$
$$= H(X_1) + H(X_2 \mid X_1) + H(X_3 \mid X_1, X_2) + \cdots + H(X_n \mid X_1, \ldots, X_{n-1}).$$

Let P and Q be two probability distributions over a countable set $\mathcal{X}$ with probability mass functions p and q. Then the *Kullback–Leibler divergence* or *relative entropy* of P and Q is

$$D(P \| Q) = \sum_{x \in \mathcal{X}\,:\, p(x) > 0} p(x) \log \frac{p(x)}{q(x)}.$$

Since $\log x \leq x - 1$,

$$D(P \| Q) = -\sum_{x \in \mathcal{X}\,:\, p(x) > 0} p(x) \log \frac{q(x)}{p(x)} \geq -\sum_{x \in \mathcal{X}\,:\, p(x) > 0} p(x) \left(\frac{q(x)}{p(x)} - 1 \right) \geq 0.$$

Hence, the relative entropy is always nonnegative and equals 0 if and only if $P = Q$. This simple fact has some interesting consequences. For example, if $\mathcal{X}$ is a finite set with N elements, X is a random variable with distribution P, and we take Q to be the uniform distribution over $\mathcal{X}$, then $D(P \| Q) = \log N - H(X)$, and therefore the entropy of X never exceeds the logarithm of the cardinality of its range. Another immediate consequence of the nonnegativity of the relative entropy is the so-called *log-sum inequality*, which states that if $a_1, a_2, \ldots$ and $b_1, b_2, \ldots$ are nonnegative numbers with $A = \sum_i a_i$ and $B = \sum_i b_i$, then

$$\sum_i a_i \log \frac{a_i}{b_i} \geq A \log \frac{A}{B}.$$

Let now P and Q be distributions over an n-fold product space $\mathcal{X}^n$, and for $t = 1, \ldots, n$ denote by

$$P_t(x_1, \ldots, x_{t-1}) = \sum_{x_t, x_{t+1}, \ldots, x_n} P(x_1, \ldots, x_n)$$

and

$$Q_t(x_1, \ldots, x_{t-1}) = \sum_{x_t, x_{t+1}, \ldots, x_n} Q(x_1, \ldots, x_n)$$

the marginal distributions of the first $t - 1$ variables. Then the *chain rule for relative entropy* (a straightforward consequence of the definition) states that

$$D(P \| Q) = \sum_{t=1}^{n} \sum_{x_1, \ldots, x_{t-1}} D(P_{|x_1, \ldots, x_{t-1}} \| Q_{|x_1, \ldots, x_{t-1}}),$$

where $P_{|x_1, \ldots, x_{t-1}}$ denotes the conditional distribution over $\mathcal{X}^{n-t}$ defined by

$$P_{|x_1, \ldots, x_{t-1}}(x_t, x_{t+1}, \ldots, x_n) = \frac{P(x_1, \ldots, x_n)}{P_t(x_1, \ldots, x_{t-1})},$$

and $Q_{|x_1, \ldots, x_{t-1}}$ is defined similarly.

The following fundamental result is known as *Pinsker's inequality*. For any pair of probability distributions P and Q,

$$\sqrt{\frac{1}{2} D(P \| Q)} \geq \sum_{x : P(x) \geq Q(x)} \left(P(x) - Q(x) \right).$$

Sketch of Proof. First prove the inequality if P and Q are concentrated on the same two atoms. Then define $A = \left\{ x : P(x) \geq Q(x) \right\}$ and the measures P^*, Q^* on the set $\{0, 1\}$ by $P^*(0) = 1 - P^*(1) = P(A)$ and $Q^*(0) = 1 - Q^*(1) = Q(A)$, and apply the previous result. ■

A.3 Basics of Classification

In this section we summarize some basic facts of the probabilistic theory of binary classification. For more details we refer to Devroye, Györfi, and Lugosi [88]. The problem of binary classification is to guess the unknown binary class of an observation. An observation x is an element of a measurable space $\mathcal{X}$. The unknown nature of the observation is called a *class*, denoted by y, and takes values in the set $\{0, 1\}$.

In the probabilistic model of classification, the observation/label pair is modeled as a pair (X, Y) of random variables taking values in $\mathcal{X} \times \{0, 1\}$.

The *posterior probabilities* are defined, for all $x \in \mathcal{X}$, by

$$\eta(x) = \mathbb{P}[Y = 1 \mid X = x] = \mathbb{E}[Y \mid X = x].$$

Thus, $\eta(x)$ is the conditional probability that Y is 1, given $X = x$.

Any function $g : \mathcal{X} \to \{0, 1\}$ defines a *classifier*, and the value $g(x)$ represents one's guess of y given x. An *error* occurs if $g(x) \neq y$, and the *probability of error* for a classifier g is

$$L(g) = \mathbb{P}[g(X) \neq Y].$$

The next lemma shows that the *Bayes classifier* given by

$$g^*(x) = \begin{cases} 1 & \text{if } \eta(x) > 1/2 \\ 0 & \text{otherwise} \end{cases}$$

minimizes the probability of error. Its probability of error $L(g^*)$ is called the *Bayes error*.

Lemma A.14. *For any classifier* $g : \mathcal{X} \to \{0, 1\}$,

$$\mathbb{P}[g^*(X) \neq Y] \leq \mathbb{P}[g(X) \neq Y].$$

Proof. Given $X = x$, the conditional probability of error of any decision g may be expressed as

$$
\begin{aligned}
\mathbb{P}[g(X) \neq Y \mid X = x] \\
&= 1 - \mathbb{P}[Y = g(X) \mid X = x] \\
&= 1 - \left(\mathbb{P}[Y = 1, g(X) = 1 \mid X = x] + \mathbb{P}[Y = 0, g(X) = 0 \mid X = x] \right) \\
&= 1 - \left(\mathbb{I}_{\{g(x)=1\}} \mathbb{P}[Y = 1 \mid X = x] + \mathbb{I}_{\{g(x)=0\}} \mathbb{P}[Y = 0 \mid X = x] \right) \\
&= 1 - \left(\mathbb{I}_{\{g(x)=1\}} \eta(x) + \mathbb{I}_{\{g(x)=0\}} (1 - \eta(x)) \right).
\end{aligned}
$$

Thus, for every $x \in \mathcal{X}$,

$$
\begin{aligned}
\mathbb{P}[g(X) \neq Y \mid X = x] - \mathbb{P}[g^*(X) \neq Y \mid X = x] \\
&= \eta(x)\left(\mathbb{I}_{\{g^*(x)=1\}} - \mathbb{I}_{\{g(x)=1\}} \right) + \left(1 - \eta(x) \right)\left(\mathbb{I}_{\{g^*(x)=0\}} - \mathbb{I}_{\{g(x)=0\}} \right) \\
&= \left(2\eta(x) - 1 \right)\left(\mathbb{I}_{\{g^*(x)=1\}} - \mathbb{I}_{\{g(x)=1\}} \right) \\
&\geq 0
\end{aligned}
$$

by the definition of g^*. The statement now follows by taking expected values of both sides. ∎

Lemma A.15. *The Bayes error may be written as*

$$L(g^*) = \mathbb{P}[g^*(X) \neq Y] = \mathbb{E}\left[\min\{\eta(X), 1 - \eta(X)\} \right].$$

Moreover, for any classifier g,

$$L(g) - L(g^*) = 2\mathbb{E}\left[\left| \eta(X) - 1/2 \right| \mathbb{I}_{\{g(X) \neq g^*(X)\}} \right].$$

Proof. The proof of the previous lemma reveals that

$$L(g) = 1 - \mathbb{E}\left[\mathbb{I}_{\{g(X)=1\}} \eta(X) + \mathbb{I}_{\{g(X)=0\}} (1 - \eta(X)) \right]$$

and, in particular,

$$L(g^*) = 1 - \mathbb{E}\left[\mathbb{I}_{\{\eta(X)>1/2\}} \eta(X) + \mathbb{I}_{\{\eta(X)\leq 1/2\}} (1 - \eta(X)) \right].$$

The statements are immediate consequences of these expressions. ∎

References

[1] M.A. Aizerman, E.M. Braverman, and L.I. Rozonoer. The method of potential functions for the problem of restoring the characteristic of a function converter from randomly observed points. *Automation and Remote Control*, 25:1546–1556, 1964.

[2] M.A. Aizerman, E.M. Braverman, and L.I. Rozonoer. The probability problem of pattern recognition learning and the method of potential functions. *Automation and Remote Control*, 25:1307–1323, 1964.

[3] M.A. Aizerman, E.M. Braverman, and L.I. Rozonoer. Theoretical foundations of the potential function method in pattern recognition learning. *Automation and Remote Control*, 25:917–936, 1964.

[4] P. Algoet. Universal schemes for prediction, gambling, and portfolio selection. *Annals of Probability*, 20:901–941, 1992.

[5] P. Algoet. The strong law of large numbers for sequential decisions under uncertainty. *IEEE Transactions on Information Theory*, 40:609–634, 1994.

[6] P. Algoet and T. Cover. Asymptotic optimality and asymptotic equipartition properties of log-optimum investment. *Annals of Probability*, 16(2):876–898, 1988.

[7] C. Allenberg-Neeman and B. Neeman. Full information game with gains and losses. In *Proceedings of the 15th International Conference on Algorithmic Learning Theory*, pp. 264–278. Springer, New York, 2004.

[8] J.K. Anlauf and M. Biehl. The Adatron: An adaptive Perceptron algorithm. *Europhysics Letters*, 10:687–692, 1989.

[9] N. Aronszajn. Theory of reproducing kernels. *Transactions of the American Mathematical Society*, 68:337–404, 1950.

[10] P. Auer. Using confidence bounds for exploitation-exploration trade-offs. *Journal of Machine Learning Research*, 3:397–422, 2002.

[11] P. Auer, N. Cesa-Bianchi, and P. Fischer. Finite-time analysis of the multiarmed bandit problem. *Machine Learning*, 47:235–256, 2002.

[12] P. Auer, N. Cesa-Bianchi, Y. Freund, and R. Schapire. The nonstochastic multiarmed bandit problem. *SIAM Journal on Computing*, 32:48–77, 2002.

[13] P. Auer, N. Cesa-Bianchi, and C. Gentile. Adaptive and self-confident on-line learning algorithms. *Journal of Computer and System Sciences*, 64(1), 2002.

[14] P. Auer and P.M. Long. Structural results for online learning models with and without queries. *Machine Learning*, 36(3):147–181, 1999.

[15] P. Auer and M. Warmuth. Tracking the best disjunction. *Machine Learning*, 32(2):127–150, 1998.

[16] R.J. Aumann. Subjectivity and correlation in randomized strategies. *Journal of Mathematical Economics*, 1:67–96, 1974.

[17] R.J. Aumann. Correlated equilibrium as an expression of Bayesian rationality. *Econometrica*, 55:1–18, 1987.

[18] B. Awerbuch, Y. Azar, A. Fiat, and T. Leighton. Making commitments in the face of uncertainty: How to pick a winner almost every time. In *Proceedings of the 28th ACM Symposium on the Theory of Computing*, pp. 519–530. ACM Press, New York, 1996.

[19] B. Awerbuch and R.D. Kleinberg. Adaptive routing with end-to-end feedback: Distributed learning and geometric approaches. In *Proceedings of the 36th ACM Symposium on the Theory of Computing*, pp. 45–53. ACM Press, New York, 2004.

[20] K.S. Azoury and M. Warmuth. Relative loss bounds for on-line density estimation with the exponential family of distributions. *Machine Learning*, 43(3):211–246, 2001.

[21] A. Baños. On pseudo-games. *Annals of Mathematical Statistics*, 39:1932–1945, 1968.

[22] A. Barron, J. Rissanen, and B. Yu. The minimum description length principle in coding and modeling. *IEEE Transactions on Information Theory*, 44:2743–2760, 1998.

[23] O. Bashkirov, E.M. Braverman, and I.E. Muchnik. Potential function algorithms for pattern recognition learning machines. *Automation and Remote Control*, 25:692–695, 1964.

[24] A. Beck and M. Teboulle. Mirror descent and nonlinear projected subgradient methods for convex optimization. *Operations Research Letters*, 31:167–175, 2003.

[25] S.N. Bernstein. *The Theory of Probabilities*. Gastehizdat Publishing House, Moscow, 1946.

[26] D.A. Berry and B. Fristedt. *Bandit Problems*. Chapman and Hall, New York, 1985.

[27] P. Billingsley. *Convergence of Probability Measures*. Wiley, New York, 1968.

[28] D. Blackwell. An analog of the minimax theorem for vector payoffs. *Pacific Journal of Mathematics*, 6:1–8, 1956.

[29] D. Blackwell. Controlled random walks. In *Proceedings of the International Congress of Mathematicians, 1954*, vol. III, pp. 336–338. North-Holland, New York, 1956.

[30] D. Blackwell and L. Dubins. Merging of opinions with increasing information. *Annals of Mathematical Statistics*, 33:882–886, 1962.

[31] H.D. Block. The Perceptron: A model for brain functioning. *Review of Modern Physics*, 34:123–135, 1962.

[32] A. Blum and C. Burch. On-line learning and the metrical task system problem. *Machine Learning*, 39:35–58, 2000.

[33] A. Blum and A. Kalai. Universal portfolios with and without transaction costs. *Machine Learning*, 35:193–205, 1999.

[34] A. Blum and Y. Mansour. From external to internal regret. In *Proceedings of the 18th Annual Conference on Learning Theory*, pp. 621–636. Springer, New York, 2005.

[35] A. Bordes, S. Ertekin, J. Weston, and L. Bottou. Fast kernel classifiers with online and active learning. *Journal of Machine Learning Research*, 6:1579–1619. Microtome Publishing, Brookline, MA, 2005.

[36] A. Borodin and R. El-Yaniv. *Online Computation and Competitive Analysis*. Cambridge University Press, New York, 1998.

[37] A. Borodin, R. El-Yaniv, and V. Gogan. Can we learn to beat the best stock? *Journal of Artificial Intelligence Research*, 21:579–594, 2004.

[38] B. Boser, I. Guyon, and V.N. Vapnik. A training algorithm for optimal margin classifiers. In *Proceedings of the Fifth Annual ACM Workshop on Computational Learning Theory*, pp. 144–152. ACM Press, New York, 1992.

[39] L. Bottou and N. Murata. Stochastic approximations and efficient learning. In M.A. Arbib, ed., *The Handbook of Brain Theory and Neural Networks*. Cambridge University Press, New York, 2002. 2nd edition.

[40] O. Bousquet and M. Warmuth. Tracking a small set of experts by mixing past posteriors. *Journal of Machine Learning Research*, 3:363–396, 2002.

[41] L. Breiman. Optimal gambling systems for favorable games. In *Proceedings of the Fourth Berkeley Symposium on Mathematical Statistics and Probability*, pp. 65–78. University of California Press, Berkeley, CA, 1961.

[42] G.W. Brier. Verification of forecasts expressed in terms of probability. *Monthly Weather Review*, 75:1–3, 1950.

[43] T. Bylander. Worst-case absolute loss bounds for linear learning algorithms. In *Proceedings of the 14th National Conference on Artificial Intelligence*, pp. 485–490. MIT Press, Cambridge, MA, 1997.

[44] A. Cahn. General procedures leading to correlated equilibria. *International Journal of Game Theory*, 33(1):21–40, 2004.

[45] C. Campbell, N. Cristianini, and A. Smola. Query learning with large margin classifiers. In *Proceedings of the 17th International Conference on Machine Learning*, pp. 111–118. Morgan Kaufmann, San Mateo, CA, 2000.

[46] N. Cesa-Bianchi. Analysis of two gradient-based algorithms for on-line regression. *Journal of Computer and System Sciences*, 59(3):392–411, 1999.

[47] N. Cesa-Bianchi, A. Conconi, and C. Gentile. A second-order Perceptron algorithm. *SIAM Journal on Computing*, 34(3):640–668, 2005.

[48] N. Cesa-Bianchi, Y. Freund, D. Haussler, D.P. Helmbold, R. Schapire, and M. Warmuth. How to use expert advice. *Journal of the ACM*, 44(3):427–485, 1997.

[49] N. Cesa-Bianchi, C. Gentile, and L. Zaniboni. Worst-case analysis of selective sampling for linear-threshold algorithms. In *Advances in Neural Information Processing Systems 17*, pp. 241–248. MIT Press, Cambridge, MA, 2005.

[50] N. Cesa-Bianchi, P.M. Long, and M. Warmuth. Worst-case quadratic loss bounds for prediction using linear functions and gradient descent. *IEEE Transactions on Neural Networks*, 7(3):604–619, 1996.

[51] N. Cesa-Bianchi and G. Lugosi. On prediction of individual sequences. *Annals of Statistics*, 27:1865–1895, 1999.

[52] N. Cesa-Bianchi and G. Lugosi. Minimax values and entropy bounds for portfolio selection problems. *Talk given at the First World Congress of the Game Theory Society*, 2000.

[53] N. Cesa-Bianchi and G. Lugosi. Worst-case bounds for the logarithmic loss of predictors. *Machine Learning*, 43:247–264, 2001.

[54] N. Cesa-Bianchi and G. Lugosi. Potential-based algorithms in on-line prediction and game theory. *Machine Learning*, 51:239–261, 2003.

[55] N. Cesa-Bianchi, G. Lugosi, and G. Stoltz. Minimizing regret with label efficient prediction. *IEEE Transactions on Information Theory*, 51:2152–2162, 2004.

[56] N. Cesa-Bianchi, G. Lugosi, and G. Stoltz. Regret minimization under partial monitoring. Manuscript, 2004.

[57] N. Cesa-Bianchi, Y. Mansour, and G. Stoltz. Improved second-order bounds for prediction with expert advice. In *Proceedings of the 17th Annual Conference on Learning Theory*, pp. 217–232. Springer, New York, 2005.

[58] X. Chen and H. White. Laws of large numbers for Hilbert space-valued mixingales with applications. *Econometric Theory*, 12(2):284–304, 1996.

[59] Y.S. Chow and H. Teicher. *Probability Theory*. Springer, New York, 1988.

[60] T.H. Chung. Approximate methods for sequential decision making using expert advice. In *Proceedings of the 7th Annual ACM Workshop on Computational Learning Theory*, pp. 183–189. ACM Press, New York, 1994.

[61] T.H. Chung. *Minimax Learning in Iterated Games via Distributional Majorization*. PhD thesis, Stanford University, 1994.

[62] B. Clarke and A. Barron. Information-theoretic asymptotics of Bayes methods. *IEEE Transactions on Information Theory*, 36:453–471, 1990.

[63] B. Clarke and A. Barron. Jeffrys' prior is asymptotically least favorable under entropy risk. *Journal of Statistical Planning and Inference*, 41:37–60, 1994.

[64] B. Clarke and A. Dawid. Online prediction with experts under a log-scoring rule. Unpublished manuscript, 1999.

[65] W. Cohen and Y. Singer. Context-sensitive learning methods for text categorization. *ACM Transactions on Information Systems*, 17:141–173, 1999.

[66] R. Cohn, L. Atlas, and R. Ladner. Training connectionist networks with queries and selective sampling. In *Advances in Neural Information Processing Systems 2*, pp. 566–573. MIT Press, Cambridge, MA, 1990.

[67] C. Cortes and V.N. Vapnik. Support vector networks. *Machine Learning*, 20:1–25, 1995.

[68] T. Cover. Behavior of sequential predictors of binary sequences. In *Proceedings of the 4th Prague Conference on Information Theory, Statistical Decision Functions, Random Processes*, pp. 263–272. Publishing House of the Czechoslovak Academy of Sciences, Prague, 1965.

[69] T. Cover. Universal gambling schemes and the complexity measures of Kolmogorov and Chaitin. Technical Report 12, Department of Statistics, Stanford University, Stanford, CA, 1974.

[70] T. Cover. Universal portfolios. *Mathematical Finance*, 1:1–29, 1991.

[71] T. Cover and D.H. Gluss. Empirical Bayes stock market portfolios. *Advances in Applied Mathematics*, 7:170–181, 1986.

[72] T. Cover and E. Ordentlich. Universal portfolios with side information. *IEEE Transactions on Information Theory*, 42:348–363, 1996.

[73] T. Cover and E. Ordentlich. Universal portfolios with short sales and margin. In *Proceedings of IEEE International Symposium on Information Theory*, p. 174. IEEE Press, Piscataway, NJ, 1998.

[74] T. Cover and J.A. Thomas. *Elements of Information Theory*. Wiley, New York, 1991.

[75] K. Crammer and Y. Singer. Ultraconservative online algorithms for multiclass problems. *Journal of Machine Learning Research*, 3:951–991, 2003.

[76] N. Cristianini and J. Shawe-Taylor. *An Introduction to Support Vector Machines*. Cambridge University Press, New York, 2001.

[77] N. Cristianini and J. Shawe-Taylor. *Kernel Methods for Pattern Analysis*. Cambridge University Press, New York, 2004.

[78] J.E. Cross and A. Barron. Efficient universal portfolios for past-dependent target classes. *Mathematical Finance*, 13:245–276, 2003.

[79] L. D. Davisson. Universal lossless coding. *IEEE Transactions on Information Theory*, 19:783–795, 1973.

[80] A. Dawid. The well-calibrated Bayesian. *Journal of the American Statistical Association*, 77:605–613, 1982.

[81] A. Dawid. Statistical theory: The prequential approach. *Journal of the Royal Statistical Society A*, 147:278–292, 1984.

[82] A. Dawid. Calibration-based empirical probability. *The Annals of Statistics*, 13:1251–1285, 1985.

[83] A. Dawid. The impossibility of inductive inference. *Journal of the American Statistical Association*, 80:340–341, 1985.

[84] A. Dawid. Prequential data analysis. *Current Issues in Statistical Inference*, IMS Lecture Notes – Monograph Series 17, pp. 113–126, 1992.

[85] D.P. de Farias and N. Megiddo. How to combine expert (or novice) advice when actions impact the environment. In *Advances in Neural Information Processing Systems 16*. MIT Press, Cambridge, MA, 2004.

[86] D.P. de Farias and N. Megiddo. Combining expert advice in reactive environments. In *Advances in Neural Information Processing Systems*, vol. 17, pp. 409–416. MIT Press, Cambridge, MA, 2005.

[87] E. Dekel, D. Fudenberg, and D.K. Levine. Learning to play Bayesian games. *Games and Economic Behavior*, 46:282–303, 2004.

[88] L. Devroye, L. Györfi, and G. Lugosi. *A Probabilistic Theory of Pattern Recognition*. Springer, New York, 1996.

[89] L. Devroye and G. Lugosi. Lower bounds in pattern recognition and learning. *Pattern Recognition*, 28:1011–1018, 1995.

[90] M. Drmota and W. Szpankowski. Precise minimax redundancy and regret. *IEEE Transactions on Information Theory*, 50:2686–2707, 2004.

[91] R.M. Dudley. Central limit theorems for empirical measures. *Annals of Probability*, 6:899–929, 1978.

[92] V. Fabian and J. Hannan. On Blackwell's minimax theorem and the compound decision method. *Statistica Sinica*, 7:195–209, 1997.

[93] K. Fan. Minimax theorems. *Proceedings of the National Academy of Sciences USA*, 39:42–47, 1953.

[94] M. Feder. Gambling using a finite state machine. *IEEE Transactions on Information Theory*, 37:1459–1465, 1991.

[95] M. Feder, N. Merhav, and M. Gutman. Universal prediction of individual sequences. *IEEE Transactions on Information Theory*, 38:1258–1270, 1992.

[96] W. Feller. *An Introduction to Probability Theory and its Applications, Vol. 1*. Wiley, New York, 1968.

[97] X. Fernique. Regularité des trajectoires des fonctions aléatoires gaussiennes. In *École d'Été de Probabilités de Saint-Flour, IV-1974*, vol. 480 of *Lecture Notes in Math*, pp. 1–96. Springer, New York, 1975.

[98] X. Fernique. Regularité de fonctions aléatoires non gaussiennes. In *École d'Été de Probabilités de Saint-Flour, XI-1981*, volume 976 of *Lecture Notes in Math.*, pp. 1–74. Springer, New York, 1983.

[99] B.M. Fitingof. Optimal coding for unknown and variable statistics of messages. *Problems of Information Transmission*, 2:3–11, 1966.

[100] B.M. Fitingof. The compression of discrete information. *Problems of Information Transmission*, 3:22–29, 1967.

[101] F. Forges. Correlated equilibrium in two-person zero-sum games. *Econometrica*, 58:515, 1990.

[102] J. Forster. On relative loss bounds in generalized linear regression. In *Proceedings of the 12th International Symposium on Fundamentals of Computation Theory*, pp. 269–280. Lecture Notes in Computer Science 1684, Springer-Verlag, Berlin, 1999.

[103] D. Foster. Prediction in the worst-case. *Annals of Statistics*, 19:1084–1090, 1991.

[104] D. Foster. A proof of calibration via Blackwell's approachability theorem. *Games and Economic Behavior*, 29:73–78, 1999.

[105] D. Foster and R. Vohra. Calibrated learning and correlated equilibrium. *Games and Economic Behaviour*, 21:40–55, 1997.

[106] D. Foster and R. Vohra. Asymptotic calibration. *Biometrika*, 85:379–390, 1998.

[107] D. Foster and R. Vohra. Regret in the on-line decision problem. *Games and Economic Behavior*, 29:7–36, 1999.

[108] D. Foster and P.H. Young. Learning, hypothesis testing, and Nash equilibrium. *Games and Economic Behavior*, 45:73–96, 2003.

[109] D. Foster and P.H. Young. Regret testing: A simple payoff-based procedure for learning Nash equilibrium. Technical Report 04-12-034, Santa Fe Institute, Santa Fe, NM, 2004.

[110] D.A. Freedman. On tail probabilities for martingales. *Annals of Probability*, 3:100–118, 1975.

[111] Y. Freund. Predicting a binary sequence almost as well as the optimal biased coin. In *Proceedings of the 9th Annual Conference on Computational Learning Theory*, pp. 89–98. ACM Press, New York, 1996.

[112] Y. Freund and R. Schapire. A decision-theoretic generalization of on-line learning and an application to boosting. *Journal of Computer and System Sciences*, 55:119–139, 1997.

[113] Y. Freund and R. Schapire. Adaptive game playing using multiplicative weights. *Games and Economic Behavior*, 29:79–103, 1999.

[114] Y. Freund and R. Schapire. Large margin classification using the Perceptron algorithm. *Machine Learning*, 37(3): 277–296, 1999.

[115] Y. Freund, R. Schapire, Y. Singer, and M. Warmuth. Using and combining predictors that specialize. In *Proceedings of the 29th Annual ACM Symposium on the Theory of Computing*, pp. 334–343. ACM Press, New York, 1997.

[116] Y. Freund, S. Seung, E. Shamir, and N. Tishby. Selective sampling using the query by committee algorithm. *Machine Learning*, 28(2/3):133–168, 1997.

[117] D. Fudenberg and D.K. Levine. Steady state learning and Nash equilibrium. *Econometrica*, 61:547–573, 1993.

[118] D. Fudenberg and D.K. Levine. Universal consistency and cautious fictitious play. *Journal of Economic Dynamics and Control*, 19:1065–1089, 1995.

[119] D. Fudenberg and D.K. Levine. *The Theory of Learning in Games*. MIT Press, Cambridge, MA, 1998.

[120] D. Fudenberg and D.K. Levine. An easier way to calibrate. *Games and Economic Behavior*, 29:131–137, 1999.

[121] D. Fudenberg and D.K. Levine. Universal conditional consistency. *Games and Economic Behavior*, 29:104–130, 1999.

[122] J. Galambos. *The Asymptotic Theory of Extreme Order Statistics*. R.E. Kreiger, Malabar, FL, 1987.

[123] C. Gentile. A new approximate maximal margin classification algorithm. *Journal of Machine Learning Research*, 2:213–242, 2001.

[124] C. Gentile. The robustness of the *p*-norm algorithms. *Machine Learning*, 53(3):265–299, 2003.

[125] C. Gentile and M. Warmuth. Linear hinge loss and average margin. In *Advances in Neural Information Processing Systems 10*, pp. 225–231. MIT Press, Cambridge, MA, 1999.

[126] F. Germano and G. Lugosi. Global Nash convergence of Foster and Young's regret testing. Technical report, Universitat Pompeu Fabra, Barcelona, Spain, 2004.

[127] D.C. Gilliland. Sequential compound estimation. *Annals of Mathematical Statistics*, 39:1890–1904, 1968.

[128] D.C. Gilliland and J. Hannan. On an extended compound decision problem. *Annals of Mathematical Statistics*, 40:1536–1541, 1969.

[129] J.C. Gittins. *Multi-Armed Bandit Allocation Indices*. Wiley-Interscience series in Systems and Optimization. Wiley, New York, 1989.

[130] E.M. Gold. Language identification in the limit. *Information and Control*, 10:447–474, 1967.

[131] G. Gordon. *Approximate solutions to Markov Decision Processes*. PhD thesis, Carnegie Mellon University, 1999.

[132] T. Graepel, R. Herbrich, and R.C. Williamson. From margin to sparsity. In *Advances in Neural Information Processing Systems 13*, pp. 210–216. MIT Press, Cambridge, MA, 2001.

[133] A.J. Grove, N. Littlestone, and D. Schuurmans. General convergence results for linear discriminant updates. *Machine Learning*, 43(3):173–210, 2001.

[134] P. Grünwald. A tutorial introduction to the minimum description length principle. In P. Grünwald, I.J. Myung, and M. Pitt, eds., *Advances in Minimum Description Length: Theory and Applications*. MIT Press, Cambridge, MA, 2005.

[135] L. Györfi, G. Lugosi, and F. Udina. Nonparametric kernel-based sequential investment strategies. *Mathematical Finance*, 2005. In Press.

[136] L. Györfi and D. Schäfer. Nonparametric prediction. In *Advances in Learning Theory: Methods, Models and Applications*, pp. 339–354. NATO Science Series. IOS Press, Amsterdam, 2003.

[137] A. György, T. Linder, and G. Lugosi. Efficient algorithms and minimax bounds for zero-delay lossy source coding. *IEEE Transactions on Signal Processing*, 52:2337–2347, 2004.

[138] A. György, T. Linder, and G. Lugosi. A "follow the perturbed leader"–type algorithm for zero-delay quantization of individual sequences. In *Data Compression Conference*, pp. 342–351. IEEE Computer Society Press, Los Alamitos, CA, 2004.

[139] A. György, T. Linder, and G. Lugosi. Tracking the best of many experts. In *Proceedings of the 18th Annual Conference on Learning Theory*, pp. 204–216. Springer, New York, 2005.

[140] P. Hall and C.C. Heyde. *Martingale Limit Theory and its Application*. Academic Press, New York, 1980.

[141] J. Hannan. Approximation to Bayes risk in repeated play. *Contributions to the Theory of Games*, 3:97–139, 1957.

[142] J. Hannan and H. Robbins. Asymptotic solutions of the compound decision problem for two completely specified distributions. *Annals of Mathematical Statistics*, 26:37–51, 1955.

[143] M.H. Hansen and B. Yu. Model selection and the principle of minimum description length. *Journal of the American Statistical Association*, 96:746–774, 2001.

[144] S. Hart. Adaptive heuristics. Technical Report DP-372, Center for Rationality, The Hebrew University of Jerusalem, Israel, 2004.

[145] S. Hart and A. Mas-Colell. A simple adaptive procedure leading to correlated equilibrium. *Econometrica*, 68:1127–1150, 2000.

[146] S. Hart and A. Mas-Colell. A general class of adaptive strategies. *Journal of Economic Theory*, 98:26–54, 2001.

[147] S. Hart and A. Mas-Colell. A reinforcement procedure leading to correlated equilibrium. In *Economic Essays: A Festschrift for Werner Hildenbrand*, pp. 181–200. Springer, New York, 2002.

[148] S. Hart and A. Mas-Colell. Uncoupled dynamics do not lead to Nash equilibrium. *American Economic Review*, 93:1830–1836, 2003.

[149] S. Hart and A. Mas-Colell. Stochastic uncoupled dynamics and Nash equilibrium. Technical report, The Hebrew University of Jerusalem, Israel, 2004.

[150] S. Hart and D. Schmeidler. Existence of correlated equilibria. *Mathematics of Operations Research*, 14:18–25, 1989.

[151] D. Haussler, J. Kivinen, and M. Warmuth. Sequential prediction of individual sequences under general loss functions. *IEEE Transactions on Information Theory*, 44:1906–1925, 1998.

[152] D. Haussler and M. Opper. Mutual information, metric entropy and cumulative relative entropy risk. *The Annals of Statistics*, 25:2451–2492, 1997.

[153] D.P. Helmbold, J. Kivinen, and M. Warmuth. Relative loss bounds for single neurons. *IEEE Transactions on Neural Networks*, 10(6):1291–1304, 1999.

[154] D.P. Helmbold, N. Littlestone, and P.M. Long. Apple tasting. *Information and Computation*, 161(2):85–139, 2000.

[155] D.P. Helmbold and S. Panizza. Some label efficient learning results. In *Proceedings of the 10th Annual Conference on Computational Learning Theory*, pp. 218–230. ACM Press, New York, 1997.

[156] D.P. Helmbold and R. Schapire. Predicting nearly as well as the best pruning of a decision tree. *Machine Learning*, 27(1):51–68, 1997.

[157] D.P. Helmbold, R. Schapire, Y. Singer, and M. Warmuth. A comparison of new and old algorithms for a mixture estimation problem. *Machine Learning*, 27(1):97–119, 1997.

[158] D.P. Helmbold, R. Schapire, Y. Singer, and M. Warmuth. On-line portfolio selection using multiplicative updates. *Mathematical Finance*, 8:325–344, 1998.

[159] D.P. Helmbold and M. Warmuth. Tracking the best expert. *Machine Learning*, 32(2):151–178, 1998.

[160] M. Herbster and M. Warmuth. Tracking the best linear predictor. *Journal of Machine Learning Research*, 1:281–309, 2001.

[161] W. Hoeffding. Probability inequalities for sums of bounded random variables. *Journal of the American Statistical Association*, 58:13–30, 1963.

[162] A. Hoerl and R. Kennard. Ridge regression: Biased estimation for nonorthogonal problems. *Technometrics*, 12:55–67, 1970.

[163] J. Hofbauer and W.H. Sandholm. On the global convergence of stochastic fictitious play. *Econometrica*, 70:2265–2294, 2002.

[164] M. Hutter and J. Poland. Prediction with expert advice by following the perturbed and penalized leader. Technical Report IDSIA-20-04, Istituto Dalle Molle di Studi sull'Intelligenza Artificiale, Switzerland, 2004.

[165] M. Hutter and J. Poland. Adaptive online prediction by following the perturbed leader. *Journal of Machine Learning Research*, 6:639–660, 2005.

[166] G. Iyengar. Universal investment in markets with transaction costs. *Mathematical Finance*, 15:359–371, 2005.

[167] G. Iyengar and T. Cover. Growth optimal investment in horse race markets with costs. *IEEE Transactions on Information Theory*, 46:2675–2683, 2000.

[168] P. Jacquet and W. Szpankowski. A combinatorial problem arising in information theory: Precise minimax redundancy for Markov sources. In *Mathematics and Computer science II (Versailles, 2002)*, Trends in Mathematics, pp. 311–328. Birkhäuser, Basel, 2002.

[169] J.S. Jordan. Bayesian learning in normal form games. *Games and Economic Behavior*, 3:60–81, 1991.

[170] J.S. Jordan. Bayesian learning in repeated games. *Games and Economic Behavior*, 9:8–20, 1995.

[171] S. Kakade and D. Foster. Deterministic calibration and Nash equilibrium. In *Proceedings of the 17th Annual Conference on Learning Theory*, pp. 33–48. Springer, New York, 2004.

[172] S. Kakade, M. Kearns, J. Langford, and L. Ortiz. Correlated equilibria in graphical games. In *Proceedings of the 4th ACM Conference on Electronic Commerce*, pp. 42–47. ACM Press, New York, 2003.

[173] S. Kakade and A.Y. Ng. Online bounds for Bayesian algorithms. In L.K. Saul, Y. Weiss, and L. Bottou, ed., *Advances in Neural Information Processing Systems 17*, pp. 641–648. MIT Press, Cambridge, MA, 2005.

[174] A. Kalai and S. Vempala. Efficient algorithms for the online decision problem. In *Proceedings of the 16th Annual Conference on Learning Theory*, pp. 26–40. Springer, New York, 2003.

[175] A. Kalai and S. Vempala. Efficient algorithms for universal portfolios. *Journal of Machine Learning Research*, 3:423–440, 2003.

[176] E. Kalai and E. Lehrer. Rational learning leads to Nash equilibrium. *Econometrica*, 61:1019–1045, 1993.

[177] E. Kalai, E. Lehrer, and R. Smorodinsky. Calibrated forecasting and merging. *Games and Economic Behavior*, 29:151–169, 1999.

[178] Y. Kalnishkan, V. Vovk, and M.V. Vyugin. A criterion for the existence of predictive complexity for binary games. In *Proceedings of the 15th International Conference on Algorithmic Learning Theory*, pp. 249–263. Lecture Notes in Artificial Intelligence 3244, Springer, Heidelberg, Germany, 2004.

[179] M. Kearns and Y. Mansour. Efficient Nash computation in large population games with bounded influence. In *Proceedings of the 18th Conference on Uncertainty in Artificial Intelligence*, pp. 259–266. Margan Kaufmann, San Mateo, CA, 2002.

[180] J.L. Kelly. A new interpretation of information rate. *Bell System Technical Journal*, 35:917–926, 1956.

[181] J. Kivinen and M. Warmuth. Exponentiated gradient versus gradient descent for linear predictors. *Information and Computation*, 132(1):1–63, 1997.

[182] J. Kivinen and M. Warmuth. Averaging expert predictions. In *Proceedings of the Fourth European Conference on Computational Learning Theory*, pp. 153–167. Lecture Notes in Artificial Intelligence, Vol. 1572. Springer, Berlin, 1999.

[183] J. Kivinen and M. Warmuth. Relative loss bounds for multidimensional regression problems. *Machine Learning*, 45(3):301–329, 2001.

[184] J. Kivinen, M. Warmuth, and P. Auer. The Perceptron algorithm vs. Winnow: Linear vs. logarithmic mistake bounds when few input variables are relevant. *Artificial Intelligence*, 97:325–343, 1997.

[185] N.A. Kolmogorov. Three approaches to the definition of the concept "quantity of information." *Problems of Information Transmission*, 1:3–11, 1965.

[186] R.E. Krichevsky and V.K. Trofimov. The performance of universal encoding. *IEEE Transactions on Information Theory*, 27:199–207, 1981.

[187] F.R. Kschischang, B.J. Frey, and H.-A. Loeliger. Factor graphs and the sum-product algorithm. *IEEE Transactions on Information Theory*, 47(2):498–519, 2001.

[188] S. Kulkarni and G. Lugosi. Minimax lower bounds for the two-armed bandit problem. *IEEE Transactions on Automatic Control*, 45:711–714, 2000.

[189] T.L. Lai and H. Robbins. Asymptotically efficient adaptive allocation rules. *Advances in Applied Mathematics*, 6:4–22, 1985.

[190] T.L. Lai, H. Robbins, and C.Z. Wei. Strong consistency of least squares estimates in multiple regression. *Proceedings of the National Academy of Sciences*, 75(7):3034–3036, 1979.

[191] T.L. Lai and C.Z. Wei. Least squares estimates in stochastic regression models with applications to identification and control of dynamic systems. *The Annals of Statistics*, 10(1):154–166, 1982.

[192] M. Ledoux and M. Talagrand. *Probability in Banach Spaces*. Springer, Berlin, 1991.

[193] E. Lehrer. Approachability in infinite dimensional spaces. *International Journal of Game Theory*, 31:255–270, 1997.

[194] E. Lehrer. Any inspection is manipulable. *Econometrica*, 69:1333–1347, 2001.

[195] E. Lehrer. A wide range no-regret theorem. *Games and Economic Behavior*, 42:101–115, 2003.

[196] E. Lehrer and R. Smorodinsky. Merging and learning. In *Statistics, Probability and Game Theory*, IMS Lecture Notes Monograph Series 30, pp. 147–168. Institute of Mathematical Statistics, Hayward, CA, 1996.

[197] A. Lempel and J. Ziv. On the complexity of an individual sequence. *IEEE Transactions on Information Theory*, 22:75–81, 1976.

[198] M. Li and P. Vitányi. *An Introduction to Kolmogorov Complexity and its Applications*. Springer, New York, 1997. 2nd edition.

[199] Y. Li and P.M. Long. The relaxed online maximum margin algorithm. *Machine Learning*, 46(1/3):361–387, 2002.

[200] N. Littlestone. Learning quickly when irrelevant attributes abound: A new linear-threshold algorithm. *Machine Learning*, 2(4):285–318, 1988.

[201] N. Littlestone. Redundant noisy attributes, attribute errors, and linear threshold learning using Winnow. In *Proceedings of the 4th Annual Workshop on Computational Learning Theory*, pp. 147–156. Morgan Kaufmann, San Mateo, CA, 1991.

[202] N. Littlestone, P.M. Long, and M. Warmuth. On-line learning of linear functions. *Computational Complexity*, 5(1):1–23, 1995.

[203] N. Littlestone and M. Warmuth. The weighted majority algorithm. *Information and Computation*, 108:212–261, 1994.

[204] J.E. Littlewood. On bounded bilinear forms in an infinite number of variables. *Quarterly Journal of Mathematics (Oxford) 1*, pp. 164–174, 1930.

[205] P.M. Long. On-line evaluation and prediction using linear functions. In *Proceedings of the 10th Annual Conference on Computational Learning Theory*, pp. 21–31. ACM Press, New York, 1997.

[206] G. Lugosi. Pattern classification and learning theory. In L. Györfi, ed., *Principles of Nonparametric Learning*, pp. 5–62. Springer, 2002.

[207] W. Maass and M. Warmuth. Efficient learning with virtual threshold gates. *Information and Computation*, 141(1):66–83, 1998.

[208] S. Mannor and N. Shimkin. On-line learning with imperfect monitoring. In *Proceedings of the 16th Annual Conference on Learning Theory*, pp. 552–567. Springer, New York, 2003.

[209] H. Markowitz. Portfolio selection. *Journal of Finance*, 7:77–91, 1952.

[210] B. Martinet. Perturbation des méthodes d'optimisation. Applications. *RAIRO Analyse Numérique*, 12:153–171, 1978.

[211] H.B. McMahan and A. Blum. Online geometric optimization in the bandit setting against an adaptive adversary. In *Proceedings of the 17th Annual Conference on Learning Theory*, pp. 109–123. Springer, New York, 2004.

[212] N. Megiddo. On repeated games with incomplete information played by non-Bayesian players. *International Journal of Game Theory*, 9:157–167, 1980.

[213] N. Merhav and M. Feder. Universal schemes for sequential decision from individual data sequences. *IEEE Transactions on Information Theory*, 39(4):1280–1292, 1993.

[214] N. Merhav and M. Feder. Universal prediction. *IEEE Transactions on Information Theory*, 44:2124–2147, 1998.

[215] N. Merhav, E. Ordentlich, G. Seroussi, and M.J. Weinberger. On sequential strategies for loss functions with memory. *IEEE Transactions on Information Theory*, 48:1947–1958, 2002.

[216] J.-F. Mertens, S. Sorin, and S. Zamir. Repeated games. CORE Discussion papers 9420, 9421, 9422. Louvain-la-Neuve, Belgium, 1994.

[217] S.P. Meyn and R.L. Tweedie. *Markov Chains and Stochastic Stability*. Springer-Verlag, London, 1993.

[218] K. Miyasawa. On the convergence of the learning process in a 2×2 non-zero-sum game. Technical Report 33, Economic Research Program, Princeton University, Princeton, NJ, 1961.

[219] M. Mohri. Semiring frameworks and algorithms for shortest-distance problems. *Journal of Automata, Languages and Combinatorics*, 7:321–350, 2002.

[220] D. Monderer and L. Shapley. Fictitious play property for games with identical interests. *Journal of Economic Theory*, 68:258–265, 1996.

[221] J.H. Nachbar. Prediction, optimization, and learning in repeated games. *Econometrica*, 65:275–309, 1997.

[222] J. Nash. Non-cooperative games. *Annals of Mathematics*, 54:286–295, 1951.

[223] A. Nemirovski and D. Yudin. *Problem Complexity and Method Efficiency in Optimization*. Wiley, New York, 1998.

[224] J. Neveu. *Discrete Parameter Martingales*. North-Holland, New York, 1975.

[225] A.B.J. Novikov. On convergence proofs on Perceptrons. In *Proceedings of the Symposium of the Mathematical Theory of Automata*, vol. XII, pp. 615–622. Wiley, New York, 1962.

[226] D. Oakes. Self-calibrating priors do not exist. *Journal of the American Statistical Association*, 80:339, 1985.

[227] P. Odifreddi. *Classical Recursion Theory*. North Holland, New York, 1989.

[228] M. Opper and D. Haussler. Worst case prediction over sequences under log loss. In *The Mathematics of Information Coding, Extraction, and Distribution*. Springer, New York, 1999.

[229] E. Ordentlich and T. Cover. The cost of achieving the best portfolio in hindsight. *Mathematics of Operations Research*, 23:960–982, 1998.

[230] C.H. Papadimitriou. Algorithms, games, and the Internet. In *Proceedings of the 33rd ACM Symposium on the Theory of Computing*, pp. 749–753. ACM Press, New York, 2001.

[231] C.H. Papadimitriou. Computing correlated equilibria in multiplayer games. In *Proceedings of the 37th ACM Symposium on the Theory of Computing*, pp. 49–56. ACM Press, New York, 2005.

[232] C.H. Papadimitriou and T. Roughgarden. Computing equilibria in multiplayer games. In *Proceedings of the Sixteenth Annual ACM-SIAM Symposium on Discrete Algorithms*, pp. 82–91. ACM Press, New York, 2005.

[233] F. Pereira and Y. Singer. An efficient extension to mixture techniques for prediction and decision trees. *Machine Learning*, 36:183–199, 1999.

[234] A. Piccolboni and C. Schindelhauer. Discrete prediction games with arbitrary feedback and loss. In *Proceedings of the 14th Annual Conference on Computational Learning Theory*, pp. 208–223. Springer, New York, 2001.

[235] G. Pisier. Some applications of the metric entropy condition to harmonic analysis. In *Banach Spaces, Harmonic Analysis, and Probability Theory*. Lecture Notes in Mathematics 995, pp. 123–154. Springer, 1983.

[236] J. Rissanen. Generalized Kraft's inequality and arithmetic coding. *IBM Journal of Research and Development*, 20:198–203, 1976.

[237] J. Rissanen. Modeling by shortest data description. *Automatica*, 14:465–471, 1978.

[238] J. Rissanen. Universal coding, information, prediction and estimation. *IEEE Transactions on Information Theory*, 30:629–636, 1984.

[239] J. Rissanen. Complexity of strings in the class of Markov sources. *IEEE Transactions on Information Theory*, 32:526–532, 1986.

[240] J. Rissanen. Stochastic complexity and modeling. *The Annals of Statistics*, 14(3):1080–1100, 1986.

[241] J. Rissanen. Stochastic complexity. *Journal of the Royal Statistical Society B*, 49:223–239, 252–265, 1987.

[242] J. Rissanen. Fischer information and stochastic complexity. *IEEE Transactions on Information Theory*, 42:40–47, 1996.

[243] J. Rissanen and G.G. Langdon Jr. Universal modeling and coding. *IEEE Transactions on Information Theory*, 27:12–23, 1981.

[244] H. Robbins. Asymptotically subminimax solutions of compound statistical decision problems. In *Proceedings of the Second Berkeley Symposium on Mathematical Statistics and Probability, 1950*, pp. 131–148. University of California Press, Berkeley, CA, 1951.

[245] H. Robbins. Some aspects of the sequential design of experiments. *Bulletin of the American Mathematical Society*, 55:527–535, 1952.

[246] J. Robinson. An iterative method of solving a game. *Annals of Mathematics*, 54:296–301, 1951.

[247] R.T. Rockafellar. *Convex Analysis*. Princeton University Press, Princeton, NJ, 1970.

[248] R.T. Rockafellar. Monotone operators and the proximal point algorithm. *SIAM Journal on Control and Optimization*, 14(1):877–898, 1976.

[249] F. Rosenblatt. The Perceptron: A probabilistic model for information storage and organization in the brain. *Psychological Review*, 65:386–408, 1958.

[250] F. Rosenblatt. *Principles of Neurodynamics*. Spartan Books, Washington, DC, 1962.

[251] A. Rustichini. Minimizing regret: The general case. *Games and Economic Behavior*, 29:224–243, 1999.

[252] B.Ya. Ryabko. Twice-universal coding. *Problems of Information Transmission*, 20:24–28, 1984.

[253] B.Ya. Ryabko. Prediction of random sequences and universal coding. *Problems of Information Transmission*, 24:87–96, 1988.

[254] J. Van Ryzin. The sequential compound decision problem with $m \times n$ finite loss matrix. *Annals of Mathematical Statistics*, 37:954–975, 1966.

[255] S. Saitoh. *Theory of Reproducing Kernels and Its Applications*. Longman, Harlow, U.K., 1988.

[256] E. Samuel. Asymptotic solutions of the sequential compound decision problem. *Annals of Mathematical Statistics*, 34:1079–1094, 1963.

[257] E. Samuel. Convergence of the losses of certain decision rules for the sequential compound decision problem. *Annals of Mathematical Statistics*, 35:1606–1621, 1964.

[258] A. Sandroni and R. Smorodinsky. Belief-based equilibrium. *Games and Economic Behavior*, 47:157–171, 2004.

[259] A. Sandroni, R. Smorodinsky, and R. Vohra. Calibration with many checking rules. *Mathematics of Operations Research*, 28:141–153, 2003.

[260] A. De Santis, G. Markowski, and M.N. Wegman. Learning probabilistic prediction functions. In *Proceedings of the 1st Annual Workshop on Computational Learning Theory*, pp. 312–328. Morgan Kaufmann, San Mateo, CA, 1988.

[261] N. Sauer. On the density of families of sets. *Journal of Combinatorial Theory, Series A*, 13:145–147, 1972.

[262] B. Schölkopf and A. Smola. *Learning with kernels*. MIT Press, Cambridge, MA, 2002.

[263] E. Seneta. *Non-negative Matrices and Markov Chains*. Springer, New York, 1981.

[264] R.J. Serfling. Probability inequalities for the sum in sampling without replacement. *Annals of Statistics*, 2:39–48, 1974.

[265] L. Shapley. *Some Topics in Two-Person Games*. Princeton University Press, Princeton, NJ, 1964.

[266] S. Shelah. A combinatorial problem: Stability and order for models and theories in infinitary languages. *Pacific Journal of Mathematics*, 41:247–261, 1972.

[267] Y.M. Shtarkov. Universal sequential coding of single messages. *Problems of Information Transmission*, 23:3–17, 1987.

[268] A.C. Singer, S.S. Kozat, and M. Feder. Universal linear least squares prediction: Upper and lower bounds. *IEEE Transactions on Information Theory*, 48:2354–2362, 2002.

[269] Y. Singer. Switching portfolios. *International Journal of Neural Systems*, 8:445–455, 1997.

[270] S.P. Singh, M. Kearns, and Y. Mansour. Nash convergence of gradient dynamics in general-sum games. In *Proceedings of the 16th Conference on Uncertainty in Artificial Intelligence*, pp. 541–548. Morgan Kaufmann, San Mateo, CA, 2000.

[271] M. Sion. On general minimax theorems. *Pacific Journal of Mathematics*, 8:171–176, 1958.

[272] E.V. Slud. Distribution inequalities for the binomial law. *Annals of Probability*, 5:404–412, 1977.

[273] R. Solomonoff. A preliminary report on a general theory of inductive inference. Technical Report ZTB-138, Zator Company, Cambridge, MA, 1960.

[274] R. Solomonoff. A formal theory of inductive inference, part I. *Information and Control*, 7:1–22, 1964.

[275] R. Solomonoff. A formal theory of inductive inference, part II. *Information and Control*, 7:224–254, 1964.

[276] S. Sorin. *A First Course on Zero-Sum Repeated Games*. Springer, New York, 2002.

[277] D.F. Specht. Probabilistic neural networks and the polynomial Adaline as complementary techniques for classification. *IEEE Transactions on Neural Networks*, 1:111–121, 1990.

[278] G. Stoltz and G. Lugosi. Learning correlated equilibria in games with compact sets of strategies. Manuscript, 2004.

[279] G. Stoltz and G. Lugosi. Internal regret in on-line portfolio selection. *Machine Learning*, 59:125–159, 2005.

[280] V.N. Sudakov. Gaussian measures, Cauchy measures and ε-entropy. *Soviet Mathematics Doklady*, 10:310–313, 1969.

[281] S.J. Szarek. On the best constants in the Khintchine inequality. *Studia Mathematica*, 63:197–208, 1976.

[282] W. Szpankowski. On asymptotics of certain recurrences arising in universal coding. *Problems of Information Transmission*, 34:142–146, 1998.

[283] E. Takimoto, A. Maruoka, and V. Vovk. Predicting nearly as well as the best pruning of a decision tree through dynamic programming scheme. *Theoretical Computer Science*, 261:179–209, 2001.

[284] E. Takimoto and M. Warmuth. The minimax strategy for gaussian density estimation. In *Proceedings of the 13th Annual Conference on Computational Learning Theory*, pp. 100–106. Morgan Kaufmann, San Mateo, CA, 2000.

[285] E. Takimoto and M. Warmuth. Predicting nearly as well as the best pruning of a planar decision graph. *Theoretical Computer Science*, 288:217–235, 2002.

[286] E. Takimoto and M. Warmuth. Path kernels and multiplicative updates. *Journal of Machine Learning Research*, 4(5):773–818, 2004.

[287] M. Talagrand. Regularity of Gaussian processes. *Acta Mathematica*, 159:99–149, 1987.

[288] M. Talagrand. *The Generic Chaining*. Springer, New York, 2005.

[289] S. Tong and D. Koller. Support vector machine active learning with applications to text classification. In *Proceedings of the 17th International Conference on Machine Learning*, pp. 999–1006. Morgan Kaufmann, San Mateo, CA, 2000.

[290] P. Tseng and D.P. Bertsekas. On the convergence of the exponential multiplier method for convex programming. *Mathematical Programming*, 60:1–19, 1993.

[291] Y. Tsypkin. *Adaptation and Learning in Automatic Systems*. Academic Press, New York, 1971.

[292] V.N. Vapnik. *Statistical Learning Theory*. Wiley, New York, 1998.

[293] V.N. Vapnik and A.Ya. Chervonenkis. On the uniform convergence of relative frequencies of events to their probabilities. *Theory of Probability and Its Applications*, 16:264–280, 1971.

[294] V.N. Vapnik and A. Lerner. Pattern recognition using generalized portrait method. *Automation and Remote Control*, 24:774–780, 1963.

[295] N. Vielle. Weak approachability. *Mathematics of Operations Research*, 17:781–791, 1992.

[296] J. von Neumann and O. Morgenstern. *Theory of Games and Economic Behavior*. Princeton University Press, Princeton, NJ, 1944.

[297] V. Vovk. Aggregating strategies. In *Proceedings of the 3rd Annual Workshop on Computational Learning Theory*, pp. 372–383. Morgan Kaufmann, San Mateo, CA, 1990.

[298] V. Vovk. A game of prediction with expert advice. *Journal of Computer and System Sciences*, 56(2):153–173, 1998.

[299] V. Vovk. Derandomizing stochastic prediction strategies. *Machine Learning*, 35(3):247–282, 1999.

[300] V. Vovk. Competitive on-line statistics. *International Statistical Review*, 69:213–248, 2001.

[301] V. Vovk and G. Shafer. Good randomized sequential probability forecasting is always possible. Technical Report 7, Game-Theoretic Probability and Finance Project, 2004. Available at: www.vovk.net.

[302] V. Vovk, A. Takemura, and G. Shafer. Defensive forecasting. In *Proceedings of the Tenth International Workshop on Artificial Intelligence and Statistics*, pp. 365–372. Society for Artificial Intelligence and Statistics, 2005.

[303] V. Vovk and C. Watkins. Universal portfolio selection. In *Proceedings of the 11th Annual Conference on Computational Learning Theory*, pp. 12–23. ACM Press, New York, 1998.

[304] H. Walk and S. Yakowitz. Iterative nonparametric estimation of a log-optimal portfolio selection function. *IEEE Transactions on Information Theory*, 48:324–333, 2002.

[305] M. Warmuth and A.K. Jagota. Continuous and discrete-time nonlinear gradient descent: Relative loss bounds and convergence. In *Electronic proceedings of the 5th International Symposium on Artificial Intelligence and Mathematics*, 1997.

[306] C. Watkins. Kernels from matching operations. Technical Report CSD-TR-98-07, Department of Computer Science, Royal Holloway College, University of London, 1999.

[307] M.J. Weinberger, N. Merhav, and M. Feder. Optimal sequential probability assignment for individual sequences. *IEEE Transactions on Information Theory*, 40:384–396, 1994.

[308] T. Weissman and N. Merhav. Universal prediction of binary individual sequences in the presence of noise. *IEEE Transactions on Information Theory*, 47:2151–2173, 2001.

[309] T. Weissman, N. Merhav, and Somekh-Baruch. Twofold universal prediction schemes for achieving the finite state predictability of a noisy individual binary sequence. *IEEE Transactions on Information Theory*, 47:1849–1866, 2001.

[310] B. Widrow and M.E. Hoff. Adaptive switching circuits. In *1960 IRE WESCON Convention Record*, pp. 96–104, 1960.

[311] F.M.J. Willems, Y.M. Shtarkov, and T.J. Tjalkens. The context-tree weighting method: Basic properties. *IEEE Transactions on Information Theory*, 41:653–664, 1995.

[312] Q. Xie and A. Barron. Asymptotic minimax loss for data compression, gambling, and prediction. *IEEE Transactions on Information Theory*, 46:431–445, 2000.

[313] K. Yamanishi. A decision-theoretic extension of stochastic complexity and its application to learning. *IEEE Transactions on Information Theory*, 44:1424–1440, New York, 1998.

[314] K. Yamanishi. Minimax relative loss analysis for sequential prediction algorithms using parametric hypothesis. In *Proceedings of the 11th Annual Conference on Computational Learning Theory*, pp. 32–43. ACM Press, New York, 1998.

[315] R. Yaroshinsky, R. El-Yaniv, and S. Seiden. How to better use expert advice. *Machine Learning*, 55(3):271–309, New York, 2004.

[316] P.H. Young. *Strategic Learning and Its Limits*. Oxford University Press, New York, 2004.

[317] J. Ziv. Coding theorems for individual sequences. *IEEE Transactions on Information Theory*, 24:405–412, 1978.

[318] J. Ziv. Distortion-rate theory for individual sequences. *IEEE Transactions on Information Theory*, 26:137–143, 1980.

[319] J. Ziv and A. Lempel. A universal algorithm for sequential data-compression. *IEEE Transactions on Information Theory*, 23:337–343, 1977.

[320] A.K. Zvonkin and L.A. Levin. The complexity of finite objects and the development of the concepts of information and randomness by means of the theory of algorithms. *Russian Mathematical Surveys*, 25:83–124, 1970.

Author Index

Subject Index

activation function, 90, 91, 93
Adatron, 355
aggregating forecaster, 36, 40, 52, 55–57, 250, 320, 330
algorithmic randomness, 35
all subsets kernel, 358
ALMA forecaster, 344, 356, 357
alternative fixed share forecaster, 123, 124, 127
anova kernel, 358
apple tasting, 145, 152, 174
approachable set, 197, 198, 201, 202, 204, 230
arithmetic coding, 251, 271

Bayes classifier, 140, 372
Bayes probability of error, 140, 372
bayesian mixture, 250, 330
Bennett's inequality, 362
Bernstein's inequality, 133, 361, 362
  for martingales, 74, 133, 149, 363
best reply, 184, 185, 195, 206–208, 226, 231
Beta distribution, 126, 127, 258, 323, 369
binary classification, 140
Blackwell condition, 10, 11, 34, 36, 49, 72, 82–84, 91–94, 178, 299, 357
Blackwell's approachability theorem, 3, 10, 35, 184, 197, 198, 201, 202, 226, 230, 289
Borel–Cantelli lemma, 87, 96, 135, 192, 200, 209, 231
Bregman divergence, 203, 294–296, 300, 301, 305, 307–309, 312, 313, 315, 316, 319, 329⁻
Bregman projection, 202–203, 295, 304, 307, 308, 331
Brier score, 86, 95

calibration, 3, 71, 85, 90, 93–96, 194, 226, 227
  uniform, 97
Catalan number, 127
Cauchy–Schwarz inequality, 204, 238, 239, 353, 354
chain rule for entropy, 370
chain rule for relative entropy, 167, 371
chaining, 241, 367, 369
checking rule, 71, 93–95
Chernoff's technique, 360, 362
column player, 181, 187, 190, 195–197, 204, 220, 228, 232

combinatorial expert, 99, 100
competitive analysis, 36
compound action, 99, 101–108, 124, 126, 145, 177
conditional regret, 191, 192, 229, 230
constant expert, 42, 43, 48, 63, 238, 249, 254, 256, 259, 261, 265, 269, 272–274, 283
constantly rebalanced portfolio, 277, 282, 283, 286, 288–292
context tree, 110
contraction principle, 239, 368
correlated equilibrium, 182–185, 190–196, 205, 206, 215, 226, 227, 230
  computation of, 193–194
covering number, 239, 240, 245, 265, 269–271
Cramér–Wold device, 244, 365

data compression, 2, 35, 125, 247, 249–251, 271
deterministic exploration–exploitation, 222, 232
  repeated, 224, 232
differential entropy, 328, 332
Dirichlet density, 259, 282–284, 289
discounted regret, 8, 32, 33, 36, 39, 98
distinguishing action, 155
Doeblin's condition, 211, 212
double mixture forecaster, 274
doubling trick, 17, 27, 36, 38, 39, 86, 134, 232
dual gradient update, 299, 300, 304, 308, 329, 331, 335
dual regret update, 299
dual weight, 299, 300, 314
dynamic pricing, 143, 145, 152, 175
dynamic strategy, 73, 100, 145

EG forecaster, 302, 305, 328, 355
EG investment strategy, 277, 284–287, 289, 291
empirical frequency of play, 184, 185, 190–196, 205, 215, 216, 226, 227, 229
empirical process, 239, 240
entropy, 18, 101, 295, 297, 370
ε-checking rule, 94, 98
ε-correlated equilibrium, 193
ε-Nash equilibrium, 207–209, 212, 215, 217, 227
ergodic theorem, 212

Printed in the United States
By Bookmasters